HANDBOOK OF MULTICULTURAL COUNSELING COMPETENCIES

HANDBOOK OF MULTICULTURAL COUNSELING COMPETENCIES

Edited by
Jennifer A. Erickson Cornish
Barry A. Schreier
Lavita I. Nadkarni
Lynett Henderson Metzger
Emil R. Rodolfa

WILEY

JOHN WILEY & SONS, INC.

Library of Congress Cataloging-in-Publication Data:

Handbook of multicultural counseling competencies / edited by Jennifer A. Erickson Cornish . . . [et al.] ; foreword by Derald Wing Sue.
    p. cm.
  ISBN 978-0-470-43746-9 (cloth); 978-0-470-60917-0 (ebook); 978-0-470-60919-4 (ebook); 978-0-470-60919-4 (ebook)
  1. Cross-cultural counseling. 2. Multiculturalism. 3. Minorities–Counseling. I. Cornish, Jennifer A. Erickson.
  BF636.7.C76H363 2010
  158^1.308–dc22

                                                          2009042696

Printed in the United States of America

V10011030_061119

CONTENTS

FOREWORD

In my 40 years of work in the field of psychology, I have never come across a better integrated and more groundbreaking text than *The Handbook of Multicultural Counseling Competencies* edited by Erickson Cornish, Schreier, Nadkarni, Henderson Metzger, and Rodolfa. Simply stated, it is an outstanding piece of work destined to make a major contribution to the field by (a) broadening our understanding of multicultural identities that go beyond race/ethnicity; (b) pointing out similarities and differences that distinguish many marginalized groups; (c) offering an integrated definition of multicultural counseling competencies that incorporates developmental levels; (d) presenting "best practices" guidelines in each chapter; (e) providing readers with case vignettes to illustrate real-life situations; and (f) presenting numerous helpful exercises that allow/force readers to explore their values, biases, and assumptions about human behavior (an important cultural competency foundation). What is impressive about this book is how the editors and contributors have so smoothly combined these strengths into each chapter so that it reads with clarity, insight, and lived experience. Each chapter comes to life, is filled with nuggets of insights and truths, and provides readers with valuable suggestions for working with these populations.

Although there are now numerous published works on cultural competency, this handbook does not stick to the narrow confines of a limited population, but is philosophically grounded in the assumption that multiculturalism encompasses an umbrella that includes multiple dimensions such as age, race, ethnicity, gender, immigration, linguistic background, social class, sexual orientation, size, religion, gender identities, and multiracial identities. Reading the chapters carefully leads readers to conclude that while differences between the groups are important and oftentimes unique, sociopolitical shared similarities for many marginalized groups exist.

Sizeism, for example, is an unrecognized prejudice directed toward "overweight" and "obese" people filled with stigma and possessing damaging consequences to targets. The authors of this chapter (Abakoui & Simmons) make a strong case that they prefer the term *fat* as an objective statement of size and as an attempt to destigmatize the word. When one views all groups in this chapter, it is clear they share similar dynamics and processes related to stigma, prejudice, discrimination, and the detrimental consequences of marginalization. For that reason, Chapter 15, "Developing Competency with White Identity and Privilege" (Dressel, Kerr, & Steven), has special significance to each chapter as it speaks to how helping professionals need to recognize the power differentials in their relationships with marginalized groups, how traditional systems of counseling/psychotherapy may become forms of cultural oppression, and the need to work with marginalized client populations in culturally competent ways that may challenge traditional forms of helping/healing.

The editors of the *Handbook* have attracted a talented pool of contributors, major scholars and practitioners who are experts in their fields. They write with passion, commitment, and expertise that is immediately obvious to readers. To them, multicultural counseling competence is more than an intellectual exercise, and requires helping professionals to develop not only the knowledge base of counseling and the information related to a particular population they hope to understand, but also the attitudes, awareness, and skills needed to function in an increasingly pluralistic society. Nearly all authors emphasize the need to go beyond a cognitive understanding of groups, to exploring their own assumptions about human behavior, biases, and emotions related to the groups they hope to help. To me, this is especially important as increasing research now reveals that cultural competence may increase with training, but that unconscious biases and "nested negative" feelings toward certain marginalized groups remain unchanged unless training programs directly confront them.

Little doubt exists in my mind that *The Handbook of Multicultural Counseling Competencies* will become a standard and perhaps a classic in the field. It is destined to become a part of the knowledge base of counseling competence, and should be used as a major text in multicultural counseling courses and other social science disciplines. It brings together recent advances in the fields of cultural competence and multicultural populations, and is extremely relevant not only to the helping professionals but to general fields in the social sciences. Few texts on multicultural counseling present cutting-edge information in such a scholarly manner, translate cultural perspectives and methodologies in ways that have meaning to scholars and practitioners, and do such a fine job in involving readers in the real-life experiences of the populations addressed in this text.

I commend the editors and authors for producing this much-needed and valuable piece of work. You have done a great service to the profession.

—Derald Wing Sue, PhD
Professor of Psychology and Education
Teachers College, Columbia University

ACKNOWLEDGMENTS

The editors would like to express our sincere gratitude to Derald Wing Sue for writing the Foreword to this volume. We could have no higher aspiration for our work than that it live up to his gracious expectations. We also want to offer our appreciation to the authors for their thoughtful contributions, to Bethany Kasdon for the countless hours she spent reviewing the chapters from a student's perspective, and to Marquita Flemming, our editor at Wiley, for her endless patience and support. Finally, the Association of Counseling Center Training Agencies (ACCTA) deserves particular thanks for multicultural leadership and for growing this book: For this reason, all royalties from the sales of the Handbook will go to support ACCTA's leadership in training psychology's newest professionals in multiculturally competent practice.

In addition, we want to thank our partners, friends, and families for their personal support to each of us: Tom Birkenholz; the Erickson Cornish family; the Henderson and Metzger families, respectively and collectively (with special thanks to Linda, Steve, Galen, and Landon, Luke, Ashley, and Elizabeth); the sugarloafers; and Maya and Michael Wilson.

CHAPTER 1

AN OVERVIEW OF MULTICULTURAL COUNSELING COMPETENCIES

Lynett L. Henderson Metzger, Lavita I. Nadkarni, and Jennifer A. Erickson Cornish

INTRODUCTION

The November 2008 election of the first African American U.S. President signaled for many a "dramatic change in attitudes toward race in America" (Turner, 2009). Others, however, placed significant caveats on the apparent gains made by some traditionally disenfranchised groups in this country:

> Throughout this election season, where the 3 strongest candidates—a senior citizen, a woman and an African American—were "non-traditional," we were reminded that an individual's differences are too often viewed as weakness rather than strength. We were reminded that while diversity is today a fact of life, there is still much work to be done to create a culture of inclusion where a person's age, gender, ability, race, religion or any other defining characteristic—whether physical or cultural—adds to the creativity, innovation and commitment that leads to the kind of breakthrough thinking required to solve the most seemingly intractable problems. (Crider, 2008, p. 2)

Mental health practitioners, researchers, and educators who value inclusivity and social justice likewise walk a fine line between celebrating the laudable strides made by the field in recent decades and acknowledging the enormity of the distance left to go. Much of this work lies within the arenas of race, ethnicity, and culture; much lies beyond the scope of traditionally defined "multiculturalism" and focuses on individuals whose places at the diversity table to date have been limited to folding chairs in the corner of the room. This textbook represents a small gesture of welcome toward a few of these historically overlooked groups.

MULTICULTURALISM IN PRACTICE: MUCH PROGRESS, MUCH TO BE DONE

If, as the saying goes, the journey of 1,000 miles begins with a single step, then surely the climb toward a richer definition of multicultural competence rests on the innumerable handholds placed by those with the vision, courage, and eloquence to define a paradigm—and shatter it. The seminal works of Cross, Parham, and Helms (see, e.g., Cross, Parham, & Helms, 1991; Helms, 1990), McIntosh (2008), D. W. Sue and D. Sue (1990, 2008), and so many others form the scaffolding upon which modern American multicultural discourse is built. Early (and continuing) efforts to operationalize White and non-White identity development, understand privilege and combat oppression,[1] and create a

[1] As used throughout this textbook, *oppression* means the process by which individuals from historically higher-status groups knowingly or unwittingly, with or without any conscious effort on their parts, utilize the entitlements inherent in their status, thus perpetuating a status quo in which individuals from other groups have by definition lower status, with fewer attendant opportunities, and so on (see Rothenberg, 2004, who has described oppression as "the flip side of privilege," p. 106).

CASE VIGNETTE 1.1

Mariana Prader, PhD, directs Progressive State College (PSC)'s clinical training program. The Provost has called for across-the-board budget cuts, and all program directors have been asked to submit proposals reducing expenditures by 10 percent. Dr. Prader knows next year's spreadsheet includes two big-ticket proposals from her program. One is the installation of an elevator system connecting the parking garage to the PSC Mental Health Clinic waiting area. Currently, an uncovered ramp winds from a service entrance on the far side of the building to a hallway several doors down from the waiting room entrance. The ramp is steep, ices over in winter, and (Dr. Prader thinks to herself) is a lawsuit waiting to happen. However, as no client in a wheelchair has ever utilized the Clinic, she reasons there must not be much need for disability services in the PSC community. The second item is a 5-day "SafeZone" training colloquium for all PSC personnel. Dr. Prader believes the training would be helpful in educating faculty and staff about issues facing gay, lesbian, and bisexual students, especially in light of some homophobic graffiti found on campus recently. Although she *personally* values diversity, Dr. Prader is aware that several faculty members have been very vocal in their opposition to the proposed colloquium; politically, the best thing for all concerned might be if the idea died a regrettable—but unavoidable—death from *acute budgetitis.*

Across town, Etienne Lamont, LCSW, also faces a dilemma: bran muffins, or jelly doughnuts? Eti (as his clients call him) conducts an evening parenting skills group for single fathers. Most of the men come to the two-hour group straight from work—some will return for extra hours or head to second jobs afterward—and Eti likes to offer a few snacks to tide them over. He frowns, tabulating an appropriate ratio of healthy to not-so-healthy items, and mentally runs through a quick checklist of his clients' dietary constraints. Ted and Kyle have heart conditions (bran for them). Roger has diabetes (sugar-free angelfood cake), and Vaughn has some unpronounceable gastrointestinal affliction; he probably won't eat anything, anyway. The 8 men in the group have between them 11 kids, 9 jobs, 6 functional vehicles (if you count Colin's old truck, which runs about half the time), 5 mortgages (including a pending foreclosure and an eviction notice), close to $100k in outstanding debt, and an average blood pressure of 140/90. Eti remembers taking a graduate course on "gender issues," and his feelings of indignation over the historical and ongoing oppression of women worldwide. He pauses, checks in with himself. He still feels that anger, is still aware of his privilege and that of other men—but there is a story to be told here, too. He struggles to think of a way to speak *both* truths to the men in his group. Eti sighs. *Men may run the world,* he thinks, sticking a couple of bananas in the basket, *but, man, it runs them, too.*

At that exact moment, Dae-sun Yi sits at her computer and thoughtfully compares college Web sites. She is considering majoring in psychology, and would like an intellectually rigorous program with some clinical training opportunities in the community. She hopes to attend graduate school, perhaps earning a PsyD with an emphasis on working with older adults. One program, offered at a nearby school, looks pretty good. There are some interesting electives, the teachers appear to be well-respected, and the program utilizes a nationally recognized competency-based diversity training model. Dae-Sun hesitates, finger poised above the button on the mouse. *Diversity—is that important?*, she wonders. *Is that* me?

shared knowledge base and minimal expectations of multicultural competencies (see, e.g., American Psychological Association [APA], 2003) provide a critical starting point for understanding what it means to be an effective and ethical practitioner in an increasingly diverse world.

But what constitutes "effective" and "ethical" may evolve over time and with developmental level. Consider the examples discussed in Case Vignette 1.1 on the preceding page.[2]

The scaffolding is there—but, as the previous vignette illustrates, it is by no means complete. Increasingly nuanced understandings of the interplay between target status and day-to-day reality are emerging from current explorations of racial *microaggressions* (the insidious and pervasive staccato of invalidating and disempowering messages with which persons of color are almost continually bombarded) (Sue, Capodilupo, & Holder, 2008; Sue et al., 2007), *intersectional identity theory* (see, e.g., Shuddhabrata Sengupta's 2006 article, "I/Me/Mine," in which she describes multiple identities as "minefields," and observes, "it's just that we don't know which mine (as in 'weapon' and as in 'first-person possessive singular personal pronoun') will claim which part of me," p. 634), *contemporary racism* (Smith, Constantine, Graham, & Dize, 2008, for example, note that clinicians risk hitting a "developmental ceiling unless they simultaneously refine their understanding of the operations of racism within their own and their clients' conceptual worlds" [p. 337], including forms of oppression much more subtle than those encountered during the civil rights era), and myriad other issues at the forefront of social justice scholarship.

Nor are racial, ethnic, and cultural themes the only overlooked aspects of diversity. By way of example, a cursory search for the term *racism* appearing in publication titles over the last 20 years yields 58 results; once *racism* is excluded, the terms *ageism, sexism, ableism, sizeism,* and *transphobia* appear in only 19 journal titles *combined* over the same period of time, with sexism

accounting for all but one of these.[3] In decrying the 96 percent failure rate in summary judgment on employment discrimination suits based on multiple claims (cases in which the plaintiff argues that she was discriminated against based on, e.g., her age, gender, *and* religious affiliation), Kotkin (2009) questions whether "the realities of today's workplace" suggest that "diversity is tolerated or may even be valued up to a point," but that "too much difference" leads to "disparate treatment" (p. 3). When the provision of psychotherapy services itself risks becoming inherently "disparate" due to a lack of clinical expertise in the core issues that impact hundreds of millions of people (or, if considered in the aggregate, every human being), the time has come for a reconsideration of what the field means by basic "cultural competence."

Practitioners and researchers alike recognize gaps in therapists' awareness and experience in effectively meeting the needs of clients whose multicultural identities fall outside of the syllabi of most three-credit graduate "diversity" courses. Recent articles question the competency of counseling training program graduates to offer services to differently abled clients (Cornish et al., 2008; Smart & Smart, 2006) and argue that even among those with positive attitudes toward diversity in general, college "faculty members may not consider disability as an aspect of diversity" (Barnard, Stevens, Oginga Siwatu, & Lan, 2008, p. 173). Similarly, Bartoli (2007) argues that training in the areas of religion and spirituality "continues to be scarce and inadequate," suggesting that "recent, and not so recent, graduates are left on their own to seek further training and develop relevant competencies," a reality that renders it "dubious whether psychologists currently meet the needs of religious and spiritual clients adequately" (p. 54). In promulgating its "Guidelines for Psychological

---

[2] All vignettes represent amalgams of the authors' experiences and do not depict any actual person or situation.

[3] PsycARTICLES search conducted July 28, 2009. *Ageism* appeared in one journal article title; *ableism, sizeism,* and *transphobia* yielded no results for the timeframe searched. *Sexism* and *racism* appeared together in three titles.

Practice with Girls and Women," the American Psychological Association (APA, 2007) acknowledged that "many psychologists and members of the general public may believe that women's issues in psychology were dealt with and resolved in the 1970s and 1980s" (p. 949), while the needs of female clients in today's changing social and economic context remain unmet. In an increasingly pernicious double-bind, older adults chronically underutilize therapy services, while "mental health issues relevant to older individuals continue to be underrepresented in the research literature and underemphasized in psychology, medical, and other health care provider training programs" (Smith, 2007, p. 277). Popular media and the counseling and training literature are full of similar examples of a profound disconnect between the needs of the mental health field's constituent communities and the functional expertise of its providers. The Surgeon General's office, for example, has documented disparities along ethnic and racial lines in both mental health access and service delivery (U.S. Department of Health and Human Services, 2001). Leigh, Powers, Vash, and Nettles (2004) could be speaking of a broad range of categories of difference when they acknowledge that the inclusion of "disability culture" in coursework "remains incidental. Psychologists typically have minimal or no training that will prepare them to deal appropriately with people with disabilities" (p. 49). And, as Garrett et al. (2001) note,

> Research has shown that persons of color tend to underutilize counseling services, terminating at a rate of greater than 50% after the first session (Priest, 1994; D. W. Sue & D. Sue, 1999). This overwhelming rate of early termination, according to Sue and Sue, has been attributed to the biased nature of services and the lack of sensitivity and understanding for the life experiences of the culturally different client (p. 148).

Without an adequate foundation upon which to build functional competencies, professionals working with the individuals and groups described in the following chapters may, too often, find themselves participating in this very lack of awareness of how best to serve the needs of those different from themselves.

WHAT THIS BOOK IS

The list of underserved—and, too often, under-acknowledged—categories of difference includes a number of dimensions explored in this *Handbook*: age, size, sex, and social class; spiritual/religious, racial, ethnic, and multiracial identification; immigration, linguistic, ability, and gender-identity status; sexual orientation; and White identity/privilege. This introductory text offers clinicians and clinicians-in-training an overview of these issues with an emphasis on the practical application of theory and technique to real-world case examples. In keeping with the "basic assumption" in the field of psychology that "the path toward proficiency is developmental" (Stoltenberg, 2005, p. 858), detailed, developmentally relevant competency categories will be examined, with resources and exercises geared toward students, instructors, and practitioners at various levels of experience and expertise. The topics covered in this *Handbook* represent a cross-section of diversity characteristics and best-practice guidelines rarely addressed in depth in textbooks of this kind. These guidelines (discussed as applicable in the following chapters) are geared toward the APA Board of Educational Affairs Council of Chairs of Training Counsels (2007) benchmarks and reflect principles shared by professional organizations throughout the mental health field (see, e.g., APA, 2007). Think of this *Handbook* as a multicultural "sampler" consisting of common clinical issues *uncommonly* included in professional training protocols.

WHAT THIS BOOK IS NOT

A seven-course meal. This *Handbook* does not comprehensively address any single topic, nor does it purport to provide an exhaustive overview of *all* (or even most) multicultural competencies. The coverage is selective and, in some ways, eclectic—by design. Excellent and detailed examinations of what might be considered foundational diversity concepts exist already in the canon of the field (see, e.g., Atkinson & Hackett, 1998; Atkinson, Morten, & Sue, 1998; Constantine & Sue, 2005, 2006; Helms & Cook, 1999; Pederson, 2001; Ponterroto, Casas, Suzuki, & Alexander, 2001; Sue, Arredondo, & McDavis, 1992; D. W. Sue & D. Sue, 1990; D. W. Sue & D. Sue, 2007;). Many of these documents provide a foundation for the comments of the authors included here. This text, however, is designed to bridge the gaps in what we *don't* know we don't know—helping us to examine and, in turn, reduce our multicultural blind spots in areas that we may not even recognize *as* diversity.

For this reason, chapter topics may be grouped (or singled out) in ways that initially seem counterintuitive. However, we believe it is well worth considering "otherness" from this broad perspective. The organizing principle behind *these* contributions to the conversation on multiculturalism is, "What is missing?" The authors whose work appears within these pages have each attempted to tell the stories of those about whom the "dialogue on diversity" has been largely silent. The need to understand is real—but what constitutes "competency" in this broad context, and how can the developmental needs of mental health professionals best be met?

Competency in Practice

Competency "is generally understood to mean that a professional is qualified, capable, and able to understand and do things in an appropriate and effective manner" (Rodolfa et al., 2005, p. 348), while professional competency is the "habitual and judicious use of communication, knowledge, technical skills, clinical reasoning, emotions, values, and reflection in daily practice for the benefit of the individual and community being served" (Epstein & Hundert,

2002, p. 277). Competencies are "complex and dynamically interactive clusters" that include "knowledge . . . skills . . . attitudes, beliefs, and values" and other important characteristics (Rubin et al., 2007, p. 453). Competency ensures that "a professional is capable (i.e., has the knowledge, skills, and values) to practice the profession safely and effectively" (Rodolfa et al., 2005, p. 349).

The "culture of competence" (Roberts, Borden, Christiansen, & Lopez, 2005, p. 356) refers to a pedagogical shift in mental health education from learning *objectives* to learning *outcomes*. The movement away from students learning to practice by accumulating hours and toward students demonstrating competent practice started within medical and nursing education (e.g., Association of American Medical Colleges, 1998). The history of the competencies movement among education and health professions (including psychology) has been well documented by Kaslow et al. (2007). As a brief summary, within psychology, the National Council of Schools and Programs in Professional Psychology (NCSPP) (Peterson, Peterson, Abrams, & Stricker, 1997) first delineated six core competencies of psychological practice, including relationship, assessment, intervention, consultation and education, and management and supervision. NCSPP subsequently expanded these ideas, which currently include relationship, assessment, intervention, diversity, research/evaluation, management/supervision, and consultation/education (see http://www.ncspp.info/model.htm). In addition to identifying competencies to be taught in a core curriculum, NCSPP "highlighted that each competency is composed of the knowledge, skills, and attitudes necessary for professional functioning" (Kaslow et al., 2007, p. 701). NCSPP recently released its *Competency-Based Education for Professional Psychology* handbook (Kenkel & Peterson, 2009), outlining a training model that emphasizes five components: psychological science and education, integrative pedagogy, core curriculum and the professional core competency areas, elements of practice, and social responsibility, diversity, and gender. Other training councils, including scientist-practitioner clinical psychologists (Belar & Perry, 1992), counseling psychologists (e.g., Stoltenberg et al., 2000), and clinical scientists (http://psych.arizona.edu/apcs/apcs.html) have also outlined competency-based education and training approaches. The APA Committee on Accreditation (http://www.apa.org/ed/accreditation/) and Canadian Psychological Association Accreditation Panel (http://www.cpa/ca/accreditation/) implemented competency-based approaches to accreditation of academic and internship programs beginning in the 1990s. Various organizations have developed guidelines related to competencies, including multicultural competencies (e.g., APA, 2003).

The 2002 Competencies Conference: Future Directions in Education and Credentialing in Professional Psychology, was organized by the Association of Psychology Postdoctoral and Internship Centers (APPIC), together with the APA and 33 related organizations, to move the competency movement forward. Each sponsoring organization sent a delegate; other participants were chosen based on their areas of expertise. A preconference survey resulted in consensus around eight core competency domains: scientific foundations of psychology and research; ethical, legal, public policy/advocacy, and professional issues; supervision; psychological assessment; individual and cultural diversity; intervention; consultation and interdisciplinary relationships; and professional development. A "competency cube" (Rodolfa et al., 2005) was developed at the conference that included foundational competency (reflective practice/self-assessment; scientific knowledge and methods; relationships; ethical and legal standards and policy issues; individual and cultural diversity; interdisciplinary systems), functional competency (assessment/diagnosis/conceptualization; intervention; consultation; research/evaluation; supervision/teaching; management/administration), and developmental stages (graduate education; practica/internship; postgraduate supervision; residency/fellowship; and continuing competency). Within each professional stage, specialty education was recommended

via parameters of practice that differentiate specialties, including populations served.

Following the Competencies Conference in 2002, the APA Board of Educational Affairs (BEA) began to focus on the assessment of competencies, the Association of Directors of Psychology Training Centers developed an outline of competencies for graduate field placements (Hatcher & Lassiter, 2007), and a Benchmarking Conference was held by the BEA in 2007. Rubin and colleagues (2007) have described a current "national zeitgeist focusing on competencies and their assessments" (p. 453). Obviously, the competency and assessment of competency movements are beyond the scope of this *Handbook*. The goal of each of our chapters, however, is to help clinicians enhance not only their ability to provide services to the populations specifically described, but also their general multicultural competency. Some of the populations included in this *Handbook* have received considerable attention in the literature, and others little scrutiny at all. As previously discussed in this chapter, the list of topics addressed in this book is not meant to be exhaustive, but does represent many of the target groups we feel have experienced discrimination in the United States and can be treated and supported more competently by well-trained mental health professionals.

Certainly, every mental health professional cannot be expected to possess all of the knowledge, skills, attitudes, and values necessary to work optimally with each of these populations, particularly since each includes many different subpopulations, each of which is itself subject to constantly changing contexts. However, we hope this volume will give the reader a general overview of the basic aspects of competency, with many resources and references provided for further information.

D. W. Sue and D. Sue (2008) describe culturally competent counselors, in part, as being aware of their own assumptions, values, and biases; understanding the worldview of culturally diverse clients; and using appropriate intervention strategies and techniques. These criteria correspond with the attitudes/values, knowledge, and skills typically used to define competence in general.

Knowledge has been defined as "facts [and] information . . . acquired . . . through experience or education; the theoretical or practical understanding of a subject" (*The New Oxford American Dictionary*, 2005, p. 938). Thus knowledge of a specific diverse population will include such information as the definition of the population, including its various segments, and the history of oppression the population has experienced.

Skill has been defined as "proficiency, ability or dexterity" (*Webster's*, 2005, p. 1058) and "the ability to do something well; expertise" (*The New Oxford American Dictionary*, 2005, p. 1589). For the diverse populations in this *Handbook*, clinical/counseling skills are outlined relevant to functional categories, including assessment, diagnosis, case conceptualization, intervention, relationship, collaboration, referral, and supervision and training.

Attitude is "a settled way of thinking or feeling about someone or something, typically . . . that is reflected in a person's behavior" (*The New Oxford American Dictionary*, 2005, p. 102), while a *value* is "a principle, standard, or quality considered inherently worthwhile or desirable" (*The American Heritage Dictionary*, 1983, p. 749). One of the most difficult aspects for a mental health counselor working with diverse populations is to overcome his or her own *isms*, including racism, heterosexism, and ageism (Henderson Daniel, Roysircar, Abeles, & Boyd, 2004); however, those who do engage in such self-assessment craft a more reflective and likely more effective practice.

Multicultural Counseling Competency

Consistent across various definitions of multicultural competence has been the view that the competencies are not static, but ever changing. In his 2004 keynote address to the Teachers College Winter Roundtable on Cultural Psychology and Education, Parham (as cited in Hanson et al., 2006) described the process of becoming a multiculturally competent psychotherapist as a complex and lifelong journey.

Implicit in this understanding is that the psychotherapist is engaging in an active process of personal and social change. *Multicultural competence* can be defined as the extent to which a psychotherapist is actively engaged in the process of self-awareness, obtaining knowledge, and implementing skills in working with diverse individuals (Arredondo et al., 1996; Constantine, Hage, Kindaichi, & Bryant, 2007; Sue, Arredondo, & McDavis, 1992).

The domains within this multicultural counseling competencies model can be thought of from either a fixed-goal or process perspective (Collins & Pieterse, 2007). The fixed-goal perspective implies that the eventual competency outcome is seen through demonstrable behaviors, whereas the process perspective requires internal engagement and change. Within the *knowledge* domain, multicultural counseling competence may consist of obtaining information about "various worldview orientations, histories of oppression endured by marginalized populations, and culture-specific values that influence the subjective and collaborative experience of marginalized populations" (Constantine et al., 2007, p. 24). *Skill development and implementation*, within the multicultural counseling competency, requires that the psychotherapist act in a way that "draws from an existing fund of cultural knowledge to design mental health interventions that are relevant to marginalized populations" (Constantine et al., 2007, p. 24). The process dimension or domain of *self-awareness* requires that the multiculturally competent counselor is "cognizant of one's attitudes, beliefs and values regarding race, ethnicity, and culture along with one's awareness of the sociopolitical relevance of cultural group membership in terms of issues of cultural privilege, discrimination, and oppression" (Constantine et al., 2007, p. 24).

History of Multicultural Counseling Competency in Mental Health

The integration of multiculturalism into graduate clinical and counseling psychology curricula, training, and research has been a 30-year endeavor. There has been widespread agreement that the United States has become increasingly diverse over the past several decades and that mental health practitioners have been, and will be, providing counseling to clients who may have different worldviews from their own. Yet, there remains some debate as to what form of service delivery is deemed to be culturally relevant and what constitutes multiculturally competent psychotherapy.

For example, various iterations of a multicultural counseling competencies model have been proposed since the early 1980s. The American Counseling Association (ACA) and the APA both supported the creation of and endorsed the multicultural counseling competencies and multicultural guidelines, respectively (see, e.g., Arredondo & Perez, 2006). Sue et al. (1982) were the first to propose a model that addressed counselor competency with respect to racial and ethnic groups. The model delineated three broad competency areas: therapist's awareness of her or his own assumptions, values, and biases; understanding the worldview of culturally different others; and developing appropriate intervention strategies and techniques. These three areas are reflected in a therapist's attitudes, knowledge, and skills. The second iteration of the multicultural counseling competencies (Sue et al., 1998) added competencies at the organizational/systemic level. These 31 multicultural counseling competencies were operationalized through the addition of 119 explanatory statements, and the introduction of a model highlighting multiple identity dimensions within a contextual framework (Arredondo et al., 1996). In 2003, the Association for Multicultural Counseling and Development, a division within ACA, produced an updated version of the multicultural counseling competencies (Roysircar, Arredondo, Fuertes, Ponterotto, & Toporek, 2003). Similarly, the APA has produced aspirational guidelines to promote competent research, assessment, and clinical practice with diverse populations. At present, there are APA practice guidelines for working with gay, lesbian, bisexual, and transgender populations, older adults, girls and women, and ethnic, linguistic,

and culturally diverse populations (examined in more detail within the relevant chapters in this volume). In 2003, guidelines with respect to multicultural education, training, research, practice, and organizational change were adopted by the APA. A list of Multicultural Competency Guidelines proposed by the APA and other organizations is included below.

Multicultural Competency Guidelines

The following Web sites provide links to the core multicultural competency guidelines for most major professional organizations in the United States (please see individual chapters for additional information and topic-specific resources):

APA Ethics Code (2002)
http://www.apa.org/ethics/code/index,aspx

APA Guidelines for Psychotherapy with Older Adults (2004)
http://www.apa.org/practice/guidelines/older-adults.pdf

APA Guidelines on Multicultural Education, Training, Research, Practice and Organizational Change for Psychologists (2002)
http://www.apastyle.org/manual/related/guidelines-multicultural-education.pdf

APA Guidelines for Psychotherapy with Lesbian, Gay and Bisexual Clients (2000)
http://www.apapracticecentral.org/ce/guidelines/glbt.pdf

APA Guidelines for Psychological Practice with Girls and Women (2007)
http://www.apa.org/about/division/girlsandwomen.pdf

American Counseling Association Ethics Code
http://www.counseling.org/Resources/CodeOfEthics/TP/Home/CT2.aspx

National Association of Social Workers Cultural Standards (2006)

http://www.socialworkers.org/practice/stan
dards/NASWCulturalStandardsIndicators
2006.pdf

National Association of Social Workers Code
of Ethics
http://www.socialworkers.org/pubs/code/
code.asp

American Psychiatric Association Ethics Code
http://www.psych.org

AMCD Multicultural Counseling Competencies
http://www.counseling.org/Files/FD .ashx?
guid=735d18d6-2a6e-41bf-bd4a-5f4ce48
a100

As a result of widespread acceptance of the
multicultural counseling competencies among
professional organizations and accrediting bodies (such as the APA, The Council for Accreditation of Counseling and Related Educational
Programs [CACREP], etc.), most graduate programs have incorporated at least one course in
multicultural issues into their training models.
Several authors have assessed the implementation of these competencies and guidelines across
curricula and practica experiences, and within
supervision (Smith, Constantine, Dunn, Dinehart, & Montoya, 2006; Vereen, Hill, & McNeal,
2008). Despite such attention to multicultural
education, research has shown that there appear
to be some gaps between beliefs and practice, and
that skill development and implementation will
require further efforts on the part of training
institutions and psychotherapists at all levels of
training (Hanson et al., 2006; Henderson Daniel,
Roysircar, Abeles, & Boyd, 2004).

In addition to widespread endorsement, the
multicultural counseling competencies have also
received criticism, leading to a rich debate within
the various fields. Weinrach and Thomas
(2002) and Thomas and Weinrach (2004) have
questioned the imposition of the multicultural
counseling competencies on mental health professionals, and believe them to have created
potential ethical concerns for practitioners.

They argue that the competencies are exclusive
in nature, with an undue emphasis on racial identity and who defines such, that dissimilar identity
constructs are given the same weight, that the
terms *multicultural* and *diversity* are used interchangeably, and that the competencies are dated
based on their source material. Their arguments
have received support from Vontress and Jackson
(2004) and Patterson (2004), who propose a
universal system of counseling, grounded in
empiricism and theory, that requires respect,
genuineness, empathic understanding—coupled
with communication of these concepts—and
structure. Yet, in their 20-year content analysis
of empirical research on the multicultural counseling competencies (MCC), Worthington, Soth-
McNett, and Moreno (2007) concluded that "the
existing empirical MCC process/outcome research has shown consistently that counselors
who possess MCCs tend to evidence improved
counseling processes and outcomes with clients
across racial and ethnic differences" (p. 358).

OVERVIEW OF HANDBOOK

Our goal is to describe the knowledge, skills, and
attitudes/values necessary to work with diverse
populations, focusing on the following areas of
diversity: age, disability, ethnicity, immigration,
language, men, multiracial individuals, race, sexual orientation, size, social class, spirituality/reli-
gion, transsexual/intersex/transgender identity,
White identity/privilege, and women. We present
the groups in alphabetical order by subject for ease
of reference, although we acknowledge that members of certain groups have experienced differential levels of oppression at specific historical times.

Each chapter synthesizes the existing literature into the competencies of practical *knowledge,
skills,* and *attitudes/values* necessary for clinical
work with that particular target group. In addition, references and resources relevant to each
population group are included. A developmental
approach is utilized throughout, generally based
on the June 2007 *Benchmarks* document (APA,
Board of Educational Affairs & Council of
Chairs of Training Councils, 2007). Although

each chapter is written using the same general outline, each is designed to function either as a stand-alone resource or in conjunction with the remaining material for a more comprehensive examination of these issues. Each chapter is briefly summarized below.

Age and Diverse Older Adults

Given that the population of the United States is aging as well as becoming increasingly diverse, it is vital that all health-care providers receive adequate education on adult development, aging, and multiculturalism, as well as the intersection between these topics. This chapter presents the demographics of today's aging population, examines important concepts such as the sociocultural/ psychological dynamics of aging, and outlines common misconceptions and ageist beliefs when treating diverse older adults. Appropriate skills needed for effective assessment and intervention with this population are described.

Disability

In this chapter, the concept of disability as a multicultural issue is examined. Various models for understanding disabilities are explored, including explanations of types of disability, historical and legal considerations, developmental concerns, multiple minority status, and current issues and skills needed to treat individuals with disabilities.

Ethnicity

Ethnicity is an often-overlooked and even more often misunderstood cornerstone of self-identification for many individuals. This chapter clarifies terms and explores issues involved in the examination of ethnic differences through the lens of personal experience as well as current research. Using a developmental approach to explore the multicultural competencies needed by practitioners at various points along the developmental continuum, this chapter describes competent psychotherapeutic work with clients from diverse ethnic backgrounds.

Immigration

Immigration imposes significant pressures on members of immigrant communities as it necessitates a psychological restructuring against the backdrop of multiple cultural contexts. Understanding immigrants' experiences and competently serving their mental health needs becomes imperative. This chapter highlights the requisite knowledge and skills needed to work with a specific group, Asian Indians, who have immigrated to the United States.

Language

The importance of training future mental health practitioners to become competent in issues of language acquisition development related to the areas of assessment and intervention is undeniable (e.g., U.S. Census data from 2000 reports that 18% of the population speaks a language other than English). This chapter focuses on self-awareness about English-language learners and knowledge related to second-language acquisition. Vignettes guide the reader to turn this knowledge into competent practice.

Men

The chapter on psychotherapy with men serves as a primer for the conceptual and clinical issues that therapists experience when treating male clients. Many training models fail to recognize how male socialization and male identities influence the process of psychotherapy. Pertinent knowledge, skills, and values/attitudes are examined, with an emphasis on the core concepts, historical and present-day realities, and clinical dynamics that inform the provision of services to male clients.

Multiracial Identities

There are a growing number of individuals who identify as multiracial or of mixed race. Individuals of racially diverse ancestry have faced a long history of oppression and marginalization in this country. Typically the identity development trajectories and self-conceptualizations of multiracial people differ in important ways from those of individuals with a single racial identification. Therefore, mental health practitioners must increase their understanding of the unique characteristics and needs of this population to provide competent services for these individuals. This chapter provides guidelines and resources to enhance professionals' awareness of their own values and attitudes, knowledge of ecological issues, and skills in developing competency in working with persons of mixed ancestry.

Race

Understanding the concept of race, the unique challenges and opportunities of racial identity formation in the face of historical and ongoing racism, and the needs of racially diverse individuals represents a core multicultural counseling competency. This chapter provides an introduction to the basic terms, identity development concepts, historical contexts, and assessment and intervention models relevant to providing competent and effective services to people of color in the United States.

Sexual Orientation

A proliferation of research and scholarly writing regarding the development of sexual orientation and identity has occurred over the past 30 years since the removal of homosexuality from the *Diagnostic and Statistical Manual of Mental Disorders*. This chapter helps mental health practitioners familiarize themselves with the professional literature, educate themselves regarding gay, lesbian, and bisexual culture, examine their own beliefs and attitudes, and synthesize this information into an effective therapeutic stance to provide competent clinical treatment.

Size

Currently there is a "war on obesity" being fought in the media, in medical and mental

health consulting rooms, and in our homes, with research typically focused on treatment for obesity and the stigma of being fat. This chapter outlines the importance of size as an aspect of diversity and how size-acceptance in conjunction with treatment from a *health-at-every-size* perspective can improve mental and physical health for our clients. This chapter provides tools to create a respectful and supportive therapeutic environment to help clients reach their therapeutic goals.

Social Class

This chapter examines the clinical and training goals necessary for mental health practitioners to integrate social class and an awareness of classism into their work. Using the Social Class Worldview model, the authors review relevant literature and provide suggestions for how best to become a competent mental health practitioner in the arenas of social class and classism.

Spirituality and Religion

The chapter on spiritual and religious aspects of counseling outlines knowledge, skills, and attitudes/values necessary to provide sensitive services to individuals who hold a range of spiritual and religious worldviews. The authors provide a summary of central elements of major world religions, a comprehensive resource guide, and training and practice suggestions to enhance practitioners' competency in religious and spiritual development.

Transsexual/Intersex/Transgender

This chapter addresses identities located along both the biologically influenced continuum of sex identity and the more socially constructed continuum of gender identity. Working with individuals who present with identities outside the traditional dichotomous framework of gender and sex can be intimidating for mental health practitioners because they are often conflated with sexual orientation as well as with each other. For each of the topics presented in this chapter, a rationale for its emphasis in mental health training, a summary of current knowledge and scholarship in the area, key definitions and terms, and recommendations for necessary skill development and self-awareness are provided.

White Identity and Privilege

The understanding of White privilege is a crucial element in becoming a culturally sensitive mental health provider. For White mental health practitioners, this understanding must go beyond a cognitive processing and encompass an affective experience of self. This chapter emphasizes the need for a lifelong commitment to an understanding of privilege and describes the knowledge, skills, and values/attitudes necessary to incorporate this understanding into competent practice.

Women

This chapter focuses on women's gender within the context of multiple identities, noting that in an increasingly global world, and one that adheres almost universally to patriarchal social structures, it is important for therapists to understand the strengths demonstrated and challenges experienced by women by virtue of being female. A selected review of the historical backdrop and the literature on the psychology of women is discussed, and practitioners are provided with an overview of the knowledge, skills, and values/attitudes necessary for competent practice when treating women.

SUMMARY

While this book provides practical guidelines for working with 15 categories of difference not commonly addressed in training manuals of this type, many topics remain unexplored. Areas for further study include disparate treatment based on geographic location/geography of origin

among individuals born in the United States (including, e.g., stereotypes and assumptions based on a person hailing from "the South," "the West Coast," etc.); political affiliation (expressed or assumed); level of educational attainment (as distinct from professional identity and socioeconomic status); marital status and traditional versus nontraditional family structures (cohabitation, adoption, unpartnered individuals, work-related issues, etc.); veteran status and military service experience or affiliation; educational issues (e.g., providing services to students who utilize American Sign Language or other assisted-learning modalities); and a whole host of other areas ripe for exploration. Even within the broad topics covered here, it is clear that the field would benefit from a more in-depth focus on specific permutations of human experience (the dynamics of traumatic brain injury, for example) and a greater range of coverage of these and additional categories (e.g., the challenges facing *younger* adults as a function of age or perceived age). This list could clearly extend indefinitely.

Notwithstanding the rich body of work yet to be done, however, we hope within these chapters to have assembled a useful, relevant, and timely exploration of issues fundamental to multicultural competency at each stage of professional development. Below we provide a selection of resources designed to serve as a general introduction to the experiential possibilities of multicultural awareness and diversity training. These resources do not focus on a particular population or set of competencies, but, rather, on the process of increasing one's recognition of the way diversity issues influence day-to-day life as well as mental health practice. Each of these activities can be modified depending on the goal, size of the group, or type of setting. These resources represent a starting point for discussing the principles and concepts presented in greater detail throughout the remainder of this book. The authors hope that these materials will prove useful in facilitating ongoing dialogues about multicultural competence in all its permutations—a dialogue in which they feel very honored to have taken some small part.

RESOURCES

The following resources are provided as suggestions for further inquiry and as tools students, clinicians, trainees, and supervisors can utilize to help improve the quality of the services they provide.

EXERCISE 1.1: THE "NAME GAME"

Ideal as an icebreaker or group-bonding experience, this activity involves each group participant simply writing her or his full name on a chalkboard, dry-erase surface, or large piece of paper and explaining what she or he knows about the source and meaning of each component.

As can be seen in the example below, participants do not need to have a particularly sophisticated knowledge of the linguistic derivations of their names or genealogies to generate interesting avenues for discussion and exploration of a variety of personal identities:

Lynett	Lee	Henderson Metzger
My father, a police officer, came across this name on a file while my mother was pregnant with me. She tells me that she does not know the type of case involved, but assures me that it was not "murder or anything really bad."	My father's middle name; growing up, it was important to me that it was the "boy spelling" for this reason.	My partner and I took the same combined name: Henderson (my mother's family name, not an uncommon practice in the South; space no hyphen) Metzger ("butcher" in German; especially meaningful to preserve because many of his Jewish extended family members were killed in the Holocaust).

Variations include having group members write down the *meanings* of their names (without the names attached), collecting these, and having group members match meanings with names, or recall exercises in which group members are asked to remember particular names and meanings.

While generally perceived as a relatively nonthreatening way to open a discussion around sociocultural issues, this exercise should be approached thoughtfully in terms of accessibility issues (e.g., are there obstacles that make it impossible or awkward for some participants to get to the front of the room, write their names, etc.) and with the awareness that names and the act of naming are charged topics in their own right. For example, those with limited access to their own biographical information (through adoption or removal from the home, family secret-keeping, etc.), whose names are inextricably linked with oppressive or imperialistic historical realities (e.g., those with family "slave names," descendents of immigrants who anglicized their names upon arrival to this country), and who have undergone or are in the process of undergoing identity transitions (as in divorce, emancipation, gender realignment surgery, or other significant life changes) may find this exercise particularly challenging.

Facilitators are encouraged begin with a disclaimer allowing anyone who chooses to do so to opt out of the exercise (and to structure the exercise in such a way that it is not immediately obvious who has and has not participated), to be alert to cues that participation may be distressing to some individuals, and to intervene appropriately if any aspect of the activity has the effect of perpetuating oppression, increasingly marginalization, or otherwise limiting open and productive communication. When participants do choose to discuss these types of issues, however, the experience can be an especially rich and rewarding one for all those involved.

EXERCISE 1.2: SAMPLE SOCIOCULTURAL IDENTITY WHEEL

In this exercise, participants are provided with (or draw) a circle with a circle inside it; the two circles are connected by lines, thus creating several smaller compartments. Participants are asked to write down one of their sociocultural identities in each segment, and perhaps to circle "two or three" that are the most salient. Those who wish to do so are then invited to share a salient identity. In the course of the discussion, attention may be directed to helpful concepts—for example, which identities typically reflect a degree of personal choice (e.g., political affiliation, social group membership) and which represent more or less immutable factors (e.g., visual racial/ethnic group status, some types of differential ability)—and questions may be raised regarding thought-provoking response patterns (e.g., "What do we make of the fact that no White participants identified race or ethnicity as a salient sociocultural identity?"). This exercise can be structured to take only a few minutes or can incorporate substantial additional material and analysis.

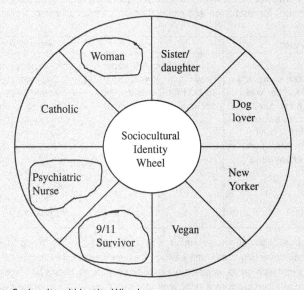

Figure 1.1   Sociocultural Identity Wheel

In the figure, the participant self-identifies as a sister/daughter, a dog lover, a New Yorker, a vegan, a 9/11 survivor, a psychiatric nurse, a Catholic, and a woman. She has selected "9/11 survivor," "psychiatric nurse," and "woman" as her three most salient identities, as indicated by the circle around each identity. Note that, in this example, participants are asked to highlight 8 sociocultural identities; however, any number could be selected.

Variations on This Theme:

- Asking participants to identify ways in which they are members of a "target group" (traditionally disenfranchised, marginalized, or oppressed individuals—e.g., women, persons of color, and those who are differently abled) or "non-target group" (traditionally empowered individuals—e.g., men, White people, those with high socioeconomic status) [see below for a more detailed description of these concepts]

- Examining the intersection between multiple identities (e.g., What does it mean to be a bisexual Latina mother?)

- Exploring relationships between salient life experiences and these identities (i.e., each participant might be asked to complete a Life Experiences Wheel similar to the Sociocultural Identity Wheel and comment on how, for example, socioeconomic status has impacted his or her career choice and professional development; what affirming and invalidating messages she or he has gotten based on racial and ethnic identification; to what extent gender-based violence has impacted past and present relationships, etc.)

EXERCISE 1.3: "KNAPSACK OF PRIVILEGES" EXERCISE

Peggy McIntosh (2008) famously "unpacked" the invisible "knapsack" of White privilege (p. 239), acknowledging the unearned and largely unrecognized collection of entitlements, presumptions in their favor, and cultural cache of which White individuals in American society are the unspoken beneficiaries on a daily basis (for more information on White privilege specifically, please see Chapter 15). This concept has been expanded to include a broad range of privilege categories (e.g., heterosexual privilege; McIntosh, 2002), and can be useful in assisting those for whom this may be a new perspective in thinking through how the dual dynamics of privilege and oppression play out in everyday experiences. Along with those discussed elsewhere in this volume, identified privileges might include items such as the following:

- As a White person, I do not worry that I have (or that my child has) been invited to a party or social event as the token representative of my race to demonstrate the inclusivity and open-mindedness of the host.

- As a White student or employee, my image is not routinely used on marketing materials, in photos, etc., as evidence of the organization's diverse enrollment or hiring practices.

- As a person of an accepted faith-based denomination, I can rest assured that my religion will not be associated with terrorism.

- As a person who is traditionally abled, I can assume I will be able to attend a class such as this (find suitable transportation; be able to gain access to the building; find a comfortable seat; and participate fully in the activities of the semester) without undue hardship.

- As a heterosexual woman, I do not have to worry that people will assume I am a child molester if I am around young children.

- As a young adult, I can expect that not being able to recall a memory does not reflect anything about my age.

- As a person with a culturally validated body shape, I do not have to fear that people will roll their eyes, groan, complain, or ask to move when I am assigned a seat next to them on an airplane.

- As a native English speaker, I can question a sales assistant, service provider, or government official about a confusing or unclear item, bill, or policy without him or her assuming that I do not understand enough to have a valid concern.

- As a cisgender individual, I am addressed by others using titles and pronouns that fit my concept of my own identity. I am never referred to by derogatory terms such as "s/he" or "it."

One simple exercise involves printing a variety of these types of privileges on strips of paper, dividing participants into small discussion groups, and having each group member randomly select a privilege to read and discuss. The individual may hold the privilege (i.e., be a member of a group that benefits from the privilege) or may not hold the privilege (i.e., be a member of a group that lacks the privilege). Ideally, each discussion group will be composed of individuals from a

(continued)

(*continued*)

variety of privileged/nonprivileged statuses. The specific items used in the exercise can be tailored to reflect areas of particular salience for the participants or venue. Participants may also be asked to generate ideas about ways in which they are privileged in their particular identities or settings.

EXERCISE 1.4: SALIENCY EXERCISES

Another way to begin talking about a broad variety of multicultural issues involves asking participants to think through various scenarios, evaluating the salient sociocultural considerations in each. There are obviously innumerable ways to present this material, from providing clinical vignettes (all vignettes, as with all clinical experiences—and, indeed, all human interactions—include diversity, power, and privilege components, some more explicitly than others) to deconstructing popular media images and themes or asking participants to bring in real-life examples of situations in which they noticed an exercise of privilege, were aware of an identity status, reacted to a power differential, observed (or perpetrated) an act of microaggression, and so forth.

One specific type of exercise involves examining the implications of our assumptions in particular circumstances. These are the ways in which our minds fill in the blanks when certain sociocultural cues are ambiguous or missing. For example, participants might be given the following instructions:

In each of the following scenarios consider your reactions to the basic narrative—and then ask yourself how your perspective changes when additional information is provided or sociocultural statuses are clarified. What assumptions did you make initially? Did those change; if so, how? How would these assumptions likely impact the situation?

Scenario #1: I have just walked 6 blocks to the police station. I arrive, exhausted and out of breath, to report that I have just been robbed. I describe my assailant as a young male, probably in his 20s, and state that he took all of my money, credit cards, and identification. I can't remember any other details of his appearance or the incident. [Additional information: At 74 years old, I am the oldest person in the police station.]

Scenario #2: I have just been called into my boss's office on a charge of sexual harassment. A co-worker has claimed that I made sexually inappropriate and derogatory comments. This is the third accusation the worker has brought against me, and the head of my employer's HR department is telling me that I could lose my job and face a civil lawsuit or even criminal prosecution. [Additional information: At 350 pounds and 5 feet 7 inches tall, my body type is considered "morbidly obese."]

Scenario #3: Two workers, a man and a woman, have just arrived at my home from the Department of Social Services. They tell me they are here because my brother, who is 12 years old, told his teacher I touched him in his "private place." I have never been in trouble before, and I do not know what is going to happen. [Additional information: At 54, my estimated IQ places my cognitive abilities within the range defined as "moderate mental retardation."]

These and similar exercises can serve as a jumping-off point to discuss positive and negative stereotypes (see Chapter 2 for a discussion of the impact of positive and negative stereotypes associated with older adults, for example), institutionalized and systemic *isms*, and the importance of self-reflection in clinical practice. Along similar lines, participants might be invited to engage in the following visualization exercise:

If you are comfortable doing so, close your eyes. Notice your breathing—a deep breath in; slowly out. Deep, easy, breaths—in; out. Relax into your chair. Let the sounds of the room fall away. Now imagine that you have been arrested. You are in the [fill in the appropriate city or county] jail, awaiting arraignment. Sit with that idea for a moment. Think about what it would be like, being you, in the jail cell. Notice your surroundings. What do you see, hear, smell? What thoughts go through your mind? What are your expectations? Your fears? What feelings are you aware of in your body at this moment?

Now imagine the same scenario: You have been arrested, and you are you, just as you are here today, everything the same, *except* change one salient sociocultural identity. If you are a male, for example, you could imagine yourself as a female; if you are traditionally abled, as someone differently abled; if you are from a lower-SES background, as being wealthy, and so on. You can give yourself more or less privilege. You can change a status that is apparent to others, or a status only you would know about. Now ask yourself—what has changed? Do you have different thoughts, fears, expectations? Do you notice different aspects of your environment? What are your feelings now?

Participants can then explore personally and with the group their thoughts and reactions as they "experienced" the process of surrendering or taking on a more privileged status.

Note that the preceding examples were adapted from course curricula utilized with graduate students in a master's-level forensic psychology training program. The specific situations could, of course, be tailored to reflect common scenarios encountered in any discipline (e.g., Scenario #3 could be introduced with, "As a social worker, how would you react if . . . " and adapted accordingly; the visualization exercise could be modified to involve walking into a new classroom setting or employment situation).

As participants become more familiar with the concepts and language of diversity, many find it beneficial to complete Target Journey and Non-Target Journey exercises. Sample instructions are included below:

EXERCISE 1.5: TARGET AND NON-TARGET JOURNEYS

The basic concept of the *Target Journey* involves reviewing your life and recognizing ways in which you have experienced oppression as a member of a "target" (nonprivileged) group or as a result of a target status or experience. A few examples of potential target groups or statuses are:

- Persons of color
- Persons with gay, lesbian, or bisexual affectional orientations
- Transgender individuals
- Differently abled persons
- Women
- Persons with non-majoritarian religious affiliations or spiritual beliefs
- Persons from lower socioeconomic backgrounds
- Persons whose first language is not English (in American culture), or who speak nonstandard English
- Persons who were not born in this country
- Persons who face discrimination based on their age or perceived age
- Persons who do not fit into the current cultural "ideal" of beauty
- Persons with limited access to educational opportunities

(*continued*)

(*continued*)

This list is by no means exhaustive. Your personal experience may not fit into one of these categories, or it may fit into several. It is your choice as to which group or groups on which to focus. You may choose to focus on one or two experiences in great detail, or to provide a narrative exploring how these issues have impacted you throughout your life.

Note that each individual's experience is different; thus, many of us may have experienced only "moments" of awareness of our target status; many others may have been aware of our nonprivileged status on a daily basis for a lifetime.

Conversely, the basic concept of the *Non-Target Journey* involves reviewing your life and recognizing ways in which you have oppressed others as a member of a "non-target" (or privileged) group. A few examples of potential non-target groups or statuses are:

- White persons
- Heterosexual persons
- Persons with traditionally accepted gender identification
- Traditionally abled persons
- Men
- Persons with majoritarian religious affiliations or spiritual beliefs
- Persons from middle- and upper-class socioeconomic backgrounds
- Persons whose first language is English (in American culture), or who speak standard English
- Persons who were born in this country
- Persons who do not face discrimination based on their age or perceived age
- Persons who fit into the current cultural ideal of beauty
- Persons with greater access to educational opportunities

Again, this list is by no means exhaustive, and your personal experience may fit into none or several of these categories. You may choose to focus on one or two instances in which you have displayed discrimination or acted in an oppressive manner, or you may provide a narrative exploring various ways in which you have done so throughout your life.

The Journeys can be written, shared orally, or a combination of both. Additional research is not generally required; however, participants may be encouraged to include quotations, excerpts, music or video selections, or other materials if doing so would enrich their Journeys. If information from the Journeys is shared in a group format (a powerful and moving experience for most participants), care should be taken to outline basic rules of "safe sharing" in this context. Those listening should be aware that their role is to bear witness to the Journey and affirm the individual's experience of sharing; it is not necessary that they agree with the person sharing, understand his or her perspective, or even "get it."

REFERENCES

American Psychological Association. (2000). Guidelines for psychotherapy with lesbian, gay and bisexual clients. *American Psychologist*, *55*(12), 1440–1451.

American Psychological Association. (2003). Guidelines on multicultural education, training, research, practice, and organizational change for psychologists. *American Psychologist*, *58*, 377–402.

American Psychological Association. (2004). Guidelines for psychotherapy with older adults. *American Psychologist*, *59*(4), 236–260.

American Psychological Association. (2007). Guidelines for psychological practice with girls and women. *American Psychologist, 62,* 949–979.

American Psychological Association, Board of Educational Affairs & Council of Chairs of Training Councils. (2007, June). *Assessment of Competency Benchmarks Work Group: A developmental model for the defining and measuring competence in professional psychology.* Washington, DC: Author. Retrieved August 24, 2009, from http://www.apa.org/ed/graduate/comp_benchmark.pdf

The American heritage dictionary (2nd College ed.). (1983). Boston MA: Houghton Mifflin.

Arredondo, P., & Perez, P. (2006). Historical perspectives on the multicultural guidelines and contemporary applications. *Professional Psychology: Research and Practice, 37*(1), 1–5.

Arredondo, P., & Toporek, R. (2004). Multicultural counseling competencies = ethical practice. *Journal of Mental Health Counseling, 26*(1), 44–55.

Arredondo, P., Toporek, R., Brown, S. P., Jones, J., Locke, D. C., Sanchez, J., et al. (1996). Operationalization of the multicultural counseling competencies. *Journal of Multicultural Counseling and Development, 24,* 42–78.

Association of American Medical Colleges. (1998). Learning objectives for medical student education: Guidelines for medical schools. Available at: https://services.aamc.org/publications/showfile.cfm?file=version87.pdf&prd_id=198&prv_id=239&pdf_id=87

Atkinson, D. R., & Hackett, G. (1998). *Counseling diverse populations* (2nd ed.). New York: McGraw-Hill.

Atkinson, D. R., Morten, G., & Sue, D. W. (1998). *Counseling American minorities* (5th ed.). New York: McGraw-Hill.

Barnard, L., Stevens, T., Oginga Siwatu, K., & Lan, W. (2008). Diversity beliefs as a mediator to faculty attitudes toward students with disabilities. *Journal of Diversity in Higher Education, 1,* 169–175.

Bartoli, E. (2007). Religious and spiritual issues in psychotherapy: Training the trainer. *Psychotherapy: Theory, Research, Practice, Training, 44,* 54–65.

Belar, C., & Perry, N. (1992). The National Conference on Scientist-Practitioner Education and Training for the Professional Practice of Psychology. *American Psychologist, 47,* 71–75.

Collins, N. M., & Pieterse, A. L. (2007). Critical incident analysis based on training: An approach to developing an active racial/cultural awareness. *Journal of Counseling and Development, 85,* 14–23.

Constantine, M. G., Hage, S. M., Kindaichi, M. M., & Bryant, R. M. (2007). Social justice and multicultural issues: Implications for the practice and training of counselors and counseling psychologists. *Journal of Counseling & Development, 85,* 24–29.

Constantine, M. G., & Sue, D. W. (Eds.). (2005). *Strategies for building multicultural competence in mental health and educational settings.* Hoboken, NJ: Wiley.

Constantine, M. G., & Sue, D. W. (Eds.). (2006). *Addressing racism: Facilitating cultural competencies in mental health and educational settings.* Hoboken, NJ: Wiley.

Cornish, J. E., Gorgens, K., Monson, S., Palombi, B., Olkin, R., & Abels, A. (2008). Perspectives on ethical practices with people who have disabilities. *Professional Psychology: Research and Practice, 39,* 488–497.

Crider, G. (2008, November 5). Reflections on Election '08: Progress & opportunity. Available at: http://www.diversitybestpractices.com/pdf/gwenLttr_election.pdf

Cross, W., Parham, T., & Helms, J. (1991). The stages of black identity development: Nigrescence models. In R. Jones (Ed.), *Black psychology* (3rd ed., pp. 319–338). Berkley, CA: Cobb & Henry.

Cynkar, A. (2007). The changing gender composition of psychology. *Monitor on Psychology, 38*(6), p. 46.

Epstein, R. M., & Hundert, E. M. (2002). Defining and assessing professional competence. *Journal of the American Medical Association, 287,* 226–235.

Fowers, B. J., & Davidov, B. J. (2006). The virtue of multiculturalism: Personal transformation, character, and openness to the other. *American Psychologist, 61*(6), 581–594.

Garrett, M. T., Borders, L. D., Crutchfield, L. B., Torres-Rivera, E., Brotherton, D., & Curtis, R. (2001). Multicultural SuperVISION: A paradigm of cultural responsiveness for supervisors. *Journal of Multicultural Counseling and Development, 29,* 147–158.

Hanson, N. D., Randazzo, K. V., Schwartz, A., Marshall, M., Kalis, D., Frazier, R., et al. (2006). Do we practice what we preach? An exploratory survey of multicultural psychotherapy competencies. *Professional Psychology: Research and Practice, 37*(1), 66–74.

Hatcher, R. L., & Lassiter, K. D. (2007). Initial training in professional psychology: The practicum competencies outline. *Training and Education in Professional Psychology, 1*(1), 49–63.

Hays, D. G. (2008). Assessing multicultural competence in counselor trainees: A review of instrumentation and future directions. *Journal of Counseling and Development, 86,* 95–101.

Helms, J. (Ed.). (1990). *Black and white racial identity: Theory, research, and practice.* Westport, CT: Praeger.

Helms, J. H., & Cook, D. A. (1999). *Using race and culture in counseling and psychotherapy: Theory and process.* Needham Heights, MA: Allyn & Bacon.

Henderson Daniel, J., Roysircar, G., Abeles, N., & Boyd, C. (2004). Individual and cultural-diversity competency: Focus on the therapist. *Journal of Clinical Psychology, 60,* 755–770.

Kaslow, N., McCarthy, S., Rogers, J., & Summerville, M. (1992). Psychology postdoctoral training: A developmental perspective. *Professional Psychology: Research and Practice, 23,* 369–375.

Kaslow, N., Rubin, N., Bebeau, M., Leigh, I., Lichtenberg, J., Nelson, P., et al. (2007). Guiding principles and recommendations for the assessment of competence. *Professional Psychology: Research and Practice, 38,* 441–451.

Kenkel, M. B., & Peterson, R. L. (Eds.). (2009). *Competency-based education for professional psychology.* Washington, DC: American Psychological Association.

Kotkin, M. (2009). Diversity and discrimination: A look at complex bias. *William & Mary Law Review, 50,* 1–57. Available at: http://works.bepress.com/minna_kotkin/18

Leigh, I. W., Powers, L., Vash, C., & Nettles, R. (2004). Survey of psychological services to clients with disabilities: The need for awareness. *Rehabilitation Counseling, 49,* 48–54.

McIntosh, P. (2002). White privilege: Unpacking the invisible knapsack. In P. S. Rothenberg (Ed.), *White privilege: Essential readings on the other side of racism* (pp. 97–102). New York: Worth.

McIntosh, P. (2008). White privilege and male privilege: A personal account of coming to see correspondences through work in women's studies. In M. McGoldrick, & K. Hardy (Eds.), *Re-visioning family therapy: Race, culture, and gender in clinical practice* (2nd ed., pp. 238–249). New York: Guilford.

The new Oxford American dictionary (2nd ed.). (2005). New York: Oxford University Press.

Patterson, C. H. (2004). Do we need multicultural counseling competencies? *Journal of Mental Health Counseling, 26*(1), 67–73.

Pederson, P. B. (2001). *A handbook for developing multicultural awareness* (3rd ed.). Alexandria, VA: American Counseling Association.

Peterson, R. L., Peterson, D. R., Abrams, J. C., & Stricker, G. (1997). The National Council of Schools and Programs of Professional Psychology educational model. *Professional Psychology: Research and Practice, 28*(4), 373–386.

Ponterroto, J. G., Casas, J. M., Suzuki, L. A., & Alexander, C. M. (2001). *Handbook of multicultural counseling* (2nd ed.). Thousand Oaks, CA: Sage.

Priest, R., (1994). Minority supervisor and majority supervisee: Another perspective on clinical reality. *Counselor Education and Supervision, 34,* 152–158.

Roberts, M. C., Borden, K. A., Christiansen, M. D., & Lopez, S. J. (2005). Fostering a culture shift: Assessment of competence in the education and careers of professional psychologists. *Professional Psychology: Research and Practice, 36,* 355–361.

Rodolfa, E., Bent, R., Eisman, E., Nelson, P., Rehm, L, & Ritchie, P. L. (2005). A cube model for competency development: Implications for psychology educators and regulators. *Professional Psychology: Research and Practice, 36*(4), 347–354.

Rothenberg, P. S. (2004). *White privilege: Essential readings on the other side of racism* (2nd ed.). New York: Worth.

Roysircar, G., Arredondo, P., Fuertes, J. N., Ponterotto, J. G. & Toporek, R. L. (2003). *Multicultural counseling competencies 2003.* Alexandria, VA: Association of Multicultural Counseling and Development.

Rubin, N. J., Bebeau, M., Leigh, I. W., Lichtenberg, J. W., Nelson, P. D., Portnoy, S., et al. (2007). The competency movement within psychology: An historical perspective. *Professional Psychology: Research and Practice, 38,* 452–462.

Sengupta, S. (2006). I/me/mine: Intersectional identities as negotiated minefields. *Signs: Journal of Women in Culture & Society, 31*(3), 629–639.

Sherry, A., Whilde, M. R., & Patton, J. (2005). Gay, lesbian, and bisexual training competencies in American Psychological Association accredited graduate programs. *Psychotherapy: Teaching, Research, Practice, and Training, 42*(1), 116–120.

Smart, J. F., & Smart, D. W. (2006). Models of disability: Implications for the counseling profession. *Journal of Counseling and Development, 85,* 20–40.

Smith, H. (2007). Psychological services needs of older women. *Psychological Services, 4,* 277–286.

Smith, L., Constantine, M., Graham, S., & Dize, C. (2008). The territory ahead for multicultural competence: The "spinning" of racism. *Professional Psychology: Research and Practice, 39,* 337–345.

Smith, T. B., Constantine, M. G., Dunn, T., Dinehart, J. M. & Montoya, J. A. (2006). Multicultural education in the mental health professions: A meta-analytic review. *Journal of Counseling Psychology, 53,* 132–145.

Stoltenberg, C. (2005). Enhancing professional competence through developmental approaches to supervision. *American Psychologist, 60,* 857–864.

Stoltenberg, C., Pace, T. M., Kashubeck-West, S., Biever, J. L., Patterson, T., & Welch, I. D. (2000). Training models in counseling psychology: Scientist-practitioner versus practitioner-scholar. *The Counseling Psychologist, 28,* 622–640.

Sue, D., & Sue, D. M. (2007). *Foundations of counseling and psychotherapy: Evidence-based practices for a diverse society.* Hoboken, NJ: Wiley.

Sue, D. W., Arredondo, P., & McDavis, R. J. (1992). Multicultural counseling competencies and standards: A call to the profession. *Journal of Counseling and Development, 70,* 477–483.

Sue, D. W., Bernier, J. B., Durran, M., Feinberg, L., Pederson, P., Smith, E., et al. (1982). Position paper: Cross-cultural counseling competencies. *The Counseling Psychologist, 10,* 45–52.

Sue, D. W., Capodilupo, C., & Holder, A. (2008). Racial microaggressions in the life experiences of Black Americans. *Professional Psychology: Research and Practice, 39*(3), 329–336.

Sue, D. W., Carter, R. T., Casas, J. M., Fouad, N. A., Ivey, A. E., Jensen, M., et al. (1998). *Multicultural counseling competencies: Individual and organizational development.* Thousand Oaks, CA: Sage.

Sue, D. W., Capodilupo, C., Torino, G., Bucceri, J., Holder, A., Nadal, K., et al. (2007). Racial micro-aggressions in everyday life: Implications for clinical practice. *American Psychologist, 62,* 271–286.

Sue, D. W. & Sue, D. (1990). *Counseling the culturally different: Theory and practice.* New York: Wiley.

Sue, D. W., & Sue, D. (1999). *Counseling the culturally diverse: Theory and practice* (3rd ed.). New York: Wiley.

Sue, D. W., & Sue, D. (2008). *Counseling the culturally diverse: Theory and practice* (5th ed.). Hoboken, NJ: Wiley.

Thomas, K. R., & Weinrach, S. G. (2004). Mental health counseling and the AMCD multicultural counseling competencies: A civil debate. *Journal of Mental Health Counseling, 26*(1), 41–43.

Turner, A. (2009, November 5). Election 2008; Historic first; fulfillment of a dream; for some, Obama's victory signals a move toward equality and a dramatic change in attitudes toward race in America. *The Houston Chronicle,* p. B1. Available at: http://www.chron.com/disp/story.mpl/chronicle/6095679.html

U.S. Department of Health and Human Services. (2001). *Mental health: Culture, race, and ethnicity—A supplement to mental health: A report of the Surgeon General.* Rockville, MD: U.S. Department of Health and Human Services, Public Health Office, Office of the Surgeon General.

Vereen, L. G., Hill, N. R., & McNeal, D. T. (2008). Perceptions of multicultural counseling competencies: Integration of the curricular and the practical. *Journal of Mental Health Counseling, 30* (3), 226–230.

Vontress, C. E., & Jackson, M. L. (2004). Reactions to the multicultural counseling competencies debate. *Journal of Mental Health Counseling, 26*(1), 74–80.

Webster's eleventh new collegiate dictionary (3rd ed.) (2005). Boston/New York: Houghton Mifflin.

Weinrach, S.G., & Thomas, K.R. (2002). A critical analysis of the multicultural counseling competencies: Implications for the practice of mental health counseling. *Journal of Mental Health Counseling, 24,* 20–35.

Worthington, R. L., Soth-McNett, A. M., Moreno, M. V. (2007). Multicultural counseling competencies research: A 20-year content analysis. *Journal of Counseling Psychology, 54*(4), 351–361.

CHAPTER 2

THE COMPETENT TREATMENT OF THE DIVERSE OLDER ADULT

CARMEN INOA VAZQUEZ

INTRODUCTION

The definition of the *diverse older adult* encompasses aspects of the general description of aging, and additional specific categories that relate to diversity, and includes issues of identity, gender, spirituality or religious affiliation, social class, race or ethnicity, place of residence (e.g., whether urban or rural), health status, and sexual orientation (American Psychological Association, 2004; Angel & Hogan, 2004; Levant, 2005; Mehrotra & Wagner, 2009; D. W. Sue & D. Sue, 2003). This list is by no means exclusive, but serves to highlight the broad range of diversity that exists among the U.S. older adult population. This is a list that is, by all accounts, a growing one. Different sources inform us that the population of the United States will be more racially and ethnically diverse, as well as much older, by mid-century (Federal Interagency Forum on Aging Related Statistics, 2004; Harris, 1998; Mehrotra & Wagner, 2009; National Institute on Aging 2006; U.S. Census, 2008; Weinberger, 2007). It is important to note that the first Baby Boomers will reach age 65 in 2011, while the last of the baby-boom population will reach age 65 in the year 2029. This population is projected to double to 62 million by 2050. The Asian and Pacific Islander population is expected to reach 41 million by 2050, maintaining its status as the fastest-growing racial group. On the other hand, the projections of growth for the Latino/Hispanic-origin population indicate an increase of 39 percent from 2000 to 2010, 45 percent from 2010 to 2030, and 60 percent from 2030 to 2050. (In this chapter, the terms *Hispanic* and *Latino* are used interchangeably.) It is also reported that the elderly are the fastest-growing group among Latino/Hispanics, with a population growing at a faster rate than that among African Americans and a projected population of 12 million by 2050 (Angel & Hogan, 2004).

These changes are due in part to the increased longevity of the U.S. population. The Centers for Disease Control and Prevention (CDC) National Center for Health Statistics (2008) reports an impressive growth in the average life span in the United States overall. Between 2003 and 2004, life expectancy increased for males and females, and for both the White and African American populations. Life expectancy increased by 0.5 years (from 72.6 to 73.1) for African American individuals, and by 0.4 year (from 77.9 to 78.3) for White individuals. Both males and females in each racial group experienced increases in life expectancy between 2003 and 2004. The greatest increase was experienced by African American males, with a gain of 0.6 year (from 68.9 to 69.5). Life expectancy increased by 0.4 year for African American females (from 75.9 to 76.3), for White females (from 80.4 to 80.8), and for White males (from 75.3 to 75.7).

With the expectation of such a broad representation of life expectancy in the relatively near future, the provision of appropriate and competent treatment to diverse older populations is not only challenging but requires an understanding of the concept of "diversity" as it relates to the older adult. This understanding begins with a comparison of those who have historically been regarded as "typical" older adults in North American society and the growing populations of diverse older adults in this country.

The purpose of this chapter is to provide mental health-care providers, students, trainers, and trainees with a reference point that will guide them in the competent treatment of diverse older individuals. Guidelines and existing resources focused on relevant and specific aspects of the aging process as it relates to diversity will be explored. The chapter includes the basic information necessary for understanding differences and similarities between diverse and less diverse clients, and incorporating this understanding into the effective provision of services in the areas of assessment, intervention, consultation, training, social welfare, assisted living, general health, and long-term care. Key themes will be developed in each of these areas, for example, the importance of and challenges related to the incorporation of family members within the treatment context, with an understanding of cultural changes that may have developed unevenly among family members. Clinicians will be provided with resources offering guidance in terms of attitudes and general knowledge of the diverse older adult, as well as the specifics of aging. The need to consult with other professionals and the specifics of training to provide culturally competent services will also be emphasized (Barrio et al., 2003; Department of Health and Human Services [DHHS], 2003; Harris, 1998; National Center for Health Statistics, 2009).

DEFINITIONS OF THE DIVERSE OLDER ADULT

Briefly, *diversity* (widely defined throughout this book) refers to the vast range of human experience related to differences shared by a group of people that affect how they are treated by members from other groups as well as by members of their own group (R. J. Angel & J. L. Angel, 2006; Angel & Hogan, 2004; He, Sengupta, Velkoff, & DeBarros, 2005; Mehrotra & Wagner, 2009).

Aging or *senescence* is a term derived from the Latin word *senex*, which translates into old or advanced age (Eyetsemitan, 2007). Old age entails changes that are both biological and physical and have been categorized into primary and secondary aging. *Primary aging* includes the universal and unavoidable physical changes associated with old age; *secondary aging* directly relates to the changes resulting from the individual's sociocultural environment and varies according to the cultural and social interpretation of the process. These definitions frame an understanding of the aging process in the *diverse older adult* that includes physical declines affecting health and overall wellbeing, and specific cultural and social perceptions of aging (Westerhof, Katzko, Dittmann-Kohli, & Hayslip, 2001; Whitbourne, 1985).

The diverse older adult shares similarities with older adults in general, and these can include characteristics experienced by individuals at any age (Abeles et al., 1998; Butler, Lewis, & Sunderland, 1991). These shared characteristics range

from adaptational problems resulting from a serious illness or encountering a disability status to work-related issues, retirement, and per-sonal responses to the many stressors faced by individuals in their daily lives, along with many others. While some aspects of aging can vary in either intensity or manifestation, it is also true that the diverse older population has specific characteristics that are predicated on gender, marital status, living arrangements, trauma history (experienced by self or family members), participation in the labor force and retirement, values, acculturation, language, socio-economic status (SES), education, and literacy. Fluctuation in literacy and reading levels are bound to place the older adult from a diverse background at a disadvantage (Gazmararian et al., 1999; Robinson, Novelli, Pearson, & Norris, 2007). These characteristics exist within a wide range of differences among and between diverse groups. However, it should be understood that problems such as health care, poverty, and inadequate housing are both exacerbated by being older and experienced differentially based on ethnicity, race, and gender. Socioeconomic issues place minority women, for example, at a disadvantage that can manifest itself in the inability to maintain good health, forcing women who are unable to physically continue working into earlier "retirement" than desired, if this option exists, or into chronic unemployment and poverty, if it does not (Angel & Whitfield, 2007; Flippen, 2005; Hayward, Crimmins, Miles, & Yu, 2000; Hayward, Warner, & Crimmins, 2007; Kelley-Moore & Ferraro, 2004; Smith & Kington, 1997; Warner & Hofmeister, 2006).

In terms of gender, according to the International Labour Office of the United Nations (2006), the older population is primarily female. A 2006 survey of Africa, Asia, Europe, Latin America, Northern America, and Oceania placed the population of women aged 60 or over at 378 million, versus 310 million for men. That equates to 1.2 women for each man in this age range in the most developed regions.

It is also known that acculturation, language, and literacy issues are more prevalent among older adults from a diverse background and can lead to important differences in the assessment, treatment, and provision of general services to this population (He, 2002; Kagitcibasi, 1997; Trans, 1990). The degree to which environmental factors impact acculturation may be increasingly fluid, becoming less pronounced as a result of the influence of the Western value system. Acculturation consists of three separate but potentially interactive dimensions: (1) the *Global Dimension*, which refers primarily to the biological components of aging and death; (2) the *Developed Dimension*, which relates to the Western value dominance described above and affects perception of aging and the elderly; and (3) the *Developing Dimension*, which incorporates cultural values and practice inherent to the inhabitants of specific areas. While these dimensions all affect the aging process, the Developing Dimension includes important aspects of the group in question, such as native medicine and spiritualism, local languages, education, different technological experiences, and *collectivism*, or a focus on the members of a society rather than the individual (Eyetsemitan, 2002).

Different groups will manifest different levels of acculturation, and it is not always clear in which category that specific individual or family member belongs. Although age of arrival in this country roughly translates into level of acculturation, in that the younger a person arrives in a new country, the more opportunity he or she has to adapt to it, a direct correlation of these events is not always present. This is the case because many immigrant groups travel back and forth to their countries of origin or can function within their communities without the need to have contact with members of the larger population. Consequently, the level of acculturation of an individual is not always easily recognized, as illustrated in Case Vignette 2.1. It should be noted that the names and specific circumstances of the individuals used in examples throughout this chapter have been changed to protect their identities.

In order to recommend appropriate services for Belinda, the clinician must have a thorough knowledge of Belinda's history, including an understanding that she is a diverse older adult who matured in a different cultural context. Belinda was born in Ethiopia, but lived in Manila from an early age to middle adulthood. The only language she learned was Filipino, her mother's primary language. Her history of immigration both in the Philippines and in the United States is relevant for test selection, administration, and norming, as well as for evaluation of her

CASE VIGNETTE 2.1

Belinda Martinaso has lived in New York City since she moved from Manila at the age of 39. She worked as a seamstress in a clothing company and put her two sons through college. Now 87 and a widow, she has been having fainting spells and has been referred for a neuropsychological evaluation. Belinda communicates in English poorly because her primary language is Filipino. For the 48 years she has lived in this country, she has socialized solely with family and a few friends. These friends have either died or moved to other areas with their own families, which causes Belinda to complain of isolation and depression. She was encouraged to become involved with a senior center in her neighborhood, but she refused.

language skills and to inform recommendations for services. If time spent in the Unites States is taken as a proxy for her level of acculturation, then it would be assumed that she has reached a level in her acculturation process that in reality she has not attained. Belinda has spent most of her life socializing almost exclusively with friends from the Philippines who speak Filipino. She lived in areas in which stores were owned by Filipinos, read a Filipino newspaper, and returned to Manila for 15 years after her children were grown. In fact, Belinda moved back to the United States only within the past 10 years. Thus, if Belinda were asked only when she *arrived* in the United States, any follow-up regarding these important issues would be missed. For example, to assume that there is something wrong cognitively with Belinda because she does not speak English (as most educated people in the Philippines speak both English and Filipino, the official languages of the Republic of the Philippines since the 1987 Constitution of the Philippines; see Lewis, 2009) would be to inaccurately understand her history of immigration. It is good practice not to make assumptions regarding the variables of a group, whether referring to SES, gender issues, language, or acculturation levels of individuals. For example, in terms of minorities, it is sometimes assumed that a greater number are poor than may be the case. According to the U.S. Census Bureau's Poverty Rates by Race for 2003 to 2005, approximately one-quarter of African Americans were living in poverty; this means three-quarters were presumably not (U.S. Census Bureau, 2006). Similarly, it cannot be assumed that older diverse adults living alone are represented in great numbers within the poverty level or are disabled, although the income of many older adults living by themselves may place them on the low end of the socioeconomic continuum. The level of education among diverse older adults is quite varied, which translates into different levels of income, life expectancy, and language literacy. These are important components when treating older adults who may have a range of needs and behavioral challenges, such as suggested changes in eating habits (Barrow,

1992; Williams, 2005). The variability among individuals indicates that it is very difficult to have a clear picture of the "diverse" older adult, and suggests that it is not possible to infer the characteristics of one group or another.

Assumptions about groups or race or any concept that falls under a stereotypical definition must be avoided, in particular when working with individuals who are different in terms of cultures, language, and values (Sue, 1998). One good approach to the assessment and treatment of diverse older adults is to ask the individual and/or family members directly about their views on health, treatment issues, and any other relevant factors. This practice may provide the clinician with useful information about the person being served and his or her specific cultural and familial context.

Knowledge

Mental health providers treating the diverse older adult must acquire a knowledge base that both overlaps with and transcends that generally required to obtain an accurate psychological assessment for the older adult population overall. This includes recognizing the physical and biological changes associated with the aging process, as well as individuals' adaptations in psychological, social, and cultural arenas. Among these factors we find clinical problems uniquely related to late life, such as losses in the areas of familial and social attachment, familial overgeneralization, which assumes that certain groups form a close family niche automatically, loss of job, loss of friends, loss of health, isolation, depression, medication, and end-of-life issues (Lowenstein, Katz, & Gur-Yaish, 2007; Palinkas et al., 2006; Williams, Baker, & Allman, 2008).

These important factors require the understanding of a series of specific considerations that can vary within the diverse older adult population and can be affected by ethnicity and culture, such as health and behavior (Kelty et al., 2000). Many professionals understandably welcomed the 1992 American Psychological Association (APA) Guidelines for Psychological Practice with Older Adults, a set of scientifically informed recommendations that represent consensus among some members of the field of psychology on how best to help older adults from diverse backgrounds (APA, 2004). These suggestions are listed here:

Attitudes

Guideline 1: Psychologists are encouraged to work with older adults within their scope of competence, and to seek consultation or make appropriate referrals when indicated.

Guideline 2: Psychologists are encouraged to recognize how their attitudes and beliefs about aging and about older individuals may be relevant to their assessment and treatment of older adults, and to seek consultation or further education about these issues when indicated.

General Knowledge about Adult Development, Aging, and Older Adults

Guideline 3: Psychologists strive to gain knowledge about theory and research in aging.

Guideline 4: Psychologists strive to be aware of the social/psychological dynamics of the aging process.

Guideline 5: Psychologists strive to understand diversity in the aging process, particularly how sociocultural factors such as gender, ethnicity, socioeconomic status, sexual orientation, disability status, and urban/rural residence may influence the experience and expression of health and of psychological problems in later life.

Guideline 6: Psychologists strive to be familiar with current information about biological and health-related aspects of aging.

Clinical Issues

Guideline 7: Psychologists strive to be familiar with current knowledge about cognitive changes in older adults.

Guideline 8: Psychologists strive to understand problems in daily living among older adults.

Guideline 9: Psychologists strive to be knowledgeable about psychopathology within the aging population and cognizant of the prevalence and nature of that psychopathology when providing services to older adults.

Assessment

Guideline 10: Psychologists strive to be familiar with the theory, research, and practice of various methods of assessment with older adults, and knowledgeable of assessment instruments that are psychometrically suitable for use with them.

Guideline 11: Psychologists strive to understand the problems of using assessment instruments created for younger individuals when assessing older adults, and to develop skill in tailoring assessments to accommodate older adults' specific characteristics and contexts.

Guideline 12: Psychologists strive to develop skill at recognizing cognitive changes in older adults, and in conducting and interpreting cognitive screening and functional ability evaluations.

Intervention, Consultation, and Other Service Provision

Guideline 13: Psychologists strive to be familiar with the theory, research, and practice of various methods of intervention with older adults, particularly with current research evidence about their efficacy with this age group.

Guideline 14: Psychologists strive to be familiar with and develop skill in applying specific psychotherapeutic interventions and environmental modifications with older adults and their families, including adapting interventions for use with this age group.

(continued)

(*continued*)

Guideline 15: Psychologists strive to understand the issues pertaining to the provision of services in the specific settings in which older adults are typically located or encountered.

Guideline 16: Psychologists strive to recognize issues related to the provision of prevention and health promotion services with older adults.

Guideline 17: Psychologists strive to understand issues pertaining to the provision of consultation services in assisting older adults.

Guideline 18: In working with older adults, psychologists are encouraged to understand the importance of interfacing with other disciplines, and to make referrals to other disciplines and/or to work with them in collaborative teams and across a range of sites, as appropriate.

Guideline 19: Psychologists strive to understand the special ethical and/or legal issues entailed in providing services to older adults.

Education

Guideline 20: Psychologists are encouraged to increase their knowledge, understanding, and skills with respect to working with older adults through continuing education, training, supervision, and consultation.

Source: American Psychological Association (2004).

While the guidelines are not standards of treatment, they offer a helpful framework for clinicians providing mental health services to the older population in general.

It should be noted that these guidelines are expected to be revised in 2010. The awareness that few psychologists receive formal training in the psychology of aging requires the development of a set of goals that will guide clinicians working with elderly adults in a variety of settings. The guidelines emphasize the importance of understanding that competent clinical work with the older adult includes knowledge of developmental issues specific to late life, generational perspectives and preferences, physical illnesses that may change behavior and outlook on life (and which may require using multiple medications), cognitive and sensory impairments, and the existence of previous medical or mental disorders. Similarly, it is also recommended that clinicians consider consultation with other professionals sharing the same culture or group of reference in their work with the diverse older adult. Working with a diverse older population presents challenges that require acquiring knowledge in general aspects of the culture along with the individual's values, language, and educational

issues, socioeconomic levels, health and religious beliefs, and personal history, behaviors, and customs.

It is not possible for any clinician to have an exhaustive knowledge of all cultures and the factors unique to each, but it is very important to recognize that there are differences among groups in terms of values, beliefs, and the application of both. Rather than seeing the learning process as overwhelming, it is recommended that clinicians aim to attain a basic level of cultural competence through readings, training, supervision, and consultation. In this regard, APA's Guidelines on Multicultural Education, Training, Research, Practice, and Organizational Change for Psychologists (2003) can also serve as a guide for the practicing clinician serving a diverse population. In addition, the Veteran's Administration Technical Advisory Group in Geropsychology (TAGG) has developed recommendations that refer to the knowledge and skills required of psychologists working with older adults (Molinary et al., 2003).

Using the APA guidelines listed earlier can help interested clinicians in their treatment of older adults in general; the focus of the remainder of this chapter, however, will be an exploration of Guideline 5, which reads:

Psychologists strive to understand diversity in the aging process, particularly how sociocultural factors such as gender, ethnicity, socioeconomic status, sexual orientation, disability status, and urban/rural residence may influence the experience and expression of health and of psychosocial problems in later life. (APA, 2004, p. 237)

Notice that Guideline 5 does not refer to the importance of issues such as immigration, acculturation, language, and culture-specific values. Despite these omissions, these concepts must be included in the assessment, diagnosis, and treatment of the diverse older adult.

SKILLS

Assessment and Diagnosis

The treatment of the older adult in mental health services begins with a thorough assessment that should include place of birth, history of immigration, and cultural or self-identification, including but not limited to ethnic, racial, and gender-related concepts. The process of differential diagnosis should address the multiple problems typical of many older adults, including emotional distress, cognitive impairment, chronic physical conditions, and changes in environment or social network; these constitute important parts of the assessment of the diverse older adult, as well (Gatz & Knight, 1998). In general, the assessment of individuals from other cultures is a balancing act for the clinician. He or she should not miss any culturally relevant information, but must simultaneously understand that not all diverse older adults are traditional or hold similar values, and that groups such as Latin Americans, Asian/Pacific Islanders (APIs), and others are very diversified.

The reader can refer to the Resources section at the end of this chapter and other references throughout this book to consult and expand on specific and relevant topics. A few key topics have been highlighted here:

Health Beliefs—The assessment/diagnosis of the diverse older adult requires an understanding and inclusion of the individual's belief about the causes, cures and prevention of illnesses. This will be helpful both in the assessment and diagnosis of the presenting problem, as well as in the treatment that may follow a diagnosis and the expected adherence to a treatment regime. As an illustration, the concept of Ayurvedic Medicine refers to a healing system that originated in India and may include using herbs as a treatment (Panganamala & Plummer, 1998). Similar practices exist in many other countries. The following example (Case Vignette 2.2) illustrates the importance of knowledge of behaviors and customs when working with older adults from a diverse background around issues of health.

Case Vignette 2.2 shows that mental health practitioners evaluating older adults must routinely ask clients from regions of Asia and other countries in which herbs are commonly used as treatments, whether they are using these or other types of medications. Obviously, this requires that the clinician first establish a connection of trust and open communication with the individual seeking treatment. In order to establish this communication there must be a basic knowledge of the behaviors and linguistic characteristics

CASE VIGNETTE 2.2

Simin Wong, 67, sought treatment at a clinic in a major hospital. Her presenting symptoms included stomach discomfort, disorientation, forgetfulness, anxiety, and depression. The approach used during the intake evaluation included asking Simin whether she was taking any herbs. The response was positive and the clinician referred her immediately for blood work, which indicated she had high levels of lead in her body. Knowledge of cultural behaviors that include taking alternative herbs, creams, and other self-treatment methods alerted the clinician to seek further, rather than assuming Simin had a mood disorder.

that correspond to the specific culture in question. In this regard, understanding the normative associations of behavior within a particular group can be helpful. Again, however, this understanding is to be tempered with a recognition that not all individuals will conform to cultural group expectations.

Culture and Language. Culture and language are also essential components of the assessment and diagnosis of the diverse older adult. Cultural values such as beliefs in the afterlife are held by most elderly from traditional cultures who believe in spiritually preparing the soul for life after death. Speaking about death can relate to a philosophical, rather than depressive, perspective. Many elderly people prepare for events following their deaths by making funeral arrangements, selecting burial clothing, choosing a coffin, and so forth, as a way of "being ready." These values can again present a challenge to the clinician who is trying to ascertain whether the elderly person is speaking from a cultural and spiritual position, as opposed to expressing the effects of depression. In cases like this, it is always recommended to consult with relatives or with an expert from the group in question. Cultural beliefs can interfere with the assessment of a mental condition; for example, some elderly individuals see mental illness as possible possession of the "evil eye" (Kalavar, 1999). Understanding these beliefs can help the individual, the family, and the mental health practitioner in the formulation of a diagnosis and in conducting a full assessment.

Another challenge facing the clinician working with the diverse older adult is that, in many cultures, mental illness is considered a source of shame. This might require an approach that is respectful in explaining in a culturally sensitive manner the reason for visiting a clinic or for administering a battery of tests. Mental health practitioners should recognize that the diverse older adult may feel very uncomfortable with certain questions, such as asking about suicidal ideation or thoughts. The diverse older adult may also present symptoms in ways not familiar to clinicians from other backgrounds. For example, diverse patients may not present with a classic picture of depression, instead presenting a constellation of somatic complaints such as headaches and muscle or stomach pain. In these instances, the observation of nonverbal behavior is very helpful to the clinician in the formulation of an appropriate diagnosis. It is suggested that the clinician monitor the mannerisms and intonations on the part of the diverse older adult (Kalavar, 1999).

Effective assessment of these clients may involve the patient, the family, and the mental health practitioner, along with others as needed. In addition, the problem as presented by the patient might require a specific understanding of the role of culture, language, and literacy. The presentation of somatic complaints could mean a true physical condition, for example, but such symptoms could also represent a socially recognized signal of illness or a culturally sanctioned way of revealing psychological problems. The reverse could also be true, in that a patient may initially present psychological problems in such a manner that they are missed by the clinician. This could include behaviors of compliance, such as saying what they think therapists want to hear—or not saying what they think therapists do *not* want to hear, which may include the stoic avoidance of admission of pain (Ibrahim, Burant, Mercer, Siminoff, & Kwoh, 2003). I have found the technique called The Netting Effect on Assessment proposed by Wen-Shing Tseng (2001) to be very useful. This technique can be best described as "fishing with a net": Ask the patient as much as possible (in other words, "fish" for information), with the understanding that, the wider the net, the more you get and the bigger the fish.

Cultural differences between the mental health practitioner and the patient raise the stakes around administering a neuropsychological examination in an informed, effective way. Misdiagnosis and misinterpretation can be present, for example, when the clinician is seeking a neuropsychological examination to rule out dementia or other memory problems. In these cases, it is important to screen older adults from diverse backgrounds for English-language difficulties (please see Chapter 6 for more information on this topic), literacy skills, and educational attainment. The main purpose of the neuropsychological evaluation in these situations is to evaluate the presence or absence of cognitive abnormalities, assess a decline in functioning or severity of dementia, or assist in determining appropriate rehabilitation techniques, placement options, and treatment protocols. But when the assessment involves an adult from a diverse background, it is very important to understand the culture of the individual, including linguistic factors, family values, and educational experience (Irvine & Berry 1988; Mungas, Marshall, Weldon, Haan, & Reed, 1996).

Given that there are limited instruments for the appropriate assessment of the older adult from a diverse background, the clinician must be cognizant of these important variables; otherwise, the possibility exists that normal aging processes or cultural and linguistic variables could make average performance seem deficient and lead to an inaccurate diagnosis (Perez-Arce & Puente, 1996; Schaie, 1994). The use of nonverbal tests does not fully address this concern, because the possibility of a cultural bias can still exist (Jacobs et al., 1997; Loewenstein, Arguelles, Barker, & Duara, 1993; Lopez & Taussig, 1991). Translating a test into the language of the individual who does not speak English is not the answer, either, as there must be specific awareness of the relevant cultural concepts of the language in question (Ardila, 1995).

Many diverse older adults may not speak English and may need a health-care interpreter. Use of an appropriately trained interpreter is recommended to obtain an accurate picture of the individual being assessed and to establish good therapeutic rapport (Derose & Baker, 2000; Ginsberg, Martin, Andrulis, Shaw-Taylor, & McGregor, 1995; Jacobs et al., 2004; Marcos, 1979; Solis, Marks, Garcia, & Shelton, 1990; Vazquez & Javier, 1991; Woloshin, Bickell, Schwartz, Gany, & Welch, 1995).

In summary, it is best to take a broad approach similar to the Netting Effect proposed by Wen-Shin Tseng (2001) and previously mentioned within this chapter during the assessment process, which includes a thorough evaluation of the individual's health values and beliefs, family issues, SES, eating habits, medication, immigration history, and level of acculturation. Mental health practitioners should also ask clients about the state of their health, their attitudes and values around end-of-life issues, notable changes in family relations, and concerns regarding the loss of friends and jobs. In addition, the clinician should assess the client's levels of isolation and depression and follow up with questions related to any other diagnostically relevant factors. It is often helpful to begin the interview with a social interchange, such as:

- How would you like me to address you? [*Make the person feel comfortable by waiting patiently for a response.*]
- Tell me what brings you here today. [*Validate his or her feelings. Sometimes older adults complain about pain and old age not being so golden. Support for presented losses or life changes can often be provided just by listening or giving a look of understanding.*]

The individual's response to these overtures will give the mental health practitioner an idea of what types of interpersonal skills may be the most effective in working with the client. For example, it may be helpful to be more engaging when encountering a traditional older adult who feels disloyal discussing family issues outside of the family context. Expressing feelings of being rejected or put aside can likewise be a source of confusion, anxiety, and shame to many older individuals. It is also important to assess the existence of self-neglect and abuse since these are issues of concern for the elderly population (Filippo, Reiboldt, White, & Hails, 2007).

Interventions

While this type of work shares some components with work focused on younger adults in general, it also involves recognizing specific issues commonly associated with older adult populations, such as dementia and comorbidity, and may involve rendering opinions on functional abilities and the need for placement or institutional care (Knight, Hinrichsen, Qualls, & Duffy, 2009). There are also differences in the manner conditions such as depression, anxiety, alcohol abuse, psychosis, and personality disorders present in the older adult (Alexopoulos et al., 2002; Sheikh, 2005; Sorocco & Ferrell, 2006).

Chronic medical conditions are not the sole domain of the older adult, of course, but the abundance of these conditions in later life requires a nuanced understanding of the interaction of physical and psychological experiences. This understanding must also often incorporate knowledge of the effects of medication on clients at both a physical and a psychological level. Mental health practitioners can begin the process of gaining expertise in these areas through readings and training in the health psychology of late-life medical disorders (Aldwin, Park, & Spiro, 2007; Frazer, 1995; Haley, 1996) and the effects of medical and psychological conditions on functional ability in older adults (Knight et al., 2009).

Another specific component of work with older adults focuses on the interface between clinicians and various significant systems within the adult's life. These may include family, residential facilities such as nursing homes and assisted-living facilities (and/or planning for these types of placements), health care, and community providers serving older adults. Meeting these needs often requires direct interactions on the part of the clinician with the individual family and staff members involved (Hyer & Intrieri, 2006; Lichtenberg et al., 1998; Molinari, 2000; Rosowski, Casciani, & Arnold, 2008).

Different levels of acculturation attained by members of a family can be misunderstood by the older adult and may need explanation, the involvement of different family members, and the incorporation of workable solutions for those concerned. In these situations, involving the family members can be helpful, as in Case Vignette 2.3.

CASE VIGNETTE 2.3

Doña Juanita, a 75-year-old Costa Rican woman, was suffering from late-onset diabetes and felt that, despite her age, it was totally unfair that her health was so poor. She had come from Costa Rica to live with her only son and his family, and the most difficult aspect of her illness was not being given the attention that she would have received back home. Her daughter-in-law, who was North American, was as sensitive as she could be, but there were many cultural differences with which both she and her mother-in-law had to come to terms. Doña Rosita, for example, covered all the mirrors whenever it rained because she had been taught to believe that mirrors attract lightning. She also wanted to "sanitize" the eggs by washing the shells when she took them out of the carton, and all food had to be cooked extensively in order to kill the germs.

She couldn't understand why her family was "too busy" to tend to her. Even when she tried to help with cooking or sewing, what she produced was not to her grandchildren's liking. The only thing she herself truly enjoyed was eating; because of her condition, however, she could no longer eat the sweet things she loved most, such as the delicious custard called dulce de leche (made with boiled milk and sugar) and her childhood favorite, melcocha (made from raw sugar). Not only was she in despair, but she was also making life extremely difficult for her son, who had to listen to all her complaints about her plight, her poor health, and her uncaring grandchildren, in addition to his wife's expressions of frustration about the situation.

Involving all the family members, including the daughter-in-law from another culture and the grandchildren, was very helpful in the treatment of Doña Juanita. Her son was advised to inform his wife about Doña Juanita's cultural customs, and the daughter-in-law was grateful to understand her mother-in-law's cultural values and beliefs. In order to ameliorate Doña Juanita's isolation, it was recommended that she participate in a church group at which she could meet others her age. She was also provided with information on how to make her favorite dessert with a tasty sugar substitute for herself and the church group. The grandchildren were also able to see a different picture, which afforded better quality of communication with their grandmother.

Research

Research is an important component of competent treatment of the diverse older adult. As Mehrotra and Wagner (2009) note, "research helps us understand human behavior and this understanding, in turn, suggests ways to improve people's lives" (p. 33). There is, however, a scarcity of research describing the quality of care offered to a growing, diverse older adult population (Mehrotra & Wagner, 2009). This is puzzling when we look at the significant changes projected by the Census 2000. Research informs us about the significance of ethnic differences among diverse older adults, for example, in terms of a wide range of utilization issues, including assessment, treatment, and the equitable allocation of supportive services (Aday, Andersen, & Fleming, 1980; Aday, Fleming, & Andersen, 1984).

One significant component of research literacy is a better understanding of how cultural values inform concepts that can affect the services being provided. This is because certain behaviors, beliefs, or practices do not equally translate across cultures (Teresi, Stewart, Morales & Stahl, 2006). People's perceptions of the world are based largely on their cultural upbringings, and individuals from different backgrounds may process information differently. For example, elders who grew up in Asian cultures might process information more holistically (Nisbett & Masuda, 2003). In light of these complexities, many relevant issues need additional exploration and clarification, such as identifying the proper tools to evaluate the true cognitive decline of the older adult from a diverse background. The utilization of suitable interpreters and appropriate translation methods will help the clinician to get a clearer picture of appropriate placement options, with less risk of over- or under-pathologizing clients based on inter- or intra-cultural miscues. This is important, because it cannot be assumed that cohorts share characteristics based on their national and ethnic status without determining related causes (Kagitcibasi, 1979). Variables such as education, place of residence (e.g., rural or urban), income, values, and type of employment can vary across groups. For example, data suggest that an elderly Latino individual is more likely to have grown up in another culture and to have completed fewer than eight years of formal education—potentially significant variables in assessing functioning among members of this population (Crum, Anthony, Bassett, & Folstein, 1993; Mouton & Esparza, 2001; Mouton, Johnson, & Cole 1995; Mungas et al., 1996). The lack of clear guidelines and information regarding clinical characteristics within the diverse older adult population underscores the need to develop instruments that will help clinicians perform assessments for diagnoses such as depression in a competent manner (Golding & Aneshensel, 1989; Golding, Aneshensel, & Hough, 1991; Radloff, 1977). More research is also needed in the area of fear of dependence or expectations of familial support, particularly when assessing the suitability of placement for the older adult.

Researchers at the University of California at San Francisco (UCSF) have reported findings on the benefits of physical activities for the older adult and the need to adapt research in accordance with the population at hand. One of these projects, The Community Healthy Activities Model Program for Seniors (CHAMPS) (UCSF, 2004), found that using the telephone was an effective method to obtain quantitative survey data. CHAMPS is a public health model program conducted by UCSF Institute for Health & Aging that encourages physical activity appropriate for different health needs. Two different research projects (CHAMPS I and II) form the bases for this program. The results of these research projects have led to the development of a model program (CHAMP III), which is geared to reach minorities to benefit from physical activities (mostly Latino and African American), as well as lower-income, elderly individuals.

Ethical Considerations in Research with Diverse Older Adults

When obtaining informed consent for research involving members of the diverse older adult population, it is critical that investigators demonstrate flexibility and sensitivity to level of acculturation. Likewise, differences in levels of acculturation and language skills among participants from diverse backgrounds require the adaptation and appropriate translation of instruments. This may mandate the inclusion of content suitable for and meaningful to the participant's culture. Stewart and Napoles-Springer (2000) recommend the use of focus groups as a way of developing concepts that can be relevant in multiple languages and with different cultural groups.

Research-Based Interventions

Various research- and practice-based therapeutic approaches recognize the importance of cultural context (Knight, 2003). Effective interventions tend to reflect three major concepts: congruence (or genuineness), unconditional positive regard, and empathy (Burns, 2008). Specific techniques such as reminiscence, reflective listening, validation, support, and guidance have been found to be useful with the diverse older adult population. Reminiscence therapy, for example, has been found to be successful in decreasing depression among institutionalized, rural-dwelling elderly individuals. This technique has also proven to be effective in the early stages of dementia and in dealing with adaptation following loss and other painful experiences (Kunz, 1991, 2002; Kunz & Florence, 2007). Music therapy and looking at pictures from magazines can be very useful for residents of facilities in the process of reminiscence (Burns, 2008). Cognitive-behavioral, brief psychodynamic, interpersonal psychotherapeutic, and psychoeducational approaches have similarly been found to be effective with diverse older adults and members of their families. The inclusion of alternative therapies such as meditation, massage, and aromatherapy, in conjunction with other forms of treatment, has also proven helpful.

Research findings on the cognitive effects of aging remain mixed, with some documented declines in areas such as speed of mental processes, working memory, and capacity to inhibit irrelevant information while other cognitive abilities appear less severely affected as a result of the natural aging process. Effective interventions are being developed to assist older adults struggling with cognitive deficits or declines such as cognitive training. Cognitive skills have been found to improve with exercises that are often used in cognitive training, such as crossword puzzles; these types of activities also appear to have a rehabilitative effect following strokes or other brain injuries. Cognitive training is designed to improve functioning in specific cognitive areas. Although cognitive training has proliferated in recent years and has been applied to all ages, there is a need to demonstrate its effectiveness. Sherry Willis and colleagues (2006) conducted the first multi-site, randomized control study entitled the Advance Cognitive Training for Independence and Vital Elderly (ACTIVE). This research project looked at the effects of cognitive training on specific cognitive functions, including verbal episodic memory, inductive reasoning, and speed of processing. Positive findings on the effectiveness of cognitive training were reported, including specific improved abilities among older adults maintained through five years. However, the main question of the study—which asked whether evidenced improvement would generalize to everyday living and prevent aging-related declines—was not supported, and the need to conduct similar research efforts with the diverse older population remains (Mehrotra & Wagner, 2009). The mental health practitioner seeking information about the diverse older adult can refer to a database of research publications containing information on existing studies and specifics on how to conduct research with this population. Such sites include PubMed, a service of the U.S. National Library of Medicine with over 17 million citations from MEDLINE and other journals, which can be accessed at www. pubmed.gov. PsyINFO, the online database of psychological research, can be accessed through most university libraries or privately at http://www.apa.org/psycinfo. The Centers for Disease Control (CDC) provides a Web site with information on healthy aging, along with health statistics and research. The CDC Web site is http://www.cdcgov/aging.

TRAINING AND SUPERVISION

Training Skills

In the course of their daily practices, most mental health practitioners will encounter the need to evaluate and treat members of the growing population of older adults from a diverse background (Devries & Ogland-Hand, 2007; Janson & Mueller, 1983). Yet only a small number of these clinicians believe that their academic or clinical training has adequately prepared them to provide these services in a competent manner, with the necessary understanding of ethnic differences essential for the rendering of accurate diagnosis and treatment (Sakauye, 1996).

The main challenge faced by mental health practitioners is the provision of services and the rendering of opinions and recommendations within their scope of professional competence.

Graduate programs and internships have increased focus on the treatment of older adults in general, but this work continues to be challenging for most clinicians, given the variability and complexity of the issues presented and because there is no comprehensive model of training to prepare clinicians to serve older adults (Knight et al., 2009). Several training models have been proposed or are in development, however, and two of these are explored in greater detail in the following.

Ethnogeriatrics: Treatment Plan Specifics for Older Adults

As regards the diverse older adult, a curriculum in *ethnogeriatrics* designed to serve as a generic model was created by members of the Collaborative of Ethnogeriatric Education with the support of the Bureau of Health Professions, Health Resources and Services Administration in 1999 and 2000 at Stanford School of Medicine (Yeo, 2001). A group of faculty from 31 Geriatric Education Centers throughout the United States, serving as regional resource centers for geriatric education for multiple health-care disciplines, revised the curriculum.

The program offers a series of modules with ethnic-specific information included as examples of the concepts. At the moment there are five modules of training being applied at Stanford Education Center at Stanford University School of Medicine. The ethno-specific modules cover specific groups representing older adults from diverse backgrounds, including African Americans, American Indians/Alaska Natives, Hispanic/Latino, Asian/Pacific Islander, Asian Indian, Chinese, Filipino, Japanese, Korean, Native Hawaiian/PI, Pakistani, and Southeast Asian. Each module can be used separately, but the authors recommend inclusion of all modules if at all possible. A few of the suggestions for culturally appropriate geriatric care are outlined here (Yeo, 2001):

- Older persons should be addressed by their last name by the denomination of Mrs., Señora,

Mr., or Señor, or another that corresponds to the culture in question.

- It is important to show an accepting and patient attitude.
- It is important to include family members and to value their input.
- Include the individual in treatment planning and decision making, whenever possible.
- Inquire as to what is the most worrying thing about the client's illness and what is most on his or her mind.
- Find out what the individual thinks of his or her illness.

The complete curriculum can be found online at: http://www.stanford.edu/group/ethnoger.

The Pikes Peak Model: Competencies for Training

Another model of training geared to the work with the older adult is the Pikes Peak Model for training in professional geropsychology, which proposes that specific training in geropsychology is not necessary for all psychologists who work with older adults (Knight et al., 2009). Although aspirational in nature, this model suggests the attainment of a competencies-based approach—that is, training clinicians by allowing entry points at multiple levels of professional development, including doctoral programs and internships, and through postdoctoral training.

The Pikes Peak model was guided by outcomes of the 2002 Competencies Conference: Future Directions in Education and Credentialing in Professional Psychology (Kaslow, 2004; Kaslow et al., 2004; Rodolfa et al., 2005) and is also based on the APA Guidelines for Psychological Practice with Older Adults (APA 2004). There is consensus in the field that there are limitations in the present models of training for most programs (Knight et al., 2009). The existing norm for training involves multiple programs at different levels, including graduate, internship, postdoctoral, and post licensure. The Pikes Peak Model for Training recognizes and requires the

inclusion of education, training, and credentialing within professional psychology and includes the categories of attitudes, general knowledge about adult development, aging and older adults, clinical issues, assessment, intervention, consultation and other service provision, and continuing education focusing on work with older adults, including the recognition of individual diversity (Knight et al., 2009)

Development of Competencies Across Levels of Training

The Pikes Peak Model for Training has identified six components of training considered essential in the training of a geropsychologist (Qualls, 2009):

1. Normal aging is taught so that students have a basis for understanding abnormal aging experiences.
2. Bona fide professional geropsychologists using observational methods are employed as supervisors in geropsychology training programs so that students can develop appropriate skills in working with older adults.
3. Training in geropsychology includes facilitated experiences to gain self-awareness about one's responses to aging that vary by health status (e.g., frail as well as healthy aging), cultural and individual identities (e.g., wealthy or poor, rural or urban, ethnic identity, gender identity, sexual orientation, religious identity, disability status), and also diverse historical cohort experiences.
4. Experiential professional training with older adults is provided across a variety of settings. Trainees need experience in diverse settings (e.g., nursing homes, assisted living, primary care medical practice, hospitals, clients' homes).
5. Interprofessional team training is an essential part of professional geropsychology training. Trainees must learn about the knowledge base, scope of practice, and distinct professional work styles of other disciplines.

6. The distinct ethical and legal issues and practice standards that are part of practice with older adults are included in professional geropsychology training programs. Examples include late-life decision making and functional capacities, advance care planning and surrogate decision making, communication with caregiving families in a manner that respects the confidentiality of the older client, and end-of-life care.

Supervision

According to Hinrichsen (2006), training for graduate students who provide assessment and treatment services to diverse older adults should ideally be incorporated into existing curricula and supervisory sessions. Effective supervision in this context requires guiding the supervisee as he or she works to attain competency in both intervention skills and understanding the impact of diversity on many aspects of the aging process. Special attention should be paid to sociocultural factors such as gender, ethnicity, socioeconomic status, immigration status, acculturation, sexual orientation, disability status, and urban/rural residence; as noted previously, these factors in particular may influence the expression of health and of psychological problems in later life. Additional factors include the client's cultural and linguistic context in general (as well as the cultural framework of the family), considerations related to the aging process, and aspects of ability status and losses as they relate to diversity issues.

As demands for mental health services among members of this population increase, supervisors must become better informed about the practical implications of ethnic differences in providing these services—in order to minimize patients dropping out of treatment prematurely, for example. Low utilization rates can be reduced by understanding the components of diversity. (Knight, Kaskie, Shurgot, & Dave, 2006). One of the main reasons patients leave treatment is misunderstanding of values, particularly for those in the older population who may be more fixed in their beliefs. It becomes challenging for clinicians working with older adults from diverse backgrounds when they are confronted with myriad different values and beliefs ranging from differing understandings of family and community roles (Kikuzawa, 2006) to disparate expressions of chronic pain (Ibrahim et al., 2003). Perception of aging also varies among different groups, based in part on influences of acculturation and generational perspectives (Filipo, Reiboldt, White, & Hails, 2007).

Supervisors and supervisees alike must be cognizant of the potential barriers that may complicate the process for the diverse older adult seeking treatment. These include linguistic and cultural barriers, including unfamiliarity with traditional health services on the part of the diverse older adult, and the perception of mental health services as a source of weakness and shame. In many cultures, the need for mental health services is seen as related to psychosis or to "being crazy." This may be particularly concerning to elderly individuals who may adhere to more traditional beliefs. In these cultures, the path to health includes family, friends, faith healers, herbalists, pastors, priests, or other religious heads and the primary physicians, but not mental health professionals.

Supervision of assessment and/or treatment with diverse older adults requires helping the supervisee to understand salient differences that can affect coping with changes occasioned by pain, illnesses, loneliness, physical limitations, and the cognitive changes associated with late life. While these changes exist in the general older population as well, supervisees working with diverse older clients need specific types of scientific, clinical, and cultural knowledge (discussed throughout this chapter) to assist in differentiating those that are part of the normal aging process and those that are not.

The role of the supervisor is, therefore, to guide the supervisee in integrating all aspects of the diverse older adult. In this respect, it is very useful to be familiar with the most recent findings in the field of general gerontology and to be well-versed in current research related specifically to the diverse older adult. New information regularly challenges existing perceptions about the aging process. For example, recent studies looking at the cognitive and psychosocial development of the functioning of the brain indicate that from age 60 to 80 both sides of the brain are used equally, suggesting the existence of a higher level of functioning in later adult years than was previously known (Cohen, 2005; Kunz & Florence, 2007). Lawrence-Lightfoot (2009) informs us of the significance of a distinct developmental stage that places the older adult in general in a very positive phase, a factor relevant to both assessment and treatment. These new findings can provide information that potentially reduces stereotypes about aging and presents factual and useful information that helps in the understanding of the older adult.

Framing the Issues in Supervision

There are many questions that can facilitate an enlightening dialogue between supervisors and supervisees, such as:

- What is the importance of dealing with loneliness?
- How can faith impact adjustment of the older adult?
- Is sexuality considered a taboo topic among some older adults? How is one to know?
- What are the different coping mechanisms that older adults from diverse backgrounds present to the clinician?
- What are the results of missing important variables that affect the mental health of the elderly?

Facilitating these types of conversations will also help the supervisee in his or her understanding of available options for coping with loneliness or in finding solutions to benefit diverse older adults. Supervisees must be guided to reflect on their own feelings about aging and diversity. An exploration into the supervisee's counter-transferential feelings regarding the diverse older adult can make a significant impact toward providing an effective

treatment that preserves the client's dignity, improving the likelihood that he or she will return to receive additional services.

However, these are not always easy conversations to have. Many trainees struggle with understanding losses and perceptions of end-of-life issues within the traditional values of a specific culture. Concepts such as the ability to adapt and to go on with one's life can be very difficult propositions for trainees, particularly at the beginning of their work with older adults. In some cultures, the value placed on what is expected of the individual—"social role identity"—carries significant weight in relation to how one reacts to a physical illness, for example. The evolving roles of family, community, and institution-based care require adaptation geared to understanding each group and setting as it applies to the individual client's context.

The reality is that it is not possible to have knowledge of all the cultural specifics, language needs, or values endorsed by older adults from diverse backgrounds as they face these types of issues and decisions. What *is* important is the understanding that differences exist both within and between groups. This level of understanding can assist clinicians in smoothing over certain conflicts resulting from different expectations among family members, some of whom may hold more or less traditional beliefs and values around, for example, nursing home placement (Butler & Lewis, 1982; Fitzgerald, Mullavey-O'Byrne, & Clemson, 2001; Henderson, 1992; Kosloski & Karner, 1999). Many families who adhere to traditional values find it very difficult to place an older relative in a nursing home. Treatment specifically geared to address cultural values that create guilt and disagreement among family members (who may be at different level of acculturation or may be from other cultures, but members of the family through marriage) could be helpful in such a situation.

As you will see in Case Vignette 2.4, an understanding of the cultural mandates that Ramona was facing allowed the mental health practitioner to approach the problem in a way that helped Ramona to feel understood and open to the idea

CASE VIGNETTE 2.4

Ramona Ranudo, a 65-year-old woman, came for an evaluation because her 90-year-old mother was suffering from Alzheimer's disease, and the responsibility of caring for her mother was falling on Ramona alone. Although her mother had other children, Ramona, as the only daughter, automatically became her mother's caregiver. However, the other siblings were willing to place their mother in a nursing home, likely the most sensible arrangement given that Ramona's health was very poor and it was not realistic or helpful to the mother to be cared for by her daughter. The other siblings were willing to help with the details.

of communicating with her siblings. The main work in this case was supporting Ramona's culturally mandated sense of herself as a dutiful daughter. The intervention consisted of providing a great deal of support and meeting with all of the siblings as a group based on the therapist's recognition that these cultural mandates were guiding Ramona's behavior. The use of empathic listening, exploratory inquiry, and clarifications based on cultural values and these unconscious determinants was applied and proved to be very useful to all the members of the family.

VALUES AND ATTITUDES

Kite and colleagues (2005) conducted a meta-analysis of over 100 studies and concluded that attitudes toward older adults in general were negative since there were more negative stereotypes toward older than younger adults. In fact, this "culture of youth" is exemplified in magazines, movies, greeting cards portraying growing old in a mocking way, and the media in general presenting white hair and wrinkles as negative stereotypes in particular for women. A study conducted by Clarke and Griffin (2008) examined how older women felt and responded to their experience of *ageism* (discrimination against older individuals) as it related to their physical appearances. Women between the ages of 50 and 70 years indicated that they felt they were fighting invisibility by using cosmetics and other methods that could diminish the appearance of aging. Ageism has been described as falling on the

continuum of oppression; as with categories such as sexism and racism, ageism involves individuals being rejected and humiliated based on status—in this case, the fact that they have lived past the age idealized by popular culture (Butler, 1975; Butler & Lewis, 1982). Among the misconceptions surrounding ageism is that of placing all older adults in the same category without recognizing diversity. That includes the tendency to define older adults as lonely, sick, depressed, rigid, and frail. These definitions represent myths (Hinrichsen, 2006). In fact, aside from the dementias, the prevalence of psychological disorders appears to be lower in older adults than in adults in general. Older adults for the most part have also developed higher degrees of resilience than their younger counterparts, and this translates into a lower prevalence rate of the development of new psychological disorders in old age (Gatz & Knight, 1998).

It is known that ageism is found in the workplace (see, e.g., Finkelstein, Burke, & Raju, 1995; McCann & Giles, 2002; Rosen & Jerdee, 1976). It is also present in health-care facilities (Caporael & Culbertson, 1986; DePaola, Neimeyer, Lupfer, & Fiedler, 1992). Although some individuals feel depressed and despondent when they retire, there is also evidence that many adapt to changes quite well (Lawrence-Lightfoot, 2009). We can see ageism in treatment facilities in which the cognitive capabilities of older individuals are misunderstood, and this can translate into disempowering the older adult in terms of treatment recommendations and decision making (Adelman, Greene,

Friedmann & Charon, 1991; Greene, Hoffman, Charon, & Adelman, 1987).

Mental health practitioners as well as clients themselves are bound to have personal perceptions of the aging process that can affect treatment. Consequently, clinicians need to examine their own feelings, values, and attitudes toward old age, as well as those of their patients. One of the recommendations of the APA multicultural guidelines is thus recognizing that, as cultural beings, people tend to hold attitudes and beliefs that can affect their perceptions of and interactions with those who are different from themselves in terms of race and ethnicity (APA, 2003). Mental health practitioners working with diverse older adults need to reflect on their own values and attitudes and consider the essentials of providing competent psychological services to this population. These essentials include understanding life span and developmental issues, recognizing the historical experience for each individual in relation to their cultural or group membership(s), acknowledging the common problems experienced by older people (potentially including loss of health, friends, and relationships), and being aware of the circumstances of their lives in general (Knight, 2004). Part of the self-reflective work of the clinician is to pragmatically analyze and balance the realistic declines of many older adults against misconceptions based on prejudices. This involves also understanding that old age can include positive expectations of a productive life that fits within the developmental stage of the individual. Although research and clinical experience inform us that different ethnic groups hold different views of their older adults, which can include respect and appreciation of their experiences and wisdom, there are also negative attitudes against older adults in many other cultures, as well (Mehrotra & Wagner, 2009). We need to be cognizant of the effect of the differences and similarities existing among the diverse older adults requesting our services on a daily basis in order to provide culturally competent services to this population.

SUMMARY

The purpose of this chapter is to provide mental health-care providers, students, trainers, and trainees in this area with a reference point to guide them in the competent treatment of the diverse older adult, a large and growing population in the United States. The chapter provides basic information necessary for the understanding and incorporation of critical differences between diverse and less-diverse older adult populations, while also highlighting the many ways in which older adults may demonstrate similar developmental needs Clinical issues of treatment, including assessment, intervention, consultation and training, general health care and social services, assisted-living services, long-term care, and incorporation of the family with an understanding of cultural changes that may have developed unevenly among family members were also explored and discussed.

This chapter emphasized the need for expanded and improved training, supervision, and research opportunities focused on this population. To provide competent, culturally relevant services to older adults, service providers in the mental health field must be familiar with a variety of general gerontological issues, as well as concepts specific to members of the individual groups with which they work.

RESOURCES

The following resources are provided as suggestions for further inquiry and as tools students, clinicians, trainees, and supervisors can utilize in improving the quality of the services they provide to diverse older individuals.

Suggested Readings on Cultural Diversity are provided by Council on Social Work Education Geriatric Education Center, National Center for Gerontological Social Work Education, Geriatric Social Work Initiative on Cultural Diversity—Human Behavior and the Social Environment (HBSE).

Ajrouch, K., Antonucci, T., & Janevic, M. (2001). Social networks among blacks and whites: The interaction between race and age. *Journals of Gerontology, 56B,* S112–S118.

Allaire, J. C., & Whitfield, K. E. (2004). Relationships among education, age, and cognitive functioning in older African Americans: The impact of desegregation. *Aging, Neuropsychology, and Cognition, 11*(4), 443–450.

American Psychological Association. (2004). Guidelines for psychological practice with older & adults. *American Psychologist, 59,* 237.

Angel, J., & Angel, R. (2003). Hispanic diversity and health care coverage. *Journal of Aging and Public Policy, 13,* 8–12.

Angel, J., Angel, R., & Markides, K. S. (2002). Stability and change in health insurance among older Mexican Americans: Longitudinal evidence from the Hispanic established populations for epidemiologic study of the elderly. *American Journal of Public Health, 92,* 1264–1271.

Angel, J., Frisco, M., Angel, J., & Chiriboga, D. (2003). Financial strain and health among elderly Mexican-origin individuals. *Journal of Health and Social Behavior, 44,* 536–551.

Angel, J., & Hogan, D. (2004). Population aging and diversity in a new era. In K. E. Whitfield (Ed.), *Closing the gap: Improving the health of minority elders in the new millennium.* Washington, DC: The Gerontological Society of America.

Aranda, M. P. (2006). Older Latinos: A mental health perspective. In B. Berkman, (Ed.), *Handbook of aging in health and social work.* New York: Oxford.

Aranda, M. P., Lee, P., & Wilson, S. (2001). Correlates of depression in older Latinos. *Home Health Care Services Quarterly, 20,* 1–20.

Aranda, M. P., Villa, V. M., Trejo, L., Ramirez, R., & Ranney, M. (2003). The El Portal Latino Alzheimer's Project: A model program for Latino caregivers of Alzheimer's disease-affected persons. *Social Work, 48,* 259–272.

Asian American Justice Center and Asian Pacific American Legal Center. (2006). *A community of contrasts: Asian and Pacific Islanders in the United States.* Washington, DC: Author.

Baldridge, D. (2001). Indian elders: Family traditions in crisis. In D. Infeld (Ed.), *Disciplinary approaches to aging, Vol 4: Anthropology of aging.* New York: Routledge.

Barker, V., & Giles, H. (2003). Integrating the communicative predicament and enhancement of aging models: The case of older Native Americans. *Health Communication, 15*(3), 255–276.

Barusch, A. (2006). Native American elders: Unique histories and special needs. In B. Berkman (Ed.), *Handbook of aging in health and social work.* New York: Oxford.

Beyene, Y., Becker, G., & Mayen, N. (2002). Perception of aging and sense of well-being among Latino elderly. *Journal of Cross-Cultural Gerontology, 17,* 155–172.

Bonder, B., Martin, L., & Miracle, A. (2001). Achieving cultural competence: The challenge for clients and healthcare workers in a multicultural society. *Generations, 25,* 35–43.

Braun, K. L., & Browne, C. (1998). Cultural values and caregiving patterns among Asian and Pacific Islander Americans. In D. E. Redburn and L. P. McNamara (Eds.), *Social gerontology.* Westport, CT: Greenwood Press.

Braun, K. L., Yang, H., Onaka, A. T., & Horiuchi, B. Y. (2000). Asian and Pacific Islander mortality difference in Hawaii. In K. Braun, J. Pietsch, & P. Blanchette (Eds.), *Cultural issues in end-of-life decision making.* Thousand Oaks, CA: Sage Publications.

Braun, K. L., Yee, B., Browne, C., & Mokuau, N. (2004). Native Hawaiian and Pacific Islander elders. In K. E. Whitfield (Ed.), *Closing the gap: Improving the health of minority elders in the new millennium.* Washington, DC: The Gerontological Society of America, 55–68.

Burton, L. M., & Whitfield, K. E. (2003). "Weathering" towards poorer health in later life: Comorbidity in urban low-income families. *Public Policy and Aging Report, 13,* 13–18.

Calasanti, T. (1996). Incorporating diversity: Meaning, levels of research and implications for theory. *The Gerontologist, 36,* 147–156.

Calderon, R. V., Morrill, A., Change, B. H., & Tennstedt, S. (2002). Service utilization among disabled Puerto Rican elders and their caregivers: Does acculturation play a role? *Journal of Aging Health, 1,* 3–23.

Choi, N. G. (1999). Living Arrangements and Household Compositions of Elderly Couples and Singles: A Comparison of Hispanics and blacks. *Journal of Gerontological Social Work, 31*(1/2), 41–62.

Choi, N. G. (2001). Frail older adults in nutrition supplement programs: A comparative study of African American, Asian American and Hispanic participants. *Journal of Gerontological Social Work, 36,* 187–207.

Chow, J., Jaffee, K., & Snowden, L. (2003). Racial/ ethnic disparities in the use of mental health services in poverty areas. *American Journal of Public Health*, *93*, 792–797.

Cohen, E. S. (2001). The complex nature of ageism: What is it? Who does it? Who perceives it? *The Gerontologist*, *41*(5), 576–577.

Conway-Turner, K. (1999). Older women of color: A feminist exploration of the intersections of personal, familial and community life. *Journal of Women and Aging*, *11*(2/3), 115–130.

Crimmins, E. M., & Sato, Y. (2001). Trends in healthy life expectancy in the United States: Gender, racial and educational differences. *Social Science and Medicine*, *52*, 1629–1641.

Curry, L., & Jackson, J. (2003). The science of including older ethnic and racial group participants in health-related research. *The Gerontologist*, *43*, 15–17.

Dilworth-Anderson, P., Williams, I.-C., & Gibson, R. E. (2002). Issues of race, ethnicity, and culture in caregiving research: A 20-year review. *The Gerontologist*, *42*, 237–272.

Ferraro, F. R. (2001). Assessment and evaluation issues regarding Native American elderly adults. *Journal of Clinical Geropsychology*, *7*, 311–318.

Ferraro, K., Thorpe, R., McCabe, G., Kelley-Moore, J., & Jiang, Z. (2006). The color of hospitalization over the adult life course: Cumulative disadvantage in black and white? *Journals of Gerontology*, *61B*, S299–S306.

Freeman, H. T., & Payne, R. (2000). Racial injustice in health care. *New England Journal of Medicine*, *11*, 17–20.

Groger, Lisa. (2002). Coming to terms: African-Americans' complex ways of coping with life in a nursing home. *International Journal of Aging and Human Development*, *55*(3), 183–206.

Hayward, M. D., Crimmins, E., Miles, T., & Yang, Y. (2000). The significance of socioeconomic status in explaining the racial gap in chronic health conditions. *American Sociological Review*, *65*, 910–930.

He, W. (2002). The older born foreign-born populations in the United States: 2000. *Current Population Reports P23–211*. Washington, DC: U.S. Bureau of the Census.

Henderson, J., & Henderson, L. (2002). Cultural construction of disease: A "supernormal" construct of dementia in an American Indian tribe. *Journal of Cross-Cultural Gerontology*, *17*, 197–212.

Hikoyed, N., & Wallace, S. (2001). Do ethnic-specific long-term-care facilities improve resident quality of life? Findings from the Japanese American community. *Journal of Gerontological Social Work*, *36*, 83–106.

Hong L. (2004). Barriers to and unmet needs for supportive services: Experiences of Asian-American caregivers. *Journal of Cross-Cultural Gerontology*, *19* (3), 241–261.

Hudson, R. (2002). Getting ready and getting credit: Populations of color and retirement security. *Public Policy and Aging Report*, *12*, 1–2.

Hurdle, D. E. (2002). Native Hawaiian traditional healing: Cultural based interventions for social work practice. *Social Work*, *47*, 183–192.

Jackson, J. S. (2002). Conceptual and methodological linkages in cross-cultural groups and cross-national aging research. *Journal of Social Issues*, *58*, 825–835.

Jackson, P. (2005). Health inequalities among minority populations. *Journals of Gerontology*, *60B*, 63–67.

Jang, Y., Borenstein-Graves, A., Haley, W., Small, B., & Mortimer, J. (2003). Determinants of a sense of mastery in African American and white older adults. *Journals of Gerontology*, *58B*, S221–S224.

Janson, P., & Mueller, K. J. (1983). Age, ethnicity and well-being: A comparative study of Anglos, blacks, and Mexican Americans. *Research and Aging*, *5*(3), 353–367.

John, R. (2004). Health status and health disparities. In K. Whitfield (Ed.), *Closing the gap: Improving the health of minority elders in the new millennium*. Washington, DC: Gerontological Society of America.

Kelley-Moore, J. A., & Ferraro, K. F. (2004). The black/white disability gap: Persistent inequality in later life? *Journals of Gerontology Series B: Psychological Sciences and Social Sciences*, *59B*(1), 34–44.

Kessler, R. C., Mickelson, K. D., & Williams, D. R. (1999). The prevalence, distribution, and mental health correlate of perceived discrimination in the United States. *Journal of Health and Social Behavior*, *40*, 208–230.

Kuo, T., & Torres-Gil, F. (2001). Factors affecting utilization of health services and home and community-based care programs by older Taiwanese in the United States. *Research on Aging*, *23*, 14–37.

LaVeist, T. A. (2003). Pathways to progress in eliminating racial disparities in health. *Public Policy and Aging Report*, *13*(3), 19–22.

Lewis, P. M. (Ed.). 2009. *Ethnologue: Languages of the world* (16th ed.). Dallas, TX: SIL International. Retrieved August 12, 2009, from http://www.ethnologue.com/.

Lincoln, K. D., Chatters, L. M., & Taylor, R. J. (2005). Social support, traumatic events and depressive symptoms among African Americans. *Journal of Marriage and Family*, *67*(3), 754–766.

Lincoln, K. D., Taylor, R. J., & Chatters, L. M. (2003). Correlates of emotional support and negative interaction among older black Americans. *Journals of Gerontology, 58B*, S225–233.

Lopez, S. (2002). Mental health care for Latinos: A research agenda to improve the accessibility and quality of mental health care for Latinos. *Psychiatric Services, 53*, 1569–1573.

Markides, K., & Eashbach, K. (2005). Aging, migration and mortality: Current status of research on the Hispanic paradox. *Journals of Gerontology, 60B*, 68–75.

Martinez, I. L. (2003). The elder in the Cuban American family: Making sense of the real and ideal. *Journal of Comparative Family Studies, 33*, 359–370.

McDonald, P., Brennan, P., & Wykle, M. (2005). Perceived health status and health-promoting behaviors of African American and white informal caregivers of impaired elders. *Journal of National Black Nurses Association, 16*, 8–17.

McDonald, P., & Wykle, M. (2003). Predictors of health-promoting behavior of African American and white caregivers of impaired elders. *Journal of National Black Nurses Association, 14*, 1–12.

Mikuls, T. R., Mudano, A. S., Pulley, L. V., & Saag, K. G. (2003). Association of race/ethnicity with the receipt of traditional and alternative arthritis-specific health care. *Medical Care, 41*, 1233–1239.

Mills, T. L., & Edwards, C. (2002). A critical review of research on the mental health status of older African-Americans. *Ageing and Society, 22*(3), 273–305.

Mills, T. L., & Henretta, J. C. (2001). Racial, ethnic, and sociodemographic differences in the level of psychosocial distress among older Americans. *Research on Aging, 23*(2), 131–153.

Min, J. (2005). Preference for long-term care arrangement and its correlates for older Korean-Americans. *Journal of Aging and Mental health, 17*, 363–395.

Min, J., & Moon, A. (2006). Older Asian Americans. In B. Berkman (Ed.), *Handbook of social work in health and aging*. New York: Oxford.

Min, J., Moon, A., & Lubben, J. (2005). Determinants of psychological distress over time among older Korean Americans and non-Hispanic white elders. Evidence from a two-wave panel study. *Aging and Mental Health, 9*, 210–222.

Mui, A., & Kang, S.Y. (2006). Acculturation stress and depression among Asian immigrant elders. *Social Work, 51*, 243–255.

Mui, A., Kang, S. Y., Chen, L. M., & Domanski, M. (2003). Reliability of the geriatric depression scale for use among elderly Asian immigrants in the USA. *International Psychogeriatrics, 15*, 253–271.

Nandan, M. (2005). Adaptation to American culture: Voices of Asian Indian immigrants. *Journal of Gerontological Social Work, 44*, 175–203.

O'Rand, A. M. (1996). The precious and the precocious: Understanding cumulative disadvantage and cumulative advantage over the life course. *The Gerontologist, 36*, 230–238.

Ozawa, M. N., & Choi, Y. (2002). The relationship between pre-retirement earnings and health status in old age: Black-white differences. *Journal of Gerontological Social Work, 38*(4), 19–38.

Palloni, A., & Arias, E. (2004). Paradox lost: Explaining the Hispanic adult mortality advantage. *Demography, 41*, 385–415.

Peek, C., Koropeckyj-Cox, T., Zsembik, B. A., & Coward, R. T. (2004). Race comparisons of the household dynamics of older adults. *Research on Aging, 26*(2), 179–202.

Peng, T., Navaie-Waliser, M., & Feldman, P. (2003). Social support, home health use and outcomes among four racial-ethnic groups. *The Gerontologist, 43*, 503–513.

Pinquart, M., & Sorensen, S. (2005). Ethnic differences in stressors, resources, and psychological outcomes of family caregiving: A meta-analysis. *The Gerontologist, 45*, 90–106.

Robison, J., Gruman, C., Gaztambide, S., & Blank, K. (2002). Screening for depression in middle-aged and older Puerto Rican primary care patients. *Journals of Gerontology, 57A*, M308–314.

Rooks, R., & Whitfield, K. (2004). Health disparities among older African Americans: Past, present and future perspectives. In K. Whitfield (Ed.), *Closing the gap: Improving the health of minority elders in the new millennium*. Washington, DC: Gerontological Society of America.

Roubideaux, Y. (2002). Perspectives on American Indian health. *American Journal of Public Health, 92*, 1401–1403.

Salgado de Snyder, V., & Diaz-Guerrero, R. (2003). Enduring separation: The psychological consequences of Mexican migration to the United States. In L. Adler & U. Gielen (Eds.), *Migration: Immigration and emigration in international perspective*. Westport, CT: Praeger.

Smedley, B., Stith, A., & Helson, A. (2003). *Unequal treatment: Confronting racial and ethnic disparities in health care*. Washington, DC: National Academy Press.

Stokes, S. D., Thompson, L., Murphy, S., & Galla-gher-Thompson, D. (2002). Screening for depression in immigrant Chinese American elders: Results of a pilot study. In N. Choi (Ed.), *Social work practice with the Asian American elderly*. New York: Haworth Press.

Takeuchi, D., & Gage, S. (2003). What to do with race? The changing conceptions of race in the social sciences. *Culture, Medicine and Psychiatry, 27*, 435–445.

Taylor, R. J., Lincoln, K. D., & Chatters, L. M. (2005). Supportive relationships with church members among African Americans. *Family Relations, 54*, 501–511.

Torres, G., & Moga, K. (2001). Multiculturalism, social policy and the new aging. *Journal of Gerontological Social Work, 36*(3/4), 12–32.

Whitbourne, S., & Sneed, J. (2002). The paradox of well being, identity processes and stereotype threat: Ageism and its potential relationships to the self in later life. In Nelson, T. (Ed.), *Ageism: Stereotyping and prejudice against older persons* (pp. 247–276). Cambridge: MIT Press.

Whitfield, K. E., & Hayward, M. (2003). The landscape of health disparities among older adults. *Public Policy and Aging Report, 13*(3), 1, 3–7.

Williams, D. R. (2000). Race, stress, and mental health. In C. Hogue, M. Hargraves, and K. Scott-Collins (Eds.), *Minority health in America*. Baltimore: Johns Hopkins University Press.

Williams, D. R. (2004). Racism and health. In K. E. Whitfield (Ed.), *Closing the gap: Improving the health of minority elders in the new millennium*. Washington, DC: The Gerontological Society.

Williams, D. R. (2005). The health of U.S. racial and ethnic populations. *Journals of Gerontology, 60B*, 53–62.

Williams, D. R., & Rucker, T. D. (2000). Understanding and addressing racial and ethnic disparities in health care. *Health Care Financing Review, 21*, 75–90.

Williams, D. R., & Wilson, C. M. (2001). Race, ethnicity and aging. In R. A. Binstock, & L. K. George (Eds.), *Handbook of aging and the social sciences* (5th ed.). New York: Academic Press.

Williams, S. W., & Dilworth-Anderson, P. (2002). Systems of social support in families who care for dependent African American elders. *Gerontologist, 42*(2), 224–237.

Wilmoth, J., & Chen, P. (2003). Immigrant status, living arrangements and depressive symptoms among middle-aged and older adults. *Journals of Gerontology, 58B*, S305–313.

Zauszniewski, J., Picot, S.Roberts, Debanne, S., & Wykle, M. (2005). Predictors of resourcefulness in African American women. *Journal of Aging and Health, 17*, 609–33.

Zhang, R., & Snowden, L. (1999). Ethnic characteristics of mental disorders in five U.S. communities. *Cultural Diversity and Ethnic Minority Psychology, 5*, 134–46.

WEB SITES/VIDEOS ON AGING

National Institute on Aging (NIA)

The Gerontology Society of America (GSA): offers opportunity to improve quality of life to providers, researchers, and educators; http://geron.org.

The American Society on Aging (ASA): a diverse and multidisciplinary association geared to promote the knowledge and skills of individuals who aim to enhance the quality of life of older adults; http://www.asaing.org/index.cfm.

Films and videos on aging are an excellent resource to learn about the older population from a diverse background. Educational videos in adult development and aging offer more than 200 videos on adult development and aging, including diversity.

Aging and the Cinema: http://apadiv20.phhp.ufl.edu/cinema.doc.

Aging in the Americas—The Years Ahead: a video covering topics ranging from immigration through losses from tornados.

Grandparents Raising Grandchildren: focuses on grandparents raising their grandchildren, the emotions and problems attached.

Silent Pioneers—Gay and Lesbian Elders: a documentary about lesbian and gay aging.

The Open Road—America Looks at Aging: a documentary exploring the future of the Baby Boomers.

COMPETENCY BENCHMARK TABLES

The purpose of the Competency Benchmarks (Tables 2.1-2.4) is to develop developmental models for defining and measuring competencies in professional psychology; each chapter in this *Handbook* applies the diversity competence for mental health practitioners in their work with a particular diverse population.

Table 2.1   Developmental-Level Competencies I

READINESS LEVEL—ENTRY TO PRACTICUM	
Competencies	Learning Process and Activities
Knowledge Students are gaining knowledge in: • Theories and skills relevant to mental health in general. • Codes of ethics. • Multiculturalism and guidelines for practice. • The specifics of the aging process in psychology and society. • Understanding of factors that vary across different groups within biological, psychological, and sociopolitical realities and their effects on mental health. • Relevance of identification with the process of aging.	The learning process of mental health practitioners at this level of development incorporates initial knowledge in the development of skills, values and attitudes required by their discipline. This stage is considered a beginning stage in which the students are exposed to the principles of the profession and the practice of their discipline. The emphasis in most training curricula is on core areas such as the literature on multiculturalism, ethics, basic mental health treatment, and scientific knowledge, as well as an understanding of the importance of self-awareness and reflection.
Skills Skills in the following areas are beginning to develop: • The ability to demonstrate empathic listening skills, respect, and interest when talking with the diverse older adult. • Awareness of need to consult with supervisors, in particular around issues of placement, assessment, and how to understand the different cultural behaviors and language issues that may arise in the process of intake or treatment. • An ability to conceptualize and make formulations regarding the presenting problems of the older adult.	The recommended mode of teaching skills is to infuse in the entire curriculum issues of relevance to the diverse older adult. This should be done in all courses, supervision, and consultation. Differences and similarities should be highlighted and students and trainees should be assisted in looking at the diverse older adult in a balanced manner, with an eye toward distinguishing real cognitive declines from the results of prejudice and ageism.
Values and Attitudes Students demonstrate: • The ability and motivation to practice self-exploration regarding their attitudes about old age and the differences that this population may present. These differences may require a conscious understanding on the part of the clinician. • Willingness to engage in self-exploration about their stereotypes and biases (negative and positive) regarding old age. • Intellectual curiosity and flexibility. • Ability to value expressions of diverse viewpoints and belief systems. • Capacity to examine their own fears of aging and how these may interfere with their assessment of the diverse older adult.	It might be helpful to provide students with resources that include readings, videos, movies, novels, and psychological literature to expand their knowledge and perceptions of this population.

Table 2.2   Developmental-Level Competencies II

READINESS LEVEL—ENTRY TO INTERNSHIP	
Competencies	Learning Process and Activities
Knowledge Students have: • General knowledge about adult development, including the social construction of age, psychological dynamics of the aging process, and ageism. Knowledge of relevant research, cognitive changes, problems in daily living, expression of health and psychological problems in daily life. General understanding of the heterogeneity of the diverse older adult population and how this impacts the assessment and treatment process. • Familiarity with the process of primary and secondary aging and the social perceptions of aging. • An understanding of cultural and language-based elements in psychological assessment, diagnosis, theory, and treatment modalities. • An understanding of developmental issues specific to late life, as well as generational perspectives and preferences. Recognition of the impact of physical illnesses, which may change behavior and outlook on life, require multiple medications, and produce cognitive and sensory impairments. • Awareness of the general principles of culturally competent assessment and treatment. • Awareness of APA's *Guidelines for Psychological Practice with Older Adults*.	At this stage of development, students are building on their educational and applied experiences (such as supervised practicum) to attain a core set of foundational competencies. They can then begin applying this knowledge to professional practice. As a result of being exposed to didactic training and close supervision, students attain multicultural values and attitudes appropriate to their level of development. Foundational knowledge and multicultural values and attitudes are becoming well-established, but more specific skills in work with the diverse older adult are still developing at this juncture. Learning occurs through multiple modalities: • Some students may choose to train in clinical settings geared primarily to providing services to the diverse older adult and also to work in clinics, hospital units, or institutions that serve a geriatric population. • Knowledge and experience in issues pertaining to diverse older adults can be attained through training programs containing seminars focused on multiculturalism, as well as courses on the older adult specifically and on the development, assessment, and treatment of diverse older individuals.
Skills Skills in the following areas are beginning to develop: • The ability to enact the basic elements of assessment and treatment with a recognition of the differences and specifics of the diverse older adult, including individual cultural, language-based, acculturation, and immigration issues, along with resulting specific behaviors. • The ability to conceptualize the diverse older adult in terms of general issues when faced with differences in culture, language, adjustment to illnesses, and other changes. • The ability to more fluidly establish a therapeutic alliance with the diverse older adult by including empathy, patience, and general understanding of the challenges faced by the diverse older adult. • The ability to formulate treatment plans that include individual health beliefs, history in relation to place in society and within the family, health status, and issues relevant to present development stage. • The ability to find existing strengths in the individual that will foster self-esteem.	Clinicians can also apply the skills obtained formally in their training programs and seek supervision and obtain additional knowledge. • Conducting research or participating in research projects that will shed light on differences and similarities among these populations and the specifics of diagnosis and treatment efficacy. Topics to be covered in didactic training include: • The importance of the aging process as a component of multicultural competency. • The relationship of the aging process to individual and cultural differences. • Basic research literature describing the relevance of the diverse older adult's relationship to wellness, and physical and mental health. • The social construction of the aging process and its impact on the diverse older adult.

READINESS LEVEL—ENTRY TO INTERNSHIP	
Competencies	**Learning Process and Activities**
	• The ability to recognize whether students' own views of the aging process may impact the provision of services to the diverse older adult.	
Values and Attitudes	Students demonstrate: • An understanding that aging is an important component of multicultural diversity • Awareness of self perceptions of existing factors such as ethnicity, SES, old age, and others. • An awareness of their own and others' expressions and acts of ageism. • A commitment to engage in self-exploration around personal perceptions of aging. • A commitment to engage in self-exploration around own stereotypes and biases (negative and positive) regarding the diverse older adult.	

Table 2.3   Developmental-Level Competencies III

READINESS LEVEL—ENTRY TO PROFESSIONAL PRACTICE	
Competencies	**Learning Process and Activities**
Knowledge	Practitioners have: • Knowledge of the literature on the heterogeneity of the diverse older adult population, relevance and importance of cultural values, language barriers, and impact of acculturation on the diverse older adult's mental and physical health. • A good understanding of the relevance of inclusion of the individual's belief in the cure and prevention of illnesses as perceived through the lens of different cultural values and beliefs. • A good understanding of the limitations of norms, significance of language barriers, and impact of culture in psychological assessment, diagnosis, theory, and treatment modalities. • A good understanding of the general principles of culturally competent mental health treatment. • Knowledge of specific components of assessment, diagnosis, and treatment with older adults, including dementia, comorbidity of illnesses, and chronic conditions. • Knowledge of the range of possible mental health and physical issues for the diverse older adult. • Increasing knowledge of specific subgroups of the diverse older population and the impact of membership in these groups on treatment and assessment of individuals. • Knowledge of community resources, such as day programs for the diverse older adult, nursing homes, assisted-living programs, meal services, adult day care, and in-home respite.	At the beginning stages of training, students strengthened their professional knowledge base and attained appropriate values and attitudes vis-à-vis the development and amplification of refined clinical skills. It is expected that mental health practitioners reaching the level of Entry to Professional Practice have mastered the full range of competencies in the domains expected of all independent practitioners. This level of competency is achieved through closely supervised clinical work, professional reading to keep up with the latest scientific additions and findings in the profession, personal exploration, and other continuous training opportunities such as professional development and training seminars. In order to develop clinical competency with the aging process, supervisees should be offered the opportunity to self-disclose in a nonjudgmental atmosphere in which they can present their clinical work, receive training in assessment, case conceptualization, and treatment planning, and examine their countertransference reactions, biases, and values. Supervisors can guide this process by creating a safe place for supervisees to express frightening feelings induced by the client or by their own life experiences. *(continued)*

Table 2.3 Developmental-Level Competencies III (*continued*)

READINESS LEVEL—ENTRY TO PROFESSIONAL PRACTICE		
Competencies		Learning Process and Activities
Skills	Skills are demonstrated by the ability to: • Perform the basics of culturally competent therapy appropriately. • Perform a thorough analysis that integrates multiple aspects of the individual, including values, beliefs, immigration history, health behaviors, family perceptions, and language, along with all of the basics of a traditional intake or assessment necessary to rule out dementia or to formulate other specific diagnostic categories. • Form diagnostic impressions with the awareness of what the normal aging process entails, and utilize diagnoses to assist and empower clients. • Formulate appropriate treatment plans that are sensitive to the client's aging process and acculturation experience. • Identify the limits of one's own competency with certain issues that affect the aging diverse adult. • Develop a therapeutic alliance with the individual that will foster appropriate communication based on trust and respect. • Use supervision/consultation to enhance skills that are geared toward providing appropriate assessment and treatment of the diverse older adult. • Establish effective consultation relationships with treatment centers and institutions that provide services for the diverse older adult, such as nursing homes, assisted-living facilities, primary care medical practices, hospitals, and clients' homes. • Create a climate in which supervisees and trainees feel safe to talk about their countertransference issues, possibly including fear of aging and the implications brought by the loss of youth.	Additional methods by which practitioners can attain competency with the diverse older adult at this level include: • Seeking opportunities to provide therapy to a diverse range of older adult clients. • Supervision/consultation provided by supervisors knowledgeable and skilled in working with issues pertinent to diverse older adults. • Self-directed study and professional development opportunities. • Internship and postdoctoral seminar training in issues relevant to diverse older adults. • Presenting and participating in clinical case conferences that include discussion of cases of diverse older adults. • Follow existing models of training such as the Pikes Peak model, which is geared to different entry points. • Consult an ethnogeriatric curriculum such the one offered by the Stanford University School of Medicine.
Values and Attitudes	Practitioners have: • Increased understanding of the complexity of multiple dimensions of the aging process, including health issues, losses, the need to make decisions about one's own life in arenas such as placement in an institution. • Increased awareness of their own and others' ageist assumptions. • Increased awareness of how their own experiences, culture, and socialization with older adults (whether in their own family or in the society in general) impact their approach to clients. • Commitment to lifelong learning and self-knowledge regarding the aging process. Awareness of perceptions of losses in this stage of development and the fear and anxiety that they may generate in the individual and in the therapist.	

Table 2.4   Developmental-Level Competencies IV

READINESS LEVEL—ADVANCED PRACTICE AND SPECIALIZATION	
Competencies	Learning Process and Activities
Knowledge Extensive knowledge of: • The range of experiences and similarities evidenced by the diverse older adult and the impact of these in their daily functions and conflicts. • The intersection of multiple dimensions of adaptation to changes and losses. • Meaning of the developmental changes of aging and the impact of life experiences on the older adult. • The connection between diversity, age, and mental health. • The various diagnostics categories experienced by older adults, and the relationship between these and gender, SES, immigration history, culture, and language-based issues. • The impact of media on ageism and the perceptions and misperceptions of the diverse older adult.	Application of different modalities of treatment and techniques will be acquired according to the training of the therapist and relevance to the population(s) served. Areas that can be helpful include professional reading (e.g., information about diverse older individuals in general, developmentally appropriate behaviors and functions, and literature on the different groups that form the overall population of diverse older adults). Continued education opportunities, whether they include conferences, professional conventions, lectures, or workshops. • Ethnic studies, medical rounds, sociology, feminist studies, training, conferences, anthropological lectures, courses on older adults or the history and customs of different countries. • Movies, videos, and documentaries. • Teaching. • Attending and leading educational workshops. • Peer consultation groups. • Consultation with knowledgeable mental health professionals and experts on different cultures.
Skills Advanced skills in: • Assessment and diagnosis geared to address the specific issues of the diverse older adult. • Providing culturally sensitive therapy that addresses the full range of issues presented by the diverse older adult. • Providing therapy that takes into consideration the multiple realities of the diverse older adult, including health, medication, acculturation, losses, loneliness, and functioning in particular settings (e.g., an institution). • Finding respectful ways in which to promote and encourage the choices of the diverse older adult. • Managing boundary issues in a nuanced manner that takes the diverse older adult's needs and circumstances into account. • Helping supervisees to process their own biases as they relate to their work with clients.	
Values and Attitudes Well-integrated values and attitudes demonstrated by the following: • Independently monitors own biases, fears, and ageism in relation to work with others. • Continually assesses and reassesses own biases and expectations of the diverse older adult client. • Continuous engagement in professional development through the broadening of knowledge of existing resources relating to the diverse older adult.	

REFERENCES

Abeles, N., Cooley, S., Deitch, I., Harper, M. S., Hinrichsen, G., Lopez, M. A., et al. (1998). What practitioners should know about working with older adults. *Professional Psychology: Research and Practice, 29*, 413–427.

Aday, L., Andersen, R. M., & Fleming, G. (1980). *Health care in the U.S.: Equitable for whom?* Beverly Hills, CA: Sage.

Aday, L., Fleming, G., & Andersen, R. M. (1984). *Access to medical care in the U.S.: Who has it and who doesn't?* Chicago: Pluritus.

Adelman, R. D., Greene, M. G., Charon, R., & Friedmann, E. (1991). The content of physician and elderly patient interaction in the medical primary care encounter. *Communication Research, 19*, 370–380.

Aldwin, D. M., Park, C. L., & Spiro, A. (Eds.). 2007. *Handbook of health psychology and aging.* New York: Guilford Press.

Alexopoulos, G. S., Borson, S., Cuthbert, B. N., Devanand, D. P., Mulsant, B. H., Olin, J. T., et al. (2002). Assessment of late life depression. *Society of Biological Psychiatry, 52*, 164–174.

American Psychological Association. (2003). Guidelines on multicultural education, training, research, practice, and organizational change for psychologists. *American Psychologist, 58*, 377–402.

American Psychological Association. (2004). Guidelines for psychological practice with older adults. *American Psychologist, 59*, 236–260.

Angel, J. L., & Hogan, D. P. (2004). Population aging and diversity in a new era. In K. E. Whitfield (Ed.), *Closing the gap: Improving the health of minority elders in the new millennium.* Washington, DC: The Gerontological Society of America.

Angel, J. L., & Whitfield, K. E., (Eds.). (2007). *The health of aging Hispanics: The Mexican-origin population.* New York: Springer.

Angel, R. J., & Angel, J. L. (2006). Diversity and aging in the United States. In R. H. Binstock & L.K. George (Eds.) *Handbook of aging and the social sciences* (6th ed., pp. 94–106). Burlington, MA: Elsevier Academic Press.

Ardila, A. (1995). Directions of research in cross-cultural neuropsychology. *Journal of Clinical and Experimental Neuropsychology, 17*, 143–150.

Barrio, C., Yamada, A. M., Hough, R., Hawthorne, W., Garcia P., & Jeste, D. V. (2003). Ethnic disparities in utilization of public mental health care management services among clients with schizophrenia. *Psychiatric Services, 54*, 1264–1270.

Barrow, G. M. (1992). *Aging, the individual, and society* (5th ed.). St. Paul, MN: West.

Burns, S. U. (2008). Geropsychology practice: One psychologist's experience in long-term care. *Psychological Services, 5*(1), 73–84.

Butler, R. (1975). *Why survive? Being old in America.* New York: Harper & Row.

Butler, R., & Lewis, M. (1982). *Aging and mental health* (3rd ed.). St. Louis, MO: C. V. Mosby.

Butler, R. N., Lewis, M. I., & Sunderland, T. (1991). *Aging and mental health: Positive psychosocial and biomedical approaches* (4th ed.). New York: Merrill.

Caporael, L., & Culbertson, G. H. (1986). Verbal response modes of baby talk and other speech at institutions for the aged. *Language & Communication, 6*(1–2), 99–112.

Centers for Disease Control and Prevention, National Center for Health Statistics. (2008). Health, United States, 2008. Retrieved August 13, 2009, from http://www.cdc.gov/nchs/data/hus/hus08.pdf#026

Clarke, L. H., & Griffin, M. (2008). Visible and invisible ageing: Beauty work as a response to ageism. *Ageing & Society, 28*, 653–674.

Cohen, G. (2005). *The mature mind.* New York: Basic Books.

Crum, R. M., Anthony, J. C., Bassett, S. S., & Folstein, M. F. (1993). Population-based norms for the mini-mental state examination by age and educational level. *Journal of American Medical Association, 269*, 2386–2391.

DePaola, S. J., Neimeyer, R. A., Lupfer, M. B., & Fiedler, J. (1992). Death concern and attitudes toward the elderly in nursing home personnel. *Death Studies, 16*, 537–555.

Department of Health and Human Services (DHHS). (2003). *President's New Freedom Commission on Mental Health, No. SMA-03-3832.* Rockville, MD.

Derose, K. P., & Baker, D. W. (2000). Limited English proficiency and Latinos' use of physician services. *Med. Care Res. Rev., 57*, 76–91.

DeVries, H. M., & Ogland-Hand, S. M. (2007). Crisis with older adults. In F. M. Dattilio, & A. Freeman, *Cognitive-behavioral strategies in crisis intervention* (3rd ed., pp. 377–396). New York: Guilford Press.

Eyetsemitan, F. (2002). Suggestions regarding cross-cultural environment as context for human development and aging in non-Western cultures. *Psychological Reports, 90*, 823–833.

Eyetsemitan, F. (2007). Perception of aging in different cultures. In M. Robinson, W. Novelli, C. Pearson, L. Norris (Eds.), *Global health & global aging* (pp. 58–67). San Francisco: Jossey Bass.

Federal Interagency Forum on Aging Related Statistics. (2004).

Filippo, S. M. S., Reiboldt, W., White, B., & Hails, J. (2007). Perception of elderly self-neglect: A look at culture and cohort. *Family & Consumer Sciences Research Journal, 35*(3), 215–231.

Finkelstein, L. M., Burke, M. J., & Raju, N. S. (1995). Age discrimination in simulated employment contexts: An integrative analysis. *Journal of Applied Psychology, 80,* 652–663.

Fitzgerald, M. H., Mullavey-O'Byrne, C., & Clemson, L. (2001). Families and nursing home placements: A cross-cultural study. *Journal of Cross-Cultural Gerontology, 16*(4), 333–351.

Flippen, C. A. (2005). Minority workers and pathways to retirement. In R. Hudson (Ed.), *The new politics of old age policy* (pp. 129–157). Baltimore: Johns Hopkins University Press.

Frazer, D. (1995). The medical issues in geropsychology training and practice. In B. G. Knight, L. Teri, P. Wohlford, & J. Santos (Eds.), *Mental health services for older adults: Implications for training and practice in geropsychology* (pp. 63–72). Washington, DC: American Psychological Association.

Gatz, M., & Knight, B. G. (1998). Psychotherapy with older adults. In G. P. Koocher, J. C. Norcross, & S. S. Hill, (Eds.), *Psychologists' desk reference* (pp. 370–373). Oxford University Press.

Gazmararian, J. A., Baker, D. W., Williams, M. V., Parker, R. M., Scott, T. L., Green, D. C., et al. (1999). Health literacy among Medicare enrollees in a managed care organization. *JAMA: The Journal of the American Medical Association, 281,* 545–551.

Ginsberg, C., Martin, D., Andrulis, D., Shaw-Taylor, Y., & McGregor, C. (1995). *Interpretation and translation services in health care: A survey of U.S. public and private teaching hospitals* (pp. 1–49). Washington, DC: National Public Health and Hospital Institute.

Golding, J. M., & Aneshensel, C. S. (1989). Factor structure of the Center for Epidemiologic Studies Depression Scale among Mexican Americans and non-Hispanic whites. *Psychological Assessment: A Journal of Consulting and Clinical Psychology, 1,* 163–168.

Golding, J. M., & Aneshensel, C. S., & Hough, R. L. (1991). Responses to depression scale items among Mexican-Americans and non-Hispanic whites. *Journal of Clinical Psychology, 47*(1), 61–75.

Greene, M. G., Hoffman, S., Charon, R., & Adelman, R. (1987). Psychosocial concerns in the medical encounter: A comparison of the interactions of doctors with their old and young patients. *The Gerontologist, 27,* 164–168.

Haley, W. E. (1996). The medical context of psychotherapy with the elderly. In S. H. Zarit & B. G. Knight (Eds.), *A guide to psychotherapy and aging: Effective clinical interventions in a life-stage context* (pp. 221–240). Washington, DC: American Psychological Association.

Harris, H. L. (1998). Ethnic minority elders: Issues and interventions. *Educational Gerontology, 24,* 309–323.

Hayward, M. D., Crimmins, E. M., Miles, T. P., & Yu, Y. (2000). The significance of socioeconomic status in explaining the racial gap in chronic health conditions. *American Sociological Review, 65,* 910–930.

Hayward, M. D., Warner, D. F., & Crimmins, E. M. (2007). Does longer life mean better health? Not for native-born Mexican Americans in the Health and Retirement Study. In J. L. Angel & K. E. Whitfield (Eds.), *The health of aging Hispanics: The Mexican-origin population* (pp. 85–95). New York: Springer.

He, W. (2002). The older foreign-born population in the United States: 2000. *Current Population Reports.* Series p. 23–211. *United States Census Bureau.* Washington, DC: U.S. Government Printing Office.

He, W., Sengupta, M., Velkoff, V. A., & DeBarros, K. A. (2005, December). *65+ in the United States: 2005.* Washington, DC: U.S. Government Printing Office, pp. 23–209.

Health Care Strategic Manager. (1995). Need for interpreter/translation services critical in hospitals and other clinical settings. *Health Care Strategic Manager, 13,* 15.

Henderson, J. N. (1992). The power of support: Aging. [Publication Nos. 363–364]. Washington, DC: U.S. Department of Health and Human Services, Administration on Aging, pp. 24–31.

Hinrichsen, G. A. (2006). Why multicultural issues matter for practitioners working with older adults. *Professional Psychology: Research and Practice, 37*(1), 29–35.

Hyer, L., & Intrieri, R. C. (2006). *Geropsychological interventions in long-term care.* New York: Springer.

Ibrahim, S. A., Burant, C. J., Mercer, M. B., Siminoff, L. A., & Kwoh, C. K. (2003). Older patients' perceptions of quality of chronic knee or hip pain: Differences by ethnicity and relationship to clinical variables. *Journals of Gerontology: Series A: Biological Sciences and Medical Sciences, 58A(5)*, 472–477.

International Labour Office (ILO) database on labor statistics—LABORSTA. Retrieved November 12, 2006, from http://laborsa.ilo.org

Irvine, S. H., & Berry, J. W. (1988). *Human abilities in cultural contexts* (pp. 87–104). New York: Cambridge University Press.

Jacobs, D. M., Sano, M., Albert, S., Schofield, P., Dooneief, G., & Stern, Y. (1997). Cross-cultural neuropsychological assessment: A comparison of randomly selected, demographically matched cohorts of English- and Spanish-speaking older adults. *Journal of Clinical and Experimental Neuropsychology, 19*, 331–339.

Jacobs, E. A., Shepard, D. S., Suaya, J. A., & Stone, E. L. (2004). Overcoming language barriers in health care: Costs and benefits of interpreter services. *American Journal of Public Health, 94*, 866–869.

Janson, P., Mueller, K. J. (1983). Age, ethnicity and well-being: A comparative study of Anglos, blacks, and Mexican Americans. *Research and Aging, 5*, 353–367.

Kagitcibasi, C. (1997). *Individualism and collectivism*. In J. W. Berry, M. H. Segall, & C. Kagitcibasi (Eds.), *Handbook of cross-cultural psychology, Vol. 3: Social behavior and applications* (pp. 1–51). Boston: Allyn & Bacon.

Kalavar, J. M. (1999, July 10–16). Intergenerational relations and service utilizations: The experience of Asian Indian elderly in the United States. [Research abstract]. Bethesda, MD: National Institute on Aging, Summer Institute on Aging Research.

Kaslow, N. J. (2004). Competencies in professional psychology. *American Psychologist, 59*, 774–781.

Kaslow, N. J., Borden, K. A., Collins, F. L., Jr., Forrest, L., Illfelder-Kay, J., Nelson, P. D., et al. (2004). Competencies conference: Future directions in education and credentialing in professional psychology. *Journal of Clinical Psychology, 60*, 699–712.

Kelley-Moore, J. A., & Ferraro, K. F. (2004). The black/white disability gap: Persistent inequality in later life? *Journal of Gerontology: Social Sciences, 59B*, S34–S43.

Kelty, M. E, Hoffman, R. R., III, Ori, M. G., & Harden, T. J. (Eds.) (2000). *Behavioral and Sociocultural aspects of aging, ethnicity, and health* (pp. 139–158). Mahwah, NJ: Lawrence Erlbaum Associates Publishers.

Kikuzawa, S. (2006). Multiple roles and mental health in cross-cultural perspective: The elderly in the United States and Japan. *Journal of Health and Social Behavior, 47*, 62–76.

Kite, M. E., Stockdale, G. D., Whitley, B. E., Jr., & Johnson, B. T. (2005). Attitudes toward younger and older adults. An updated meta-analysis review. *Journal of Social Issues, 61(2)*, 241.

Knight, B. G. (2003). Psychotherapy and older adults resource guide. American Psychological Association, Office on Aging. Available at: http://www.apa.org/pi/aging/psychotherapy.html

Knight, B. G. (2004). *Psychotherapy with older adults* (3rd ed.). New York: Sage.

Knight, B., Karel, M., Hinrichsen, G., Qualls, S., & Duffy, M. (2009, April). Pikes Peak model for training in professional geropsychology. *American Psychologist, 64(3)*, 205–214.

Knight, B. G., Kaskie, B., Shurgot, G. R. & Dave, J. (2006). Improving mental health of older adults. In J. E. Birren & K. W. Schaie (Eds.), *The handbook of psychology of aging* (6th ed., pp. 407–424). San Diego: Academic Press.

Kosloski, K., Montgomery, R., & Karner, T. (1999). Differences in the perceived need for assistive services by culturally diverse caregivers of dementia patients. *Journal of Applied Gerontology, 18*, 239–256.

Kunz, J. (1991). Case Reports: Counseling approaches for disoriented older adults. *Illness Crisis and Loss, 1* (2), 91–96.

Kunz, J. (2002). *The joys and surprises of telling your life story*. Superior: Center for Continuing Education/Extension, University of Wisconsin-Superior.

Kunz, J. A., & Florence, G. S. (Eds.) (2007). *Transformational reminiscence life story work*. New York: Springer.

Lawrence-Lightfoot. (2009). *The third chapter: Passion, risk and adventure in the 25 years after 50*. New York: Sarah Crichton Books, Farrar, Straus & Giroux.

Levant, R. F. (2005). Evidence-based practice in psychology, *American Psychologist, 36(2)*. President's column.

Lewis, P. M. (Ed.). 2009. *Ethnologue: Languages of the world* (16th ed.). Dallas, TX: SIL International. Retrieved August 12, 2009, from http://www.ethnologue.com/

Lichtenberg, P. A., Smith, M., Frazer, D., Molinari, V., Rosowski, E., Crose, R., et al. (1998). Standards for psychological services in long-term-care facilities. *The Gerontologist, 38*, 122–127.

Lowenstein, A., Katz, R., Gur-Yaish, N. (2007). Reciprocity in parent-child exchange and life satisfaction among the elderly: A cross-national perspective. *Journal of Social Issues, 63*(4), 865–883.

Loewenstein, D. A., Arguelles, T., Barker, W. W., & Duara, R. (1993). A comparative analysis of neuropsychological test performance of Spanish-speaking and English-speaking patients with Alzheimer's Disease. *Journal of Gerontology: Psychological Sciences, 48,* 142–149.

Lopez, S., & Taussig, I. M. (1991) Cognitive intellectual functioning of Spanish-speaking impaired and non-impaired elderly: Implications for culturally sensitive assessment. *Psychological Assessment, 3,* 448–454.

Marcos, L. R. (1979). Effects of interpreters on the evaluation of psychopathology in non-English speaking patients. *American Journal of Psychiatry, 136,* 171–174.

McCann, R., & Giles, H. (2002). Ageism in the workplace: A communication perspective. In T. D. Nelson (Ed.), *Ageism: Stereotyping and prejudice against older persons* (pp. 163–199). Cambridge, MA: MIT Press.

Mehrotra, C. M., & Wagner, L. S. (2009). *Aging and diversity: An active learning experience* (2nd ed.). New York, London: Routledge Taylor & Francis Group.

Molinari, V. (Ed.). (2000). *Professional psychology in long term care.* New York: Hatherleigh Press.

Molinary, V., Karel, M., Jones, S., Zeiss, A., Cooley, S. G., Wray, L., et al. (2003). Recommendations about the knowledge and skills required of psychologists working with older adults. *Professional Psychology: Research and Practice, 34,* 435–443.

Morgan, A. C. (2003). Psychodynamic psychotherapy with older adults. *Practical Geriatrics, 54,* No. 12, 1592–1594.

Mouton, C., & Esparza, Y. B. (2001). Ethnicity and geriatric assessment. In J. Gallo, T. Fullmer, G. J. Paveza, & W. Reichel (Eds.), *Handbook of geriatric assessment* (pp. 13–28). Gaithersburg, MD: Aspen.

Mouton, C. P., Johnson, M. S., & Cole, D. R. (1995) Ethical considerations with African-American elders. *Clinics in Geriatric Medicine, 11,* 113–129.

Mungas, D., Marshall, S. C., Weldon, M., Haan, M., & Reed, B. R. (1996). Age and education correction of the mini-mental state exam for English and Spanish-speaking elderly. *Neurology, 46,* 700–706.

National Center for Health Statistics. (2009). Online. Retrieved July 2009, from http://www.cdc.gov/aging

National Institute on Aging. (2006, March). Dramatic changes in U.S. aging highlighted in new census. NIH Report: *Impact of Baby Boomers anticipated.*

Nisbett, R. E., & Masuda, T. (2003). *Culture and point of view. Proceedings of the National Academy of Sciences of the United States of America, 100*(19), 11163–11170.

Palinkas, L. A, Criado, V., Fuentes, D., Shepherd, S., Milian, H, Folsom, D., et al. (2006). A qualitative study of unmet needs for services for older adults with mental illness: Comparison of views of different stakeholder groups. *American Journal of Geriatric Psychiatry, 15,* 530–540.

Panganamala, N. R., & Plummer, D. L. (1998). Attitudes toward counseling among Asian Indians in the United States. *Cultural Diversity and Mental Health, 4*(1), 55–63.

Perez-Arce, P., & Puente, A. E. (1996). Neuropsychological assessment of ethnic minorities: The case of assessing Hispanics living in North America. In R. J. Sbordone (Ed.), *Ecological validity of neuropsychological testing* (pp. 283–300). Delray Beach, FL: GR Press/St. Lucie Press.

Qualls, S. H. (2009). Pikes Peak model for training in professional geropsychology. *American Psychologist 2009, American Psychological Association, 46*(3), 205–214.

Radloff, L. S. (1977). The CES-D Scale: A self-report depression scale for research in the general population. *Applied Psychological Measurement, 1,* 385–401.

Robinson, M., Novelli, W., Pearson, C., & Norris, L. (2007). Perception of aging in different cultures. In F. E. Eyetsemitan (Ed.), *Global health and global aging* (pp. 58–67). San Francisco: Jossey-Bass.

Rodolfa, E., Bent, R., Eisman, E., Nelson, P., Rehm, L. & Ritchie, P. (2005). A cube model for competency development: Implications for psychology educators and regulators. *Professional Psychology: Research and Practice, 33,* 435–442.

Rosen, B., & Jerdee, T. H. (1976). The influence of age stereotypes on managerial decisions. *Journal of Applied Psychology, 61,* 428–432.

Rosowski, E., Casciani, J. M., & Arnold, M. (2008). *Geropsychology and long term care: A practitioner's guide.* New York: Springer.

Sakauye, K. (1996). *Ethnocultural aspects in comprehensive review of geriatric Psychiatry, Vol. II* (2nd ed.).

In J. Sadavoy, L. W. Lazarus, L. F. Jarvik, & G. T. Grossberg (Eds.), *Comprehensive review of geriatric psychiatry—II* (2nd ed.), (pp. 197–221). Washington, DC: American Psychiatric Association.

Schaie, K. W. (1994). The course of adult intellectual development. *American Psychologist, 49,* 304–313.

Sheikh, J. I. (2005). Investigations of anxiety in older adults: Recent advances and future directions. *Journal of Geriatric Psychiatry and Neurology, 18,* 59–60.

Smith, J. P., & Kington, R. (1997). Demographic and economic correlates of health in old age. *Demography, 34,* 159–170.

Solis, J., Marks, G., Garcia, M., & Shelton, D. (1990). Acculturation, access to care, and use of preventive service by Hispanics: Findings from HHANES 1982-84. *American Journal of Public Health, 80,* 11–19.

Sorocco, K. H., & Ferrell, S. W. (2006). Alcohol use among older adults. *The Journal of General Psychology, 133,* 453–467.

Stewart, A. L., & Napoles-Springer, A. (2000). Health-related quality-of-life assessments in diverse population groups in the United States. *Medical Care,* 38 (Suppl. 9) 11102–11124.

Sue, D. W., & Sue, D. (2003). Counseling the culturally diverse: Theory and practice (4th ed.). Hoboken, NJ: Wiley.

Sue, S. (1998). In search of cultural competence in psychotherapy and counseling. *American Psychologist, 27,* 722–742.

Teresi, J. A., Stewart, A. L., Morales, L. S., & Stahl, S. M. (2006). Measurements in a multiethnic society: Overview to the special issue. *Med Care, 44* (11 Suppl. 3), S3–4.

Trans, T. V. (1990). Language acculturation among older Vietnamese refugee adults. *The Gerontologist, 30,* 94–99.

Tseng, W.-S. (2001). *Handbook of cultural psychiatry.* San Diego: Academic Press.

University of California, San Francisco, Institute for Health & Aging. (2004). CHAMPS: Community Healthy Activities Model Program for Seniors. Available at: http://sbs.ucsf.edu/iha/champs.

U. S. Census Bureau, Population Division—Population estimate 2008.

U. S. Census Bureau. (2006). Current population survey, 2004 to 2006 annual social and economic supplements. Retrieved August 13, 2009, from http://www.census.gov/hhes/www/poverty/poverty05/table5.html

Vazquez, C., & Javier, R. (1991). The problem with interpreters: Communicating with Spanish-speaking patients. *Hospital Community Psychiatry, 42,* 163–165.

Warner, D. F., & Hofmeister, H. (2006). *Late career transitions among men and women in uncertainty and late careers in society.* London: Routledge, pp. 141–181.

Weinberger, M. B. (2007). Population aging: A global overview. In M. Robinson, W. Novelli, C. Pearson, & L. Norris (Eds.), *Global health & global aging* (pp. 15–30). San Francisco: Jossey-Bass.

Westerhof, G. J., Katzko, M. W., Dittmann-Kohli, F., & Hayslip, B. (2001). Life contexts and health-related selves in old age. *Journal of Aging Studies, 15,* 105–127.

Whitbourne, S. K. (1985). *The aging body.* New York: Springer.

Williams, B. R., Baker, P. S., & Allman, R. M. (2008). Nonspousal family loss among community-dwelling older adults. *Journal of Death and Dying, 51*(2), 125–142.

Williams, D. R. (2005). The health of U.S. racial and ethnic populations. *Journals of Gerontology, Series B: Psychological Sciences and Social Sciences, 60B* (Special Issue 2), 53–62.

Willis S. L., Tennstedt, S. L., Marsiske, M., Ball, F.K., Elias, J., Koepke, K.M., et al. (2006) Long-term effects of cognitive training on everyday functional outcomes in older adults. *Journal of American Medical Association, 296*(23), 2805–2814.

Woloshin, S., Bickell, N., Schwartz, L., Gany, F., & Welch, G. (1995). Language barriers in medicine in the United States. *JAMA,* 724–728.

Yeo, G. (Ed.). (2001). *Curriculum in ethnogeriatrics* (2nd ed.). Retrieved July 21, 2009, from http://www.stanford.edu/group/ethnoger.

CHAPTER 3

DISABILITY: MULTIPLE AND INTERSECTING IDENTITIES— DEVELOPING MULTICULTURAL COMPETENCIES

Barbara J. Palombi

INTRODUCTION

Disability is a complex and multifaceted issue that transcends all social groups, including race/ethnicity, sexual orientation, gender, religion, and class strata (McDonald, Keys, & Balcazar, 2007). Signs of oppression toward persons with disabilities (PWDs) are apparent within our society by inaccessible structures, higher rates of poverty and unemployment, continued biomedical categorization of difference as deviance, and social rejection of "disabled other" by persons both within and outside the disability community (Kinavey, 2006). Due to emphasis on medical concerns and the focus on "individual-centered deficits and impairments" (McDonald et al., 2007, p. 146), it has been easy to ignore the societal attitudes toward persons with disabilities.

Many members of our society assume that everyone is or should be "normal," and believe that being healthy is normal and that illness is a "deviance" (Weeber, 1999; Wendell, 1997). Those who are not disabled might assume they are superior to people with a disability. This attitude is labeled *ableism*, a form of prejudice and bigotry that labels people with a disability as "less than" people without disabilities (Weeber, 1999, p. 20). An underlying root of ableism is that individuals often fear disability and the possibility of themselves becoming disabled (Hirschberger, Florian, Mikulincer, 2005; Taylor, 2001).

Because of these attitudes, it has been difficult for PWDs to see themselves as a political group having power and influence. Most PWDs live in families and communities that have little understanding or provide little support regarding the prejudice and discrimination that they experience (Gill, 2001; Olkin, 2002; Weeber, 1999). This allows PWDs to become isolated and labeled as weak, needy, and incompetent by their families and colleagues (Gill, 2001; Weeber, 1999). Similarly, minority communities and progressive political groups may also contribute to oppression of PWDs (Gill, 2001). Groups who organize against racism, sexism, homophobia, and other dimensions of oppression have at times expressed negative attitudes regarding disability. PWDs of color and PWDs who are gay, for instance, have reported marginalization within all of their minority communities (Tsao, 1998; Vernon, 1998).

Within multicultural counseling, PWDs represent one of the largest diversity groups (Olkin, 2002). According to the Council on Disability Awareness, over 51 million Americans are classified as disabled, representing 18 percent of the population (retrieved June 29, 2009, from http://www.disabilitycanhappen.org/chances_disability/disability_stats.asp). Yet PWDs struggle to be acknowledged as experiencing oppression and discrimination as do other groups who have been marginalized (Gill, 2001; Olkin, 2002). Due to this lack of recognition by mental health practitioners concerning multicultural issues among PWDs, competencies and interventions for this population are sparse (Taliaferro, 2004). The absence of this material parallels the invisibility of disability issues in mental health (Olkin & Taliaferro, 2005).

This chapter will (a) define terms and concepts that will assist practitioners to expand their understanding and awareness regarding PWDs; (b) provide the historical overview regarding the models used and the legislation affecting PWDs; (c) discuss the multicultural issues related to those PWDs with multiple identities; (d) explore issues and challenges related to diagnosis, assessment, and case conceptualization; and (e) give an overview of the elements of competency to include knowledge and values/attitudes/skills.

It is important to understand that research conducted regarding disability has been disability specific. When working with PWDs, it is important that mental health practitioners recognize the limitations of research that is disability specific. Also, it is important to consider that each individual with a disability has a unique and personal experience of disability. Therefore, this chapter will not address disabilities from an individual perspective, specific categories of disability (i.e., cognitive impairment, emotional impairment, hearing impaired, etc.), or specific groups of individuals with disabilities (children, adolescents, elderly, etc.).

TERMS AND CONCEPTS

Disability Language

The term *person with a disability* (*PWD*) is being used in this chapter and the proper etiquette in talking about persons with disabilities is to refer to the person first, not the disability. For example, "the person who uses a wheelchair" or "the person with arthritis" is preferred over "the wheelchair person" or "the arthritic." This last term especially defines the disability as the person rather than as one aspect of his or her life. This general rule may be different within some communities, such as those who are blind or deaf. Individuals in these groups often self-identify as "blind person" or "deaf person." Even though individuals who are blind or deaf may self-identify as a "blind person" or a "deaf person," they may consider it culturally insensitive for a mental health practitioner to use this same terminology (retrieved June 19, 2009, from http://www .unitedspinal.org/pdf/DisabilityEtiquette.pdf). The best way to proceed when referring to disability in a clinical session is to ask clients what terminology they would feel comfortable using when referring to their disability.

Defining *Disability*

It is difficult to identify a clear and universal definition of *disability* (Olkin, 1999), and identifying who are PWDs is not necessarily a straightforward question (Marks, 2008). Marks further states that the definition of disability is associated with a conglomerate of theories regarding the body, society, and psyche. The lack of consensus regarding the definition of disability is observed throughout the literature. Nagi (1991) defined disability as "a form of inability or limitation in performing roles and tasks expected of an individual within a social environment." Pope and Tarlov (1991) defined disability as "the expression of a physical or mental limitation in a social context—the gap between a person's capabilities and the demands of the environment." M. R. Hulnick and H. R. Hulnick (1989) characterized *disabled* as *differently abled*, referring to functional limitation in terms of one's physical body, psyche, or emotions. From a medical perspective, the definition of *disability* tends to focus on the limitations on physical abilities and the etiology of the corresponding diagnosis (Pledger, 2003). In contrast, the Social Security Administration's definition of disability is based on one's inability to work. Individuals are considered disabled under Social Security rules if: (a) They are unable to accomplish the work they had previously performed, (b) are unable to adjust to other work because of medical concerns, and (c) the disability lasts for at least one month or could result in the end of one's life (retrieved June 24, 2009, from http:// www.ssa.gov/disability/step4and5.htm).

A frequently used definition comes from the 1990 Americans With Disabilities Act, which defines individuals with disabilities as "any individual that has a physical or mental impairment that substantially limits one or more major life activities or a person on record or regarded by others as having such an impairment" (retrieved June 28, 2009, from http://www.ada.gov/cguide .htm#anchor62335). Examples of major life activities include seeing, hearing, walking, being able to care for oneself, breathing, and so on.

It is important to recognize the distinction between disability and other protected categories, such as race, in that disability is not necessarily a permanent characteristic. It is possible for people to completely recover from some types of disabilities (e.g., a broken leg, cancer, etc.). Other types of disabilities are characterized by periods of recovery and remission (e.g., depression, multiple sclerosis, etc.). Mental health practitioners providing services to PWDs should further understand that agencies providing social services to this population, researchers, educators, and the general public may differ in their understanding of the meaning of the term *disability*.

Some may view a visible disability as a person in a wheelchair, perhaps because the international symbol for disability is depicted as such. In reality, there are many different types of disability categories, such as visible and invisible (spinal cord injury, paralysis, major depression, learning disability), permanent and temporary (blindness, deafness, broken arm), and acquired and congenital (traumatic brain injury, amputation, cerebral palsy) (Smart, 2001).

The following is a case vignette (3.1) about Tom, a PWD. The focus of the vignette is the definition of disability, which may shift according to the social context and environmental and functional demands.

CASE VIGNETTE 3.1

Tom is a 26-year-old partnered gay male living in the suburbs of Chicago. In his freshman year of college, he was in an automobile accident that resulted in a closed head injury and left Tom with severe memory loss and a seizure disorder. After a year-long rehabilitation process and with the assistance of the State of Illinois Office of Vocational Rehabilitation, he returned to college. During his first semester, he met with the Office for Students with Disabilities and identified himself as a student with a disability. After five years of study, he earned a BS degree in information technology. He continued his education and will graduate with an MS in Computer Science. He has already secured a job with the IT department at a local hospital located in the inner city of Chicago. Because of his seizure disorder and not being seizure free, he is unable to drive. He plans to take the train into the city and then transfer to a city bus to reach his destination. He feels excited and fulfilled that many of his life dreams are coming true.

Discussion Questions:
- Does Tom have a disability?
- If yes, on what definition are you basing your decision?
- If no, on what are you basing your decision?
- How might Tom consider himself disabled or not disabled?
- How might the following view Tom as having or not having a disability?
  - Tom's partner
  - Illinois Vocational Rehabilitation system
  - University he attended
  - Chicago transportation system
  - Hospital where he will be employed

BARRIERS TO COMPETENCY IN ISSUES REGARDING DISABILITY

Charged by ethical codes and practice guidelines to practice in a multiculturally sensitive manner, mental health practitioners may find it difficult to incorporate factors related to disability into treatment for a number of reasons. Many mental health practitioners feel unprepared to address disability-related issues in counseling. Most practitioners have never received any academic instruction or training in the area of disability (Hogben & Waterman, 1997; Kemp & Mallinckrodt, 1996; Olkin & Taliaferro, 2005; Rubino, 2001).

It is virtually impossible for mental health practitioners not to have been exposed to the biases and attitudes of our society and not to have internalized these attitudes and biases. Therefore, they may also feel uncomfortable with the topic because they may not have explored or may be unaware of their own biases and attitudes toward PWDs (Kemp & Mallinckrodt, 1996; Olkin, 1999).

Many mental health practitioners have had little exposure or interaction with PWDs. Therefore, they may question their competency and whether they can be of assistance. Mental health practitioners may also reflect the common concerns that the general public have in regard to disability: (a) uncertainty about what to do/not do; (b) wondering what a person with a disability can do/not do; (c) questions about what to do in a crisis; (d) uneasiness about being depended upon; (e) inability to see a PWD as a person; (f) making assumptions without asking; (g) resentment of "special treatment;" and (h) confusion about hidden disabilities—even wondering if that disability is real (e.g., learning disabilities, mental and emotional disabilities, illness that may involve chronic fatigue and/or pain, such as fibromyalgia, lupus, chronic fatigue syndrome, etc.). Since few mental health practitioners have an understanding of the prejudice and discrimination that PWDs face, they may be hesitant to engage with PWDs. As a result,

mental health practitioners will seldom ask clients: (a) whether they may have a disability, if so, (b) for how long, (c) what was the cause, and (d) how it may affect their lives. The lack of awareness about these issues and hesitancy to address the topic of disability may leave a client who has a disability feeling further marginalized and invalidated (Kemp & Mallinckrodt, 1996; Leigh, Powers, Vash, & Nettles, 2004).

Elements of Competency

Mental health professionals in the fields of rehabilitation psychology and rehabilitation counseling have focused on PWDs with the primary emphasis on developing employment skills and returning the client to the workplace. Drawing upon the work of these professionals, other mental health practitioners have begun to contribute to the social work, counseling, and psychological literature to clarify elements of competency when working with PWDs. In the next few sections, we will outline knowledge, skills, attitudes, and values essential to competent mental health practice. Four levels of competencies have been defined when working with PWDs, using the levels described in the Assessment of Competency Benchmark document (2007): Entry to Practicum, Entry to Internship, Entry to Professional Practice, and Advanced Practice and Specialization levels, which are Tables 3.1 through 3.4 in the Resources section of this chapter.

Knowledge

Counseling PWDs requires mental health practitioners to have an expansive knowledge base. Knowledge concerning intersecting identities (racial, gender, GLB [gay, lesbian, and bisexual], and socioeconomic status) is crucial information, yet focuses only on the personal aspect of disability. Mental health practitioners need to be knowledgeable about external aspects that affect the lives and mental health of PWDs. This section will also include knowledge regarding societal models of disability, legislative initiatives, definition of reasonable accommodations, personal experiences of harassment and abuse, and intersecting identities.

Models of Disability

There are numerous models of disability. This section will focus on the Moral, Medical, and the Minority or Social Models of disability. Mental health practitioners need to be cognizant of PWDs' understanding of these models and how they influence society's response to disability. For example, models of disability provide a basis for defining disability and offering a structure for how society and government can strive to meet the needs of this population. On the other hand, models of disability are sometimes criticized for being unrealistic, narrow in focus, and nonspecific in creating action steps (Olkin, 2002). Models of disability do influence PWDs' response to their disability. For example, youths with disabilities are especially vulnerable to "internalize the stigmatized reflection that society holds up for them and begin to see themselves . . . through the stigmatized lens" (Kinavey, 2006, p. 1093).

Perhaps the oldest framework for disability is the Moral Model (Mackelprang & Salsgiver, 1999; Olkin, 1999). The Moral Model of Disability views disability as a type of punishment placed on a person or family by some type of spiritual force. The disability may be a consequence of wrongs done by the individual, family, or community member, or even an act committed in a previous life. Disability is often associated with the notion of sin, and promotes feelings of shame and guilt, even to a point where families will keep PWDs hidden. Under the Moral Model, entire families may be ostracized, stigmatized, and experience social exclusion. In contrast, some may view disability under this model as a required affliction that must be endured before a future reward can be obtained, and portray PWDs as being inspirational and a blessing to others who could not endure such afflictions (Mackelprang & Salsgiver, 1999;

Olkin, 1999; D. W. Sue & D. Sue, 2003). Within this model, terms such as *lame, dumb, mad, feeble,* and *imbecile* were used to describe disability.

The Medical Model has historically dominated the development of disability policy. Disability is defined in the medical model as the physical and psychological experiences of biological impairments stemming from any number of illnesses or injuries within the bodies of the affected person. This approach postulates that disability results from a person's physical or mental limitations, and is not associated with social or environmental barriers (Smart, 2001). The Medical Model places the origin of the problem within the PWD and places an emphasis on finding a cure for the PWD or helping the PWD become more "normal" (Mackelprang & Salsgiver, 1999; Olkin, 1999). If a "cure" is not possible, the only available option is to accept the disability and provide the necessary care to support the PWD.

Many PWDs do not support this model because they reject the notion of being abnormal. It is perceived as promoting a sense of dependence, segregation, and institutionalization of PWDs. This model limits PWDs' opportunities to achieve their fullest potential and sense of control over their lives (I. Prilleltensky & O. Prilleltensky, 2003). At times, individuals may ignore the advice of medical professionals if the recommendations reflect the negative images propagated in the culture about PWDs, such as using a wheelchair instead of walking with crutches and braces (Kinavey, 2006).

The Minority Model of Disability, sometimes referred to as the Social Model of Disability, was an outgrowth of the strategies used by African Americans in the 1960s. From observing the actions used by African Americans during the civil rights movement, PWDs became aware of the need to advocate for their civil rights (Middleton, Rollins, & Harley, 1999). The Minority Model of Disability looks at disability as being the consequence of environmental, social, and attitudinal barriers that inhibit PWDs from full participation in society (Hahn, 1997). From a sociopolitical perspective, this model suggests that disability is a consequence of society's inability to meet the needs and goals of PWDs (J. F. Smart & D. W. Smart, 2006). Therefore, if barriers exist within society and the environment, society and the environment must be altered. For example, if a person who is blind cannot read a book in print, the printed material needs to be changed so that the person who is blind can successfully read the material. In the Minority Model, the person is not actually disabled in an environment where he or she can gain access to and use information in the same way that someone without a disability is able to access it. Less participation by PWDs is not due to the disability; rather, it is barriers that prevent full participation (Olkin, 1999).

Under the Minority Model, if social, environment, and attitudinal barriers are eliminated, the lives of PWDs will be enhanced. PWDs will also have equal and equitable access to the same opportunities as are experienced by other members of society. This model places responsibility on the society for change while appreciating the individual needs of PWDs (J. F. Smart & D. W. Smart, 2006). Yet, members of the dominant culture have been hesitant to acknowledge the legitimacy of a disability culture and have responded in a "hostile, dismissive, and patronizing" manner (Barnes & Mercer, 2001, p. 523).

Legislation

A study by Stageberg, Fischer, and Barbut (1996) found that college students with disabilities were unfamiliar with major pieces of civil rights legislation. Without crucial information about their civil rights, PWDs may be subjected to discrimination or treated as second-class citizens. This section will focus on two major pieces of disability civil rights legislation: the Rehabilitation Act of 1973 and the Americans With Disabilities Act (ADA).

Due to PWDs' long history of being marginalized by members of society, legislation has been enacted to assist PWDs to overcome barriers to integration (Stageberg, Fischer, & Barbut, 1996). A fundamental piece of civil rights legislation was the Rehabilitation Act of 1973, which disallows

discrimination on the basis of disability in programs operated by the federal government, in obtaining federal funding, in federal employment, and in public institutions of higher education.

The Americans with Disabilities Act of 1990 is often cited as the most significant piece of civil rights legislation since the 1964 Civil Rights Act. The ADA provides extensive civil rights protection and ensures equal access and opportunity for PWDs. The ADA (a) assures that PWDs have equal opportunity to participate in the full range of employment activities and reasonable accommodations; (b) prohibits discrimination in all aspects of the work environment; (c) ensures that PWDs have equal access to all services that are provided to nondisabled persons, including education, employment, and public transportation systems; (d) obligates newly constructed and modified facilities (e.g., restaurants, retails stores, hotels, etc.) to be accessible to PWDs; and (e) mandates television and telephone access for people with hearing and speech disabilities.

In 2008, the ADA was amended, and the ADA Amendment Act (ADAAA) went into effect in 2009. The ADAAA better defines what it means to have a disability and may be the foundation for overturning previous court decisions about disability. For additional information regarding legislation and disability, visit the government's Web site regarding the ADA at http://www.ada.gov/ and other legislation.

Reasonable Accommodations

The 1990 Americans with Disabilities Act (ADA) and the Rehabilitation Act of 1973 require that organizations make reasonable accommodations for workers with disabilities who ask for assistance. The Rehabilitation Act focuses on both the work environment and access to educational programs (K–12 and higher education). The ADA emphasizes three categories of "reasonable accommodations": modifications or adjustments to (1) a job application and (2) the work environment, and (3) "a current work environment that

CASE VIGNETTE 3.2

Reasonable Accommodations

Maria is an international student from Mexico enrolled in her junior year of undergraduate study at a university in California. English is not her first language, and she has been blind since birth. She is taking a film class as a general elective for her liberal arts degree. Two days ago, the professor in the class announced he is requiring the entire class to visit a cultural theater that is showing a 1960s black-and-white international French film that has English captioning. The last day to view the film at the theater is tomorrow. A five-page paper is required in conjunction with viewing the film.

Discussion Questions

- What might be some reasonable accommodations you could encourage Maria to ask for given the scenario without making her feel "different, special, or given an unfair advantage"?
- If you were Maria, how would you potentially advocate with the professor for reasonable accommodations?
- What are other resources Maria might call upon for assistance at the university, in the community, in the international student office, and so on, given the scenario?
- How might other students in the class react to Maria if she is provided "reasonable accommodations"?

would enable a current employee with a disability to enjoy equal benefits and privileges of employment as are enjoyed by other employees without disabilities" (retrieved June 20, 2009, from http://www.eeoc.gov/policy/docs/accommodation.html#general).

Case Vignette 3.2 focuses on reasonable accommodations; the lack of such accommodations is a major source of stress and frustration for PWDs. Mental health practitioners need to assist their clients with disabilities in identifying reasonable accommodations that would allow them to have full participation in all aspects of daily living.

Societal Attitudes: Prejudice/Hate Crimes/ Abuse

Mental health practitioners have been trained to be sensitive to issues related to discrimination and prejudice regarding different aspects of diversity. Yet due to the lack of training received by mental health practitioners regarding prejudice

and discrimination faced by PWDs, these issues are frequently overlooked in therapy (Olkin, 2002). Individuals with disabilities are perceived by the public with conflicting positive and negative emotions (Gill, 2001). Open devaluation of disabled people conflicts with our society's prevailing values of protection, charity, and nurturance. Consequently, disabled prejudice is seldom expressed overtly in the way racial bigotry or antigay views are often communicated (Hahn, 1997). PWDs frequently lack the preparation to be conscious of their minority status especially in comparison to those growing up in a racial/ethnic community (Gill, 2001). Persons with disabilities: (a) are targets of negative and inaccurate ascriptions and have few guideposts to define their social treatment, (b) rarely encounter the clarity of contempt associated with racism and homophobia because others consciously suppress negative sentiment, (c) are rejected based on appearance due to their disability even though they are not necessarily defined by their disability, and (d) find it difficult to recognize their marginalized membership within society because it is often perpetrated by family members and fellow associates (Gill, 2001).

A study by McCaughey and Strohmer (2005) explored stereotypes toward those with disabilities and found that participants described persons with schizophrenia as "dangerous and harmful to self or others," persons with mental retardation were considered "helpless and slow learners," and persons with physical disabilities were seen as "dependent, isolated, and emotionally unstable" (p. 92). Such stereotypical views allow others to develop decreased role expectations, serve as reasons for not hiring and employing PWDs, and provide justification for not developing personal relationships with PWDs (McCaughey & Strohmer, 2005). These attitudes and stereotypes make PWDs more vulnerable to disability harassment, hate crimes, and emotional, sexual, and physical abuse (Grattet & Jenness, 2001; McCaughey & Strohmer, 2005; McMahon, West, Lewis, Armstrong, & Conway, 2004).

Many acts of discrimination/harassment are subtle, may be unnoticed, and are not acknowledged by members of society (Grattet & Jenness, 2001; Holzbauer & Berven, 1996). Consequently, PWDs who experience discrimination and/or harassment may perceive that it was their fault, feel humiliated and ashamed, and be unable to talk about their experience (Crocker, 1983). Due to their marginal status, PWDs also have difficulty gaining access to the criminal justice system. Subsequently, many of these crimes are underreported (McMahon et al., 2004). Perpetrators of crimes against people with disabilities have included personal assistants, family members, neighbors, and acquaintances (Curry, Hassouneh-Phillips, & Johnston-Silverberg, 2001).

Women with disabilities are especially at risk to be victims of abuse and, in most studies, experience higher incidences of abuse than women without disabilities (Hassouneh-Phillips & Curry, 2002). Women with disabilities are vulnerable to abuse due to their lack of economic independence (Nosek, Howland, & Hughes, 2001), are susceptible to entering and remaining in abusive relationships, experience abuse for longer duration than women without disabilities (Hassouneh-Phillips & Curry, 2002; Swedlund & Nosek, 2000), and may not recognize abuse or have their experience regarded as abuse (Nosek et al., 1997; Womendez & Schneiderman, 1991).

PWDs are especially vulnerable to abuse and harassment due to their lack of power and personal control (Curry et al., 2001). Yet mental health practitioners may overlook issues of harassment and abuse with PWDs. If PWDs are not asked about possible abuse and harassment, mental health practitioners may unintentionally perpetuate society's discounting these concerns.

Multiple Identities

As previously mentioned, disability touches individuals of all races, ethnicities, sexual orientation, genders, religions, and social class. Those with membership in multiple marginalized groups experience being "a minority within a minority" (McDonald et al., 2007, p. 148). It is crucial for mental health practitioners to understand that having a disability and being a member of a marginalized group creates a unique living experience for the individual. Gaining a greater understanding of disability can better enable mental health practitioners to understand the intersection between disability and other multicultural identities.

Disability identity is a cultural-developmental phenomenon by which the PWD will "incorporate into his or her self-definition his or her own disability-related differences and regards that difference as a resource for participation in normative activities of his or her society" (Mpofu & Harley, 1981, p. 16). Individuals with disabilities who encompass multiple identities may find it difficult to determine which identities are of importance and how to integrate and categorize the experiences that encompass these multiple identities. This section will identify some of the challenges that those with multiple identities may experience. Due to space limitations, mental health practitioners may want to refer to other resources such as D. W. Sue and D. Sue (2003) for additional background information regarding different aspects of multiple identities.

Cultural Construct of Disability

The term *disability* is "culturally constructed through ways of talking and treating and writing" (Whyte, 1995, p. 268). As an example, the personal belief about independence and interdependence is a culturally influenced concept (Szymanski et al., 1996). Also, a society's social, moral, and economic values influence the response and treatment of PWDs, shape the attitudes and behaviors toward PWDs, and have a direct impact on the opportunities available to PWDs (Alur, 2002; Chan, Lee, Yuen, & Chan, 2002; Chen, Brodwin, Cardoso, & Chan, 2002; Lam, 1993; Wilhite, 1995). According to Cuellar and Arnold (1988): "culture can influence (a) the beliefs about causes, (b) the conditions that qualify as sickness, (c) the expectations about what the affected person should do, and (d) the actions of others in response to that person's condition" (Mumford, 1981, (p. 37).

Individuals who have a disability and also represent multiple identities may struggle with acculturation stress, created when environmental or internal demands tax a person's ability to cope and adapt (J. F. Smart & D. W. Smart, 1994). A high level of acculturative stress may impact PWDs in a negative manner by impairing (a) physical health and recovery from illness and injury, (b) decision making, (c) occupational functioning, (d) adaptation to acceptance of disability, and (e) the counselor–client relationship (J. F. Smart & D. W. Smart, 1993). Therefore, mental health practitioners need to develop an awareness of the cultural context that has influenced PWDs' beliefs about self, limitations imposed by the disability, and what their potential is for independent living, economic self-sufficiency, and type and quality of interpersonal relationships.

Disability and Racial/Ethnic Minorities

Asian Americans, Hispanics, African Americans, Native Americans, and other marginalized racial groups all have shared experiences of exclusion from the opportunities of the dominant culture (Szymanski, Trevino, & Fernandez, 1996). African Americans and American Indians represent the highest percentages of PWDs (Fassinger, 2008), and American Indians between the ages of 16 and 64 have one of the highest rates of disability (27%) for any racial group (U.S. Census Bureau, 2002). Meaning of disability, racial identity and acculturation, language, role models, types of interventions, structural factors and opportunity structures, gender and ethnicity interaction are all part of the experience of PWDs who represent ethnic/racial diversity (Szymanski et al., 1996). Being a PWD may isolate individuals from others within their racial/ethnic group and/or may keep the individual segregated from other people with disabilities (Alston, Bell, & Feist-Price, 1996; Mpofu & Harley, 1981). Racial identity development may be context specific (Mpofu & Harley, 1981). In the presence of individuals of similar ethnic/racial backgrounds, individuals with disabilities may be more inclined to examine their racial identity. Conversely, if these individuals are in a social situation with PWDs, ethnic differences may recede and the focus may center on disability, thereby lowering common social barriers based on racial criteria (McDonald et al., 2007).

PWDs of color experience a minority status of both racial discrimination and disability (Feist-Price & Ford-Harris, 1994). Mental health practitioners need to recognize that belonging to either group has traditionally been associated with prejudice that obstructs involvement in various life activities compared to nondisabled, nonminority persons.

Disability and Gender

Women and men differ in terms of types and prevalence of disabling conditions. Four times as many men become disabled from trauma as compared to women (Nosek & Hughes, 2003). Yet, women have a greater prevalence of physically disabling conditions overall. Gender disparities are also present regarding different mental health conditions. Women are twice as likely as men to experience depression (McGrath, Keita, Strickland, & Russo, 1990), report higher levels of stress (Noonan et al., 2004), and are more likely to live in poverty (Schleiter, Statham, & Reinders, 2006). Also, women receive "more treatment for acute illnesses, chronic illnesses, and mental health problems and have one third more physician visits, greater use of prescription and nonprescription drugs, and more time lost from work due to minor disabilities than men" (Stark-Wroblewski & Chwalisz, 2003, p. 309).

Men with disabilities have been found to be pessimistic and struggle with what they perceive as gender role incompatible—requiring assistance and accommodations, which is in conflict with their self-perception of needing to be strong and independent (Martinez & Sewell, 2000). Men with disabilities may be perceived as unable, incompetent, or inept in meeting the cultural standard of masculinity defined as capable and strong (Barnes & Mercer, 2001; Marini, 2001; McDonald et al., 2007).

Women with disabilities are often perceived as weak and dependent, and receive more conflicting social messages (Barnes & Mercer, 2001; Nosek, Howland, & Hughes, 2001). Cultural perceptions regarding women with disabilities include being asexual, and unable to work, to nurture, or to be mothers (McDonald et al., 2007), or what Fine & Asch (1988) labeled as *rolelessness* (p. 234). Mental health practitioners need to be aware of the gender differences when working with PWDs. For example, men with disabilities may subscribe to the traditional male role of not needing assistance, whereas a woman with a disability may have increased difficulty in defining her role within society.

A group of individuals who are frequently overlooked and their needs not met are transgender individuals with disabilities (C. Beighley & M. Ford, personal communication, July 29, 2009). Because of the changes that these individuals may encounter in adapting to/taking on their target gender, they remain vulnerable to psychological and physiological trauma. These traumas may inadvertently create situations that limit their opportunities and ability to fully participate in today's society. Mental health practitioners need to be aware of the life experiences that affect the mental and physical health of transgender individuals.

Lesbian, Gay, and Bisexual (LGB) Populations

In the literature, disability and sexual orientation have been viewed as separate entities. Little is known about the experience and sexual identity of LGB people with disabilities (Harley, Nowak, Gassaway & Savage, 2002). Receptiveness of LGBs with disabilities differs within various communities. The disability community often accepts sexual minorities, whereas the LGB community frequently does not accept disability (Appleby, 1994; McDaniel, 1995; Thompson, 1994). For example, gay males with disabilities complained about "lookism" (e.g., discrimination based on physical appearance) (Harley et al., 2002). Lesbian individuals with disabilities report that other lesbians may assume that they are asexual (Harley et al., 2002) and childlike (Whitney, 2006). Many LGB individuals with disabilities experience a lack of community support that leaves them feeling exhausted and isolated, and leads to internalized ableism and homophobia (Harley et al., 2002; Whitney, 2006).

It is important to remember that LGB individuals are both similar and diverse. They share common experiences as sexual minorities and the joint issues of marginalization, discrimination, and heterosexism (Harley et al., 2002). Yet, LGB individuals with disabilities differ across disability, race and ethnicity, age, immigration status, and other identity issues (Harley et al., 2002). Harley and colleagues (2002) stressed that "sexual orientation and disability must be perceived as interconnected rather than as parallel occurrences because there is clearly reciprocity of influence" (p. 525). LGB persons with disabilities are vulnerable to the oppression felt by those who are sexual minorities and those who are disabled (Stuart, 1994). Because of multiple identities, LGB persons may often experience dual, triple, or even quadruple oppression (Harley et al., 2002). It is important for mental health practitioners to remember that LGB clients with disabilities face barriers in coming to terms with their sex orientation that nondisabled LGBs do not (Whitney, 2006). Mental health practitioners need to be aware that this interpersonal struggle faced by LGB clients with disabilities leaves them especially vulnerable to isolation, exhaustion, and "internalized ableism and homophobia" (Whitney, 2006, p. 40).

Social Class and Disability

Social class, often identified by current economic resources, is less understood than race/ethnicity, gender, or sexual orientation in relation to disability (McDonald et al., 2007; J. B. Turner & R. J. Turner, 2004). In reviewing the economic status of PWDs, the poverty rate is about 24 percent, compared with 9 percent for people without disabilities (APA, 2007). Three times as many PWDs as their nondisabled peers have household incomes below $15,000 (National Organization on Disability-NOD, 2004) and are five times more likely than their nondisabled counterparts to be involuntarily unemployed (J. B. Turner & R. J. Turner, 2004). Employment rates are considerably lower for people of color with disabilities than for White men with disabilities (Fabian & Liesener, 2005). The impact of social class leaves PWDs vulnerable to continual marginalization and institutionalized discrimination due to fewer economic and social resources (McDonald et al., 2007).

The presence of disability predisposes an individual to lower levels of income (Bowe, 1981; D. W. Smart & J. F. Smart, 1997). Membership in an ethic minority compounds the effect of a disability upon economic status (J. F. Smart & D. W. Smart, 1992). If the minority individual with a disability is a woman, she belongs to three categories that predispose her to poverty: disability, ethnic group, and sex.

There is a danger of confusing culture with socioeconomic level (J. F. Smart & D. F. Smart, 1992). A client may appear to be indecisive and uncooperative when in fact he or she may feel helpless, powerless, and frustrated due to economic deprivation and its resulting disadvantages. Such a client may drop out of counseling due to the lack of economic resources. Some of the client's problems might be mistakenly diagnosed as internal in origin, such as anxiety and passivity, when in reality the problem is external. Indeed, poverty may lie at the root of many behaviors that could be misdiagnosed as having an internal locus (Castro, Furth, & Karlow, 1984). If mental health practitioners are unaware of the socioeconomic stresses faced by PWDs, it is easy to make erroneous assumptions regarding clients' behavior. These assumptions also make it difficult for mental health practitioners to build strong therapeutic alliances with clients with disabilities.

Assessment, Diagnosis, and Case Conceptualization

Assessment and diagnosis serves as the clinical foundation for mental-health care. Without an accurate and thorough assessment, mental health practitioners may misdiagnose and, therefore, use clinical interventions that may be inappropriate and may even be detrimental to the mental health of PWDs. Clinical assessment is a complex and multidimensional process, especially considering the lack of research and knowledge regarding *evidence-based practice* (*EBP*) and assessment instruments with PWDs (Olkin & Taliaferro, 2005). Though PWDs may have similar problems as others, they also face unique challenges not typically addressed by EBP, including "the pervasive prejudice, stigma, and discrimination that individuals with disabilities encounter in every sphere: housing, restaurants, transportation, employment, health care, recreational sites and activities, social and intimate interactions," problems that are external to the person (Olkin & Taliaferro, 2005, p. 357). Additionally, the symptoms associated with some disabilities—"pain, uncertainty, fatigue, weakness, daily hassles, misunderstanding by others, and a lack of sympathy for the disability experience—carry psychological ramifications that might need addressing" (Olkin & Taliaferro, 2005, p. 357).

Conventional assessment instruments are frequently used to assist mental health practitioners with diagnosis or to clarify clients' clinical concerns. Yet disability bias often occurs with conventional assessment instruments. These instruments usually do not have norms for PWDs. Because of symptoms related to their disabilities, PWDs may endorse items that inflate scores (Olkin & Taliaferro, 2005). To develop better skills in assessing mental health and personal concerns for PWDs, mental health practitioners would improve their competency by viewing concerns from both a social justice and an interpersonal perspective (Palombi & Matteson Mundt, 2006). The clinical assessment serves as the foundation for mental health practitioners to formulate the case, identify treatment options, and determine how treatment interventions are implemented and how the effects of treatment interventions are assessed (Olkin, 1999). When a mental health practitioner lacks a comprehensive view of clients' issues and concerns, and how they are impacted by outside forces, the practitioner may be inadvertently unable to appropriately assess mental health and personal concerns.

Ethical and Legal Issues

Most mental health professions have written in their ethics codes a requirement that practitioners become competent in working with multiculturally diverse clients. Many ethical standards (American Counseling Association [ACA], 2005; APA, 2002; National Association of Social Workers [NASW], 1996) specifically include disability as an element of diversity. Each of these organizations' Web sites includes a search engine that connects the reader to changes in the ethics codes regarding disability and other disability resources.

When compared to other oppressed groups, including women, racial/ethnic minorities, and sexual minorities, there are no ethical standards that assist practitioners on the mental health treatment of PWDs. To rectify the lack of ethical standards, the American Counseling Association has developed *Multicultural–Social Justice Counseling and Advocacy Competencies* (retrieved June 19, 2009, from http://www.counseling.org/Publications/CounselingTodayArticles.aspx?AGuid=47bfe1ea-cee2-43d2-957e-ec6e60baa479). The APA Task Force on Assessment and Treatment of Persons with Disabilities (in review) has created *The Guidelines for Assessment of and Intervention with Individuals Who Have Disabilities* for use by the memberships. These documents will fill a void within the mental health community

Mental health practitioners also need to be concerned about the ethical and competent clinical practice of the students and trainees whom they supervise. If students and trainees are unaware of the multicultural issues affecting those with disabilities, they may unknowingly perpetuate the marginalization of persons with disabilities (Palombi, 2008). Practitioners unaware of disability culture and issues may be unable to provide ethical and culturally competent practice to PWDs (Kemp & Mallinckrodt, 1996; Olkin & Taliaferro, 2005). Thus, most able-bodied therapists are currently doing cross-cultural counseling with clients with disabilities without requisite training (Olkin, 2002).

SKILLS

Assessing Accessibility

An important component of the Rehabilitation Act and the ADA is *accessibility*. Accessibility not only refers to buildings and public transportation, but also to educational and employment programs. The following are questions to consider regarding accessibility. Since many mental health practitioners do not have to struggle with issues regarding accessibility, these concerns are frequently overlooked or ignored.

Consider an environment where you are employed, participate in educational experiences, or volunteer your time. Consider the following questions and assess the accessibility of the venue:

Transportation

- Where is the nearest public transportation system to your location?
- How would you give directions to your site for different types of disabilities (e.g., vision impairment, mobility impairment, etc.)?
- If there is no public transportation system available, what will you suggest to the person who wants to come to your office?

Web Site

- If you have a Web site, is it accessible for persons who use screen-reading software?
- If you are unsure, how will you find out if the Web site is or is not accessible?
- What resources might you access to help your agency ensure that all information is accessible to all people?

Facilities

- Is your facility accessible with ramps, and doors that are wide enough for carts and wheelchairs?
- Is there a disability-accessible restroom available?

Special Accommodations

- If someone needs special accommodations, how will the person know where to find local assistance, and whom to ask for help? If someone is hearing impaired and needs an interpreter, how will you arrange this? If someone cannot see or write to fill out required forms, how will this be accomplished?

Assessing Client's Model of Disability

Assessing the Client's Model of Disability (Olkin, 1999; chart at the bottom of this page) contains a list of questions that a mental health practitioner can use to determine which model of disability is predominantly subscribed to by the client. According to Olkin (1999), the model used by the client reflects "how the problem is conceived and how it's presented, the locus of the problem and the goals for the treatment . . . the disability model permeates the clinical work from the first interaction with the client" (p. 52). It is important for PWDs to develop an understanding of how the models of disability influence their personal perception regarding their disability. Having an understanding of these models also allows PWDs to determine which model they feel most comfortable with, and which model works for them and provides "the greatest degree of satisfaction and contentment with self and others" (Olkin, 1999, p. 172).

Assessing the Client's Model of Disability

Moral Model	Do you feel shame or embarrassed about your disability?
	Do you feel you bring dishonor to your family?
	Do you try to hide and minimize the disability as much as possible?
	Do you try to make as few demands on others as possible, because it's "your problem" and hence your responsibility?
	Do you try to make your disability inconspicuous?
	Do you think your disability is a test of your faith, or is a way for you to prove your faith?
	Do you think your disability is a punishment for your or your family's failing?
Medical Model	Do you think that life for persons with disabilities has improved tremendously?
	Do you think a public figure, such as the president, wouldn't have to hide his or her disability today?
	Do you try to make as few demands as possible, because you think you should be able to find a way to do it yourself?
	Do you dress in ways that maximize your positive features and minimize the visibility of the disability?
	Do you believe that persons with disabilities do best when they are fully integrated into the nondisabled community?

(continued)

Assessing the Client's Model of Disability (*continued*)

Minority Model	Do you identify yourself as part of a minority group of persons with disabilities?
	Do you feel kinship and belonging with persons with disabilities?
	Do you think that not enough is being done to ensure rights of persons with disabilities?
	When policies and legislation are new, do you evaluate them in terms of their effects on persons with disabilities?
	Do you think the major goal of research should be to improve the lives of persons with disabilities by changing policies, procedures, funding, and laws?
	Do you think that persons with disabilities do best when they are free to associate in both the disabled and nondisabled communities, as bicultural people?

Relationship Skills

It is important for mental health practitioners to recognize that personal stereotypes and prejudice may impact the relationship-building process with PWDs (Feist-Price & Ford-Harris, 1994). Counselors need to have an awareness of their countertransference reactions to clients with disabilities. Therefore, in order to provide effective treatment interventions, mental health practitioners need to (a) establish a secure working relationship, (b) understand the client's experience, (c) determine the client's treatment needs, and (d) collaborate with the client to formulate a viable treatment plan (Danek, 1992).

Mental health practitioners need to recognize that, for PWDs, a considerable amount of personal energy is spent on fitting in, and forms of discrimination may be overlooked or ignored (Gill, 2001). This pattern of interaction with others may erode PWDs' self-esteem and sense of personal worth. Living in a culture that values physical beauty, work productivity, and financial success also affects PWDs' self-perception and sense of self-worth (Kemp & Mallinckrodt, 1996).

Whether a disability is invisible or visible, PWDs fear that their disability may serve as a reason for them to be ignored, rejected, or discredited as an individual (Galvin, 2005; Shelton & Matthews, 2001). Because of these fears, PWDs may not share that they have a disability and/or disclose issues related to their disability (Shelton & Matthews, 2001). Mental health practitioners need to be receptive to these fears and address them in an immediate and proactive manner (Olkin, 1999).

Assessment Skills

A model that may assist mental health practitioners in assessment and delineate possible areas for interventions is the Community Model of Embeddedness, Interdependence, Intradependence, & Evolution (CMEIIE), as outlined by Palombi and Matteson Mundt (2006). The CMEIIE model encourages the mental health practitioner to be aware of individuals' connection to their community, focusing on embeddedness, interdependence, intradependence, and evolution.

In the dimension of embeddedness, mental health practitioners need to access how the client is embedded into the community, including all aspects of multiculturalism and community living (employment, education, social/economic, etc.) and all clinical services interventions provided to other marginalized populations. The principle of embeddedness encourages mental health practitioners to become advocates for clients and assures that PWDs receive needed services and become members of their communities (Hunt, Matthews, Milsom, & Lammel, 2006). To provide accurate assessments and interventions for PWDs, mental health practitioners must validate PWDs, view their inclusion as important, and ensure the accessibility of the services and program that they sponsor and support (D. W. Sue & D. Sue, 2003).

The second dimension of this model is interdependence, which emphasizes PWDs' connections to other individuals within society. Since PWDs are frequently ignored and/or discounted, they may be hesitant to develop interpersonal relationships with those with whom they may associate. Failing to do so maintains their sense of isolation and alienation (Palombi & Matteson Mundt, 2006). Interdependence also focuses on the relationship between the client and therapist. Mental health practitioners reflect the prejudices of the culture and may not be aware of how these beliefs manifest themselves in therapy (Leigh et al., 2004). These prejudices create therapeutic distance between the client and the therapist and may not allow for a strong therapeutic alliance to develop.

Intradependence focuses on the unique clinical and personal stressors that are currently affecting PWDs. For those with disabilities, stress is a central part of everyday lives (Iwasaki & Mactavish, 2005) and they are exposed to a wider range of stressors than their able-bodied counterparts (Bramston & Fogerty, 2000). The stress that PWDs experience is of a chronic nature, intensified by disability-related factors (Turk & Monarch, 2002), and at multiple levels: personal, social, economic, societal/structural, cultural, and political (Noonan et al., 2004; Yorkston et al., 2003). Due to the complex and multiple causes of these stressors, stress may impact these individuals' health, well-being, and quality of life (Janssen, Schuengel, & Stolk, 2002). Iwasaki and Mactavish (2005) identified four major areas of stress: (1) disability (i.e., added demands in daily living, including the extra energy, effort, time, and care required to fulfill daily responsibilities and the complications of disability and aging); (2) health; (3) interpersonal relationships; and (4) the inability to meet expectations. They also found that there were additional series of stressors that "emanate from broader social-structural levels of society" (p. 204): (a) exclusionary social systems and structures, (b) lack of accessibility, (c) employment accessibility, and (d) marginality. These sources of stress tend to create a cycle that increases personal trauma and contributes to social exclusion. These stressors may be unique to the personal experience of PWDs, which many clinicians and other members of society do not have to either acknowledge or struggle with (Palombi & Matteson Mundt, 2006).

The last phase of the model emphasizes evolution. Evolution focuses on changes that may occur in personal/physical/social dimensions, advances in medical treatment and technology, and new research findings. To be aware of societal, medical, and technological developments and changes, mental health practitioners need to continue to educate themselves through reading and personal contact with PWDs (Hunt et al., 2006). The model allows mental health practitioners to prepare for the many challenges and modifications created by the changing nature of the community and the field of counseling and mental health services that may affect PWDs (Palombi & Matteson Mundt, 2006).

Case Vignette 3.3 (on page 71) is regarding an Asian woman with a disability. In order to provide a viable treatment plan, a thorough assessment

A Community Model of Embeddedness, Interdependence, Intradependence, and Evolution

Embeddedness	Interdependence	Intradependence	Evolution
Community	Friends	Dependence/independence	Changes in health
Family	Acquaintances with other people with disabilities	Aging Congenital or acquired disability	Changes in treatment regimens
Work	Friends only with those who are able-bodied	Time management	Changes in relationship
Organizations	Support groups	Vulnerability	Economic changes
Exclusionary social systems and structures	Clubs	Societal messages and beliefs	Loss of paid assistance *(continued)*

(*continued*)

Embeddedness	Interdependence	Intradependence	Evolution
Physical accessibility	Hobbies and fellow colleagues	Self-concept/competency	Changes in employment
Health/medical care	Personal caregivers	Dealing with limits/reality testing	Needing additional equipment or different equipment
Housing	Health/medical care providers	Empowerment	
Economic support	Transportation providers	Career development	
Insurance	Teachers/professors/fellow students	Economic	
Education	Supervisors and co–workers	Relationships/sexuality/ rolelessness/sexlessness Extra energy, effort, time, and care	
		Poor health	

interview needs to be conducted that includes exploration of clinical and personal concerns, possible cultural influences, issues related to multiple identities, and environmental structures. For some mental health practitioners, the purpose of the assessment interview is to indentify clinical symptoms that will meet the criteria outline in the *DSM IV-TR* (2000) for the initial diagnosis. Due to the multifaceted issues related to a disability, an evaluation focused only on presenting symptoms may not provide an accurate assessment of the client and his or her issues. It may also prevent the mental health practitioner from developing an understanding of how the client's personal stressors (added demands in daily living, including the extra energy, effort, time, and care required, health concerns, inability to meet expectations, exclusionary social systems and structures, lack of accessibility, employment accessibility, and marginality) all contribute to the client's psychological distress. These stressors may be unique to the personal experiences of PWDs, which many clinicians do not have to acknowledge or experience.

Another issue to consider in conducting an assessment with a PWD is how the interviewer's biases and perceptions can distort the process of asking questions and interpreting answers. The CMEIIE provides a structure for the mental

health practitioner to access clients from a community model of engagement. In order to gather information for each of the four dimensions, the interviewer has to expand the type of questions asked, understand how the answers may be interpreted, and consider what follow-up information and questions are required to develop a thorough understanding of the client's concerns. This process usually provides more in-depth information and understanding of how the presenting concern may impact the individuals' health, wellbeing, and quality of life.

Case Vignette 3.3 uses the CMEIIE as the format to complete the assessment. Listed below is a list of questions that the mental health practitioner may use to explore the four dimensions of CMEIIE.

Embeddedness—Connection to the Community:

- What is your role in the community mental health center?
- What is your current level of interface with your medical community?
- How integrated do you feel you are with your Asian community?
- How supported are you by your health/medical care providers?
- Is your home and the home of friends and relatives accessible?

CASE VIGNETTE 3.3

Pearl is an 18-year-old, first-generation Asian female who lives in a neighborhood nearby the community mental health center. Pearl uses an electric wheelchair for mobility and has limited range of motion with her arms and hands. As Pearl shares her concerns, it becomes apparent that her breathing is labored and that she requires considerable physical effort to articulate her concerns. Due to the extent of her physical disability, Pearl relies on a personal attendant to dress and bathe her in the morning and to prepare her for bed in the evenings.

In the session, Pearl shares that she is three months' pregnant. The father of the child is her personal attendant. Due to her physical disability, her pregnancy is considered high risk. Pearl will spend the last five months of pregnancy in bed, lying on her back, and using a respirator to assist her with breathing. Her physician has expressed concern about Pearl's pregnancy and how it may be detrimental to her physical health.

Pearl also expressed concern about her extended family's reaction to her pregnancy. Her extended family has considered her disability to be a burden on the family. Now, her being pregnant and unmarried will also mar the family's reputation within the community. Pearl's parents are aware of and concerned about her pregnancy. They have expressed their belief that Pearl should give the baby up for adoption. Pearl acknowledges her family's wishes, yet she wants to keep the baby and raise it herself. Pearl is excited about her pregnancy since she has always wanted to be a mother. Pearl wants to focus on her pregnancy, deal with her parents' wishes, find means to provide financial security for the baby, and identify a career that will allow her to be financially independent.

- Are you able to socialize with friends and family members in local restaurants?
- Is there accessible transportation available for your travel in the city?
- Have you ever considered employment opportunities for yourself in the community?
- What community recreational activities are available for you to participate in?

Interdependent—Connection to Others, Relationship with Therapist, Therapist's Possible Reactions to:

- How do you feel about working with a client with such a severe physical disability?
- Do you have any reactions to the client being sexually active?
- How do you feel about her attendant being both her attendant and her sexual partner?
- What are your feelings regarding your client's willingness to endure such a high-risk pregnancy?
- What is your reaction to the client's excitement about being pregnant?
- Do you feel your client has the right to raise her baby?

- Do you find yourself either focusing on the disability as the only experience of the individual or ignoring the client's disability?

Other Relationships Connected to Client and Her Concerns:

- What type of a relationship do you have with your personal attendant?
- How would you describe your relationship with your parents?
- Do you have strong relationships with members of your extended family?
- With your primary medical provider and nursing staff, do you feel comfortable asking for additional information regarding your health?
- If assigned a case manager, how would you see a case manager as being helpful?

Intradependent—Clinical and Personal Stressors:

- Would you please tell me about your disability? How has your disability affected your life? How do you feel about having your disability?

- Do you see your relationship with your personal attendant as long term?
- Would you feel comfortable sharing with me information regarding your previous sexual experiences?
- How did the sexual relationship between you and your attendant begin?
- What are your thoughts and feelings about being a mother? Do you foresee any possible barriers in being a mother?
- What does it mean in your culture to be a woman with a disability? What are your culture's expectations of a woman with a disability?
- If you could create "the perfect future" for yourself, what would it look like? If you could have any career, what would it be? What would you need to do to achieve these dreams?
- Are you concerned about the health risks associated with you pregnancy?
- Are you aware of the medical costs associated with your disability and/or with your pregnancy?
- Do you have other financial resources available, such as Social Security Disability, family resources, etc.?
- Have you considered whether your personal attendant wants to exercise his rights as a parent?
- How do you feel about having your baby adopted?
- How do you handle the conflict between you and your parents regarding your baby?
- How do the members of your community view your pregnancy? What feedback have you received regarding keeping the baby or placing it for adoption?

Evolution—Changes in Personal/Physical Dimensions, Advances in Treatment and Technology, and New Research Findings:

- Have you noticed any personal changes since the birth of your baby?
- How do you feel about your attendant as the father of your baby?

- How is the quality of your health since having your baby?
- Have you made any decisions regarding your education and/or career?
- Is the medical care that you are receiving meeting your needs?
- Are you concerned about your financial security?
- Since you have had your baby, where do you plan to live? Does your place of residence have adequate space for you and your baby?
- Sometimes women may struggle with postpartum depression after having a baby. How are you feeling since having the baby?
- I have given you some information regarding new technologies that may increase your independence and ability to care for the baby. Are you interested in exploring some of these options?

Issues to Consider:

- Do you have any countertransference reactions, either positive or negative?
- What assessment questions regarding client's disability will you ask?
- What are the potential ethical issues in this case—relationship with attendant, medical risks of pregnancy, parenting skills? How might you resolve them?
- Should you consult with parents, medical professionals, rehabilitation professionals, the father of her child, community leaders?
- What issues do you feel competent to address, and what issues do you not feel you are able to address?
- Do you feel that it is appropriate for you to provide her with counseling? If not, what is your treatment plan?

Using the information gathered from completing the four dimensions of the CMEIIE, organize and prioritize the client's concerns to develop treatment goals. From the initial assessment of the client, the following might be possible treatment goals:

Therapy Goal:

- Gain informed consent from client for including her disability as a topic within therapy.
- Assist the client in making a self-care plan to ensure a healthy pregnancy and after the pregnancy.
- Assist with her decision of whether to keep the child and raise the child herself.
- Clarify the client's relationship with her attendant and with her parents.
- Assess her beliefs regarding her disability, being a mother, and future goals for herself.
- Assist the client in finding a career direction that meets her interest and provides an adequate level of economic support.
- Assist her in developing more interpersonal connections with individuals within her interpersonal environment.
- Consult with knowledgeable colleagues and rehabilitation professionals as needed.
- Refer client to rehabilitation professional (if appropriate) to discuss her concerns regarding disability and securing possible employment.
- Draw upon client's strengths, including her ability to make difficult personal decisions, decision to have the baby, willingness to consider being a mother, and future personal goals.
- Assist client in reconnecting to her community and developing new interpersonal relationships.

Intervention Skills

Mental health practitioners have historically focused on helping PWDs adjust to their disability, grieve the loss of their functioning, and develop strategies for coping with their disability (Marks, 2008). There has been a longstanding inaccurate assumption that the primary clinical issue PWDs want and need to address in therapy is their disability (Olkin & Taliaferro, 2005). In fact, disability is only one of a spectrum of characteristics that comprise the identity of PWDs. PWDs, like all other people, possess multiple identities and need assistance with issues that affect their career, education, relationships, personal identity, sexuality, spirituality, and so on (J. F. Smart & D. W. Smart, 2006).

Danek (1992) suggests that the counseling process should be active, present oriented, and include the following foci: (a) counter deficit thinking/negative self-talk regarding client's disability or personal concerns; (b) teach self-management skills and flexible coping strategies, focus on self-efficacy in order to overcome the powerlessness that a client may feel; (c) emphasize choice, assist client in identifying and exploring personal options; (d) develop strategies to overcome isolation, encourage client to join support groups where issues regarding disabilities could be addressed; (e) develop a positive self-image incorporating disability and other parts of self, help the client see that personal self-worth is not dependent on one's ability; (f) learn new problem-solving strategies to implement treatment goals, challenge the client to set personal goals and develop strategies to achieve them; and (g) concentrate on system change strategies, acknowledge that the client may experience oppression and encourage client to be a self-advocate.

Hunt and colleagues (2006) identified several themes as being crucial to successful clinical interventions in a study that interviewed lesbians with disabilities. Mental health practitioners need to: (a) Be aware of their own thoughts and feelings regarding multiple identities and disability in order to be cognizant of any misperceptions and biases that can influence their work with clients; (b) intervene from a multidimensional perspective working with the client as a whole person; (c) make the effort to learn as much as they can about issues related to their client's disability and/or other multiple identities outside of session, rather than place the responsibility of educating on the client; (d) set a tone of openness and affirmation, because appearing neutral may be viewed as maintaining the status quo of prejudice, discrimination, and oppression; (e) be proactive in addressing multiple-identity and disability issues with clients by directly asking about a client's disability and multiple-identity experiences; and (f) be patient with clients who are confrontational and questioning since some clients may test mental health practitioners

CASE VIGNETTE 3.4

A therapist noticed that her female client who was being treated for depression had a slight limp when she walked. It would have been clinically acceptable for the therapist to disregard the client's limp and focus on other clinical issues. Yet the therapist made a therapeutic decision to ask the client about her limp. By noticing the limp and asking about it, she gave the client permission to share with the therapist that she had a degenerative muscle disorder. This information allowed the therapist to develop a better understanding of the client's struggles with her negative self-image and feelings of being inferior, worthless, and dependent. The negative messages regarding her disability also affected her relationships with others to the extent that she feared that if her boyfriend knew about her disability, he would terminate their relationship. This additional piece of information altered the focus of therapy and allowed the counselor to be a more effective practitioner.

to determine whether it is safe to discuss complicated life issues. These findings may also be applicable for PWDs with other multiple identities.

The mental health practitioner as an advocate is critical when issues of program accessibility and awareness are considered. Mental health practitioners need to raise the awareness and sensitivity of mainstream programs to include issues of accessibility (Danek, 1992), while simultaneously encouraging PWDs to advocate for themselves by helping them with assertiveness training and decision-making skills (Hunt et al., 2006).

Speaking from a social work practice perspective, Marks' (2008) notion of an integrative approach to disability may be beneficial for mental health practitioners. The mental health practitioner can learn from the individual with a disability about the physical consequence of the person's experience, has the opportunity to gain understanding about the mental and emotional experience, and can have an awareness of the social guidelines and institutional framework (see Case Vignette 3.4).

Collaboration and Referral Skills

Due to the multifaceted nature of disabilities and related physical and psychological concerns, including pain, fatigue, weakness, the uncertainty associated with a disability, and frustration with the medical system, PWDs may seek additional assistance from alternative health providers. Alternative health practices such as aquatic exercise, stretching, light exercise, yoga, tai chi, acupuncture, massage, and self-hypnosis may also be helpful in lessening the symptoms associated with the disability. Mental health providers need to be aware of community resources and programs that offer such services.

Also, it is not uncommon for persons of color with disabilities to seek treatment from Eastern therapeutic methods and traditional healing ceremonies (Lomay & Hinkebein, 2006). The use of traditional healing methods may help to restore a sense of balance with the PWD and family, and may promote adherence to mainstream medical and therapeutic interventions. Therefore, traditional healing can improve the quality of life for a PWD at the emotional, social, and spiritual level and may complement and benefit mainstream methods of treatment (Marbella, Harris, Diehr, G. Ignace, & G. T. Ignace, 1998). Mental health practitioners need to capitalize on the trusting relations and influence indigenous healers have with their clients (Helms & Cook, 1999). Indigenous healers should be given the same respect for their knowledge, training, and healing credentials within their cultures as Western therapists expect to receive in their own culture (Lomay & Hinkebein, 2006).

CASE VIGNETTE 3.5

Traci is a 42-year-old single (divorced with 2 children, ages 10 and 12) African American heterosexual female who holds a Protestant faith system. She started to progressively lose her vision at age 19, secondary to a history of macular degeneration. She is "quantified" as being blind/legally blind by the Social Security Administration. At age 34, this client experienced a series of strokes that required emergency brain surgery. She was in a coma for two weeks after the surgery. The client participated in a year-long rehabilitation program following this experience. The only observed lingering functional effect of the strokes and surgery appears to be slower informational processing speed and periodic struggles to find the "right words" when speaking, and depressed mood. Because of the client's visual impairment, her guide-dog Buffy accompanies her to each session. Unemployed since her health issues began, she is dependent on social services to financially assist her. She lives with her male partner of 2 years who abuses several different substances. At intake she did not definitively respond to the counselor's inquiry whether she had ever experienced abuse or domestic violence. Her presenting concerns relate to wanting to return to college to finish a bachelor's degree in chemistry. She worries about her capacity to succeed academically because of being blind. She was referred for therapy by a state agency providing services to individuals with disabilities. At the first session, the client asks to feel the counselor's face as a means of becoming introduced.

Discussion Questions

- Given the case scenario, what are some of the treatment considerations for the mental health practitioner?
- What type of accommodation may need to be made, given the client's disability?
- How may your approach to treatment be impacted by the presence of the client's disability?
- What are some thoughts and feelings this client may be experiencing?
- What are some thoughts, feelings, and reactions you as the professional have to this client?
- Is the therapist required to contact Child Protective Services due to the partner's substance abuse?
- What thoughts and feelings arise regarding Tracy's request to touch the therapist's face?
- Knowing that women with disabilities are frequently abused by their partners, how may this issue be explored in therapy?
- What are some ethical concerns considering this case vignette?

In the resources section of this chapter, there is an extensive list of organizations that provide information and services related to specific types of disabilities. Mental health practitioners may want to either visit these Web sites or refer clients for additional information and resources.

Supervision and Training Skills

In spite of PWDs being the largest diversity group within the United States, practitioners in the field of mental health are seldom trained to work with clients with disabilities (Olkin, 2002; Strike, Skovholt, & Hummel, 2004). Practitioners are unaware of disability culture and issues, receive little or no training regarding disabilities, and thus may be unable to provide culturally competent practice to PWDs (Kemp & Mallinckrodt, 1996; Olkin & Taliaferro, 2005). Students in mental health training programs receive fewer hours of training for disability than for other minority groups (Hogben & Waterman, 1997; Kemp & Mallinckrodt, 1996; Rubino, 2001).

Even those who receive training in the area of disability and view themselves as competent also struggle. Strike and colleagues (2004) studied mental health practitioners concerning disability competence and found that they lacked (a) knowledge about specific types of disabilities, (b) the clinical competency to work with persons with disabilities,

and (c) clinical skills in areas such as accurate case conceptualization (see Case Vignette 3.5).

Currently, mental health practitioners are encouraged to gain additional training and expertise to be effective multicultural professionals. Training on issues related to disability should include education on (a) the cultural history of people with disabilities; (b) stereotypes and biases; (c) related potential mental health issues, such as alienation, discrimination experiences, and relationship issues; and (d) training in effective counseling strategies (Kemp & Mallinckrodt, 1996). Receiving training in issues related to disability allows mental health practitioners to feel more at ease and competent in meeting the mental health needs of PWDs (Olkin, 2002).

IMPLICATIONS FOR SUPERVISORS

- *Assessment Approaches:* Encourage supervisees to ask open-ended questions about whether disability is a salient feature in the client's experience, beliefs, and presenting concerns.

- *Individual and Cultural Differences:* Encourage supervisees to examine their own beliefs and values, reflect on their own experiences, explore how disability relates to cultural beliefs, and to the society's social, moral, and economic values, and how they influence the response and treatment of PWDs.

- *Interpersonal Assessment:* Help supervisees work through their potential countertransference issues. Suggest use of family genogram to help supervisees make sense of the own personal heritage regarding disability and explore ways in which their experiences may affect their work.

- *Theoretical Orientation:* Encourage supervisees to know what their chosen theoretical orientation assumes and teaches about disability and assist supervisees in constructing effective interventions that are consistent with their chosen orientation to (a) counter deficit thinking, (b) teach self-management skills, (c) emphasize choice, (d) develop strategies to overcome isolation, (e) develop a positive self-image incorporating disability, (f) learn new problem-solving strategies to implement their goals, and (g) concentrate on system change strategies.

- *Problem Conceptualization:* Address strengths of disability orientation and bring attention to how economic disadvantage, attitudinal barriers, discrimination, inaccessible transportation, and housing are some examples of the challenges PWDs may be experiencing related to their disability.

- *Selecting Treatment Goals and Plans:* Help supervisees develop treatment goals and plans that are compatible with clients' beliefs, values and practices and address disability-related concerns. Refer supervisees to professional publications, rehabilitation professionals, and writing on disability to enhance supervisees' range of understanding.

- *Ethics:* Train supervisees to work with clients with disabilities in an ethical manner by informing them of the ethical guidelines and codes that pertain to clients with disabilities and disability issues.

- *Intervention Skills:* Incorporate discussion of psychotherapy techniques to help supervisees examine their own understanding of disability and the usefulness of psychotherapy interventions.

Source: Adapted from Aten and Hernandez (2004).

VALUES AND ATTITUDES

It is important for mental health practitioners to recognize that they are members of a society that continues to discriminate against and marginalize PWDs. It is virtually impossible for mental health practitioners not to have been exposed to the biases and attitudes of the society and not to have internalized these attitudes and biases. Research indicates that those without disabilities do not necessarily want to engage with those with disabilities. They may ignore, evade, or discredit in order to avoid communicating or interacting with PWDs. Studies investigating communications between nondisabled and disabled interactions confirm patterns of avoidance, strain, and depersonalizing (Asch, 1984). Therefore, mental health practitioners need to have a heightened sensitivity to how these prejudices and biases may affect and/or influence their therapy with PWDs. Kemp and Mallinckrodt (1996) studied counselors' attitudes toward clients with disabilities. They found that therapists may (a) encourage dependency, (b) expect a client to hold an inferior societal status and accept a sick role, (c) maintain low expectations of client capability, (d) impose their own personal values that may not match client values, and (e) fail to address the disability at all. It is crucial for mental health practitioners to assess for the possible effects of "social stigma, culturally inferior status, pejorative treatment, feelings of belongingness, and discrimination experiences" (Kemp & Mallinckrodt, 1996, p. 381). The lack of awareness about these issues may leave a client who has a disability feeling further marginalized and invalidated (Kemp & Mallinckrodt, 1996; Leigh et al., 2004). Due to the lack of knowledge, skills, and understanding regarding working with PWDs, clinicians are apt to make therapeutic mistakes. These mistakes include (a) dispense the cure, (b) identify through personal experience, (c) have lower expectations for the client, (d) provide meaningless encouragement, (e) propose too many helpful solutions, (f) participate in client's denial of disability, and (g) treat the client with special care or "just like anyone else" (Esten & Willmott, 1993).

SUMMARY

The purpose of this chapter has been to provide mental health practitioners, students, trainers, educators, and supervisors with guidelines and resources for expanding their competencies in assessing and working with PWDs. We have outlined requisite areas of knowledge (individual and cultural diversity, assessment, diagnosis and case conceptualization, and ethical and legal standards); skills (relationship, assessment, intervention, referral, and supervision and training); and the attitudes and values necessary to provide multiculturally sensitive services to individuals with disabilities. Providing mental health services to PWDs encourages mental health practitioners to develop new clinical competencies through didactic education (seminars, lectures, specialized courses in disability service delivery, etc.) and field experiences. To develop clinical competencies, mental health practitioners need to acknowledge their own personal feelings concerning disability and those with disabilities.

Mental health practitioners can assist PWDs in identifying and developing community and personal interventions that empower them and assist in their personal growth; ensure that the issues and concerns of PWDs are embedded into multiculturalism and included in all dialogues, research, and development of clinical interventions; and confront the barriers for PWDs caused by society's prejudice and discrimination that prohibit equality and social justice. Through the case vignettes, examples, and resources provided, we hope that the reader has deepened his or her repertoire of knowledge, skills, and methods for integrating disability into competent training practice.

RESOURCES

The following resources and Web sites are provided as suggestions for further inquiry and as tools students, clinicians, trainees, and supervisors can utilize to help improve the quality of the services they provide.

GENERAL DISABILITY

People with Disabilities Foundation (PWDF)	http://www.pwdf.org
National Organization for Rare Disorders, Inc. (NORD)	http://www.rarediseases.org
Equip for Equality, Inc. (EFE)	http://www.equipforequality.org
Association on Higher Education and Disability (AHEAD)	http://www.ahead.org
Disability Information for Students and Professionals (DISP)	http://www.abilityinfo.com
Health Resource Center	http://www.heath.gwu.edu/
National Disabled Students Union (NDSU)	http://www.disabledstudents.org
National Center for the Dissemination of Disability Research (NCDDR)	http://www.ncddr.org
Online Disability Information System Database (ODIS)	http://www.umaine.edu/cci/
Disability Information for Students (DIS)	http://www.abilityinfo.com
Libraries without Walls (Equal Access to Software and Information [EASI])	http://www.rit.edu/~easi/lib/csun96bc.htm
Access E-Bility	http://www.ebility.com/index.php
National Center for Education Statistics: An Institutional Perspective on Students with Disabilities in Postsecondary Education	http://www.nces.ed.gov/pubs99/1999046.pdf
EmployAbilities	http://www.employabilities.ab.ca/

ADHD/ADD

College and ADD	http://www.add.org/content/legal/college.htm
Children and Adults with Attention Deficit Disorders (CHADD)	http://www.chadd.org
SAALD (Student Alliance on ADD)	http://www.adult-add.org

AMPUTEES

Amputee Coalition of America	http://www.amputee-coalition.org

ARTHRITIS

Road Back Foundation (Arthritis)	http://www.roadback.org

ASPERGER'S SYNDROME

Asperger Syndrome Coalition of the U.S. (ASC-U.S.)	http://www.asperger.org

ASTHMA

Asthma and Allergy Foundation of America	http://www.aafa.org
AllAllergy	http://www.allallergy.net

AUTISM

Autism National Committee — http://www.autcom.org

BLIND/VISUALLY IMPAIRED

American Council of the Blind — http://www.acb.org
Recording for the Blind & Dyslexic — http://www.rfbd.org
National Federation of the Blind — http://www.nfb.org
Guide Dogs for the Blind, Inc. — http://www.guidedogs.com

CANCER

American Cancer Society, Inc. — http://www.cancer.org
Women's Cancer Resource Center (WCRC) — http://www.givingvoice.org

CEREBRAL PALSY

United Cerebral Palsy — http://www.ucpnyc.org
Inter-American Conductive Education Association (IACEA) — http://www.iacea.org
Cerebral Palsy Information Central — http://www.geocities.com/aneecp/index2.html

DEAF & HARD OF HEARING

Alexander Graham Bell Association for the Deaf and Hard of Hearing — http://www.agbell.org
The National Association of the Deaf — http://www.nad.org
The Midwest Center for Postsecondary Outreach — http://www.mcpo.org
Deaf Women Against Violence — http://www.dwav.org
Deaf Resource Library (DRF) — http://www.deaflibrary.org/
Deaf Queer Resource Center (DQRC) — http://www.deafqueer.org/
Deafblind Online — http://www.ssco.esu.k12.oh.us/ocdbe/index.html
Midwest Center on Law and the Deaf — http://www.mcld.org

DIABETES

American Diabetes Association — http://www.diabetes.org/home.jsp
International Diabetes Foundation — http://www.idf.org

EPILEPSY

The Epilepsy Foundation of America — http://www.efa.org
American Epilepsy Society (AES) — http://www.aesnet.org

FIBROMYALGIA & CHRONIC FATIGUE SYNDROME

American Fibromyalgia Syndrome Association, Inc. — http://www.afsafund.org
Shasta CFIDS — http://www.shasta.com/cybermom
The Unify Coalition — http://www.cssa-inc.org/_unify/rebuilding.htm
Guillain-Barre — http://www.gbs.org/

HEADACHE SUFFERERS

Migraine Awareness Group (MAGNUM) — http://www.migraines.org/disability
National Headache Foundation (NHF) — http://www.headaches.org

(continued)

(continued)

HIV/AIDS AND IMMUNE DISORDERS

Health Info	http://www.uhfpres.org/health.htm
AIDS Healthcare Foundation	http://www.aidshealth.org
Immune Deficiency Foundation	http://www.primaryimmune.org

LEARNING DISABILITIES

About Dyslexia	http://www.interdys.org/index.jsp
Recording for the Blind & Dyslexic	http://www.rfbd.org
Learning Disabilities Association of American (LDA)	http://www.ldanatl.org
The International Dyslexia Association	http://www.interdys.org

MENTAL ILLNESS

National Alliance for the Mentally Ill (NAMI)	http://www.nami.org
National Mental Health Association	http://www.nmha.org
World Fellowship for Schizophrenia and Allied Disorders (WFSAD)	http://www.world-schizophrenia.org
Anxiety Disorders Association of America (ADAA)	http://www.adaa.org
National Foundation for Depressive Illness, Inc. (NAFDI)	http://www.depression.org/index
National Association for Anorexia Nervosa and Associated Disorders (ANAD)	http://www.anad.org
NY Society for the Study of Multiple Personality and Dissociation (NYSSMP&D)	http://www.nyssmpd.org

MULTIPLE SCLEROSIS

Multiple Sclerosis Association of America	http://www.msaa.com
National Multiple Sclerosis Society	http://www.nmss.org

PARALYSIS/SPINAL CORD INJURIES

National Spinal Cord Injury Association	http://www.spinalcord.org
Spinal Cord Injury Resource Guide at MGH	http://www.neurosurgery.mgh.harvard.edu/spine/lnkspine.htm
Spinal Cord Injury Network International	http://www.sonic.net/~spinal

REFLEX SYMPATHETIC DYSTROPHY/COMPLEX REGIONAL PAIN SYNDROME

The American RSDHope Group	http://www.rsdhope.org
RSDS Association	http://www.rsds.org

RESTLESS LEG SYNDROME

Restless Leg Syndrome (RLS) Foundation, Inc.	http://www.rls.org

SPINA BIFIDA

Spina Bifida Association of America	http://www.sbaa.org
Education Resources for People with Disabilities, Carnegie	http://www.carnegielibrary.org/subject/disabled/edu.html

STROKE

The Stroke Network, Inc.	http://www.strokenetwork.org

STUTTERING

The National Center for Stuttering   http://www.stuttering.com
National Multiple Sclerosis Society   http://www.nmss.org

TOURETTE SYNDROME

Tourette Syndrome Association, Inc. (TSA)   http://www.tsa-usa.org
Spinal Cord Injury Resource Guide at MGH   http://www.neurosurgery.mgh.harvard.edu/spine/
                                               Inkspine.htm
Spinal Cord Injury Network International   http://www.sonic.net/~spinal

TRAUMATIC BRAIN INJURY/TUMORS

Perspectives Network On-Line   http://www.tbi.org
American Brain Tumor Association   http://www.hope.abta.org/site/PageServer

---

DISABILITY MULTIPLE IDENTITIES SEMINAR

Topics and Activities

Trainers and clinicians may select activities from among the following suggestions.

A. Knowledge gained through didactic training and independent study:

1. Relation of disability competency to multicultural competency

2. Individual and cultural differences (including age, gender, sexual orientation, social-economic status [SES], ethnicity) relating to disability issues

3. Literature describing the relevance of disability to wellness, physical health, mental health and economic health

4. Definitions of disability

5. Cultural attitudes toward disability (Western, non-Western, and indigenous)

6. Cultural practices regarding disability

7. Models of disability: moral, medical, minority

8. Types of disabilities: congenital/acquired, visible/invisible disabilities

9. Legislation focused on disability

10. Disability assessment methods; diagnosis, case conceptualization, and treatment planning

11. Experiences related to discrimination, marginalization, and isolation

12. Psychological and social ramifications of disability

13. Disability coping styles and problem-solving style (self-directing, deferring, collaborative)

14. Theoretical orientation of psychotherapy—view of disability

15. Disability intervention techniques; risks and benefits; contraindications to using disability interventions

16. Therapy issues that frequently have a disability component: grief, abuse recovery, sexual identity development, aging, death and dying, addiction, career development

(continued)

(*continued*)

17. Transference and countertransference issues

18. Ethical/legal standards: informed consent to provide disability interventions, potential dual roles, and legal mandates regarding disability

19. Roles of psychotherapists, rehabilitation professionals, minister/religious or spiritual leaders, alternative health providers

20. Resource information: consumers representing different disabilities, community advocate leaders, rehabilitation professionals, medical providers, alternative health providers, psychotherapists specializing in therapy with PWDs

B. Awareness of own attitudes and values—may use one or more of the following techniques to explore one's own beliefs, attitudes, and experiences:

- Genogram focusing on disability within a family
- Journaling
- Family member interview
- Disability lifeline

Questions for examining beliefs and attitudes include:

What are your first memories of learning about persons with disabilities?

What were the disability beliefs and values in your household?

To what degree have you subscribed to those same beliefs?

What factors have affected the degree to which you have subscribed to these disability beliefs throughout the course of your life?

C. Activities to build knowledge, awareness, and skills:

1. Visit a service connected with assisting persons with disabilities:

   a. Independent-living center

   b. Social Security Administration—state

   c. Office of vocational rehabilitation

2. Write a paper describing the beliefs and practices of two disability traditions.

3. Invite community leaders with disabilities to the seminar.

4. Participate in group discussions of disability related issues.

5. Participate in hospital grand rounds in a rehabilitation facility relating to visible/invisible disabilities.

6. Discuss therapy case examples and disability issues scenarios. Identify possible therapeutic interventions, transference and countertransference issues, and ethical dilemmas.

7. Choose a model of disability and research how it is addressed in societal attitudes.

8. Explore disability concepts through reading books describing personal experiences regarding disability, viewing films focused on individuals with disabilities, and reviewing current media regarding treatment of disability.

9. Participate in disability experiences (e.g., book readings, movie festivals, disability speaker events, lobbying for disability civil rights, etc.).

INTEGRATION OF DISABILITY ISSUES INTO THE TRAINING CURRICULUM

- Human growth and development courses (connection of cognitive, social, and moral development with the development of disability beliefs, attitudes and practices).
- Social and cultural foundations (multicultural coursework).
- Helping relationships courses (interviewing skills, counseling skills).
- Group therapy (create an environment of mutual respect; demonstrate and use role-play techniques to use with disability dilemmas).
- Career and lifestyle development (examine influence of disability issues on career decision making, starting with one's own exploration of personal values).
- Appraisal (assess disability issues during intake process, then use more specific disability assessment if appropriate).
- Research and program development (study of disability literature).
- Ethics (understanding of ethical issues relevant to disability issues).

COMPETENCY BENCHMARK TABLES

The purpose of the Competency Benchmarks (Tables 3.1-3.4) is to develop developmental models for defining and measuring competencies in professional psychology; each chapter in this *Handbook* applies the diversity competence for mental health practitioners in their work with a particular diverse population.

Table 3.1   Developmental-Level Competencies I

	READINESS LEVEL—ENTRY TO PRACTICUM	
Competencies		Learning Process and Activities
Knowledge	The student is gaining knowledge in: • Multiculturalism—the student is engaged in the process of learning that all individuals, including themselves, are cultural beings with worldviews that shape and influence their attitudes, emotions, perceptions, and experiences. • The importance of reflective practice and self-awareness. • Core counseling skills and theories. • Ethics code.	At this stage of development, the emphasis in psychotherapist education is instilling knowledge of foundational domains that provide the groundwork for subsequent attainment of functional competencies. Students at this stage become aware of the principles and practices of the field, but they are not yet able to apply their knowledge to practice. Therefore, the training curriculum is focused on knowledge of core areas, including literature on multiculturalism, ethics, basic counseling skills, scientific knowledge, and the importance of reflective practice and self-awareness.
Skills	The student is: • Beginning to develop the ability to demonstrate empathic listening skills, respect, and interest when talking with individuals expressing different values and belief systems. • Learning to critically examine the diversity literature.	It is important that throughout the curriculum, trainers and teachers define individual and cultural differences broadly, to include disability differences. This should enable students to have a developing awareness of how to extrapolate their emerging multicultural competencies to include the realm of individuals with disabilities and cultural differences of those with disabilities. Most students, through their life experiences,
Values and Attitudes	The student demonstrates: • Willingness to engage in self-exploration—to consider own motives, attitudes, behaviors. and effect on others.	*(continued)*

Table 3.1   Developmental-Level Competencies I (*continued*)

READINESS LEVEL—ENTRY TO PRACTICUM	
Competencies	Learning Process and Activities
• Intellectual curiosity and flexibility. • Ability to value expressions of diverse viewpoints and belief systems.	would be expected to have basic knowledge of at least one person with a disability, awareness of the definitions of *disability/handicapped/cripple*, and personal awareness of their cultural experience regarding disability.

Table 3.2   Developmental-Level Competencies II

READINESS LEVEL—ENTRY TO INTERNSHIP		
Competencies		Learning Process and Activities
Knowledge	The student has: • General understanding of the traditions, beliefs, and practices of several of cultures regarding disability. • Understanding of potential ethical dual roles possible in disability counseling. • Knowledge that working with disability issues in therapy may be contraindicated in certain circumstances, though not yet well understood. • Understanding of the importance of consulting with supervisors and others when presented with unfamiliar client issues and disability.	At this level of development, students are building on their education and applied experiences (such as supervised practicum experiences) to attain a core set of foundational competencies. They can then begin applying this knowledge to professional practice. As a result of being exposed to didactic training and close supervision, students attain the multicultural values and attitudes appropriate to their level of development. Foundational knowledge and multicultural values and attitudes are becoming well established, but skills in working with disability issues would be expected to be rudimentary at this level of development.
Skills	Skills in the following areas are beginning to develop: • Discerning personal limits of openness to beliefs and attitudes toward disability and PWDs and, after consultation with supervisors, referring clients to appropriate resources if not able to work with them. • Building therapeutic alliance to create a trusting, safe, and open therapeutic climate to discuss disability issues, if indicated. • Learning to use the *DSM-IV-TR* diagnostic categories related to disabilities, including Axis III.	Learning occurs through multiple modalities: • Receiving disability didactic training in academic programs may occur in multicultural courses, culture-specific courses (e.g., women's issues, Latino/a, and GLB courses) and it may be infused into the core curriculum (e.g., ethics, assessment, multicultural, career counseling, research, human growth and development, and clinical courses). (See an example of curriculum infusion in the Resources section of this chapter.) • Providing therapy, under supervision, to clients representing diversity of disability beliefs in practicum experiences. • Receiving supervision from psychotherapists knowledgeable and skilled in working with disability issues. • Seeking additional study and professional development opportunities. Topics to be covered in didactic training include: • Relation of disability competency to multicultural competency. • Relationship of disability worldviews to individual and cultural differences (e.g.,
Values and Attitudes	The student demonstrates self-awareness and appropriate cultural and multicultural attitudes as evidenced by the following: • Understands that disability is an aspect of multicultural diversity and touches individuals and families throughout the world. • Awareness of own intersecting individual dimensions (gender, ethnicity, SES, sexual orientation, ability, etc.) and ability to discern clients' intersecting identities.	

READINESS LEVEL—ENTRY TO INTERNSHIP	
Competencies	Learning Process and Activities
• Commitment to examine and challenge own attitudes and biases concerning disability and PWDs. • Willingness to admit own limitations in ability to be open to some expressions of disability beliefs. • Demonstrates genuine respect for varying personal experiences and responses others have toward PWDs and PWDs have toward others.	including age, gender, sexual orientation, SES, and ethnicity). • Basic research literature describing the relevance of disability to wellness, physical health, mental health. • Definitions of *disability, handicapped, cripple, marginalize, rolelessness, harassment,* etc. • Trainers and teachers could offer students enrolled in multicultural diversity courses an option to research disability issues as a project for the class. Possible topics are cited in the Disability Issues Seminar outline in the Resources section of this chapter.

Table 3.3   Developmental-Level Competencies III

READINESS LEVEL—ENTRY TO PROFESSIONAL PRACTICE		
Competencies		Learning Process and Activities
Knowledge	Knowledge of: • Literature on the relationship between disability beliefs and mental and physical health; knowledge of the range of possible client issues and disability. • Expressions, concepts, and vocabulary pertaining to the persons with disabilities with whom one works. • Beliefs and behaviors that are considered normative and healthy within client's cultural tradition regarding disability. • Community resources, including disability leaders from various religions and faith traditions, spiritual healers, and psychotherapists specializing in disability therapy. • Understanding that working with disability is an aspect of multicultural counseling competency.	In the earlier stages of training, students solidified their professional knowledge base and attained appropriate values and attitudes while developing increasingly sophisticated clinical skills. At the level of Entry to Professional Practice, psychotherapists have attained the full range of competencies in the domains expected of all independent practitioners. Preparation for this level of competency takes place through closely supervised clinical work, augmented by professional reading, personal exploration, and training opportunities such as professional development and training seminars. Clinical supervisors observe students' clinical work, provide training in assessment, case conceptualization, and treatment planning, and challenge supervisees to examine their countertransference reactions, biases, and values to develop their supervisees' clinical competency with disability issues.
Skills	Skills are demonstrated by the ability to: • Perform a basic assessment of clients' beliefs and worldviews to assess the relevance of disability to therapy; assess for contraindications. • Diagnose and formulate appropriate treatment plans that are sensitive to the client's disability, including how multiple systems and individual differences impact client. • Identify the limits of one's own competency with disability issues and refer appropriately. • Form a trusting therapeutic relationship with clients so that clients may express disability	Additional methods by which students can attain disability competency at this level include: • Seeking opportunities to provide therapy to clients representing disability diversity. • Supervision provided by supervisors knowledgeable and skilled in working with disability issues. • Self-directed study and professional development opportunities.

(continued)

Table 3.3   Developmental-Level Competencies III (*continued*)

READINESS LEVEL—ENTRY TO PROFESSIONAL PRACTICE	
Competencies	Learning Process and Activities
concerns if relevant and provide basic therapeutic interventions focused on disability. • Use supervision to enhance disability skills. • Avoid dual roles and boundary violations regarding disability. • Establish effective consultation relationships with community leaders with expertise in area of disability. • Create climate in which supervisees and trainees feel safe to talk about disability issues.	• Internship and postdoctoral seminar training in disability issues. • Presenting and participating in clinical case conferences that include discussion of disability aspects of cases.
Values and Attitudes Awareness of own worldview and associated biases regarding disability, willingness to continually broaden self-knowledge, and commitment to expanding knowledge of disability belief systems as part of multicultural competency enhancement.	

Table 3.4   Developmental-Level Competencies IV

	READINESS LEVEL—ADVANCED PRACTICE AND SPECIALIZATION	
	Competencies	Learning Process and Activities
Knowledge	Extensive knowledge of: • Disability literature. • Disability development models. • Impact of disability experiences upon human development. • Disability belief traditions.	Psychotherapists who have a particular interest in disability aspects of diversity as they apply to clinical work may seek to attain advanced levels of competency. Learning activities will vary depending on the psychotherapist's unique background, established competencies, and interest areas. For example, psychotherapists working in hospital treatment settings may wish to focus on interventions for this population. Similarly, psychotherapists working in a hospice setting may choose to focus on the disability and issues related to acquired disabilities, or visible and invisible disabilities.
Skills	Advanced skills in: • Providing a variety of disability interventions. Integrating knowledge of disability concepts (discrimination, harassment, marginalization, and rolelessness from psychological and societal perspectives) into treatment. • Proactively sharing knowledge of disability issues in the work setting with members of other mental health professions. • Performing differential diagnosis of disability-related issues versus viewing them as pathology. • Differentiating between healthy and unhealthy adjustment to disability with full knowledge of the wide range of multicultural-appropriate expressions of disability-related concerns.	Regardless of the focus area, learning activities can include: • Professional reading (information about diverse disability beliefs; empirical studies, and literature on theory and practice). • Teaching. • Attending and leading educational workshops. • Peer consultation groups. • Consultation with knowledgeable mental health professionals and leaders with disabilities.

READINESS LEVEL—ADVANCED PRACTICE AND SPECIALIZATION	
Competencies	Learning Process and Activities
Addressing growth-restricting beliefs and attitudes regarding disability. • Provide effective supervision to trainees working with client with disabilities or disability-related issues.	• Participation in unfamiliar disability experiences (e.g., visiting nursing home, rehabilitation facility, classroom specialized to students with disabilities, Para Olympics, Special Olympics, Disability Student Services at your university, Veterans hospital).
Values and Attitudes Well-integrated values and attitudes demonstrated by the following: • Continually engages in broadening knowledge of disability resources for continuing professional development. • Actively cultivates relationships with community leaders with disabilities. • Involved in local and national groups and organizations relevant to disabilities issues. • Independently and proactively provides ethical and legal consultation and supervision to trainees and other professionals. • Works for social justice to enhance understanding among individuals without disabilities to understand the personal experience of PWDs. • Independently monitors own disability identity in relation to work with others with awareness and sensitivity to varying disability experiences.	

REFERENCES

Alston, R. J., Bell, T. J., & Feist-Price, S. (1996). Racial identity and African Americans with disabilities: Theoretical and practical considerations. *Journal of Rehabilitation*, 11–15.

Alur, M. (2002). Status of disabled people in India: Policy and inclusion. *Exceptional Education Canada*, *12*, 137–167.

American Counseling Association. (2005). Multicultural-social justice counseling and advocacy competencies. *Counseling Today Online: Dignity, Development & Diversity*. Retrieved June 20, 2009, from http://www.counseling.org/Publica tions/CounselingTodayArticles.aspx?AGuid=47bf e1ea-cee2-43d2-957e-ec6e60baa479

American Psychiatric Association. (2000). *Diagnostic and statistical manual of mental disorders DSM-IV-TR*. Washington, DC: American Psychiatric Association.

American Psychological Association. (2002). *Ethical principles of psychologists and code of conduct*. Washington, DC: American Psychological Association.

American Psychological Association. (2007). Report of the APA Task Force on Socioeconomic Status. Washington, DC: American Psychological Association. Available at: www2.apa.org/pi/SES_task _force_report.pdf

American Psychological Association. (In review). *Proposed guidelines for assessment of and intervention with individuals who have disabilities*. Washington, DC: American Psychological Association.

Americans with Disabilities Act. (1990). Retrieved January 29, 2009, from http://www.ada.gov/pubs/ada .htm

Appleby, Y. (1994). Out in the margins. *Disability & Society*, *9*(1), 19–32.

Asch, A. (1984). The experience of disability: A challenge for psychology. *American Psychologist Association*, *39*(5), 529–536.

Asch, A., & Fine, M. (1988). Introduction: Beyond pedestals. In M. Fine & A. Asch (Eds). *Women with disabilities: Essays in psychology, culture, and politics* (pp. 1–37). Philadelphia: Temple University Press.

Assessment of Competencies Benchmark Work Group: Competencies Benchmark Document (2007). American Psychological Association Board of Educational Affairs in collaboration with the Council of Chairs of Training Councils.

Aten, J. D. & Hernandez, B. C. (2004). Addressing religion in clinical supervision: A model. *Psychotherapy: Theory, Research, Practice, Training, 41*(2), 152–160.

Barnes, C., & Mercer, G. (2001). Disability culture: Assimilation or inclusion? In G. L. Albrecht, K. D. Seelman, & M. Bury (Eds.), *Handbook of disability studies* (pp. 515–535). London, Sage.

Barton, L. (1998). Society, disability studies and education: Some observations. In T. Shakespeare (Ed.), *The disability reader: Social science perspectives* (pp. 53–64). London: Cassell.

Bowe, F. (1981). *Demography and disability: A chartbook for rehabilitation*. Hot Springs: Arkansas Rehabilitation and Training Center.

Bramston, P., & Fogerty, G. (2000). The assessment of emotional distress experienced by people with an intellectual disability: A study of different methodologies. *Research in Developmental Disabilities, 21*, 487–500.

Castro, J. C., Furth, P., & Karlow, H. (1984). The health beliefs of Mexican American and Anglo American women. *Hispanic Journal of Behavioral Sciences, 6*(4), 365–383.

Chan, C., Lee, T., Yuen, H., & Chan, F. (2002). Attitudes toward people with disabilities between Chinese rehabilitation and business students: An implication for practice. *Rehabilitation Psychology, 47*, 324–338.

Chen, R. K., Brodwin, M. G., Cardoso, E., & Chan, F. (2002). Attitudes toward people with disabilities in the social context of dating and marriage: A comparison of American, Taiwanese, and Singaporean college students. *Journal of Rehabilitation Psychology, 47*, 324–338.

Crocker, P. L. (1983). An analysis of university definitions of sexual harassment. *Signs: Journal of Women in Culture & Society, 8*, 696–707.

Cuellar, I., & Arnold, B. R. (1988). Cultural considerations and rehabilitation of disabled Mexican Americans. *Journal of Rehabilitation, 54*(3), 35–41.

Curry, M., Hassouneh-Phillips, D. & Johnston-Silverberg, A. (2001). Abuse of women with disabilities: An ecological model and review. *Violence against Women—An International and Interdisciplinary Journal, 7*(1), 60–79.

Danek, M. M. (1992). The status of women with disabilities revisited. *Journal of Applied Rehabilitation Counseling, 23*(4), 7–13.

Erickson Cornish, J. A., Gorgens, K. A., Monson, S. P., Olkin, R., Palombi, B., & Abels, A. (2008). Toward ethical practice with people who have disabilities. *Professional Psychology: Research and Practice, 39*, 488–492.

Esten, G., & Willmott, M. (1993). Double bind messages: The effects of attitude towards disability on therapy. In M. Willmuth & L. Holcomb (Eds.), *Women with disabilities: Found voices* (pp. 29–42). New York: Haworth.

Fabian, E. S., & Liesener, J. J. (2005). Promoting the career potential of youth with disabilities. In S. D. Brown and R. W. Lent (Eds.), *Career development and counseling: Putting theory and research to work* (pp. 551–572). New York: Wiley.

Fassinger, R. E. (2008). Workplace diversity and public policy: Challenges and opportunities for psychology. *American Psychologists, 63*(4), 252–268.

Feist-Price, S., & Ford-Harris, D. (1994). Rehabilitation counseling: Issues specific to providing services to African American clients. *Journal of Rehabilitation, 60*(4), 13–19.

Fine, M., & Asch, A. (1988). *Women with disabilities: Essays in psychology, culture, and politics*. Philadelphia: Temple University Press.

Galvin, R. D. (2005). Researching the disabled identity: Contextualizing the identity transformations which accompany the onset of impairment. *Sociology of Health and Illness, 27*(3), 393–413.

Gill, C. J. (2001). Divided understanding: The social experience of disability. In G. L. Albrecht, K. D. Seelman, & M. Bury (Eds.), *Handbook of disability studies* (pp. 351–372). Thousand Oaks, CA: Sage Publication.

Gold, S. (2002). Beyond pity and paternalism: Even progressive persons committed to social justice are unable to embrace the disability rights movement: Are we afraid of something? *The Other Side, 38*(5), 16–21.

Grattet, R., & Jenness, V. (2001). Criminology: Examining the boundaries of hate crime law: Disabilities and the "dilemma of difference." *Journal of Criminal Law & Criminology, 91*(3), 653–697.

Hahn, H. (1997). The political implications of disability definitions and data. In R. P. Marinelli & A. E. Dell Orto (Eds.), *The psychological & social impact of disability* (pp. 3–11). New York: Springer.

Harley, D. Q., Nowak, T. M., Gassaway, L. J., & Savage, T. A. (2002). Lesbian, gay, bisexual, and transgender college students with disabilities: A look at multiple cultural minorities. *Psychology in the Schools, 39*(5), 525–538.

Hassouneh-Phillips, D., & Curry, M. A. (2002). Abuse of women with disabilities: State of the science. *Rehabilitation Counseling Bulletin, 45*(2), 96–104.

Helms, J. E., & Cook, D. A. (1999). *Using race and culture in counseling and psychotherapy: Theory and process.* Needham Heights, MA: Allyn & Bacon.

Hirschberger, G., Florian, V., & Mikulincer, M. (2005). Fear and compassion: A terror management analysis of emotional reactions to physical disability. *Rehabilitation Psychology 50*(3), 246–257.

Hogben, M., & Waterman, C. K. (1997). Are all of your students represented in their textbooks? A content analysis of coverage of diversity issues in introductory psychology textbooks. *Teaching of Psychology, 24*(2), 95–100.

Holzbauer, J. J., & Berven, N. L. (1996). Disability harassment: A new term for a long-standing problem. *Journal of Counseling and Development, 74*, 478–483.

Hulnick, M. R., & Hulnick, H. R. (1989). Life's challenges: Curse or opportunity? Counseling families of persons with disabilities. *Journal of Counseling & Development, 68*, 166–170.

Hunt, B., Matthews, C., Milsom, A., & Lammel, J. A. (2006). Lesbians with physical disabilities: A qualitative study of their experiences with counseling. *Journal of Counseling and Development, 84*, 163–173.

Ingstad, B., & Whyte, S. R. (1995). *Disability and culture.* Berkley, CA: University of California Press.

Iwasaki, Y., & Mactavish, J. B. (2005). Ubiquitous yet unique: Perspectives of people with disabilities on stress. *Rehabilitation Counseling Bulletin, 48*(4), 194–209.

Janssen, C. G. C., Schuengel, C., & Stolk, J. (2002). Understanding challenging behaviour in people with severe and profound intellectual disability: A stress-attachment model. *Journal of Intellectual Disability Research, 46*, 445–453.

Kaplan, D. (n.d.). The definition of disability. Retrieved April 22, 2009, from http://www.accessiblesociety.org/topics/demographicsidentity/dkaplanpaper.htm

Kemp, N. T., & Mallinckrodt, B. (1996). Impact of professional training on case conceptualization of clients with a disability. *Professional Psychology: Research and Practice, 27*(4), 378–385.

Kinavey, C. (2006). Explanatory models of self-understanding in adolescents born with spinal bifida. *Qualitative Health Research, 16*(8), 1091–1107.

Lam, C. S. (1993). Cross-cultural rehabilitation: What Americans can learn from their foreign peers. *Journal of Applied Rehabilitation Counseling, 24*(3), 26–30.

Lambert, M., & Barley, D. E. (2001). Research summary on the therapeutic relationship and psychotherapy outcome. *Psychotherapy, 38*, 357–361.

Lee, B. A. (1996). Legal requirements and employer response to accommodating employees with disabilities. *Human Resource Management Review, 6*, 231–251.

Leigh, I. W., Powers, L., Vash, C., & Nettles, R. (2004). Survey of psychological services to clients with disabilities: The need for awareness. *Rehabilitation Counseling, 49*(1), 48–54.

Lomay, V. T., & Hinkebein, J. H. (2006). Cultural considerations when providing rehabilitation services to American Indians. *Rehabilitation Psychology, 51*(1), 36–42.

Mackelprang, R., & Salsgiver, R. (1999). *Disability: A diversity model approach in human service practice.* Pacific Grove, CA: Brooks/Cole.

Marbella, A. M., Harris, M., Diehr, S., Ignace, G., & Ignace, G. T. (1998). Use of Native American healers among Native American patients in an urban Native American health center. *Archives of Family Medicine, 17*, 182–185.

Marini, I. (2001). Cross-cultural counseling issues of males who sustain a disability. *Journal of Applied Rehabilitation Counseling, 32*, 36–41.

Marks, D. (2008). Physical disability. In M. Davies (Ed.), *The Blackwell companion to social work* (pp. 41–49). Malden, MA: Blackwell.

Martinez, R., & Sewell, K. W. (2000). Explanatory style in college students: Gender differences and disability status. *College Student Journal, 34*(1), 72–78.

McCaughey, T. J., & Strohmer, D. C. (2005). Prototypes as an indirect measure of attitudes toward disability groups. *Rehabilitation Counseling Bulletin, 48*(2), 89–99.

McDaniel, J. (1995). *The lesbian couples' guide: Finding the right woman and creating a life together.* New York: HarperCollins.

McDonald, K. E., Keys, C. B., & Balcazar, F. E. (2007). Disability, race/ethnicity and gender: Themes of cultural oppression, acts of individual resistance. *American Journal of Community Psychology, 39*(1–2), 145–161.

McGrath, E., Keita, G. P., Strickland, B. R., & Russo, N. E. (1990). *Women and depression: Risk factors and treatment issues: Final report of the American Psychological Association's National Task Force on Women and Depression.* Washington DC: American Psychological Association.

McMahon, B. T., West, S. L., Lewis, A. N., Armstrong, A. J., & Conway, J. P. (2004). Hate crimes and disability in America. *Rehabilitation Counseling Bulletin, 47*(2), 66.

Michigan Disability Rights Coalition. (2005). Models of disability. Retrieved April 10, 2009, from http://www.copower.org/leader/models.htm.

Middleton, R. A., Harley, D. A., Rollins, C. W., & Solomon, T. (1998). Affirmative action, cultural diversity, and disability policy reform: Foundation to the civil rights of persons with disability. *Journal of Applied Rehabilitation Counseling, 29*(3).

Middleton, R. A., Rollins, C. W., & Harley, D. A. (1999). The historical and political context of the civil rights of persons with disabilities: A multicultural perspective for counselors. *Journal of Multicultural Counseling & Development, 27,* 105–114.

Morris, J. (1993). *Independent lives? Community care and disabled people.* London: Macmillan.

Mpofu, E., & Harley, D. A. (2006). Racial and disability identity: Implications for the career counseling of African Americans with disabilities. *Rehabilitation Counseling Bulletin, 50*(1), 14–23.

Mumford, E.(1981). Culture: Life perspectives and the social meaning of illness. In R. C. Simon and H. Pardes (Eds.). *Understanding human behavior in health and illness.* Baltimore, MD: Williams and Wilkins.

Nagi, S. Z. (1991). Disability concepts revised: Implications for prevention. In A. M. Pope & A. R. Tarlov (Eds.), *Disability in America: Toward a national agenda for prevention.* Washington, DC: National Academy Press.

National Association of Social Workers (1996). *Code of ethics.* Retrieved January 14, 2010, from http://www.socialworkers.org/pubs/code/code.asp

National Council on Disability. (2004). *Harris survey of Americans with disabilities.* Washington, DC: National Council on Disability.

National Organization on Disability – NOD (2004). Landmark disability survey find pervasive disadvantages. Retrieved January 15, 2010 from http://www.nod.org/index.cfm?fuseaction=Feature.showFeature&FeatureID=1422

Noonan, B. M., Gallor, S. M., Henseler-McGinnis, N. F., Fassinger, R. E., Wang, S., & Goodman, J. (2004). Challenge and success: A qualitative study of the career development of highly achieving women with physical and sensory disabilities. *Journal of Counseling Psychology, 51*(1), 68–80.

Nosek, M. A., Howland, C. A., & Hughes, R. B. (2001). The investigation of abuse and women with disabilities. *Violence against Women, 7,* 477–499.

Nosek, A., Howland, C.A., Rintala, D. H., Young, E. M., & Chanpong, G. F. (1997). *National study of women with physical disabilities: Final report.* Houston: Center for Research on Women with Disabilities.

Nosek, M. A., & Hughes, R. B. (2003). Psychosocial issues of women with physical disabilities: The continuing gender debate. *Rehabilitation Counseling Bulletin 46*(4), 224–233.

O'Keefe, J. (1993). Disability, discrimination and the Americans with Disabilities Act. *Consulting Psychology Journal, 45*(2), 3–9.

Oliver, M. (1996). A sociology of disability or a disablist sociology? In L. Barton (Ed.), *Disability and society* (pp. 18–42). London: Longman.

Olkin, R. (1999). *What psychotherapists should know about disability.* New York: Guilford Press.

Olkin, R. (2002). Could you hold the door for me? Including disability in diversity. *Cultural Diversity and Ethnic Minority Psychology, 8*(2), 130–137.

Olkin, R. (2004). Making research accessible to participants with disabilities. *Multicultural Counseling and Development, Extra* 2004, *32,* 332–343.

Olkin, R., & Taliaferro, G. (2005). In J. Norcross, L. Beutler, & R. Levant (Eds.), *Evidence-based practices in mental health: Debate and dialogue on fundamental questions.* Washington DC: American Psychological Association.

Palombi, B. (2008). Focus on disability: It's about time. *Professional Psychology: Research and Practice, 39,* 494–495.

Palombi, B. J., & Matteson Mundt, A. (2006). Achieving social justice for college women with disabilities: A model for inclusion. In T. Israel and R. Toporek (Eds)., *Social justice handbook.* Thousands Oak, CA: Sage.

Parr, H., & Butler, R. (1999). New geographies of illness, impairment and disability. In R. Butler & H. Parr (Eds.), *Mind and body spaces: Geographies of illness, impairment and disability* (pp. 1–24). New York: Routledge.

Pledger, C. (2003). Discourse on disability and rehabilitation issues: Opportunities for psychology. *American Psychologist, 58*(4), 279–284.

Pope, A. M., & Tarlov A. R. (1991). *Disability in America: Toward a national agenda for prevention.* Washington DC: National Academy Press.

Prilleltensky, I., & Prilleltensky, O. (2003). Synergies for wellness and liberation in counseling psychology. *The Counseling Psychologist, 31*(3), 273–281.

Rintala, D. H., Hart, K. A., & Fuhrer, M. J. (1996). Perceived stress in individuals with spinal cord injury. In D. M. Krotoski, M. A. Nosek, & M. A. Turks (Eds.), *Women with physical disabilities: Achieving and maintaining health and well-being* (pp. 223–242). Baltimore: Brookes.

Rogers, C. (1951). *Client centered therapy.* Boston: Houghton Mifflin.

Rubino, M. J., III. (2001). Psychologists' clinical judgment about a female client with a visible disability, hidden disability, or no disability. [Unpublished doctoral dissertation]. California School of Professional Psychology, Berkeley/Alameda.

Schleiter, M. K., Statham, A., & Reinders, T. (2006). Challenges faced by women with disabilities under TANF. *Journal of Women, Politics & Policy, 27*(3), 81–95.

Shelton, M. W., & Matthews, C. K. (2001). Extending the diversity agenda in forensics: Invisible disabilities and beyond. *Argumentation and Advocacy, 28* (2), 121–130.

Smart, D. W., & Smart, J. F. (1997). The racial/ethnic demography of disability. *Journal of Rehabilitation,* 9–15.

Smart, J. F. (2001). *Disability, society and the individual.* Gaithersburg, MD: Aspen.

Smart, J. F., & Smart, D. W. (1992). Cultural issues in the rehabilitation of Hispanics. *Journal of Rehabilitation, 23*(2), 29–37.

Smart, J. F., & Smart, D. W. (1993). Acculturation, biculturalism, and the rehabilitation of Mexican Americans. *Journal of Applied Rehabilitation Counseling, 24,* 46–51.

Smart, J. F., & Smart, D. W. (1994). Rehabilitation of Hispanics: Implications for training and educating service providers. *Rehabilitation Education, 8*(4), 360–368.

Smart, J. F., & Smart, D. W. (2006). Models of disability: Implications for the counseling profession. *Journal of Counseling & Development, 84,* 29–40.

Social Security Administration. (2009). What we mean by disability. Retrieved February 6, 2009, from http://www.ssa.gov/dibplan/dqualify4.htm

Stageberg, D., Fisher, J., & Barbut, A. (1996). University students' knowledge of civil rights laws pertaining to people with disabilities. *Journal of Applied Rehabilitation Counseling, 27*(4), 25–29.

Stark-Wroblewski, K., & Chwalisz, K. (2003). Adjustment to illness. In M. Kopala & M. A. Keital (Eds.), *Handbook of counseling women* (pp. 309–322). London: Sage.

Strike, D. L., Skovholt, T. M., & Hummel, T. J. (2004). Mental health professionals' disability competence measuring self-awareness, perceived knowledge, and perceived skills. *Rehabilitation Psychology, 49*(4), 321–327.

Stuart, C. K. (1994). Homophobia: Are rehabilitation counselors in the closet? *Journal of Applied Rehabilitation Counseling, 25,* 41–44.

Stuart, O. (1993). Double oppression: An appropriate starting-point? In J. Swain, V. Finkelstein, S. French, & M. Oliver (Eds.), *Disabling barriers: Enabling environments* (pp. 93–100). London: Sage.

Sue, D. W., & Sue, D. (1990). *Counseling the culturally different: Theory and practice* (2nd ed.). New York: Wiley.

Sue, D. W., & Sue, D. (2003). *Counseling the culturally diverse: Theory and practice* (4th ed.). New York: Wiley.

Swedlund, N., & Nosek, M. (2000). An exploratory study on the work of independent living centers to address abuse of women with disabilities. *Journal of Rehabilitation, 66*(4), 57–64.

Szymanski, E. M., Trevino, B., & Fernandez, D. (1996). Rehabilitation career planning with minorities. *Journal of Applied Rehabilitation Counseling, 27,* 45–49.

Taliaferro, G. (2004). *Empirically supported treatments and disability.* [Manuscript submitted for publication].

Taylor, C. (2001). Who goes there and how: Lesbians and disability. Retrieved May 28, 2009, from http://www.womenwriters.net/may2001/taylor.htm

Thompson, D. (1994). The sexual experience of men with learning disabilities having sex with men: Issues for HIV prevention. *Sexuality and Disability*, *12*, 221–242.

Tsao, G. (1998). Growing up Asian American with a disability. Retrieved June 26, 2009, from http://www.colorado.edu/journals/standards/V7N1/FIRSTPERSON/tsao.html

Turk, D. C., & Monarch, E. S. (2002). Biopsychosocial perspective on chronic pain. In D. C. Turk & R. J. Gatchel (Eds.), *Psychological approaches to pain management: A practitioner's handbook* (pp. 3–29). New York: Guilford Press.

Turner, J. B., & Turner, R. J. (2004). Physical disability, unemployment, and mental health. *Rehabilitation Psychology*, *49*(3), 241–249.

U.S. Census Bureau. (2002). The American Indian and Native Alaskan population: 2000. Retrieved January 15, 2009, from http://www.censwus.gov/2002pubs/c2kbr01-15.pdf

U.S. Equal Employment Opportunity Commission. (2002). Enforcement guidance: Reasonable accommodation and undue hardship under the Americans With Disabilities Act. Retrieved June 7, 2009, from http://www.eeoc.gov/policy/docs/accommodation.html#general.

Vernon. A. (1998). Multiple oppression and the disabled people's movement. In T. Shakespeare (Ed.), *The disability reader* (pp. 201–210). London: Cassell.

Waxman, B. (1994). Up against eugenics: Disabled women's challenge to receive reproductive services. *Sexuality and Disability*, *12*(2), 155–171.

Weeber, J. E. (1999). What could I know of racism? *Journal of Counseling and Development*, 77, 20–23 +.

Wendell, S. (1997). Toward a feminist theory of disability. In L. J. Davis (Ed.). *The disability studies reader* (pp. 260–278). New York: Routledge.

Wendell, S. (2001). Unhealthy disabled: Treating chronic illnesses as disabilities. *Hypatia*, *4*, 17–33.

Whitney, C. (2006). Intersections in identity: Identity development among queer women with disabilities. *Sexuality and Disability*, *24*(1), 39–52.

Whyte, S. R. (1995). Disability between discourse and experience. In B. Ingstad and S. R. Whyte (Eds.), *Disability and culture*. Berkley: University of California Press.

Wilhite, B. C. (1995). Daily life experiences of Japanese adults with physical disabilities. *International Journal of Rehabilitation Research*, *18*, 146–150.

Womendez, C., & Schneiderman, K. (1991). Escaping from abuse: Unique issues for women with disabilities. *Sexuality and Disability*, *9*, 273–279.

Yorkston, K. M., Johnson, K., Klasner, E. R., Amtmann, D., Kuehn, C. M., & Dudgeon, B. (2003). Getting the work done: A qualitative study of individuals with multiple sclerosis. *Disability and Rehabilitation*, *25*, 369–379.

CHAPTER 4

BROACHING ETHNICITY COMPETENTLY IN THERAPY

DELIDA SANCHEZ, ALICIA DEL PRADO, and CLAYTIE DAVIS III

Delida

In a recent dinner I had with a colleague and fellow *Puertorriqueña*, we discussed our plans for the academic break. My colleague was going to Puerto Rico to spend time with her family and I planned to spend the break in New York City with my family. Our conversation took place in both English and Spanish at a Latin restaurant. From the "outside," one might assume upon hearing us that our ethnic experiences are similar. While both my colleague and I claim Puerto Rican roots (e.g., *tenemos raíces Puertorriqueñas*), our ethnic (and racial) experiences are significantly different—including our physical features (hers more European and mine more African), the dominant language used in most contexts (hers Spanish, mine English), our cultural values (more collective versus individualistic), and so forth. However, there remains a very strong connection between us as Puerto Ricans and Latinas that is unlike the connection I feel with other ethnic groups, whether born in the United States or elsewhere. My experience ethnically is similar to many second-generation Americans. There is a sense of neither fully belonging to my family's island of origin (my *Americanizada*) nor fully identifying with the dominant American culture.

Alicia

My ethnicity often confuses people. My dark-brown hair, tanned skin, pointed nose, and other phenotypic attributes have led others to misperceive my ethnicity. I have been ethnically misidentified by others as Mexican, Native American, and Guamanian. Ethnically, I identify as Filipina and Italian. I am a mixed-race person, a woman of color, and an American with Filipino and Italian ancestry. Ethnicity is an important part of my identity, but its saliency lies in my own self-descriptors and phenomenological perspective. When others have made false assumptions about me based on who they think I am, I have felt invalidated, embarrassed, angry, and surprised. My personal experiences with ethnicity contribute to my professional commitment to appropriately conceptualizing and discussing ethnicity in clinical work.

Claytie

As a Black man, I have often thought about my racial identity more than my ethnic identity. That all changed with the birth of my daughter, who is biracial, or more specifically, *bi-ethnic* (African American and Chinese American). Alexandra has brown skin, almond-shaped eyes, and curly, long brown hair, and strangers seem to enjoy asking me, "What is she?," meaning, what ethnicity is her mother? Before I can answer the what-is-she question with "Beautiful," they usually like to guess "Filipino? Indian?" I think about what it means for her to attend Chinese school on Sundays where no one looks like her. I also wonder how her African American peers will interact with her, knowing there is history of discrimination based on skin color, hair, and just general appearance. Thus, each time I look in my daughter's eyes I see the complexity of the construct *ethnicity*. It is my hope that readers will take something from this chapter that helps them work with individuals of various ethnic groups, including bi-ethnic folks.

INTRODUCTION

We decided to open this chapter with personal snapshots of our ethnic experiences to illustrate that what you see physically upon meeting us (our race) does not capture the complexity of our ethnic experiences. Our ethnicity is more than just our physical features and its accompanying privilege or lack thereof. Rather, it is a complex matrix of factors, of which race is only one piece. As the U.S. population continues to become more ethnically diverse, it is incumbent upon mental health practitioners to receive the necessary training to provide ethnically competent services. When learning a client's ethnicity, a mental health practitioner obtains valuable information about culture, beliefs, values, and behavior patterns that can be used for the benefit of creating a culturally competent therapeutic process and client experience. The practitioner can apply the knowledge he or she has about the client's ethnicity in order to inform rapport building, case conceptualization, and treatment planning.

In this chapter we provide an overview of the current empirical and theoretical literature on ethnicity and ethnic counseling competencies, highlight current barriers to effective multicultural counseling training, and review models for addressing ethnicity in education, training, and clinical practice. We share a developmental approach to teaching and demonstrating ethnic counseling competency necessary for clinical work. Case examples and training tools for clinicians at varying levels of education and training are provided.

KNOWLEDGE

Unpacking Ethnicity: Definitions and Distinguishing Ethnicity from Race

The terms *race* and *ethnicity* are often used interchangeably in the mental health literature. Both terms have evolved from mostly biological and demographic categorizations to definitions that include socially constructed meanings (Quintana, 2007). The following are operational definitions of each term as defined by Markus (2008):

Race:
A dynamic set of historically derived and institutionalized ideas and practices that 1) sorts people into groups according to perceived physical and behavioral human characteristics; 2) associates differential value, power and privilege with these characteristics and establishes a social status ranking among the different groups; and 3) emerges when groups are perceived to pose a threat (political, economic, or cultural) to each other's worldview or way of life; and/or b) to justify the denigration and exploitation (past, current, or future) of, and prejudice toward, other groups. (p. 654)

Ethnicity:
A dynamic set of historically derived and institutionalized ideas and practices that 1) allows people to identify or to be identified with groupings of people on the basis of presumed (and usually claimed) commonalities including language, history, nation or region of origin, customs, ways of being, religion, names, physical appearance, and/or genealogy or ancestry; 2) can be a source of meaning, action and identity; and 3) confers a sense of belonging, pride and motivation. (p. 654)

The differentiation between race and ethnicity is based on perceived differences associated with power and social hierarchies (race) and with meanings, values, and ways of living (ethnicity) (Markus, 2008).

An important component of ethnicity is the cultural patterns that distinguish groups from one another. *Culture* is defined as learned skills, attitudes, and behaviors that are transmitted from generation to generation, usually within the confines of a physical-social environment (Carter, 1995). Tradition is a significant and important aspect of culture and is expressed via unwritten customs, taboos, and sanctions. It provides people with a mind-set that can have a powerful influence on their moral system for judging what is right or wrong, good or bad, desirable or undesirable (Harris & Moran, 1991) and includes protocol regarding food, dress, and behavior. Cultural values may be seen as underpinning, shaping,

and justifying individuals' affect, behaviors, and cognitions (Schwartz, 2003).

Ethnic Groups

Unlike the small number of racial categorizations recognized by the U.S. Census, that is, White ($N = 211,460,626$); Black/African American ($N = 34,658,190$); Asian ($N = 10,242,998$); Hispanic/Latino ($N = 35,305,818$); American Indian/Alaska Native ($N = 2,475,956$); Native Hawaiian/Other Pacific Islander ($N = 398,835$); and Biracial/Multiracial ($N = 6,826,228$), the number of ethnicities exceeds this exponentially (U.S. Census Bureau, 2000). The following is a chart of ethnic groups listed by U.S. Census racial groups (U.S. Census Bureau, 2000):

Ethnicities Listed by U.S. Census Racial Groups

White	Black or African-American	Asian	Hispanic/Latino/a	American Indian and Alaska Native	Native Hawaiian and Other Pacific Islander
Afghani	Algerian	Asian Indian	Argentinean	Alaskan	Fijian
Arabic	Angolan	Bangladeshi	Bolivian	Athabascan	Guamanian or Chamorro
Armenian	Cameroonian	Cambodian	Chilean	Aleut	Melanesian
Assyrian	Congolese	Chinese	Colombian	Apache	Micronesian
Australian	Côte d'Ivoire	Filipino	Costa Rican	Blackfeet	Native Hawaiian
Belgian	Ethiopian	Hmong	Cuban	Cherokee	Polynesian
British	Gambian	Indonesian	Dominican	Cheyenne	Samoan
Canadian	Ghanaian	Japanese	Ecuadorian	Chickasaw	Tongan
Czech	Liberian	Korean	Guatemalan	Chippewa	
Dutch	Libyan	Laotian	Honduran	Choctaw	
Egyptian	Malian	Malay	Mexican	Colville	
French	Namibian	Pakistani	Nicaraguan	Comanche	
Finnish	Nigerian	Sri Lankan	Panamanian	Cree	
German	Somalian	Taiwanese	Paraguayan	Creek	
Greek	South African	Thai	Peruvian	Crow	
Hungarian	Sudanese	Vietnamese	Puerto	Delaware	
Icelander	Tunisian		Rican	Eskimo	
Iranian	Ugandan		Salvadoran	Houma	
Irish	Zimbabwean		South	Iroquois	
Israeli	Zambian		American	Kiowa	
Italian			Spaniard	Latin American Indian	
Jewish			Uruguayan	Lumbee	
Kurdish			Venezuelan	Menominee	
Latvian				Navajo	
Lebanese				Osage	
Lithuanian				Ottawa	
Middle-Eastern				Paiute	

(*continued*)

Ethnicities Listed by U.S. Census Racial Groups (*continued*)

White	Black or African-American	Asian	Hispanic/ Latino/a	American Indian and Alaska Native	Native Hawaiian and Other Pacific Islander
Near Easterner				Pima	
New Zealander				Potawatomi	
Norwegian				Pueblo	
Palestinian				Puget Sound Salish	
Polish				Seminole	
Portuguese				Shoshone	
Russian				Sioux	
Saudi Arabian				Tlingit-Haida	
Scottish				Tohono O'Odham	
Slovak				Ute alone	
Swedish				Yaqui	
Syrian				Yuman	
Turkish					
Turkmen					
Uzbeck					
Welsh					
Yemeni					
Yugoslavs					

Ethnic Identity

Ethnic identity is one's subjective sense of ethnic group membership. It refers to the level of attachment an individual has to his or her ethnic group, and the correlated knowledge, understanding, values, behaviors, and pride that are direct implications of that ownership. According to Chang and Kwan (2009), "an ethnic group can form the basis for an ethnic identity when individuals begin the process of deciding that they belong to that ethnic group and use their ethnic group membership to establish a sense of who they are" (p. 115). One's ethnic identity provides a central frame of reference through which social interactions are experienced and interpreted (Outlaw, 1990).

Within the United States, ethnic identity is significantly impacted by the larger dominant Euro-American macroculture—a context that is shaped largely by racial factors. A powerful dominant cultural value and assumption in the United States is the focus on individualism and autonomy. American culture encourages independence and the development of personal preferences, goals, and perspectives (Markus, 2008). The individual is assumed to be the source of all thought, feeling, and action (Moya & Markus, in press). The concern for others is intentional and voluntary, not necessarily obligatory (Adams, Anderson, & Adonu,). Overall, American cultural values are often tied with success in education and work, potentially leading to a higher social class and acceptance into "mainstream culture."

Ethnicity seems to have different connotations and consequences for White Americans, particularly those who have been in the United States for several generations, than for members of immigrant and ethnic minority groups. Waters (1999) observed that for Whites in the United States, ethnicity seems to be an optional aspect of the individual's identity, which may or may not be claimed. In fact, "symbolic ethnicity" characterizes ethnicity among White Americans (Gans, 1979), because many do not have knowledge of their ancestral culture or speak the language—a result of broken-down cultural ties to their ancestors through intermarriage, assimilation, and social mobility. Individuals can choose when and how they wish to identify with their ethnic groups without having to pay the cost of actual membership or incorporate it into their everyday lives. When working with White American clients, mental health practitioners should be open to the possibility that ethnicity may or may not be a salient aspect of their identity.

Compared to White Americans, immigrant, and ethnic minority groups often experience their ethnicity as an imposed identity equated with subordination, inferiority, minority status, and marginalization (Trimble, Helms, & Root, 2003). Experiences with discrimination, immigration, or minority standing in society may influence one's level of ethnic identification (Phinney, 1996). Ethnicity may be a source of distress and conflict for many immigrants and ethnic minority groups and may place individuals at risk for developing certain psychological disorders such as depression, eating disorders, and suicide (Hovey, 1998, 2000). *Culture shock* often results subsequent to a series of disorienting encounters that occur when an individual's basic values, beliefs, and patterns of behavior are challenged by a different set of values, beliefs, and behaviors (Lynch, 2004). This occurs when the strategies that the individual uses to solve problems, make decisions, and interact positively are not effective, and when the individual feels an overwhelming sense of discomfort in the environment. When working with different ethnic groups, it is important to gauge for culture shock via questions, surveys, and other forms of assessment. Symptoms of depression, anxiety, and even psychosis can mask culture shock, and if only the symptoms are treated, the underlying cause will not be addressed.

Ethnic identification may also serve as a buffer against stress, particularly for immigrant/ first-generation ethnic groups (See Inman and Tummala-Narra, Chapter 5 in this *Handbook*). This buffer may be activated by the acculturative stress stemming from learning about and adapting to the dominant Euro-American U.S. culture (Kim, 2009). Thus, maintaining one's original culture may be a protective mechanism against psychological and social stress that the dominant culture exerts on immigrant and ethnic minority individuals on a continual basis.

The extent to which the experience of immigration and/or minority ethnic group membership will impact an individual's identity and psychological state depends on many factors, such as the history and present status of one's group in society; one's personal experiences with prejudice; and one's responses to perceptions of stereotypes and discrimination. Thus, when developing competencies among mental health practitioners, it is important to consider the following: level of *acculturation*—individual and group-level changes in cultural patterns as a consequence of contact with the ethnic majority (Chun, Organista, & Marin, 2003; Roysircar-Sodowsky & Maestas 2000); *enculturation*—the degree to which the individual learns about and is (re)socialized into the norms of his or her ancestral culture (Kohatsu, 2005); and *assimilation*—the adaptation of the new (host) culture's beliefs, values, and norms and rejection of one's original cultural identity (Lustig & Koester, 1996); generational status in the United States; and experiences with and impact of socioracial (oppression and discrimination) forces on the development and advancement (and lack of advancement) of certain ethnic groups in the United States. Additionally, practitioners may find it beneficial to a client's wellbeing to process aspects of a client's ethnic culture that contribute to a client's strength and resiliency.

Ethnic Identity Development

A strong ethnic identity is important for healthy adaptation and wellbeing in society. In cases where one's ethnic group is not valued in the larger context, a positive ethnic identity may be hard to achieve, and self-esteem is in jeopardy. Phinney (1996) proposed an ethnic identity model comprised of the following dimensions: self-categorization (self-identity with a particular ethnic group); commitment and attachment to one's ethnic group (sense of belonging); exploration (range of activities, such as reading and talking to people); learning cultural practices, and attending cultural events; behavioral involvement (speaking the language, eating the food, associating with members of one's group); ingroup attitudes (private regard, positive attitudes toward one's ethnic group); ethnic values and beliefs; importance or salience of group membership; and,- ethnic identity in relation to national identity (Phinney & Ong, 2007). The ethnic identity model (Phinney, 1996) assumes that those individuals growing up between cultures can experience identity confusion and adaption problems if they perceive a lack of appreciation for the skills, knowledge, and feelings that are typical of their cultural background.

Quintana (2007) summarized the empirical research on ethnic identity and concluded the following: (a) ethnic identity exploration is heightened during adolescence, (b) ethnic prejudice and discrimination tends to trigger this exploration, and (c) high levels of positive regard toward one's ethnic group are associated with positive adjustment and can be a buffer against stress. For example, among youth, it has been shown that strength of ethnic identification made a greater contribution to academic achievement than just the ethnic labels used among adolescents from diverse backgrounds (Fuligni, Witkow, & Garcia, 2005). Mental health practitioners who work with adolescents and college students should be especially aware of this research. For example, referral of clients of color to multicultural centers and organizations may help foster positive feelings toward their ethnic group and provide a buffer against stress related to ethnicity. Mental health practitioners may identify that a treatment goal is to foster the student of color's positive regard toward his or her ethnic group. They may ask about experiences of discrimination, and/or when hearing about acts of discrimination, recall that this may lead to ethnic identity exploration.

There are other ethnic identity models that have been developed based on Phinney's work that are important for mental health practitioners to be familiar with, such as Poston's (1990) Biracial Identity Development Model and Root's (1996) Stages of Biracial and Bicultural Identity Development. These models, which are explored by Dixon-Peters in greater detail in Chapter 8 of this *Handbook*, highlight the various phases, stages, or experiences bi-ethnic and bicultural groups (immigrant and U.S. born) may go through in the process of identity development. These models focus on how an internalization of two cultures informs and influences one's identity, and certain social cues and cultural contexts become important in how ethnic identity is defined and integrated into one's sense of self (Cheryan & Tsai, 2007).

Barriers to Competency

The mental health field is based on Western philosophical and cultural thought and most theoretical orientations posit that agency for change mainly resides within the person. Moreover, the standards of individualism and autonomy are purported by the dominant ethnic majority to be neutral and basic. While applicable to certain population groups, namely White Americans, the language, behaviors, and societal expectations associated with the dominant White American culture are often in conflict with immigrant and ethnic minority groups' cultural values. Specifically, the emphasis on individuality and individuation may go against the more collectivistic cultural values of non-European ethnic minority groups. Immigrant and ethnic minority groups may place more emphasis on relationship to others and social influence—a more collective and interdependent approach (D. W. Sue & D. Sue, 2003). These behaviors, such as deferring to authority figures, seeking attention and approval from friends and family, and valuing the feelings of others over oneself, might be mistakenly misdiagnosed as pathological when in fact they might be resources of resiliency and healthy ways of coping.

Another barrier to cultural competency around ethnicity is the assumption that White ethnic groups and ethnic minority groups share similar acculturation and assimilation patterns. Differences in historical circumstances, structural barriers in access to resources, and most important, in terms of their acceptance by the White majority, have a differential impact on the ethnic identity development of White ethnic groups and ethnic minority groups such as African Americans, Asians, Latinos, and American Indians (Markus, 2008). Simply making ethnic comparisons across ethnic groups with different levels of racial power and privilege can be misleading and hurtful to clients who might be experiencing ethnic related discrimination and stress.

Similarly, another barrier to cultural competency is stereotype bias. *Stereotyping* is defined as "a fixed or conventional notion or conception, as of a person, group idea, etc., held by a number of people, and allowing for no individuality, or critical judgment" (*Merriam-Webster Online Dictionary*, 2009). It is comprised of two cognitive processes—categorization and generalization—that allow individuals to organize a vast amount of information on a daily basis to facilitate their learning and social interactions (Hays, 2001). Hays posits that stereotypes serve two key functions: *Descriptive stereotypes* define how most people in a particular group behave, what they prefer, and where their competency lies. They exert control because they create a starting point for peoples' expectations. *Prescriptive stereotypes* define "how certain groups *should* think, feel, and behave" (Hays, 2001, p. 22).

Misinformation and a lack of awareness are the foundation of many stereotypes and failures in cross-ethnic counseling dyads. Stereotype bias can be reflective of practitioners' good intent to connect with their ethnically different client— usually of an ethnic background they have little experience or knowledge about. In some cases, tereotypes can guide us toward more accurate hypotheses and a quicker understanding of someone. However, in other situations, stereotypes may lead to inaccurate and rigid assumptions. For example, the stereotype that there is no variation among White ethnic groups (this is also true for Black, Asian, Latino, and Native American ethnic groups) may result in overlooking important cultural differences among Whites. While they may share certain privileges associated with being White, such as access to resources and power, the differing immigration/emigration histories and cultural and religious values and patterns of various White ethnic groups may reflect different ethnic worldviews and experiences in the United States. For example, the ethnic experiences of a fifth-generation person of Irish ancestry will be very different from a newly immigrated person from the Czech Republic, or an ethnically identified Jew whose grandparents were survivors of the Holocaust.

The process of stereotyping is automatic, and unconscious assumptions are very powerful. It is not something that can be shut off or ignored (Hays, 2001). However, the deeper and broader a practitioner's knowledge of and experience with a client's ethnicity and culture, as well as the deeper the understanding of the practitioner's own ethnicity and culture, the more accurate and relevant these hypotheses and questions will be and the more they can lead to an increase in clients' trust and confidence in the practitioner.

Colonialism and Colonial Mentality

What happens when a person automatically rejects anything from his or her own ethnic culture and uncritically prefers anything from the host culture? This question captures the concept of *colonial mentality* and is a variable that is important to consider when providing counseling services to clients from ethnic groups who have experienced colonization. Colonial mentality, or *internalized colonialism*, includes a perception of ethnic inferiority that is believed to be a consequence of centuries of colonization by external powers (David & Okazaki, 2006a).

When colonialism began in Africa, the Americas, Asia, and the Pacific Islands in the late 1400s (Nadal, 2009), colonizing countries (e.g., Great Britain, France, Japan, the Netherlands, Portugal, Spain, and the United States) exerted power and control through slavery and annihilation of indigenous peoples as well as maintaining cruel and harsh treatment toward remaining indigenous populations over the areas they colonized (Helms & Cook, 1999; Rodriguez, 1995). The emphasis on the superiority of the colonizers was reflected in a wide range of racial/caste classification systems (Rodriguez, 1995), mainly based on skin color, that had clear implications for social class and social standing.

While many of the aforementioned countries are now governed independently, colonialism continues to psychologically impact individuals of ethnic groups from colonized countries living in the United States. Colonial mentality is expressed in various ways, including self-deprecation of one's identity, body, and culture; discrimination against other members of one's ethnic group who are less Americanized; and tolerance of current oppression of one's ethnic group (David & Okazaki, 2006a). For example, eyelid surgery in Asian communities and hair straightening in Latino and African American communities can be reflective of a colonial mentality.

Colonial mentality appears to be associated with poor mental health. David and Okasazi (2006b) found higher levels of depression and lower personal and collective self-esteem among Filipino Americans with colonial mentality than among those without it. For a mental health practitioner, appropriately exploring how colonial mentality might play a role in a client's distress might help his or her progress in therapy.

SKILLS

How practitioners take into account ethnic issues and how they discuss them with clients is key to a successful therapeutic outcome (Maxie, Arnold, & Stephenson, 2006). Practitioners should be able to talk about how their ethnic identity impacts the therapeutic relationship with a client of a similar or a different ethnicity. They should also be able to discuss the ethical issues involved in determining whether they are competent to work with individuals ethnically different from themselves. Competency skills involve monitoring and applying knowledge of ethnicity in assessment, treatment, and consultation work with others. This encompasses career and personality assessments and mental-status exams, as well as providing outreach and consultation services.

Mental health practitioners should know how to implement assessment questions, interventions, and empathic statements about ethnicity

in a way that is supportive and nonjudgmental. Important issues concerning ethnic identity center on questions such as the following:

1. In what situations does one's ethnicity become salient?
2. In cases of mixed ethnicity, how does one decide which ethnic group to identify with, and how does this change according to the situation and over time?
3. What cultural patterns behaviors does the client endorse?
4. What thoughts, feelings, and attitudes does the client have toward her ethnicity and others from her ethnic group and outside her ethnic group?

Categorical self-descriptions of ethnicity (e.g., on an intake form) can be a starting point and help a mental health practitioner with initial, tentative hypotheses regarding aspects of the client's identity and history. In sessions, being able to explore the client's subjective perspective of his or her ethnicity provides more depth using the broaching technique (Day-Vines et al., 2007). Appropriate use of enculturation and acculturation measures in clinical settings offers a way ethnicity can be talked about tangibly in the counseling session.

Practically speaking, when working with clients around ethnicity, it is important to keep in mind the following questions:

1. What meaning does the client's ethnicity have for him/her?
2. What are your automatic assumptions, beliefs, and stereotypes about what it means to be Indian/Italian/African American/Peruvian, and so on?

D. W. Sue and D. Sue (2003) challenge the fallacy of colorblind counseling—good counseling is good counseling—that ignores the role of ethnicity in clinical interpretation. They emphasize the importance of knowing the worldview perspective of the client using an *emic* and *etic* continuum. An emic orientation takes into account the client's

CASE VIGNETTE 4.1

Corey is a 17-year-old African American high school student, who presents at his school counselor's office reporting anxiety about applying to college. He shares that both of his parents are lawyers and he has an older sister in graduate school. He currently attends a predominantly White high school but applied only to HBCUs (historically Black colleges/universities) so that he would have the opportunity to meet more African Americans. However, following a recent visit to one of the universities, he reports that he regrets the decision to attend an HBCU, as he believes he does not have much in common with most other African-Americans and doesn't talk "like they do." Corey tells his counselor, "I feel like a sellout and like I was born in the wrong skin. What's wrong with me?"

ethnic background and how different disorders are perceived and manifested within his or her culture. An etic orientation proposes that mental health and mental illness transcend culture. That is, ethnicity and culture are less important—depression is depression, regardless of one's skin color and family background, and therefore can be treated using a standard protocol.

Taking a look at Case Vignette 4.1, an universal perspective (etic) might focus on the fact that the client has achieved much success and comes from a high-achieving family and therefore must be content with his academic identity. However, an emic (culturally relative) orientation might note this level of achievement but question whether there has been a cost for this achievement. It has been noted by several scholars (Fordham & Ogbu, 1986) that for many African-Americans, academic achievement is not always perceived positively in school. Conversely, if this student was a member of certain Asian-American groups (e.g., Chinese American), an emic perspective might lead to a discussion of parental or peer pressures to excel. Neither perspective is wrong, and mental health practitioners are encouraged to question both; however, without the knowledge of cultural values and norms of a particular ethnic group as well as an understanding of one's own belief system, it is difficult to hold a complex conceptualization of a client, such as the one described above.

Practitioners who have had limited experience working with certain ethnic groups or perhaps with individuals from their own ethnic group might be encouraged to seek out those opportunities. They might be asked to become familiar with the traditions of these ethnic groups in order to more comprehensively and sensitively account for their presenting concerns. These types of experiences are different from a traditional multicultural seminar or class in that the focus is on individual training needs rather than assuming that everyone is at the same place, with the same needs.

Broaching Ethnicity as a Multicultural Competence Skill

Day-Vines et al. (2007) proposed an empirically supported conceptual framework for addressing ethnicity (and race) in the counseling process. The framework, called *broaching*, is defined as "the counselor's ability to consider the relationship of ethnic [and racial] factors into the client's presenting problems and inviting the client to explore these factors in treatment using an ongoing attitude of openness and genuine commitment" (p. 404). The onus of responsibility is on the counselor to initiate ethnic-related dialogues; otherwise, ethnic issues might remain unexamined during the counseling process. The following is an example of broaching behavior: "We're both from different ethnic backgrounds; I'm wondering how you feel about working with an Indian American/Dominican/Irish woman/man on your concerns."

Day-Vines et al.'s (2007) broaching framework includes five broaching styles, ranging from lower to more advanced levels of engaging clients in ethnic-related dialogues in counseling: (1) avoidant, (2) isolating, (3) continuing/

incongruent, (4) integrated/congruent, and (5) infusing. Practitioners demonstrating *avoidant* behaviors do not broach the topic of ethnicity and maintain an ethnic (and race) neutral, or even resistant or defensive perspective toward issues related to ethnicity. Practitioners demonstrating *isolating behaviors* broach the topic of ethnicity superficially and simplistically—acknowledging cultural differences between the practitioner and client on a single occasion and never seriously considering how ethnic factors may affect the client's wellbeing. *Continuing/incongruent* broachers invite clients to explore the relationship between their presenting problems and issues related to ethnicity and may ask about it several times in treatment. They are well intentioned and often display ethnic magazines and artwork in their offices and demonstrate a healthy appreciation of their client's ethnic worldview. However, they may experience difficulty translating their appreciation of cultural difference into effective counseling strategies and interventions. They may only be able to examine the cultural features of clients' lives in a stereotypic fashion by making assumptions about the client on the basis of the values and preferences of an entire ethnic or cultural group rather than the client's ethnic experience.

Integrated/congruent counselors not only broach the subject of ethnicity effectively during the counseling process but have integrated this behavior into their professional identity. They accept and encourage their clients to make culture-specific interpretations of their counseling concerns. They do not apply their understanding of culture in a stereotypic fashion, and can distinguish between culture-specific behaviors and unhealthy human functioning, recognize complexities associated with ethnicity, and acknowledge the vast heterogeneity that characterizes culturally diverse clients. *Infusing* practitioners have a somewhat similar profile as integrated/congruent practitioners; however, infusing broachers broach as way of being and not just a professional obligation. This lifestyle orientation requires a complex comprehension of sociopolitical issues and a commitment toward social justice and equality that transcends the bounds of professional identity. Such infusing practitioners are seen as systemic change agents since they petition for change at the institutional and organizational level (Day-Vines et al., 2007).

Mental health practitioners who display advanced levels of broaching and possess heightened levels of ethnic identity functioning are likely to promote trusting and open relationships with their clients and accommodate a range of social and cultural experiences. On the other hand, counselors with low levels of broaching behavior and ethnic identity functioning have the potential to foster threatening and apprehensive relationships and might even refuse to

CASE VIGNETTE 4.2

Lorelei is a 20-year-old, second-generation Filipina pre-med biology major in her second year at a public university. She indicates that her presenting concerns are career indecision and family issues. Specifically, she is unsure of whether being a doctor is what she wants given her interests in interior decorating and design. As she continues therapy with you, she shares that she dislikes her skin coloring, "flat" nose, and short stature. Lorelei recalls that her mother put a clothespin on her nose in an attempt to elongate it and used skin-bleaching soap in order to prevent Lorelei from becoming any darker. As you empathize with the pain (perhaps shame, embarrassment, anger, sadness) that is likely associated with Lorelei's body dissatisfaction, she further shares about other family members' influence on her life. Lorelei's grandmother encouraged Lorelei to avoid joining the Filipino Student Association at her college because "many Filipinos don't come from 'good families.'" Lorelei's older brother makes fun of Filipinos who speak with a Filipino accent and/or who recently immigrated to the United States.

acknowledge the significance of ethnicity in a client's life.

Using the broaching method for Case Vignette 4.2 (shown on the previous page), a mental health practitioner may introduce dialogues around ethnicity regarding Lorelei's negative self-appearance and body image by first exploring how she feels talking to an ethnically similar/different mental health practitioner. Knowing Lorelei has a Filipina ethnicity might conjure certain hypotheses about the cause and treatment of her presenting problems. Questions to consider for Lorelei are: What is Lorelei's enculturation level? What is Lorelei's ethnic identity? What role, if any, does colonial mentality play in Lorelei's presenting issues? What role, if any, does acculturative stress play in Lorelei's concerns? If the practitioner is familiar with the Philippines' history of colonization from Spain, Japan, and the United States (reflective of an integrative/congruent or infusing broaching level), the practitioner may postulate how this history plays a role in Lorelei's body and facial dissatisfaction. For example, Lorelei's and her mother's idealization of Caucasian physical characteristics (e.g., fair skin, pointy nose, and tall stature) demonstrate an aspect of colonial mentality. Understanding of Filipino cultural values that strongly influence appropriate social interactions, such as *amor propio* ("personal dignity"), *hiya* ("shame"; "sense of social propriety"), and ("getting along with others"), may further contribute to an ethnically competent conceptualization and intervention around Lorelei's experiences.

The preceding hypotheses and possible interpretations made by the mental health practitioner are proposed under the premise that the mental health practitioner has been engaging in self-awareness, working through prejudices, and challenging ethnocentric attitudes. It is important that practitioners allow space for all levels of ethnic identification among their clients. While it may be very clear and easy for some individuals to identify their ethnicity, others may struggle with this issue. Similarly, it is possible that thinking about ethnicity may bring up issues regarding

early childhood and/or family of origin that may be very painful. Thus, practitioners need to be mindful of creating a safe therapeutic environment that is conducive for ethnic self-exploration.

VALUES/ATTITUDES/AWARENESS

A first step in the process of better preparing mental health practitioners to work with diverse populations is to ensure that they gain insight into their own ethnicity, ethnic identity, experiences or lack thereof with immigration and acculturation, colonial mentality, and so forth, and learn how to be more skilled in understanding and responding to issues of ethnicity (Sanchez-Hucles & Jones, 2005). It is important for practitioners to know their belief systems regarding the importance (or not) of ethnic influences of behavior.

An essential component of developing ethnic self-awareness is beginning to articulate how one's own ethnic group membership influences who one is and how one relates to other people. This can be accomplished through coursework and participation in conferences and workshops, where one has the opportunity to start engaging in ethnic self-exploration through group experiences and exercises such as journaling and cultural sharing. Individuals can be either asked to describe what their ethnicity means to them in class or asked to reflect upon this between classes (and either write an essay about it or be prepared to discuss in the next class). Mental health practitioners can also be encouraged to take the Multigroup Ethnic Identity Measure (Phinney, 1992), which measures the affective dimension of ethnic identification as well as other group attitudes. This instrument can be completed in less than five minutes. Sample items include, "I have a clear sense of my ethnic background and what it means for me," and "I sometimes feel it would be better if different ethnic groups didn't try to mix together."

The *ADDRESSING* framework is one way to begin thinking about the influence that ethnicity has had on one's identity development (Hays, 2001). Since ethnicity is comprised of several factors, including language, history, region of origin, customs, religion, physical appearance, and so forth, understanding the saliency of these various influences is important to explore. The ADDRESSING framework is a self-reflective exercise that involves writing the acronym ADDRESSING (*A*ge/generational influences, *D*evelopmental or acquired *D*isabilities, *R*eligion and spiritual orientation, *E*thnicity, *S*ocio-economic status, *S*exual orientation *I*ndigenous heritage, *N*ational origin, and *G*ender) and, next to each category, recording a brief description of the influences (growing up and current) one considers salient for oneself.

The following are more specific questions that can be used with the ADDRESSING framework aimed at exploring how ethnically related values affect one's work with clients:

1. How have these ethnic influences shaped who I am, how I see myself, and how others (e.g., clients) see me?
2. How do these influences affect my comfort level in certain ethnic groups and my feelings about particular clients?
3. What is the relationship between my visible identity and my self-identification, and how is this influenced by my ethnic context?
4. What kinds of assumptions are others likely to make about me based on my ethnicity?

Some practitioners may have difficulty identifying their ethnicity and may use race inadvertently. For example, when thinking about ethnicity, one may respond with "I'm Asian" or "Asian-American." Individuals should be aware that Asian is a race and that there are many ethnic groups that fall under that race. Addressing the delicacy of, and distinction between, stereotypes and between-group differences may be a fruitful area of exploration.

SUPERVISION AND TRAINING

Overall, training and supervision should result in a level of multicultural competency where a practitioner is able to independently address complex individual and cultural diversity issues as they inform all foundational and functional competencies. Trained practitioners actively contribute to individual and cultural diversity understanding in work settings and in the profession. They integrate an understanding of individual and cultural diversity when performing all functional competencies such as assessment, treatment, supervision, and consultation. They demonstrate how individual and cultural diversity sensitivity informs and is informed by all foundational competencies by taking responsibility for continuing professional development of knowledge, skills, and attitudes in relation to individual and cultural diversity.

Continuous engagement in self-exploration around ethnicity is expected and strongly encouraged as part of supervision and training. Through coursework, students can obtain basic knowledge of the scientific, theoretical, and contextual issues related to ethnicity as they apply to professional psychology. Included in this are learning definitions of ethnicity, colonialism, ethnocentrism, language, assimilation, acculturation, enculturation, immigration/migration, prejudice and oppression, learning about ethnocentrism in psychology (in the United States in particular), and ethnic identity models. There are several models in the literature regarding ethnic identity, including but not limited to: Phinney's (1992) Ethnic Identity Model, the Cultural Identity Development Model by D. W. Sue and D. Sue (1999), the Cross (1991) Model of African-American Development, and the Ruiz (1990) Model for Latino Identity Development.

Structured-Cultural Interview

The structured-cultural interview, where facilitated by someone trained in the process, is comprised of a detailed set of questions provided for students to answer and explore more deeply the ethnic messages and values learned throughout their development (Carter, 2003). Specifically, students are asked to consider the messages they were taught growing up by their family, peers, and school. They are asked if their personal identification with their ethnic group membership differs from that of their family. They also have an opportunity to explore areas that they have not come to terms with regarding their ethnicity. The cultural interview also helps students to consider how their ethnicity and that of their clients impact their work as a mental health practitioner. Students have a chance to re-evaluate their ethnic-cultural patterns from a more complex level given their internalization of earlier course material on ethnicity and begin to engage in exploration of the intersections of ethnicity with other reference groups such as race, gender, sexual orientation, social class, ability/disability, and so on.

More advanced-level practitioners are expected to independently apply knowledge, skills, and attitudes regarding intersecting dimensions of diversity—such as age, gender, enculturation, and sexual orientation—to professional work. For example, the experience of having a disability may differ significantly given ethnic group membership. Many groups of color and non-American White cultural groups tend to attribute disability to karma and religious or spiritual reasons, whereas White Americans are more inclined to see the origin as biological or genetic. The cultural influences of religion often play a big role in shaping one's attitudes toward disability.

Advanced-level ethnically competent practitioners should also demonstrate readiness to specialize in working with specific populations and problems. Some examples are (a) advanced-level clinical practice and research with victims of post-9/11 ethnic profiling; (b) HIV intervention with South Asian male cab drivers; (c) sexual health among African American and Latino youth; and (d) knowledge of immigration laws and their impact on acculturative experiences among Mexicans and Vietnamese, or the mental health needs of Pueblo Indians in the Southwest. The ability to develop and maintain specialization is based on regular, independent use of knowledge of self to monitor and improve effectiveness as a professional. Mental health practitioners at this level are able to critically evaluate feedback and initiate consultation when uncertain about diversity issues with specific populations and problems.

CONCLUSION

In sum, ethnic competency, as with knowledge itself, is an ongoing process and does not reach an end point. We began our chapter with self-reflection regarding our own experiences with ethnicity. Self-awareness of one's own ethnicity, as well as intrapsychic exploration regarding others' ethnicities, is a pivotal part of the multicultural learning process. Engaging in ongoing introspective work about ethnicity sets the stage for being able to competently broach ethnicity in therapy with clients. Through the lens of openness that arises from self-exploration, mental health practitioners can appropriately metabolize the meaning of ethnicity and its related constructs (e.g., ethnic identity, enculturation, colonial mentality) as well as conceptualize and integrate the complex construct of ethnicity into their work. It is our hope that the increase in ethnic diversity in our population—client, trainer, educator, and practitioner—allows for continued evolution and growth in the field of mental health.

RESOURCES

The following resources are provided as suggestions for further inquiry and as tools students, clinicians, trainees, and supervisors can utilize to help improve the quality of the services they provide.

ADDRESSING FRAMEWORK

Investigating Your Own Cultural Heritage[1]

One way to begin thinking about the influence that diverse cultural factors have had on you is

[1] Excerpt from Hays (2001).

by doing the following exercise (Hays, 2001): First, take a ruled piece of paper; on the left side, write the acronym ADDRESSING vertically, leaving space to the right of and below each letter. Next, record a brief description of the influences you consider salient for yourself in each category. If current influences are different from those that influenced you growing up, note the salient influences and identities in relation first to your upbringing, and then to your current contexts. Also, fill in every category, even those for which you hold a dominant cultural identity, because this too is meaningful information.

The following general questions can help elicit the meanings of age and generational influences during the self-evaluation:

- When I was born, what were the social expectations for a person of my identity?
- When I was a teenager, what were the norms, values, and gender roles supported within my family, by my peers, in my culture, and in the dominant culture?
- How was my view of the world shaped by the social movements of my teenage years?
- When I was a young adult, what educational and occupational opportunities were available to me? And now?

More specific questions aimed at exploring how culturally related values affect one's work with students include the following:

- How have these cultural influences shaped who I am, how I see myself, and how others (students) see me?
- How do these influences affect my comfort level in certain groups and my feelings about particular students?
- What kinds of assumptions are others (students) likely to make about me based on my visible identity, my sociocultural context, and what I choose to share about myself?
- How might my areas of privilege affect my work (e.g., my clinical judgments, theoretical preferences, view of students, beliefs about

education, beliefs about access to resources, beliefs about families)?[2]

Addressing Framework

Cultural Influence	Self-Assessment
Age and generational influences	
Developmental or acquired disabilities	
Religion and spiritual orientation	
Ethnicity	
Socioeconomic status	
Sexual orientation	
Indigenous heritage	
National origin	
Gender	

Note: Mark with an asterisk (*) the areas in which you hold dominant cultural identity.

Example of Cultural Self-Assessment Using Addressing Framework[3]

Cultural Influence	Example
*Age and generational influences	52 years old; third-generation U.S. American; member of politically active generation of Chicanos and Chicanas in California; first generation affected by post–Civil Rights academic and employment opportunities in the 1970s.
Developmental or acquired disabilities	Chronic knee problems since early adulthood, including multiple surgeries; sometimes uses crutches to walk.
*Religion and spiritual orientation	Mother is a practicing Catholic, father non-practicing Presbyterian; my current beliefs are a mixture of Catholic and secular; I don't attend mass.

(continued)

---

[2] From Hays (2001).
[3] Hays (2001).

(continued)

Cultural Influence	Example
Ethnicity	Mother and father both of mixed Mexican (Spanish and Indian) heritage, both U.S. born; my own identity is Chicana; I speak Spanish, but my primary language is English.
*Socioeconomic status	Parents urban, working, lower-middle-class members of an ethnic minority culture; however, my identity is as a university-educated Chicana; I identify with working-class people, although my occupation and income are middle class.
*Sexual orientation	Heterosexual

Cultural Influence	Example
Indigenous heritage	My maternal grandmother was Indian and immigrated to the United States from Mexico with my grandfather when they were young adults; what I know about this part of my heritage came from her, but she died when I was 10.
*National origin	U.S., but deep understanding of the immigration experience from my grandparents.
Gender	Woman, Chicana, divorced, mother of two children.

Note: * = holds dominant cultural identity.

TRIANDIS SURVEY: ARE YOU AN INDIVIDUALIST OR A COLLECTIVIST?[4]

Cultures differ in their emphases on collectivism and individualism. Collectivists place some collective (family, work group, country) in a central position regulating social life. Individualists place the individual in the center of things. For example, when there is a conflict between the goals of a collective and an individual, in collectivist cultures it is obvious that the collective *should* "win," whereas in individualist cultures it is obvious that the individual should "win."

This questionnaire can help you find out if you are a collectivist or an individualist by asking you to answer questions about your own circumstances and lifestyle. Where you stand on these tendencies will be determined by summing up "points."

Under C (collectivism) and I (individualism), you should enter a rating on a 0 to 10 scale, following the instructions under each question.

For example, suppose you are asked: Do you feel a part of any group, so if you were expelled by that group you would feel that your life has ended? If the answer is "Yes, very definitely, absolutely true," you should enter 10 under C. On the other hand, if it is not at all true, you might use a zero.

You will be asked questions that either reflect individualism, so you should enter a number between 0 and 10 next to I =, or collectivism, so you should enter a number between 0 and 10 next to C = . After you answer all the questions, add all the points you have given to C and separately the points you have given to I. You will then get an idea of how high you are in these tendencies.

Please follow the instructions carefully and faithfully, so you will get an accurate estimate of your individualism and collectivism.

1. Individualists tend to be concerned with their personal success, even if that does not help their family. Collectivists often choose family over personal goals. On the whole, how close do you feel to your family? C =

    The closer you feel the higher should be your collectivism rating.

    To remind you: Enter numbers from 0 to 10.

    0 = no trace   5 = quite a bit   10 = the maximum possible

    (continued)

[4] From Triandis (1995).

(*continued*)

2. There are probably other groups to which you feel very close. These might be co-workers, neighbors, people of your own religion, race, nationality, political orientation, civil rights views, personal rights views, environmental views, social standing, people with similar aesthetic standards, etc. Now select the three or four groups that you feel closest to and enter an average collectivism rating, indicating how close you feel to these groups.   C =

3. The younger people are, the more they like to explore new ideas and do things that do not necessarily fit what their groups want them to do. But that is not constant with age. Young children often want to do what their parents want them to do; in some cultures teenagers want to do what their friends want them to do; old people often want to do what their own children and grandchildren want them to do. *Now think how free you are from group influences.* If you feel *totally* free, enter a 10. Otherwise, use a lower number.   I =

4. Individuals who travel a lot or change residences frequently do not feel that they must necessarily do what their neighbors want them to do. How free do you feel from the influences of your neighbors? If you feel totally free, enter a 10.   I =

5. The smaller the community in which you live, the more people (fellow neighbors) know what you are doing, and you may feel that you must pay attention to their ideas about your lifestyle. If you feel that you are paying maximum attention to the ideas that people in your community have about your lifestyle, enter a 10.   C =

6. You have probably picked up a lot of ideas about how you should live from your parents, and they from their parents. So it is likely that traditions that were in the families of your grandparents are still very influential in your own life. If these traditions are maximally influential in your life, use a 10.   C =

7. Think of your grandparents and parents in terms of how much they have been influenced by individualistic cultures such as those of the United States, England, Canada, Australia, and New Zealand, or collectivist cultures such as those of Africa, East Asia, and Latin America.

   One clue is the kind of child rearing. When the child rearing you have experienced was warm-controlling, in other words, your parents adored you as long as you did what they told you to do, you are most likely to have become a collectivist; on the other hand, if the child rearing was warm-independent, that is, your parents adored you and encouraged you to be independent, self-reliant, exploratory, it was okay to get into trouble, and they would help you get out of trouble, you are likely to have become an individualist. If your child rearing was cold and neglected, you would also be an individualist; if it was cold and controlling, you would be a collectivist, but these relationships are weaker, so do not give too many points in this rating. Try to estimate how individualistic you are, taking into account who your parents and other important influences (e.g., relatives, teachers) were and also how influential each of them was while you were growing up. If you feel you were influenced so as to become an extreme individualist, enter a 10; if, on the other hand, you were influenced not to be individualistic, enter a 0.   I =

8. Think of the people (e.g., close friends) you socialized with when you were growing up. In the previous question the influences from the different cultures were present, but they did not necessarily influence you directly. *Now we are talking about direct influence.* Did the people you socialized with come from different cultures and traditions? The more diverse they were, the more likely it is that yon are an individualist. Rate yourself on I = by giving yourself a 10 if most of your friends and influential adults (e.g., teachers) when you were growing up were from different ethnic groups.   I =

9. How interdependent are you in your finances? Some people cannot make any decisions about how to spend their money without consulting others, either because they have too little money or because they have important financial obligations. If you cannot spend even small amounts of money without considering what that will do to other people, give yourself a 10.   C =

10. How much education do you have? The more education you have, the more you can consider different points of view from different parts of the world, and you have to decide for yourself what is right and wrong, and so you become more of an individualist. Rate the maximum a 10.   I =

11. How much formal traditional education did you have? This is education about your ethnic group (e.g., Sunday school, language school) covering the language, religion, history, rituals, and traditions of your ethnic group. The more traditional education you have had, the higher you should rate yourself on C =.   C =

12. How much have you traveled alone abroad? If you have traveled that way a lot, enter I = 10 because you have seen many countries and met people from all over the world, and you had to decide for yourself what lifestyle is best for you, and so you must have become more of an individualist. If you traveled with your own group, you maintained your home culture while you were abroad, so you did not have to face the question of lifestyles. In that case, give few points or a 0.   I =

13. Did you live abroad for more than 6 months? The chances are that if you did, you had to decide for yourself whether the way of life of the host people was the kind of life you wanted for yourself, and so you would have become more individualistic. If you have not lived abroad, enter a 0; if you lived in different countries every few years, enter 10.   I =

14. Are you partnered? Generally, partnered people have to live in a way that pays attention to the needs of their significant other and that makes them more collectivist. How collectivist do you feel because of your marital status? If you are not married, enter a 0.   C =

15. Did you grow up in a large family, with many siblings and other relatives, in which you had to pay attention to the needs of others? In that case you may have become a collectivist. Rate yourself accordingly.   C =

16. Television, movies, and magazines often expound an individualistic viewpoint (e.g., boy meets girl, they fall in love and get married, though sometimes this upsets their family and friends). How much exposure to such media did you experience? The more exposure, the greater the I.   I =

17. Do you approve or disapprove of the stories in the media mentioned in the previous question? The more you disapprove the more collectivist you may be. If you strongly condemn these stories, enter a 10.   C =

18. Are your jobs or most of your activities allowing you to "do your own thing" (e.g., you are writing novels as you see fit) or do you have to act so as to take into account the needs and views of others? The more you have to take other people into account the more collectivist you are likely to be.   C =

19. What percent of your time do you work alone? If you work alone almost all the time, you do not have to pay attention to the needs of others; thus enter a 10.   I =

20. Do you enjoy doing fun things alone (e.g., taking a walk alone), or must you do things with others? The more you must have others with you in order to have fun, the more collectivist you are. Rate yourself on that.   C =

(continued)

(continued)

21. Would you say that most of the time you do "your own thing," paying no attention to whether it fits customs and "proper" behavior? If you do your own thing all the time, enter a 10. I =

22. How much do you value your privacy? If you value your privacy very much, enter a 10 below; if you think that privacy is unimportant, rate I = 0. I =

23. Is your occupation or job such that you *can* make decisions while ignoring the needs and views of others? The more you can do that, the larger should be the number below. I =

24. Finally, in your occupation or job, do you generally pay a lot of attention to the views and needs of others? The more you pay such attention, the higher the score. C =

Self- Scoring

Now add all the C and I scores and look at your grand total. A score of 60 is average. The more you deviate from 60, the more (or less) of that quality you have.

ENTER HERE   C = _____   I = _____

COMPETENCY BENCHMARK TABLES

The purpose of the Competency Benchmarks (Tables 4.1-4.4) is to create developmental models for defining and measuring competencies in professional psychology; each chapter in this *Handbook* applies the diversity competence for mental health practitioners in their work with a particular diverse population.

Table 4.1   Developmental-Level Competencies I

READINESS LEVEL—ENTRY TO PRACTICUM	
Competencies	Learning Process and Activities
Knowledge	The student is gaining: • Knowledge of concepts and theories of ethnicity, ethnic identity, colonial mentality, acculturation, enculturation, etc. • Knowledge of the distinction among, and relationship between, multicultural language such as ethnicity, nationality, and culture. • Familiarity with many ethnicities in the United States. • Knowledge of the APA Multicultural Guidelines (APA, 2003). • Understanding of how power, oppression, injustice, and privilege can impact the experiences of people from marginalized ethnicities (NCSPP, 2007). • Beginning knowledge of differing ethnicities' alternative theories and models of healing. • Basic knowledge of ethical principles and guidelines that address professional relationships and issues related to ethnicity (NCSPP, 2007).	At this stage of development, students are challenging themselves to learn about the complexity of ethnicity as well as its relationship to counseling and psychological variables. Students must demonstrate openness to exploring their own ethnicity so that they can identify how their own identity as ethnic beings influences work with their clients. Students are beginning to learn how to broach ethnicity in their clinical work. Students at this developmental level may benefit from participating in the activities below. Educators and trainers should use their clinical and multicultural judgment when deciding which activities will be most appropriate for their students. Experiential learning may include: • Students can create a "two-sided mask" by using a paper plate with holes cut out for eyes.

READINESS LEVEL—ENTRY TO PRACTICUM	
Competencies	Learning Process and Activities

| Skills | The student has the:

• Ability to articulate one's own ethnicity (NCSPP, 2007), including how ethnicity intersects with other aspects of one's identity and diversity.
• Ability to hear clients share about their ethnicity in session.
• Ability to establish rapport with individuals from diverse ethnic groups.
• Ability to recognize and discuss the impact of racism, ethnocentrism, and other forms of social injustice that pertain to people of marginalized ethnicities.
• Ability to consult and research about ethnicities in the United States when unfamiliar with such ethnic groups.
• Beginning of ability to implement assessment questions, interventions, and empathic statements about ethnicity in a way that is supportive and nonjudgmental. | Students decorate the outside of the mask with items they think people see when they look at them, and decorate the inside of the mask with objects or drawings of how they see themselves.
    Discussions of the activity can focus on the differences and similarities between the two sides; issues of acculturation and discrimination may be explored (Roysircar-Sodowsky, 2007).

• Students answer and process the questions (Jaipal, 2001): What significance does being _____ (e.g., Haitian, Israeli American, Dominican, Japanese, etc.) have for me? What aspects of my ethnic background(s) do I like/do I dislike?
• Students can conceptualize ethnicity, acculturation, enculturation, ethnic identity, and/or colonial mentality through a sand tray exercise. The portrayal in the sand tray can be a present, past, and/or future representation of ethnicity. |
| Values and Attitudes | The student demonstrates:

• Acknowledgment of ethnicity as important in understanding human behavior and in the provision of clinical services.
• Willingness to explore one's own ethnic group membership and engage in self-examination of biases and stereotypes (favorable and unfavorable) toward members of various ethnic groups.
• Openness and curiosity regarding one's own and others' power, oppression, and privilege as it pertains to ethnicity and how it impacts clinical work (NCSPP, 2007).
• Openness and willingness to take initiative regarding learning about issues related to ethnicity.
• Willingness to make active attempts to interact with, and provide clinical services to, persons of ethnically diverse backgrounds.
• Investment in behaving in an ethical and respectful manner with people of all ethnicities. | |

Table 4.2   Developmental-Level Competencies II

READINESS LEVEL—ENTRY TO INTERNSHIP	
Competencies	Learning Process and Activities

| Knowledge | The student has:
• Understanding of an individual's ethnicity as an integration with other multiple identities, including, but not limited to, race, gender, sexual orientation, etc. | At this level of development, students have a base of educational knowledge and applied experiences that allow them to understand, as well as constructively critique, the ethnicity literature and theories. Students demonstrate their

<div align="right">*(continued)*</div> |

Table 4.2   Developmental-Level Competencies II (*continued*)

READINESS LEVEL—ENTRY TO INTERNSHIP	
Competencies	Learning Process and Activities
<ul><li>Knowledge of assessments of acculturation, enculturation, ethnic identity, colonial mentality, etc.</li><li>Knowledge of the limitations of mainstream theories and interventions for clients from diverse ethnic groups (NCSPP, 2007).</li><li>Understanding of how power, oppression, and privilege impact the client experience, clinical presentation, and professional relationship of/ with a person with a marginalized ethnicity (NCSPP, 2007).</li><li>Knowledge of differing ethnicities' alternative theories and models of healing (NCSPP, 2007).</li></ul>	comprehension of ethnicity as an identity that is not in existence in isolation, but rather integrated with other multicultural identities. They are beginning to integrate their ethnicity competencies in multiple clinical arenas, including assessment, treatment planning, and individual, group, and couples interventions. Furthermore, students are asked to appropriately broach issues pertaining to ethnicity in nonclinical professional situations, such as in supervision and in seminars. In other words, foundational knowledge and multicultural values and attitudes are becoming well established, but skills in working with ethnic issues would be expected to be basic at this level of development.
Skills The student displays the:<ul><li>Ability to introduce and explore the concept of ethnicity in session with clients and examine how ethnicity may play a role in clients' presenting issues and influence therapeutic alliance.</li><li>Ability to work effectively with clients from similar and different ethnicities from yourself, and be able to monitor how you are similar and different from these clients.</li><li>Ability to self-reflect and process the role of one's ethnicity in clinical work.</li><li>Ability to apply and integrate ethnicity concepts and terminology to clinical conceptualization, treatment planning, and intervention.</li><li>Ability to recognize and discuss the impact of ethnocentrism, and other forms of social injustice on an individual of marginalized ethnicity(ies) in case material.</li><li>Ability to communicate with professional peers and supervisors about one's ethnicity in appropriate ways.</li></ul>	Experiential learning may include:<ul><li>Taking acculturation, ethnic identity, and colonial mentality instruments with the aim to increase self-awareness and to dialogue about how clients might experience taking such instruments.</li><li>Partaking in events that celebrate the diversity of ethnic groups (e.g., fairs, festivals, theater).</li><li>Conducting an ethnography (Roysircar-Sodowsky, 2007).</li><li>Participating in academic conferences that are dedicated to ethnic diversity and/or ethnic groups.</li></ul>
Values and Attitudes The student demonstrates (NCSPP, 2007):<ul><li>Openness to feedback on issues related to ethnicity.</li><li>Appreciation of the need to stay current of ethnicity-related scholarship that informs professional development.</li><li>Openness to integration of ethnicity in case conceptualization, treatment planning, assessment, and intervention.</li><li>Openness to integrating a client's ethnically indigenous models of healing into interventions when indicated.</li><li>Committed to understanding and incorporating the importance of ethnicity into personal ethical values and into ethical principles in all professional activities.</li></ul>	

Table 4.3   Developmental-Level Competencies III

READINESS LEVEL—ENTRY TO PROFESSIONAL PRACTICE	
Competencies	Learning Process and Activities
Knowledge The new professional can demonstrate the following: <ul><li>Understanding of how the knowledge base regarding ethnicity continues to evolve, requiring a commitment to lifelong learning (NCSPP, 2007).</li><li>Understanding of indigenous and emic bodies of knowledge that extend beyond Western psychological literature.</li><li>Recognition that professional and institutional roles interact with one's ethnic identity, which impacts professional work (NCSPP, 2007).</li><li>Understanding of certain ethnic populations in depth, or as an emphasis area, while also knowing areas where growth of knowledge is needed.</li><li>Understanding of the need to impact systems that perpetuate oppression of marginalized ethnicities and privilege of majority ethnicities (NCSPP, 2007).</li><li>Understanding of how ethical guidelines and their implementation are influenced by the ethnicity of stakeholders.</li></ul>	At the level of Entry to Professional Practice, mental health practitioners are expected to be able to independently practice ethically in regard to ethnic issues, which includes knowing when to consult on areas outside their realm of ethnic competency. Mental health practitioners at this developmental level obtain ongoing professional development regarding ethnicity. Ongoing professional development may include: <ul><li>Collaborating with professionals who have expertise in ethnic issues.</li><li>Engaging in self-directed study and professional development opportunities, such as attending conferences on ethnic diversity.</li><li>Partaking in active membership of professional organizations dedicated to ethnic issues (e.g., American Psychological Association's Division 45 Society for the Psychological Study of Ethnic Minority Issues).</li><li>Subscribing and reading academic journals and literature dedicated to ethnic issues.</li></ul>
Skills The new professional has the: <ul><li>Ability to appropriately apply the knowledge, values, perceptions, strengths, assumptions, and biases that result from one's ethnicity to clinical, professional, and scholarly work.</li><li>Ability to evaluate, critique, and modify traditional models of intervention and assessment to best fit ethnically diverse populations (NCSPP, 2009).</li><li>Ability to work concurrently with alternative theories and models of healing from a client's ethnic background.</li><li>Ability to routinely integrate ethnicity information in development of case conceptualization, treatment planning, and intervention.</li><li>Ability to seek out consultation and continuing education related to social justice for people of marginalized ethnicities.</li><li>Ability to seek consultation regarding ethnicity when needed.</li></ul>	
Values and Attitudes The new professional demonstrates: <ul><li>Commitment to lifelong learning related to ethnicity (NCSPP, 2007).</li><li>Pursuit of active, ongoing self-reflection of how one's ethnicity plays a role throughout one's personal and professional life.</li></ul>	

(continued)

Table 4.3   Developmental-Level Competencies III (*continued*)

READINESS LEVEL—ENTRY TO PROFESSIONAL PRACTICE	
Competencies	Learning Process and Activities
• Awareness of limits, and need for consultation, when working with clients from ethnicities you are not fully competent with. • Commitment to remaining informed of and to contribute to scholarship pertaining to ethnicity (NCSPP, 2007). • Belief that one's practice is ethical only if it includes decision making that integrates ethnicity (NCSPP, 2007).	

Table 4.4   Developmental-Level Competencies IV

READINESS LEVEL—ADVANCED PRACTICE AND SPECIALIZATION		
Competencies		**Learning Process and Activities**
Knowledge	The professional has extensive knowledge of: • Specialized research and knowledge of clinical practice with specific ethnic groups.	When in Advanced Practice and Specialization, mental health practitioners often maintain multiple roles (e.g., supervisors, directors, consultants, trainers) and possess some institutional and organizational power. At this developmental level, practitioners can be an advocate for ethnic diversity issues. For example, as a director of an agency, a practitioner can prioritize programming that integrates or focuses on ethnic diversity. As a director of a program (e.g., training, group), a practitioner can design a curriculum that embeds ethnic diversity content. In supervisory roles, practitioners can emphasize developing their supervisees' clinical competency with issues related to ethnicity.
Skills	The professional has advanced skills as demonstrated in the: • Ability to effectively supervise psychologists in training regarding issues of ethnicity. • Development of an area of emphasis (specialization) with a specific ethnic group(s). • Ability to consult with those outside the field of psychology on ethnicity-related topics. • Ability to integrate ethnicity issues into ethical decision making. • Ability to integrate community healers/leaders of various ethnicities and negotiate professional roles to include ethnically indigenous health practices (NCSPP, 2007). • Ability to reflect on and responsibly use own experiences of power, oppression, and privilege in professional roles to promote social justice for people of marginalized ethnicities (NCSPP, 2007).	Relevant professional development activities will vary depending on the mental health practitioner's unique background, established competencies, work setting, and professional role. Professional development activities can include: • Participating in peer consultation groups that are committed to multicultural competency. • Serving as a mentor in ethnic diversity organizations. • Attending and facilitating workshops, seminars, retreats, and classes dedicated to ethnicity issues.
Values and Attitudes	Well-integrated values and attitudes are demonstrated by the following: • Independent, active, ongoing self-monitoring of one's ethnicity. • Commitment to the critique and modification of traditional models of intervention used with ethnically diverse populations (NCSPP, 2007). • Confident expression of, and consistent commitment to, the promotion of social justice of ethnically marginalized persons in all professional roles (NCSPP, 2007; e.g., organizational consultant, supervisor, colleague, therapist).	

REFERENCES

Adams, G., Anderson, S. L., & Adonu, J. K. (2004). The cultural grounding of closeness and intimacy. In D. J. Mashek & A. Aron (Eds.), *Handbook of closeness and intimacy* (pp. 321–342). Mahwah, NJ: Erlbaum.

American Psychological Association (2003). Guidelines on multicultural education, training, research, practice, and organizational change for psychologists. *American Psychologist, 58*, 377–402.

Carter, R. T. (1995). *The influence of race and racial identity in psychotherapy: Toward a racially inclusive model.* New York: John Wiley & Sons.

Carter, R. T. (2003). Becoming racially and culturally competent: The racial-cultural counseling laboratory. *Journal of Multicultural Counseling and Development, 31*(1), 20–30.

Chang, T., & Kwan, K. K. (2009) Asian American racial and ethnic identity. In N. Tewari & A. N. Alvarez (Eds.), *Asian American psychology: Current perspectives* (pp. 113–134). New York: Psychology Press.

Cheryan, S., & Tsai, J. L. (2007). Ethnic identity. In F. T.L. Leong, A. G. Inman, A. Ebreo, L. Kinoshita, & L. H. Yang (Eds.), *Handbook of Asian American psychology* (2nd ed., pp. 125–139). Thousand Oaks, CA: Sage Publications.

Chun, K., Organista, P., & Marin, G. (2002). *Acculturation: Advances in theory, measurement and applied research.* Washington, DC: American Psychological Association.

Cross, W. E. (1991). *Shades of black: Diversity in African American identity.* Philadelphia: Temple University Press.

David, E. J. R., & Okazaki, S. (2006a). Colonial mentality: A review and recommendation for Filipino American psychology. *Cultural Diversity & Ethnic Minority Psychology, 12*(1), 1–16.

David, E. J. R., & Okazaki, S. (2006b). The Colonial Mentality Scale (CMS) for Filipino Americans: Scale construction and psychological implications. *Journal of Counseling Psychology, 53*(2), 241–252.

Day-Vines, N. L., Wood, S. M., Grothaus, T., Craigen, L., Holman, A., Dotson-Blake, K., et al (2007). Broaching the subjects of race, ethnicity and culture during the counseling process. *Journal of Counseling & Development, 85*, 401–409.

Fordham, S., & Ogbu, J. U. (1986). Black students' school success: Coping with the "burden of 'acting' white." *The Urban Review, 18*(3), 176–206.

Fuligni, A. J., Witkow, M., & Garcia, C. (2005). Ethnic identity and the academic adjustment of adolescents from Mexican, Chinese, and European backgrounds. *Developmental Psychology, 41*, 799–811.

Gans, H. J. (1979). Symbolic ethnicity: The future of ethnic groups and cultures in America. *Ethnic and Racial Studies, 2*, 1–20.

Harris, P. R., & Moran, R. T. (1991). *Managing cultural differences: High-performance strategies for a new world of business* (3rd ed.). Houston: Gulf Publishing.

Hays, P. A. (2001). *Addressing cultural complexities in practice: A framework for clinicians and counselors.* Washington, DC: American Psychological Association.

Helms, J. E., & Cook, D. A. (1999). *Using Race and culture in counseling and psychotherapy: Theory and process.* Needham Heights, MA: Allyn & Bacon.

Hovey, J. D. (1998). Acculturative stress, depression, and suicidal ideation among Mexican American adolescents: Implications for the development of suicide prevention programs in schools. *Psychological Reports, 83*(1), 249–50.

Hovey, J. D. (2000). Acculturative stress, depression, and suicidal ideation in Mexican Immigrants. *Cultural Diversity and Ethnic Minority Psychology, 6*(2), 134–151.

Kim, B. S. K. (2009). Acculturation and enculturation of Asian Americans: A primer. In N. Tewari & A. N. Alvarez (Eds.), *Asian American psychology: Current perspectives* (pp. 97–112). New York: Psychology Press.

Kohatsu, E. L. (2005). Acculturation: Current and future directions. In R. T. Carter (Ed.), *Handbook of racial-cultural psychology and counseling, Vol. 1* (pp. 26–40). Hoboken, NJ: Wiley.

Lustig, M. W., & Koester, J. (1996). *Intercultural competence: Interpersonal communication across cultures* (2nd ed.). New York: HarperCollins College.

Lynch, E. W. (2004). Conceptual framework: From culture shock to cultural learning. In E. W. Lynch & M. J. Hanson (Eds.), *Developing cross-cultural competence: A guide for working with young children and their families* (pp. 23–45). Baltimore: Paul H. Brookes.

Markus, H. R. (2008). Pride, prejudice, and ambivalence: Toward a unified theory of race and ethnicity. *American Psychologist*, 651–670.

Maxie, A. C., Arnold, D. H., & Stephenson, M. (2006). Do therapists address ethnic and racial differences in cross-cultural psychotherapy? *Psychotherapy: Theory, Research, Practice, Training, 43*(1), 85–98.

McGoldrick, M., Gerson, R., & Shellenberger, S. (1999). *Genograms: Assessment and intervention* (2nd ed.). New York: Guilford Press.

Merriam-Webster Online Dictionary. (2009). Stereotype. Retrieved July 19, 2009, from http://www.merriam-webster.com/dictionary/stereotype.

Moya, P., & Markus, H. R. (in press). Doing race: A conceptual overview. In H. R. Markus & P. Moya (Eds.), *Doing race: 21 essays for the 21st century*. New York: Norton.

Nadal, K. L. (2009). Colonialism: Societal and psychological impacts on Asian Americans and Pacific Islanders. In N. Tewari & A. N. Alvarez (Eds.), *Asian American psychology: Current perspectives* (pp. 153–172). New York: Psychology Press.

National Council of Schools and Programs in Professional Psychology (2007, August 15). Competency developmental achievement levels (DALS) of the National Council of Schools and Programs in Professional Psychology (NCSPP). Retrieved February 10, 2008, from http://www.ncspp.info/DAL of%20NCSPP%209-21-07.pdf

Outlaw, L. T. (1990). Towards a critical theory of race. In D. Goldberg (Ed.), *Anatomy of racism* (pp. 58–82). Minneapolis: University of Minnesota.

Phinney, J. (1992). The multigroup ethnic identity measure: A new scale for use with adolescents and young adults from diverse groups. *Journal of Adolescent Research, 7,* 156–176.

Phinney, J. (1996). When we talk about American ethnic groups, what do we mean? *American Psychologist, 51,* 918–927.

Phinney, J., & Ong, A. D. (2007). Conceptualization and measurement of ethnic identity: Current status and future directions. *Journal of Counseling Psychology, 54,* 271–281.

Poston, W. S. C. (1990). The biracial identity development model: A needed addition. *Journal of Counseling & Development, 69,* 152–155.

Quintana, S. M. (2007). Racial and ethnic identity: Developmental perspective and research. *Journal of Counseling Psychology, 54,* 259–270.

Roysircar-Sodowasky, G. (2007). The two-sided mask. National Council of Schools and Programs in Professional Psychology. Retrieved from http: www.multiculturalcenter.org/exercises/Two-SidedMask.pdf

Rodriguez, C. E. (1995). Racial themes in the literature: Puerto Ricans and other Latinos. In G. Haslip-Viera & S. L. Baver (Eds.), *Latinos in New York: Communities in transition.* Notre Dame, IN: University of Notre Dame Press.

Root, M. P. P. (1996). *The multiracial experience: Racial borders as the new frontier.* Thousand Oaks, CA: Sage Publications.

Roysircar-Sodowasky, G. (2007). The two-sided mask. National Council of Schools and Programs in Professional Psychology.Retrieved from http://www.multiculturalcenter.org/exercises/Two_SidedMask.pdf

Roysircar-Sodowsky, G., & Maestas, M. V. (2000). Acculturation, ethnic identity, and acculturative stress: Evidence and measurement. In R. H. Dana (Ed.), *Handbook of cross-cultural and multicultural personality assessment* (pp. 131–171). Mahwah, NJ: Erlbaum.

Ruiz, A. S. (1990). Ethnic identity: Crisis and resolution. *Journal of Multicultural Counseling and Development, 18,* 29–40.

Sanchez-Hucles, J., & Jones, N. (2005). Breaking the silence around race in training, practice, and research. *The Counseling Psychologist, 33,* 547–558.

Schwartz, S. (2003). Mapping and interpreting cultural differences around the world. In H. Vinken, J. Soeters, & P. Ester (Eds.), *Comparing cultures: Dimensions of culture in a comparative perspective.* Leiden, The Netherlands: Brill.

Sue, D. W., & Sue, D. (1999). *Counseling the culturally different: Theory and practice* (3rd ed.). New York: John Wiley & Sons.

Sue, D. W., & Sue, D. (2003). *Counseling the culturally diverse: Theory and practice* (4th ed.). New York: John Wiley & Sons.

Triandis, H. C. (1995). *Individualism and collectivism.* Boulder, CO: Westview Press.

Trimble, J. E., Helms, J. E., & Root, M.P.P. (2003). Social and psychological perspectives on ethnic and racial identity. In N. G. Bernal, J. E. Trimble, A. K. Burlew, & Y F. T. L. Leong (Eds.), *Handbook of racial and ethnic minority psychology* (pp. 239–275). Thousand Oaks, CA: Sage.

U.S. Census Bureau. (2000). *Racial and ethnic classifications used in Census 2000 and beyond.* Retrieved December 12, 2008, from http://www.census.gov/population/www/socdemo/race/racefactcb.html.

van den Berghe, P. L. (1981). *The ethnic phenomenon.* New York: Elsevier North Holland.

Waters, M. (1999). *Black identities: West Indian immigrant dreams and American realities.* Cambridge: Harvard University Press.

CHAPTER 5

CLINICAL COMPETENCIES IN WORKING WITH IMMIGRANT COMMUNITIES

ARPANA G. INMAN and PRATYUSHA TUMMALA-NARRA

INTRODUCTION

Immigration imposes significant pressures on foreign-born or immigrant communities as it necessitates a psychological restructuring against the backdrop of multiple cultural contexts (Inman, 2008). Within this framework, understanding immigrant experiences and serving their mental health needs through culturally competent means become imperative. Through use of case examples and vignettes, this chapter highlights the requisite knowledge, values/attitudes, and skills needed to work with a specific group of immigrants—South Asians—in the United States. It is hoped that many of the overarching concepts related to immigration issues generally will assist mental health practitioners working with members of immigrant communities from various backgrounds.

Although the United States has seen many waves of emigrants (e.g., individuals or families leaving their countries to live elsewhere temporarily) and immigrants (e.g., individuals or families entering a country to settle there; Potocky-Tripodi, 2002) since the sixteenth and seventeenth centuries (Pedraza & Rumbaut, 1996), the Immigration and Naturalization Family Reunification Act of 1965 resulted in a greater influx of immigrants to the United States. While the initial immigrant groups were from Europe, the post-1965 landscape changed dramatically. The United States saw more immigration from countries in Asia and South/Latin America. Since 2000, the number of individuals naturalized in the United States has been steadily increasing. For instance, individuals naturalized in the United States increased 58 percent from 660,477 in 2007 to 1,046,539 in 2008 with the greatest number of immigrants coming from Asia (36.6%), Mexico and Latin America (27.2%), and Europe (15.3%; U.S. Department of Homeland Security, 2008). This increase certainly suggests a strong need to examine the issues pertinent to this community.

DEFINITION OF TERMS

The emigrational status of an individual is an important precursor to the kind of adjustment and transition they will experience as they acculturate to the new home environment. Therefore, before discussing issues pertinent to immigrant communities, it is important to distinguish *immigrants* from *refugees*. Simply put, *immigrants* are foreign-born individuals who leave their countries on a

The authors would like to acknowledge Aubrey DeCarlo for her excellent assistance with this chapter.

voluntary basis. Typically in search of better economic opportunities and upward mobility, these individuals have the freedom to return to or visit their countries without difficulties. *Refugees*, on the other hand, while also foreign-born, are involuntarily displaced from their countries. Forced to leave their countries because of political unrest, human rights violations, or other chaotic situations, they are exiled from their own lands. Unable to return to their own countries, they seek asylum elsewhere (Fong, 2004; Potocky-Tripodi, 2002).

While *refugees* may have temporary protective status that allows them short- or long-term legal residence in a new country, ~~immigrants or sojourns~~ (tourists, students) typically enter the country with planful legal documentation (e.g., visas). However, this status can change with immigrants becoming undocumented if they enter the country without proper authorization or if they violate the terms of their visa and stay in the country beyond the expiration date. Furthermore, if legal documentation is maintained, the status of a foreign-born individual (whether refugee or immigrant) can change after a year. Specifically, after a year, these individuals are eligible to become permanent residents and receive what is termed a "green card." After five years, permanent residents are eligible to become naturalized citizens of the United States. A naturalized citizen is someone who is born in another country but acquires citizenship in the new country of residence and becomes a national of this new country. Anyone who is not a citizen of the United States is termed an "alien."

Irrespective of the type of migration, the legal or illegal status of an individual can have a profound impact on family functioning and adjustment issues in the new country. As indicated by the definitions, issues pertinent to immigrant and refugee communities are vast and distinct. As such, because of the parameters of our chapter, our intent is to focus primarily on the experience of immigrants.

THEORIES RELATED TO IMMIGRANT ISSUES

Several theories have been proposed regarding the reasons for people's immigration from one country to another. One classic theory is that immigration occurs because of the "push-pull" phenomenon (Lee, 1966). This theory suggests that people leave their countries because factors such as lack of opportunities, discrimination, or economic conditions "push" them from their country of origin. Conversely, factors such as better economic opportunities "pull" people to migrate to other countries. A second theory

is related to neoclassical economic theory (Malmberg, 1997), which posits that people make informed decisions and weigh the economic advantages and disadvantages of staying or migrating to another country. The assumption underlying this theory is that such rational thinking allows all individuals (rich or poor) to migrate, yet statistics show that only two percent of the world's population is able to migrate (Faist, 1997). In light of this, other theories have been postulated that provide a more comprehensive perspective and highlight the complex nature of immigration.

Currently, there is a recognition that migration occurs due to a dialectic intersection of three factors or levels: the *macro* or structural level, the *meso* or relational level, and the *micro* or the individual level (Faist, 1997; Malmberg, 1997). The *macro* or structural level refers to political, economic, cultural, and geographic forces that are implicated in the push-pull theory. Political forces include issues related to political freedoms and stability, as well as favorable immigration policies; economic forces relate to standard of living and job opportunities; cultural forces include elements such as ethnic composition and language accessibility; and geographic forces entail climate and distance between countries. Typically there is an assumption that people tend to migrate to countries that have political stability, economic opportunities, geographic proximity, and cultural similarity.

The second factor or level, the *meso* or the relational level, involves family/social networks and ties to ethnic, religious, and social associations, with the assumption that strong family ties and social networks make it harder for people to migrate. The final level highlights *micro* or individual factors such as age, education, ethnicity, religion, and financial assets, which are also important considerations. For example, literature shows that older people are not only less likely to immigrate as compared to younger individuals, but also have greater difficulties adjusting to a new place (Akhtar, 1999).

The complexity of the immigration process is further exemplified by the different phases or stages that it entails: pre-migration, the journey or transit, and the adjustment to entering a new environment (Berger, 2000; Drachman, 1992; Fong, 2004; Potocky-Tripodi, 2002). Each of these stages comes with its own issues and requires a restructuring or remaking of one's identity. The pre-migration phase consists not only of the decision to immigrate but also the departure itself. Although the departure is planned for immigrants, the separation from family and friends, and the potential loss and the resultant pain that comes from this separation, can be immense (Inman, Howard, Beaumont, & Walker, 2007). Sometimes this loss may be overshadowed by the potential journey itself. The anticipation of a new adventure can be both exciting and overwhelming. Navigating visa issues and the logistics of making a long journey may be fraught with new beginnings and discoveries. Finally, as immigrants enter a new country there is a process of resettlement that occurs— typically an ongoing, lifelong process. Against the backdrop of multiple cultures, immigrants have to forge a new identity that selectively incorporates aspects of the culture of origin as well as the new environment (Prathikanti, 1997). Within this context, immigrants experience a push from the country of origin and pull to the country of immigration (Segal, 2002).

While immigrants typically have been raised in cultures with fairly consistent and functional values and practices, transitioning into a new cultural environment requires a reevaluation of cultural practices, within the context of a lack of a social structure that supports their cultural priorities and needs (Inman, Howard et al., 2007). This can result in conflicting loyalties and generational dissonance (Inman, Constantine, & Ladany, 1999; Inman, Ladany, Constantine, & Morano, 2001). For example, feelings of ambivalence toward the adopted country may be heightened for an immigrant parent with an adolescent child who engages in a behavior (e.g., dating) that is incongruent with his or her culture of origin. Although the parent may have developed a strong connection with the mainstream context in the adopted country

(Tummala-Narra, 2001), the mourning of various types of losses (e.g., elder guidance, social and community supports) may play a critical role in shaping the immigrant identity and experience (Akhtar, 1999; L. Grinberg & R. Grinberg, 1989; Inman, Howard et al., 2007). The ability to mourn the distance from one's country of origin, and the ability to recreate aspects of home within the new cultural environment, are thought to be critical for psychological wellbeing and identity transformation (Ainslie, 1998; Akhtar, 1999).

Akhtar (1999) has described four interrelated tracks of identity transformation that should be considered in the immigration process: (1) movement from love or hate of either the country of origin or the adopted country to feelings of ambivalence; (2) the negotiation of physical distance from the country of origin, which may occur through re-creation of aspects of one's cultural environment in the adopted country; (3) the negotiation of past, present, and future, when an individual may fantasize about returning to the country of origin; and (4) reconciling a feeling of separateness from the adopted land to a feeling of participation and a sense of "we-ness" within the larger social context of the adopted country (p. 97). Each of these trajectories needs to be considered within the context of sociocultural issues specific to both the country of origin and the adopted country.

BARRIERS TO COMPETENCY IN WORKING WITH IMMIGRANTS

Although immigrant communities experience a range of difficulties including interpersonal, familial, and intergenerational issues, health, identity, and racism (Inman, 2006; Inman & Yeh, 2007; Tewari, Inman, & Sandhu, 2003; Tummala-Narra, Inman, & Ettigi, in progress), several individual, sociocultural, and structural/institutional barriers influence help-seeking attitudes and behaviors (Fong, 2004). For instance, at the individual level, immigrants may lack knowledge of or exposure to Western mental health treatment, and may have misconceptions about professional counseling (Akutsu, 1997; Kagawa-Singer & Chung, 2002). This may be closely related to their immigration history (Takaki, 1998), length of stay in the United States, and level of acculturation. Other individual variables such as gender (Nolen-Hoeksema, 2002), age (Leong & Lau, 2001), limited language proficiency (Kagawa-Singer & Chung, 2002), history of previous treatment (Solberg, Choi, Ritsma, & Jolly, 1994), and client–counselor ethnic matching may also influence help-seeking behaviors (Uba, 1994).

At the sociocultural level, cultural values and views of mental health (e.g., separation of mind and body or a holistic integrated perspective), stigmatization of the mentally ill and the use of mental health services, expression of distress (e.g., physical, emotional, spiritual), and availability of alternative healing practices contribute to the underutilization of mental health services (Hilton et al., 2001; Inman, Yeh, Madan-Bahel, & Nath, 2007; Mullatti, 1995; Yeh, Inman, Kim, & Okubo, 2006).

At the structural or institutional level, conflicting Western mental health systems values and social norms (e.g., self-disclosure, expression of emotions, individual goals) and immigrant values (e.g., keeping personal issues in the family, collectivistic orientation to problems) may keep immigrants from seeking professional help (Leong, & Lau, 2001; Leong, Wagner, & Tata, 1995; Tummala-Narra, 2001; Yeh Inman, Kim, & Okubo, 2006). Inaccurate evaluations or misdiagnoses due to therapist's cultural biases or culturally incongruent scales may create significant difficulties in perceived counselor credibility and competence (Leong & Lau, 2001; Uba, 1994). Other systemic issues such as access to services (e.g., financial, transportation, child care) can further deter mental health services use. A lack of knowledge and understanding of these issues may deter mental health practitioners from providing competent mental health services.

Mark's vignette (5.1) illustrates how a lack of knowledge and understanding of these issues may deter mental health professionals from providing competent mental health services. Specifically, this vignette highlights how psychological interpretations that are either premature and/or inaccurate may be experienced by immigrant clients.

Although Mark's conceptualization of the underlying meaning of headaches may have been partly accurate, it did not address Joseph's

CASE VIGNETTE 5.1

Mark, a mental health practitioner, conducted an initial intake evaluation with a client, Joseph, who was referred to psychotherapy by his primary care physician. Joseph is a married man in his mid-30s who immigrated from Sri Lanka about five years prior to meeting with Mark. He is fluent in Tamil and English, and describes himself as a devout Christian. In his first session, Joseph expressed that he needed help coping with headaches that began about one year following his relocation to the United States from Sri Lanka. He experienced these headaches more frequently in the past two months, during a period of increasing verbal conflict with his wife. Joseph told Mark that he understood that there was no physical evidence for the headaches, but didn't know how a psychotherapist could help him. In response to his questions, Mark indicated that he believed that Joseph's conflicts with his wife were most likely the reason for his headaches. At the end of the session, Joseph thanked the therapist, but did not return for another meeting with Mark following this first session. Mark felt confused about Joseph's discontinuation of psychotherapy, because he believed that he had a positive interaction with Joseph.

understanding and experience of psychotherapy, and/or validate Joseph's real experience of headaches and how they may be interfering with his life. Additionally, Mark made an assumption that the sole cause of the headaches was the conflict between Joseph and his wife, without attending to the fact that Joseph began experiencing the headaches following his immigration to the United States. Mark, then, should have considered a more complete examination of Joseph's immigration experience, and possibly his religious beliefs, by asking some of the following questions: (a) What is your and your family's understanding of why you have headaches? How would these headaches be understood in Sri Lanka? (b) How do you tend to deal with difficulties? What has helped you deal with emotional or physical difficulties in the past? (c) What does your religion say about how one should handle problems? These questions are aimed at inquiring about Joseph's experiences from his point of view rather than imposing traditional Western psychotherapeutic concepts prematurely. Unfortunately, in using an ethnocentric perspective in session, Mark and Joseph may have enacted Joseph's experience of not feeling understood in the larger mainstream context—an aspect of the encounter that may have contributed to Joseph's decision to not return to psychotherapy.

ELEMENTS OF COMPETENCE

To begin addressing the barriers, mental health practitioners need to have some basic elements of competency when working with immigrants. Because of the distinct experience of immigrants, we have chosen to focus on one group of immigrants, South Asians, as a framework for considering broader work with members of immigrant groups. Drawing on the extant literature, we highlight the requisite knowledge (history, individual and cultural diversity, intersection of immigration and mental health issues, and ethical and legal standards), skills (conceptual framework, assessment, diagnosis, intervention), as

well as the attitudes and values necessary to provide multiculturally sensitive services needed to work with this group of immigrants. Finally, recommendations for supervision and training in this area are provided. This conceptual structure highlights issues common to the immigration process in general, while the content areas delineated below serve both as a reference guide for working with individuals from South Asian countries specifically and as a practical starting point for identifying issues of possible salience for individuals from other regions of origin. As noted earlier, those interested in working with individuals from other backgrounds must, of course, recognize the unique personal, historical, and cultural factors relevant to each client, and must take care to avoid overgeneralizations based on the experiences of others.

KNOWLEDGE

Brief History of South Asian Immigration

As with other groups of settlers throughout U.S. history, within the waves of South Asian immigration to the United States there has been great variation in terms of country of origin (i.e., India, Pakistan, Bangladesh, Sri Lanka, Nepal, Bhutan, and the Maldives), age at immigration, and reasons for immigration. Other differences relate to the level of intergenerational conflict prior to immigration, immigration status on entry to the United States (voluntary or involuntary), length of stay in the United States, and exposure to Western values prior to immigration. Finally, varying levels of community support, educational and skill levels, socioeconomic status/social class in the country of origin and current status, and religiosity have also been noted in the different waves of immigrants to the United States (Tewari et al., 2003).

Although there were some immigrants from South Asia in the 1800s, the first substantial wave of immigrants came to the United States as *sojourns* in the early 1900s. Following changes in U.S. immigration law, a second wave of immigrants came in 1946, primarily to be united with their families. The first two waves consisted of laborers who were not formally educated and who came primarily from the northern part of rural India (e.g., Punjab). The third and largest wave came post-1965, with the majority being highly educated, urban professionals. The two subsequent decades (i.e., 1980s and 1990s) saw a shift in the type of immigrants. Not as highly educated and perhaps from a lower socio-economic status, these individuals were relatives of these who had immigrated in the post-1965 wave (Gupta, 1999). Further, while the majority of the immigrants have historically been from India, there is currently an increase in immigration from Bangladesh and Pakistan. Additionally, it is important to note that throughout their immigration history, South Asians have not been immune from the discriminatory and exclusionary immigration policies (e.g., restricted immigration, access to land ownership, citizenship, and anti-miscegenation laws) accorded to immigrants in the United States. These are significant factors that need to be considered in understanding the adjustment and socialization of the South Asian immigrant (Almeida, 1996; Hines, Garcia-Preto, McGoldrick, Almeida, & Weltman, 1992).

Diversity, Cultural Identity, and the South Asian Immigrant Experience

Heterogeneity

Demographically, South Asians are the fourth-largest ethnic subgroup, with a population approximating 2,963,999 in the United States (U.S. Census Bureau, 2000). Among South Asian Americans, Asian Indian Americans tend to dominate, representing about 1,678,795 of the total South Asian population in the United States, followed by individuals from Pakistan, Bangladesh, Sri Lanka, Bhutan, Nepal, and the Maldives (U.S. Census Bureau, 2000). The term *South Asian* denotes a common identity, bringing together diverse populations on the basis of a shared ancestry and culture, yet it is important to note that this

term is a political construct that is accepted more by later generations in the United States. (Shankar & Srikanth, 1998).

Despite a shared culture and history, people from South Asia differ in their languages, religions, customs, beliefs, traditions, and foods. The primary languages spoken by South Asians include Hindi in India, Urdu in Pakistan and Bangladesh, and Singhalese in Sri Lanka, with English (due to Britain's colonization) also spoken in most countries. However, there are approximately 30 regional languages and over 400 dialects spoken in the various parts of South Asia. These include Gujarati, Punjabi, Bengali, Marathe, Tamil, Telegu, Kannada, and Malayalam, to name just a few. South Asian Americans also vary in their religious and spiritual philosophies. The primary religion among Indians is Hinduism (82%), followed by Islam (12%), Christianity (2.5%), Sikhism (2%), Buddhism (0.7%) Jainism (0.5%), Zoroastrianism/Parsi (0.01%), and Judaism (0.005%). Pakistanis and Bangladeshis, on the other hand, are primarily Muslim and Sri Lankans are mostly Buddhist (Tewari et al., 2003). Because of these differences, whether South Asians live abroad or in their country of origin, they tend to identify in terms of national, linguistic, or religious ties (Shankar & Srikanth, 1998).

Enculturation and Acculturation

In understanding the South Asian immigrant experience, it is important to consider the constructs of enculturation and acculturation. *Enculturation* involves being socialized within one's own ethnic culture (e.g., values, attitudes, and behaviors), whereas *acculturation* involves socialization to the "host culture" thorough an involvement in the host culture's values, attitudes, and behaviors (Berry, 1980). To facilitate success, South Asians have been noted to selectively acculturate to certain U.S. cultural norms (e.g., speaking English, career goals, dress) while holding onto fundamental ethnic cultural values related to family interactions, intimate relations, sex-role/gendered expectations, and religion (Dhruvarajan, 1993; Naidoo, 1985; Prathikanti,

1997). Particularly true of first-generation immigrants, these South Asians may not fully identify with the American culture. Conversely, it is important to note that South Asians who are born in the United States (i.e., second generation) may take on an American identity and strongly identify with mainstream American culture before (or in lieu of) identifying with the South Asian culture. Alternatively, there may be those who have a strong dual identification equally to both the American and the South Asian culture (Liebkind, Jasinskaja-Lahti, & Solheim, 2004). In noting these realities, we need to challenge the traditional conceptualization of acculturation (Uba, 2002). The individual differences and identities that evolve from these various levels of acculturation and enculturation are important issues in contextualizing the complexities of South Asian American individuals and their cultural identities.

Ethnicity and Race

Ethnicity is defined by one's shared cultural values, traditions, and customs within an ethnic community, whereas *race* refers to an externally imposed arbitrary classification system based on one's position of power and privilege within society (Inman & Alvarez, 2009). In the United States, both ethnicity and race are central frames of references through which social interactions are experienced and interpreted (Outlaw, 1990). Thus, developing an ethnic and racial identity becomes important in maintaining visibility and navigating relationships within both the culture of origin and the dominant culture (Inman, 2006). Within this context, a critical dilemma that emerges for South Asians is the extent to which one can value and retain one's ethnic identity (Inman, 2006; Kwan & Sodowsky, 1997).

Given these dilemmas, ethnic identity has been found to function differently for U.S.-born South Asians versus foreign-born South Asians. For instance, Inman (2006) found that ethnic identification was a greater buffer against stress for foreign-born first-generation South Asians than for U.S.-born second-generation South Asians. Furthermore, because of a bicultural influence, South Asian Americans internalize two cultures that inform and influence their lives—the South Asian identity and the American identity. Although being "American" is not consistent with an ethnic identity (Cheryan & Tsai, 2007), identifying with an American identity and being seen as American provides South Asians with a sense of legitimacy as well as the cultural competence needed to access resources and navigate interactions effectively (Phinney, Horenczyk, Liebkind, & Vedder, 2001; Ying, Lee, Tsai, Yeh, & Huang, 2000). Furthermore, how particular aspects of identity may operate in particular situations is influenced by social cues that South Asian Americans experience (LaFromboise, Coleman, & Gerton, 1993) as well as exposure and connection to a cultural context (e.g., visiting Asia or lack of contact with Asia; Cheryan & Tsai, 2007), with some aspects being seen as more salient than others. These factors become important in how ethnic identity is defined (e.g., including all cultural heritages and not just based on one's country of origin) and integrated into one's sense of self (Cheryan & Tsai, 2007).

While the construct of ethnicity has been easier to own, the concepts of race and racism have been hard to pin down for South Asian Americans. For instance, ethnicity and notion of shared customs and cultural values have been important elements in the continuation of culture for South Asians. Perpetuating cultural traditions and values provides a sense of legitimacy and belongingness for South Asians in their community (Inman et al., 1999). Conversely, despite a long history of racism (e.g., denial of land ownership and citizenship, anti-miscegenation laws, targets of racial slurs and violence), and recent events such as the backlash against South Asians following the terrorist attacks of September 11, 2001 (Ahmed, Nicolson, & Spencer, 2000; Inman, Yeh et al., 2007; Kibria, 1998), acceptance of these issues has varied from within and outside of this community. Factors that have influenced this invisibility have been related to the model minority myth (Alvarez, Juang, & Liang, 2006; Wu, 2001), the lack of racial socialization or a language to speak to these issues among new immigrants (Inman, Howard et al., 2007), and the economic and educational successes of this community (Inman & Alvarez, 2009). Furthermore, recent research (Tummala-Narra et al., in progress) has revealed that, for South Asians, race and ethnicity seem to hold overlapping yet distinct meanings. For example, Asian Indians in the United States seemed to experience race as salient in situations when they experienced racial discrimination, whereas they appeared to experience ethnicity as salient when they were involved with religious and cultural activities within the Asian Indian community in the United States. At the same time, in further describing race and ethnicity, they indicated experiencing both feelings of otherness and alienation as well as feelings of pride and connection to their Asian Indian heritage, suggesting an ambivalent relationship with the constructs of race that tend to be interpreted as ethnicity and vice versa. Furthermore, second-generation Asian Indians tended to report higher levels of racism-related stress and viewed their position as racial minorities as more significant to their conception of race than first-generation Asian Indians, who emphasized experiences of discrimination in their conceptions of race (Tummala-Narra et al., in progress). These findings highlight the importance of considering intersections of ethnic and racial identities when working with South Asian Americans.

Gender Roles

Traditional South Asian culture has been strongly influenced by religious teachings and views masculine and feminine characteristics to be intrinsic and complementary to each other. Although this allows for greater variability in the notions of masculinity for South Asian men when compared to White men, the South Asian culture has typically been patriarchal. As such, while both men and women are expected to be family oriented and to fulfill their parents' expectations, men have traditionally been the breadwinners and decision makers and women have been the caretakers of children in the family

(Tewari et al., 2003). Furthermore, men tend to be held to less stringent expectations in relation to sexual behaviors and intimacy, whereas South Asian women have typically experienced greater community censures in relation to gender roles and intimacy issues. Relatedly, they bear a disproportionate burden with regard to cultural responsibilities, including that of passing on cultural traditions (Dasgupta, 1998).

However, within the context of a bicultural socialization, South Asian men and women have needed to negotiate competing cultural representations of masculinity or femininity. This has been further complicated by role reversals as a function of immigration (Uba, 1994), significantly influencing South Asian family roles and expectations. In particular, the emphasis on dual-income families has pulled women into the workforce, with men having to take on more child-care responsibilities, which may result in tensions in male–female roles and relationships. This has important implications as South Asian men and women manage their gender roles.

Sexuality and Sexual Identity

Although one's sexuality and being attracted to another individual is a fundamental part of human interactions, social and religious influences have been restrictive, creating a silence surrounding the issue of sexuality in the South Asian community (S. D. Dasgupta & S. Dasgupta, 1996; Inman & Sandhu, 2002). These restrictions have resulted from socially sanctioned fears surrounding the implications of dating and sexuality, parental roles in mate selection, and pressures that children marry within the community, have their own children, and perpetuate the cultural traditions (S. D. Dasgupta & S. Dasgupta, 1996; Inman, Howard et al., 2007). This attitude takes on greater significance within the context of homosexuality (Inman & Alvarez, 2009). Perceived as a Western concept (Chung & Katayama, 1998) and as a "White disease" (Leupp, 1995), homosexuality is seen as unnatural. Although acculturation to U.S. values may create positive attitudes toward sexuality and sexual identity issues (Pope, 1995), familial and cultural influences may trump these attitudes. As South Asian American sexual minorities develop their identities, and experience pressures related to marriage, the fear of familial rejection may be a major hindrance in the ownership of their identities and the coming-out process (Chan, 1989; Pope & Chung, 1999). Similarly, religion (e.g., Christianity, Islam, Hinduism) also plays a significant role in the negative valence surrounding sex and homosexuality. Religious teachings (e.g., Hinduism) tend to subscribe to a balance between female (Shakti) and male (Shiva) attributes with a focus on heterosexual relationships. As such, sex is to occur only within the constraints of a marital relationship and any leaning toward homosexuality is considered undesirable and perverse (Pope & Chung, 1999).

It is important to recognize that South Asians negotiate multiple identities within the context of their immigrant experience. The developmental processes related to the different identities may occur simultaneously or one may follow the other. In this context it becomes salient to ask some important questions: What is the relative importance of each identity for the individual? How do the identities intersect or interact at different points in one's life? How does this influence the negotiation of the minority identities? (Inman & Alvarez, 2009). Case Vignette 5.2 reflects the negotiation of some of these questions related to the complex nature of identity formation for South Asians, and more broadly for members of immigrant groups as a whole.

Poonam's struggle with adjusting to her new cultural environment in the context of her marriage is shared by many immigrants who face developmental transitions without preparation in the country of origin. Her conflicts further exemplify challenges within and outside of the family context that concern the simultaneous

CASE VIGNETTE 5.2

Poonam is a 28-year-old woman married to a second-generation Asian Indian man, born and raised in the United States. She immigrated from a rural part of India when she got married at the age of 24. Poonam sought psychotherapy with the support of a family friend who was concerned about her depressed mood. In psychotherapy, Poonam described her family in India as supportive, and stated that she missed feeling like she had a home. In India, she felt taken care of by her parents and extended family, and at the same time, experienced herself as rebellious as she left for college in an urban setting some distance away from her parents. Poonam's marriage to her husband was arranged by her family and she met her husband a few times in person and got to know him through phone calls and e-mails prior to getting married. She reported a positive relationship with her husband, whom she described as loving and responsible. She admired the way he managed his work life, friendships, and family life. However, she felt increasingly lonely and isolated as he worked long hours. She had completed her Bachelor's degree in India in finance, but had experienced difficulty in navigating her professional identity in the United States. She also found it difficult to socialize with her husband's friends as she experienced them as more "Westernized" than she, and often felt "out of place" in his social circles. As an example, Poonam expressed that she was unaccustomed to other Indian women socializing more freely with men in dinner parties she attended with her husband. She found herself comparing her relatively sexually modest style of clothing with the clothing style of her peers in the United States, and became anxious about her husband's sexual interest in her. She noted her difficulty in communicating her feelings to her husband at times, when she felt as though he could not understand her experience.

renegotiation of gender roles and cultural norms (e.g., sexual expression). Whereas Poonam experienced herself as a progressive woman in India, she felt as though she lacked a sense of belonging in her husband's "Westernized" circles. These shifts in identity contributed to her feelings of sadness and a wish to feel reconnected with her family and friends in India.

The Intersection of Immigration and Mental Health Among South Asians in the United States

Intergenerational Conflicts

Several authors (Inman, Howard et al., 2007; Prathikanti, 1997; Ramisetty-Mikler, 1993; Sodowsky & Carey, 1987) have discussed intergenerational conflicts as a major source of stress for South Asian immigrants. Because of the selective acculturative practices in the South Asian community (Prathikanti, 1997), most immigrant families try to maintain their traditional patterns, but parental expectations may change based on their length of stay in North America. Thus, children may be allowed more freedom in the United States than if they were in India due to the parents being influenced by cultural values and norms of the host culture. Alternatively, the fear of children becoming more "Americanized" (S. D. Dasgupta & S. Dasgupta, 1998; Sodowsky & Carey, 1988) may result in restrictive parenting practices. The struggle for many South Asians to understand, incorporate, and fit into the American culture while still maintaining their ethnic values, attitudes, and traditions can create different choices for parents and their children, resulting in conflict and tension for both parties (Inman, 2008; Tewari et al., 2003).

Discrimination/Oppression

As with most immigrants, discriminatory experiences have played a significant role in the lives of South Asians. Research on racial and ethnic discrimination and its relationship to mental health among South Asians indicates that racial and ethnic discrimination, including perceived

prejudice in social/professional settings (being of a minority status) and negative stereotyping (math geniuses, snake worshippers, bride burners, etc.), contributes to depression, anxiety, and suicidal ideation (Bhugra, 2002; Bhui et al., 2005; Ramisetty-Mikler, 1993). Differences in clothing style, accents, and physical appearance, perceived negative stereotyping, non-majority status, and feelings of isolation may be sources of stress. Such acculturation stress can lead to immigrants becoming defensive, internalizing feelings of inferiority, or developing prejudice against the majority culture (Ramisetty-Mikler, 1993). In addition, the experience of discrimination seems to vary with respect to the immigrant generation. Specifically, studies have revealed that second-generation Asian Indians experience higher levels of racism-related stress when compared with first-generation Asian Indians (e.g., Tummala-Narra et al., in progress). This finding coincides with those of other studies that report better mental health among foreign-born immigrants than U.S.-born immigrants (Takeuchi et al., 2007).

Trauma

Much of what we know about trauma in the South Asian community in the United States has been gained through research conducted in the area of intimate partner violence (Dasgupta, 1998; Raj & Silverman, 2003). As research on domestic violence within the South Asian community has expanded in recent years, several studies have documented the relatively low rate of reporting domestic violence among immigrant women (Krishnan, Hilbert, & VanLeeuwen, 2001). Some studies on coping with violence among immigrant women suggest that they tend to report abuse incidents and seek help only when the violence reaches a crisis or severe level (Abraham, 2000; Huisman, 1996), whereas other studies indicate that women experiencing more severe abuse may be the least likely to disclose the abuse to others (Yoshioka, Gilbert, El-Bassel, & Baig-Amin, 2003). These divergent findings may be accounted for, at least in part, by the prevalent use of shelter samples, and the tendency

CASE VIGNETTE 5.3

Asma is a 45-year-old Pakistani American married woman who sought psychotherapy to address her conflicts with her college-age daughter. She was worried about her daughter's involvement with her White, European American boyfriend. She was ambivalent about her daughter dating and her choice of partner. Asma expressed feeling a deep level of anxiety about her daughter's safety and any potential loss of cultural identity as a result of her relationship. In the course of psychotherapy, she discussed her own childhood history of being sexually abused by a male neighbor, which she eventually revealed to her parents. Her parents responded by protecting her, but struggled with not knowing how to help her cope with her anxiety, which continued to affect her functioning throughout her childhood and adolescence. Asma's concerns over safety were further complicated after immigrating to the United States. As an adult she continued to feel like a foreigner after experiencing various incidents of discrimination by some White Americans. Asma never told her husband or her daughter about her childhood trauma, as she feared that this would create an unnecessary burden for them. At the same time, her careful attention to her daughter's needs led, at times, to an overprotective approach to her parenting. This was accentuated by her concerns about preserving Pakistani cultural traditions and values in her family life and guarding against discrimination. Asma's daughter expressed on several occasions to her mother that she did not understand her constant concern for her safety, and that she wished that her mother was more supportive of her relationship.

to lump together groups of ethnically diverse women (i.e., using a Vietnamese sample to represent Asian Americans as a group).

While research on domestic violence in the South Asian community has begun to expand, research on other types of interpersonal trauma, such as sexual abuse, physical abuse, rape, and political trauma in South Asian communities, as among other immigrant communities, is virtually nonexistent. However, it has been noted in the clinical literature that traumatic experiences complicate immigrants' identifications with both the country of origin and the adopted country, and can manifest in culturally specific ways, such as anxiety that is expressed through somatic symptoms (Tummala-Narra, 2001). The ways in which many South Asian Americans cope with traumatic experiences should be considered through a sociocultural lens as well. Coping strategies that may promote resilience in one cultural context may be experienced as a liability in another cultural context (Tummala-Narra, 2007a). For example, a South Asian immigrant may express his or her resiliency in the face of trauma as he or she

engages in prayer or seeks the help of an older member within his or her community (Inman, Yeh, et al., 2007).

Asma's case, shown in Case Vignette 5.3, reveals the complexity of mental health issues as they are influenced by various immigration-related factors, some of which include the experience of discrimination, intergenerational conflicts, and interpersonal violence. It is clear that her negotiation of acculturation is complicated by her traumatic experience and her role as a parent in an adopted land. The multiple roles involved in her adjustment to a new cultural environment (an adjustment characterized in part by hostility), coupled with her early experiences of sexual trauma, contribute to the difficulty involved with establishing a sense of safety for herself and her daughter. The ways in which she copes with these various adjustments involve a culturally congruent approach in that she preserves her identity as a protective and loving wife and mother, although this approach may in some ways constrict her ability to explore the sources of her anxiety more openly. These types of conflicts between internal and external demands are an inherent part of emotional adjustment in the course of immigration.

Ethical and Legal Standards

The American Psychological Association (APA) provides clear guidelines for the provision of psychological services to ethnically, linguistically, and culturally diverse populations (APA 1993; APA, 2003). These are highlighted later in this section. Despite these guidelines, working with South Asian immigrant communities (as with other communities of individuals from diverse backgrounds) can raise significant ethical dilemmas. Therefore, being attuned to these issues becomes important.

For instance, not only do mental health practitioners encounter clients with different cultural norms, but also different legal issues. Rather than becoming "mental health cops" (Chung, Bemak, Ortiz, & Sandoval-Perez, 2008, p. 314) and being linear in their application of legal statutes, mental health practitioners are encouraged to evaluate each situation through intentionality and informed decisions. For example, clinicians are required to report any signs of physical abuse in children. While the duty to report such abuse is intended to protect children, the nature of what is considered abuse varies across cultural contexts. For example, in the case of many South Asian homes, physical discipline such as spanking children is generally not considered to be harmful to children. Rather, it is considered a parental responsibility to help socialize children so that children bridge their senses of identity to a larger family and community context. This perspective, however, does not negate the fact that physical abuse, distinct from physical discipline, does occur in some South Asian homes. It is important that these issues be explicitly discussed with clients in order to clarify the clients' understanding of family interactions, and related legal and ethical implications. This example suggests a need to conduct a comprehensive cultural assessment around, in this case, a cultural practice intended to help rather than abuse

a child (Chung et al., 2008). These types of issues often underscore significant dilemmas to be worked through in the clinical setting.

Another important issue to consider is the role of the mental health practitioner. Given the range of client needs, authors (e.g., Chung et al., 2008; D. W. Sue & D. Sue, 2003) have noted the need for clinicians to fulfill a broad range of counselor roles. Specifically, roles have been divided into direct service roles, advocacy roles, and consultant roles. With regard to direct services, mental health practitioners can play the role of helper (e.g., one who uses intervention strategies, counseling skills, and assessment tools to evaluate and facilitate client change), outreach worker (e.g., someone who goes into the client community to work with clients), educator (e.g., someone who provides tutoring, mentoring, modeling of behaviors, and psychoeducation), caregiver (e.g., one who provides direct support, encouragement, and hope to clients), caseworker/manager (e.g., one who helps connect clients with services, acts as liaison among different professionals, takes clients to appointments, etc.), and crisis worker (e.g., one who works with clients in cases of emergency). With regard to advocacy, mental health practitioners can function as brokers (e.g., one who helps clients find and use services), advocates (e.g., one who champions and defends clients' causes and rights), mobilizers (e.g., one who organizes client and community support in order to provide needed services), and community planners (e.g., one who designs, implements, and organizes new programs to serve client needs). Finally, as consultants, mental health practitioners seek and offer knowledge, support other professionals, and meet clients and community groups to discuss and solve problems. Since 9/11, taking on the advocacy and consultancy roles has become all the more important within immigrant communities due to potential community reactions or the "culture of fear" (Chung et al., 2008) that has been created by the media. Furthermore, due to the perception of counseling as a Western phenomenon, trust in the helper may be increased through the use of these alternative roles (Inman, Yeh et al., 2007). Providing

APA Guidelines

The Guidelines represent general principles that are intended to be aspirational in nature and are designed to provide suggestions to psychologists in working with ethnically, linguistically, and culturally diverse populations.

1. Psychologists educate their clients to the processes of psychological intervention, such as goals and expectations; the scope and, where appropriate, legal limits of confidentiality; and the psychologists' orientations.

2. Psychologists are cognizant of relevant research and practice issues as related to the population being served.

3. Psychologists recognize ethnicity and culture as significant parameters in understanding psychological processes.

4. Psychologists respect the roles of family members and community structures, hierarchies, values, and beliefs within the client's culture.

5. Psychologists respect clients' religious and/or spiritual beliefs and values, including attributions and taboos, since they affect worldview, psychosocial functioning, and expressions of distress.

6. Psychologists interact in the language requested by the client and, if this is not feasible, make an appropriate referral.

7. Psychologists consider the impact of adverse social, environmental, and political factors in assessing problems and designing interventions.

8. Psychologists attend to as well as work to eliminate biases, prejudices, and discriminatory practices.

9. Psychologists attend to culturally relevant forms of resilience in assessing their clients' emotional adjustment.

10. Psychologists working with culturally diverse populations should document culturally and sociopolitically relevant factors in the records.

Source: Modified from American Psychological Association (APA, 1993, pp. 46–47). *Guidelines for providers of psychological services to ethnic, linguistic, and culturally diverse populations.*

education and advocacy services for community members can reduce preconceived notions and biases that may exist within the community. The ability to navigate each of these roles effectively is key in becoming a culturally competent mental health practitioner.

SKILLS

Conceptual Framework

In culturally attuned therapy, it is important to align the conceptualization of the problem to the multiple contexts in which the individual exists. In capturing the complexity of an immigrant's life, assessing the relative significance of various relationships (families, friends), systems (school, work), and environments (immigration, racism), and the intersection of the three, becomes even more important (Inman, Rawls, Meza, & Brown, 2002). In order to work competently and effectively with South Asian immigrant communities, a conceptual framework based in these various complexities is proposed. This framework is not intended to take the place of the mental health practitioner's theoretical orientation. Rather, it is expected to enhance the therapeutic work by allowing the therapist to consider complex cultural systems and contexts that South Asian immigrants must negotiate within a pluralistic society such as the United States. Further, this framework will hopefully allow mental health practitioners to also acknowledge their own influence in the therapeutic process (Inman et al., 2002). These principles may be customized to address the context of other immigrant groups.

Consistent with recent perspectives related to the immigrant experience (Faist, 1997; Malmberg, 1997), we propose an approach that is based in an ecological framework (Bronfenbrenner, 1989; Harvey, 2007) and focuses on two key issues: The first is the interplay of different contexts (individual-family, cultural-migration, structural-racial relations in society); the second focuses on the mental health practitioner's role in facilitating the therapeutic process (Keeney, 1983). Given the unique needs and issues pertinent to South Asian immigrant communities, it is important to understand how the nature of their interactions within these multiple contexts shape and influence their lives (Furuto, 2004).

Based in an ecological framework, the interactions between person and environment are important in understanding an immigrant's experience (Bronfenbrenner, 1989; Harvey, 2007; Tummala-Narra, 2007a). Specifically, the ecological perspective emphasizes the role of resiliency, where individuals negotiate and influence, and are affected by, various contexts (Harvey, 2007; Riger, 2001). This bidirectional influence of person and environment is central to the understanding of how immigrants engage with the physical and psychological adjustment to separation from their country of origin and living in the adopted country. Thus, it becomes necessary to examine the pre-immigration and current life circumstances, as the interaction of both with the environment becomes increasingly salient. In order to understand these different circumstances, however, it is equally important to examine the various systems within which South Asian immigrants exist.

Throughout their life span, South Asians, like other immigrants, either directly or indirectly negotiate a complex web of interconnecting systems (individual, and micro-, meso-, exo-, and macrosystems; Bronfenbrenner, 1989; Yakushko & Chronister, 2005). At the center of this ecological model is the individual, whose characteristics (e.g., age, gender, personality traits, coping

styles) play an important role. The *microsystem* refers to the immediate environment (e.g., family, occupational status, acculturation, racial and ethnic composition of neighborhood). The *mesosystem* refers to the quality of relationships and linkage between two or more systems (e.g., the relationship between South Asian immigrant families and the school or families and the mental health setting). The *exosystem* encompasses environmental processes and events (e.g., discrimination) within specific social structures (e.g., neighborhood, workplace) that indirectly impact the immigrant (e.g., familial interactions in the home). Finally, the *macrosystem* includes the overarching cultural variables, societal values (e.g., messages from the media, political policies, laws, societal norms) that exert influence within the different levels (micro, meso, exo) and define one's identity and resources. Acknowledging and utilizing the different levels and cultural contexts are important considerations in delivering comprehensive culturally sensitive psychological services to these individuals and families, regardless of specific country of origin or ethnic background.

In addition to the various systems within the ecological model, the mental health practitioner's role is an important link to the provision of competent services. Specifically, within the therapeutic relationship the therapist must address socially based differences (e.g., cultural, religious, class, sexual orientation) and similarities that may exist between himself or herself and the client. The development of this skill is even more important when working with South Asian immigrant communities who are similarly balancing their development and experience in the larger society on a daily basis (Inman et al., 2002).

In particular, this ecological perspective highlights the individual's place as a part of an interrelated system (e.g., the client and the client's family), along with the notion that one cannot observe a behavior of another without changing it or having an impact on it. When a mental health practitioner functions as an outside observer and occupies a position of power over the client, an incongruent hierarchical structure can result (Madanes, 1981), reflecting the unequal power differentials faced by immigrants (Altman, 2000; Tummala-Narra, 2001). This type of environment fails to foster the culturally supportive atmosphere needed to work successfully with immigrants. On the other hand, therapists can participate as agents rather than directors of change (R. J. Becvar & D. S. Becvar, 1994; Daniels & White, 1994; Hoffman, 1990). They are "involved-observers" by being not only a part of the system but also a part of what must change. This second-order change perspective allows for an environment that embraces the cultural and social ideology of the client, while facilitating adjustment to the mainstream cultural context as directed by the individual client (Ogbu, 1995).

Assessment and Diagnosis

To perform competent clinical assessment and diagnosis, mental health practitioners must have knowledge of a range of possible immigrant issues. Specifically in developing an assessment plan, clinicians need to be able to explore the following areas:

• *Pre-immigration experience:* Understand the South Asian pre-immigration environment and life circumstances as it pertains to cultural norms, family relationships, socioeconomic status, education, resources, and supports.
• *Conditions for departure:* Inquire about the specific conditions under which South Asians departed from their countries. Within this context, ask questions related to reasons for immigration, potential losses experienced (e.g., jobs, relationships), and other systemic issues navigated (e.g., visa issues).
• *Situation at arrival:* Gain knowledge of circumstances surrounding their arrival. Have an understanding of how different cohorts and time period of arrival may have influenced the different immigrant waves. For example, having arrived in the 1960s or 1970s, when there were minimal support

systems, is significantly different from the experience of recent South Asian immigrants (1980–2000). Issues related to culture shock, cultural transitions, extent of change in resources, social status, and negotiations are important to explore.
• *Current conditions:* Assess current life circumstance related to number of generations in the country, number of years in the country, acculturation levels, language barriers and/or fluency in English, homesickness, reception by the mainstream cultural context (e.g., discrimination), socioeconomic conditions, current legal status of the immigrant group, interactions with different systems (e.g., schools, work, neighborhoods), extent of family support, extent of community resources, and level of education. These are important pieces of information that can help contextualize the immigrant experience.
• *Developmental issues:* Explore intrapsychic and interpersonal issues that are relevant to developmental transitions that co-occur in the context of migration. Examples include an immigrant child who is adjusting to a new school environment or his or her separation from extended family, or an adult immigrant who is coping with the death of a parent who resided in the country of origin, or an immigrant who experiences physical illness or disability post-migration, affecting his or her ability to visit the country of origin.
• *Assessing resilience:* Assess resilience from a multidimensional perspective in which South Asians may cope with psychological distress in ways that are culturally congruent. This may promote a positive cultural identity and adjustment to the adopted country. Assessing both individual and collective expressions of resilience becomes important given the collectivistic culture of South Asians (Harvey, 2007; Tummala-Narra, 2007a).
• *Culture-bound syndromes:* Become familiar with and appropriately apply diagnoses of culture-bound syndromes, as indicated in the *DS-IV-TR* (American Psychiatric Association, 2000).

Arriving at a diagnosis can be compounded by several factors. Given that the cultural background and values influence a client's conceptualization of a problem, applying a diagnosis from the *DSM-IV-TR* indiscriminately can result in overdiagnosis and pathologizing (Potocky-Tripodi, 2002). Therefore, it becomes important to (a) tune into any cultural explanations that clients might give for their presenting issues, (b) consider any cultural factors that may be related to the psychosocial environment and level of functioning, (c) identify language issues that may be reflective of how concerns are being presented, and (d) avoid confusing behaviors that arise out of sociocultural conflicts with pathology (*DSM-IV-R*, APA, 2000). Finally, cultural differences between the client and the mental health practitioner are key to a competent diagnosis and need to be thoroughly examined (e.g., within supervision).

Assessment and Intervention

Given the complexities of the South Asian immigrant experience, mental health practitioners need to develop competencies in several areas. In particular, assessment and interventions need to occur at multiple levels (e.g., individual, and micro-, macro-, meso-, and exosystems). However, it is important to note that "developmental processes and life experiences are not represented in one ecological system" (Yakushko & Chronister, 2005, p. 293). In fact, processes tend to overlap with a dialectical interaction between systems. This section highlights the specific areas that should be considered in the assessment and development of clinical and community interventions when working with South Asian immigrants (again, these guidelines may be adapted to inform assessment and treatment planning strategies with clients from a wide variety of cultural perspectives):

• *Individual level:* Assessment at this level includes attention to pre-immigration experiences and beliefs. In particular, it is important to explore pre-migration stress and/or mental health issues, age at immigration, type of migration (e.g.,

voluntary), expectations related to migration, language skills, cognitive flexibility, coping styles and beliefs, immigration stress, physical health, history and degree of trauma, cultural views of psychological distress and healing, and developmental transitions (e.g., losses). Because of the emphasis on building rapport, interventions at this level emphasize a collaborative relationship with the client that facilitates a safe therapeutic environment, and involves a sense of validation and curiosity regarding sociocultural issues as relevant to the client's psychological distress.

• *Microsystemic level:* Assessment at this level involves examining the immediate environment. Because migration can produce significant psychological distress (Rumbaut, 1991), this can include understanding the family composition, occupational status, acculturation level, environmental stressors related to racial and ethnic composition of neighborhood, access to resources as a function of migration (individual-familial, physical, economic, institutional, sociopolitical, sociocultural), and experiences in the nuclear or extended family due to relocation (e.g., client's relationship with his or her family in country of origin and in the United States, and with ethnic and religious communities). These issues can provide information about potential loyalties, conflicts, and relational expectations. Interventions may involve the inclusion of family members, if appropriate, and/or interpreters. Further, exploring cultural values and practices as strengths while sifting through and teasing out values that are important in daily functioning and ongoing relationships allows for a strength-based approach that considers culturally congruent sources of individual and collective resiliency (Tummala-Narra, 2007b). These interventions would also include the client's access to "refueling" (Akhtar, 1999), or contact with their culture of origin in some form (e.g., temple, mosque, church, grocery stores, restaurants, phone calls to relatives in country of origin, visits to country of origin).

• *Mesosystemic level:* Assessment at this level involves examining the interpersonal and interactional issues between the immigrant and the different support systems within the micro-system. It involves exploring how individuals ne-gotiate multiple roles and cultural contexts in the formation of identity. Thus, this may involve examining issues such as intergenerational con-flicts, management of shifts in gender roles, ability to continue cultural traditions, and shifts in employment status. The extent to which South Asians are able to negotiate a successful identity may be influenced by support networks as well as pre-migration relationships. Interventions need to occur at an interpersonal level with a focus on family, significant others, friends, neighbors, and co-workers. It may also be valuable to explore areas of strength from which they can draw. One example of a strength-focused approach involves including other care providers in the process of intervention. This may be especially helpful when the client is engaged in indige-nous healing practices (e.g., Ayurvedic or ho-meopathic medicine) that may be seen as culturally consistent coping mechanisms (Fong, 2004; Inman, Yeh et al., 2007). This collaboration between care providers and heal-ers across different cultural traditions is often important for the client's ability to establish trust with the mental health practitioner, and for a more complete understanding of the cli-ent's experience.

• *Macrosystemic and exosystemic levels:* These levels are viewed as encapsulating the overarching cultural/societal values and structural/systemic forces that can influence the immigrant expe-rience. Some examples include issues such as stereotyping, discrimination, prejudice, sexism, and imposition of Western psychological the-ories and other cultural values that can limit access (e.g., economic, political, legal). Psycho-therapy and community interventions that increase awareness of discrimination and prej-udice, or educate immigrants about relevant laws, can help to empower immigrant clients in coping with potential hostility in the main-stream context. Being aware of one's own priv-ilege and power, and critically evaluating the theories and approaches used in therapy, are important steps, as they influence assessment, diagnosis, and treatment.

Relatedly, immigrant communities are at risk for internalizing mainstream cultural values due to negative experiences related to their own culture (Yakushko & Chronister, 2005). Mental health practitioners may also need to explore factors that push for assimilation versus holding onto one's cultural identity. Likewise, increas-ing access to resources within the mainstream context (such as legal and medical services) and other forms of advocacy can often be helpful in building increased support. Interventions may also be more preventive in nature and can include engaging in outreach presentations that inform immigrant communities of availa-ble mental health services and their potential benefits.

Finally, assessing resiliency as it is expressed across all of the above areas is an important component in helping immigrant clients. Resil-iency in the face of psychological distress, within the South Asian context, could involve an indi-vidual's internal resources, such as ability to self-soothe or professional success (individual level), attending to the needs of a family member (interpersonal level), and engaging in ways to combat negative systemic realities, such as dis-crimination (macrosystemic level).

VALUES/ATTITUDES

The development of effective psychotherapeutic interventions with immigrants, and related train-ing in psychology, must consider the role of values and attitudes held by both the client and the mental health practitioner. Specifically, the ther-apist should actively work to increase his or her level of awareness regarding his or her own social context, including areas such as culture, religion, social class, sexual orientation, and physical abil-ity, and how this may interact with that of the client. Often, specific values and attitudes mani-fest in transference and countertransference, and, if left unexplored, contribute to impasses in the psychotherapy process. This is particularly salient in addressing the therapist's potential stereotyping of the client's social background.

Additionally, the client and the mental health practitioner may have varying expectations of psychotherapy based on cultural worldviews. For instance, a South Asian client with a history of severe loss and trauma may expect the duration of therapy to be no more than a few sessions, whereas the mental health practitioner may feel that the client would benefit from long-term psychotherapy. There may also be differences in expectations of the therapeutic relationship. For example, a South Asian client may feel reluctant to express anger and frustration directly toward the therapist as a way to maintain a more harmonious sense of connection with the

therapist. The mental health practitioner, on the other hand, may actively encourage the client to express negative emotions more directly in their work together. In other instances, there may be significant differences in the therapist's and the client's perceptions of boundaries. This is evident when a South Asian client gives the mental health practitioner a gift as a way of appreciating what he or she has provided. The therapist may or may not feel comfortable in receiving such gifts, based on his or her Western training. Each of these examples poses challenges to traditional conceptualizations of the therapeutic relationship, and highlights the importance of attending to cultural values and attitudes as they either consciously or unconsciously influence the therapeutic relationship. Therefore, the mental

CASE VIGNETTE 5.4

Manav is a 29-year-old Asian Indian immigrant from a rural part of India. He sought psychotherapy on his own, after experiencing increasing anxiety in his workplace. Manav moved to the United States about two years prior to seeking help. He had minimal knowledge of how psychotherapy might benefit him, but had heard from an extended family member in the United States that working with a therapist could help him cope with his anxiety. Manav left his immediate family in India (parents and three siblings) and moved to the United States in the hope of gaining more income to help support his family, who are from a low-income background. Manav worked over 50 hours per week in a relatively low-paying job in a parking garage, but managed to save some money to send back to his family on a monthly basis. He expressed uncertainty about his immigration status, and this became a source of concern since moving to the United States. Recently, his family suggested that he return to India to get married, as he was at a customary age for marriage. Manav described his conflictual feelings about getting married, and trying to secure his immigration status. He reported that he increasingly felt burdened by the various roles he held for his family and by his own desire to take care of their needs.

In the United States, he formed a few friendships with other Asian Indian immigrants and maintained ties with extended family in a different part of the country, but felt uncomfortable, generally, with socializing outside of his ethnic community. Prior to his immigration, Manav imagined that he would make friends in the United States as readily as he had in India. He expressed not anticipating as many changes through the immigration process as he had actually experienced after moving to the United States. In addition to his separation from his family and friends in India, he missed the warm climate and familiar surroundings. Manav found himself less engaged with his longtime interest in reading fiction and watching films. He fantasized about returning to live in India, but felt as though this would be counterproductive to his goal of attaining resources for his family.

health practitioner's awareness of and engagement with the cultural specifics of intervention are required for effective therapeutic work—irrespective of the client's culture of origin.

Manav's case vignette (5.4, shown on the previous page) illustrates an ecological approach that considers the examination of the client's and mental health practitioner's values and attitudes in psychotherapy as central to working with immigrant clients.

In psychotherapy, Manav wondered if his Indian American therapist (second author) could truly understand his wish of wanting to return to India, despite the fact that he had sought an Indian American therapist. He stated in one session, "You sound like you are used to things here. Your family probably came a long time ago. I don't know if you even go to India anymore." His questions led to an examination of transference and countertransference issues related to his sense of belonging both as an Indian in the United States, and an Indian in India. He assumed that the therapist was more "Westernized" than he, and that she did not share his vision of India, although he was reassured by the fact that she had a similar ethnic background. The therapist expressed to him that they probably both shared some experience of India, but also had very unique experiences. Working through this conflict over ethnic similarity and difference in the therapeutic relationship was ultimately helpful in attending to Manav's struggles with acculturation and his mourning of his separation from India. Eventually, he was able to consider the possibility of engaging with people from unfamiliar backgrounds, and find ways to access familiar surroundings such as meeting other Asian Indians in a local temple or watching Indian films in a local theater. He was also able to communicate his wish to postpone plans for marriage to his parents, and sought help from an immigration attorney to address his concerns over his immigration status. All of these components of the treatment contributed to his ability to cope with his anxiety and sadness.

Manav's case illustrates the ways in which psychotherapy can effectively address the complexity of immigration. It was through attention to all of the levels of the ecological approach (individual, family, and systems) that Manav was able to address the internal and external realities of his experience. The individual factors included Manav's own internal pre- and post-immigration experiences, his sense of connection to his family and friends, and his desire to achieve financial success in the United States. Family or microsystem factors involved his interactions with his family as well as his connection with his ethnic and religious community. Systemic issues that were addressed in psychotherapy included increasing connection with legal assistance, coupled with social supports within and outside of his ethnic community. Manav's ability to reconnect with a sense of resiliency through increased social interaction and engagement with his longstanding interests was also an essential component of psychotherapy. Finally, each of these issues was explored in the context of a collaborative therapeutic relationship in which issues of transference and countertransference informed important aspects of Manav's psychological functioning and related coping. It is clear that attending to potential conflicts in values and attitudes between the therapist and client can play an important role in creating a safe therapeutic space for such exploration to be possible.

SUPERVISION AND TRAINING

Cultural demographics and increasing immigration to the United States have heightened the need for culturally competent mental health practitioners. Literature has revealed positive outcomes with culturally responsive supervision and training. For instance, culturally responsive supervision and effective psychotherapeutic intervention have been shown to relate to an increase in counselor multicultural competence (Inman, 2006), inclusion of cultural issues in case conceptualization (Ladany, Inman, Constantine, & Hofheinz, 1997), and greater discussion and incorporation of cultural issues (e.g., racial and cultural dynamics) in supervision (Burkard et. al., 2006; Dressel,

Consoli, Kim, & Atkinson, 2007; Tummala-Narra, 2004). Furthermore, supervisors who have a higher racial consciousness (Bhat & Davis, 2007; Ladany et al., 1997) or have incorporated a feminist identity (Szymanski, 2005) have been better equipped to create a culturally receptive environment, revealing that supervisor multicultural identity is an important precursor to effective supervisory and training practices. Because of the central role that supervisors play in developing professional and clinical competence, Ancis, Ladany, and Inman (in progress) have proposed a model of multicultural supervision that highlights six domains that supervisors need to attend to in supervision: (1) supervisor's own awareness of personal cultural values, biases, and worldview; (2) supervisee's self-awareness of personal values and biases in her- or himself; (3) facilitating multicultural client conceptualizations; (4) guiding supervisees in the utilization of culturally appropriate skills and interventions with clients; (5) attending to multicultural processes in supervision (e.g., discussing cultural differences between the supervisor and supervisee); and (6) effectively evaluating the supervisee's multicultural competencies.

In addition, training (e.g., coursework, seminars) that complements supervision by increasing the trainee's clinical competence through enhanced cultural awareness, knowledge, and skills becomes critical. Cultural issues (e.g., sociopolitical influences, immigration policies, pre-immigration experiences, post-immigration challenges, access to mental health services) should be incorporated into all aspects of curricula with different instructional techniques. For instance, to increase knowledge, trainees can read about identity development (Ibrahim, Ohnishi, & Sandhu, 1997) and culture-bound and class-bound values of traditional psychotherapies (Ancis & Ali, 2005; Kakar, 1982). Furthermore, reacting to critical incidents in cross-cultural interactions (i.e., Intercultural Sensitizer; Leong & Kim, 1991) and teaching students to perceive situations from the perspectives of the "other community members"

(Intercultural Assimilator Model; Fielder, Mitchell, & Triandis, 1971) is an effective means of identifying the complexity inherent in immigrant experiences. In doing so, it is important to consider that instructors should also engage in cross-cultural learning experiences on an ongoing basis, as training in multicultural competence involves an element of mutual influence between students and instructors (Tummala-Narra, 2009).

Beyond knowledge and skills, self-awareness is an important aspect of cultural competence. Building self-awareness can entail utilizing consultation and ongoing dialogue with peers and colleagues regarding immigration issues. It can also be enhanced through activities such as cultural genograms (Hardy & Laszloffy, 1995), autobiographical essays (Arredondo & Arciniega, 2001), and self-reflective journals (Burnett & Meacham, 2002) that highlight a trainee's own family immigration history and help personalize issues salient to immigrants in general. Activities such as cultural immersion exercises (Arredondo et al., 1996), the triad training model (Pedersen, 1994), and racial-cultural labs (Carter, 2003) can also help increase self- and other awareness with regard to biases and stereotypes held in different situations.

CONCLUSION

Working with immigrant clients requires an understanding of the interaction between individual experience and systemic realities. Mental health practitioners should carefully consider the complex history of immigration of different ethnic groups in the United States, which has contributed to the tremendous heterogeneity in immigrant experience within any given ethnic community. Throughout this chapter, the interaction between internal and external challenges inherent to the immigration process have been illustrated through the various case vignettes of South Asian immigrants. Therapists must continue to examine the immigrant's resiliency in the face of these challenges. But above all, the mental health practitioner's attention to his or her values and attitudes rooted in his or her own sociocultural background and their influence on the therapeutic relationship is critical in helping immigrant clients.

RESOURCES

In this section, we provide resources for building competencies through self-assessment activities and assessment tools, as well as resources for finding additional information. Appendix A provides different self-reflective training activities

that can be engaged in within the context of masters- or doctoral-level courses, supervised clinical training at various levels, or for independent professional development. Appendix B provides assessment tools that may be used within clinical practice. Appendix C provides additional resources (e.g., films, Internet resources, and books) that may supplement professional competence.

APPENDIX A: EXPERIENTIAL EXERCISES FOR MENTAL HEALTH PRACTITIONERS

SELF–REFLECTIVE ACTIVITIES

1. Reflect on your own ethnicity, gender, social class, sexual identity, and physical ability, in the context of your or your family's experience with immigration. What would your experience have been like if social identity issues differed in some way, such as if you were of a different gender or social class background?

2. Examine the history of your ethnic group in relation to its reception by the mainstream U.S. context. What are some implications for racial politics and dynamics that relate to your ethnic group or groups of belonging? How might this be similar to or different from that of South Asians in the United States?

3. Attend a South Asian cultural, religious, or political event. What did you think and feel while you attended the event? Did this contrast in any way with what you had expected to think and feel? What did you notice about the interactions you had within this context, both about yourself and others?

4. Interview a South Asian immigrant about his or her understanding of psychological distress and illness, and help seeking. What are some explanations regarding psychological distress and health within this indigenous perspective? How do these perspectives compare to Western theories of psychology and psychopathology?

5. Explore various South Asian communities via the Web. For a start, you may want to read the discussion forums on South Asians Leading Together (www.saalt.org). What are your reactions to the postings? What resonates with you? Is there anything that is unfamiliar to you? How are these views similar to or different from the perspectives to which you have been exposed?

6. Interview a first-generation South Asian individual and a second-generation South Asian individual about the effects of immigration in their lives. Reflect on similarities and differences across these two individuals' experiences, and on your own values and assumptions related to acculturation

APPENDIX B: ASSESSMENT TOOLS

Assessment Based on an Ecological Framework

Individual-Level Assessment (Goals: establish rapport; create respectful and safe climate)

- Express curiosity about culture.
- Ask about life experience prior to migration (pre-migration history).
- Ask about experience migrating to the United States (migration experience, share story of migration).
- Ask about expectations of the immigration process (pre-migration).
- Ask about initial experience at arrival (post-migration experience).
- Ask about nature and effects of transitions.
- Ask about potential coping styles used to deal with stressors.
- Ask about physical health and wellbeing pre- and post-immigration.

Microsystemic-Level Assessment (Goals: understanding of psychotherapy attitudes and understanding of immediate environmental stressors)

- Find out about which family members came to the United States and which stayed back.
- Find out reasons for migration for those who came and for not migrating for those who did not.
- Find out conditions under which migration occurred (provides info about expectations, optimism).
- Assess health beliefs and cultural explanations of psychological distress.
- Ask about religious beliefs.
- Explore expectations of treatment and the role of the therapist.
- Assess need for interpreter.
- Assess acculturation level by asking about:
  - Ability to negotiate multiple cultures (potential barriers, push toward assimilation, acceptance of cultural identity).
  - Composition of neighborhood and interaction with larger community.

Mesosystemic-Level Assessment (Goal: identification of resiliency and supports/availability of bilingual staff)

- Inquire about quality of relationships between:
  - Family and school.
  - Family and work.
  - Family and ethnic and/or religious community.
- Inquire about supports within the above systems.
- Inquire about supports within country of origin.
- Inquire about communication and coping skills within systems.
- Use nontraditional healers.

Exo- and Macrosystemic-Level Assessment (Goal: identification and advocacy of systematic supports and barriers)

- Assess community needs and concerns.
- Assess service gaps and barriers.
- Inquire about interactions with individuals outside of ethnic/religious community.

- Assess availability of community resources.
- Provide policy and program advocacy.
- Provide community consultation.
- Provide health education.
- Ask about experiences of discrimination.
- Assess issues related to immigration status and need for legal help.
- Assess financial needs, limitations, and resources.

Adapted from Potocky-Tripodi (2002); Yakushko & Chronister (2005).

Genograms

General Information

A *genogram* is a family tree that includes social data. It is a graphic picture of family history and patterns and includes basic structure, family demographics, functioning, and relationships. This tool is especially salient and effective with immigrants as it allows families and clients to look at generational issues. It is virtually impossible to remove culture from this assessment.

- Strengths:

  - Best tool for tracking family life cycle when used with chronology.
  - Organizes large amount of information in a concise and time-efficient manner.
  - Has had a positive effect in enlarging the focus from just mothers to broader network of relationships.
  - Can be helpful in predicting and understanding reactions of family members at different points in the life cycle.
  - Many clinicians find that the best stories are shared while constructing a genogram.
  - Lends itself to a cooperative therapeutic alliance.
  - Valuable with aging clients who might experience themselves as a central link to past and future generations.
  - Adoption situations—natural parents can offer something to a child they have given to adoption.

  Note: Genograms can also bring out issues that are "family secrets," bringing some painful memories to light. Clients who lack this information or come upon it without much support may find it distressing.

- Genogram: interview
- Index person, children, and partners, family of origin:

  - Name, DOB, occupation
  - Name/sex/age of significant partner, name/sex/age of children with each partner
  - Dates of abortions, miscarriages, separations, divorces, births, deaths
  - Miscarriages, stillbirths, adopted and foster children
  - Causes of death, occupations, education
  - Who lives in household now?

  Note: Clients can perceive this line of inquiry as invasive. Addressing this information in a sensitive and empathic manner is most helpful.

- Ethnicity:

  - Ethnic/religious background and languages spoken

- Major moves
- Significant others:

  - Others who lived with or are important to the family

- Serious medical, behavioral, or emotional problems
- Job problems
- Drug or alcohol problems
- Problems with the law
- For all individuals listed, indicate any who were:

- Especially close
- Distant or conflictual
- Cut off from each other
- Overly dependent on each other

Note: important to recognize that degree of family involvement can vary in cultural appropriateness

Genogram: Interpretive Categories

- *Category 1: Family Structure*

  - Household composition
  - Intact nuclear household
  - Single-parent household
  - Remarried family household
  - Three-generation household
  - Household including non-nuclear family member

- *Category 2: Life Cycle Fit*

  - Specific tasks and responsibilities
  - Developmental Issues
  - Emotional Processes
  - Scheduled and off-schedule events

- *Category 3: Pattern Repetition across Generations*

  - Patterns of functioning
  - Patterns of relationship
  - Repeated structural patterns

- *Category 4: Life Events and Family Functioning*

  - Coincidences of life events
  - Impact of life changes, transitions, and traumas
  - Anniversary reactions
  - Social, economic, and political events

- *Category 5: Relational Patterns and Triangles*

  - Parent–child triangles
  - Common couple triangles
  - Divorce and remarried family triangles
  - Triangles in families with foster/adopted children
  - Multigenerational triangles
  - Relationships outside the family

- *Category 6: Family Balance and Imbalance*

  - Family Structure
  - Roles
  - Level and style of functioning
  - Resources

Web sites to Download Free Software to Create Genograms

- http://www.Smartdraw.com
- http://www.Interpersonaluniverse.net

Ecomaps

General Information

Developed by Ann Hartman (1995), an *ecomap* is a social "solar system" that maps family and community systems' relationships and processes over time. The family is typically at the center and other important people (priest) and institutions (school, work, religious settings, cultural organizations) are depicted with circles around the family. An ecomap is a depiction of the family's relationship to environmental systems. It can be used with individuals, couples, and families. Ecomaps and genograms should be seen as complementary and can be used with families from diverse backgrounds. The emphasis of ecomaps is on current functioning.

- Strengths:

  - In an outcome-based managed-care climate, it offers a timely transition to interventions.
  - A solutions-based approach encourages clients to see what is going "right."
  - Intergenerational deficits are not the primary area of concern so it is good to use with clients who are skeptical about exploring past functioning.
  - Easy to learn—practice on self and friends and you will be ready to use with clients.
  - Primary value is its visual impact and ability to organize and present a great deal of info.
  - Connections, themes, and quality-of-life issues jump off the page.
  - Brings up new info (possibly not considered before).

- ○ Focuses on thoughts, feelings, and behaviors rather than problems.
- ○ Lends itself to a cooperative therapeutic alliance.
- Additional use: can help counselor trainees understand their own backgrounds in order to be aware of biases and assumptions.

Web site to Download Free Ecomaps

- http://www.smartdraw.com/specials/ecomap .htm

APPENDIX C: FILMS, INTERNET RESOURCES, BOOKS

Films

Films about Family Relationships and Identity

Knowing Her Place (1990)

An Indian woman looks at her life, her marriage, and her role in contemporary society, both in India and the United States. A film by Indu Krishnan.

Desi: South Asians in New York (2000)

Presents dozens of first- and second-generation New Yorkers who share their insights, reflections, and experiences to illustrate the wide spectrum of Pakistanis, Indians, Bangladeshis, Sri Lankans, Nepalese, and other South Asians who have become an integral part of the city.

Bend It Like Beckham (2002)

A movie about an Asian Indian family, coming-of-age, interracial relations, and gender issues.

Namesake (2006)

Based on the book by Jumpha Lahari (New York: Houghton Mifflin, 2004); about names, identity, and Asian Indian family relations.

American Desi (2001)

Romantic comedy about Indian American youth in a college setting. Presents peer interactions within ethnic community.

Bhaji on the Beach (1993)

A group of British women of South Asian descent travel together on a day trip. The women are of different age backgrounds, with a range of traditional and nontraditional South Asian cultural values and attitudes. Issues such as domestic violence, interracial relationships, and racism are highlighted.

Monsoon Wedding (2001)

Set in India, a family prepares for a traditional Hindu wedding. The story invo-lves tension among family relationships, and issues of childhood sexual abuse.

Voices Heard Sisters Unseen (1995)

This is a documentary by Grace Poore, focused on issues of domestic violence within the South Asian community.

The Children We Sacrifice (2000)

This is a documentary by Grace Poore, focused on incest and sexual violence within the South Asian diaspora.

Films about Sexuality

Chutney Popcorn (1999)

A movie about an Asian Indian lesbian estranged from her parents who agrees to carry a child for her infertile sister, much to chagrin of her partner and parents.

Khush (1991)

Interviews with South Asian lesbians and gay men in Britain, North America, and India concerning the intricacies of being gay and of color.

Fire (1996)

Story of gender, marriage, and homosexuality in the lives of two married women in India.

Films about Race Relations

Mistaken Identity: Sikhs in America (2004)

An investigation of attitudes toward Sikhs in the United States following the events of September 11, 2001, and an exploration of the religion, culture, and history of Sikhs in America, highlighting contributions Sikh Americans have made to the American society and economy for over 100 years.

Raising Our Voices: South Asian Americans Address Hate (2002)

A film developed to raise awareness about hate crimes and bias incidents affecting South Asians living in America, with particular reference to their increase since the terrorist attacks of September 11, 2001.

The Way Home (1998)

A documentary about women (of different racial groups) and race relations.

Mississippi Masala (1991)

Story of an Asian Indian family who is expelled from Uganda, and relocates to Mississippi. Acculturation, intergenerational conflicts, and interracial relationships (Indian and African American) are highlighted.

Films about Religion

In the Name of God (2007)

This documentary by a South Asian filmmaker shows the political/religious movement prior to the destruction of the Barbari Mosque in UP.

On Common Ground: World Religions in America (1997)

Diana L. Eck and the Pluralism Project at Harvard University capture the fundamental beliefs and practices of different faiths and the transformation of old traditions within new settings.

Internet Resources

- Asian American Psychological Association: http://www.aapaonline.org
- Chai: http://www.chaicounselors.org/
- South Asians Leading Together: http://www.saalt.org
- South Asian Psychological Networking Association: http://www.oursapna.org
- Garam Chai: http://www.garamchai.com

Books

Asian Women United of California (Eds.). (1989). *Making waves: An anthology of writings by and about Asian American women.* Boston: Beacon Press.

Bahri, D., & Vasudeva, M. (1996). *Between the lines: South Asians and postcoloniality.* Philadelphia: Temple University Press.

Bhatia, S. (2007). *American Karma: Race, culture, and identity in the Indian Diaspora.* New York: New York Press.

Dasgupta, S. D. (1998). *A patchwork shawl: Chronicles of South Asian women in America.* New Brunswick, NJ: Rutgers University Press.

Gupta, S. R. (1999). *Emerging voices: South Asian American women redefine self, family and community.* Walnut Creek, CA: Altamira Press.

Khandelwal, M. S. (2002). *Becoming American, being Indian: An immigrant community in New York City. (The anthropology of contemporary issues).* New York: Cornell University Press.

Nguyen, T. (2005). *We are all suspects now: Untold stories from immigrant communities after 9/11.* Boston: Beacon Press.

Prashad, V. (2000). *The Karma of brown folks.* Minneapolis: University of Minnesota Press.

Purkayastha, B. (2005). *Negotiating ethnicity: Second-generation South Asian Americans traverse a transnational world.* Piscataway, NJ: Rutgers University Press.

Rangaswamy, P. (2000). *Namasté America: Indian immigrants in an American Metropolis.* University Park, PA: Pennsylvania State University Press.

Shankar, L. D., & Srikanth, R. (1998). *A part, yet apart: South Asians in Asian America*. Philadelphia: Temple University Press.

Shukla, S. (2003). *India abroad: Diasporic cultures of postwar America and England*. Princeton, NJ: Princeton University Press.

Women of South Asian Descent Collective (2008). *Our feet walk the sky: Women of the South Asian Diaspora*. San Francisco, CA: Aunt Lute Books.

COMPETENCY BENCHMARK TABLES

The purpose of the Competency Benchmarks (Tables 5.1–5.4) is to develop developmental models for defining and measuring competencies in professional psychology; each chapter in this *Handbook* applies the diversity competence for mental health practitioners to their work with a particular diverse population.

Table 5.1   Developmental-Level Competencies I

READINESS LEVEL—ENTRY TO PRACTICUM	
Competencies	**Learning Process and Activities**
Knowledge The student is gaining knowledge in: • Multiculturalism—students are engaged in the process of learning that all individuals, including themselves, are cultural beings with worldviews that shape and influence their attitudes, emotions, perceptions, behaviors, and experiences. • The importance of reflective practice and self-awareness when working with immigrant clients. • Core counseling skills and theories helpful to building a strong therapeutic alliance with immigrant clients. • Ethics code.	At this stage of development, the emphasis in mental health practitioner education is on instilling knowledge of foundational domains that provides the groundwork for subsequent attainment of functional competencies. Students at this stage become aware of the principles and practices of the field, but they are not yet able to apply their knowledge to practice. Therefore, the training curriculum is focused on knowledge of core areas, including literature on multiculturalism, ethics, basic counseling skills, scientific knowledge, and the importance of reflective practice and self-awareness.
Skills The student is: • Beginning to develop the ability to demonstrate empathic listening skills, respect, and interest when talking with individuals expressing different values and belief systems. • Learning to critically examine the literature with regard to immigration and legal policies and advocate for the needs of this community. • Recognizing heterogeneity in experience that may exist across different waves of immigration and generations of immigrants.	It is important that, throughout the curriculum, trainers and teachers define individual and cultural differences broadly, to include immigrant identity. This should enable students to have a developing awareness of how to extrapolate their emerging multicultural competencies to include the immigrant identity realm of individual and cultural differences.
Values and Attitudes The student demonstrates: • Willingness to engage in self-exploration—to consider own motives, attitudes, behaviors and effect on others. • Intellectual curiosity and flexibility about the attitudes that society holds about immigration and immigrants. • Ability to value expressions of diverse viewpoints and belief systems of various immigrant groups.	Most students, through their life experiences, would be expected to have basic knowledge of the important terms and definitions used when discussing immigrant experiences, awareness of the impact of discrimination in immigrant's lives, and personal awareness of how multiple identities may intersect with an immigrant identity.

Table 5.2 **Developmental-Level Competencies II**

READINESS LEVEL—ENTRY TO INTERNSHIP	
Competencies	**Learning Process and Activities**
Knowledge The student has:	At this level of development, students are building upon their education and applied experiences (such as supervised practicum experiences) to attain a core set of foundational competencies. They can then begin applying this knowledge to professional practice. As a result of being exposed to didactic training and close supervision, students attain the multicultural values and attitudes appropriate to their level of development. Foundational knowledge and multicultural values and attitudes are becoming well established, but skills in working with immigrant issues would be expected to be rudimentary at this level of development.
• General understanding of the research data on immigration and health.	
• General understanding of traditions, beliefs, and practices of immigrant groups.	
• Understanding of the differences and similarities between different groups of immigrants (e.g., assessment, diagnosis).	
• Knowledge of the family, social support, acculturation, enculturation, and other factors influencing the mental health of immigrants.	
• Understanding the intersections of diversity in the context of immigration, such as the role of race, gender, social class, religious identity, sexual orientation, and physical disability.	
• Knowledge of majority and minority dynamics, and the role of discrimination in the lives of immigrants.	Learning occurs through multiple modalities:
• Understanding the importance of consulting with supervisors and others when presented with unfamiliar immigrant client issues.	• Receiving didactic training on immigrant issues in academic programs may occur in multicultural courses and culture-specific courses (e.g., Asian American, Latino/a courses) and it may be infused into the core curriculum (e.g., ethics, assessment, multicultural, career counseling, research, human growth and development, and clinical courses).
• Understanding of the ethical guidelines and standards of care in the field pertaining to work with immigrant communities.	
Skills Skills in the following areas are beginning to develop:	• Providing therapy, under supervision, to clients representing diverse immigrant experiences in practicum settings.
• The ability to conceptualize immigrant issues within the context of sociopolitical and historical factors.	• Receiving supervision from psychotherapists knowledgeable and skilled in working with immigrant communities.
• The ability to conceptualize immigrant issues within an ecosystemic lens (micro, meso, macro, etc).	• Seeking additional study and professional development opportunities (e.g., to attain knowledge of common counseling issues when working with immigrant communities).
• The ability to recognize generational and individual differences within any particular immigrant community.	
• Building therapeutic alliance by using basic counseling skills, as well as the ability to empathize with clients who may be dealing with societal discrimination and prejudice.	Topics to be covered in didactic training include:
• Learning to use the *DSM-IV-TR* diagnostic categories of culture-bound syndromes and understanding the ways these diagnoses can be pathologizing of clients' experiences.	• Relation of immigrant experience to multicultural competency.
	• Relationship of immigrant identity to individual and cultural differences (e.g., including age, gender, sexual orientation, SES, and ethnicity).
• The ability to formulate treatment plans that empower immigrant communities to access opportunities, while at the same time not imposing own values on the client.	• Basic research literature describing the relevance of immigrant identity to wellness, physical health, mental health.
• The ability to illuminate strengths in the client and utilize these in therapy.	• An understanding of differences between refugee and immigrant experiences.
	• Trainers and teachers could offer students enrolled in multicultural diversity courses an option to research immigrant issues as a class project.

READINESS LEVEL—ENTRY TO INTERNSHIP	
Competencies	**Learning Process and Activities**
• Ability to include indigenous treatment approaches along with traditional approaches to treatment.	• Possible topics could use the media resources listed in Appendix C of this chapter to supplement learning and structure discussions.
Values and Attitudes Demonstrates self awareness and appropriate cultural and multicultural attitudes as evidenced by the following: • Understands that immigrant identity is an important dimension of cultural identity. • Identifies stereotypes and biases toward immigrants and is committed to exploring and challenging these assumptions. • Recognizes own intersecting individual dimensions (gender, ethnicity, socioeconomic status (SES), sexual orientation, ability, etc.) and has ability to discern clients' intersecting identities. • Shows willingness to admit own limitations working with immigrant communities. • Demonstrates genuine respect for the immigrant experience.	

Table 5.3   Developmental-Level Competencies III

READINESS LEVEL—ENTRY TO PROFESSIONAL PRACTICE	
Competencies	**Learning Process and Activities**
Knowledge Knowledge of: • Literature on the relationship between immigrant identity and physical health; knowledge of the range of issues immigrant clients may have. • The current debate on immigration policies and its impact on access to health care. • APA guidelines for providers of psychological services to ethnically, linguistically, and culturally diverse populations. • Community resources, including support groups and activist organizations, and indigenous treatment approaches people use (and ability to access these resources). • Relationship between working with immigrants and multicultural counseling competency.	In the earlier stages of training, students solidified their professional knowledge base and attained appropriate values and attitudes while developing increasingly sophisticated clinical skills with immigrant communities. At the level of Entry to Professional Practice, psychotherapists have attained the full range of competencies in the domains expected of all independent practitioners with regard to immigrant identity and its intersection with other dimensions of culture (e.g., race/gender). Preparation for this level of competency takes place through closely supervised clinical work, augmented by professional reading, personal exploration, and training opportunities such as professional development and training seminars. Clinical supervisors observe students' clinical work, provide training in assessment, case conceptualization, and treatment planning, and challenge supervisees to examine their countertransference reactions, biases, and values
Skills Skills are demonstrated by the ability to: • Perform a basic assessment of clients' immigrant issues related to therapy.	

(continued)

Table 5.3 Developmental-Level Competencies III (*continued*)

READINESS LEVEL—ENTRY TO PROFESSIONAL PRACTICE

Competencies		Learning Process and Activities
	<ul><li>Diagnose and formulate appropriate treatment plans that are sensitive to the client's worldview and understanding of their own immigrant identity, including how multiple systems and individual differences impact client.</li><li>Identify the limits of one's own competency with immigrant issues and refer appropriately.</li><li>Form a trusting therapeutic relationship with clients so that clients may express immigration-related concerns if relevant and provide basic affirmative explorations of immigrant identity.</li><li>Use supervision to enhance skills with immigrant clients.</li><li>Assess the client's environment to determine safety concerns and sources of oppression and discrimination.</li><li>Work to address such concerns by creating safety plans, identifying more inclusive work and community environments, and building upon internal and external resources.</li><li>Create climate in which supervisees and trainees feel safe to talk about immigration related issues.</li><li>Be able to communicate about the multiple roles mental health practitioners have in counseling (e.g., gatekeepers, advocate, liaison, case manager).</li><li>Engage in ongoing efforts to learn about the experiences of different immigrant communities.</li></ul>	to develop their supervisees' clinical competency with immigrant identities. Additional methods by which students can attain competency with immigrant individuals at this level include: <ul><li>Seeking opportunities to provide therapy to clients who identify as immigrants.</li><li>Supervision provided by supervisors knowledgeable and skilled in working with immigrant communities.</li><li>Self-directed study and professional development opportunities.</li><li>Internship and postdoctoral seminar training in immigrant issues.</li><li>Presenting and participating in clinical case conferences that include discussion of immigrant identity aspects of cases.</li><li>Seeking opportunities to increase knowledge about immigrant communities that are less familiar.</li></ul>
Values and Attitudes	Be reflective and aware of assumptions made about clients based on immigration status; understand the practice implications of these assumptions; and commit to expanding knowledge of immigrant identity as part of multicultural competency enhancement.	

Table 5.4 Developmental-Level Competencies IV

READINESS LEVEL—ADVANCED PRACTICE AND SPECIALIZATION

Competencies		Learning Process and Activities
Knowledge	Extensive knowledge of: <ul><li>Immigrant literature.</li><li>Models of practice with immigrant individuals.</li></ul>	Psychotherapists who have a particular interest in immigrant issues as they apply to clinical work may seek to attain advanced levels of competency.

READINESS LEVEL—ADVANCED PRACTICE AND SPECIALIZATION	
Competencies	Learning Process and Activities
<ul><li>Impact of immigrant identity upon human development.</li><li>Local national, and Internet immigrant community resources; current sociopolitical climate and the impact on immigrant communities.</li><li>Advocacy initiatives on immigrant concerns (e.g., employment discrimination; access to health care).</li><li>Information and resources to educate colleagues and trainees to increase their knowledge base with immigrant individuals.</li></ul>	Learning activities will vary depending on the mental health practitioner's unique background, established competencies, and interest areas. For example, practitioners working in college counseling settings may wish to ensure how individual issues (e.g., acculturation), cultural issues (e.g., family environment), and systemic issues (e.g., discrimination) may impact the immigrant experience. Similarly, mental health practitioners working with youth should use their knowledge of immigrant identity to seek to understand, support, and affirm their experience and potential intergenerational conflicts that may occur for this community.
Skills Advanced skills in: <ul><li>Assessment of whether immigrant concerns are primary or secondary concerns in counseling. If there are comorbid mental health concerns (e.g., depression), be able to work collaboratively on treatment planning.</li><li>Advocacy for change in social, economic, educational, and political structures within which clients live.</li><li>Assisting colleagues and trainees in identifying salient treatment concerns and interventions with immigrant clients.</li><li>Responding to and integrating the interpersonal, intrapersonal, social, and cultural identities of clients, and addressing experiences of oppression and discrimination.</li><li>Advocacy for clients to their families and communities. Providing effective supervision to trainees working with immigrant client issues.</li></ul>	Regardless of the focus area, learning activities can include: <ul><li>Professional reading (information about immigration and immigrants; empirical studies, and literature on theory and practice)</li><li>Teaching</li><li>Attending and leading educational workshops</li><li>Peer consultation groups</li><li>Consultation with knowledgeable mental health professionals, immigrant leaders</li><li>Participation in community events related to supporting the immigrant community (e.g., opposes legal policies that hurt the immigrant experience).</li></ul>
Values and Attitudes Well-integrated values and attitudes demonstrated by the following: <ul><li>Continually engages in broadening knowledge of immigrant resources and for continuing professional development.</li><li>Actively cultivates relationships with immigrant community leaders.</li><li>Seeks involvement in local and national groups and organizations relevant to immigrant issues</li><li>Independently and proactively provides ethical and legal consultation and supervision to trainees and other professionals on immigration issues.</li><li>Works for social justice to enhance understanding among individuals.</li><li>Independently monitors own identity and privilege in relation to work with others with awareness and sensitivity.</li></ul>	

REFERENCES

Abraham, M. (2000). Isolation as a form of marital violence: The South Asian immigrant experience. *Journal of Social Distress and the Homeless, 9,* 221–236.

Ahmed, B., Nicolson, P., & Spencer, C. (2000). The social construction of racism: The case of second-generation Bangladeshis. *Journal of Community and Applied Psychology, 10,* 33–48.

Ainslie, R. C. (1998). Cultural mourning, immigration, and engagement: Vignettes from the Mexican experience. In M. Suarez-Orozco (Ed.), *Crossings: Immigration and the socio-cultural remaking of the North American space* (pp. 283–300). Cambridge, MA: Harvard University Press.

Akhtar, S. (1999). *Immigration and identity: Turmoil, treatment, and transformation.* Northvale, NJ: Jason Aronson, Inc.

Akutsu, P. D. (1997). Mental health care delivery to Asian Americans: Review of the literature. In E. Lee (Ed.), *Working with Asian Americans: A guide for clinicians* (pp. 464–447). New York: Guilford Press.

Almeida, R. (1996). Hundu, Christian, and Muslim families. In M. McGoldrick, J. Giordano, & J. K. Pearce (Eds.), *Ethnicity and family therapy* (2nd ed., pp. 395–423). New York: Guilford Press.

Altman, N. (2000). Black and white thinking: A psychoanalyst reconsiders race. *Psychoanalytic Dialogues, 10,* 589–605.

Alvarez, A. N., Juang, L. P., & Liang, C.T.H. (2006). Asian Americans and racism: When bad things happen to "model minorities." *Cultural Diversity & Ethnic Minority Psychology, 12,* 477–492.

American Psychiatric Association (1993). Guidelines for providers of psychological services to ethnic, linguistic, and culturally diverse populations. *American Psychologist, 48,* 45–48.

American Psychiatric Association. (2000). *Diagnostic and Statistical Manual of Mental Disorders (DSM-IV-R; 2000).* (4th ed.). Washington, DC: American Psychiatric Association.

American Psychological Association. (2003). Guidelines on multicultural education, training, research, practice, and organizational change for psychologists. *American Psychologist, 58,* 377–402.

Ancis, J. R., & Ali, S. R. (2005). Multicultural counseling training approaches: Implications for pedagogy. In C. Z. Enns & A. L. Sinacore (Eds.), *Teaching and social justice: Integrating multicultural and feminist theories in the classroom* (pp. 85–97). Washington, DC: American Psychological Association.

Ancis, J., Ladany, N., & Inman, A. G.(in progress). A multicultural framework for counselor supervision: Knowledge and skills. In N. Ladany & L. Bradley (Eds.), *Counselor Supervision* (4th ed.). New York: Routledge.

Arredondo, P., & Arciniega, G. M. (2001). Strategies and techniques for counselor training based on the multicultural counseling competencies. *Journal of Multicultural Counseling & Development, 29,* 263–273.

Arredondo, P., Topreck, R., Brown, S. P., Jones, J., Locke, D. C., Sanchez, J., et al. (1996). Operationalization of the multicultural counseling competencies. *Journal of Multicultural Counseling & Development, 24,* 42–78.

Becvar, R. J., & Becvar, D. S. (1994). The ecosystemic story: A story about stories. *Journal of Mental Health Counseling, 16,* 22–32.

Berger, R. (2000). When remarriage and immigration coincide: The experience of Russian immigrant stepfamilies. *Journal of Ethnic and Cultural Diversity in Social Work, 8,* 75–96.

Berry, J. W. (1980). Acculturation as varieties of adaptation. In A. M. Padilla (Ed.), *Acculturation: Theory, models, and some new findings* (pp. 9–25). Boulder, CO: Westview Press.

Bhat, C. S., & Davis, T. E. (2007). Counseling supervisors' assessment of race, racial identity, and working alliance in supervisory dyads. *Journal of Multicultural Counseling and Development, 35,* 80–91.

Bhugra, D. (2002). Suicidal behavior in South Asians in the UK. *Crisis, 23,* 108–113.

Bhui, K., Stansfeld, S., McKenzie, K., Karlsen, S., Nazroo, J. and Weich, S. (2005). Racial/ethnic discrimination and common mental disorders among workers: Findings from the empiric study of ethnic minority groups in the United Kingdom. *American Journal of Public Health, 95,* 496–501.

Bronfenbrenner, U. (1989). Ecological systems theory. *Annals of Child Development, 6,* 187–249.

Burkard, A. W., Johnson, A. J., Madson, M. B., Pruitt, N. T., Contreras-Tadych, D. A., Kozlowski, J. M., et al. (2006). Supervisor cultural responsiveness and unresponsiveness in cross-cultural supervision. *Journal of Counseling Psychology, 53,* 288–301.

Burnett, P. C., & Meacham, D. (2002). Learning journal as a counseling strategy. *Journal of Counseling & Development, 80,* 410–415.

Camarota, S. (2000). Our new immigration predicament. *American Enterprise Institute for Public Policy Research, 11*, 26–29.

Carter, R. T. (2003). Becoming racially and culturally competent: The racially-cultural counseling laboratory. *Journal of Multicultural Counseling & Development, 31*(1), 20–30.

Chan, C. S. (1989). Issues of identity development among Asian-American lesbians and gay men. *Journal of Counseling & Development, 68*, 16–20.

Cheryan, S., & Tsai, J. L. (2007). Ethnic identity. In F. T.L. Leong, A. G., Inman, A. Ebreo, L. Kinoshita, & L. H. Yang (Eds.), *Handbook of Asian American psychology* (2nd ed., pp. 125–139). Thousand Oaks, CA: Sage Publications.

Chung, R. C., Bemak, F., Ortiz, D. P., & Sandoval-Perez, P. A. (2008). Promoting the mental health of immigrants: A multicultural/social justice perspective. *Journal of Counseling & Development, 86*, 310–317.

Chung, Y. B., & Katayama, M. (1998). Ethnic and sexual identity development of Asian American lesbian and gay adolescents. *Professional School Counseling, 1*, 21–25.

Daniels, M. H., & White, L. J. (1994). Human systems as problem-determined linguistic systems: Relevance for training. *Journal of Mental Health Counseling, 16*, 105–119.

Dasgupta, S. D. (1998). Gender roles and cultural continuum in the Asian Indian immigrant community in the United States. *Sex Roles, 38*, 953–974.

Dasgupta, S. D., & Dasgupta, S. (1996). Public face, private space: Asian Indian women and sexuality. In N. B. Maglin & D. Perry (Eds.), *Bad girls, good girls: Women, sex, and power in the nineties* (pp. 226–243). New Brunswick, NJ: Rutgers University.

Dasgupta, S. D., & Dasgupta, S. (1998). Women in exile: Gender relations in the Asian Indian community in the United States. In S. Maira & R. Srikanth (Eds.), *Contours of the heart: South Asians map North America* (pp. 381–400). New York: The Asian American Writers' Workshop.

Dhruvarajan, V. (1993). Ethnic cultural retention and transmission among first generation Hindu Asian Indians in a Canadian prairie city. *Journal of Comparative Family Studies, 24*, 63–79.

Drachman, D. (1992). A stage-of-migration framework for service to immigrant populations. *Social Work, 37*, 68–72.

Dressel, J. L., Consoli, A. J., Kim, B. S. K., & Atkinson, D. R. (2007). Successful and unsuccessful multicultural supervisory behaviors: A Delphi poll. *Journal of Multicultural Counseling and Development, 35*, 51–64.

Faist, T. (1997). The crucial meso-level. In T. Hammar, G. Brochmann, K. Tamas, & T. Faist (Eds.), *International migration, immobility, and development: Multidisciplinary perspectives* (pp. 187–218). New York: Berg.

Fielder, F. E., Mitchell, T., & Triandis, H. C. (1971). The culture assimilator: An approach to cross-cultural training. *Journal of Applied Psychology, 55*, 95–102.

Fong, R. (2004). *Culturally competent practice with immigrants and refugee children and families*. New York: Guilford Press.

Furuto, S. B. C. L. (2004). Theoretical perspectives for culturally competent practice with children and families. In R. Fong (Ed.), *Culturally competent practice immigrants and refugee children and families* (pp. 19–38). New York: Guilford Press.

Grinberg, L., & Grinberg, R. (1989). *Psychoanalytic perspectives on migration and exile*. New Haven, CT: Yale University Press.

Gupta, S. R. (1999). *Emerging voices: South Asian American women redefine self, family and community*. Walnut Creek, CA: Altamira Press.

Hardy, K. V., & Laszloffy, T. A. (1995). The cultural genogram: Key to training culturally competent family therapists. *Journal of Marital and Family Therapy, 21*, 227–237.

Hartman, A. (1995). Diagrammatic assessment of family relationships. *Families in Society, 76*, 111–122.

Harvey, M. R. (2007). Towards an ecological understanding of resilience in trauma survivors: Implications for theory, research, and practice. *Journal of Aggression, Maltreatment & Trauma, 14*, 9–32.

Hernandez, M., & Isaacs, M. (1998). *Promoting cultural competence in children's mental health services*. Baltimore: Brooks/Cole.

Hilton, B. A., Grewan, S., Popatia, N., Bottorff, J. L., Johnson, J. L., Clarke, H., et al. (2001). The Desi ways: Traditional health practices of South Asian women in Canada. *Health Care for Women International, 22*(6), 553–567.

Hines, P. M., Garcia-Preto, N., McGoldrick, M., Almeida, R., & Weltman, S. (1992). Intergenerational relationships across cultures. *Families in Society, 73*, 323–338.

Hoffman, D. M. (1990). Beyond conflict: Culture, self and intercultural learning among Iranians in the United States. *International Journal of Intercultural Relations, 14*, 275–299.

Huisman, K. A. (1996). Wife battering in Asian American communities: Identifying the service needs of an overlooked segment of the U.S. population. *Violence Against Women, 2*, 260–283.

Ibrahim, F., Ohnishi, H., & Sandhu, D. S. (1997). Asian American identity development: A culture specific model. *Journal of Multicultural Counseling and Development, 25*, 34–50.

Inman, A. G. (2006). South Asian women: Identities and conflicts. *Cultural Diversity and Ethnic Minority Psychology, 12*, 306–319.

Inman, A. G. (2008). Counseling South Asian immigrant communities. *Psychotherapy Bulletin, 48*, 5–9.

Inman, A. G., & Alvarez, A. N. (2009). Individuals and families of Asian descent. In D. C. Hays & B. T. Erford (Eds.), *Developing multicultural counseling competency: A systems approach* (pp. 246–276). Boston, MA: Pearson Merrill Prentice Hall.

Inman, A. G., Constantine, M. G., & Ladany, N. (1999). Cultural value conflict: An examination of Asian Indian women's bicultural experience. In D. S. Sandhu (Ed.), *Asian and Pacific Islander Americans: Issues and concerns for counseling and psychotherapy* (pp. 31–41). Commack, NY: Nova Science.

Inman, A. G., Howard, E. E., Beaumont, R. L., & Walker, J. A. (2007). Cultural transmission: Influence of contextual factors in Asian Indian immigrant parents' experiences. *Journal of Counseling Psychology, 54*, 93–100.

Inman, A. G., Ladany, N., Constantine, M. G., & Morano, C. K. (2001). Development and preliminary validation of the Cultural Values Conflict Scale for South Asian women. *Journal of Counseling Psychology, 48*, 17–27.

Inman, A. G., Rawls, K. N., Meza, M. M., & Brown, A. L. (2002). In F. W. Kaslow (Ed.), *Comprehensive handbook of psychotherapy: Interpersonal/humanistic/existential*, Vol. 3 (pp. 153–178). Hoboken, NJ: John Wiley & Sons.

Inman, A., & Sandhu, D. S (2002). Cross-cultural perspectives on love and sex. In L. D. Burlew & D. Capuzzi (Eds.), *Sexuality Counseling* (pp. 41–61). Hauppauge, NY: Nova Science Publishers.

Inman, A. G., & Yeh, C. J. (2007). Asian American stress and coping. In F.T.L. Leong, A. G. Inman, A. Ebreo, L. Kinoshita, & L. H. Yang (Eds.), *Handbook of Asian American psychology* (2nd ed., pp. 323–339). Thousand Oaks, CA: Sage Publications.

Inman, A. G., Yeh, C. J., Madan-Bahel, A., & Nath, S. (2007). Bereavement and coping of South Asian families post 9/11. *Journal of Multicultural Counseling and Development, 35*, 101–115.

Kagawa-Singer, M., & Chung, R. C. (2002). Toward a new paradigm: A cultural systems approach. In K. S. Kurasaki, S. Okazaki, & S. Sue (Eds.), *Asian American mental health: Assessment theories and methods. International and cultural psychology series* (pp. 47–66). New York: Academic/Plenum.

Kakar, S. (1982). *Shamans, mystics, and doctors: A psychological inquiry into India and its healing traditions.* New Delhi, India: Oxford University Press.

Keeney, B. (1983). *Aesthetics of change.* New York: The Guilford Press.

Kibria, N. (1998). The racial gap: South Asian American racial identity and the Asian American movement. In L. D. Shankar & R. Srikanth (Eds.), *A part, yet apart: South Asians in Asian America* (pp. 69–78). Philadelphia: Temple University Press.

Krishnan, S. P., Hilbert, J. C., & VanLeeuwen, D. (2001). Domestic violence and help-seeking behaviors among rural women: Results from a shelter-based study. *Family & Community Health, 24*, 28–38.

Kwan, K. L. K., & Sodowsky, G. R. (1997). Internal and external ethnic identity and their correlates: A study of Chinese American immigrants. *Journal of Multicultural Counseling & Development, 25*, 51–67.

Ladany, N., Inman, A. G., Constantine, M. G., & Hofheinz, E. W. (1997). Supervisee multicultural case conceptualization ability and self-reported multicultural competence as functions of supervisee racial identity and supervisor focus. *Journal of Counseling Psychology, 44*, 284–293.

LaFromboise, T., Coleman, H. L. K., & Gerton, J. (1993). Psychological impact of biculturalism: Evidence and theory. *Psychological Bulletin, 114*, 395–412.

Lee, E. (1966). A theory of migration. *Demography, 3*, 37–57.

Leong, F. T. L., & Kim, H. H. W. (1991). Going beyond cultural sensitivity on the road to multiculturalism: Using the Intercultural Sensitizer as a counselor training tool. *Journal of Counseling & Development, 70*, 112–118.

Leong, F. T. L., & Lau, A. S. L. (2001). Barriers to providing effective mental health services to Asian Americans. *Mental Health Services Research, 3*, 201–214.

Leong, F. T. L., Wagner, N. S., & Tata, S. P. (1995). Racial and ethnic variations in help-seeking attitudes. In J. G. Ponterotto, J. M. Casas, L. A. Suzuki, & C. M. Alexander (Eds.), *Handbook of multicultural counseling* (pp. 415–438). Thousand Oaks, CA: Sage Publications.

Leupp, G. (1995). *Male colors: The construction of homosexuality in Tokugawa Japan.* Berkeley, CA: University of California Press.

Liebkind, K., Jasinskaja-Lahti, I., & Solheim, E. (2004). Cultural identity, perceived discrimination and parental support as determinants of immigrants' school adjustment: Vietnamese youth in Finland. *Journal of Adolescent Research, 19,* 635–656.

Madanes, C. (1981). *Strategic family therapy.* San Francisco: Jossey Bass.

Malmberg, M. (1997). Time and space in international migration. In T. Hammar, G. Brochmann, K. Tamas, & T. Faist (Eds.), *International migration, immobility, and development: Multidisciplinary perspectives* (pp. 21–48). New York: Berg.

Mullatti, L. (1995). Families in India: Beliefs and realities. *Journal of Comparative Family Studies, 26,* 11–25.

Naidoo, J. C. (1985). Contemporary South Asian women in the Canadian mosaic. *International Journal of Women's Studies, 8,* 338–350.

Nolen-Hoeksema, S. (2002). Gender differences in depression. In I. H. Gotlin & C. L. Hammen (Eds.), *Handbook of depression* (pp. 492–509). New York: Guilford Press.

Ogbu, J. U. (1995). Origins of human competence: A cultural-ecological perspective. In N. R. Goldberger & J. Bennet (Eds.), *The culture and psychology reader* (pp. 245–275). New York: New York University Press.

Outlaw, L. T. (1990). Towards a critical theory of race. In D. Goldberg (Ed.), *Anatomy of racism* (pp. 58–82). Minneapolis: University of Minnesota.

Pedersen, P. (1994). Simulating the client's internal dialogue as a counselor training technique. *Simulation & Gaming, 25,* 40–50.

Pedraza, S., & Rumbaut, R. (1996). *Origins and destinies: Immigration, race, and ethnicity in America.* Belmont, CA: Wadsworth.

Phinney, J., Horenczyk, G., Liebkind, K., & Vedder, P. (2001). Ethnic identity, immigration, and well-being: An interactional perspective. *Journal of Social Issues, 57,* 493–510.

Pope, M. (1995). The "salad bowl" is big enough for us all: An argument for the inclusion of lesbians and gay men in any definition of multiculturalism. *Journal of Counseling & Development, 73,* 301–304.

Pope, M., & Chung, Y. B. (1999). From bakla to tongzhi: Counseling and psychotherapy with gay and lesbian Asian and Pacific Islander Americans. In D. S. Sandhu (Ed.), *Asian and Pacific Islander Americans: Issues and concerns for counseling and psychotherapy* (pp. 283–300). Commack, NY: Nova Science Publishers.

Potocky-Tripodi, M. (2002). *Best practices for social work with refugees and immigrants.* New York: Columbia University Press.

Prathikanti, S. (1997). East Indian American families. In Lee. E. (Ed.), *Working with Asian Americans: A guide for clinicians* (pp. 79–100). New York: Guilford Press.

Raj, A., & Silverman, J. G. (2003). Immigrant South Asian women at greater risk for injury from intimate partner violence. *American Journal of Public Health, 93,* 435–437.

Ramisetty-Mikler, S. (1993). Asian Indian immigrants in America and sociocultural issues in counseling. *Journal of Multicultural Counseling and Development, 21,* 36–49.

Riger, S. (2001). Transforming community psychology. *American Journal of Community Psychology, 29,* 69–78.

Rumbaut, R. G. (1991). The agony of exile: A study of the migration and adaptation of Indochinese refugee adults and children. In L. Ahearn Jr. & J. L. Athey (Eds.), *Refugee children: Theory, research, and services: The Johns Hopkins series in contemporary medicine and public health* (pp. 53–91). Baltimore: Johns Hopkins University Press.

Segal, U. (2002). *A framework for immigration: Application to Asians in the United States.* New York: Columbia University Press.

Shankar, L. D., & Srikanth, R. (1998). *A part, yet apart: South Asians in Asian America.* Philadelphia: Temple University Press.

Sodowsky, G. R., & Carey, J. C. (1987). Asian Indian immigrants in America: Factors related to adjustment. *Journal of Multicultural Counseling and Development, 15,* 129–114.

Sodowsky, G. R., & Carey, J. C. (1988). Relationship between acculturation-related demographics and cultural attitudes of Asian Indian immigrants. *Journal of Multicultural Counseling and Development, 16,* 117–136.

Solberg, V. S., Choi, K., Ritsma, S., & Jolly, A. (1994). Asian-American college students: It is time to reach out. *Journal of College Student Development, 35,* 296–301.

Sue, D. W, & Sue, D. (2003). *Counseling the culturally diverse: Theory and practice* (4th ed.). Hoboken, NJ: John Wiley & Sons.

Szymanski, D. M. (2005). Feminist identity and theories as correlates of feminist supervision practices. *The Counseling Psychologist, 33,* 729–747.

Takeuchi, D. T., Zane, N., Hong, S., Chae, D. H., Gong, F., Gee, G. C., et al. (2007). Immigration-related factors and mental disorders among Asian Americans. *American Journal of Public Health, 97*(1), 84–90.

Takaki, R. T. (1998). *Strangers from a different shore.* Boston: Little, Brown.

Tewari, N., Inman, A. G., & Sandhu, D. S. (2003). South Asian Americans: Culture, concerns and therapeutic strategies. In J. Mio & G. Iwamasa (Eds.), *Culturally diverse mental health: The challenges of research and resistance* (pp. 191–209). New York: Brunner-Routledge.

Tummala-Narra, P. (2001). Asian trauma survivors: Immigration, identity, loss, and recovery. *Journal of Applied Psychoanalytic Studies, 3,* 243–258.

Tummala-Narra, P. (2004). Dynamics of race and culture in the supervisory encounter. *Psychoanalytic Psychology, 21,* 300–311.

Tummala-Narra, P. (2007a). Conceptualizing trauma and resilience across diverse contexts: A multicultural perspective. *Journal of Aggression, Maltreatment & Trauma, 14,* 33–53.

Tummala-Narra, P. (2007b). Trauma and resilience: A case of individual psychotherapy in a multicultural context. *Journal of Aggression, Maltreatment & Trauma, 14,* 1–18.

Tummala-Narra, P. (2009). Teaching on diversity: The mutual influence of students and instructors. *Psychoanalytic Psychology, 26*(3), 322–334.

Tummala-Narra, P., Inman, A. G., & Ettigi, S. (in progress). *Race, ethnicity and racism-related stress in the Asian Indian community.*

Uba, L. (1994). *Asian Americans: Personality patterns, identity, and mental health.* New York: Guilford Press.

Uba, L. (2002). *A postmodern psychology of Asian Americans: Creating knowledge of a racial minority.* Albany, NY: State University of New York Press.

U.S. Census Bureau. (2000). *Table DP-1: Profile of general demographic characteristics: 2000 Census of population and housing (May 1, 2001).* Washington DC: U.S. Department of Commerce.

U.S. Department of Homeland Security. (2008). *Yearbook of immigration statistics.* Washington, DC: U.S. Department of Homeland Security, Office of Immigration Statistics.

Wu, F. H. (2001). *Yellow: Race in America beyond black and white.* New York: Basic Books.

Yakushko, O., & Chronister, K. (2005). Immigrant women and counseling: The invisible others. *Journal of Counseling and Development, 83,* 292–298.

Yeh, C. J., Inman, A. C., Kim, A. B., & Okubo, Y. (2006). Asian American families' collectivistic coping strategies in response to 9/11. *Cultural Diversity and Ethnic Minority Psychology, 12,* 134–148.

Ying, W., Lee, P. A., Tsai, J. L., Yeh, Y., & Huang, J. S. (2000). The conception of depression in Chinese American college students. *Cultural Diversity and Ethnic Minority Psychology, 6*(2), 183–195.

Yoshioka, M. R., Gilbert, L., El-Bassel, N., & Baig-Amin, M. (2003). Social support and disclosure of abuse: Comparing South Asian, African American, and Hispanic battered women. *Journal of Family Violence, 18*(3), p. 171–180.

CHAPTER 6

COMPETENCY WITH LINGUISTICALLY DIVERSE POPULATIONS

HENRIETTA PAZOS and LAVITA I. NADKARNI

INTRODUCTION

Language is powerful, as it can affect us in many ways, from the simple to the dramatic. For example, language is one of the primary means by which family history is passed from generation to generation, with stories and songs creating lasting intergenerational memories. Culture and language are necessarily interconnected concepts; one might say that language, in a very literal sense, gives voice to culture, and that culture gives meaning to language. Certainly, "language is among the most important carriers of group identity" (Eide, 2000, p. 12). For mental health practitioners, language per se represents an important topic for exploration in its own right, given its impact on cognitive and psychological processes and the unique role it plays in individual and group behavior.

Unfortunately, for those who do not speak the dominant language in a particular geographic area, language differences can also become obstacles to full participation in society. In the United States, individuals not fluent in English have historically faced marginalization or worse (see, e.g., "Immigrants Face Struggle to Live without English," 1992). Language can be seen as a barrier to accessing mental health care and services (U.S. Department of Health and Human Services,). Linguistically isolated households, in which no adolescent or adult speaks English well, have the additional challenges of limited job prospects, difficulties communicating with educators, and restricted ability to seek medical or emergency assistance.

This chapter will thus explore the challenges and realities of providing ethical, legal, and competent services to culturally and linguistically diverse individuals. The importance of expanding training and education around these issues in the various mental health fields can hardly be overstated. As Santiago-Rivera and Altarriba (2009) have noted with regard to Spanish-English bilingual clients in particular, "the reality is that more training is needed to produce culturally competent psychologists who understand the dynamics of language" (p. 30). They go on to add that, irrespective of the theoretical orientation employed in providing services, "understanding the role of language in therapy is central to effective treatment" (p. 30).

For many mental health practitioners, the question of what constitute "best practices" for linguistically diverse clients is not a theoretical one—or, at least, will not remain so for long. According to the U.S. 2000 Census, nearly 20 percent of the U.S. population over the age of five spoke a language other than English at home, which represents a dramatic increase over the past two decades (U.S. Census Bureau, 2002). Bancroft () reported that there are over 300 languages spoken in the United States (p. 4), with Spanish being the most commonly spoken after English (Shin & Bruno, 1998, Table 1, p. 4).

The implications for the provision of mental health services are clear. While the likelihood of contact with a client whose primary language is not English varies somewhat depending on the region of the country in which the mental health practitioner resides, the landscape is changing. California has the largest percentage of households (42.5%) in which a language other than English is spoken at home (U.S. Census Bureau, 2002). However, many regions of the country that have not traditionally seen an influx of immigrant groups have begun to experience this transition, as well. For example, between 1990 and 2000 the number of English language learners (ELLs) served at the elementary school level

(continued)

increased by 163 percent in Colorado, by 264 percent in South Dakota, and by 350 percent in Nebraska (Flynn & Hill, 2005, p. 2). Overall, the proportion of school-age children considered to be ELLs has increased by nearly 140 percent in the past 30 years (National Center for Education Statistics, 2009). By the year 2010, it is estimated that over 30 percent of all school-age children will reside in homes in which the primary language is not English (http://www.bnkst.edu). As such, children may be the primary target for service delivery considerations. Addressing the mental health and educational needs of these linguistically diverse populations will be the next challenge for all educators and mental health practitioners.

This chapter seeks to provide mental health practitioners at all levels of training with guidelines and resources for expanding their competencies in working with clients who are linguistically diverse. Explanations of the terminology used historically and currently for individuals whose first language is not Standard American English (SAE) will be presented as a starting point, followed by a discussion of elements of competency in this area and barriers to competency in working with linguistically diverse populations. In examining competency, the substantive areas of knowledge (individual and cultural diversity, assessment, diagnosis and case conceptualization, intervention, and ethical and legal standards) will be discussed. Next, the linguistic considerations necessary to effectively utilize the skills for mental health service delivery (such as relationship building, assessment, intervention, referral, and supervision and training) will be introduced. Finally, explorations of the attitudes and values necessary to provide multiculturally sensitive services to linguistically diverse populations will be presented. Although space limitations prohibit exploration of all possible variations of language issues within this chapter, certain topics will be explored in greater detail (such as international students, the use of interpreters, and special issues in assessment). This chapter will include case vignettes and examples, pertinent questions to ask during various stages of service delivery and supervision, and exercises for evaluating and increasing self-awareness related to language biases. It is hoped that this information will assist mental health practitioners in providing more competent services to linguistically diverse populations.

TERMINOLOGY

Second language acquisition (SLA) is the process by which an individual acquires a language other than his or her first language. A *second language learner* (SLL) is someone who is learning a language other than his or her first language; in the United States, someone whose first language is not English is often referred to as an *English language learner* (ELL) (Rhodes, Ochoa, & Ortiz, 2005). Other terms used to describe someone learning English as a second language have been *limited English proficient* (LEP) or *non–English proficient* (NEP) (Rhodes et al., 2005), although ELL is the most widely used in the recent literature. From a strength-based perspective, an ELL could be described as "an individual who is _____ dominant" (fill in the blank with the individual's first or dominant language). This shift may more accurately represent the process of language acquisition than outdated terms

emphasizing deficits rather than strengths. Similarly, the term *culturally and linguistically diverse* is also currently used because it underscores the interrelation between culture and language. An individual's *first language* is the language initially acquired, usually in early development, and it can be referred to as "native language" or "L1." Conversely, an individual's *second language* could be referred to as "target language" or "L2."

ELLs also differ in the context in which SLA takes place and in their reasons for learning a second language. For instance, someone who was exposed to a second language after developing their first language is thought to have *sequential bilingual ability* (Valdés & Figueroa, 2003). Usually, these individuals either migrated from another country or grew up in a monolingual home in the United States before entering the school system. Someone who learns both languages at the same time, such as an individual who grows up in a household in which two languages are spoken, is said to have *simultaneous bilingual ability* (Valdés & Figueroa, 2003).

The motivation for developing two sets of language skills has also been described as a factor that differs among bilingual individuals, leading to the terms *circumstantial* or *elective bilinguals* (Valdés & Figueroa, 2003). For instance, someone who has to learn a second language to survive in a new country or circumstance is thought to be developing *circumstantial bilingualism*. These individuals tend to find themselves in situations in which their first language is not the dominant or most powerful language in their new circumstances. A large number of students in the public school system are likely *circumstantial bilinguals* (Rhodes et al., 2005). Individuals who have chosen to learn a second language are called *elective bilinguals* (Valdés & Figueroa, 2003). These individuals typically continue to conduct the majority of their daily lives in their primary language. Lastly, other differences within ELL populations include their SLA developmental stage and processes, and their level of proficiency in both the first and second language.

ELEMENTS OF COMPETENCY

To address the varied needs of linguistically diverse people, mental health practitioners must possess the requisite levels of awareness, knowledge, and skill-based functioning. But what are the expectations regarding professional competence in these areas? The multicultural counseling competencies (Arrendondo et al., 1996), the Competency Benchmarks Document (APA, 2007), and the recent literature on competencies in professional psychology (Kaslow et al., 2007; Rodolfa et al., 2005) offer mental health practitioners a general description of competence rooted in this knowledge and these skills, values, and attitudes.

In this chapter, scholarship primarily related to SLA is provided and integrated with linguistic competence at the four levels described in the Competency Benchmarks Document (APA, 2007): (1) Entry into Practicum; (2) Entry into Internship; (3) Entry into Professional Practice; and (4) Entry into Advanced Practice and Specialization (see Tables 6.1 through 6.4).

KNOWLEDGE

As one of the multiple identities an individual holds, linguistic affiliation influences values, behaviors, experiences, worldview, and self-concept. Mental health practitioners providing services to culturally and linguistically diverse individuals need a knowledge base related to core competencies in the areas of individual and cultural diversity, the SLA process, assessment, diagnosis, case conceptualization, intervention, adherence to ethical and legal standards, supervision, and teaching. Specific principles relating to each of these concepts will be outlined in the following sections.

Language and Culture

Mental health practitioners must have the ability to communicate in a language that is understandable to their clients, of course, but they must also be able to use constructs that are understandable in the clients' cultures. Health and mental health concepts do not have equivalent meaning in English and other languages, and vary widely among cultures (Bolten & Tang, 2002). Spielberger, Moscoso, and Brunner (1994) noted the difficulty of assessing emotion and personality across cultures, commenting that "languages differ in the connotations of words used to describe feeling and cognitions associated with different emotional states and personality traits" (p. 347). Learning a second language is a transformative experience, and it is crucial that mental health practitioners understand both the process itself and its impact on the SLL.

Second Language Acquisition

According to Cummins (1983), "many of the difficulties minority students experience in school are the result of both inappropriate pedagogy and misconceptions about the nature of bilingualism among educational professionals" (p. 384). Specialized knowledge, in conjunction with fluency in a student's first language, is needed to provide "linguistically competent" services to ELLs (Ortiz, 2002).

Krashen and Terrell (1997) proposed an approach to the teaching of a second language (the Natural Approach) that was based on an empirically grounded theory of second language acquisition. The second principle of the Natural Approach, which posits that production of speech emerges in stages, appears to have been adapted by others (e.g., Hill & Flynn, 2006) in a more formal articulation of stages of SLA. According to Krashen and Terrell (1997), SLLs typically progress from nonverbal communication to responses

on the development of receptive and expressive language skills that can be used in both social and academic settings. Each stage is associated with a particular timeline, with Advanced Language Fluency being reached approximately 5 to 7 years after exposure to the second language, and identifies characteristics common to individuals within the stage. Other research shows that fluency in a second language can even take up to 7 to 10 years, especially if a student has limited to no schooling in his/her native language (Thomas & Collier, 2006, in Haynes, 2007).

Stages of Second Language Acquisition Theory: An Overview

Stages	Duration	Characteristics
Stage 1: The Silent/Receptive or Preproduction Stage	Approximate length of time: 0 to 6 mos.	Silent period/mostly receptive language.
Stage 2: The Early Production Stage	Approximate length of time: 6 mos. to 1 year.	1,000 "receptive/active" words; one- to two-word phrases; can respond with short answers to simple *yes, no, either/or,* or *who/where* questions.
Stage 3: The Speech Emergence Stage	Approximate length of time: 1 to 3 years.	3,000+ words; can use short phrases and ask simple questions; grammatical errors can interfere with communication.
Stage 4: The Intermediate Language Fluency Stage	Approximate length of time: 3-5 years.	6,000+ words; beginning to make complex statements, express strong opinions, ask for clarification, share thoughts, and speak in longer sentences.
Stage 5: The Advanced Language Proficiency Stage	Approximate length of time: 5-10 years.	Specialized content-area vocabulary; can benefit from grade-level content with support; grammar and vocabulary comparable to same-age native English speakers.

Adapted from Krashen & Terrell (1997); Haynes (2007); Hill & Flynn (2006); and Thomas & Collier (2006).

consisting of a single word, then to combinations of two or three words, then phrases; eventually, they begin to communicate in complete sentences and increasingly complex forms of discourse (p. 20). The authors note that while adults may be quicker in their initial rate of SLA, children tend to ultimately acquire more language, thus appearing to be similar to native speakers.

The five stages of SLA adapted by Hill and Flynn (2006) from Krashen and Terrell's (1997) seminal work include: Preproduction, Early Production, Speech Emergence, Intermediate Language Fluency, and Advanced Language Fluency stages (see the table above). These stages focus

The *Preproduction Stage,* commonly called the "silent period," usually develops from 0 to 6 months after exposure to the second language. The duration of this stage may depend on the situation and the age of the individual. The individual at this stage cannot verbally express him- or herself in the L2 (second language) but is receptively processing information in the L2. Some of the characteristics of this stage of language proficiency include: zero to limited verbal output in L2, with gradual use of one-word responses; the individual may appear apprehensive and display low confidence, and may communicate primarily with nonverbal responses. During this stage there is an especially high potential for someone to be: (a) inappropriately referred for an evaluation, (b) misdiagnosed, or (c) erroneously placed in special education. Due to the silent, often unresponsive nature of the individual, common misdiagnoses could be Selective Mutism, Autism, Learning and/or Language disability, or cognitive or social/emotional delay. This stage may be relatively brief in nature, but may have a longer duration for some individuals due to exacerbating factors such as difficulties with acculturation, trauma related to migration, low-risk-taking characteristics, and/or performance anxiety.

In the second stage, the *Early Production Stage*, the individual begins to use and develop expressive language skills by communicating with one- to two-word phrases, responding to simple *yes* and *no* questions, and providing simple responses to *who/where* questions. In comprehending spoken language, ELLs tend to focus on main ideas and various key words, and to rely on cues that provide context to language. They are very dependent on environmental cues, such as visual cues, social context, and the nonverbal communication gestures of others to continue their learning of the second language. This stage usually lasts up to 1 year after exposure to the target language (L2).

The third stage is the *Speech Emergence Stage*, which can last up to 3 years after exposure to the L2. Characteristics of SLLs at this stage are that they: (a) produce words that have been heard and understood with high frequency, (b) can speak with short phrases and/or ask simple questions, and (c) may show mispronunciation of words and grammatical errors.

The fourth stage is the *Intermediate Language Fluency Stage*, with a 3 to 5 year duration, which can last up to another year or two after the Speech Emergence Stage. The characteristics common to this stage are the ability to: (a) speak in longer and more complex sentences; and (b) share thoughts and opinions and ask for clarification, while still developing fluency in the academic language (such as in reading and writing).

The final stage, the *Advanced Language Fluency Stage*, which requires the most amount of time to develop, can last from 5 to 10 years Achievement of this stage connotes that the individual is able to speak and understand the second language with the same fluency as a native speaker and also has the ability to benefit from grade-level academic instruction with support. The individual's grammar and vocabulary are comparable to those of native speakers of the second language.

Second Language Acquisition Instructional Models

According to the literature on the provision of services to ELLs, knowledge about models of second language instruction and principles of teaching SLLs is required to provide culturally and linguistically appropriate assessment services (Rhodes et al., 2005), and classroom interventions (Harris & Goldstein, 2007). Various types of SLA programs are currently utilized nationwide. These include native language instruction, English language development (ELD or ESL), English immersion with sheltered English instruction, and dual language or two- way bilingual programs. English immersion with no support for SLA is also utilized, but it offers minimal support for ELLs to learn in their second language (Echevarria, Vogt, & Short, 2004; Miramontes, Nadeau, & Commins, 1997; Roseberry-McKibbin & Brice, 2005). The following are the most widely utilized instructional models.

1. *Native Language Instruction.* In the United States, the most common native language instruction for ELLs is delivered in Spanish, such that students who are dominant in Spanish receive their literacy and instruction in other subjects in Spanish. However, most programs also include specific instruction time focused on developing the student's English language skills, while allowing the student to simultaneously learn in his or her native language (see, e.g., Cloud, 2007; Rhodes et al., 2005).

2. *Sheltered English Instructions.* Sheltered English instruction is an empirically based model of teaching that can be utilized to make the English language more comprehensible for ELLs while

they are developing their English language skills (Echevarria et al., 2004). Under this approach, students receive their literacy training and instruction in other subjects exclusively in English. The students learn in a classroom with other ELLs or a combination of ELLs and native English speakers. Sheltered English instruction strategies are used in the classroom by a trained and certified teacher to support the student who is learning in his or her second language. These strategies include integrating language and content goals into grade-level curriculum. The student's level of English language proficiency is strategically considered when planning and delivering instruction; concepts are made comprehensible through various strategies such as "the use of visual aids, modeling, demonstration, graphic organizers, vocabulary previews, predictions, adapted texts, cooperative learning, peer tutoring, multicultural content, and native language support" (Echevarria et al., 2004, p. 14).

Connections between the student's past learning and background and the content area being taught are explicitly made. Teachers strike a balance between focusing on factual information and assisting students in understanding how to accomplish academic tasks, develop study skills, and utilize learning strategies (e.g., note taking, self-monitoring of comprehension). Teachers who implement sheltered English instruction also consider the students' emotional needs and diverse learning styles. They consider students' multiple intelligences (Gardner, 1993) and allow for students to learn and demonstrate their learning utilizing these unique qualities.

3. *Dual Language or Two-Way Bilingual Programs.* Instruction is provided for students in both the students' first and second languages and usually there is an even distribution of students in the classroom who are learning in both their first and second languages (Rhodes et al., 2005). In the United States, for example, the most common languages utilized within such programs are English and Spanish, and students are typically evenly distributed between native English and Spanish speakers.

4. *English Immersion.* In this model, ELLs are placed in classrooms with native English speakers and receive both literacy and content instruction in only English with no additional support. Research has shown that this sink-or-swim approach to second language learning is not effective compared to other methods of instruction. For example, Rhodes et al. (2005) cite various studies that show English immersion to be less effective than instruction that provides support for ELLs via native language instruction, dual-language instruction, or English instruction with support.

5. *English Language Development.* This program, usually provided in conjunction with one of the other models mentioned above, involves students receiving direct instruction in English, within the school day, (length of ELD time per day varies and may be guided by State Education Law) in specific areas of focus such as vocabulary building, oral language, survival vocabulary, and development of reading skills.

When evaluating the possibility of learning disability or other cognitive or academic concerns, it is crucial that mental health professionals assessing an ELL understand the model of learning in which the client is being instructed and the likely advantages and limitations of the model. As noted, the least amount of support is provided in a sink-or-swim modality, in which the student is immersed in English instruction with no English language development or sheltered English instruction strategies. A higher level of support is provided by English language instruction that includes sheltered English instruction strategies implemented by qualified teachers. Native language instruction can provide the highest level of support if it is delivered through maintenance or dual-language models, which allow students to maintain their first language while learning the second language.

Three large-scale studies (Ramirez, Yuen, & Ramney, 1991; Thomas & Collier, 2006, 1997) have been cited as addressing two factors not previously addressed in bilingual education research—namely, the effectiveness of bilingual education by type of program and the long-term consequences of bilingual education. This research concluded that ELL students instructed within a maintenance or dual-language program outperform ELL students who receive native language instruction through a transitional/early exit program (described as a program in which the child is initially taught in English and his or her native language, but is transitioned to only English within a brief period; Rhodes et al., 2005).

Individual and Cultural Diversity among English Language Learners

ELLs share one common characteristic: By definition, English is not their first, native and/or primary language. Because of this commonality, ELLs are often referred to as if they constitute a single entity (even within the confines of this chapter). In reality, however, ELLs are a diverse group of individuals, and this diversity needs to be considered in the provision of services to this population. ELLs come from different countries and linguistic backgrounds, speak different dialects, and exhibit different levels of acculturation, all of which can affect the rate of SLA and subsequent academic, occupational, and social- emotional functioning. ELLs' academic histories and individual personality characteristics, including

"language anxiety and willingness to communicate in the second language, and motivation, and attitudes toward learning a second language" (Mitchell & Myles, 2004, pp. 27–28), as well as immigration, medical status, and psychological histories, are all factors that can impact the rate of SLA and learning. Consider the following examples in Case Vignette 6.1.

What differences might each of these individuals face in terms of the SLA process? What variables may play into the relative ease or difficulty with which they adapt into the linguistic contexts in which they find themselves? What specific challenges may each face?

As the reader considers these questions, it may be helpful to note that, in relation to differences in languages and dialects, it is important to be aware that the level of difficulty experienced in acquiring English as a second language may vary depending on the individual's primary language. Consider, for example, the difficulties inherent in learning, not just a new language, but a new alphabet or symbol structure—a challenge faced by Aygul and Karl. In addition, even individuals from the same country may speak in different dialects depending on the region of the country from which they migrated and social group to which they belonged. Note that Aygul's experience as a member of a disenfranchised ethnic

CASE VIGNETTE 6.1

Modu, a 29-year-old Nigerian engineer, recently relocated to the United States to complete graduate studies at a prestigious Ivy League PhD Program. He has studied English (the official language of Nigeria) since he was 3 years old, along with his parents' ancestral language of Hausa. Modu completed his undergraduate degree at Cambridge University in England in an exclusively English-based curriculum.

Aygul, a 47-year-old Uighur attorney from Xinjiang province, China, recently applied for asylum due to ethnic unrest and violence in her native country. She studied English as part of her primary schooling and speaks some conversational English; however, she lacks knowledge of technical and legal terms specific to her field.

Karl, a Siberian-born skilled laborer who immigrated to the United States from a rural region of Russia, has been referred for ESL courses by his employer, an urban roofing company based in the northwestern United States. He has received no formal training or education in English, but has picked up some construction terms from his coworkers, most of whom speak either English or Spanish, or a combination of both.

group may have impacted her opportunities and experiences in her homeland. Level of acculturation is also a factor that is important to consider for all ELLs, as the rate of acculturation may differ between ELLs due to individual and/or social-cultural factors. The relationship between acculturation and language deserves special mention and will be covered in a subsequent section of this chapter.

Another individual characteristic to consider among ELLs is history of language instruction; specifically, it is important to obtain information about the level and quality of formal education received in the home country, as a strong foundation in formal education in one's first language is considered an important factor for successful learning in a second language (Echevarria et al., 2004). As an attorney and an engineer, respectively, Aygul and Modu likely achieved a different level of educational attainment than Karl; these distinctions may carry over into the SLA process, as well. Consistency of language instruction is another factor that has been shown to affect SLA and learning in a second language. For instance, an individual who has been alternately instructed in English and his or her first language (usually Spanish in the United States), with no theory to guide these changes, could have difficulties with learning.

Acculturation

As discussed in Chapter 5 of this text, the literature in this arena offers numerous definitions of acculturation and descriptions of the lifelong psychosocial process by which acculturation occurs (Berry, 1997; Padilla & Perez, 2003; Roysircar & Maestas, 2002). The common threads among all are that: (a) acculturation is a process that results from continuous contact between at least two different cultures (Garcia-Vázquez, 1995); (b) one culture is usually more dominant than the other; (c) the less dominant culture typically makes the most changes; and (4) changes can include behavior, values (Szapocznik, Scopetta, Kurtines, & Arnalde 1980), language (Szapocznik &

Kurtines, 2005), cognition, and affect (Cuellar, Arnold, & Maldonado, 1995). Language is one of the most widely used factors in measuring acculturation, and may vary depending on context. For example, individuals from the same linguistic group may speak English at school or work, yet prefer to communicate with one another in their native language when at home or in their community. Choices around language use and preference may suggest awareness of what is adaptive for different contexts or may reflect personal identity structure. Within the linguistic and psychological literature, there is consensus on the interdependence of acculturation and language (Mantero, 2007; Vazquez-Nuttal et al., 2007;), acculturation and literacy skills (Garcia-Vázquez, 1995), and the effect of acculturation on cognitive test performance (Kestemberg, Silverman, & Emmons, 1983). According to Collier, Brice, and Oades-Sese (2007), language proficiency is one of the acculturation variables thought to affect special education placement. Perhaps not surprisingly, strength in one or both first and second language skills was identified as a critical factor affecting the degree of acculturation (Cummins, 1984; Knoff, 1983; Szapocznik & Kurtines, 2005). Collier and colleagues (2007) describe a model that depicts some of the different responses of students to the acculturation process within a school system/culture, referred to as the Acculturation Matrix (outlined in the following).

Assimilation Home/heritage replaced by school/new culture/language	Integration Home/heritage blended with school/new culture/language
Deculturation (Marginalization) Acceptance of neither home/heritage nor school/new culture/language	Rejection Intentional rejection of home/heritage for school/new culture/language OR intentional rejection of school/new culture/language for home/heritage

Acculturation Matrix (Collier, Brice, & Oades-Sese, 2007).

The model reflects the authors' view that the process of acculturation and SLA can develop simultaneously. The four quadrants of the Acculturation Matrix represent types of adaptation to the process of acculturation, and are as follows (pp. 364–366): *Assimilation* (the home/heritage replaced by school/new culture/language); *Integration* (home/heritage blended with school/new culture/language); *Deculturation* (acceptance of neither home/heritage nor school/new culture/language); and *Rejection* (intentional rejection of home/heritage for school/new culture/language or intentional rejection of school/new culture/language for home/heritage).

Collier and colleagues (2007) further discuss the potential for *acculturative stress*, the effects of which can include "heightened anxiety, confusion in locus of control, code-switching, silence or withdrawal, distractibility, response fatigue, and other indications of stress response" (p. 357). For mental health practitioners, it is important to note that these side effects may be incorrectly perceived as indicators of learning disabilities. They suggest the *Acculturation Quick Screen* (AQS, Collier, 2000) as an aid in identifying varying levels of acculturation of students to public school (from significantly less acculturated to highly acculturated), as it is not specific to any one language or ethnic group. These disparate levels also demand different types of interventions, ranging from the use of relaxation techniques and identification of coping skills to assistance with the acculturation process and certain types of second language instructional strategies. Although discussing the multitude of interventions described at each level of acculturation is beyond the scope of this chapter, the reader is referred to the work cited for more detailed information.

Assessment, Diagnosis, and Case Conceptualization

Knowledge regarding these cultural and linguistic factors is relevant in assessment, diagnosis, and case conceptualization in that it provides the assessor with information regarding normative second language development processes and reactions, as well as the most widely accepted and best-researched methods in which to effectively teach ELLs. This information allows the assessor to view SLA-related referral concerns through a cultural and linguistic lens. In addition, it is important for a professional assessing an ELL to have knowledge about these different processes, as they impact decisions regarding language of assessment, interpretation, conceptualization, and recommendations derived from the assessment. Skills and values related to these topics are discussed in the relevant sections that follow.

According to Ortiz (2002), "linguistic competence," requires a "knowledge base related to first and second language development and instructional methodology and pedagogy" (p. 1324) in addition to speaking the ELL's first language fluently. Although the majority of mental health practitioners do not meet the second criteria, most can work toward meeting the first. Once knowledge in these areas has been obtained, the next step is to utilize this knowledge to guide decision making on issues such as the language of assessment and/or intervention and to guide interpretation of assessments that will lead to appropriate conceptualizations, diagnoses, and recommendations. The mental health practitioner must use caution to ensure that information obtained through the clinical interview is not viewed as pathology when it may be a reflection of linguistic differences.

Ethical and Legal Implications

In 2001, recognizing that culture and language affect the service delivery of health and mental health care, the U.S. Department of Health and Human Services, Office of Minority Health, created a set of national standards for the provision of culturally and linguistically appropriate services (CLAS). Four of the 14 standards are related to Language Access Services. Standards 4 to 7 (as described in more detail later) are based on Title IV of the Civil Rights Act of 1964.

National Standards for Provision of Culturally and Linguistically Appropriate Services

Title IV: Requires all federally funded/assisted entities to ensure that limited English proficient (LEP) individuals have meaningful access to the health services provided.

Standard 4: Health care organizations must offer and provide language assistance services, including bilingual staff and interpreter services, at no cost to each patient/consumer with LEP at all points of contact, in a timely manner during all hours of operation.

Standard 5: Health care organizations must provide to patients/consumers in their preferred language both verbal offers and written notices informing them of their right to receive language assistance services.

Standard 6: Health care organizations must assure the competence of language assistance provided to LEP patients/consumers by interpreters and bilingual staff. Family and friends should not be used to provide interpretation services (except on request by the patient/consumer).

Standard 7: Health care organizations must make available easily understood patient-related materials and post signage in the languages of the commonly encountered groups and/or groups represented in the service area.

—*Adapted from U.S. Department of Health and Human Services ().*

In reviewing the mental-health-care standards, the National Association of Social Workers (NASW, 2007) outlined 10 standards to be considered in the provision of culturally competent social work practice. Standard 9 refers to language diversity: "Social workers shall seek to provide and advocate for the provision of information, referrals, and services in the language appropriate to the client, which may include the use of interpreters" (p. 39). The NASW language standard (2007, p. 41) also denotes that culturally competent social workers:

- Demonstrate an understanding that language is an important aspect of an individual's identity and that clients have the right to receive information/referrals/services/resources in their own language in an accessible manner.
- Advocate for the preservation and promotion of language diversity among clients.
- Improve their own linguistic ability with clients while staying within the bounds of their professional skill levels.
- Ensure accurate communication, recognizing that there are variations in dialect, word usage, and colloquialisms.
- Prepare to work effectively with translators and interpreters, including those providing American Sign Language interpretation.

Ethical guidelines for psychologists have also been developed to reinforce the importance of providing culturally and linguistically appropriate services within the field of psychology; these include the Guidelines on Multicultural Education, Training, Research, Practice, and Organizational Change for Psychologists (American Psychological Association, 2003). The Standards for Educational and Psychological Testing, promulgated by the American Educational Research Association (AERA), American Psychological Association (APA), and National Council on Measurement in Education (NCME) (AERA, APA, & NCME, 1999) also addressed the issue of discriminatory assessment of ELLs by stating that any test that includes language is, by default, also measuring language proficiency, a fact that could "introduce construct-irrelevant components to the testing process" and misrepresent the characteristics and/or abilities being measured (Abedi, 2006, p. 2283). It thus becomes "important to consider language background in developing, selecting, and administering tests and in interpreting test performance (Abedi, 2006, p. 2283). Finally, Ortiz (2002) outlines three major tenets within the APA's (1990) Guidelines for Providers of Psychological Services to Ethnic, Linguistic, and Culturally Diverse Populations that should be considered when working with culturally and linguistically diverse (CLD) individuals (Ortiz, 2002, p. 1322):

1. "The influence of language and culture on behavior when working with diverse groups"

2. "The validity of the methods and procedures used to assess minority groups"
3. "The importance of interpreting resultant psychological data within the context of the individual's linguistic and cultural characteristics."

ELLs face significant potential for biased and discriminatory assessment practices, given that most formal and informal assessment tools are based on language (most often English) and developed according to U.S. mainstream culture. Nondiscriminatory assessments are vital to the academic, economic, professional, and personal success of those assessed. The negative effects of discriminatory and/or biased assessment practices on ELLs could include misdiagnosis and potential contratherapeutic interventions and recommendations. It could also result in overrepresentation of ELL students in special education and underrepresentation of ELL students in gifted and talented programs. This in turn could affect student, teacher, and parent expectations and accessibility to standard and/or enriched education. Research suggests that these outcomes do, in fact, occur. For example, various studies have shown that ELLs are overrepresented in special education (Gottlieb & Hamayan, 2007; National Educational Association and National Association of School Psychologists, 2007; Rhodes et al., 2005). Numerous incidents of discriminatory assessment practices directed toward CLD students have led to consent decrees, as well as court rulings and federal law (Rhodes et al., 2005). Legally, according to the Individuals with Disabilities Education and Improvement Act of 2004, students who are being assessed for special education eligibility must be assessed in their "native language or other mode of communication and in the form most likely to yield accurate information on what the child knows and can do academically, developmentally, and functionally, unless it is clearly not feasible to provide or administer" (IDEIA, 2004); (b) tests selected must not be discriminatory based on cultural or racial factors; (c) a "variety of assessment tools and strategies" should be utilized "to gather

relevant functional, developmental, and academic information about the child, including information provided by the parent" (IDEIA, 2004).

Knowledge in Supervision and Training

Competency-based supervision is defined by Falender and Shafranske (2007) as "an approach that explicitly identifies the knowledge, skills, and values that are assembled to form a clinical competency and develops learning strategies and evaluation procedures to meet criterion-referenced competence standards in keeping with evidence-based practices and requirements of the local clinical setting" (p. 233).

According to the Competency Benchmarks Document (APA, 2007), certain competencies need to be reached within the supervisory role. For instance, a supervisor needs to be aware of supervision models and be able to express how these models can be applied within everyday practice. While other diversity aspects are gradually being incorporated into multicultural supervision, language is often overlooked (Biever et al., 2002). A framework for understanding issues involved in supervising bilingual mental health services is provided by Fuertes (2004), but these recommendations assume that the supervisees are bilingual. In relation to multicultural assessment supervision models, and more specifically multilingual assessment supervision models, there is very limited literature to guide mental health practitioners who hold supervisory positions. However, Allen (2007) describes a "Multicultural Assessment Supervision Model" that could be applied to the supervision of multilingual assessments. Allen's (2007) model is competency-based in that it focuses on eight competencies that supervisors and supervisees need to obtain and utilize in providing appropriate multicultural assessment. The eight competencies are knowledge in: "(1) measurement theory and construct validity relevant to culture and skills; (2) multicultural collaborative assessment; (3) culturally appropriate interviewing and culturally congruent assessment services practices; (4) acculturation status assessment; (5) culturally grounded test interpretation; (6) use of local norms and tests; (7) multicultural report writing; and (8) multicultural assessment ethical decisions." (P. 250)

Following are knowledge-specific competencies based on Allen's (2007) model applied to multilingual assessment competencies and based on research cited previously in this chapter. The competencies described in Allen's model are also relevant to linguistically diverse individuals, as culture based on multiple identities (i.e., gender, sexual orientation, ethnicity, race, socioeconomic status, disability) is also very much part of the linguistically diverse individual's identity. These competencies therefore complement those outlined earlier in the Multicultural Assessment Supervision Model (Allen, 2007).

1. Knowledge in ethical and legal mandates and professional guidelines on the provision of assessment services to English language learners
2. Knowledge in the development of first and second language and related processes and instructional models and guidelines on second language acquisition pedagogy (Ortiz, 2002)
3. Knowledge in the use of interpreters and attendant ethical guidelines

While knowledge in each of these areas represents an essential component to effective supervision in the arena of language diversity, knowledge in the abstract is by no means enough to ensure an ethical and effective supervisory relationship. Specific skills and values related to this aspect of professional practice will be explored in the following sections, as well.

SKILLS

Knowledge of SLA instructional models and guiding pedagogical principles is relevant in that an assessor must be aware of the research-based principles and strategies that have been shown to be effective for the academic success of ELLs (Echevarria et al., 2004). This knowledge is important in placing the experience of the ELL in context, understanding important dynamics that may impact the referral question, and developing effective and relevant recommendations. This section addresses practical applications of knowledge in these areas, as well as specific methods and considerations when putting this knowledge into practice.

Assessment Skills

An ELL's proficiency in his or her native language and in English needs to be considered prior to deciding on whether an assessment should occur in English or the client's first language. It is important to note that any one word in English may be conveyed by many words with varying connotations in the client's language (Ji, Zhang, & Nisbett, 2004), and that regional variations/cultural referents can further affect the utility of an instrument. In addition, instruments may vary on their *semantic* or *linguistic equivalence*—the degree to which an instrument retains its meaning across cultures and after translation (Marsella, 2001).

During a clinical interview, the client may be unable to fully explain the symptoms experienced or ask questions related to treatment, which affects his or her ability to actively participate in the process. Thus, the more structured the clinical interview, the less likely the mental health practitioner will misinterpret the responses due to communication barriers (Aklin & Turner, 2006). In addition, body language, which can sometimes convey affective tone, varies from culture to culture and may be misperceived by the mental health practitioner; similarly, due to language barriers, a client may pay closer attention to a mental health practitioner's nonverbal expressions. According to Aklin and Turner (2006), factors such as language barriers and/or dialect and language capabilities can influence the course of a clinical interview. Certain subgroups, such as children and international students, may require increased awareness on the part of the mental health practitioner. These types of factors may be present for a broad age range of students, from preschool to college age. Bagnato and Neisworth (2005) studied professionals' views of the difficulties in using traditional assessment measures of intelligence with preschool children, and found that the primary reasons for determining that a child was untestable included the child's language deficits and language demands of the standardized measures.

While there was initially a decrease in enrollment after September 11, 2001, universities have seen a steady increase in the enrollment of international students in recent years. According to the Institute of International Education, recent figures suggest that there are nearly 624,000 international students in the United States (Bhandari, 2009). India reportedly sent the most students, followed by China and South Korea (Chow & Marcus, 2008). These international students may face a number of psychological concerns in addition to trying to maintain their academic load. While beyond the scope of this chapter, please see Singaravelu and Pope (2003) for a thorough review of the psychological issues in counseling of international students.

As mentioned earlier, different regional dialects, cultural referents, and colloquialisms can affect the utility of any assessment tool. The World Health Organization (WHO) has identified guidelines that assist in developing different language versions of English assessment tools considered to be conceptually equivalent in each of the target countries/cultures (http://www.who.int). The process recommended by WHO for development of these types of assessments includes forward translation, expert panel back translation, pre-testing and cognitive interviewing, and then creation of the final version of the measure. Despite guidelines for the translation of assessment tools, Vazquez-Nuttal et al. (2001) advise mental health practitioners to remain mindful that the "constructs, procedures, tools, and standards used in the process were conceived, developed, and designed from the vantage point of a particular culture" (p. 266).

Determination of Language of Assessment

Language assessment for SLLs is governed by case law, federal law, and professional guidelines (see, e.g., Rhodes et al., 2005). Specifically, an individual must be assessed in the language or mode of communication in which he or she is most proficient, if such a test is available (IDEIA, 2004). The assessment could be conducted either by an assessor who is proficient in the individual's first language or through the use of an interpreter.

When determining language proficiency for individuals, it is important to differentiate between social and academic language. Cummins (1984) coined the terms Basic Interpersonal Communication Skills (BICS) and Cognitive Academic Language Proficiency (CALP) to distinguish proficiencies in these two areas. BICS is the language learned and utilized within social contexts and usually develops between 2 and 3 years after exposure to the second language, while CALP takes 5 to 7 years to develop and is the language required to succeed in academic settings with little support or context (Martines & Rodriguez-Srednicki, 2007; Miramontes, Nadeau, & Commins, 1997; Ortiz & Ochoa, 2005; Rhodes et al., 2005). Other research has shown that it can take up to 7 to 10 years to develop CALP, depending largely on formal education background in one's native language (Thomas & Collier, 2006 in Haynes, 2007).

Language of assessment of a student should be determined and/or results be interpreted considering the student's level of CALP, as opposed to his or her BICS, if the content being assessed is highly academic (i.e., cognitive and academic tests). There are students whose BICS are advanced in their second language; this may lead to a false assumption that the student should also do well academically and test well in that language. However, the student's level of CALP would be the best indicator of the appropriate language in which to conduct formal and norm-referenced or standardized assessment, as most such tests measure academic language proficiency, not the social/conversational language abilities encompassed by the student's BICS. It is important to note, however, that academic testing in a student's first language will only yield valid results if the student has or is being instructed in his/her first language. If the student has or is not receiving instruction in his/her first language, the student's level of CALP and exposure to the second language instruction should be considered when making interpretations and recommendations. In addition, Rhodes et al. (2005) recommend that language proficiency be measured through multiple means, including formal and informal measures of both oral and academic language and receptive/expressive language skills. If possible, these assessments should be conducted in both languages. Relatedly, in the 1990s a National Educational Goals Panel comprised of experts in early childhood development and assessment established six general principles and recommendations to guide assessment practices for professionals and lawmakers (Shepard, Kagan, & Wurtz, 1992, p. 5). Recognizing that all assessments are, to some extent, measures of language, the panel recommended that assessments be linguistically appropriate.

Examples of formal language proficiency tests in both languages are the Woodcock-Muñoz Language Survey—Revised (WMLS-R; Woodcock, Muñoz-Sandoval, Ruef, & Alvarado, 2009) (assesses in both Spanish and English), the Basic Inventory of Natural Language (BINL; Herbert, 1986) (available in various languages), and the Bilingual Verbal Ability Test (BVAT; Muñoz-Sandoval, Cummins, Alvarado, & Ruef, 1998) (available in various languages). In addition, currently all states within the United States are mandated by the No Child Left Behind Act of 2001 to assess the English language proficiency of all public school students in third through eighth grade in the areas of speaking, listening, reading, writing, and comprehension skills (http://www.learningpt.org/pdfs/qkey5.pdf; retrieved November 30, 2008). These state proficiency tests are meant to assess both oral and academic language and could be utilized in combination with other methods to develop a more complete picture of a student's overall linguistic ability.

As alluded to earlier, because of the numerous limitations of language proficiency testing, Rhodes et al. (2005) suggest conducting informal assessments of language proficiency in conjunction with formal testing. Informal methods described by the authors include observations of a student's use of both languages in academic as well as social settings, the use of parent questionnaires (such as the Bilingual Language Proficiency Questionnaire; Mattes and Santiago, 1985), and teacher questionnaires (e.g., the Student Oral Language Observation Matrix—SOLOM; Rhodes et al., 2005). Other methods noted are storytelling, story retelling, cloze techniques (oral or written fill-in-the-blank exercises), and analyzing language samples for "structural mistakes and pragmatic features" (Rhodes et al., 2005, p. 145).

One of these techniques, storytelling, can be a particularly accessible way to informally assess students' levels of proficiency. Students may be asked to tell about favorite books or movies in the language in which they are most proficient, and then asked to retell the same story in English. Close attention is paid to sentence length, grammar, and vocabulary use in both languages, as well as the ability to tell a story with sufficient detail and in proper sequence. Rhodes et al. (2005) provide a list of questions recommended by Roseberry-McKibbin (2002) to assist in the evaluation of the quality of the student's story (p. 144). The questions are:

1. Does the student organize the story in such a way that it can be easily understood?
2. Is the information in the story comprehensible to the listener?
3. Does the student give elaborated comments, opinions, and explanations that are relevant to the story?
4. Does the student include all the major details of the story?
5. If questioned, can the student remember specific details from the story?

The following vignette (6.2) highlights some of the questions raised by this process.

CASE VIGNETTE 6.2

Melham, a 12-year-old boy who immigrated with his parents to the United States from Lebanon approximately 6 weeks ago, is referred to you for an evaluation of classroom placement. Melham's family's language of origin is Arabic; in addition, he and his siblings speak French fluently. You are told by school administrators that his English is "shaky," but that he "gets by" in the classroom and appears to communicate fairly well in English with his two brothers and sister (who attend the same school). According to his teachers, he rarely initiates verbal contact with peers or others outside of his family, but answers questions when asked directly. Records indicate that Melham's academic performance was high average prior to his family's relocation.

Questions:
1. In Melham's case, what language(s) of assessment would you utilize?
2. What informal and formal measures would you utilize to obtain information about Melham's conversational and academic language proficiency?

As this example illustrates, in thinking through the dynamics of assessment, mental health practitioners must consider a variety of factors that may impact the assessment process, and carefully determine which assessment tools are likely to obtain the most accurate and useful information.

Assessors also need to be aware of certain language processes that typify second language development, such as Interference, Interlanguage, Silent Period, Code Switching, and Language Loss (Roseberry-McKibbin, 2002). Characteristics and clinical implications of each of these processes are outlined in the following chart; each term is discussed in more detail in the text following.

Interference errors, according to Krashen and Terrell (1997), occur when the individual falls back on his or her first language when a language rule for the second language is lacking. *Code-switching* to one's second language, in a

Language Processes, Characteristics, and Clinical Relevance

Language Process	Characteristics	Relevance to Practice
Interference	• Language or some form of communication in first language (L1) presents itself in the second language (L2). • Usually occurs in the academic setting. • *Example:* When an ELL wants to communicate to a peer to "have a seat." In Spanish, this would be stated as "tome una silla." *Tome una silla* literally translates to "take a seat." (Rhodes et al., 2005)	• Important to rule out interference as a cause for errors in second language.
Interlanguage	• Transitory • ELL develops a personal set of rules of language composed of a combination of L1 and L2, which eventually more closely resembles L2. • It is a hypotheses testing process for ELLs as they navigate through learning a second language.	• Important to rule out interference as a cause for errors in second language.

(continued)

Language Processes, Characteristics, and Clinical Relevance (*continued*)

Language Process	Characteristics	Relevance to Practice
Silent Period	• First stage within Krashen's stages of second language acquisition. • Significantly limited verbal communication. • ELL more of an observer than a participant.	• Important to rule out Silent Period as the reason for an ELL's lack of verbalizations or interactions with others and passivity, to reduce misdiagnoses of selective mutism, autism, and cognitive/language disability.
Code-Switching	• Switching from one language to another during conversation, most commonly between sentences. • *Example:* "Yo fui al Mercado" ("I went to the grocery store"). "I bought my favorite candy." • Could also be utilized as an acceptable mode of communication within a cultural group, despite developed proficiency in both languages.	• Important to rule out code-switching as a cause for errors in second language. • Important to assess whether code-switching is an acceptable mode of communication within individual's culture.
Language Loss	• Loss of first language (L1) due to exposure to second language (L2) and limited opportunity to adequately develop first language. • Could include lack of development of L1, and presence of deficits in L1 and L2.	• Important to rule out language loss as a cause for errors in second language.

Adapted from Rhodes et al. (2005); Roseberry-McKibbin (2002).

therapeutic setting, may be used by the client to address issues that might be upsetting when discussed in his or her first language (Santiago-Rivera & Altarriba, 2009). *Language loss* may also be a normal part of acquiring a second language and usually involves the loss of the first language due to exposure to the second language, coupled with limited opportunity to continue developing the first language. Two forms of language loss that could occur as part of the normal process of acquiring a second language are: *subtractive bilingualism*, which is lack of development of L1, and *semilingualism*, which refers to the presence of deficits in both L1 and L2 (Schiff-Myers, 2002). Individuals who experience language loss in their native languages may eventually develop *additive bilingualism*, which is the development of fluency in both L1 and L2 (Schiff-Myers, 2002). One or all of these processes can occur in the normal course of development of a SLL. The following vignette highlights the importance of ruling out normal SLA processes as a major factor contributing to

the presenting problems when an ELL is referred for assessment.

In considering how you might respond to Case Vignette 6.3, review the stages of SLA described previously. To determine if the student's behavior is related to issues other than language acquisition, you might consider questions regarding the length of time the student has been exposed to the second language and information about the student's overall social-emotional functioning. Individuals who know the student well might be able to provide information about whether this behavioral presentation is also seen at home and was evident prior to SLA. You may want to consider the constant effort that is required to listen and speak in a new language when evaluating the student's behavior.

Diagnostic and Conceptualization Skills

Once the relevant information has been obtained as described earlier, the next step involves framing the client's presenting problems in a useful and

CASE VIGNETTE 6.3

You are conducting a classroom observation of an ELL student. You observe that the student is passive and does not verbally interact with his peers or teachers. When he is asked a question in English, he simply stares or puts his head down and seems sad.

Questions:
1. What language process would you want to rule out in this scenario?
2. What type of questions could you ask to determine whether the student's behaviors are likely a result of a typical second language acquisition process?

culturally relevant way. This includes evaluating the degree to which confounding factors (such as individual and cultural diversity, the impact of the SLA learning process and attendant variables, etc.) impact the individual's current functioning and referral behavior. Consideration should also be given to the extent that the ELL's language acquisition process is impacted by environmental and other external factors. This analysis is an essential component of accurate diagnosis. The following is a list of cultural and linguistic factors that could impact learning for ELLs:

- History of inconsistent language of instruction.
- Current instruction delivered in student's less dominant language, as determined by informal and formal language assessments in both languages, and without sheltered English instruction.
- Student is not receiving instruction on a daily basis to develop English language skills.
- It is the student's first or second year of second language instruction.
- The student migrated from a country where the experience of trauma is likely.
- The student has limited opportunity to practice the second language.
- The student is experiencing stress related to acculturation and/or bicultural-biracial/multicultural identity development.

Based on these factors, there are a series of questions that the first author developed to aid in ruling out SLA factors as reasons for an ELL's learning problems (Cultural and Linguistic

Checklist; Pazos, 2009; please see the Resources section).

In considering responses to Case Vignette 6.4, the reader is referred to the stages of SLA. Information about Mercy's individual characteristics, such as her native language, migration history, and acculturation process, also needs to be considered. It would be important to take into account the fact that, for older children such as Mercy, there may be a difference between interacting with native English speakers on the playground and interacting effectively in a classroom setting. Additionally, this vignette is an example of a student who has developed her BICS, but is still developing her CALP. This presentation can be misleading to teachers and others because her academic work is so discrepant from her oral presentation in less academically demanding tasks. This information is useful to share with teachers, especially if they do not have training in SLA, as it provides them with a different framework in which to analyze their ELL students' academic progress.

Finally, although beyond the scope of this chapter to address in detail, it is important to be aware of the wide range of systemic variables that may be impacting the referral issues and Mercy's life experiences. Issues of bias and marginalization should be addressed, and mental health practitioners should explore the assumptions, beliefs, and reactions at play in the dynamic—including their own and those of the referral source. A recent story featured on National Public Radio, for example, highlighted differential expectations held by school

CASE VIGNETTE 6.4

Mercy is a 12-year-old girl from Somalia who arrived in the United States approximately $1\frac{1}{2}$ years ago. She is currently being instructed in English with sheltered English instruction and English language development. Mercy often seems distracted, inattentive, and fatigued, and displays low motivation and self-confidence. Academically, she is falling behind all the other ELLs in the classroom. Mercy initially presented as nonverbal and unresponsive, but is now slowly utilizing English in the classroom setting and is often seen in the playground and nonacademic settings speaking English well when conversing with her peers. Her teacher strongly feels that Mercy has a learning disability because she is able to speak English well, and at times translates for other ELL students, but is not showing this proficiency in her academics.

Questions:
1. What stage of second language acquisition is Mercy experiencing?
2. What individual and cultural identity factors should you consider in your assessment?
3. What may be some cultural and linguistic factors impacting this referral (e.g., personal factors, second language and cultural learning effects, learning environment, assessor's beliefs)?
4. How might you address the teacher's concerns about Mercy's discrepant abilities in the use of English in academic versus social settings?

administrators and educators regarding Chinese-American versus Dominican-American students ("At School, Lower Expectations of Dominican Kids," July 31, 2009). The current national debate on immigration, ongoing "achievement gaps" between students of color and White students (see, e.g., Teske, Brodsky, & Medler, 1978), and myriad other contextual factors form the societal backdrop against which ELLs live, attend school, work, and function on a day-to-day basis. While difficult to quantify at the individual level, the influence of these dynamics on mental health functioning and clinical presentation is undoubtedly profound.

Intervention Skills

Although Spanish is the most commonly spoken language other than English in the United States (Borsato & Padilla, 2008), mental health practitioners may be presented with clients who speak other languages. In 2007, according to the Department of Homeland Security, the leading countries of nationality for refugee admissions were Burma (Myanmar) (29%), Somalia (14%), and Iran (11%). The leading countries of nationality for granted-asylum cases were China (25%), Columbia (8.6%), and Haiti (6.6%).

From the service-delivery perspective, there is a shortage of bilingual mental health practitioners. In an investigation of the current practices of school psychologists, Ochoa, Riccio, Jimenez, Garcia de Alba, and Sines (2004) found that only 33 percent of the school psychologists who assess ELLs are bilingual; of the 78 percent who reported using an interpreter during such assessments, only half had previously received training on working with interpreters.

The Use of Interpreters in Mental Health Practice

In light of these statistics, it is likely that more mental health practitioners will need to utilize the services of interpreters. Typically, interpreters are bilingual individuals who are used to facilitate communication between those who do not speak the same language. Thus, working with interpreters is an intervention skill that is needed to ensure competency when working with linguistically diverse clients.

The addition of an interpreter significantly alters the relationship between the mental health practitioner and client. As a function of convenience/resources, mental health practitioners may use untrained interpreters (such as family members or individuals from the same cultural community). However, the use of family is considered problematic (Prendes-Lintel, 2001), as the family member may minimize and/or magnify the client's symptoms based on a personal agenda. While immigrant communities often use children as interpreters for the older generation, the potential for emotional harm is heightened within a mental health setting. The use of children as interpreters may make it difficult for the adult (parent/relative) to openly discuss personal information and may certainly further disrupt the parent–child boundary by having the parent rely on the child for identification and resolution of mental health difficulties.

For example, in Case Vignette 6.5, how might the mental health practitioner structure the clinical interview in a way that minimizes the emotional harm to the child (although now an adult) and maximizes the ability of the client to disclose aspects of her trauma? What other factors, besides language, would influence your decision? Are there legal/ethical concerns about which to make the parties aware prior to and/or during the clinical interview?

Trained interpreters should possess empathy, good interpersonal skills, and a reasonable degree of psychological mindedness (see Resources section for a link to training suggestions for interpreters and therapists; Miletic et al., 2006). One issue for mental health practitioners to consider when working with interpreters is the level of trust and attachment between the interpreter and client. According to Miller, Martell, Pazdirek, Caruth and Lopez (2005), therapists may initially feel a sense of discomfort and/or feel excluded. The authors note that feelings of uncertainty or competition may arise between the mental health practitioner and the interpreter. It may take longer for the therapist–client relationship to unfold when an interpreter is present.

Interpreters were once regarded as a kind of "black box," in that any personal aspects the interpreter brought into the therapy room were not seen as clinically relevant unless they adversely interfered with therapy (Westermeyer, 2007). More recently, interpreters have been understood to provide an essential cultural context for a client's ideas and behaviors. Those who interpret for refugee populations face the added potential complexity of dealing with psychological trauma, multiple losses, and re-traumatization, as the stories they are interpreting may be similar to their own life experiences.

Hays (2001), for example, recommends conducting pre- and post-sessions between the therapist and the interpreter to learn about the interpreter's background, establish rapport, and address the goals of the session/interview/treatment. Miller and colleagues (2005) also provide recommendations for the type of training therapists should receive on working effectively with interpreters. They suggest that therapists receive the following training in their skills development (p. 36):

CASE VIGNETTE 6.5

You are a mental health practitioner at a community mental health clinic, and are conducting a clinical interview on a 33-year-old Spanish-speaking female. She is accompanied by her 18-year-old daughter, who is serving as the translator. The daughter explains that her mother has been tearful, has had difficulty sleeping, is not eating, and complains of somatic symptoms. In elaborating on the details of her symptoms, the mother starts to explain that she has a trauma history previously unknown to the daughter.

CASE VIGNETTE 6.6

An English-speaking Caucasian mental health practitioner is assessing the need for services for a Bosnian Muslim client. The interpreter is a Bosnian Serb. Both interpreter and client have been in the country for more than 2 years, and they did not know each other in Bosnia. Approximately one hour into the interview, the client expresses some distrust of the interpreter due to the past ethnic conflict between the groups.

Questions:
1. Do you think the client's distrust affected the quality of the information being conveyed?
2. How would your knowledge of the Bosnian conflict have changed your assessment of the client's initial behavior (vagueness, silence, seeming annoyance)?
3. How might you have managed the interview structure to better facilitate the client feeling supported and accepted by the interpreter?
4. Have you asked your questions using simple terms and language, such that they can be easily interpretable?

1. Knowing and applying the different models of interpretation and the benefits and limitations of each
2. Developing a level of comfort necessary to allow the client's attachment to the therapist to develop after the client's attachment to the interpreter has been established
3. Allowing interpreters to interpret material in either the first or the third person
4. Holding regular debriefing meetings with interpreters to allow the processing of emotional material
5. Explaining therapy techniques to interpreters before their use in session to avoid confusion

Applying Principles of Second Language Instruction

Understanding the principles of second language learning, as detailed earlier, is imperative in providing services to ELLs. In Case Vignette 6.7 (on the following page), the reader is asked to examine the impact of the SLA process on the client's presentation, and to consider SLA instructional models when making recommendations.

Case Vignette 6.7 points the reader again to the stages of SLA to gain a better understanding of Juan's instructional needs. At this point, Juan

is still developing his academic language in English and therefore may be exhibiting learning difficulties that may or may not be associated with a learning disability. It will be important to obtain information about the level of support Juan is receiving by asking what types of English language instruction strategies have been utilized. This will also guide the consultant in providing recommendations for Juan's instruction. Finally, it will be important to obtain information about Juan's prior learning experience, in his first language. Did he exhibit learning difficulties in his native language or are his difficulties new to his profile?

Learning Environment

In addition to quality instruction for ELLs, effective SLA also depends in part on the learning environment. The level of support an ELL receives in the environment is crucial to success in SLA. This support could take the form of meaningful discussions in the classroom about similarities and differences between cultures; it should also include the development of policies, procedures, and curricula that reflect respect for the student's language(s) and culture(s) (Miramontes et al., 1997). Students need to

CASE VIGNETTE 6.7

Juan is a 10-year-old boy who migrated from Central America 2 years ago. He is currently receiving English instruction and has a history of formal education in his first language. When interacting with his peers, he often utilizes his first language (Spanish). However, in the classroom he seldom speaks, primarily in English. Overall, when he does speak, he speaks in short and incomplete sentences, exhibits grammatical errors, and often switches languages between sentences. Juan has been referred to you because his teacher is concerned that he has a learning disability.

Questions:
1. How would you use information about Juan's stage of SLA to guide your recommendations for instruction?
2. Is there any other information you want to obtain about Juan?
3. What teaching guidelines would you recommend be used in Juan's classroom?

feel a certain level of comfort and safety in their classrooms in order to take risks in speaking and learning in a second language (Miramontes et al., 1997).

A corollary to this theme is the increased support available to students when schools and teachers actively encourage and maintain family involvement (Delgado-Gaitan, 2004). There are numerous areas within this topic that are beyond the scope of this chapter (i.e., forming school-wide parent-involvement programs or school-family-community partnerships); however, there are some general steps that can be taken to increase family involvement in an ELL's learning process. These steps include, but are not limited to: (a) demonstration of acceptance of family's interactions in the school, (b) discussions of the school's expectations of the parents and the parents' expectations of school, and (c) the school's valuing of the parents' cultural/ethnic/language backgrounds and inclusion of these factors into classroom and homework activities. If a parent/caregiver is not dominant in the language of instruction or has limited academic proficiency, it is important that information be disbursed to parents in a manner that they can understand so that they can contribute to the learning process at home. For example, one creative solution recently implemented by Denver Public Schools

(DPS), a district in which Spanish is spoken in the home by 40 percent of students' families, is a weekly radio talk show broadcast in Spanish (Garcia, 2009). This outreach program, described as the first of its kind in the country, is explicitly geared toward increasing engagement between Spanish-speaking parents and the school district in a culturally relevant and accessible way.

Following is list of best practices that have been noted in the literature on assessment of ELLs (Guajardo Alvarado, 2006; Lopez, Lamar, & Scully-Demartini, 1992; Ortiz, 2002; Ortiz & Dynda, 2005; Ortiz & Ochoa, 2005; Rhodes et al., 2005):

1. Assess in most proficient language(s).
2. If possible and applicable, assess in both language(s); this is especially helpful in ruling out a potential learning disability.
3. Rule out cultural and linguistic factors (i.e., low English proficiency, acculturation, effects of learning a second language and culture, quality and quantity of formal education, and SLA models of instruction).
4. Include a written statement within the body of the report about any nonstandardized administration practices and the limitations of the current test concerning cultural and linguistic factors.

5. Report on cultural and linguistic factors and how these impact the presenting problem.
6. Indicate whether an interpreter and/or cultural consultant was utilized and any information gathered from these sources relevant to testing behavior and assessment results.
7. Include recommendations and interventions that address cultural and linguistic factors, instructional methodology or strategies designed to increase the ELL's comprehension of second language instruction, and home and environmental factors that can support second language learning of the student.

You may wish to utilize the sample report provided by the first author to help inform your report writing practices. The report concerns a Spanish-dominant student receiving Spanish instruction (see Resources section).

Skills in Supervision and Training

In addition to the knowledge required to provide appropriate supervision in this area, a number of skills-based competencies further clarify the Multicultural Assessment Supervision Model (Allen, 2007) discussed earlier. These include:

1. Skills in multicultural collaborative assessment, including collaboration with cultural consultants and/or interpreters
2. Skills in culturally and linguistically based interpretation of formal and informal assessment results
3. Skills in integrating assessment data and reporting data in a culturally and linguistically relevant context

4. Skills in providing recommendations that address the environmental/external factors, cultural and linguistic factors, and individual factors that contribute to the presenting problem
5. Skills in applying knowledge of second language acquisition and acculturation to supervisees who are practicing in their second language

Specific suggestions for supervisory exercises may be found in the Resources section of this chapter.

VALUES AND ATTITUDES

In examining the role of language within psychotherapy and psychological assessment, it is important to note that nondiscriminatory practices involve more than just selecting the best standardized tool. Mental health practitioners need to be aware of their own personal and professional biases when interpreting clinical interview and assessment data. In fact, the questions asked during interviews—and even the specific behaviors observed (or attended to)—may be influenced by preconceptions held. In Case Vignette 6.8, what are your thoughts as to how these various groups of students might present in the classroom? With their peers? With teachers? With you as a therapist?

In order to provide culturally and linguistically responsive services to SLLs, one needs to be aware of one's values and attitudes around bilingualism and become knowledgeable regarding the "myths and realities" of SLA. For example,

CASE VIGNETTE 6.8

You are a newly hired psychologist in a suburban middle school. The school population is diverse, with children who vary in their background, skills, and past experiences. Some students attended school in their home country, but their literacy and academic skills are in another language. Some students have come as refugees where they did not have the opportunities for consistent schooling.

Ortiz (2002) describes a process of non-discriminatory assessment focused on conceptualizing referral concerns/behaviors as being results of external or environmental factors, as opposed to intrinsic factors (p. 1323). This type of hypothesis setting is meant to reduce the *confirmatory bias* of the assessor, which is defined as bias in test/data selection and interpretation as a result of "preconceived notions of dysfunction or discriminatory misattributions of performance or behavior" (Ortiz, 2002, p. 1323). Assessor's beliefs about the ability of the individual being assessed could influence the assessments selected and subsequent interpretations (Vazquez-Nuttal et al., 2002), along with diagnostic and placement decisions (Gonzalez, Bauerle, Black, & Felix-Holt, 1999). An assessor's beliefs and attitudes about an ELL could influence that assessor's choices in the type and range of data collected, the manner in which testing is conducted, and the interpretation of results. In order to reduce this potential for bias, it is important for assessors to understand cultural and linguistic factors that might impact SLA, learning, and social-emotional and behavioral functioning, in addition to being aware of their own beliefs, attitudes, and values.

Listed at the end of this chapter are questions that mental health practitioners can ask themselves and/or their supervisees to determine their values and attitudes surrounding these issues (see Resources).

It is also helpful to explore the origins of such values and attitudes. Therefore, it becomes important to be aware of common myths versus the realities of SLA (Haynes, 2002; Haynes, 2007). For example, one commonly held belief is that children learn a second language more quickly than adult SLLs. In fact, although children tend to outperform older individuals in the realm of pronunciation, adults and teenagers have language-learning strategies that enable them to learn a second language more readily than their younger counterparts (Haynes, 2002). A corollary myth involves the perception that previous generations of immigrants to the United States

learned English well, got jobs, and achieved success in this country with no specialized education or support. Again, the reality is somewhat different. The types of jobs available to prior immigrant cohorts tended to be industrial in nature, requiring minimal education and communication in English; even in 1911, however, the U.S. Immigration Service found that children of immigrants struggled in the educational system, with 77 percent of Italian, 60 percent of Russian, and 51 percent of German immigrant children at least one grade level behind their peers (compared to 28% of American-born children) (Haynes, 2002; Haynes, 2007). Included in the Resources section is a questionnaire that can be filled out to assess one's level of knowledge of these dimensions of SLA. Following the questions are the correct responses with explanations provided to inform the reader of the rationale behind the response (Haynes, 2007).

Increasing sensitivity to SLA also involves becoming aware of the experience of learning a second language. This could include taking a class in a language other than one's L1 or participating in other experiential activities that provide insight into the experience of communicating in a language in which one is less proficient. One exercise that could be used is the "communication game," which is useful in providing some insight into the emotional experience of having communication barriers (Haynes, 2002) (see Resources).

Values and Attitudes in Supervision and Training

In addition to the supervision-related knowledge and skills outlined earlier, the Competency Benchmarks Document (APA, 2007) stresses supervisory competency as it relates to the supervisor's level of awareness around how his or her own "self" influences the supervisory relationship and the provision of services to diverse individuals. Falender and Shafranske (2007) use the term *metacompetence* to describe a supervisor's ability to be aware of his or her level of knowledge and skills and to be cognizant of the knowledge and skills not yet obtained. The authors suggest that such metacompetence is developed through self-assessment. Although no self-assessment tool specific to this area appears to have been developed to date, a few self-assessment questionnaires addressing multicultural competence do exist. These include the Multicultural Counseling Inventory (Sodowsky, Taffe, Gutkin, & Wise, 2007), the California Brief Multicultural Competence Scale (Gamst et al., 2004), and the Multicultural Supervision Inventory (Pope-Davis, Toporek, & Ortega-Villalobos, 2003) These, along with the self-assessment of knowledge and skills related to multilingual assessment noted earlier, could be utilized for the supervisor as well as the supervisee.

One way to assure that cultural and linguistic issues are acknowledged within the supervisory process is for the supervisor to develop or utilize a set of questions to bring forth an awareness of the supervisee's beliefs around culturally and linguistically diverse individuals. This is especially important because of the influence of evaluators' beliefs and backgrounds on test selection, administration, and interpretation, which have been well documented (Ortiz, 2002). Gonzalez and colleagues (1999) developed a set of questions to aid evaluators in becoming more aware of their "beliefs about cognitive-linguistic development and measures" (p. 295). Questions for exploration include:

1. According to your knowledge, how does intelligence develop in culturally and linguistically diverse (CLD) children?
2. According to your knowledge, how does language develop in CLD children?
3. According to your view, what is the role that culture plays in the development of intelligence?
4. Is language development similar or different in majority and CLD children?
5. Is the development of intelligence similar or different in majority and CLD children?
6. What are your views about assessing CLD children?

7. What are your views about standardized assessments?

It is important for supervisors to recognize the impact of the supervisory relationship in terms of clinical efficacy and supervisee growth. Allen (2007) terms this a "parallel process" in that a supervisor's focus on cultural issues during supervision could impact the attention the supervisee places on these issues when actually conducting the assessment. This could be applied to linguistic issues as well. Allen (2007) adds that the "working alliance" between supervisors and supervisees and the ability of supervisors to supervise students from diverse cultural backgrounds are also skills required for effective multicultural supervision. This is especially true if a supervisor is supervising someone who is from a different cultural background than that of the supervisor and may be practicing in his or her second language. Consider, for example, the dynamics at work in Case Vignette 6.9.

As is clear from this vignette, the supervisor needs to be aware of his or her own biases and values concerning bilingualism so as not to impose these in the evaluation process. In addition, SLA and acculturation variables need to be considered when supervising a student who is practicing in his or her second language. For instance, a psychology student writing assessment reports in her second language may require more time to complete the reports if her fluency in writing technical and psychological reports is stronger in the first language. This is not a function of competency in the focus skill, but rather a function of the SLA process. Verdinelli and Biever (1994) reported that bilingual supervisees may also feel burdened (e.g., due to the additional work of providing assessment reports in two languages), exploited, and isolated; they might need guidance in expressing theoretical and psychological concerns in Spanish.

Relational Values and Attitudes

Finally, in working with linguistically diverse clients, the competent mental health practitioner

CASE VIGNETTE 6.9

Loritza is a psychology student from Venezuela who recently migrated to the United States. She obtained her bachelor's degree in psychology in Venezuela with high academic marks and had some experience working in the local mental health clinic in her town before coming to the United States. Loritza is now in an academic program in the United States to obtain a master's-level degree in psychology. Loritza's supervisor is U.S. born and is a native English speaker.

Questions:
1. What difficulties might both Loritza and her supervisor encounter during supervision?
2. What steps could the supervisor take to problem-solve or address these potential difficulties?

must be able to form a positive therapeutic relationship with the client, a task made more difficult if the language of communication differs. In doing so, the professional must cultivate and maintain an attitude of respectful, humble, open-minded inquiry. Awareness that some languages do not easily differentiate between constructs such as "thinking" and "feeling" (Okawa, 2008) and that nonverbal behavior (body language such as facial expressions, eye contact, shrugs, and hand gestures, for example) varies from culture to culture allows the mental health practitioner to display linguistic/cultural sensitivity with clients. In working with individuals from diverse linguistic backgrounds, this awareness and willingness to meet the client in his or her comfort zone often assumes particular importance. Aviera (n.d.), for example, notes that many Latino clients will view a relationship as positive in part when it has elements of being mutual and reciprocal. The *compromiso* (commitment) that develops brings expectations of mutual behavior such as "responsiveness," *respeto* (respect), *confianza* (trust), *dignidad* (dignity), as well as an allowance for ample space and time. Mutual self-disclosure is expected, and *personalismo* (being personable) is a part of the foundation of the relationship.

These values and attitudes, in short, form the basis of the trusting therapeutic relationship— "one of the goals, or rather requirements, of therapy" (Aviera, n.d.)—and a critical component of the provision of mental health services across settings, language groups, and client populations.

SUMMARY

The knowledge base, skill set, and values/attitudes necessary to provide competent services to English language learners and others from diverse language backgrounds are complex and require a sophisticated understanding of the dynamics of second language acquisition, models of language instruction, strengths and limitations of assessment protocols of various types, specific diagnostic considerations and confounds, and particularized intervention strategies. To the extent that mental health professionals embrace the challenging and rewarding process of personal reflection, self-examination, and professional growth required to cultivate meaningful, effective, and culturally sensitive relationships with the CLD individuals they serve across all language groups, they facilitate a literal and metaphorical dialogue critical to both the field and the broader community.

RESOURCES

The following resources are provided as suggestions for further inquiry and as tools students, clinicians, trainees, and supervisors can utilize to help improve the quality of the services they provide.

SUGGESTED EXERCISES AND ACTIVITIES

EXERCISE 6.1: MYTHS AND REALITIES

Myths of Second Language Acquisition

Answer each of the following statements with true or false.

1. Adults learn second languages more quickly and easily than young children.   T   F

2. According to research, students in ESL-only programs, with no schooling in their   T   F
native language, take 7–10 years to reach grade-level norms.

3. Many immigrant children have learning disabilities, not language problems. They   T   F
speak English just fine but they are still failing academically.

4. Previous generations of immigrants learned how to speak English without all the   T   F
special language programs that immigrant children receive now. It was sink or
swim and they did just fine!

5. English language learners will acquire English faster if their parents speak English   T   F
at home.

6. The more time students spend soaking up English in the mainstream classroom,   T   F
the faster they will learn the language.

7. Once students can speak English, they are ready to undertake the academic tasks   T   F
of the mainstream classroom.

8. Cognitive and academic development in native language has an important and   T   F
positive effect on second language acquisition.

9. The culture of students doesn't affect how long it takes them to acquire English.   T   F
All students learn language the same way.

---

1. **Adults learn second languages more quickly and easily than young children. True:** This
question is more complex than it seems. In controlled research where children have been
compared to adults and teenagers in second language learning, it was found that the adults
and teenagers learned a second language more readily. Yes, children do outperform adults in
the area of pronunciation. Children appear to acquire social language more easily. There is an
old myth that says that children are superior to adults in language learning because their
brains are more flexible. This hypothesis has been much disputed. The differences in ability to
learn languages may be social rather than biological. Children may have more occasions to
interact socially with others. Their requirements for communication are much lower. They
have much less to learn in order to interact in the school setting with their peers. Teenagers
and adults have acquired language learning strategies.

2. **According to research, students in ESL-only programs, with no schooling in their native
language, take 7–10 years to reach grade-level norms. True:** In the Thomas/Collier studies
it was found that in U.S. schools where all instruction is given through the second language
(English), nonnative speakers of English with no schooling in their first language take 7 to 10
years or longer to reach age- and grade-level norms of their native English–speaking peers.
Immigrant students who have had 2 to 3 years of first language schooling in their home
country before they come to the United States take at least 5 to 7 years to reach typical
native-speaker performance. This pattern exists across many student groups, regardless of the
particular home language that students speak, country of origin, socioeconomic status, and
other student background variables.

3. **Many immigrant children have learning disabilities, not language problems. They speak
English just fine but they are still failing academically. False:** We often see children in the

playground who appear to speak English with no problem. Yet when they are in a classroom situation, they just don't seem to grasp the concepts. Many people fail to realize that there are different levels of language proficiency. The language needed for face-to-face communication takes less time to master than the language needed to perform in cognitively demanding situations such as classes and lectures. It takes a child about 2 years to develop the ability to communicate in a second language on the playground, but it takes 5 to 7 years to develop age-appropriate academic language. Many immigrant children have been misdiagnosed in the past as "learning disabled," when in fact the problem was that people misunderstood their fluency on the playground, thinking that it meant they should be able to perform in class as well. Actually, they still needed time and assistance to develop their academic English skills (Cummins, 1984).

4. **Previous generations of immigrants learned how to speak English without all the special language programs that immigrant children receive now. It was sink or swim and they did just fine! False:** Like present-day immigrants, many earlier immigrants had trouble in school. In 1911, the U.S. Immigration Service found that 77 percent of Italian, 60 percent of Russian, and 51 percent of German immigrant children were one or more grade levels behind in school compared to 28 percent of American-born children. Also, the level of education needed to get a job has changed. When immigrants came to this country in the earlier part of this century, they were able to get industrial jobs with relatively little education and not much English. Currently, the job market holds little promise for those without a college education. Low-skilled jobs are being done by machines and computers, or moved to other countries, and jobs in the service industry and high-tech communications are expanding. A final point to keep in mind is that earlier immigrants came mainly from Europe. They came from cultures that were similar in many ways to mainstream U.S. culture. It was easier for them to assimilate into American society because, once they abandoned their home language, they looked like any other "American." Today, many immigrants come from Asia, Latin America, and other non-European countries. They have clear physical attributes that mark them as different from White Americans. Long after they have learned English and acquired jobs in this country, they are still subject to discrimination.

5. **English language learners will acquire academic English faster if their parents speak English at home. False:** Research shows that it is much better for parents to speak in native language to their children. This language will be richer and more complex. It doesn't matter in what language basic concepts are developed. Children will eventually translate that learning to English. So if a child is being read to in native language, parents will spend more time discussing the story, and asking questions. I encourage parents to read in both languages if they can. Never instruct a parent to speak only English at home. If you were in Japan, would you be able to speak only Japanese to your own children after a few months?

6. **The more time students spend soaking up English in the mainstream classroom, the faster they will learn the language. False:** Children need comprehensible input. Imagine that you are sitting in a room of Japanese speakers. You have no idea what they are talking about. You could sit there for a long time and learn very little unless someone helped make that input comprehensible. Language is not "soaked up."

7. **Once students can speak English, they are ready to undertake the academic tasks of the mainstream classroom. False:** Children can speak and socialize way before they can use language for academic purposes. BICS are acquired first. This is social language such as the language needed to interact in the playground and in the classroom. It usually takes students from 1 to 3 years to completely develop this social language. Then children will develop CALP skills. This is the language needed to undertake academic tasks in the mainstream classroom. It includes content-specific vocabulary. It usually takes students from 3 to 7 years or longer to develop CALP.

(continued)

(continued)

8. **Cognitive and academic development in native language has an important and positive effect on second language acquisition. True:** In the Collier/Thomas examination of large data sets across many different research sites, they found that the most significant student background variable is the amount of formal schooling students have received in their first language. Across all program treatments, we have found that nonnative speakers being schooled in a second language for part or all of the school day typically do reasonably well in the early years of schooling (kindergarten through second or third grade). But from fourth grade on through middle school and high school, when the academic and cognitive demands of the curriculum increase rapidly with each succeeding year, students with little or no academic and cognitive development in their first language do less and less well as they move into the upper grades.

9. **The culture of students doesn't affect how long it takes them to acquire English. All students learn language the same way. False:** Culture can affect how long it takes children learn English. Do your students come from modern, industrialized countries or rural, agricultural societies? Do your students come from language backgrounds using a different writing system? These factors will affect how long it takes them to learn English. Previous schooling and school expectations will also affect language learning. Also, the more culture shock experienced by the child, the longer it will take him or her to learn a new language.

Haynes (2002, 2007) provided the responses to Myths of Second Language Acquisition.

EXERCISE 6.2: STATE YOUR POINT OF VIEW

This activity explores the audience's interpretation of multicultural issues and allows participants to see the continuum of cultural perceptions (Haynes, 2007).

1. Set up a continuum by using squares of paper taped to the wall in various parts of the room. Each square should display one of the following statements:

   Agree

   Somewhat Agree

   Somewhat Disagree

   Disagree

2. The facilitator reads a statement and asks the participants to stand in front of the sign that best reflects their views. Some of the sample statements are below.

   • I think the United States should adopt English as the official language so that English would be the only language used by state and federal agencies.

   • It should take our second language learners about 1 year to learn a language (Haynes, 2002).

   • My (great) grandparents came to this country and no one helped them learn English. This is what today's immigrants should be doing.

   • When you become fluent in a foreign language, you should be able to "think like a native."

   • Culture is a broad concept that embraces all aspects of human life. It is everything that humans have learned (Haynes, 2002).

   • A smile means the same thing in every language (Haynes, 2002).

   • Deep down, everyone in the world is just the same (Haynes, 2002).

   • "We will be able to achieve a just and prosperous society only when our schools ensure that everyone commands enough shared background knowledge to be able to communicate effectively with everyone else."

3. Have participants get into groups based on where they are along the continuum and defend their point of view. Encourage participants to change their place at any time. Do not impose your point of view on the participants, but use this activity to see where you may need to present more information.

Source: Haynes (2002, 2007).

EXERCISE 6.3: THE COMMUNICATION GAME

1. Each participant chooses a partner that he or she doesn't know very well.
2. Randomly assign the labels "Person A" and "Person B" to each person in each partnership.
3. Person A is asked to think of an important fact about him- or herself that Person B would be unlikely to know. Neither person may talk.

   Person A is asked to convey the message using gestures or drawings. He or she is not allowed to write words or numbers.

   Person B is not allowed to make gestures. Person B has a paper and pencil to write down the message he or she thinks is being conveyed. (It is important, however, that Person A not see this message). Person A writes down how it feels to try to convey the message without language.
4. At the end of the exercise all participants come back to together. Then each Person B reads what he or she thought the message was and each Person A then has to tell what he or she was trying to convey.

   Very few messages are correctly interpreted. Most understand a few central ideas or words but misinterpret the message. Participants after conducting this exercise sometimes voice feelings of frustration and helplessness due to an inability to communicate effectively. This is a good exercise to help others put themselves in the shoes of second language learners.

   Ideas for messages are as follows:

Last year, I was sick. I had surgery on my___. I hurt myself. . . .

During the vacation I went to___.

A funny thing happened in my class the other day. . . .

It makes me feel uncomfortable when people___.

Last night I dreamt that. . . .

Something I really like to do in my spare time is___.

Source: Haynes (2002); Everythingesl.net.

USEFUL TOOLS AND INSTRUMENTS

Cultural and Linguistic Checklist

Cultural/Linguistic Questions	YES	NO
Is the student instructed in his or her dominant language? (As per formal and informal language assessment of L1 and L2.)	Conduct an assessment in student's dominant language and compare student's rate of learning with peers with same language proficiency in language of instruction.	Proceed to next question.

(continued)

Cultural and Linguistic Checklist (*continued*)

Cultural/Linguistic Questions	YES	NO
Has the student received inconsistent language of instruction?	Consider inconsistent language of instruction as a major factor contributing to rate of learning.	Document how information was obtained. You can rule out inconsistent language of instruction as a major factor impacting rate of learning. Proceed to next question.
Has the student had *limited* exposure to formal education in home country?	Consider limited exposure as a major factor impacting rate of learning.	Document how information was obtained. You can rule out limited exposure as a major factor contributing to reduction in learning rate.
Is the student at the Silent, Preproduction, or Speech Emergence stage of second language acquisition?	Consider this as a major factor impacting rate of learning. Consider the level of stage of language acquisition and determine if presenting behaviors are secondary to characteristics common to the stage.	Consider the level of stage of language acquisition and determine if presenting behaviors are secondary to characteristics common to the Intermediate Fluency stage. If the student has received the Advanced Fluency stage, then conduct assessment of student in the dominant language as determined by informal and formal language tests in both languages.
Is the student exhibiting a higher level of English skills when conversing in the playground or in other informal settings compared to academic settings? Is the student receiving curriculum instruction to develop English language on a daily basis?	This is a typical pattern because students' Basic Interpersonal Conversational Skills (BICS) in L2 develop faster than their Cognitive Academic Language Proficiency (CALP) in L2. Document curriculum used and student progress in class.	If the student is exhibiting difficulties in both after an adequate amount of exposure to L2, then consider other factors impacting rate of second language acquisition. Consider limited exposure to L2 development as a major factor impacting low rate of learning. Implement an English Language Development curriculum and monitor student's rate of learning.
Is there a match between the home language and language of instruction?	Proceed to next question.	Provide caregivers information about student's academic material in the home language so that caregivers can provide support for learning at home. Consider after-school tutoring.
Did the student migrate from a country where exposure to trauma is likely?	Consider social-emotional functioning as a major factor contributing to low rate of learning, secondary to trauma.	Document how this was determined.

Source: Pazos (2009).

SAMPLE REPORT

The following is an example of a report that highlights many of the recommendations mentioned earlier for report writing for ELLs.

Psychological Findings

Referral/Background Information:

Student A is a 6-year-old girl of Latino descent, born in the United States, who reportedly is predominantly Spanish speaking. She was referred for cognitive and academic testing, in Spanish, to aid in her special education initial evaluation and in education planning.

In regard to Student A's English language proficiency, there were no English Language Proficiency Scores available at the time of referral. Therefore, there is no formal information about Student A's Academic and Oral English language proficiency. However, other information was obtained in the referral form, which provides informal information about Student A's oral language skills in Spanish. According to the "Student Oral Language Observation Matrix," completed by Student A's long-term substitute teacher, Ms. Olivera, Student A exhibits good language abilities, in Spanish, in the areas of comprehension, fluency, vocabulary, pronunciation, and grammar. According to the Linguistic and Conceptual Development Checklist, Student A had a good amount of exposure and practice of language skills in Spanish. However, she has not had the opportunity for long-term exposure to standard-English models.

Academic history revealed that Student A has been receiving instruction in her native language (Spanish) since Kindergarten and this year in first grade. Information on the referral form noted that Student A has been exhibiting below-grade-level academic functioning since the end of Kindergarten. She was placed in an intervention group, where she received small-group literacy instruction. Despite this intervention, Student A is reportedly still functioning below grade level in reading and writing. Math was reported to be her relative strength. Pronunciation difficulties were also noted to be a concern voiced from Student A's teacher and mother. Student A was described as a student who seems to have good self-confidence and a good sense of humor, and to be helpful with peers and others; she completes her work and tasks and displays good social skills.

Testing Observations:

Student A was tested with Wechsler Intelligence Scale for Children—Fourth Edition—Spanish (WISC-IV S).

Student A presented as happy and cooperative. She did not wear any hearing or visual aids. In a one-to-one situation, Student A displayed inconsistent attention and concentration. She needed some redirection from the examiner. This may have been partly due to the length of testing time and the level of difficulty during testing. However, Student A seemed to exhibit difficulties with concentration throughout most of the testing session. Multiple breaks were given during testing and stickers were given as tangible rewards to maintain motivation. Despite Student A's apparent difficulty with attention, she appeared to want to cooperate with the testing situation. Student A completed paper-and-pencil tasks with her right hand. Her pencil grasp seemed normal.

In relation to language, Student A spoke only Spanish. During conversation, Student A was asked some basic questions in English. Student A exhibited a limited understanding of

(*continued*)

(continued)

questions and usually responded with one- to two-word statements. She was also observed to require a long time to respond to questions in English. These difficulties were not observed in Spanish. Student A did exhibit significant pronunciation difficulties, in Spanish, which made it difficult to understand her during testing. However, repetition of words and knowledge of the context of the words by the examiner, aided in completing the testing in a valid manner. Finally, Student A was observed to have some difficulty differentiating between letter sounds in spoken language in both Spanish and English.

The WISC-IV Spanish was administered in Spanish. Some failed items on the WISC-IV S testing were also repeated in English. However, this was discontinued when it was evident that Student A was unable to fully understand the questions in English. The remainder of the testing was conducted in Spanish.

Scores are merely an estimate because of the nonstandardized translation, administration, and scoring of the WISC-IV S. Scores may be a slight underestimate due to Student A's observed attention difficulties during testing.

Cognitive/Academic Functioning:

Overall results from this testing indicated that Student A's intellectual functioning was measured to be in the Average range. Her verbal and nonverbal thinking and reasoning skills, as well as her visual/spatial-organization skills, were measured to be age appropriate. Student A was measured to have a significant strength on a measure of visual short-term memory, rapid visual scanning, and visual motor coordination. Student A's performance on the test revealed that she has a relative strength in visual processing speed and visual short-term memory. On the other hand, she was measured to have a weakness in auditory working memory.

In regard to cognitive and academic strengths and weaknesses, Student A showed a good ability to use visual details to guide her during academic tasks and her visual processing speed and short-term memory were also measured to be strengths on cognitive testing. Her area of measured weakness on the cognitive testing was in auditory working memory. Her ability to retell stories and to follow oral directions were also measured to be significantly low for Student A on the academic testing. Therefore, auditory working memory and the ability to comprehend and/or process oral language seemed to be areas of weakness for Student A, which could be impacting her learning.

Second Language Acquisition:

In relation to Student A's second language acquisition development, Student A seemed to be in the beginning stages of English language proficiency since she seemed to have limited understanding of English during conversation and she usually answered in one- to two-word sentences in English. *A formal measure of Student A's English language proficiency, however, should be one of the major sources of information to determine her English language proficiency.* Student A's oral language score on the Bateria III seemed to suggest that Student A may have limited receptive and expressive language abilities in Spanish. This may increase the time for Student A to acquire her second language. Currently, she is instructed in Spanish; however, academic scores and teacher report suggest that Student A is functioning below grade level in her first language. This may make Student A's transition to English instruction more difficult since academic proficiency and literacy skills in the first language are usually good predictors of success in a second language.

ADDITIONAL RESOURCES

Knowledge

OELA's National Clearinghouse. "Authorized under Title III of the *No Child Left Behind Act of 2001* (NCLB). (OELA)The Office of English Language Acquisition.

"OELA's National Clearinghouse is authorized to collect, analyze, synthesize, and disseminate information about language instruction educational programs for limited-English-proficient children, and related programs. Priority is given to information on academic content and English proficiency assessments and accountability systems." Taken from http://www.nclea.gwv.edu/.

Teaching Diverse Learners (TDL). A Web site for teacher development in the areas of cultural competent pedagogy with English Language Learners. This Web site includes: information on publications, educational tools, and focuses on the ongoing work of experts in cultural competence that advances the academic achievement for English Language Learners (ELL'S). Taken from http://www.alliance.brown.edu/tdl/.

Everything ESL.net (http://www.everythingesl.net/). This is a Web site that includes various publications and information on SLA learning and teaching. It also provides various exercises to increase awareness and knowledge on SLA and cultural diversity.

Center for Research on the Education of Students Placed at Risk (CRESPAR; http://ww.csus.jhu.edu/crespar/index.htm). This is a Web site that provides publications and information on academic achievement and English language learners and other populations at risk of academic difficulties.

Center for Applied Linguistics (http://www.cal.org/topics/ri/background). Provides information about refugee groups and may include topics such as the history and culture and characteristics of the refugee population.

National Association of the Deaf (http://www.nad.org\).

Vernon, M. (2006). The APA and deafness. *American Psychologist, 61*(8), 816–824.

Williams, C. R., & Abeles, N. (2004). Issues and implications of deaf culture in therapy. *Professional Psychology: Research and Practice, 35*(6), 643–648.

Skills

Center for Applied Linguistics (2007). Foreign Language Assessment Directory (http://www.cal.org/CALWcbDB/FLAD). A searchable database with assessments in 90 different languages.

Cross-Cultural Communication Systems, Inc. (http://www.ccc.sorg.com). Specializes in translation services and interpretation.

International Test Commission (ITC) Test Adaptation Guidelines. Provides excellent recommendations of methods and procedures for cross-cultural adaptation of educational and psychological tests.

COMPETENCY BENCHMARK TABLES

The purpose of the Competency Benchmarks (Tables 6.1–6.4) is to create developmental models for defining and measuring competencies in professional psychology; each chapter in this *Handbook* applies the diversity competence for mental health practitioners in their work with a particular diverse population.

Table 6.1   Developmental-Level Competencies I

READINESS LEVEL—ENTRY TO PRACTICUM	
Competencies	**Learning Process and Activities**
Knowledge The student is gaining knowledge in: • Multiculturalism—the student is engaged in the process of learning that all individuals, including themselves, are cultural beings with worldviews that shape and influence their attitudes, emotions, perceptions, and experiences. • Learning that language is an aspect of diversity, and understanding the historical context of bilingual education. • Understanding that emotions are expressed differently in different languages, and that there may not be words for certain emotions. • The importance of reflective practice and self-awareness of one's cultural identities and those of others, including facility with language use. • Core counseling skills and theories, particularly as they pertain to the value of diversity. • Ethics code and relevant legal standards. **Skills** The student is: • Beginning to develop the ability to demonstrate empathic listening skills, respect, and interest when talking with individuals expressing different values and belief systems. • Beginning to develop an understanding that the tools needed to work with second language learners may be different, and beginning to acquire those skills (such as interacting with interpreters). • Learning to critically examine the diversity literature and implications for treatment interventions. **Values and Attitudes** The student demonstrates: • Willingness to engage in self-exploration, to consider own motives, attitudes, behaviors and effect on others. • Willingness to consider their own comfort level and beliefs around bilingualism and/or ethnolinguism. • Intellectual curiosity and flexibility. • Ability to value expressions of diverse viewpoints and belief systems.	At this stage of development, the emphasis in psychotherapist education is instilling knowledge of foundational domains that provide the groundwork for subsequent attainment of functional competencies. Students at this stage become aware of the principles and practices of the field, but they are not yet able to apply their knowledge to practice. Therefore, the training curriculum is focused on knowledge of core areas, including literature on multiculturalism (including second language learners), ethics, basic counseling skills, scientific knowledge, and the importance of reflective practice and self awareness. It is important that throughout the curriculum, trainers and teachers define individual and cultural differences broadly, to include language ability and language acquisition differences. This should enable students to have a developing awareness of how to extrapolate their emerging multicultural competencies to include language differences in the process of therapy and assessment. Most students, through their life experiences, would be expected to have basic knowledge of language acquisition (based on their own experiences), but may not have considered the process for individuals who are acquiring English as a second language. Many students may have attempted to learn a second language merely as a requirement of their education, so may not have accessed this process as part of their diversity self-awareness and knowledge base.

Table 6.2   Developmental–Level Competencies II

READINESS LEVEL—ENTRY TO INTERNSHIP	
Competencies	Learning Process and Activities
Knowledge The student has: • General understanding and knowledge of the stages and models of language acquisition. • Knowledge of the intersection of culture and language, and the various dialects. • Knowledge of when it is appropriate to consider the addition of language to Axis IV. • Understanding the importance of consulting with supervisors and others when presented with language issues in therapy and/or assessment.	At this level of development, students are building on their education and applied experiences (such as supervised practicum experiences) to attain a core set of foundational competencies. They can then begin applying this knowledge to professional practice. As a result of being exposed to didactic training and close supervision, students attain the multicultural values and attitudes appropriate to their level of development. Foundational knowledge and multicultural values and attitudes are becoming well established, but skills in working with language diversity would be expected to be rudimentary at this level of development.
Skills Skills in the following areas are beginning to develop: • Discerning personal limits of openness to language diversity and attitudes surrounding such and, after consultation with supervisors, referring clients to appropriate resources if not able to work with them. • Building therapeutic alliance to create a trusting, safe, and open therapeutic climate to discuss issues, and recognizing that this therapeutic alliance may be affected by the dynamic of the triad (interpreter). • Genuine respect for the difficulty of second language acquisition.	Learning occurs through multiple modalities: • Receiving secondary language acquisition didactic training in academic programs may occur in multicultural courses and possibly developmental psychology courses (e.g., language acquisition in children). It may also be infused into the core curriculum (e.g., ethics, assessment, multicultural, career counseling, research, human growth and development, and clinical courses). • Providing therapy, under supervision, to clients who may be at different stages of secondary language acquisition, during which an interpreter may or may not be present. • Receiving supervision from mental health professionals knowledgeable and skilled in working with individuals whose primary language is not English, and who may be secondary language learners themselves. • Seeking additional study and professional development opportunities (e.g., to improve effectiveness in working with interpreters and knowledge of assessments available in multiple languages).
Values and Attitudes Demonstrates self-awareness and appropriate cultural and multicultural attitudes as evidenced by the following: • Understands that language is an aspect of diversity. • Awareness of own intersecting individual dimensions (gender, ethnicity, socioeconomic status (SES), sexual orientation, ability, etc.) and ability to discern clients' intersecting identities. • Commitment to examine and challenge own attitudes and biases about bilingual education, and belief about English as the "official" language. • Willingness to admit own limitations in ability to converse in client's language, and that second language acquisition is difficult. • Demonstrates genuine respect for people who acquire English as a second language.	Topics to be covered in didactic training include: • Relation of language competency to multicultural competency. • Relationship of language diversity to individual and cultural differences (e.g., including age, gender, sexual orientation, SES, and ethnicity). • Basic research literature describing the relevance of language to mental health and wellbeing (ability to seek education and employment opportunities).

(continued)

Table 6.2 Developmental-Level Competencies II (*continued*)

READINESS LEVEL—ENTRY TO INTERNSHIP	
Competencies	Learning Process and Activities
• Acknowledge the power differential in the therapy when it is being conducted in the client's second language, even if the client's language ability seems to be proficient	• Trainers and teachers could offer students enrolled in multicultural diversity courses an option to research language issues as a project for the class, and provide resources through which students can be exposed to/experience language diversity (including American Sign Language, international student experiences).

Table 6.3 Developmental-Level Competencies III

READINESS LEVEL—ENTRY TO PROFESSIONAL PRACTICE		
	Competencies	Learning Process and Activities
Knowledge	Knowledge of: • Literature on the relationship between language acquisition and mental and physical health, and overall wellbeing. • Literature on integration of language processes with identity issues. • Understanding of system dynamics if members of a family are at different stages of language acquisition. • Beliefs and behaviors that are considered normative and healthy within second language learners (and other communities in which there is language diversity). • Community resources, including leaders from various linguistically diverse groups. • Understanding that working with clients who present with differing levels of language ability is an aspect of multicultural counseling competency	In the earlier stages of training, students solidified their professional knowledge base and attained appropriate values and attitudes while developing increasingly sophisticated clinical skills. At the level of Entry to Professional Practice, psychotherapists have attained the full range of competencies in the domains expected of all independent practitioners. Preparation for this level of competency takes place through closely supervised clinical work, augmented by professional reading, personal exploration, and training opportunities such as professional development and training seminars. Clinical supervisors observe students' clinical work, provide training in assessment, case conceptualization and treatment planning, and challenge supervisees to examine their countertransference reactions, biases, and values to develop their supervisees' clinical competency with language issues.
Skills	Skills are demonstrated by the ability to: • Perform a basic assessment of clients' comfort with their language ability and assess the relevance of language to therapy and assessment. • Diagnose and formulate appropriate treatment plans that are sensitive to the client's language ability, including how multiple systems and individual differences impact client. • Be aware of dual roles and boundary issues when the therapeutic relationship becomes a triad instead of a dyad. • Identify the limits of one's own competency with language issues and refer appropriately. • Form a trusting therapeutic relationship with clients so that clients may express concerns over language issues that present in therapy.	Additional methods by which students can attain language diversity competency at this level include: • Seeking opportunities to provide therapy to clients representing linguistic diversity. • Supervision provided by supervisors knowledgeable and skilled in working with language diversity issues. • Self-directed study and professional development opportunities. • Internship and postdoctoral seminar training in working with bilingual clients or with populations in which second language acquisition is the norm.

READINESS LEVEL—ENTRY TO PROFESSIONAL PRACTICE

Competencies	Learning Process and Activities
	• Facilitating self-confidence in clients who may experience societal messages that denounce their lack of English fluency. • Use supervision to enhance skills in working with interpreters. • Establish effective consultation relationships with bilingual providers in the community. • Create climate in which supervisees and trainees feel safe to talk about language issues.	• Presenting and participating in clinical case conferences that include discussion of language diversity aspects of cases.
Values and Attitudes	• Awareness of own language abilities and biases, willingness to continually broaden self-knowledge, and commitment to expanding knowledge of systemic language oppression as part of multicultural competency enhancement.	

Table 6.4   Developmental-Level Competencies IV

READINESS LEVEL—ADVANCED PRACTICE AND SPECIALIZATION

Competencies		Learning Process and Activities
Knowledge	Extensive knowledge of: • Language diversity and acquisition–related literature and resources. • Language acquisition development models, and application to various groups (including immigrant, international students, hearing impaired, and refugee). • Impact of oppressive language laws on health and human development.	Mental health practitioners who have a particular interest in language aspects of diversity as they apply to clinical work may seek to attain advanced levels of competency. Learning activities will vary depending on the mental health practitioner's unique background, established competencies, and interest areas. For example, mental health practitioners working in school-based settings may wish to focus on language issues relevant to immigrant and refugee students and their families (as well as assisting teachers with tools to enhance the level of student learning). Regardless of the focus area, learning activities can include:
Skills	Advanced skills in: • Providing a variety of interventions with linguistically diverse clients. • Integrating knowledge of language concepts into treatment. • Proactively sharing knowledge of working with interpreters and working with linguistically diverse clients with other mental health professionals. • Differentiating between healthy and unhealthy behaviors related to secondary language acquisition. • Advocating for clients to receive equitable and quality medical and psychological care regardless of language abilities. • Provide effective supervision to trainees working with client language issues, and who may themselves be second language learners.	• Professional reading (information about language acquisition; empirical studies, and literature on theory and practice). • Teaching. • Research. • Attending and leading educational workshops. • Peer-consultation groups. • Consultation with knowledgeable mental health professionals, bilingual researchers, and other experts.

(continued)

Table 6.4   Developmental-Level Competencies IV (*continued*)

READINESS LEVEL—ADVANCED PRACTICE AND SPECIALIZATION	
Competencies	Learning Process and Activities
Values and Attitudes Well-integrated values and attitudes demonstrated by the following: • Continually engages in broadening knowledge of language resources and for continuing professional development. • Actively cultivates relationships with bilingual providers in the community. • Involved in local and national groups and organizations relevant to language issues. • Independently and proactively provide ethical and legal consultation and supervision to trainees and other professionals. • Work for social justice to enhance understanding among professionals and communities about linguistic diversity. • Independently monitor own bilingual language acceptance in relation to work with others.	

REFERENCES

Abedi, J. (2006). Psychometric issues in the ELL assessment and special education eligibility. *Teachers College Record, 108*(11), 2282–2303.

Abedi, J., Hofstetter, C. H., & Lord, C. (2004). Assessment accommodations for English language learners: Implications for policy-based empirical research. *Review of Educational Research, 74*(1), 1–28.

Aklin, W. M., & Turner, S. M. (2006). Toward understanding ethnic and cultural factors in the interviewing process. *Psychotherapy: Theory, Research, Practice, Training, 43*(1), 50–64.

Allen, J. (2007). A multicultural assessment supervision model to guide research and practice. *Professional Psychology: Research and Practice, 38*(3), 248–258.

American Educational Research Association, American Psychological Association, & National Council on Measurement in Education. (1999). *Standards for educational and psychological testing.* Washington, DC: American Educational Research Association.

American Psychological Association. (1990). Guidelines for providers of psychological services to ethnic, linguistic, and culturally diverse populations. Washington, DC.

American Psychological Association. (2003). Guidelines on multicultural education, training, research, practice, and organizational change for psychologists. *American Psychologist, 58*, 377–402.

American Psychological Association. (2007). Assessment of competency benchmarks work group: A developmental model for defining and measuring competence in professional psychology. Product of the Assessment of Competency Benchmarks Work Group convened by the APA Board of Educational Affairs in collaboration with the Council of Chairs of Training Councils (CCTC).

Arrendondo, P., Toporek, R., Brown, S. P., Jones, J., Locke, D. C., Sanchez, J., et al. (1996). Operationalization of the multicultural counseling competencies. *Journal of Multicultural Counseling and Development, 24*, 42–78.

Aviera, A. (n.d.). Culturally sensitive and creative therapy with Latino clients. Retrieved August 13, 2009, from http://www.apadiv31.org/Coop/CulturallySensitiveTherapyWithLatinos.pdf.

Bagnato, S. J., & Neisworth, J. T. (1994). A national study of social and treatment invalidity of intelligence testing for early intervention. *School Psychology Quarterly, 9*, 81–102.

Bancroft, M. (2005). Retrieved August 10, 2009, from http://www.hablamosjuntos.org/resources/pdf/The_Interpreter's_World_Tour.pdf.

Berry, J. W. (1997). Immigration, acculturation, and adaptation. *Applied Psychology: An International Review, 46*(1), 5–34.

Bhandari, R. (2009). *Shifting trends in global student mobility: Who is going where?* Institute of International Education. Retrieved on August 27, 2009 from http://opendoors.iienetworking.org

Biever, J. L., Castano, M. T., de las Fuentes, C., Gonzalez, C., Servin-Lopez, S., Sprowls, C., et al. (2002). The role of language in training psychologists to work with Hispanic clients. *Professional Psychology: Research and Practice, 33*, 330–336.

Bolten, P., & Tang, A. (2002). An alternative approach to cross-cultural function assessment. *Social Psychiatry and Psychiatric Epidemiology, 37*, 537–543.

Borsato, G. N., & Padilla, A. M. (2008). Educational assessment of English-language learners. In L. A. Suzuki & J. G. Ponterotto (Eds.), *Handbook of multicultural assessment: Clinical, psychological and educational applications* (3rd ed., pp. 471–489). San Francisco: Jossey-Bass.

Chow, P., & Marcus, R. (2008). International student mobility and the United States: The 2007 Open Doors Survey. *International Higher Education, 50.* Retrieved December 6, 2008, from http://www.bc.edu.

Cloud, N. (2007). Bilingual education practices. In G. B. Esquivel, E. C. Lopez, & S. G. Nahari (Eds.), *Handbook of multicultural school psychology: An interdisciplinary perspective* (pp. 201–221). Mahwah, NJ: Lawrence Erlbaum Associates.

Collier, C. (2000). *Acculturation Quick Screen.* Ferndale, WA: Cross Cultural Developmental Educational Services.

Collier, C., Brice, A. E., & Oades-Sese, G. V. (2007). Assessment of acculturation. In G. B. Esquivel, E. C. Lopez, & S. G. Nahari (Eds.), *Handbook of multicultural school psychology: An interdisciplinary perspective* (pp. 353–380). Mahwah, NJ: Lawrence Erlbaum Associates.

Cuellar, I., Arnold, B., & Maldonado, R. (1995). Acculturation rating scale for Mexican Americans-II: A revision of the original ARSMA Scale. *Hispanic Journal of Behavioral Sciences, 17*(3), 275–304.

Culturally sensitive and creative therapy with Latino clients. Retrieved August 13, 2009, from http://www.apadiv31.org/Coop/CulturallySensitiveTherapyWithLatinos.pdf

Cummins, J. (1983). Bilingualism and special education: Program and pedagogical issues. *Learning Disability Quarterly, 6*, 373–386.

Cummins, J. (1984). *Bilingualism and special education: Issues in assessment and pedagogy.* San Diego, CA: College-Hill.

Delgado-Gaitan, C. (2004). *Involving Latino families in schools: Raising student achievement through home-school partnerships.* Thousand Oaks, CA: Corwin Press.

Echevarria, J., Vogt, M. E., & Short, D. J. (2004). *Making content comprehensible for English language learners: The SIOP Model* (2nd ed.). Boston: Pearson/Allyn-Bacon.

Eide, A. (2000). United Nations, Commission on Human Rights, Sub-Commission on Promotion and Protection of Human Rights, Working Group on Minorities Commentary to the Declaration on the Rights of Persons Belonging to National or Ethnic, Religious, and Linguistic Minorities. Retrieved August 10, 2009, from http://www.unhchr.ch/Huridocda/Huridoca.nsf/e06a5300f90fa0238025668700518ca4/8ccd90477d0010bd802568eb003d3e32/$FILE/G0013692.pdf

English language learner: Working with children for whom English is a new language. Retrieved on November 23, 2008, from http://www.bankst.edu/literacyguide/ell.html

Falender, C. A., & Shafranske, E. P. (2007). Competence in competency-based supervision practice: Construct and application. *Professional Psychology: Research and Practice, 38*(3), 232–240.

Flynn, K., & Hill, J. (2005). *English language learners: A growing population [policy brief].* Aurora, CO: Midcontinent Research for Education and Learning.

Fradd, S. H. (2007). Integrating English language learners in general education. In G. B. Esquivel, E. C. Lopez, & S. G. Nahari (Eds.), *Handbook of multicultural school psychology: An interdisciplinary perspective* (pp. 223–244). Mahwah, NJ: Lawrence Erlbaum Associates.

Fuertes, J. N. (2004). Supervision in bilingual counseling: Service delivery, training, and research. *Journal of Multicultural Counseling and Development, 32*, 84–94.

Gamst, G., Dana, R. H., Der-Karabetian, A., Aragon, M., Arellano, L., Morrow, G., et al. (2004). Cultural competency revised: The California Brief Multicultural Competency Scale. *Measurement and Evaluation in Counseling Development, 37*(3), 163–183.

Garcia, N. (2009, August 27). DPS starts Spanish talk show. Retrieved August 27, 2009, from http://www.9news.com/news/article.aspx?storyid=122142&catid=188.

Garcia-Vazquez, E. (1995). Acculturation and academics: Effects of acculturation on reading achievement among Mexican-America students. *The Bilingual Research Journal, 19*(2), 305–315.

Gardner, H. (1993). *Multiple intelligences: The theory in practice.* New York: Basic Books.

Gonzalez, V., Bauerle, P., Black, W., & Felix-Holt, M. (1999). Influence of evaluators' beliefs and cultural-linguistic backgrounds on their diagnostic and placement decisions for language-minority children. In V. Gonzalez (Ed.), *Language and cognitive development in L2 language learning: Educational implications for children and adults* (pp. 269–297). Needham Heights, MA: Allyn & Bacon.

Gottlieb, M., & Hamayan, E. (2007). Assessing oral and written language proficiency: A guide for psychologists and teachers. In G. B. Esquivel, E. C. Lopez, & S. G. Nahari (Eds.), *Handbook of multicultural school psychology: An interdisciplinary perspective* (pp. 245–264). Mahwah, NJ: Lawrence Erlbaum Associates.

Guajardo Alvarado, C. (2006). Best practices in the special education assessment of culturally and linguistically diverse (CLD) students. Retrieved November 29, 2008, from http://www.fasp.org/PDF_Files/Cultural_&_Linguistic_Diversity/Best PracticesLCD.pdf

Harris, K. C., & Goldstein, B. S. C. (2007). Implementing culturally sensitive interventions in classroom settings. In G. B. Esquivel, E. C. Lopez, & S. G. Nahari (Eds.), *Handbook of multicultural school psychology: An interdisciplinary perspective* (pp. 159–178). Mahwah, NJ: Lawrence Erlbaum Associates.

Haynes, J. (2002) The Communication Game. Retrieved November 28, 2008, from http://www.everythingesl.net

Haynes, J. (2007). *Getting started with English language learners: How educators can meet the challenge.* Alexandra, VA: Association for Supervision and Curriculum Development.

Hays, P. (2001). *Addressing cultural complexities in practice.* Washington, DC: American Psychological Association.

Herbert, C. H. (1986). *Basic inventory of natural language.* San Bernardino, CA: CHECpoint Systems.

Hill, J. D., & Flynn, K. M. (2006). *Classroom instruction that works with English language learners.* Alexandria, VA: Association for Supervision and Curriculum Development.

Hirsch, E. R., Jr. (1987). *Cultural literacy: What every American needs to know.* Boston: Houghton Mifflin.

Individuals with Disabilities Education Improvement Act (IDEIA) (2004). Retrieved January 2, 2009, from http//idea.ed.gov.

Ingraham, C. L. (2007). Focusing on consultees in multicultural consultation. In G. B. Esquivel, E. C. Lopez, & S. G. Nahari (Eds.), *Handbook of multicultural school psychology: An interdisciplinary perspective* (pp. 99–118). Mahwah, NJ: Lawrence Erlbaum Associates.

Jeffreys, K. L., & Martin, D. C. (2008). *Refugees and asylees: 2007.* Washington, DC: U.S. Department of Homeland Security.

Ji, L., Zhang, A., & Nisbett, R. E. (2004). Is it culture or is it language? Examination of language effects in cross-cultural research on categorization. *Journal of Personality and Social Psychology, 87*(1), 57–65.

Kaslow, N. J., Borden, K. A., Collins, F. L., Forrest, L., Illfelder-Kaye, J., Nelson, P. D., et al. (2004). Competencies conference: Future directions in education and credentialing in professional psychology. *Journal of Clinical Psychology, 60,* 699–712.

Kestemberg, L. B., Silverman, M. T., & Emmons, M. R. (2007). Neuropsychological assessment of culturally and linguistically diverse children: A review of relevant issues and appropriate methods. In G. B. Esquivel, E. C. Lopez, & S. G. Nahari (Eds.), *Handbook of multicultural school psychology: An interdisciplinary perspective* (pp. 309–329). Mahwah, NJ: Lawrence Erlbaum Associates.

Knoff, H. M. (1983). Effect of diagnostic information on special education placement decisions. *Exceptional Children, 49,* 440–444.

Krashen, S. D., & Terrell, T. D. (1983). *The natural approach: Language acquisition in the classroom.* Englewood Cliffs, NJ: Alemany Press/Prentice Hall.

Lopez, E. C., Lamar, D., & Scully-Demartini, D. (1997). The cognitive assessment of limited English proficient children: Current problems and practical recommendations. *Cultural Diversity and Mental Health, 3*(2), 117–130.

Los Angeles Times (1992, May 11). Immigrants face struggle to live without English. Retrieved August 10, 2009, from http://articles.latimes.com/1992-05-11/news/mn-1285_1_limited-english.

Mantero, M. (2007). *Identity and second language learning: Culture, inquiry and dialogic activity.* Charlotte, NC: Information Age Processing.

Marsella, A. J. (2001). Measurement issues. In E. Gerrity, T. M. Keane, & F. Tuma (Eds.), *The mental health consequences of torture* (pp. 277–290). New York: Kluwer.

Martines, D., & Rodriguez-Srednicki, O. (2007). In G. B. Esquivel, E. C. Lopez, & S. G. Nahari (Eds.), *Handbook of multicultural school psychology: An interdisciplinary perspective* (pp. 381–405). Mahwah, NJ: Lawrence Erlbaum Associates.

Mattes, L. J., & Santiago, G. (1985). *Bilingual Language Proficiency Questionnaire*. Oceanside, CA: Academic Communication Associates.

Miletic, T., Piu, M., Minas, H., Stankovska, S., Stolk, Y., & Klimidis, S. (2006). *Guidelines for working effectively with interpreters in mental health settings*. Victorian Transcultural Psychiatry Unit.

Miller, K. E., Martell, Z. L., Pazdirek, L., Caruth, M., & Lopez, D. (2005). The role of interpreters in psychotherapy with refugees: An exploratory study. *American Journal of Orthopsychiatry*, 75(1), 27–39.

Miramontes, O. B., Nadeau, A., & Commins, N. L. (1997). *Restructuring schools for linguistic diversity: Linking decision making to effective programs*. New York: Teachers College Press.

Mitchell, R., & Myles, F. (2004). *Second language learning theories* (2nd ed.). New York: Arnold.

Muñoz-Sandoval, A. F., Cummins, J., Alvarado, C. G., & Ruef, M. L. (1998). *The Bilingual Verbal Ability Test*. Chicago: Riverside.

National Association of Social Workers. (2007). *Indicators for the achievement of the NASW standards for cultural competence in social work practice*. Washington, DC: NASW Press.

National Center for Education Statistics. (2009). *The condition of education 2009*. Retrieved August 27, 2009, from http://nces.ed.gov/programs.coe/2009/section1/table-lsm-1,asp

National Education Association and National Association of School Psychologists. (2007). *Truth in labeling: Disproportionality in special education*. Washington, DC: National Education Association.

Ochoa, S. H., Riccio, C. A., Jimenez, S., Garcia de Alba, R., & Sines, M. (2004). Psychological assessment of limited English proficient and/or bilingual students: An investigation of school psychologists' current practices. *Journal of Psychoeducational Assessment*, 22, 93–105.

Okawa, J. B. (2008). Considerations for the cross-cultural evaluation of refugees and asylum seekers. In L. A. Suzuki & J. G. Ponterotto (Eds.), *Handbook of multicultural assessment: Clinical, psychological and educational applications* (3rd ed., 165–194). San Francisco: Jossey-Bass.

Ortiz, S. O. (2002). Best practices in nondiscriminatory assessment. In A. Thomas & J. Grimes (Eds.), *Best practices in school psychology IV* (pp. 1321–1336). Washington, DC: NASP.

Ortiz, S. O., & Dynda, A. M. (2005). Use of intelligence tests with culturally and linguistically diverse populations. In D. P. Flanagan & P. L. Harrison (Eds.), *Contemporary intellectual assessment: Theories, tests, and issues* (pp. 545–556). New York: Guilford Press.

Ortiz, S. O., & Ochoa, S. H. (2005). Advances in cognitive assessment of culturally and linguistically diverse individuals: A nondiscriminatory approach. In D. P. Flanagan & P. L. Harrison (Eds.), *Contemporary intellectual assessment: Theories, tests, and issues* (pp. 234–250). New York: Guilford Press.

Padilla, A. M., & Perez, W. (2003). Acculturation, social identity, and social cognition: A new perspective. *Hispanic Journal of Behavioral Sciences*, 25(1), 35–55.

Pope-Davis, D. B., Toporek, R. L., & Ortega-Villalobos, L. (2003). Assessing supervisors' and supervisees' perceptions of multicultural competencies in supervision using the Multicultural Supervision Inventory. In D. B. Pope-Davis, H. L. K. Coleman, W. M. Liu, & R. L. Toporek (Eds.), *Handbook of multicultural competencies in counseling and psychology* (pp. 211–224). Thousand Oaks, CA: Sage Publications.

Prendes-Lintel, M. (2001). Important issues in counseling recent refugees. In J. Ponterotto, M. Casas, L. Suzuki, & C. Alexander (Eds.), *Handbook of multicultural counseling* (2nd ed., pp. 729–752). Thousand Oaks, CA: Sage.

Ramirez, J. D., Yuen, S. D., & Ramney, D. R. (1991). *Final report: Longitudinal study of structured English immersion strategy, early-exit and late-exit transitional bilingual programs for language-minority children: Executive summary*. San Mateo, CA: Aguirre International.

Rhodes, R. L., Ochoa, S. H., & Ortiz, S. O. (2005). *Assessing culturally and linguistically diverse students: A practical guide*. New York: Guilford Press.

Rodolfa, E., Bent, R., Eisman, E., Nelson, P., Rehm, L., & Ritchie, P. (2005). A Cube model for competency development: Implications for psychology educators and regulators. *Professional Psychology: Research and Practice*, 36(4), 347–354.

Roseberry-McKibbin, C. (2002). *Multicultural students with special language needs* (2nd ed.). Oceanside, CA: Academic Communications Association.

Roseberry-McKibbin, C., & Brice, A. (2005). What's "normal," what's not: Acquiring English as a second language. Retrieved November 29, 2008, from http://www.colorincolorado.org/article/5126?theme=print

Roysircar, G., & Maestas, M. L. (2002). Assessing acculturation and cultural variables. In K. S. Krasaki, S. Okazaki, & S. Sue (Eds.), *Asian American mental health: Assessment theories and methods* (pp. 77–94). New York: Kluwer Academic/Plenum.

Sanchez, Claudio. (2009, July 31). At school, lower expectations of Dominican kids. National Public Radio. Retrieved August 11, 2009, from http:www. npr.org/Coop/CulturallySensitiveTherapyWith-Latinos.pdf.

Santiago-Rivera, A., & Altarriba, J. (2002). The role of language in therapy with the Spanish–English bilingual client. *Professional Psychology: Research and Practice, 33,* 30–38.

Schiff-Myers, N. B. (1992). Considering arrested language development and language loss in the assessment of second language learners. *Language, Speech, and Hearing Services in Schools, 23*(1), 28–33.

Shepard, L. A., Kagan, S. L., & Wurtz, E. (1998). *Principles and recommendations for early childhood assessments.* Washington, DC: National Educational Goals Panel.

Shin, H. B., & Bruno, R. (2003). Language use and English-speaking ability: Census 2000 brief. U.S. Department of Commerce Economics and Statistics Administration, U.S. Census Bureau. Retrieved August 10, 2009, from http://www .census.gov/prod/2003pubs/c2kbr-29.pdf

Singaravelu, H., & Pope, M. (2007). *Counseling international students in the United States.* Alexandria, VA: American Counseling Association.

Sodowsky, G. R., Taffe, R. C., Gutkin, T. B., & Wise, S. L. (1994). Development of the Multicultural Counseling Inventory: A self-report measure of multicultural competencies. *Journal of Counseling Psychology, 41*(2), 137–148.

Spielberger, C. D., Moscoso, M. S., & Brunner, T. M. (2005). Cross-cultural assessment of emotional states and personality traits. In R. K. Hambleton, P. F. Merenda, & C. D. Spielberger (Eds.), *Adapting educational and psychological tests for cross-cultural assessment* (pp. 343–367). Mahwah, NJ: Erlbaum.

Szapocznik, J., & Kurtines, W. (1980). Acculturation, biculturalism and adjustment among Cuban Americans. In A. Padilla (Ed.), *Acculturation: Theory, modes, and some new findings. American Association for the Advancement of Science, Symposium Series 39* (pp. 139–159). Boulder, CO: Westview.

Szapocznik, J., Scopetta, M. A., Kurtines, W., & Arnalde, M. D. (1978). Theory and measurement of acculturation. *Interamerican Journal of Psychology, 12*(2), pp. 113–130.

Teske, P., Brodsky, A., & Medler, A. (2006, August 4). Fix the achievement gap in Colorado. *The Denver Post.* Retrieved August 12, 2009, from http://www .denverpost.com/search/ci_4133236.

Thomas, W., & Collier, V. (1997). *School effectiveness for language minority students.* Washington, DC: National Clearinghouse for Bilingual Education.

Thomas, W., & Collier, V. (2002). *A national study of school effectiveness for language minority students' long-term achievement.* Washington, DC: Center for Research on Education, Diversity and Excellence.

Understanding the No Child Left Behind Act: English proficiency. Retrieved November 30, 2008, from http://www.learningpt.org/pdfs/qkey5.pdf.

U.S. Census Bureau. (2003). Nearly 1-in-5 speak a foreign language at home. Retrieved May 1, 2009, from http://www.census.gov/Press-Release/www .releases/archives/census_2000.

U.S. Department of Health and Human Services. (2001). National standards for culturally and linguistically appropriate services in health care. Washington, DC: Office of Mental Health.

Valdes, G., & Figueroa, R. A. (1994). *Bilingualism and testing: A special case of bias.* Norwood, NJ: Ablex.

Vazquez-Nuttall, E., Li, C., Dynda, A. M., Ortiz, S. O., Armengol, C. G., Walton, J. W., et al. (2007). Cognitive assessment of culturally and linguistically diverse students. In G. B. Esquivel, E. Lopez, & S. G. Nahari (Eds.), *Handbook of multicultural school psychology: An interdisciplinary perspective* (pp. 265–288). Mahwah, NJ: Lawrence Erlbaum.

Verdinelli, S., & Biever, J. L. (2009). Experiences of Spanish/English bilingual supervisees. *Psychotherapy Theory, Research, Practice, Training, 46*(2), 158–170.

Wechsler, D. (2004). Wechsler Intelligence Scale for Children (4th ed., Spanish). New York: Pearson Education.

Westermeyer, J. (1990). Working with an interpreter in psychiatric assessment and treatment. *Journal of Nervous and Mental Disorders, 178,* 745–749.

Woodcock, R. W., Munoz-Sandoval, A. F., McGrew, K. S., & Mather, N. (2005). Bateria-III-Woodcock-Munoz. Chicago: Riverside.

Woodcock, R. W., Muñoz-Sandoval, A. F., Ruef, M., & Alvarado, C. G. (2005). *Woodcock-Muñoz Language Survey—Revised.* Chicago: Riverside.

World Health Organization (http://www.who.int).

CHAPTER 7

PSYCHOTHERAPY WITH MEN: BUILDING PRACTICE COMPETENCIES

MARK A. STEVENS and MATT ENGLAR-CARLSON

INTRODUCTION

Being in psychotherapy can be both an obstacle and opportunity for many male clients. Conversely, many psychotherapists experience male clients as difficult, resistant, or simply not the definition of an ideal client (Englar-Carlson, 2006). Some would say that the common element of difficultly is not necessarily that the client is male, but rather the problem lies with the construction of masculinity and the ways that the field of psychotherapy has, or has not, considered how masculinity influences the enactment of psychotherapy (Scher, 1990). The development of the scholarly discipline of the psychology of men has drawn needed attention to the notion that being a man *matters* to the extent that masculinity is a focal organizing principle for all aspects of a man's life (Brooks & Good, 2005; Levant & Pollack, 1995; Pollack & Levant, 1998; Scher, Stevens, Good, & Eichenfield 1987). Further, this influence extends to how he "does" psychotherapy and the expectations he has for therapy outcomes (Addis & Mahalik, 2003; Englar-Carlson & Stevens, 2006).

A masculine-sensitive therapeutic style and counseling interventions are critical to the engagement and ultimate success of mental health interventions with male clients. The examination of the differential process of psychotherapy and flexibility of interventions for men with multiple cultural identities based on traditional or nontraditional gender roles, class, education, age, physical abilities, ethnicities/culture, gender identity, and sexual orientations are essential. The goal of this chapter is to provide clear guidance about how to effectively create positive therapeutic outcomes with male clients. Some of the points suggested may cause the reader to pause and question the manner in which she or he was trained and the way she or he practices psychotherapy with male clients of all cultural identities. The authors consider this reflection a healthy way to evaluate how the mental health profession can effectively adapt to the needs of all men.

The chapter begins with two case examples to bring the reader into the room to experience two different male clients. The next section defines some important terms used in the chapter. The next three sections focus on the knowledge, attitudes and values, and the therapeutic competencies needed for effective mental health practices with male clients. Experiential exercises that can be used for trainees or in other professional development activities are described. The next section provides the reader with an extensive resource guide for working with male clients. The final section charts competencies needed for counselors at different professional developmental levels. Throughout the chapter, highlighted by text boxes, the reader will have the opportunity to reflect on a number of process questions relevant to the content of the particular section.

GETTING TO KNOW MALE CLIENTS: TWO CASE EXAMPLES

In this section, the authors present two short case examples of psychotherapy with men (Case Vignettes 7.1 and 7.2, shown on the following page). After each case vignette, questions are presented about the reader's reaction to the client. It is hoped that the reader takes time to reflect on the questions and contemplate his or her own personal and clinical judgments about the case.

CASE VIGNETTE 7.1

Shaking Up David

David is a 22-year-old Caucasian male in his final year of college. His girlfriend of 2 years strongly recommended ("or else") that he seek counseling. Reluctantly, David made a counseling appointment. David expressed that his girlfriend was unhappy with his style of communication and she thought he did not communicate well or demonstrate that he really loved her. Initial counseling sessions focused on establishing a nonjudgmental environment by discussing what it was like being given the ultimatum of coming to counseling or else. David told the "story" of his relationship and what kind of effort it has taken for them to stay together for so long. David displayed added comfort in the sessions and seemed to enjoy the chance to talk about himself without being evaluated. He liked a matter-of-fact approach to asking him questions. The fourth session was several days after a large earthquake hit Southern California. While in session, there was a rather significant aftershock. The therapist noticed that David did not budge. No facial expressions, no signs of distress. In contrast, the therapist did not display as much composure and showed signs of nervousness.

Questions for the Reader

Before you continue reading, consider answering some of these questions about this particular case example:

- What is your initial reaction to David and what brought him to counseling?
- How would you share your experience of being in the room with David?
- How would you help David become more comfortable with his vulnerability?

What actually happened in the session is described next. As the shaking stopped, the therapist asked David how he was able to keep such composure. David reported that he was raised in a military family and from an early age learned how to "not feel" during dangerous situations. As a boy he was rewarded by words of admiration for this behavior by friends, and particularly his father. The therapist continued the conversation by revealing that he was intimidated by the amount of composure David exhibited and thought David would think less of the therapist because he showed signs of nervousness. This became a turning point in David's therapy. He stated to the therapist that others (especially his girlfriend) also mentioned that at times they felt intimidated by him. Hearing it from an authority figure, and from someone with whom he had built some trust, motivated him to become curious about how he might unintentionally intimidate others.

CASE VIGNETTE 7.2

Christopher and the Residuals of Being Bullied

Christopher is an 18-year-old biracial, heterosexual identified college student living on campus. He is the oldest of three siblings. Christopher's mother is Latina and his father is Caucasian. Academically he is an above-average student. He was referred to counseling (by campus housing) because of what he described as "out-of-control anger issues" that got him in trouble with a roommate. Recently he has been having intense arguments with his father and cousin, which have almost turned physical. Significant history gained in the first session reveals that Christopher was picked on as a kid all the way through middle school because of his small size. His father had a problem with alcohol and was verbally abusive to his mother most of his childhood. Christopher utilized all of his allotted sessions and then decided to attend a relationship-oriented therapy group.

Questions for the Reader

Before you continuing reading, consider answering some of these questions about this particular case example:

- How would you try to establish a working relationship with Christopher given the fact he was "required" to come to counseling?
- How could Christopher's experience of being bullied impact his self-esteem and identity as a male?
- How are boys and men taught to show and control their anger?
- How might Christopher experience being too vulnerable in session?
- How would you (or would you not) describe to Christopher what he can expect in therapy?
- How might you work with Christopher and issues he has with his father?
- What kept Christopher wanting to continue in therapy?
- How do you think Christopher would describe his experience of being in therapy?
- How might Christopher's racial identity shape his sense of masculinity?

DEFINITION OF TERMS

Many terms used throughout the chapter need clarification and context. The authors have provided the reader a brief definition of terms commonly used when learning about men and masculinities.

Gender: Although *gender* is commonly used interchangeably with *sex* (male, female, or trans), historically in the social sciences it refers to the socialization process of a person, not one's biological makeup. As deBeauvoir (1970) observed, unlike biological sex, people are not born with a gender. Instead a man learns what is considered to be a man congruent with a particular society at a particular time. In the context of this chapter, *gender* is used as a term to indicate the process by which institutions (e.g., schools, family, consumer marketing, and religious) and media (e.g., TV, books) shape the way boys and men are suppose to behave because they are biological males.

Gender roles: *Gender roles* are the perceived norms (societal expectations) by which boys/men are supposed to behave because they are male.

Examples of typical gender role socialization expectations for men include: being the "breadwinner," not showing vulnerability, expressing anger and aggression, being able to fix things and preferring instrumental activities, and having athletic ability. In this chapter, gender roles are considered learned attitudes and behaviors that can be both beneficial and detrimental to the psychological and physical wellbeing of men.

Gender role conflict: James O'Neil (1990) defined *gender role conflict* as "rigid, sexist, or restrictive gender roles, learned during socialization, that result in personal restriction, devaluation, or violation of others or self " (p. 25). O'Neil (1981) hypothesized six patterns of masculine gender role conflict: (1) restrictive emotionality, (2) health-care problems, (3) obsession with achievement and success, (4) restrictive sexual and affectionate behavior, (5) socialized control, power, and competition issues, and (6) homophobia.

Hegemonic masculinity: In this chapter, hegemonic masculinity refers to the idea that a culturally normative and dominant ideal of male behavior exists (e.g., White, middle-class, heterosexual definitions of masculinity in the United States) and that men are strongly encouraged to attain this ideal (Connell, 1987). Not all men attempt to live it, and some oppose it by developing alternative (and subordinate) masculinities, but most men position themselves in relation to it in situations where their choices may be quite restricted.

Homosexism: George Lehne (1976) used the term *homosexism* to refer to heterosexual men's intolerance of deviation from rigid sex roles. Imbedded in this term is the concept that men judge other men based on these rigid roles, and an emotional distance from and fear of other men are often consequences.

Homophobia: First coined by George Weinberg (1972), *homophobia* is a term originally meant to indicate a fear and disliking of persons who are gay. The meaning has expanded to include the socialization process of and pressure on all boys/men to fear being seen as gay. Homophobia, therefore, can be viewed as both a discriminatory and restrictive process.

Masculinities: In *Masculinities*, Connell (1995) argues that there is not one masculinity, but many different masculinities. In this chapter, the term *masculinities* is intended to imply configurations of men's ways of being in the world, which are dynamic, depending on context and demographics.

Men's issues: In this chapter, the term *men's issues* refers to the variety of tasks, expectations, consequences, relationships, and internal processes that have a unique type of saliency for many men. Examples of common men's issues are: power, competitiveness, emotional restriction, homophobia, fathering and fathers, sexual conquest, career, money, and physical health.

Sex: In this chapter, *sex* is referred as the biological makeup of the person versus the gender (cultural) roles of the individual.

KNOWLEDGE ABOUT MEN AND MASCULINITIES

For purposes of cultural competency, it is vital for mental health practitioners to acquaint themselves with and acquire knowledge about men's issues from a variety of disciplines such as men's studies, gay/lesbian/bisexual/transgender (GLBT) studies, feminist studies, and cross-cultural studies. Over the past 30 years, there has been an increased awareness and attention given to men as clients in mental health counseling (Addis & Mahalik, 2003). This focus has highlighted that there is something unique about being a man (i.e., masculinity) that wholly influences how men experience the world both intrapersonally and interpersonally. Men's socialization into masculine roles contributes to gender identity and ways of thinking, feeling, and behaving, presenting problems, and attitudes and potential fears about being in mental health counseling. It is the saliency of masculinity for men across all facets of life that has led researchers and clinicians alike to question the influence of masculinity upon mental health, well-being, and ultimately psychotherapy itself (Englar-Carlson, 2006; Good, Gilbert, & Scher, 1990). An important step in working with men involves taking the time to learn about male culture in general and specifically about the worldview of individual male clients. This part of the chapter is about acquiring knowledge about men and masculinity and is broken into four sections:

1. Rationale for considering men and masculinities as a component of multiculturalism
2. Understanding the cultures of men and masculinities
3. Mental health help-seeking behaviors of men
4. Presenting concerns of male clients

Masculinity as a Culture: A Rationale for Male-Sensitive Psychotherapy

One of the greatest shifts in the practice of mental health care has been the increased sensitivity and awareness given to cultural diversity issues, including the influence of gender roles (D. W. Sue & D. Sue, 2008). Among other identity factors, gender is now recognized as a

ASK YOURSELF

Ask yourself the following questions and think about whether men and masculinity should be considered an important piece of multicultural counseling conversation:

- Is there a male identity?
- Are there stereotypes of masculinity?
- Has society set and sustained certain expectations of how men should behave?
- Is there internalized homosexism?
- Are there variations of masculinity across cultures?
- What is male pride?
- How does male privilege influence your consideration of masculinity as a cultural variable?

salient organizing variable of clients' lives and experiences. Addis (2008) points out, however, that the term *gender* in most psychological research is synonymous with women, rather than used as a lens to understand the unique experiences of women *and* men. Understanding the gendered nature of masculinity is an important cultural competency (Levant & Silverstein, 2005; Liu, 2005; Mellinger & Liu, 2006; Stevens, 2006a). Guidelines developed for multicultural counseling competency (APA, 2003) and for practice with girls and women (APA, 2007) offer some direction and considerations in regard to helping mental health practitioners work with men. These guidelines and principles highlight the importance of the sociocultural context in tailoring psychotherapy to embrace the diverse identities of clients. Practice guidelines for boys and men are in development; one of the difficulties in developing these guidelines is the lack of empirical studies exploring the process and outcome of psychotherapy with men. Rather, numerous authors (see Brooks & Good, 2005; Englar-Carlson & Stevens, 2006; Kiselica, Englar-Carlson, & Horne, 2008; Levant & Pollack, 1995; Pollack & Levant, 1998; Rabinowitz & Cochran, 2002) have outlined gender-based cultural adaptations that can be made within the therapy relationship to accommodate male clients of diverse backgrounds.

Despite the fact that men in positions of power have historically dominated most Western societies, the reality is that many individual men do not feel empowered in their lives, and large groups of men (e.g., African-American boys and young men, teenaged fathers, blue-collar males, noncustodial fathers, etc.; Kiselica & Woodford, 2007) are often marginalized within the greater society. Further, current and historical legacies of multiple forms of oppression affect men and women alike (Good et al., 1990). Painful and often traumatic early experiences of loss and separation overlaid by society's expectations of achievement, strength, and toughness can lead adolescent males and adult men to feel conflict, anxiety, and confusion about their identity (Robertson & Shepard, 2008). Because the traditional male role encourages men to hide more vulnerable emotions, many men often have few socially sanctioned outlets for emotional expression beyond the expression of anger or aggression. In comparison to women, men seek mental health assistance at lower rates (Addis & Mahalik, 2003; Vessey & Howard, 1993), have higher rates of substance abuse with greater consequences to themselves and society (Johnston, O'Malley, Bachman, & Schulenberg, 2006; Kessler et al., 1999), die, on average, close to 6 years younger than women and have higher rates of the 15 leading causes of death (Courtenay, 2000), are less likely to be diagnosed with anxiety- and depression-related disorders (Addis, 2008; Sachs-Ericsson & Ciarlo, 2000), are four times more likely to die from suicide attempts (Oquendo et al., 2001), and have significantly less-healthy lifestyles (Courtenay, 1998). Higher rates of alcoholism and drug addiction, violence, and successful suicide suggest that many men act out rather than verbally share their emotional pain.

It can be argued that all of psychology is the psychology of men. After all, most scholars of psychotherapy, until more recently, were men. Males have traditionally been viewed as representatives of all humanity; thus, males and their characteristics have been the object of most psychological research (Levant, 1990). However, most research has explored men in the aggregate, and never assumed individual differences. Further, ideas and theories of psychotherapy were created from a Western male view of the world, despite the fact that the majority of clients were, and continue to be, female. In general, knowledge about psychotherapy appeared to be structured from a male perspective about treating women. However, a gender-specific approach to understanding human behavior was proposed by feminist scholars in the 1970s as a way to study women's psychological development. The resulting influence from the feminist movement was the understanding that women needed to be considered within the context of role restrictions and clinically treated with gender-appropriate models that had been adapted to the experience of women. One outcome of the women's movement within psychotherapy was the creation of specific therapies and treatments that acknowledged the experience of women and outlined treatment tailored to a woman's way of experiencing the world (Brown, 2009). Building on these advances in conceptualizing both gender and psychotherapy, feminist and men's studies scholars in the 1980s also began to use a gender-specific approach to looking at masculinity as a complex and multilayered construct (Good et al., 1990). Accordingly, specific ways of working with male clients that acknowledged male socialization and development were created to meet their specific needs and psychology (see Englar-Carlson & Stevens, 2006; Levant & Pollack, 1995; Meth & Pasick, 1990; Scher

et al., 1987). The feminist movement, when paired with the movements in multicultural psychotherapy and the psychology of men, has led to the acknowledgment in current clinical practice that cultural identity and memberships not only matter, but also are considered an integral aspect of ethical and effective clinical practice (Englar-Carlson, 2006; Jordan, 2009).

Given the enormous changes in the roles of women in North American society, traditional male behaviors can no longer be accepted as a normative standard. When studied from more sophisticated psychological and sociological approaches, male behavior seems to be guided by socially constructed rules that encourage men to take charge in their relationships, at work, and in their roles as fathers and husbands (Connell & Messerschmidt, 2005). At the same time, situations calling for cooperation, interdependence, or just "being" can create internal conflict for men. The contemporary man is given many mixed messages—be strong and tough, yet be sensitive around certain social issues like homosexuality and violence toward women (Nylund, 2007). The crossfire of interpersonal and intrapersonal demands that require response flexibility may result in frustration and confusion in many men who have been shaped by traditional cultural expectations of how a man is supposed to act.

Male clients can present unique challenges to the mental health practitioner. Men are often socialized to fear core components of the therapeutic process: the language of feelings, the disclosure of vulnerability, and the admission of dependency needs. Male clients' discomfort with the developing intimacy of the counseling relationship can manifest as early termination, anger at the mental health practitioner, unproductive intellectualizing, and other forms of resistance. Masculine-sensitive psychotherapy draws needed attention to the notion that being a man *matters* to the extent that masculinity is a focal organizing principle for all aspects of a man's life (Brooks & Good, 2005; Englar-Carlson & Stevens, 2006; Levant & Pollack, 1995; Pollack & Levant, 1998).

For men, this concerted appreciation of masculinity in terms of mental health and well-being could not come at a better time. There have been some changes in societal expectations for men. Scholars have documented changing gender roles for men (Bernard, 1981; Cabrera, Tamis-LeMonda, Bradley, Hofferth, & Lamb, 2000; Kilmartin, 2009), often highlighting difficulties men have experienced when their own gender role appears outdated or out of line with the demands or behavior of contemporary society.

Understanding the Multiple Cultural Identities of Men and Masculinities

The question "What does it mean to be a man?" has no one answer that applies to all men in all contexts. At any given time in our society, there are many forms of masculinity. Masculinity varies between and within cultures (Doss & Hopkins, 1998), creating a wide variation within male cultures when multiple identities are considered (Smiler, 2004). In fact, it is common in the male gender scholarly literature to use the word *masculinities* rather than *masculinity* in exploring the various male ideologies with which men can identify (Tager & Good, 2005): by sexual orientation and geographic regions (Blazina, 1997), among different racial, ethnic, religious, age, and socioeconomic groups (Gibbons, Hamby, & Dennis, 1997), and across developmental periods (Kimmel & Messner, 2004; O'Neil & Egan, 1992; Robertson & Shepard, 2008). Masculinities account for the differing definitions and variations of masculinity that exist among men between and within various cultures (i.e., young, urban African American masculinities may take a different form from middle-aged, rural migrant Mexican American masculinities, etc).

Some scholars in this area adopt a social-learning paradigm to understand masculinity (Addis & Cohane, 2005; Smiler, 2004). This paradigm is based on the assumption that men learn gendered attitudes and behaviors from social environments where cultural values, norms, and ideologies about what it means to be a man are reinforced and modeled. The idea of a social construction of masculinity suggests that masculinity is malleable depending on the dominant social forces in a society during a certain era. Despite the emphasis on the conceptualizing of multiple masculinities, there is a widespread belief that certain forms of masculinities are more socially central and associated with authority and social power (Connell & Messerschmidt, 2005). In the United States, depending on the era, the dominant ideal of masculinity has moved from an upper-class aristocratic image to a more rugged and self-sufficient ideal (Kimmel, 2005). Therefore, traditional masculinity can be viewed as the dominant (referred to as *hegemonic*) form of masculinity and thus highly influential in what members of a culture take to be normative (e.g., White, middle-class, heterosexual definitions of masculinity in the United States).

One of the benchmarks in masculinity ideology theorizing, Brannon's (1976) *blueprint for manhood* outlined four guidelines for men within the United States. These guidelines describe how a man should act, noting that men are socialized to avoid appearing feminine ("no sissy stuff"), to gain status and respect ("the big wheel"), to appear invulnerable ("the sturdy oak"), and to seek violence and adventure ("give 'em hell"). The guidelines represent the socially determined gender role stereotypes (i.e., what a "man" should do) that many men take as their notion of appropriate male behavior and expectations. These guidelines support both adaptive and maladaptive behavior, cognitions, and affect in men. For example, Blazina, Eddins, Burridge, and Settle (2007) suggested that the consequences of adherence to traditional masculinity often result in relational failures in the lives of men. This can lead to the development of a masculine self characterized by emotional distance, avoidance of intimacy, and a defensive style of moving away from others. Further, Mahalik, Good, and Englar-Carlson (2003) noted this socialization supports characteristics such as restriction and suppression of emotions and the valuing of rationality, emphasis on independence and achievement, and avoidance of characteristics associated with femininity.

Boys and adolescent males learn about gender role expectations from parents, peers, media, and through numerous developmentally shaping experiences in which one is called to enact expected gender role norms (Robertson & Shepard, 2008). For example, most young boys get the social message that "big boys don't cry," and learn that crying is an unacceptable avenue of expression. On the flip side, the other part of this message is that "only girls cry," and so boys learn clear distinctions of gender-appropriate behavior of separating boys/men from girls/women (Good, Thomson, & Brathwaite, 2005). For boys, the common experience of injuring oneself, experiencing pain, and crying is often met with punitive responses from others for one's tears. Crying and expressing sensitive emotions becomes an indication of weakness and vulnerability associated with femininity or homosexuality. Males learn that others, particularly other males, view repressing and masking emotionality as a sign of strength.

Whereas the blueprint for manhood is a useful tool for conceptualizing masculinity, it does not capture the full range of masculinities. Liu (2002a; 2005) suggested that even though the literature on men and masculinity has grown, the understanding of masculinity among men of color has remained limited. In particular, it seems unclear how men of color navigate expectations of hegemonic masculinity. However, recent conceptualizations of masculinities have explored culturally contextualized notions and experiences of manhood (Kimmel, 2005).

The social construction of masculinity suggests that the subscription to a dominant ideal of masculinity is not linear or without resistance. Most men are socialized to adopt certain masculine ideals, behaviors, and attitudes. Yet this dominant ideology of masculinity often has inherent conflicts. For example, dominant masculinity was historically predicated on the exclusion of men who were not White, upper-class, able-bodied, and privileged (i.e., normative masculinity; Liu, 2005). Historically, men representing any other diversity were considered marginal figures and not used to define normative masculinity. Therefore, men often find themselves

negotiating between dominant masculine ideals that inherently exclude them or not subscribing to these dominant ideals and thus being marginalized. Yet marginalized men also create their own communities where they develop their own cultural standards, norms, and values that create an alternative against dominant masculinity. For instance, in racial, ethnic, or sexual minority communities, men may develop forms of resistance in action and attitude that challenge the expectations of dominant masculinity.

Many men of color who grow up outside mainstream European American, heterosexual, middle-class culture are reminded by their experiences of prejudice and oppression on a personal and institutional level that although they are men, they are less privileged and more vulnerable to forces outside of their control (Caldwell & White, 2001). Questionable stares, increased scrutiny, and automatic suspicion by peers, strangers, and police are regular occurrences for these men who live and work in the mainstream culture (Majors & Billson, 1992; Sue, Capodilupo, & Holder, 2008; Sue et al., 2007). Not only are they subjected to the stresses of traditional masculinity, they must also cope with the overlay of subtle and not-so-subtle racism. A layer of anger related to this cultural predicament is common in many men of color, even those who are trying to live by the rules of mainstream society (Franklin, 1998).

While not as obvious as skin color, there are varieties of cultural identity as well that leave men vulnerable to feelings of alienation. Men who are unemployed or who work in the blue-collar sector may feel alienated from those in white-collar jobs. Liu (2002b) discussed the social class dimensions of the masculine experience and noted how admonitions to compete and achieve economic success may be particularly salient for men of certain social classes. In particular, Liu suggested that normative masculinity inherently contains class variables such as status ideals and expectations. Hegemonic masculinity refers to being in control, being a self-made man, and being the "breadwinner" or "good provider," all of which relate to social class and status.

In many places in America, gay and bisexual men are fearful of expressing aspects of their sexual orientation in the presence of their straight counterparts. The abuse that many gay men suffer at the hands of heterosexual boys and men in early life and beyond is well documented (Pascoe, 2003; Plummer, 2001). The fear of heterosexual men, or heterophobia, may manifest as avoidance of situations in which heterosexual men are present, stress responses when obliged to interact with heterosexual males, especially in groups, and self-devaluation and shame. Additionally, heterophobia may be expressed as a gay man's wholesale devaluation of heterosexual men and heterosexuality in general (Haldeman, 2001, 2006). Jews, Muslims, Christians, and men from other religious backgrounds may also feel ambivalence about how public they should be in acknowledging their religious identities. Men with physical and psychological disabilities can be subject to unwanted scrutiny and judgment from other men.

For mental health practitioners working with men, it is crucial to note that existing models of masculinity do not always account for all men in terms of who they are and how they behave. Traditional and rigid models do not speak to or necessarily account for invisible populations and all groups of men. Furthermore, remaining myopically fixed upon traditional notions of masculinity can lead to overlooking the emotionally strong and available, involved and connected, compassionate and nurturing man who exists, but is often ignored and marginalized not only among groups of men, but within society as a whole. For example, the term "absent father" is commonly used, but how often is the term "present and involved father" used? When considering how to work with men from cultural groups other than their own, therapists can pay attention to how masculinity intersects with an individual's cultural, familial, and unique psychological makeup.

Seeking Mental Health Assistance

Men are less likely than women to seek help for both mental health and physical health concerns (Addis & Mahalik, 2003; Andrews, Issakidis, & Carter, 2001; Möller-Leimkuehler, 2002; Sandman, Simantov, & An, 2000). The discrepancy in help-seeking even exists when men and women are exhibiting comparable levels of distress (Pederson & Vogel, 2007). Reports consistently indicate that men seek professional help less frequently than women regardless of age (Husaini, Moore, & Cain, 1994), nationality (D'Arcy & Schmitz, 1979), and ethnic and racial backgrounds (Neighbors & Howard, 1987; Sheu & Sedlacek, 2004). Compared to women, men tend to hold more restrictive views of mental illness and have less confidence in mental health practitioners.

Men's relative reluctance to seek professional help stands in stark contrast to the range and severity of the problems affecting them. For example, it is estimated that over 6 million men in the United States suffer from depression every year (National Institute of Mental Health [NIMH], 2003). In terms of physical health, men are more likely than women to have gone at least 2 years since seeing a physician even though men die, on average, close to 6 years earlier than do women, have higher levels of stress, and higher rates of completed suicides (four times more; Pollack & Levant, 1998) and suffer from higher rates of heart disease, lung cancer, chronic obstructive pulmonary disease, suicide, and alcoholism than do women (Anderson, Kochanek, & Murphy, 1997; Courtenay, 2000). Men with more traditional conceptions of masculinity also hold more negative attitudes toward their use of both mental health (Addis & Mahalik, 2003; Good & Wood, 1995; Robertson & Fitzgerald, 1992) and career-related services (Rochlen & O'Brien, 2002). When looking at cultural variables, African American men have been found to be less receptive toward help-seeking than European American men (Neighbors, Musick, & Williams, 1998), men from a working class or lower income are less likely to seek psychological help than middle- to upper-class men (Hodgetts & Chamberlain, 2002), and an increased resistance to seeking help has been found in Asian immigrant (Shin, 2002) and Asian American men (Solberg, Ritsma, Davis, Tata, & Jolly,

1994). In terms of data on asking for help from medical professionals, O'Brien, Hunt, and Hart (2005) found that younger men who had not yet experienced problems were most resistant to seeking help, while older men who had been through a major illness had more open views. Conditions, once diagnosed, that may directly challenge masculine identity, such as prostate or testicular cancer, also seemed to positively affect a man's willingness to seek help.

In the case of psychotherapy, people often weigh the possible benefits and consequences and social norms related to psychotherapy and arrive at a decision based on a variety of factors. For some men, violating gender role expectations, feeling embarrassed over sharing personal information, and just general vulnerabilities over self-disclosing private information might be too much to risk seeking help.

Another factor that may restrict mental health service utilization by men is the lack of fit between conceptualizations of masculinity and the popular perception of psychotherapy and mental health services (Mahalik et al., 2003). Traditional models of psychotherapy emphasizing the language of feelings, disclosing vulnerability, and admitting dependency needs can create difficulties for men socialized to adopt traditional masculine roles (Rabinowitz & Cochran, 2002). To address this, mental health practitioners can tailor the clinical encounter to initially identify the expectations male clients have of the psychotherapist and psychotherapy and correct those that are erroneous or change the structure of psychotherapy to be more congruent for a given male client. To address the needs of men, Addis and Mahalik (2003) recommended enacting changes to clinical environments such as providing greater opportunities for reciprocity for men (e.g., with other group members or the community), increasing the perception of normativeness for particular problems, training mental health practitioners to recognize the ego-centrality of certain problems (e.g., is this problem part of me?) in order to be more sensitive to how a male may be perceiving the relevance of the concern, reducing the stigma of seeking help and of

experiencing mental health problems, and creating alternative nontraditional forms of assistance more congruent with masculine socialization (e. g., psychoeducational classes in work settings). All of these changes could help men feel more comfortable in seeking help.

Presenting Concerns

Many men face unique psychosocial and interpersonal challenges associated with masculine socialization experiences and changing cultural expectations of both male behavior and the roles of men (Brooks & Good, 2005. For example, some fathers report social pressure to be the family breadwinner (Doucet, 2004) while also increasingly being expected to assume greater interpersonal involvement as fathers, partners, and coworkers in ways that are often not encouraged through traditional masculine socialization experiences (Cabrera et al., 2000; Good & Sherrod, 2001; Levant & Pollack, 1995; Real, 2002). Further, as men pursue power and privilege in society, they often experience pain, powerlessness, poor health, and isolation (Liu, 2005). Many men do suffer from depression and anxiety-related disorders, but often it is manifested in the forms of addiction, violence, interpersonal conflict, and general irritability. For many men, their own psychic pain may not be obvious, and thus when men do come for psychotherapy, many male clients are not sure how to behave, confused about how to enter into a relationship with a counselor (or whether they really want or need to), and question how psychotherapy can really make a difference in their life (Englar-Carlson, 2006). Stevens (2005) proposed a multilevel *cultural-social-psychological* model to help explain how the influence of the institution of masculinity may show up in the therapy room (Figure 7.1). The innermost circle or core of the diagram is recognized or unrecognized privilege. The next circle is the impact of privilege on a society/institutional level. The next circle out reflects how institutional/societal bias can be experienced in men from a societal perspective.

The next-to-last circle reflects how men may experience or act out the societal pressures of masculinity. And finally, the outermost circle shows common symptoms and underlying reasons why men come to counseling. For example, male privilege can be seen as a contributing factor to homophobic beliefs. Homophobia is a contributing factor to fear of femininity. Fear of femininity is a contributing factor to emotional restriction, which in turn can show up in therapy as relationship problems or physical health concerns.

Depression is a serious, yet often-undiagnosed condition in men (Addis, 2008; Cochran, 2005; Cochran & Rabinowitz, 2000; NIMH, 2003;

Pollack, 1998; Real, 1997). Cochran and Rabinowitz (2000) noted the influence of gender role socialization, which encourages stoicism and suppression of emotion, as one of the several factors that obscures the expression of depressed mood in many men. Traditional masculine prohibitions against the experience of mood states of depression (e.g., sadness) and the behavioral expression of these mood states (e.g., crying) make clear and simple descriptions of male depression difficult. Thus the true expression of depression for many men creates a conflict. Further, since depression often becomes "masked," it is difficult for primary-care physicians and other health professionals to determine when men are actually experiencing

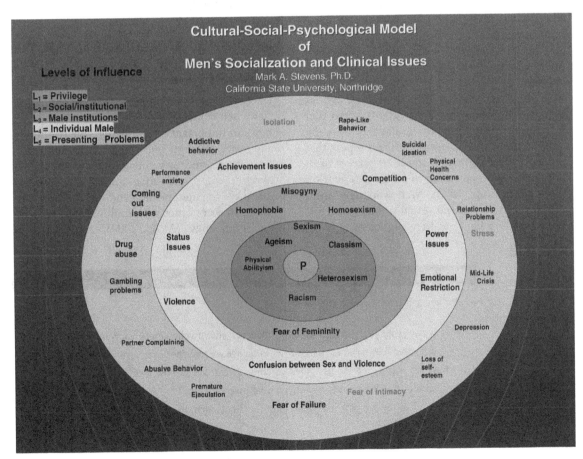

Figure 7.1 Cultural-Social-Psychological Model of Men's Socialization and Clinical Issues

Source: Mark A. Stevens, PhD, California State University, Northridge.

depressive-spectrum disorders (Cochran & Rabinowitz, 2000). Yet, many men, after experiencing interpersonal or traumatic loss, react by plunging into a depressive episode (Cochran & Rabinowitz, 1996). It is not uncommon for men to use alcohol or other mood-altering substances or activities to medicate depression (Hanna & Grant, 1997). The extremes of depression include difficulties associated with suicide and homicide. Men are more prone to an aggressive acting out of their depressed mood given their tendency toward action and externalization (Cochran & Rabinowitz, 2000). Despite reporting half the depression that women report in epidemiological surveys, men actually commit suicide three to four times more frequently than women (NIMH, 2003). This risk rises even higher with increasing age (Kennedy, Metz, & Lowinger, 1995). In addition to suicide, homicide is associated more frequently with men (U. S. Department of Justice, 2003). This, too, often occurs in conjunction with a depressive episode.

Although estimates of the sexual abuse of boys vary widely, Baker and King (2004) noted that 16 percent of adult men claim that they were the victims of child sexual abuse. Others report that at least 3 percent and as many as 20 percent of all boys have been the victim of sexual exploitation (Holmes & Slap, 1998). Men who have been verbally, physically, and sexually abused as children are more likely to have higher rates of all types of mental illness, including affective disorders, substance abuse, and certain personality disorders, and are more likely to come to the attention of clinicians (Lisak, 1994, 2001; Weeks & Widom, 1998). Violence, episodes of depression, and rates of suicide are also higher among men who have been abused or witnessed abuse in childhood (Lisak, 1994; Rosenbaum & Leisring, 2003). Because of traditional masculine gender role prohibitions on acknowledging victimization, many men do not willingly reveal the extent of their abuse to others. Homophobia is another factor related to underreporting. Many boys who have been violated by other males fear that they will be labeled "gay" if they reveal the abuse to anyone, so they keep it a secret (Cabe, 1999; Gartner, 1999).

VALUES AND ATTITUDES ABOUT MEN AND COUNSELING MEN

Liu (2005) outlined different cultural competencies when working with men. In terms of awareness, an important step is being able to identify and work through one's negative assumptions, stereotypes, and/or value conflicts pertaining to psychotherapy with men that might result in inability to understand and empathize with them. In accordance with multicultural counseling guidelines (APA, 2003), mental health

---

ASK YOURSELF

Ask yourself the following questions:

- How have your experiences with men influenced your psychotherapy work with male clients?
- How does your own gender-role journey influence your psychotherapy work with male clients?
- How has society set and sustained certain expectations of how men should behave?
- What are your stereotypes of how men *do* psychotherapy?
- What might be the potential value for male clients identifying their own masculinity from a cultural perspective?
- What do you like most about working with male clients?
- What do you like least about working with male clients?

practitioners can examine their own assumptions about men and masculinity in order to reduce subconscious attitudes that prevent or hamper male clients from opening up, being vulnerable, examining their views on what it means to be a man, or making desired changes to improve their lives. This section of the chapter gives the reader the opportunity to reflect on his or her views of men and masculinity, with the intent to examine ways to improve the therapeutic relationship with male clients.

Negative Biases Toward Male Clients?

It is possible that mental health practitioners themselves hold beliefs about men that restrict their ability to fully benefit from psychotherapy. Developing therapeutic relationships with male clients can be perceived as more difficult than with female clients (Vogel, Epting, & Wester, 2003). One of the factors underlying that perception is that men often exhibit less interpersonal openness and less confidence in the mental health profession (Leong & Zachar, 1999). A question to consider is whether male clients need to adapt their behavior to be in psychotherapy or whether psychotherapists need to adapt their beliefs and interventions to match the behavior of male clients. Clearly, mental health practitioners can take proactive steps to overcome any potential discrepancy between the male client and the process and potential benefits of psychotherapy.

To the extent that mental health practitioners hold biased views of men that label them as "perpetrators," "resistant," or "difficult," the process of developing empathy for men's struggles will be inhibited and the likelihood of forming effective therapeutic alliances will be diminished. Both male and female psychotherapists should have an awareness of the ways in which their own countertransference issues with men might influence their behavior in session (Hayes & Gelso, 2001; Scher, 2001). These reactions might take the more obvious form of negative stereotypes resulting from past experiences with men. They can also take the form of blind spots based on shared assumptions that reinforce traditional masculine expectations, such as emotional restrictiveness. Mental health practitioners who view emotional awareness and expression as gender-inappropriate for men are unlikely to successfully assist men in exploring and developing connections to their emotional selves.

ASK YOURSELF

How might these commonly held stereotypes about men perhaps restrict your full understanding of your client's experience of being a man?

- Men are chauvinistic.
- Men are Good Old Boys.
- Men don't listen well.
- Men enjoy danger.
- Men are unfeeling.
- Men are privileged.
- Men like to show off.
- Men need to control.
- Men fear being vulnerable.
- Men are competitive.

A Reframing View of Men and Masculinity: A Strength-Based Perspective

Whereas scholarly inquiry into the psychology of men has clearly raised the level of awareness of mental health professionals about the needs of men, in many ways it may also have presented men and masculinity in more restrictive and binding ways by being overly focused on deficits and the darker side of men and masculinity. When the topic of men and mental health is brought up in the popular press or in professional forums, it is often focused on the bad things that men do, or how the male socialization process scars boys and men for life, leaving them chronically flawed and in dire need of fixing (Kiselica, 2006). Most of the scholarly literature on men and mental health has overemphasized what is wrong with men and masculinity by focusing on male pathology at the expense of important data highlighting male strengths and the good things that men do. Over time, this focus on male deficits has fostered inaccurate generalizations about boys and men that are linked to potentially harmful practices by mental health practitioners working with male clients. A deficit perspective fosters the mindset that men are flawed and need to be fixed, and that they are solely at fault for the problems they bring to psychotherapy. For example, there is a tendency for mental health professionals to view males as being hypoemotional, even though the existing data on gender differences in emotion challenge the notion that men and women are emotionally different (Wester, Vogel, Pressly, & Heesacker, 2002). Heesacker and colleagues (1999) found that mental health professionals with hypoemotional stereotypes about men are more likely to blame men for the problems they bring to couples psychotherapy. It is rarely stated that most men are reasonably well-adjusted human beings, that most men recognize, experience, and express emotions within the normal range, and that most men have long traditions of acting in a prosocial manner (Kiselica, 2006). To more accurately meet the needs of men, mental health practitioners must develop a more complex and rich understanding about the emotional lives, psychological development, and behaviors of all men.

As a way of learning about the healthy aspects of men and masculinity and to incorporate a strength-based framework into psychotherapy, Kiselica, Englar-Carlson, and Fisher (2006)

ASK YOURSELF

How might these reframing attitudes about men serve you to better connect with your male clients?

Stereotypic View	Reframed View
Chauvinistic	Protects others
Good old boys	Is loyal to friends
Poor listener	Problem solves
Enjoys danger	Can be heroic
Unfeeling	Withstands pressure
Entitled privilege	Provides to others
Shows off	Takes physical risks
Need to control	Takes charge
Fear of vulnerability	Can absorb pain
Competitive	Wants to succeed

Source: Stevens (2006a).

ASK YOURSELF

How might your male clients experience being understood from a strength-based perspective?

His Behavior	Benefit to Self and Others
Responsible	Can be relied on
Clear thinking	Solutions under pressure
Conscientious	Gets work done
Strong	Others may lean on him
Self-sacrificing	Lessens danger for others
Courageous	Is rewarded by others
Physically caring	Provides security
Practical	Time efficient
Dedicated	Stays with the difficulty
Wanting to succeed	Produces results

Source; Stevens (2006a).

proposed a way of understanding men grounded in positive psychology that added a recognition of strengths and virtue over disease, weakness, and damage. In line with positive psychology, this perspective focused on building in men what is right rather than fixing what is wrong (Seligman & Csikszentmihalyi, 2000). Kiselica et al. (2006) suggested that psychotherapists include a perspective on understanding men that accentuates healthy behaviors and traditions of men. Though not exhaustive, this perspective would include focusing on and exploring male relational styles, generative fatherhood and ways fathers contribute to their children's development in beneficial ways, male ways of caring, male self-reliance, the worker/provider tradition of husbands and fathers, male daring, courage, and risk-taking, the group orientation of boys and men, and the humanitarian service of fraternal organizations.

A View of Men and Masculinity: From a Potential Cost Perspective

It is also important to acknowledge that many of the qualities and traits associated with traditional masculinity (e.g., courage, bravery, risk-taking and daring, self-reliance, personal sacrifice, and

ASK YOURSELF

Attitude and Behavior	Potential Cost
Stuffing feelings	Physical health problems
Problem-solving mode	Disconnection from others
Driven to succeed	Loss of perspective
Not admitting weakness	Limits self-learning/awareness
Avoidance of fear	Reduced emotional risk-taking
"Male pride"	Unnecessary violence
Staying strong	Missed opportunities to grieve

Source: Stevens (2006a).

protectiveness) are useful and positive only if men apply them under the right conditions and situations, and without uniformity. In that sense, the degree to which these aspects are healthy and optimal depends on the ability of a man to exercise good judgment in knowing when and how to express them (e.g., too much self-reliance can limit a man's ability to ask for help, an overemphasis on risk-taking can led to dangerous and fatal accidents, and so on).

Before moving on to the next section, consider how and when you would address some of the potential costs to your male clients regarding their behaviors and attitudes commonly associated with the male socialization process.

SKILLS FOR COUNSELING MALE CLIENTS

This section on developing competent counseling skills for working with male clients provides the reader with an opportunity to synthesize information presented in the previous sections of this chapter. Another Case Vignette (7.3) is used to

CASE VIGNETTE 7.3

Bryan and His Tearful Sessions

Bryan is a 51-year-old heterosexual identified male, born in Florida, and the only son of Polish immigrant parents. His parents came to Florida in poverty and developed a successful restaurant business. Bryan did not work in the family business, but rather got a college degree, an MBA, and started his own successful investment company. As a businessman, Bryan works hard and is an independent decision maker. At the age of 21, Bryan married his high school girlfriend, but divorced 3 years later. He remarried at age 39. After 9 years of marriage, he and his wife separated. The separation was initiated by his wife due to his long hours at work, which left her feeling unappreciated and unloved. Bryan and his wife have an 8-year-old daughter. Bryan considers himself virtually alone in the world. His father died 20 years ago, and he is not very close to his mother, who lives in another state. He does not have anyone he considers a best friend, and often relies on business acquaintances as a social outlet. Bryan has a history of alcohol abuse that began when he was in college. When his daughter was born, Bryan quit using alcohol. Bryan also struggles with some health issues such as hypertension and chronic back pain. Bryan was referred to counseling by his physician. Like many men, Bryan was embarrassed to cry in session and tried hard to hold back tears. In a half-joking manner, he blamed his therapist for his crying, noting that he rarely cried outside of the session. When asked what his crying in session meant to him, Bryan responded that it made him feel weak and out of control. Multiple times he ended sessions when he did not cry by saying, "I must be getting better, I did not cry today." Interestingly, though, when he did cry, he ended those sessions stating that he felt better and got a lot off his chest. Over time, he responded well to the therapist's statements that he respected Bryan for allowing himself to be vulnerable in session and understood how important it was for him to not feel weak or out of control. Crying in session became more comfortable for Bryan, particularly when he was able to save face. Often he would save face by making a joke, such as "Here you go again, Doc, making me cry."

Questions for the Reader

Before reading the next section, consider the following questions. How do you approach working with Bryan? What are your guiding principles? Here are a few examples of guiding principles. Do you agree with them? Why or why not?

- Men have an often-unstated strong desire and longing for deeper, more intimate, satisfying, trusting, safe, noncompetitive, heartfelt connections, yet are often too scared or lack the knowledge to attain such connections.
- Men do have a full range of feelings and are often able to sort out what the feelings are and how they may impact their relationships, although this may take some extra time and coaching.
- View men as in pain and wanting relief, yet at the same time not wanting to be vulnerable.

stimulate thinking about ways to approach counseling men. Finally, the authors present specific guidelines and approaches to work with male clients.

The wealth of scholarly research and writing in the psychology of men has demonstrated an interesting paradox. Even though most of the theoretical work in counseling, psychology, and psychotherapy is predicated on the lived experiences of men's lives, men themselves may not fully benefit from existing and accepted models of clinical treatment (Liu, 2005). Kiselica (2003) noted a fundamental mismatch between the way counseling and psychotherapy tends to be conducted and the relational styles of most males. This mismatch plays a major role in the failure of many professionals to engage men in psychotherapy. Kiselica and Englar-Carlson (2008) recalled the work of Bruch (1978), who observed that psychotherapy is a good fit for certain types of individuals, but not others. Utilizing Holland's (1973) personality theory, Bruch suggested that psychotherapy was tailor-made for people who have a "social" personality type (e.g., those who are able to easily engage others in an emotionally intimate manner, are comfortable and skilled at talking about their feelings, and enjoy self-reflection, etc.). Since psychotherapy as it is traditionally practiced and taught involves these types of interactions, those who are social personality types can more easily enter the world of psychotherapy. However, other individuals with different personality types feel out of place in traditional psychotherapy. They tend to avoid the less structured, interpersonal, and exploratory activities often employed in psychotherapy. It is not surprising that "conventional" or "realistic" personality types might feel ill-at-ease with psychotherapy as customarily practiced.

Masculine–Sensitive Approaches to Psychotherapy

Masculine-sensitive adjustments in the therapy process can be made in order to correct the mismatch between conventional psychotherapy and the relational styles of most males (Kiselica et al., 2008). Below is a synthesis of research from both clinicians and academic scholars in regard to guidelines for counseling men from a male-sensitive perspective.

Recognize, acknowledge and gently affirm the difficulty that men have with entering and being in psychotherapy. Men often believe they are being coerced into therapy (e.g., by a spouse, employer, or the law) and present with a great deal of resentment. Often men experience going to therapy with shame and fear (Levant, 1997; Park, 2006) since asking for help implies weakness and a failure to be self-sufficient. Many do not want to feel even weaker by depending on a mental health practitioner. Rather than confronting and possibly confirming a man's fears about being in therapy (and potentially causing the man to flee), it can be more helpful to recognize, acknowledge, and gently affirm the path the client has taken to get to your office, and to validate the difficulty one might experience entering into and being in counseling. During this process, reframe thoughts of personal weakness or failure as the courage and guts to reach out and work on the issue.

Help the client save "masculine face." It is important for mental health practitioners to communicate their genuine respect for their male client coming into therapy. Reflecting and contextualizing coming to therapy as a brave, courageous,

ASK YOURSELF

Consider each of the following components of masculine-sensitive approaches to psychotherapy and ask yourself what each of these would look like with your male clients. What are the ways that these components have unique saliency for men?

- Clarify confidentiality.
- Help create a "safe" environment.
- Counselor–client relationship building is essential.
- Empathize with the resistance.
- Communicate your understanding of his anger, frustration, and doubts about being in counseling.
- Be real and genuine.
- Be patient.
- Model being vulnerable and secure.
- Appreciate his vulnerability.
- Appreciate his strengths.
- Let him know (in attitude and behavior) that you are interested in getting to *know* him.

and honorable behavior is congruent with traditional male socialization (Liu & Chang, 2007; Park, 2006). For many men, acceptance as a man is needed before progressing with treatment. Normalizing a man's concern can also build therapeutic engagement. The greater the extent to which men believe a problem is normal the more likely they are to seek and receive help for that problem (Addis & Mahalik, 2003).

Educate male clients up front about the process of therapy. Most male clients don't know how the therapy process works and worry that the psychotherapist will be judgmental or discover their weaknesses (Stevens, 2006b). Some male clients have a fear of not being a "good-enough" client. They may perceive therapy as a place where they will need to become emotional, and thus don't feel ready or equipped to do what they believe will be required of them in a traditional therapy setting. It can be useful to check out his assumptions of what will be expected of him as a client and clarify your role as the mental health professional. Look to explain how one practices psychotherapy.

Set goals that match the needs of the male client. It is helpful to establish goals with the male client for the sessions, and develop an initial plan to address them. Wester and Lyubelsky (2005) suggested using male gender role conflict theory in setting up therapeutic goals with men. Implied in this discussion is that men appreciate a more explicitly goal-oriented therapy process. Eliminating stress, increasing happiness, and improving connectedness with others might be more appealing to men seeking help than an emphasis on exploring the past, expressing emotions, and sharing problems (Vogel & Wester, 2003). Empirical support for the utility of establishing goals comes from the motivational enhancement literature (e.g., Miller, Rollnick, & Conforti, 2002). Motivational approaches focus on assisting clients to resolve any ambivalence they have about making changes in their lives (Moos, 2007).

Be patient. Male clients often present a unique challenge to the psychotherapist (Englar-Carlson & Stevens, 2006). Male clients' discomfort with the developing intimacy of a psychotherapy relationship can manifest as early termination, anger at the mental health practitioner, unproductive intellectualizing, and other forms of resistance. It is important to be patient and understanding of the walls men have erected if the therapist is to be let inside. Men may slam their emotional doors and leave therapy if confrontation is used too early (Rabinowitz & Cochran, 2002). Many men often need to start therapy slowly and will resist sharing intimate personal details and feelings up front. Rituals of initial engagement through more traditional masculine means (smalltalk, good-natured humor, handshakes, and so on) are often needed (Englar-Carlson, Smart, Arczynski, Boucher, & Shepard, 2008; Kiselica, 2001). Characteristics such as dependability, benevolence, and responsiveness are seen as imperative to the development of a positive therapeutic alliance (Ackerman & Hilsenroth, 2003).

Use a therapy language and approach that is congruent with your client's gender role identity. It is important for mental health practitioners to recognize the relational style of men in contrast to their conception of how therapy should proceed (Kiselica, 2006). Male clients may want to be treated in ways that feel congruent with their masculine socialization. This can be accomplished by listening carefully, projecting warmth without appearing overly sympathetic, and tailoring the clinical work to the male client. This can mean substituting other words for *psychotherapy* (e.g., *consultation*, *coaching*, *meeting*, or *discussion*), using less jargon, being more active as counselor, and matching one's relational style to the client's needs (Englar-Carlson et al., 2008). Some men may also be reluctant to label mental health problems as *depression* or *anxiety*, but instead may want to call them *stress* (O'Brien, Hunt, & Hart, 2005). In addition, communicating an appreciation for a man's style of expression is critical at the beginning of therapy. For example, if a man uses profanity as he discusses his problems, therapists should avoid correcting this type of expression, but rather reflect back the content and emotion of his message with or without using the profanity. In an attempt to

help the therapeutic process, therapists should understand that many men have had less experience with understanding and expressing their exposed emotions (Good, 1998).

Be genuine and real. Modeling self-disclosure is another practice that can strengthen the relationship between the psychotherapist and the male client and assist in revealing personal matters (Kiselica & Englar-Carlson, 2008). When a mental health practitioner shares something about who he or she is, it can go a long way toward showing a client that he is important. Further, it can model openness and appropriate self-disclosure. Male clients often trust and are more engaged in treatment when they experience their psychologist as a "real human" who is there to help. The Latino concept of *personalismo* (Paniagua, 2005), in which male clients become more oriented toward people and warmth, seems to apply here (Englar-Carlson, 2006). Many male clients want to be treated as people first, and not as problems to be dealt with or fixed. Cusak, Deane, Wilson, and Ciarrochi (2006) found that the therapeutic bond and the perception of treatment helpfulness were more important in predicting future help-seeking by men than whether or not they were comfortable or effective with emotional expression.

Invite him to share his stories. Men have traditionally learned to express themselves through their stories (Bly, 1990) and are typically better at sharing their stories than their feelings. Sharing stories is a way for men to feel more comfortable and effective in the therapy room. Men often feel a sense of bonding with the person who listens, is interested, and can appreciate the meaning of the story. Stories can also serve as a gateway to the natural expression of his feelings (Stevens, 2006b).

FINAL THOUGHTS ON PSYCHOTHERAPY WITH MEN

We all have hopes that our clients will benefit from the experience of psychotherapy. How are your hopes different for male clients than for female clients? Below are some of the hopes the therapist had for the three case examples presented in the chapter. In thinking about your male clients, how would your list of hopes be similar or different for your male clients?

- Discover the dreams, desires, and fears of his "little boy," which has been silenced by the rules of masculinity.
- Discover that asking for help will not kill or weaken him.
- Discover how his history has impacted his current life situations.
- Discover that he can open up with others and not give up his power.
- Discover an increased value of the importance of relationships.
- Discover that vulnerability is a form of strength.
- Discover how to get to know himself.

This chapter was intended to help the reader discover or reinforce the awareness that one of the main things mental health practitioners can do is to consider and appreciate the unique concerns, needs, and difficulties that men experience in life and that are brought to and reenacted in the clinical setting. When psychotherapists are gender-aware, supportive, and male-affirming in their approach, men can have the opportunity to tell their story and make sense of what is chaotic, distilling, and conflicting. For many men, safe spaces such as this are rarely found.

RESOURCES

The following resources are provided as suggestions for further inquiry and as tools students, clinicians, trainees, and supervisors can utilize to help improve the quality of the services they provide

EXPERIENTIAL EXERCISES FOR PROFESSIONAL DEVELOPMENT

These experiential activities (7.1 and 7.2) allow the participant to explore the variety of subtle and not-so-subtle assumptions and feelings one has about counseling male clients. These activities is appropriate for all levels of counselors, as the layers associated with assumptions and feelings about working with male clients are a dynamic process.

EXPERIENTIAL EXERCISE 7.1: COUNSELING MEN: A GUIDED IMAGERY

The participants are asked to close their eyes and imagine meeting a client for the first time. Your client is male. Perhaps you knew that by the phone conversation when he made the appointment or by seeing his name. Perhaps you only found out when you walked in to meet your client in the waiting room. Regardless of how or when you found out your client is male, what are you aware of as you prepare to meet with this person? How does your body feel? How are you getting ready to meet with this client? Do you notice any resistance or hesitancy on your part? What is your level of enthusiasm to get to know this client? Are there any particular assumptions you have about this person because he is male? When you greet your client, are you different than when you greet a female client? What do you notice about how you ask questions or respond to your male client? Be aware of your subtle and not-so-subtle behaviors and assumptions.

After the guided imagery, the participants are asked to share their reactions with one another and take note of the variety of themes that emerge. Personal information about their relationships with men often is brought up, and how that influences their feelings and assumptions about counseling men. Different reactions between male and female participants are often noticed and discussed.

EXPERIENTIAL EXERCISE 7.2: MALE SOCIALIZATION PROCESS

This exercise is meant to highlight through metaphor some ways that boys have been socialized to behave, think, and feel. David and Brannon's (1976) *metaphor model* of masculinity training is used to engage the audience in memories and discussion. The intended outcome of the exercise is to increase empathy for male clients and understand how the socialization process may be a factor in how men "do" therapy.

- "No sissy stuff"—men should avoid feminine things.
- "The big wheel"—men should be successful and continually achieve.
- "The sturdy oak"—men should not show signs of weakness.
- "Give 'em hell"—men should seek adventure even at the risk of violence.

Participants are asked to identify examples of the above metaphors. Examples can be drawn from a variety of sources, including personal socialization experiences, and remembering their fathers, brothers, and other significant men in their lives or media images. After the discussion has drawn out some specific examples of how boys are taught to become men (with the understanding that there is compliance and noncompliance), the following questions can be used to stimulate discussion about men in therapy.

Questions:

1. How might the above socialization process show up in the therapy room?
2. Given these metaphors, what type of resistance might men feel about coming into therapy? How would you address the resistance in a male-friendly way?
3. How does male socialization contribute to the clinical picture of the male client?
4. How would you use this awareness about the male socialization process in your assessment and treatment plan?

MEN AND MASCULINITIES COMPETENCIES RESOURCE GUIDE

The following resources are provided as suggestions for further inquiry and as tools students, clinicians, trainees, and supervisors can utilize to help improve the quality of the services they provide.

MALE DEVELOPMENT AND THEORIES OF MASCULINITIES

Addis, M. E., & Cohane, G. H. (2005). Social scientific paradigms of masculinity and their implications for research and practice in men's mental health. *Journal of Clinical Psychology, 6*, 633–647.

Bernard, J. (1981). The good-provider role: Its rise and fall. *American Psychologist, 36*, 1–12.

Blazina, C. (1997). Mythos and men: Toward new paradigms of masculinity. *The Journal of Men's Studies, 5*, 285–294.

Brannon, R. (1976). The male sex-role: Our culture's blueprint of manhood and what it's done for us lately. In D. S. Brannon & R. Brannon (Eds.), *The forty-nine percent majority* (pp. 1–45). Reading, MA: Addison-Wesley.

Cabrera, N. J., Tamis-LeMonda, C. S., Bradley, R. H., Hofferth, S., & Lamb, M. E. (2000). Fatherhood in the twenty-first century. *Child Development, 71*(1), 127–136.

Connell, R. W., & Messerschmidt, J. W. (2005). Hegemonic masculinity: Rethinking the concept. *Gender and Society, 19*, 829–859.

Kilmartin, C. T. (2009). *The masculine self* (4th ed.). Cornwall-on-Hudson, NY: Sloan.

Kimmel, M. (2005). *Manhood in America: A cultural history* (2nd ed.). New York: Free Press.

Kimmel, M., & Messner, M. (Eds.). (2004). *Men's lives* (6th ed.). New York: Macmillan.

Nylund, D. (2007). *Beer, babes, and balls: Masculinity and sports talk radio.* Albany, NY: SUNY Press.

O'Neil, J. M., & Egan, J. (1992). Men's gender role transitions over the lifespan: Transformations and fears of femininity. *Journal of Mental Health Counseling, 14,* 305–324.

Plummer, D. C. (2001). The quest for modern manhood: Masculine stereotypes, peer culture and the social significance of homophobia. *Journal of Adolescence, 24,* 15–23.

Robertson, J., & Shepard, D. S. (2008). The psychological development of boys. In M. Kiselica, M. Englar-Carlson, & A. Horne (Eds.), *Counseling troubled boys* (pp. 3–30). New York: Routledge.

Shepard, D. S. (2005). Male development and the journey toward disconnection. In D. Comstock (Ed.), *Diversity and development: Critical contexts that shape our lives and relationships* (pp. 133–160). Belmont, CA: Brooks-Cole.

Smiler, A. P. (2004). Thirty years after the discovery of gender: Psychological concepts and measures of masculinity. *Sex Roles, 50,* 15–26.

CONSTRUCTS OF MASCULINITIES: CULTURAL CONSIDERATIONS

Caldwell, L. D. & White, J. L. (2001). African centered therapeutic and counseling interventions for African American males. In G. Brooks & G. Good (Eds.), *The handbook of counseling and psychotherapy approaches for men* (pp. 737–753). San Francisco: Jossey-Bass.

Casas, J. M., Turner, J. A., & Ruiz de Esparza, C. A. (2001). Machismo revisited in a time of crisis: Implications for understanding and counseling Hispanic men. In G. Brooks & G. Good (Eds.), *The handbook of counseling and psychotherapy approaches for men* (pp. 754–779). San Francisco: Jossey-Bass.

Franklin, A. J. (1999). Invisibility syndrome and racial identity development in psychotherapy and counseling African American men. *The Counseling Psychologist, 27,* 761–793.

Haldeman, D. C. (2006). Queer eye on the straight guy: A case of gay male heterophobia. In M. Englar-Carlson & M. Stevens (Eds.), *In the room with men: A casebook of therapeutic change* (pp. 301–318). Washington, DC: American Psychological Association.

Haldeman, D. C. (2001). Psychotherapy with gay and bisexual men. In G. Brooks & G. Good (Eds.), *The handbook of counseling and psychotherapy approaches for men* (pp. 796–815). San Francisco: Jossey-Bass.

Hammond, W. P., & Mattis, J. S. (2005). Being a man about it: Manhood meaning among African American men. *Psychology of Men and Masculinity, 6,* 114–126.

Johnson, P. D. (2006). Counseling African American men: A contextualized humanistic perspective. *Counseling and Values, 50,* 187–196.

Liu, W. M. (2002). The social class-related experiences of men: Integrating theory and practice. *Professional Psychology, 33,* 355–360.

Liu, W. M. (2002). Exploring the lives of Asian American men: Racial identity, male role norms, gender role conflict, and prejudicial attitudes. *Psychology of Men & Masculinity, 3,* 107–118.

Liu, W. M., & Chang, T. (2007). Asian American masculinities. In F. T. L. Leong, A. Ebero, L., Kinoshita, A. G. Arpana, & L. H. Yang (Eds.), *Handbook of Asian American psychology* (2nd ed.; pp. 197–211). Thousand Oaks, CA: Sage.

Majors, R. G., & Billson, J. M. (1992). *Cool pose: The dilemmas of black manhood in America.* New York: Lexington.

Park, S. (2006). Facing fear without losing face: Working with Asian American men. In M. Englar-Carlson & M.A. Stevens (Eds.). *In the room with men: A casebook of therapeutic change* (pp. 151–173). Washington, DC: American Psychological Association.

Wester, S.R. (2007). Male gender role conflict and multiculturalism: Implications for counseling psychology. *The Counseling Psychologist, 36,* 294–324.

ASSESSMENT

Cochran, S. V. (2005). Evidence-based assessment with men. *Journal of Clinical Psychology, 6,* 649–660.

Levant, R. F., & Silverstein, L. S. (2005). Gender is neglected in both evidence based practices and "treatment as usual. In J. C. Norcross, L. E. Beutler, & R. F. Levant (Eds.), *Evidence based practice in mental health: Debate and dialogue on the fundamental questions* (pp. 338–345). Washington, DC: APA books.

Liu, W. M. (2005). The study of men and masculinity as an important multicultural competency consideration. *Journal of Clinical Psychology, 6,* 685–697.

Mahalik, J. R. (1999). Incorporating a gender role strain perspective in assessing and treating men's cognitive distortions. *Professional Psychology: Research and Practice, 30,* 333–340;*39,* 240–246.

Mahalik, J. R., Good, G. E., & Englar-Carlson, M. (2003). Masculinity scripts, presenting concerns and help-seeking: Implications for practice and training. *Professional Psychology: Research & Practice, 34,* 123–131.

ASSESSMENT MEASURES FOR MEN AND MASCULINITIES

Brown, L. S. (1986). Gender role analysis: A neglected component of psychological assessment. *Psychotherapy, 23,* 243–248.

Doss, B. D., & Hopkins, J. R. (1998). The multicultural masculine ideology scale: Validation from three cultural perspectives. *Sex Roles, 38,* 719–41.

Eisler, R. M., & Skidmore, J. R. (1987). Masculine gender role stress: Scale development and component factors in appraisal of stressful situations. *Behavior Modification, 11,* 123–126.

Mahalik, J. R., Locke, B. D., Ludlow, L. H., Diemer, M. A., Scott, R. P. J., Gottfried, M., et al. (2003). Development of the Conformity to Masculine Norms Inventory. *Psychology of Men and Masculinity, 4,* 3–25.

O'Neil, J. M., Helms, B., Gable, R., David, L., & Wrightsman, L. (1986). Gender Role Conflict Scale: College men's fear of femininity. *Sex Roles, 14,* 335–350.

MASCULINE-SENSITIVE PSYCHOTHERAPY

Andronico, M. P. (1996). *Men in groups: Insights, interventions, and psychoeducational work.* Washington, DC: American Psychological Association.

Brooks, G. R. (1998). *A new psychotherapy for traditional men.* San Francisco: Jossey-Bass.

Brown, L. (2009). *Feminist therapy.* Washington, D.C.: American Psychological Association Books.

Englar-Carlson, M., & Shepard, D. S. (2005). Engaging men in couples counseling: Strategies for overcoming ambivalence and inexpressiveness. *The Family Journal, 13,* 383–391.

Englar-Carlson, M., & Stevens, M. (Eds.). (2006). *In the room with men: A casebook of therapeutic change.* Washington, DC: American Psychological Association.

Good, G. E., Gilbert, L. A., & Scher, M. (1990). Gender aware therapy: A synthesis of feminist therapy and knowledge about gender. *Journal of Counseling and Development, 68,* 376–380.

Good, G. E., Thomson, D. A., & Brathwaite, A. (2005). Men and therapy: Critical concepts, theoretical frameworks, and research recommendations. *Journal of Clinical Psychology, 6,* 699–711.

Kiselica, M. S., Englar-Carlson, M., & Horne, A. M. (Eds.). (2008). *Counseling troubled boys: A guidebook for professionals.* New York: Routledge.

Levant, R., & Pollack, W. S. (Eds.). (1995). *The new psychology of men.* New York: Basic.

Meth, R. L., & Pasick, R. S. (1990), *Men in therapy: The challenge of change.* New York: Guilford.

Pollack, W. S., & Levant, R. F. (1998). *New psychotherapy for men.* New York: Wiley.

Rabinowitz, F. E., & Cochran, S. V. (2002). *Deepening psychotherapy with men.* Washington, DC: APA.

Scher, M., Stevens, M., Good, G., & Eichenfield, E. (1987). *Handbook of psychotherapy with men.* Thousand Oaks, CA: Sage.

MEN AND EMOTIONS

Heesacker, M., Wester, S. R., Vogel, D. L., Wentzel, J. T., Mejia-Millan, C. M., & Goodholm, C. R. (1999). Gender-based emotional stereotyping. *Journal of Counseling Psychology, 46,* 483–495.

Jansz, J. (2000). Masculine identity and restrictive emotionality. In A. H. Fischer (Ed.), *Gender and emotion: Social psychological perspectives* (pp. 166–186). New York: Cambridge University Press.

Robertson, J. M., & Freeman, R. (1995). Men and emotions: Developing masculine-congruent views of affective expressiveness. *Journal of College Student Development, 36,* 606–607.

Wester, S. R., Vogel, D. L., Pressly, P. K., & Heesacker, M. (2002). Sex differences in emotion: A critical review of the literature and implications for counseling psychology. *The Counseling Psychologist, 30,* 629–651.

Wong, J. Y., & Rochlen, A. B. (2005). Demystifying men's emotional behavior: New directions and implications for counseling and research. *Psychology of Men & Masculinity, 6,* 62–72.

PSYCHOLOGICAL HELP-SEEKING

Addis, M. E., & Mahalik, J. R. (2003). Men, masculinity, and the contexts of help-seeking. *American Psychologist, 58,* 5–14.

McCarthy, J., & Holliday, E. L. (2004). Help-seeking and counseling within a traditional male gender role: An examination from a multicultural perspective. *Journal of Counseling & Development, 82,* 25–30.

Neighbors, H. W., Musick, M. A., & Williams, D. R. (1998). The African American minister as a source of help for serious personal crises: Bridge or barrier to mental health care? *Health Education & Behavior, 26,* 759–777.

Robertson, J., & Fitzgerald, L. F. (1992). Overcoming the masculine mystique: Preferences for alternative forms of assistance among men who avoid counseling. *Journal of Counseling Psychology, 39,* 240–246.

Vogel, D. L., Wester, S. R., & Larson, L. M. (2007). Avoidance of counseling: Psychological factors that inhibit seeking help. *Journal of Counseling and Development, 85,* 410–422.

MEN AND DEPRESSION

Addis, M. E. (2008). Gender and depression in men. *Clinical Psychology: Science and Practice, 15,* 153–168.

Cochran, S. V. (2005). Assessing and treating depression in men. In G. Brooks & G. Good (Eds.), *The new handbook of psychotherapy and counseling with men* (pp. 121–133). San Francisco: Jossey-Bass.

Cochran, S.V. & Rabinowitz, F.E. (2000). *Men and depression: Clinical and empirical perspectives.* San Diego, CA: Academic Press.

Real, T. (1997). *I don't want to talk about it: Overcoming the secret legacy of male depression.* New York: Fireside.

MEN, ABUSE, AND TRAUMA

Bolton, R. G., Morris, L. A., & MacEachron, A. E. (1989). *Males at risk: The other side of child sexual abuse.* Thousand Oaks, CA: Sage.

Gartner, R. B. (1999). *Betrayed as boys: Psychodynamic treatment of sexually abused men.* New York: Guilford.

Holmes, W.C., & Slap, G.B. (1998). Sexual abuse of boys: Definition, prevalence, correlates, sequelae, and management. *JAMA, 280,* 1855–1862.

Lisak, D. (1994). The psychological consequences of childhood abuse: Content analysis of interviews with male survivors. *Journal of Traumatic Stress, 7,* 525–548.

Lisak, D. (2001). Male survivors of trauma. In G. Brooks & G. Good (Eds.), *The new handbook of psychotherapy and counseling with men* (pp. 263–277). San Francisco: Jossey-Bass.

MEN AND LOSS

Cochran, S. V., & Rabinowitz, F. E. (1996). Men, loss and psychotherapy. *Psychotherapy, 33,* 593–600.

Martin, T. L., & Doka, K. J. (2000). *Men don't cry . . . women do: Transcending gender stereotypes of grief.* Philadelphia, PA: Brunner/Mazel.

MEN'S HEALTH

Courtenay, W. H. (1998). College men's health: An overview and a call to action. *Journal of American College Health, 46,* 279–290.

Courtenay, W. H. (2000). Engendering health: A social constructionist examination of men's health beliefs and behaviors. *Psychology of Men & Masculinity, 1,* 4–15.

Sandman, D., Simantov, E., & An, C. (2000). *Out of touch: American men and the health care system.* New York: Commonwealth Fund.

MEN AND SUBSTANCE ABUSE

Hanna, E., & Grant, B. (1997). Gender differences in DSM-IV alcohol use disorders and major depression as distributed in the general population:

Clinical implications. *Comprehensive Psychiatry, 38*, 202–212.

Lemle, E., & Mishkind, M. E. (1989). Alcohol and masculinity. *Journal of Substance Abuse Treatment, 6*, 213–222.

TRAINING AND SUPERVISION ISSUES

Heesacker, M., Wester, S. R., Vogel, D. L., Wentzel, J. T., Mejia-Millan, C. M., & Goodholm, C. R. (1999). Gender-based emotional stereotyping. *Journal of Counseling Psychology, 46*, 483–495.

Mellinger, T., & Liu, W. M. (2006). Men's issues in doctoral training: A survey of counseling psychology programs. *Professional Psychology: Research and Practice, 37*, 196–204.

Vogel, D. L., Epting, F., & Wester, S. R. (2003). Counselors' perceptions of female and male clients. *Journal of Counseling and Development, 81*, 131–141.

MEN AND SOCIAL JUSTICE ISSUES

Englar-Carlson, M. (2009). Men and masculinity: Cultural, contextual, and clinical considerations. In C. Ellis & J. Carlson (Eds.), *Cross cultural awareness and social justice in counseling*. New York: Routledge.

Kiselica, M. S., & Woodford, M. S. (2007). Promoting healthy male development: A social justice perspective. In C. Lee (Ed.), *Counseling for social justice* (pp. 111–135). Alexandria, VA: American Counseling Association.

TRAINING RESOURCES: MEDIA

The American Psychological Association Psychotherapy Series can be found at: http://www.apa.org/videos/. There is a specific series focused on men and masculinities, and others that are useful for working with men:

Brooks, G. R. (2008). *Working with veterans*. Washington DC: American Psychological Association.

Brown, L. S. (2005). *Working with male survivors of trauma and abuse*. Washington DC: American Psychological Association.

Englar-Carlson, M. (2010). *Engaging men in psychotherapy*. Washington DC: American Psychological Association.

Kiselica, M. S. (2009). *Positive psychology interventions with men*. Washington DC: American Psychological Association.

Stevens, M. A. (2006). *Psychotherapy with men*. Washington DC: American Psychological Association.

FILMS AND BOOKS WITH MASCULINITY THEMES

Popular motion pictures and works of fiction can provide insight into men and masculinity. Films and books provide compelling narratives about male socialization and many of different types of masculinities. Films such as *The Outsiders, Mean Creek, The Brothers* and *Stand By Me* focus on socialization experiences. Male bonding and friendships are highlighted in *Brian's Song, Bang the Drum Slowly, City Slickers, Sideways,* and *Brokeback Mountain*. The relationship between fathers and sons are explored in *The Road, Field of Dreams,* and *The Pursuit of Happyness*. Authors Sherman Alexie (*The Toughest Indian in the World, Ten Little Indians*), Richard Russo (*Nobody's Fool, Empire Falls, Straight Man*), and Cormac McCarthy (*The Road, Suttree*) capture male characters and their relationship with contemporary influences. Other books of interest include:

Beatty, P. (1996). *The white boy shuffle*. New York: Houghton Mifflin.

Bezos, M. (2006). *The testing of Luther Albright*. New York: Harper.

Ford, R. (1995). *The sportswriter*. New York: Vintage.

Iida, D. (1996). *Middle son*. New York: Algonquin.

Wolff, T. (1989). *This boy's life*. New York: Atlantic Monthly Press.

WEB SITES AND WEB RESOURCES

American Psychological Association Division 51: Society for the Psychological Study of Men and Masculinity, http://www.apa.org/divisions/div51/

The Men's Issues Page: http://www.vix.com/men/index.html

The Men's Health Network: http://www.menshealthnetwork.org/

Real Men Real Depression Campaign: www.menanddepression.nimh.nih.gov

National Organization for Men Against Sexism: www.nomas.org/

COMPETENCY BENCHMARK TABLES

The purpose of the Competency Benchmarks (Tables 7.1–7.4) is to create developmental models for defining and measuring competencies in professional psychology; each chapter in this *Handbook* applies the diversity competence for mental health practitioners in their work with a particular diverse population.

Table 7.1   Developmental-Level Competencies I

READINESS LEVEL—ENTRY TO PRACTICUM	
Competencies	Learning Process and Activities
Knowledge The student is gaining knowledge in: • Multiculturalism (inclusive of men and masculinity)—the student is engaged in the process of learning that all individuals, including themselves, are cultural beings with worldviews that shape and influence their beliefs, attitudes, emotions, perceptions, and experiences. • The importance of reflective practice and self-awareness of one's cultural identities and the cultural identities of others. • Core counseling skills and theories, particularly as they embrace and pertain to the value of multiculturalism. • Ethics code upholding professionals to develop knowledge, sensitivity, and skills in multicultural practice.	At this stage of development, the emphasis is on instilling knowledge of foundational domains that provide the groundwork for subsequent attainment of functional multicultural competencies. Students at this stage become aware of the principles and practices of the field, but they are not yet able to apply their knowledge to practice. Training curriculum is focused on knowledge of core areas, including literature on multiculturalism (inclusive men and masculinity), ethics, foundational counseling skills, scientific knowledge, and the importance of reflective practice and self-awareness. Throughout the curriculum, trainers and educators define individual and cultural differences broadly, inclusive of knowledge of socialization processes of boys and men. This should enable students to have a developing awareness of how to extrapolate their emerging multicultural competencies to include a variety of men's issues.
Skills The student is: • Developing the ability to demonstrate empathic listening skills, respect, and interest when talking with individuals expressing different values and belief systems. • Learning to critically examine the diversity literature.	Through observation and/or personal experiences, all students should be able to articulate a variety of gendered societal messages and the institutions that teach young boys how they should behave.
Values and Attitudes The student demonstrates: • Willingness to engage in self-exploration—to consider own motives, attitudes, behaviors, and effect on others. • Intellectual curiosity and flexibility. • Ability to value expressions of diverse viewpoints and belief systems.	

Table 7.2   Developmental-Level Competencies II

READINESS LEVEL—ENTRY TO INTERNSHIP	
Competencies	**Learning Process and Activities**
Knowledge	The student has: • Conceptual understanding of the various models of male gender role strain and male gender role conflict. • A basic understanding of the research associated with mental health help-seeking behaviors of men. • A basic understanding of the various intersections of masculinity with culture, class, and sexual orientation. • A basic understanding of how men may "do" therapy differently than women.	At this level of development, students are building on their education and applied experiences (i.e., supervised practicum experiences) to attain a core set of foundational competencies. They can then begin applying these competencies in professional practice. Foundational knowledge and multicultural beliefs and attitudes are becoming well established, but skills in working with men's issues are expected to be rudimentary at this level of development. Learning occurs through multiple modalities:
Skills	Skills in the following areas are beginning to develop: • Building therapeutic alliance with male clients so as to increase the likelihood the client will feel safe and welcomed. • Showing the capacity to develop intervention skills that address the resistance of male clients to therapy. • Learning to conceptualize symptoms of male clients into diagnostic framework.	• Receiving men's issues didactic training in academic programs, which may occur in multicultural courses or culture-specific courses (e.g., women's issues). It may also be infused into the core curriculum (e.g., ethics/law, assessment, multicultural, career counseling, research, human growth and development, and clinical courses). • Providing therapy, under supervision, to male clients in practicum experiences. • Receiving supervision from mental health practitioners knowledgeable and skilled in working with men's issues. • Seeking additional study and professional development opportunities (i.e., to attain knowledge of various theories about men and masculinities and personal growth networks for men).
Values and Attitudes	Demonstrates self-awareness and appropriate cultural and multicultural attitudes as evidenced by the following: • Understands that the concept of masculinity is plural. • Commitment to examine and challenge one's own beliefs about patriarchy, sexism, and negative stereotyping of men. • Willingness to examine strengths and growth edges while working with male clients.	Topics to be covered in didactic training include: • Relationship of men's issues competency to multicultural competency. • Issues of power and privilege for men. • Resistance to including men as part of the multicultural conversation. • Relationship of men's issues to individual and cultural differences (e.g., age, gender, spirituality/religion, SES, and ethnicity). • Basic research literature describing the relevance of men's issues to wellness, physical health, and mental health. • Definitions, histories, and traditions of men's studies. Trainers and educators must offer students enrolled in multicultural diversity courses an option to research men's issues as a project for the class. Furthermore, trainers and educators should provide resources and rationale through which students can better understand how men's issues belong in multicultural conversations.

Table 7.3 Developmental-Level Competencies III

READINESS LEVEL—ENTRY TO PROFESSIONAL PRACTICE

Competencies		Learning Process and Activities
Knowledge	Knowledge of: • Literature and research on counseling men from a variety of therapeutic approaches. • Literature on working with men in counseling groups. • Literature on outreach efforts to make counseling a user-friendly environment for men. • Literature pertaining to masked depression for men, substance abuse, alexthymia, men in couples counseling, men and stress and physical health, fathering, and aging.	In the earlier stages of training, students solidified their professional knowledge base and attained appropriate values, beliefs, and attitudes while developing increasingly sophisticated clinical skills. At the level of Entry to Professional Practice, mental health practitioners have attained the full range of competencies in the domains expected of all independent practitioners. Preparation for this level of competency takes place through closely supervised clinical work, augmented by professional reading, personal exploration, and training opportunities such as professional development and training seminars and attendance at local and national conferences.
Skills	Skills are demonstrated by: • Performing an assessment of how the client's masculinity training is associated with his clinical symptoms and diagnosis. • Formulating a gender-aware treatment plan. • Using therapeutic interventions that are experienced by the client as male affirmative and friendly. • Consulting with others regarding transference and countertransference issues relating to working with male clients.	Clinical supervisors observe students' clinical work, provide training in assessment, case conceptualization, and treatment planning, and challenge supervisees to examine their process-based relational reactions with clients, biases, and beliefs to develop their supervisees' clinical competency with men's issues. Additional methods by which students can attain men's issues competency at this level include:
Values and Attitudes	Demonstrates advanced levels of self-awareness and appropriate cultural and multicultural attitudes as evidenced by the following: • Willingness to further examine personal issues relating to working with male clients such as: homophobia, being a target of male violence and objectification, relationship with one's father and male siblings. • Considers one's attitudes and beliefs about male power and privilege. • Considers one's attitudes and beliefs about positive aspects of male socialization.	• Seeking opportunities to provide therapy to male clients from diverse backgrounds. • Supervision provided by supervisors knowledgeable and skilled in working with male clients. • Self-directed study and professional development opportunities through cultural immersion experiences (i.e., men's retreats, men's support groups, and professional organizations involved in issues relating to men and masculinity). • Internship and postdoctoral seminar training in men's issues. • Presenting and participating in clinical case conferences that include discussion of men's issues relating to the particular clients. • Reading professional journals related to men's issues (i.e., men's studies, fathering, psychology of men and masculinity).

Table 7.4   Developmental–Level Competencies IV

READINESS LEVEL—ENTRY TO ADVANCED PRACTICE AND SPECIALIZATION	
Competencies	Learning Process and Activities
Knowledge Extensive knowledge of: • Men and masculinities literature. • Intersections of male socialization and specific groups of men pertaining to: age, relationship status, sexual orientation, class, ethnicity, physical challenges, birthplace, and religious background. • Local and national community resources for men. • Self-help literature for men.	Mental health practitioners who have a particular interest in men's issues as it applies to clinical work, prevention, and social justice may seek to attain advanced levels of competency. Learning activities will vary depending on the mental health practitioner's unique background, established competencies, and interest areas. For example, mental health practitioners working in University Counseling Centers may wish to focus on men's issues within this broader student population. Similarly, mental health practitioners working in a hospital setting may choose to focus on the difficulties faced by men dealing with the interaction between stress and physical illness or training medical practitioners to become more aware of men's issues as they relate to being a patient.
Skills Advanced skills in: • Developing and sharing a gender-aware treatment plan. • Diagnostic assessment regarding uniqueness of depressive and anxiety symptoms for male clients. • Using masculine friendly/sensitive intervention approaches. • Integrating particular client's gender role socialization experiences with his presenting concerns. • Using self-disclosure as a tool to help deepen the exploration of male gender role issues. • Providing effective supervision to trainees working with male clients.	
Values and Attitudes Well-integrated values and attitudes as demonstrated by the following: • Continually engages in broadening knowledge of men's issues. • Actively cultivates relationships with leaders in the field of men's studies. • Involvement in local, national, or international groups and organizations relevant to men's studies. • Sharing knowledge related to men's studies through publications, workshops, or presentations. • Independently monitoring and seeking personal and professional growth as it relates to men's issues. • Willingness to mentor others interested in men's studies.	Regardless of the focus area, learning activities include: • Professional reading (information about men's studies and empirical research; literature on theory and practice). • Teaching self through the teaching of others. • Attending and leading continuing education workshops. • Peer consultation groups. • Consultation with knowledgeable mental health professionals, leaders in fields of men's studies and clinical practice. • Participation and leadership in activities that promote personal growth and awareness about one's gender role journey.

REFERENCES

Ackerman, S. J., & Hilsenroth, M. J. (2003). A review of therapist characteristics and techniques positively impacting the therapeutic alliance. *Clinical Psychology Review, 23*, 1–33.

Addis, M. E. (2008). Gender and depression in men. *Clinical Psychology: Science and Practice, 15*, 153–168.

Addis, M. E., & Cohane, G. H. (2005). Social scientific paradigms of masculinity and their implications for research and practice in men's mental health. *Journal of Clinical Psychology, 6*, 633–647.

Addis, M. E. & Mahalik, J. R. (2003). Men, masculinity, and the contexts of help-seeking. *American Psychologist, 58*, 5–14.

American Psychological Association. (2003). Guidelines on multicultural education, training, research, practice, and organizational change for psychologists. *American Psychologist, 58*, 377–402.

American Psychological Association. (2007). Guidelines for psychological practice with girls and women. *American Psychologist, 62*, 949–979.

Anderson, R. N., Kochanek, K. D., & Murphy, S. L. (1997). Report of final mortality statistics, 1995. *Monthly Vital Statistics Report, 45* (11, suppl. 2). Hyattsville, MD: National Center for Heath Statistics.

Andrews, G., Issakidis, C., & Carter, G. (2001). Shortfall in mental health service utilisation. *British Journal of Psychiatry, 179*, 417–425.

Arias, E., Anderson, R. N., Kung, H. C., Murphy, S. L., & Kochanek, K. D. (2003). *Deaths: Final data for 2001. National Vital Statistics Reports: Vol. 52, no. 3*. Hyattsville, MD: National Center for Health Statistics.

Atkinson, D. R., Bui, U., & Mori, S. (2001). Multiculturally sensitive empirically supported treatments: An oxymoron? In J. G. Ponterotto, J. M. Casas, L. A. Suzuki, & C. M. Alexander (Eds.), *Handbook of multicultural counseling* (2nd ed., pp. 542–574). Thousand Oaks, CA: Sage.

Baker, D., & King, S. E. (2004). Child sexual abuse and incest. In R. T. Francoeur & R. J. Noonan (Eds.), *International encyclopedia of sexuality* (pp. 1233–1237). New York: Continuum.

Bernal, G., & Scharrón-del-Río, M. R. (2001). Are empirically supported treatments valid for ethnic minorities? Toward an alternative approach for treatment research. *Cultural Diversity and Ethnic Minority Psychology, 7*, 328–342.

Bernard, J. (1981). The good-provider role: Its rise and fall. *American Psychologist, 36*, 1–12.

Blazina, C. (1997). Mythos and men: Toward new paradigms of masculinity. *The Journal of Men's Studies, 5*, 285–294.

Blazina, C., Eddins, R., Burridge, A., & Settle, A. G. (2007). The relationship between masculinity ideology, loneliness, and separation-individuation difficulties. *The Journal of Men's Studies, 15*, 101–109.

Bly, R. (1990). *Iron John: A book about men*. New York: Vintage Books.

Brannon, R. (1976). The male sex-role: Our culture's blueprint of manhood and what it's done for us lately. In D. S. Brannon & R. Brannon (Eds.), *The forty-nine percent majority* (pp. 1–45). Reading, MA: Addison-Wesley.

Brooks, G. (1998). *A new psychotherapy for traditional men*. San Francisco: Jossey-Bass.

Brooks, G. R., & Good, G. E. (Eds.). (2005). *The new handbook of psychotherapy & counseling with men: A comprehensive guide to settings, problems, & treatment approaches* (Rev. ed.). San Francisco: Jossey-Bass.

Brown, L. (2009). *Feminist therapy*. Washington, D.C.: American Psychological Association Books.

Bruch, M. A. (1978). Holland's typology applied to client–counselor interaction: Implications for counseling men. *The Counseling Psychologist, 7*, 26–32.

Burke, B. L., Arkowitz, H., & Dunn, C. (2001). The efficacy of motivational interviewing and its adaptations: What we know so far. In W. Miller & S. Rollnick (Eds.), *Motivational interviewing* (2nd ed., pp. 217–250). New York: Guilford.

Cabe, N. (1999). Abused boys and adolescents: Out of the shadows. In A. M. Horne & M. S. Kiselica (Eds.), *Handbook of counseling boys and adolescent males: A practitioner's guide* (pp. 199–218). Thousand Oaks, CA: Sage.

Cabrera, N. J., Tamis-LeMonda, C. S., Bradley, R. H., Hofferth, S., & Lamb, M. E. (2000). Fatherhood in the twenty-first century. *Child Development, 71*(1), 127–136.

Caldwell, L. D. & White, J. L. (2001). African centered therapeutic and counseling interventions for African American males. In G. Brooks & G. Good (Eds.), *The handbook of counseling and psychotherapy approaches for men* (pp. 737–753). San Francisco: Jossey-Bass.

Casas, J. M., Turner, J. A., & Ruiz de Esparza, C. A. (2001). Machismo revisited in a time of crisis:

Implications for understanding and counseling Hispanic men. In G. Brooks & G. Good (Eds.), *The handbook of counseling and psychotherapy approaches for men* (pp. 754–779). San Francisco: Jossey-Bass.

Cochran, S. V. (2005). Assessing and treating depression in men. In G. Brooks & G. Good (Eds.), *The new handbook of psychotherapy and counseling with men* (pp. 121–133). San Francisco: Jossey-Bass.

Cochran, S. V., & Rabinowitz, F. E. (1996). Men, loss and psychotherapy. *Psychotherapy, 33*, 593–600.

Cochran, S. V. & Rabinowitz, F. E. (2000). *Men and depression: Clinical and empirical perspectives*. San Diego: Academic Press.

Commonwealth Fund. (1998). *Women's and men's health survey*, 1998. Washington, DC: Author.

Connell, R. W. (1987). *Gender and power*. Sydney, Australia: Allen & Unwin.

Connell, R. W. (1995). *Masculinities*. Cambridge, UK: Polity Press.

Connell, R. W., & Messerschmidt, J. W. (2005). Hegemonic masculinity: Rethinking the concept. *Gender and Society, 19*, 829–859.

Courtenay, W. H. (1998). College men's health: An overview and a call to action. *Journal of American College Health, 46*, 279–290.

Courtenay, W. H. (2000). Engendering health: A social constructionist examination of men's health beliefs and behaviors. *Psychology of Men & Masculinity. 1*, 4–15.

Cusak, J., Deane, F. P., Wilson, C. J., & Ciarrochi, J. (2006). Emotional expression, perceptions of therapy, and help-seeking intentions in men attending therapy services. *Psychology of Men & Masculinity*, 7(2), 69–82.

D'Arcy, C., & Schmitz, J. A. (1979). Sex differences in the utilization of health services for psychiatric problems in Saskatchewan. *Canadian Journal of Psychiatry, 24*, 19–27.

David, D. S., & Brannon, R. (1976). *The forty-nine percent majority: The male sex role*. Reading, MA: Addison-Wesley.

deBeauvoir, S. (1970). *The second sex*. New York: Bantam.

Doss, B. D., & Hopkins, J. R. (1998). The multicultural masculine ideology scale: Validation from three cultural perspectives. *Sex Roles, 38*, 719–741.

Doucet, A. (2004). "It's almost like I have a job, but I don't get paid": Fathers at home reconfiguring work, care, and masculinity. *Fathering, 2*, 277–302.

Englar-Carlson, M. (2006). Masculine norms and the therapy process. In M. Englar-Carlson & M. A. Stevens (Eds.), *In the therapy room with men: A casebook about psychotherapeutic process and change with male clients* (pp. 13–48). Washington, DC: American Psychological Association.

Englar-Carlson, M. (2009). Men and masculinity: Cultural, contextual, and clinical considerations. In C. Ellis & J. Carlson (Eds.), *Cross cultural awareness and social justice in counseling* (pp. 89–120). New York: Routledge.

Englar-Carlson, M., & Shepard, D. S. (2005). Engaging men in couples counseling: Strategies for overcoming ambivalence and inexpressiveness. *The Family Journal, 13*, 383–391.

Englar-Carlson, M., Smart, R., Arczynski, A., Boucher, M., & Shepard, D. (2008). *The process of male sensitive psychotherapy: Qualitative analysis of cases*. Poster presentation at the annual meeting of the American Psychological Association, Washington, D.C

Englar-Carlson, M., & Stevens, M. A. (Eds.). (2006). *In the room with men: A casebook of therapeutic change*. Washington, DC: American Psychological Association.

Fischer, A. R., & Good, G. E. (1997). Men and psychotherapy: An investigation of alexithymia, intimacy, and masculine gender roles. *Psychotherapy: Theory, Research, Practice, Training, 34*, 160–170.

Franklin, A. J. (1998). Treating anger in African American men. In W. Pollack & R. Levant (Eds.), *New psychotherapy for men* (pp. 239–258). New York: Wiley.

Galdas, P. M., Cheater, F., & Marshall, P. (2005). Men and health help-seeking behaviour: Literature review. *Journal of Advanced Nursing* 49(6), 616–623.

Gartner, R. B. (1999). *Betrayed as boys: Psychodynamic treatment of sexually abused men*. New York: Guilford.

Gibbons, J. L., Hamby, B. A., & Dennis, W. D. (1997). Researching gender-role ideologies internationally and cross-culturally. *Psychology of Women Quarterly, 21*, 151–170.

Good, G. E. (1998). Missing and underrepresented aspects of men's lives. *SPSMM Bulletin, 3*(2), 1–2.

Good, G. E., Gilbert, L. A., & Scher, M. (1990). Gender aware therapy: A synthesis of feminist therapy and knowledge about gender. *Journal of Counseling and Development, 68*, 376–380.

Good, G. E., Heppner, P. P., DeBord, K. A., & Fischer, A. R. (2004). Understanding men's psychological distress: Contributions of problem-solving appraisal and masculine role conflict. *Psychology of Men & Masculinity, 5*(2), 168–177.

Good, G. E., & Mintz, L. B. (2001). Integrative psychotherapy for men. In G. Brooks & G. Good (Eds.), *The handbook of counseling and psychotherapy approaches for men* (pp. 582–602). San Francisco: Jossey-Bass.

Good, G. E., & Sherrod, N. (2001). The psychology of men and masculinity: Research status and future directions. In R. Unger (Ed.), *Handbook of the psychology of women and gender* (pp. 201–214). New York: Wiley.

Good, G. E., Thomson, D. A., & Brathwaite, A. (2005). Men and therapy: Critical concepts, theoretical frameworks, and research recommendations. *Journal of Clinical Psychology, 6*, 699–711.

Good, G. E., & Wood, P. K. (1995). Male gender role conflict, depression, and help seeking: Do college men face double jeopardy? *Journal of Counseling and Development, 74*, 70–75.

Haldeman, D. C. (2001). Psychotherapy with gay and bisexual men. In G. Brooks & G. Good (Eds.), *The handbook of counseling and psychotherapy approaches for men* (pp. 796–815). San Francisco: Jossey-Bass.

Haldeman, D. C. (2006). Queer eye on the straight guy: A case of gay male heterophobia. In M. Englar-Carlson & M. Stevens (Eds.), *In the room with men: A casebook of therapeutic change* (pp. 301–318). Washington, DC: American Psychological Association.

Hanna, E., & Grant, B. (1997). Gender differences in DSM-IV alcohol use disorders and major depression as distributed in the general population: Clinical implications. *Comprehensive Psychiatry, 38*, 202–212.

Hayes, J. A., & Gelso, C. J. (2001). Clinical implications of research on countertransference: Science informing practice. *In Session: Journal of Clinical Psychology, 57*, 1041–1051.

Heesacker, M., Wester, S. R., Vogel, D. L., Wentzel, J. T., Mejia-Millan, C. M., & Goodholm, C. R. (1999). Gender-based emotional stereotyping. *Journal of Counseling Psychology, 46*, 483–495.

Hodgetts, D., & Chamberlain, K. (2002). "The problem with men": Working class men making sense of men's health on television. *Journal of Health Psychology, 7*, 269–283.

Holland, J. (1973). *Making vocational choices: A theory of careers.* Englewood Cliffs, NJ: Prentice Hall.

Holmes, W. C., & Slap, G. B. (1998). Sexual abuse of boys: Definition, prevalence, correlates, sequelae, and management. *JAMA, 280*, 1855–1862.

Husaini, B. A., Moore, S. T., & Cain V. A. (1994). Psychiatric symptoms and help seeking behavior among the elderly: An analysis of racial and gender differences. *Journal of Gerontological Social Work, 21*, 177–195.

Jansz, J. (2000). Masculine identity and restrictive emotionality. In A. H. Fischer (Ed.), *Gender and emotion: Social psychological perspectives* (pp. 166–186). New York: Cambridge University Press.

Johnston, L. D., O'Malley, P. M., Bachman, J. G., & Schulenberg, J. E. (2006). *Monitoring the future: National survey results on drug use, 1975-2005: Vol. 1, Secondary school students* (NIH Publication No. 06-5883). Bethesda, MD: National Institute on Drug Abuse.

Jordan, J. (2009). *Relational-cultural theory.* Washington, D.C.: American Psychological Association Books.

Kennedy, G., Metz, H., & Lowinger, R. (1995). Epidemiology and inferences regarding the etiology of late life suicide. In G. Kennedy (Ed.), *Suicide and depression in late life* (pp. 3–22). New York: Wiley.

Kessler, R. C., McGonagle, K. A., Zhao, S., Nelson, C. B., Hughes, M., Eshelman, S., et al. (1994). Lifetime and 12-month prevalence of DSM–III–R psychiatric disorders in the United States: Results from the National Comorbidity Survey. *Archives of General Psychiatry, 51*, 8–19.

Kilmartin, C. T. (2009). *The masculine self* (4th ed.). Cornwall-on-Hudson, NY: Sloan Publishing.

Kimmel, M. (2005). *Manhood in America: A cultural history* (2nd ed.). New York: Free Press.

Kimmel, M., & Messner, M. (Eds.). (2004). *Men's lives* (6th ed.). New York: Macmillan.

Kiselica, M. S. (2001). A male-friendly therapeutic process with school-age boys. In G. R. Brooks & G. E. Good (Eds.), *The new handbook of psychotherapy and counseling with men* (Vol. 1., pp. 41–58). San Francisco: Jossey-Bass.

Kiselica, M. S. (2003). Transforming psychotherapy in order to succeed with boys: Male-friendly practices. *Journal of Clinical Psychology: In Session, 59*, 1225–1236.

Kiselica, M. S. (2006, August). Contributions and limitations of the deficit model of men. In M. S. Kiselica (Chair), *Toward a positive psychology of boys, men, and masculinity.* Symposium presented at the Annual Convention of the American Psychological Association, New Orleans, LA.

Kiselica, M. S., & Englar-Carlson, M. (2008). Establishing rapport with boys in individual counseling. In M. S. Kiselica, M. Englar-Carlson, & A. Horne (Eds.), *Counseling troubled boys: A guidebook for professionals* (pp. 49–65). New York: Routledge.

Kiselica, M. S., Englar-Carlson, M., & Fisher, M. (2006, August). A positive psychology framework for building upon male strengths. In M. S. Kiselica (Chair), *Toward a positive psychology of boys, men, and masculinity.* Symposium presented at the Annual Convention of the American Psychological Association, New Orleans, LA.

Kiselica, M. S., Englar-Carlson, M., & Horne, A. (2008). A positive psychology perspective on helping boys. In M. S. Kiselica, M. Englar-Carlson, & A. Horne (Eds.), *Counseling troubled boys: A guidebook for professionals.* New York: Routledge.

Kiselica, M. S., & Woodford, M. S. (2007). Promoting healthy male development: A social justice perspective. In C. Lee (Ed.), *Counseling for social justice* (pp. 111–135). Alexandria, VA: American Counseling Association.

Lehne, G. (1976). Homophobia among men. In D. David & R. Brannon (Eds.). *The forty-nine percent majority: The male sex role.* Reading, MA: Addison-Wesley.

Leong, F. T. L., & Zachar, P. (1999). Gender and opinions about mental illness as predictors of attitudes towards seeking professional psychological help. *British Journal of Guidance and Counselling, 27* (1), 123–132.

Levant, R. F. (1990). Introduction to special series on men's roles and psychotherapy. *Psychotherapy, 27,* 307–308.

Levant, R. F. (1997). The masculinity crisis. *Journal of Men's Studies, 5,* 221–231.

Levant, R. & Pollack, W. S. (Eds.). (1995). *The new psychology of men.* New York: Basic.

Levant, R. F., Richmond, K., Majors, R. G., Inclan, J. E., Rossello, J. M., Heesacker, M., et al. (2003). A multicultural investigation of masculinity ideology and alexithymia. *Psychology of Men & Masculinity, 4,* 91–99.

Levant, R. F., & Silverstein, L. S. (2005). Gender is neglected in both evidence based practices and "treatment as usual". In J. C. Norcross, L. E. Beutler, & R. F. Levant (Eds.), *Evidence based practice in mental health: Debate and dialogue on the fundamental questions.* (pp. 338–345). Washington, DC: APA books.

Lisak, D. (1994). The psychological consequences of childhood abuse: Content analysis of interviews with male survivors. *Journal of Traumatic Stress, 7,* 525–548.

Lisak, D. (2001). Male survivors of trauma. In G. Brooks & G. Good (Eds.), *The new handbook of psychotherapy and counseling with men* (pp. 263–277). San Francisco: Jossey-Bass.

Liu, W. M. (2002a). Exploring the lives of Asian American men: Racial identity, male role norms, gender role conflict, and prejudicial attitudes. *Psychology of Men & Masculinity. 3,* 107–118.

Liu, W. M. (2002b). The social class-related experiences of men: Integrating theory and practice. *Professional Psychology, 33,* 355–360.

Liu, W. M. (2005). The study of men and masculinity as an important multicultural competency consideration. *Journal of Clinical Psychology, 6,* 685–697.

Liu, W. M., & Chang, T. (2007). Asian American masculinities. In F. T. L. Leong, A. Ebero, L., Kinoshita, A. G. Arpana, & L. H. Yang (Eds.), *Handbook of Asian American psychology* (2nd ed.; pp. 197–211). Thousand Oaks, CA: Sage Publications.

Mahalik, J. R. (2001a). Cognitive therapy for men. In G. Brooks & G. Good (Eds.), *The handbook of counseling and psychotherapy approaches for men* (pp. 544–564). San Francisco: Jossey-Bass.

Mahalik, J. R. (2001b). Interpersonal therapy for men. In G. Brooks & G. Good (Eds.), *The handbook of counseling and psychotherapy approaches for men* (pp. 565–581). San Francisco: Jossey-Bass.

Mahalik, J. R., Good, G. E., & Englar-Carlson, M. (2003). Masculinity scripts, presenting concerns and help-seeking: Implications for practice and training. *Professional Psychology: Research & Practice, 34,* 123–131.

Majors, R. G., & Billson, J. M. (1992). *Cool pose: The dilemmas of black manhood in America.* New York: Lexington.

Martin, S. B., Wrisberg, C. A., Beitel, P. A., & Lounsbury, J. (1997). NCAA Division I athletes' attitudes toward seeking sport psychology consultation: The development of an objective instrument. *Sport Counselor, 11,* 201–218.

Mellinger, T., & Liu, W. M. (2006). Men's issues in doctoral training: A survey of counseling psychology programs. *Professional Psychology: Research and Practice, 37,* 196–204.

Messer, S. B., & Wampold, E. B. (2002). Let's face the facts: Common factors are more potent than specific therapy ingredients. *Clinical Psychology: Science and Practice, 9,* 21–25.

Meth, R. L., & Pasick, R. S. (1990), *Men in therapy: The challenge of change.* New York: Guilford.

Miller, W. R., Rollnick, S., & Conforti, K. (2002). *Motivational interviewing: Preparing people for change* (2nd ed.). New York: Guilford.

Möller-Leimkuehler, A. (2002). Barriers to help-seeking in men. A. review of the socio-cultural and clinical literature with particular reference to depression. *Journal of Affective Disorders, 71,* 1–9.

Moos, R. (2007). Theory-based active ingredients of effective treatments for substance use disorders. *Drug and Alcohol Dependence, 88,* 109–121.

National Institute of Mental Health. (2003). Real men. Real depression. Retrieved October 20, 2008, from http://menanddepression.nimh.nih.gov.

Neighbors, H., & Howard, C. (1987). Sex differences in professional help seeking among adult black Americans. *American Journal of Community Psychology, 15,* 403–17.

Neighbors, H. W., Musick, M. A., & Williams, D. R. (1998). The African American minister as a source of help for serious personal crises: Bridge or barrier to mental health care? *Health Education & Behavior, 26,* 759–777.

Norcross, J. C. (2001). Purposes, processes, and products of the Task Force on Empirically Supported Therapy Relationships. *Psychotherapy, 38,* 345–356.

Norcross, J. C., & Lambert, M. J. (2005). The therapy relationship. In J. C. Norcross, L. E. Beutler, & R. F. Levant (Eds.), *Evidence-based practices in mental health: Debate and dialogue on the fundamental questions* (pp. 208–218). Washington, DC: American Psychological Association.

Nylund, D. (2007). *Beer, babes, and balls: Masculinity and sports talk radio.* Albany, NY: SUNY Press.

O'Brien, R., Hunt, K., & Hart, G. (2005). It's caveman stuff, but that is to a certain extent how guys still operate: Men's accounts of masculinity and help seeking. *Social Science & Medicine, 61,* 503–516.

O'Neil, J. M. (1981). Patterns of gender role conflict and strain: Sexism and fear of femininity in men's lives. *Personnel and Guidance Journal, 60,* 202–210.

O'Neil, J. M. (1990). Assessing men's gender role conflict. In D. Moore & F. Leafgren (Eds.), *Problem solving strategies and interventions for men in conflict* (pp. 23–38). Alexandria, VA: American Association for Counseling and Development.

O'Neil, J. M., & Egan, J. (1992). Men's gender role transitions over the lifespan: Transformations and

fears of femininity. *Journal of Mental Health Counseling, 14,* 305–324.

Oquendo, M. A., Ellis, S. P., Greenwald, S., Malone, K. M., Weissman, M. M., & Mann, J. J. (2001). Ethnic and sex differences in suicide rates relative to major depression in the United States. *American Journal of Psychiatry, 158,* 1652–1658.

Paniagua, F. A. (2005). *Assessing and treating culturally diverse clients: A practical guide* (2nd ed.). Thousand Oaks, CA: Sage.

Park, S. (2006). Facing fear without losing face: Working with Asian American men. In M. Englar-Carlson & M. A. Stevens (Eds.), *In the room with men: A casebook of therapeutic change* (pp. 151–173). Washington, DC: American Psychological Association.

Pascoe, C. J. (2003). Multiple masculinities? Teenage boys talk about jocks and gender. *American Behavioral Scientist, 46,* 1423–1438.

Pederson, E., & Vogel, D. (2007, October). Male gender role conflict and willingness to seek counseling: Testing a mediation model on college-aged men. *Journal of Counseling Psychology, 54*(4), 373–384.

Plummer, D. C. (2001). The quest for modern manhood: Masculine stereotypes, peer culture and the social significance of homophobia. *Journal of Adolescence, 24,* 15–23.

Pollack, W. S. (1998). Mourning, melancholia, and masculinity: Recognizing and treating depression in men. In W. S. Pollack & R. F. Levant (Eds.), *New psychotherapy for men* (pp. 147–166). Hoboken, NJ: Wiley.

Pollack, W. S., & Levant, R. F. (1998). *New psychotherapy for men.* New York: Wiley.

Rabinowitz, F. E., & Cochran, S. V. (2002). *Deepening psychotherapy with men.* Washington, DC: APA.

Real, T. (1997). *I don't want to talk about it: Overcoming the secret legacy of male depression.* New York: Fireside.

Real, T. (2002). *How can I get through to you? Reconnecting men and women.* New York: Scribner.

Robertson, J., & Fitzgerald, L. F. (1992). Overcoming the masculine mystique: Preferences for alternative forms of assistance among men who avoid counseling. *Journal of Counseling Psychology, 39,* 240–246.

Robertson, J., & Shepard, D. S. (2008). The psychological development of boys. In M. Kiselica, M. Englar-Carlson, & A. Horne (Eds.), *Counseling troubled boys* (pp. 3–30). New York: Routledge.

Rochlen, A. B., & O'Brien, K. M. (2002). The relation of male gender role conflict and attitudes toward career counseling to interest and preferences for different career counseling styles. *Psychology of Men and Masculinity, 3,* 9–21.

Rosenbaum, A., & Leisring, P. A. (2003). Beyond power and control: Towards an understanding of partner abusive men. *Journal of Comparative Family Studies, 34,* 7–22.

Sachs-Ericsson, N., & Ciarlo, J. A. (2000). Gender, social roles, and mental health: An epidemiological perspective. *Sex Roles, 43,* 605–628.

Sandman, D., Simantov, E., & An, C. (2000). *Out of touch: American men and the health care system.* New York: Commonwealth Fund.

Scher, M. (1990). Effect of gender role incongruence on men's experience as clients in psychotherapy. *Psychotherapy, 27,* 322–326.

Scher, M. (2001). Male therapist, male client: Reflections on critical dynamics. In G. Brooks & G. Good (Eds.), *The handbook of counseling and psychotherapy approaches for men* (pp. 719–733). San Francisco: Jossey-Bass.

Scher, M., Stevens, M., Good, G. & Eichenfield, E. (1987). *Handbook of psychotherapy with men.* Thousand Oaks, CA: Sage.

Seligman, M., & Csikszentmihalyi, M. (2000). Positive psychology: An Introduction. *American Psychologist, 55,* 5–14.

Shepard, D. S. (2005). Male development and the journey toward disconnection. In D. Comstock (Ed.), *Diversity and development: Critical contexts that shape our lives and relationships* (pp. 133–160). Belmont, CA: Brooks-Cole.

Sheu, H.-B., & Sedlacek, W. E. (2004). An exploratory study of help-seeking attitudes and coping strategies among college students by race and gender. *Measurement and Evaluation in Counseling and Development, 37,* 130–143.

Shin, J. K. (2002). Help-seeking behaviors by Korean immigrants for depression. *Issues in Mental Health Nursing, 23,* 461–476.

Smiler, A. P. (2004). Thirty years after the discovery of gender: Psychological concepts and measures of masculinity. *Sex Roles, 50,* 15–26.

Solberg, V. S., Ritsma, S., Davis, B. J., Tata, S. P., & Jolly, A. (1994). Asian-American Students' severity of problems and willingness to seek help from university counseling centers: Role of previous counseling experience, gender, and ethnicity. *Journal of Counseling Psychology, 41,* 215–219.

Stevens, M. A. (2005, August). *Men and masculinity as a multicultural competency.* Presentation at the Annual Convention of the American Psychological Association, Washington, D.C

Stevens, M. A. (2006a). Engaging men in psychotherapy: Respect and challenge. In M. S. Kiselica (Chair), *Toward a positive psychology of boys, men, and masculinity.* Symposium presented at the Annual Convention of the American Psychological Association, New Orleans, LA

Stevens, M. A. (2006b). Paul's journey to find calmness: From sweat to tears. In M. Englar-Carlson & M. A. Stevens (Eds.). *In the room with men: A casebook of therapeutic change* (pp. 51–69). Washington, DC: American Psychological Association.

Sue, D. W., Arredondo, P., & McDavis, R. (1992). Multicultural counseling competencies and standards: A call to the profession. *Journal of Counseling and Development, 70,* 477–484.

Sue, D.W., Capodilupo, C., & Holder, A. (2008). Racial microaggressions in the life experience of black Americans. *Professional Psychology: Research and Practice, 39*(3), 329–336.

Sue, D.W., Capodilupo, C., Torino, G., Bucceri, J., Holder, A., Nadal, K.,et al. (2007). Racial microaggressions in everyday life: Implications for clinical practice. *American Psychologist, 62*(4), 271–286.

Sue, D. W., & Sue, D. (2008). *Counseling the culturally diverse: Theory and practice* (5th ed.). New Jersey: Wiley.

Tager, D., & Good, G. E. (2005). Italian and American masculinities: A comparison of masculine gender role norms. *Psychology of Men & Masculinity, 6,* 264–274.

Timlin-Scalera, R. M., Ponterotto, J. G., Blumberg, F. C., & Jackson, M. A. (2003). A grounded theory study of help-seeking behaviors among white male high school students. *Journal of Counseling Psychology, 50,* 339–350.

U.S. Department of Justice (2003). *Criminal victimization in the United States: 2002 statistical tables.* Retrieved on October 24, 2008, from http://www.ojp.usdoj.gov/bjs/pub/pdf/cvus0202.pdf.

Vessey, J. T., & Howard, K. I. (1993). Who seeks psychotherapy. *Psychotherapy, 30,* 546–553.

Vogel, D. L., Epting, F., & Wester, S. R. (2003). Counselors' perceptions of female and male clients. *Journal of Counseling and Development, 81,* 131–141.

Vogel, D.L., Gentile, D., & Kaplan, S. (2008, March). The influence of television on willingness to seek therapy. *Journal of Clinical Psychology, 64*(3), 276–295.

Vogel, D. L., Wade, N. G., & Haake, S. (2006). Measuring the self-stigma associated with seeking psychological help. *Journal of Counseling Psychology, 53*, 325–337.

Vogel, D. L., Wade, N. G., Wester, S., Larson, L., & Hackler, A. H. (2007). Seeking help from a mental health professional: The influence of one's social network. *Journal of Clinical Psychology, 63*(3), 233–245.

Vogel, D. L., & Wester, S. R. (2003). To seek help or not to seek help: The risks of self-disclosure. *Journal of Counseling Psychology, 50*, 351–361.

Vogel, D. L., Wester, S. R., & Larson, L. M. (2007). Avoidance of counseling: Psychological factors that inhibit seeking help. *Journal of Counseling and Development, 85*, 410–422.

Walker, L.E.A. (2001). A feminist perspective on men in emotional pain. In G. Brooks & G. Good (Eds.), *The handbook of counseling and psychotherapy approaches for men* (pp. 683–695). San Francisco: Jossey-Bass.

Wampold, B. E. (2001). *The great psychotherapy debate: Models, methods, and findings.* Mahwah, NJ: Lawrence Erlbaum.

Weeks, R., & Widom, C. S. (1998). Self-reports of early childhood victimization among incarcerated adult male felons. *Journal of Interpersonal Violence, 13*, 346–361.

Weinberg, G. (1972). *Society and the healthy homosexual.* New York: St. Martin's.

Wester, S., & Lyubelsky, J. (2005). Supporting the thin blue line: Gender-sensitive therapy with male police officers. *Professional Psychology: Research and Practice, 36*(1), 51–58.

Wester, S. R., Vogel, D. L., Pressly, P. K., & Heesacker, M. (2002). Sex differences in emotion: A critical review of the literature and implications for counseling psychology. *The Counseling Psychologist, 30*, 629–651.

Whaley, A. L., & Davis, K. E. (2007). Cultural competence and evidence-based practice: A complementary perspective. *American Psychologist, 62*, 563–574.

Zane, N., & Yeh, M. (2002). The use of culturally-based variables in assessment: Studies on loss of face. In K. S. Kurasaki & S. Okazaki (Eds.), *Asian American mental health: Assessment theories and methods* (pp. 123–138). New York: Kluwer Academic/Plenum.

CHAPTER 8

DEVELOPING MULTICULTURAL COMPETENCY IN CLINICAL WORK WITH PEOPLE OF MIXED ANCESTRY

AISHA DIXON-PETERS

INTRODUCTION

There is a growing number of mixed-race people in the United States and a growing number of individuals who identify as mixed-race or multiracial. In the last census, 6.8 million people identified as multiracial, marking more than one racial category to identify themselves or their children, with 42 percent under 18 years of age (Jones & Symens Smith, 2001). The "biracial baby boom" of the 1970s and 1980s produced a notable cohort of multiracial individuals (Bratter, 2007) and resulted in an increase in the number of mixed-race individuals from 500,000 in 1970 to nearly 7 million in 2000 (Krebs, 2000; Shih & Sanchez, 2005). Given this growing population, mental health practitioners will likely be working with increasing numbers of multiracial individuals (Kerwin, Ponterotto, Jackson, & Harris, 1993); thus, it is important for therapists and counselors to have an awareness and knowledge of the experiences of this population and to be able to transfer this awareness and knowledge into skills useful in working with multiracial individuals. Competent, ethical multicultural practice requires understanding and addressing the unique characteristics and mental health needs of this population.

This chapter will provide the reader with guidelines and resources for increasing awareness of one's own values and attitudes, knowledge of ecological issues related to people of mixed ancestry, and skills in developing competency in working with persons of mixed ancestry.

Case studies are included and will be referred to throughout the chapter to illustrate critical concepts. *Pause & Ponder* exercises will be included throughout the chapter to prompt the reader to stop, reflect, and engage in a more contemplative and dynamic way with the concepts in this text, thus increasing personal awareness and recognition of multicultural issues as they relate to people of mixed ancestry.

DEFINITIONS

In approaching discourse on multiracial identity, it is important to first acknowledge the concept of race. The APA Multicultural Guidelines (2002) note the many definitions of *race* and the philosophical discourse and debate on the questionable basis of race as biological. The definition used in these guidelines asserts that race is a social construct and "the category to which others assign individuals on the basis of physical characteristics, such as skin color or hair type, and the generalizations and stereotypes made as a result" (APA, 2002, p. 9). These physical characteristics (e.g., skin color, facial features, hair type, etc.) are referred to as *phenotype* (Roysircar-Sodowsky & Kuo, 2001, p. 219), and are frequently addressed in the literature as an important contextual consideration, the implications of which will be discussed throughout this chapter. The use of race has resulted in individuals being treated "as though they belong to biologically defined racial groups on the basis of such characteristics" (Helms & Talleyrand, 1997, p. 1247). While acknowledging that there is no one agreed-upon definition of ethnicity, these guidelines also provide a working definition of *ethnicity* as "the acceptance of the group mores and practices of one's culture of origin and the concomitant sense of belonging" (APA, 2002, p. 9).

It is also important to understand the definitions of the terms used to describe groups in this population. *Biracial* refers to an individual with parents from two different singular racial groups. For example, an individual who has one parent of Lebanese ancestry and one parent of Latino/Colombian ancestry (e.g., the famous Colombian singer Shakira) would be considered biracial. Other terms used by biracial individuals, or used to describe biracial individuals, have included *interracial* (Kerwin & Ponterotto, 1995), *mixed* (Spickard, 1992), and *half and half* (Davis, 1991). The term *hapa*, (Fulbeck, 2006) which translates to "half," has also been used to describe a person of mixed ancestry, particularly those of half-Asian or -Hawaiian descent. While this term was once considered a derogatory label, it is now embraced with pride by many biracial and multiracial people (Fulbeck, 2006).

The term *multiracial* is one that refers to individuals whose ethnic or racial heritage is comprised of multiple racial or ethnic groups and "whose parents are of different socially designated racial groups" (Root, 1996, p. ix). The multiracial descriptor also includes persons who have a parent, or both parents, of mixed racial or ethnic heritage. Consider, as an example, the children of professional golfer Tiger Woods. Their mother is Swedish and their father, Tiger Woods, refers to his own ethnic identity as "Cablinasian," of mixed African American, Dutch, Thai, and Chinese ancestry. Other terms for identifying multiracial people have included some of the same terms (e.g., *mixed*; Spickard, 1992), as well as *mixed-race* (Renn, 2008), *mixed-heritage* (Stephan, 1992), *multiethnic* (Fernandez, 1992), and *mixed-ancestry* (Fhagen-Smith, 2003). While not an exhaustive list, these terms have been widely used to describe or identify people of mixed racial and ethnic heritage. Note, however, that an individual's self-definition may vary based on familiarity with terms and familial, social, political, and cultural contexts. Moreover, individuals and communities may develop their own descriptive or affectional terms to express unique and collective aspects of identity and heritage. Some of these terms include: *Blaxican* (Black and Mexican), *Mexirican* (Mexican and Puerto Rican), *Afro-Asian* (of African and Asian descent), *Blight* (Black and White), *Latinegra/o* (Latina/o of African descent), *Filatina/o* (Filipino and Latina/o), and *Japanegro* (Japanese and African American).

In this chapter, the terms *mixed-race, multiracial, biracial,* and *of mixed ancestry* will be used interchangeably to reflect the fluidity of identity for many in this population. The term *monoracial* will be used to identify those who identify with a singular racial or ethnic group as well as those individuals who have two parents of the same racial or ethnic classification.

PAUSE & PONDER

Reflect on your reactions to the previous text. Consider your own racial/ethnic background and respond to the following questions:

- When did you realize you belonged to a particular racial or ethnic group?
- Is your racial/ethnic identification of a singular racial/ethnic group or multiple?
- Did you ever experience external or internal pressure to choose your racial/ethnic group?
- What privileges have you experienced because of your background?
- What challenges or discriminations have you experienced related to your background?
- How has your background influenced your sense of self?

CASE STUDIES

The following three case studies will be explored to provide readers with examples of how presenting problems and identity may evolve for clients of mixed ancestry. These vignettes will be referred to throughout the chapter to clarify and apply concepts. Readers are encouraged to reflect on the case studies presented and consider these vignettes while reading the concepts and models presented throughout the chapter.

CASE VIGNETTE 8.1

Justin

Justin, a 27-year-old, multiracial man, presented at a counseling center at a private liberal arts college with depression and relationship concerns. Justin's mother is a White woman (of Dutch and German ancestry), and his father is a biracial African American and White man (of African American and Swedish, ancestry). Justin's parents separated before Justin was born. Thereafter, Justin was raised by his mother, in a predominantly White, upper-middle class suburb and visited his father once per month at his father's home in a predominantly working-class, African American community. The differences in these communities were striking and Justin disliked and attempted to avoid visiting his father. Visibly, Justin presented with very light-skin complexion and features that were not readily suggestive of his African American ancestry. Justin could, and did, pass for White, a reality that brought both privileges and pain for him as he struggled to understand the complexity of his heritage. He had difficulty relating to African Americans and readily noted negative stereotypes of African Americans that he associated with his African American family members as well as his father, with whom he had a tenuous and conflicted relationship.

Raised in a predominantly White neighborhood, Justin painfully endured discriminatory remarks about African Americans made by peers and even family members. When he visited his father, in a predominantly African American neighborhood, Justin felt uncomfortable, out of place, and was called "White boy" by the kids in the neighborhood. When Justin was an adolescent, his father died of cancer. Following his father's death, there was a disconnect from his paternal family with whom he had already had a tenuous relationship. Over the course of treatment, Justin explored feelings of guilt, regret, grief, and loss from his paternal family as well as from his African American heritage. While Justin reported feeling very different from African American peers, he also reported feeling different from his White peers. For the first time, Justin chose to explicitly self-identify as "multiracial" when applying to college in hopes he would be eligible for educational programs and resources for ethnic minority students. While Justin had been in treatment with other therapists, he had avoided discussion of how his identity development and internalized racism had impacted some of his presenting concerns.

CASE VIGNETTE 8.2

Sumaya

Sumaya, an 18-year-old, first-generation college student from a working-class family, presented at a college counseling center at a private liberal arts college with concerns about

(continued)

(*continued*)

anxiety, difficulty managing stress, and social relational difficulties. Sumaya's mother is a first-generation Latina from Colombia and her father an immigrant from Lebanon. Sumaya was raised by both parents in a diverse, urban community. Sumaya identifies as biracial. Sumaya expressed frustration about frequently being asked if she were Arab, rather than being asked if she were biracial or "mixed." She struggled to find her place socially and felt most comfortable with other students of color, joining the multicultural club on campus. While navigating ethnic identity, Sumaya was simultaneously navigating cultural and religious identification, as her father is Muslim and her mother Protestant. Sumaya explored contrasts between her own values and religious beliefs in comparison to those of her father and mother. Further, issues of immigration and related trauma arose as her parents had migrated to the United States from countries that, at the time, were experiencing serious political unrest.

CASE VIGNETTE 8.3

Julie

Julie, a 26-year-old "Blackipino" lesbian, presented at a community counseling agency with relational problems. Her father is African American and her mother Filipina. Julie's parents divorced when she was a toddler and she was then raised by her mother alone in a predominantly middle-class, Asian American neighborhood. Her contact with her father and his family was very limited until mid-adolescence given the tension between her parents. She felt constrained by her Catholic, Filipino family members' beliefs and practices because of her lesbian identity, but felt accepted by them in her status as a Filipina. While Filipino peers inquired about her background because of her mixed, ambiguous physical features, they acknowledged shared commonalities with regard to culture, traditions, holidays, and language. She participated in Asian and Filipino student organizations and felt pride in her culture. She was often told by African American peers that she was "not Black enough," and she felt a sense of guilt and regret at having limited knowledge about Black culture, traditions, and history.

When Julie was an adolescent, her father got remarried to an African American woman whose adolescent daughter was of mixed African American and Korean descent. Julie bonded with her stepmother's daughter and the two identified and shared experiences of being of mixed ancestry. Julie identified this experience as being critical in allowing her to develop a strong sense of self-identity as a person of mixed ancestry. She used the term "Blackipino" to embrace her Black and Filipino heritages as well as assert her mixed-race identity, rather than succumbing to social pressures she had previously experienced to choose one over the other.

KNOWLEDGE

Identity in Context: Mixed Ancestry in a Monoracial World

Historical

As this chapter was being written, the people of the United States elected Barack Obama as their 44th President. President Obama is a biracial man, born of a Kenyan father and White mother from Kansas. His identity remained a significant point of discussion during his campaign and even well after his election. Analysts assessed whether he was Black or Black enough, White or too White, and hypothesized about the perception of Obama in the Black community, among White Americans, and among ethnic minorities in the United States and globally (Coates, 2007; Walters, 2007). The perceptions in the media, as well as his perception of himself, speak to the complexity of identity for multiracial or mixed- race people. The media spotlight was particularly intense when he referred to his identity, culture, and relationships. For example, when Obama announced his plans to adopt a dog for his children from an animal shelter and commented that the dog would be "a mutt like me," it aroused a media frenzy over his choice of language in referring to his mixed-race heritage with some believing it suggested he was comfortable in discussing racial issues while others found the term offensive (Fram, 2008; Rhee, 2008). The post-Obama zeitgeist signals a shift in the dynamics of considering and discussing race and mixed ancestry.

Well before Obama's emergence as the U.S. President, another pivotal shift occurred that forwarded the discourse and consideration of people of mixed ancestry. For the first time in history, the 2000 Census permitted respondents to identify more than one racial or ethnic category by selecting multiple racial groups. This followed efforts by mixed-race people and various advocacy and grassroots groups to lobby the Office of Management and Budget (OMB) to include a multiracial category in the next census (Rockquemore & Brunsma, 2002). This effort was met with much controversy, as some suggested it represented a means for people of mixed ancestry to de-identify with one or more of their ancestry groups or attempt to gain access to White privilege (Sundstrom, 2001). Understandably, others were concerned about the validity of the statistical procedures used to decipher the data and of implications for

lessening special efforts aimed at reducing health and education disparities for communities of color. A task force was developed to assess how to provide options for mixed-ancestry persons to identify as such, and it was ultimately recommended that, rather than giving the option of checking a "multiracial" box, respondents to the census would be permitted to check more than one racial group (Shih & Sanchez, 2005). That nearly 7 million people did report more than one racial category speaks to the shift in self-identification for many people of mixed ancestry.

Prior to census developers allowing the option of multiracial identification (i.e., from 1960 to 2000), respondents were permitted to select only one racial or ethnic category. Even earlier, respondents did not self-identify their racial category; rather, census takers determined the racial category of the respondent based on phenotype and *hypodescent* rules (Hitlin, Brown, & Elder, 2006), explained in the following.

The *hypodescent* or "one-drop" conceptualization was utilized in early U.S. history to delineate individuals with any African-descent heritage (Davis, 1991). This distinction was relied on to maintain racial inequity as well as the supposed "purity" of the White race (Rockquemore & Brunsma, 2002). Individuals with "Black blood" were qualified into categories such as *mulatto* (half Black), *quadroon* (one-quarter Black), *octoroon* (one-eighth Black), and so on. Within the context of slavery, these delineations were particularly salient. For example, well-known Black historical figures Booker T. Washington and Fredrick Douglas were labeled *mulatto*, as they were the children of mothers, who were slaves of African

PAUSE & PONDER

Reflect on the previous reading and the historical context of the hypodescent rule. Consider the impact of this historical context on your own ethnic identity and respond to the following questions:

- How has the hypodescent rule impacted you or others in your life?
- How has a monoracial conceptualization influenced how you see your own identity? That of friends? Family? Your clients?

descent, and White, slavemaster, biological fathers. However, a closer look suggests that Douglass and Washington may have had more than "half" White ancestry as their mothers were slaves who, therefore, may have also had some White ancestry (Davis, 1991). The ethnic categorizations of these men demonstrate the complexity of racial and ethnic classification in light of the hypodescent rule, as was historically applied only to people of African descent in the United States (Davis, 1991).

While multiracial individuals today are not solely those mixed-race individuals of African descent, the early conceptualizations of race based on hypodescent have influenced other mixed-race individuals of various ethnic heritages to varying degrees. Monoracial identification has been the way in which Americans have long conceptualized race, and assertion of multiracial identities challenges this conceptualization (Bratter, 2007). Hypodescent rules limit multiracial individuals' access to White identity, permitting little fluidity and flexibility for selecting between White and non-White/other identities (Bratter, 2007). Furthermore, the development of a hypodescent conceptualization of race allowed for antimiscegenistic sentiments and accordingly oppressive laws (Root, 1992).

Because of historical factors based on the rule of hypodescent, multiracial persons with African American ancestry are more likely to identify as Black/African American than multiracial or biracial (Bratter, 2007; Herman, 2004). Rules of hypodescent have influenced categorization for other mixed-race individuals, as well, with some Asian individuals tending to identify with their monoracial minority category when selecting one singular racial category (Bratter, 2007; Herman, 2004), and both African Americans and Asians being more likely to identify with their minority monoracial category if they report experiences of ethnic discrimination (Herman, 2004). These historical factors help explain the complexity of mixed-ancestry identification in a monoracial world, and its influence on concepts such as interracial marriages and fluidity in racial classification.

Interracial Marriages and Fluidity in Racial Classification

Interracial marriages were outlawed by antimiscegenation laws until 1967. These laws, and the relatively recent overturning of these laws, influenced interracial relationships and denied acknowledgment, rights, and support for interracial couples, multiracial families, and certainly the multiracial children of these unions. Since the overturning of antimiscegenation laws, interracial marriages have increased. More specifically, since 1970, interracial marriages increased at least 500 percent (Root, 2001). As a result of interracial marriages increasing, the population of persons of mixed ancestry has also increased.

There are within-group differences for interracial marriages, with some groups having higher numbers than others. It has been suggested that the variability of these rates relates to flexibility of racial identification among certain racial groups (Bratter, 2007). African Americans have the lowest rates of intermarriages, along with less fluidity in patterns of racial identification. Asians have some of the highest rates of intermarriage and relatively more flexible patterns of racial identification. Native Americans also have relatively high rates of intermarriages, though more fluidity with regard to racial identification of mixed-race offspring (Esbach, 1995). Furthermore, mixed-race youth of Native American ancestry may be more likely to switch racial self-identification over time, further supporting the assertion that racial identification may be more fluid for Native Americans and people of Native American descent (Hitlin et al., 2006).

Bratter (2007) studied 2000 Census data to gain an understanding of the racial classification of children of mixed ancestry by their parents. This researcher found complex differences in parents' identifications of their children as mixed-race or singular race based on various factors. Parents who identified their children as multiracial were more common among families in which the parents' own multiracial backgrounds did not overlap. Stated differently, parental dyads in which one parent's multiracial background was different from that of the other parent were more likely to identify their children as multiracial rather than as being a single race or ethnicity. However, parents from families in which two multiracial parents shared similar racial backgrounds with overlapping ancestry were less likely to identify their children as multiracial. Instead, these parents were more likely to identify each child as belonging to a singular racial category in which there was overlap between the two parents. For example, a child with one parent who is Chinese and White and one parent who is White and Mexican may be more likely to be identified by his or her parents as White—the overlapping racial category between the two parents. Similar to the results found by researchers in previous studies, Bratter (2007) described gender-based differences in the transmission of racial identity to children. She noted that, among families in which multiracial fathers had Asian/Pacific Islander or African American spouses, children were less likely to be classified by parents as multiracial. Further, multiracial families of African or Asian/Pacific Islander descent had the lowest rates of classifying children as multiracial. The author explored the possible rationale that parents and communities might classify Asians/Pacific Islanders of multiracial heritage as Asian as a means of sustaining the community's identity.

Hitlin and colleagues (2006) examined multiracial self-identification among adolescents between the ages of 14 and 18, and explored changes in self-identification 5 years later. These authors suggest that ethnic identity development for multiracial youth is less linear and more fluid, and may be influenced by a variety of factors across the developmental trajectory. The authors delineated six logical developmental pathways of racial self-identification, including adolescents who: (1) selected the same monoracial category at both points of measurement; (2) selected the same (multiple) categories at both points of measurement; (3) initially marked one single racial category, and then later added one or more different racial identities (termed *diversifiers*); (4) began identifying as multiracial, but later selected a singular race (termed *conso-*

lidators); (5) selected completely different multiracial identities at each point of measurement (termed *switching multiracials*); and (6) selected different singular racial identities at each point of measurement (termed *switching monoracials*).

Hitlin et al. (2006) found that diversifiers were more likely to come from backgrounds with higher education. The consolidators, who switched from a multiracial self-categorization to a singular category, were more likely to be younger, from less-educated backgrounds, and have lower self-esteem than adolescents who maintained a consistent monoracial identity. The data showed nearly twice as many adolescents who "switched" as those whose identities remained fixed over time, demonstrating fluidity in racial identification; however, youth from higher socioeconomic backgrounds, and those with higher self-esteem, were less likely to switch race categories. These authors found that switching was related to higher intelligence and suggested, in keeping with previous research, that fluidity in self-identification relates to cognitive flexibility. Individuals identified as *Switching Monoracials*, who shift predominantly between minority statuses, were found to have darker skin color, and lower self-esteem, and were less likely to live in predominantly White communities. Further, these findings highlight problems that may occur when assessing identity with multiracial individuals through an oversimplified, monoracial lens, as self-classification may vary depending on developmental stage. Without highly sensitive measures, assessments at one specific point in time may lead to oversight of the complexity of the individual's identity and misleading conclusions.

Research by Doyle and Kao (2007) also suggested that multiracials' self-identification changed over time, particularly for those identifying as Native American. These findings further highlight the fluidity of racial self-identification for multiracials, especially individuals from certain groups. More specifically, these authors found that multiracial persons with Asian and African American ancestry, when changing self-identification, tended to demonstrate an affinity for their respective minority backgrounds. In short, when Asian or African American multiracial individuals change from identifying as multiracial to monoracial, it is more likely they will self-identify in terms of their Asian or African American ancestry.

There may also be differences in how mixed-ancestry persons identify depending on the context. In a qualitative research study, Miville, Constantine, Baysden, and So-Lloyd (2005) found that participants expressed differences between public and private identity. They found that multiracial individuals tended to identify simultaneously with a singular racial or ethnic group publicly, while also identifying privately with their multiracial identity. These authors identified the *reference group* for multiracial persons as being a critical issue, as multiracial individuals rarely have accessibility to a visible multiracial group. This potentially influences the proclivity toward identification with a singular racial group for some individuals. Participants in this study also found meaningful connection in identifying as people of color (POC), and thus with a POC social reference group, with a sense of common struggle, as a buffer against oppression and racism, as well as a means for social support. Establishing connections with other communities of color was associated with a sense of pride and intimacy for these participants, who frequently perceived a sense of flexibility and adaptability in diverse groups. The authors highlighted unique strengths for multiracial people, including cognitive flexibility and openness to other groups. These strengths should be considered and affirmed when working with multiracial individuals.

Physical Appearance

Phenotype plays an important role in self-identification for people of mixed ancestry (Renn, 2008). Herman (2004) supported this notion, acknowledging that both phenotype and social context influenced the race selected by many biracial youth who endorsed a minority, as opposed to White, identification from among the options afforded by their mixed-race backgrounds. Phenotype may also affect the plausibility of identifying or not identifying with a particular aspect of one's identity (Doyle & Kao, 2007; Rockquemore & Brunsma, 2002). In fact, Doyle and Kao found that, for mixed-race persons of African American and White background, phenotypic traits explained shifts in racial self-identification over time. For example, consider the case study of Justin, who has very fair skin and features that do not appear to suggest his African ancestry. He is painfully aware that his flexibility to identify as African American has been limited given that others, including African Americans, Whites, and people of other ethnicities, do not readily identify him as African American. While in early childhood Justin identified with his mixed African American ancestry, after having to justify and explain his identity and facing disbelief from

---

PAUSE & PONDER

Consider your physical appearance: eye color, hair color, hair texture, skin color, the shape of your nose, eyes, lips, and cheek bones. Respond to the following questions considering your own experience as you read the following section:

- How would others describe your physical appearance?

- What assumptions have others made about your ethnic background based on your physical appearance? Do these assumptions tend to be accurate? Inaccurate?

- Have others (peers, colleagues, strangers, etc.) ever inaccurately assumed your racial/ethnic background based on your physical appearance? If so, what was this experience like for you?

- How does your physical appearance, and the assumptions people make based on your appearance, affect privileges? Experiences of discrimination?

peers over time, he eventually found it easier to disidentify with his African American ancestry and "passed" for White.

Light-skinned, high-yellow, red-boned, blue-black, olive, light-bright—these are all terms that have been used to describe the lightness or darkness of skin color in complex historical, cultural, and sociopolitical contexts. Skin color has historically been a charged issue in many communities of color. More specifically, privilege has been associated with lighter skin tones for members of many cultural and ethnic groups, including, Latinos, African Americans, and Asians. Hence, a number of the aforementioned terms are colloquial and the result of hypodescent rules and color stratification underlying relative differential privileges and access for people of color (Russell, Wilson, & Hall, 1992). Historically, African Americans with lighter skin tone have been granted certain privileges not accessible to those with darker skin tones (Nishimura, 2004). For instance, African American slaves with lighter complexions were more likely to work in the slavemaster's house, while slaves with darker skin were more likely to work in the fields.

Hunter (2005) discussed the well-known issue of skin-color stratification as differential perceptions of beauty based on skin color. Within this paradigm, lighter skin, closer to European/ White skin color, has been viewed within many ethnic groups as being more favorable or more beautiful, while darker skin, with more African or indigenous-looking skin tones, has been considered less

favorable and less attractive. Furthermore, skin color has also been linked to assumptions about intelligence and competence, with individuals whose skin tone is closer to that associated with skin tones of European/White individuals often being considered more intelligent and more competent than those with darker skin.

While attributes of physical appearance, including skin color, hair color, hair texture, eye color, and facial features, are particularly significant for African Americans and members of other groups of color, these same physical attributes often have a particularly defining role for people of mixed descent. The commentary on physical appearance frequently begins as early as birth, with family members or community members commenting on the skin color, hair texture, and features such as eyes, nose, and lips (which may or may not be congruent with the features of the parents, and/or the features of the respective racial groups). Being noticed, and sometimes stared at, because of physical appearance is a theme for many multiracial people and these experiences can lead to self-consciousness (Edwards & Pedrotti, 2004).

Some studies have addressed the role of physical appearance in identity development (AhnAllen, Suyemoto, & Carter, 2006; Gaskins, 1979; Rockquemore & Brunsma, 2002) and in the way mixed-race persons are perceived by others based on physical appearance (Brunsma & Rockquemore, 2001). Researchers AhnAllen and colleagues (2006) found that physical appearance was

---

PAUSE & PONDER

- What are messages you received from family, media, community, and peers about skin color and skin tone?
- What were messages about light skin tone? Dark skin tone?
- Which skin tone was considered more favorable within:

  Family?

  Community?

  Media?

  Peer groups?
- How did you internalize these messages?

significantly correlated with a sense of belonging to corresponding racial groups among multiracial Japanese European American participants. More specifically, the results indicated that Japanese physical appearance was associated with belonging in the Japanese American community, while European American physical appearance variables were associated with belonging to the European American community. These results demonstrate that physical appearance may impact one's ability to identify with and feel accepted by certain reference groups. Furthermore, monoracial self-identification was related to physical appearance as well as social variables of the respective monoracial group.

Herman (2004) found that multiracial participants who appeared White were more likely to identify as White and were also more likely to live in predominantly White communities. Again, consider the case study of Justin, who appeared White, was raised in a predominantly White suburb, and came to identify publicly as White. In fact, multiracials with Latino ancestry, when residing in a predominately White community, were more likely to self-identify as White (Herman, 2004).

Helms and Cook (1999) asserted that various racial groups have within-group differences with regard to phenotypic expression. This certainly applies to mixed-ancestry persons as well. In fact, mental health practitioners should be aware of within-group differences among multiracial individuals and their families. With regard to skin color and other phenotypic characteristics, a client's sibling group may have great variation. For example, while a client may present as light skinned with straight hair, she or he could have siblings who are of any skin color, within the range from light to dark, and hair texture from straight to wavy to tight curls. Another important consideration is that multiracial persons may come from blended families in which parents had children from other relationships prior to, or following, the birth of the client. These siblings could be from any racial group, including similar or different mixed-race backgrounds or a monoracial background consistent with the parent from the same racial group. For example, consider Case Vignette 8.3 of Julie, whose mother remarried and had children with Julie's stepfather, who is Filipino. Her younger siblings are monoracial Filipino American and, thus, have a differing experience with regards to ethnic and cultural identity development.

Ambiguity in Physical Appearance and "Passing"

Given historical racial stratification (Rockquemore & Brunsma, 2002) based on notions of superiority of certain racial groups over others and the resulting oppression, some mixed-race individuals, particularly those with more ambiguity in physical appearance, may have accepted the option of passing for White. Passing may have been seen as a viable option by which to gain access, or greater accessibility, to resources, and to avoid painful experiences of racism.

PAUSE & PONDER

Reflect on the previous readings regarding the diversity in family ethnic makeup for people of mixed ancestry. Consider your own family and respond to the following questions:

- Do your siblings have the same, or different, ethnic background as you? If so, when did you realize there were differences?
- What messages did you receive from family, peers, and/or the media about these differences?
- Are there variations in physical appearance, such as skin color, hair texture, and physical features including eyes, nose, and lip shape?
- Have siblings with different physical appearances been treated differently by peers, family members, or people in your community? If so, what meaning did this have for you?

Conversely, in more recent times, some have chosen to selectively identify, given the context, with one or more of their racial groups in order to gain access to other benefits. For example, some mixed-race individuals, or individuals who live as part of the White majority although they have mixed-race ancestry, have chosen to claim a minority racial category for college application processes or to be eligible for certain scholarships (Hitlin et al., 2006).

Exoticization

Multiracial individuals have frequently been exoticized. Individuals have noticed others staring at them in either bewilderment or awe. They have heard comments like, "Mixed people are so beautiful" or "Your kids are going to be beautiful" or "You should be a model." People of mixed ancestry may have had their background questioned and physical characteristics deconstructed by peers, colleagues, family members, or a complete stranger on the street—"What are you? . . . You don't look [it]" (Root, 2003, p. 2).

Multiracial women more frequently experience sexualized exoticization than multiracial men (Root, 1998). Root (2004) discussed the ways in which biracial women have been exoticized, considered both different and unique, with many underlying subtle and overt meanings and resulting implications. Of these underlying meanings, there is frequently a connotation of sexual difference or uniqueness (Buchanan & Acevedo, 2004). These experiences may be internalized and may influence a biracial woman's sense of self in context, particularly with regard to sexuality (Root, 2004). The effect of being exoticized may be different for certain multi-racial women, depending on many factors, particularly cohort status, the associated zeitgeist, and the resulting emphasis on physical appearance (Root, 2004).

Multiple Identities, Intersecting Identities

One's ethnic or racial identity is but one aspect of multiple, intersecting identities. Although race, particularly given the history of racism and racial oppression, is frequently identified as a key aspect of diversity, other aspects of identity should also be considered when working with any individual. Certainly, one's sense of self and affiliation with various aspects of identity and social group membership is dependent on the salience of one's multiple, intersecting identities and the context in which these identities are developed and expressed. Among these multiple identities are gender, sexual orientation, class, religious/spiritual affiliation and practices, immigration status, size, ability, and educational status. These identities, and their relative importance for the individual, must be considered as contributing factors in a client's developing sense of self within social contexts. Accordingly, issues of privilege should be considered based on social group memberships and social context.

Considering the intersection of identity between ethnicity and gender, multiracial women are sometimes considered, as are other women of color, as experiencing "double jeopardy" or "double marginalization"—that is, having to cope with stressors related to membership in multiple subordinated groups of gender and ethnicity (Edwards & Pedrotti, 2004; Nishimura, 2004). Multiracial women encounter unique stressors related to these intersecting identities with consequences of uneven distribution of power as well as inordinate emphasis on physical attractiveness. In fact, Root (1998) found that girls experienced more ridicule and rejection with regard to phenotype, including hair, body size, hair color, eye shape, and hairstyles, than did boys.

Root (2004) explained that multiracial women may present with concerns specific to their cohort. Root identified three cohorts of mixed-race women, the *exotic* women born prior to the late 1960s, the *vanguard* women born between the late 1960s and the late 1970s, and the *biracial baby boomers* born post 1980. The experiences of these cohorts of women have been influenced significantly by systemic issues of the zeitgeist such as segregation, antimiscegenation laws, racial dynamics, tensions, and changes post-WWII, and civil rights movements. Within the *exotic generation*, persons of mixed ancestry were expected to comply with the hypodescent rule and collude with efforts to maintain the so-called "purity" of Whiteness, while being simultaneously confronted with tests of authenticity by minority racial groups. Because this cohort of women was viewed as "exotic," an emphasis was placed on its members' unique physical appearances. These women may have difficulty losing status as "exotic" or unique in physical appearance both as a result of the aging process and living in a new era in which there is a growing multiracial population. While racial boundaries remained firm for women within the *vanguard generation*, the mixed-race population was on the rise and choices to identify with a singular racial group were more often motivated by proactive cognizant decision making than by ascribing solely to rules of hypodescent. Hence situational identity, in which an individual's self-identity is fluid and contextually based, is more likely for women in this cohort. Biracial women in the *biracial baby boomers* cohort may express that they experienced more opportunities to thrive, as they were beneficiaries of the civil rights movements and enjoyed a more visible cohort of mixed-race peers and figures in the media. For this cohort of women, physical appearance is likely less heavily emphasized than for women in the *exotic* cohort, given the changing sociopolitical context with regard to ethnicity, gender, and sexuality.

Environment and Experiences of Racism

Identity development, particularly along racial and ethnic dimensions, occurs within the context of a society in which certain groups hold privilege and others do not. Hence, identity development is influenced by oppression and privilege, and can be affected by discriminatory interactions (Hitlin et al., 2006). While ethnic identity development and self-identification are important aspects of development for all minority groups (Cross, 1991), exploration and subjective identification of one's racial category may often be a significant event along the developmental trajectory specific to the experience of multiracial youth (Hitlin et al., 2006). Encountering stereotypes, discrimination, and oppression can result in internalized racism and association with negative beliefs about one's

own racial group. However, researchers found that multiracial individuals who emphasize race as a social construct were less influenced by race-based stereotypes (Shih, Bonam, Sanchez, & Peck, 2007).

Internalized racism has influenced within-in-group hazing (Root, 1998) and related tests of authenticity, practices which can result in some individuals being rejected from their own social reference group (Root, 1998). Therefore, people of mixed ancestry risk the "double rejection" of being rejected from dominant society as well as their own racial or ethnic groups. For example, consider the case study of Sumaya, who reported feeling rejected, at times, by other Latino students for not being "Latina enough," and also reported feeling outcast from the dominant White culture for being a woman of color.

Multiracial people can encounter racism (Miville et al., 2005) focused on both monoracial and multiracial identities. These experiences can happen at a personal/individual level as well as at a macro/institutional level. Comments by peers, teachers, friends of parents, and extended family, can leave lasting impressions on multiracial people. Although various forms increasingly provide opportunities for individuals to more accurately and freely identify their multiracial heritage, many recall being forced to check only one box for race as an experience of institutional racism that denied their reality as a multiracial person.

Consistent with identity development models, Miville et al. (2005) found that participants also discussed critical periods along the developmental trajectory that contributed to their identity development. More specifically, elementary school emerged as a critical period in which participants began noticing differences between themselves and their peers including skin color, cultural events and celebrations, texture of hair, familial experiences, and more. Adolescence involved a time in which peer groups became an even more significant influencing factor. Participants reported an increase in freedom to self-identify with a particular social group in late adolescence and early adulthood.

The community in which a multiracial individual is raised has an influence on his or her identity development. Differences have been noted between individuals raised in predominantly White communities and those raised in predominantly minority communities. Another important factor is the degree of contact multiracials have with other minority groups in the community (Harris & Sim, 2002). Miville and colleagues (2005) also identified *critical places* in which individuals were influenced by the demographic makeup of their neighborhood. In fact, the lack of a visible, accessible multiracial community may be among the greatest challenges multiracial people face in developing a multiracial identity, as parents are often unable to provide a multiracial role model, leaving individuals to look outside of the family for guidance on how to develop a healthy sense of self.

Identity Development Models

Mental health practitioners are encouraged to develop multicultural competencies in various areas of diversity with which clients may present. One of these domains is racial/ethnic diversity. With regard to increasing knowledge of various ethnic groups, it is imperative that therapists and counselors have knowledge of ethnic identity development models. To conceptualize the experiences of clients of mixed heritage, therapists and counselors should be familiar with the various biracial/multiracial identity development models proposed over time. Therapists should also understand the differences between these models with regard to assumptions of what is the adaptive or healthy end stage, as well as how an individual progresses through stages.

Thornton and Wason (1995) outlined research approaches toward understanding multiracial identity as falling into three categories: (1) *problem approach,* (2) *equivalent approach,* and (3) *variant approach*. The *problem approach* predicted negative outcomes for biracial individuals and included such models as the "marginal man" by Stonequist (1937), which supported the idea of the "tragic mulatto" existence in which

biracial individuals were thought of as marginal, straddling two cultures without membership in either. Models encompassing the *problem approach* assumed pathology and led to conceptualizing multiracial individuals as being unable to develop a healthy identity. Perspectives of the *equivalent approach* applied preexisting models of racial identity, such as those offered by Cross (1987) and Morten and Atkinson (1983), to the identity development of biracial persons. Historically, these models followed a zeitgeist in which antimiscegenation laws were eradicated and civil rights movements had instilled racial pride in oppressed groups. More recent conceptualizations of multiracial individuals have been identified as falling into the *variant approach* category, with multiracial identity beginning to be understood as unique and differing in qualitative ways from monoracial categories. During this era, multiple identity development models have been proposed. Two researchers initially proposed specific identity development models for healthy biracial identity development utilizing clinical experience (Poston, 1990; Root, 1990) and personal experience (Root, 1990). Over time, these models have been expanded to include an ecological framework for understanding biracial and multiracial identity development within multiple contexts and beyond linear models (Renn, 2008).

In response to earlier models, which focused solely on the individual and ignored problematic social forces, Poston (1990) tentatively proposed a more positive model that acknowledged the complexity of identity development for biracial persons. Given the scarcity of research on biracial individuals, Poston looked to the already-existing models of Cross (1987) and Parham and Helms (1985) to explain how the identity development process incorporates the concepts of personal identity and reference group orientation. While there are some similarities between Poston's model and those he critiqued, significant differences exist between singular-racial and multiracial identities, specifically within the three middle stages of the model. Poston's model also explicitly recognized societal racism as an influencing factor. However, Poston's model does not consider the possibility of multiple healthy outcomes for multiracial individuals; instead, his model emphasizes integration of multiple ethnic identities. This stage of Poston's model has since been critiqued by researchers who propose there are multiple healthy identity statuses that could be developed by people of mixed racial ancestry. Poston's five-stage model approached identity development with a life-span (p. 153) focus:

1. *Personal Identity:* In one's earlier years, while one is aware of one's ethnic backgrounds, sense of self may be fairly independent from the ethnic backgrounds and orientation to social reference groups may be yet to be developed.
2. *Choice of Group Categorization:* Biracial individuals enter a state characterized by crisis and alienation in which they feel social and familial pressures to choose between identification with a social group of majority or minority status.
3. *Enmeshment/Denial:* After choosing a singular identity in the *choice* stage, individuals feel a sense of guilt, self-hatred, and confusion, and experience lack of acceptance from certain racial groups.
4. *Appreciation:* This stage is characterized by a sense of appreciation for one's multiple identities and an expanding of reference group orientation. While multiracials still tend to identify with one group among their mixed ancestry, they may begin to explore further about their multiple heritages and cultures.
5. *Integration:* This stage is characterized by wholeness and integration in one's identification with all of one's ethnic identities.

Kich (1992) also proposed a model of biracial identity development based on research with biracial adults of Japanese and White heritage, emphasizing integration and progression toward healthy self-acceptance. Kich's three-stage model (p. 305) is one in which individuals move from *dissonance* (incongruent feelings based on self-perceptions and external perceptions) toward a biracial and bicultural identity that is completely

internalized and valued. This is accomplished through efforts to gain both social acceptance and self-acceptance. According to Kich, these progressions occur according to age and relative developmental stages, with the first stage occurring between 3 and 10 years of age, the second stage typically from 8 years through young adulthood, and the final (internalized) stage between late adolescence and young adulthood. Like Poston's (1990) model, Kich's model emphasized integration of multiple ancestries as the goal for a healthy identity resolution. However, this notion has been challenged by other theorists.

Root's early model (1990) was akin to the early stages of foundational minority identity development models, though she altered the later stages of these models to account for the unique experiences of biracial individuals, particularly those with White heritage. She proposed that biracial individuals with White heritage cannot fully reject the dominant culture and immerse in the minority reference group, as was suggested would occur in the immersion-related stages of minority development models. Root explained that, during adolescence, biracial individuals experience turmoil related to not fitting completely into any one social group. Accordingly, she proposed four resolution statuses that acknowledge various ways in which biracial individuals may identify and suggested that each of these can be viewed as a potentially positive resolution. Root's model (p. 198), therefore, stands in contrast to models proposed by Poston and Kich, which suggested a specific end-goal status of integration as being more adaptive or healthy.

1. *Acceptance of the identity society assigns:* Feeling accepted by, typically, a minority racial group and alliances with family may contribute to individuals' identifying with the group to which others presume they belong. For example, in the case study of Justin, his initial self-defined identity was different from that assigned to him (White), eventually leading to Justin accepting this assigned identity.
2. *Identification with both racial groups:* An individual's ability to identify with both racial

groups is dependent on societal support and personal resilience in preserving this identity while potentially experiencing resistance from others. As an example, consider the case study of Sumaya, who identifies both with her Lebanese and Colombian racial and cultural identities. She maintained identification with both groups despite assumptions made by others about her identity.

3. *Identification with a single racial group:* As in resolution 1, the individual chooses a single racial group with which to identity; however, in this stage, the choice is independent of social forces.

4. *Identification as a new racial group:* While the individual is able to move fluidly among various racial groups, she or he most strongly identifies with other biracial individuals, without placing particular emphasis on specific heritage backgrounds.

In conceptualizing identity development for mixed-race individuals, Root considered the effect of various ecological factors in influencing identity development. These include racism, societal pressures, social support, and multiple identities. Specifically, Root suggested that gender differences contribute to identity development and may worsen or reduce the effects of racial discrimination experienced by biracial people. In her later work, Root (1999) developed an ecological metamodel for conceptualizing the varying and simultaneous resolutions of identity development that may evolve for biracial and multiracial people (see the Resources section of this chapter). Within her model, she considers a multiplicity of factors that influence identity development. She posits that inherited variables such as phenotype, extended family, parental identities, traits (i.e., temperament), coping and social skills, and socializing forces (familial, peer, and communal) are all key factors contributing to the identity development processes of multiracial individuals. Root (1999) outlines four distinct strategies, which she refers to as *border crossings*, by which identity development processes may be traversed for multiracial

individuals. These strategies contrast with models that denote one resolution as being more healthy than others, and instead propose that individuals may:

1. Develop the capacity to identify with and express multiple cultural perspectives concurrently.
2. Develop a situational identity perspective in which racial identity is shifted depending on the context.
3. Assert a multiracial orientation independent from that of peers and family.
4. Maintain a singular racial identity, depending on the particular cultural context.

Kerwin and Ponterotto's (1995) model of biracial identity development asserted that an individual's racial awareness progresses along age-based developmental indicators. The conceptual basis for this model also considers personal, societal, and environmental variables that influence an individual's process of reaching a public and private racial identity. These variables also account for the rejection or exclusion that biracial individuals may experience from both Whites and people of color. Kerwin and Ponterotto delineated five developmental stages in biracial identity development (p. 210):

1. *Preschool:* Up to age 5. Biracial children recognize physical similarities and differences; this may relate to the extent of their parents' sensitivity about race-related issues and their readiness to discuss these issues.
2. *Entry to school:* Occurs as biracial children enter school, a process that allows for an increase in contact with more social groups and through which children may be encouraged to classify themselves in terms of a monoracial label.
3. *Preadolescence:* Characterized by an increase in the awareness of social groups and social meanings based on skin tone, physical appearance, ethnicity, and religion. Environmental factors such as changes in community context from one community to another (which may be more or less diverse) as well

as direct or vicarious experiences with racist incidents that may also contribute to an increase in conscientiousness with regard to race.

4. *Adolescence:* Encountering expectations to identify with the race of a parent of color may contribute to pressures to identify with a particular group.

5. *College/young adulthood:* Characterized by a continued immersion in a singular racial group, with an acute sensitivity to race-related remarks and relevant contextual variables.

6. *Adulthood:* Biracial persons remain interested in exploring dimensions of race and culture, along with self-identification, and demonstrate increased flexibility in acclimating to diverse cultural settings.

Psychological Considerations

Continuing to consider an ecological perspective, it is important to recognize that development, expressions of personality, and psychological problems occur within a sociocultural and political context, influenced by the reality that there are privileges for some and inequity and oppressive forces for others. The ecological context is therefore unquestionably important for mental health practitioners to consider when working with people of color and, certainly, people of mixed ancestry. In fact, Root (1994, p. 456) explained that "multiraciality poses no inherent type of stress that would result in psychological maladjustment; any distress related to being multiracial is likely to be a response to an environment that has internalized racist beliefs."

Various researchers have discussed the types of psychological issues that may be encountered by persons of mixed ancestry. Shih and Sanchez (2005) identified several potential conflicts, including how one identifies and how one is identified by others, feeling pressure to justify one's choice in identification, being asked to choose when faced with forced-choice inquiries, not having multiracial role models, receiving conflicting messages from parents, peers, and community, and the "double-rejection" of being rejected by multiple groups of which one's

ancestry is comprised. These researchers conducted a review of existing studies to assess the prevalence of findings suggesting negative psychological outcomes for people of mixed ancestry. The review focused on six domains purported to be of psychological concern for multiracials: (1) racial identity development, (2) depression, (3) problem behaviors, (4) school performance, (5) peer relationships, and (6) self-esteem. In reviewing the quantitative studies, Shih and Sanchez (2005) reported that differences in findings were often attributable to methodological factors in the sample including choice of comparison groups (i.e., whether multiracial adolescents were being compared with majority or minority monoracial adolescents) and whether the sample was clinical or nonclinical. These authors also found that the direction of an outcome was frequently determined by which measures were utilized and by the type of outcome being considered. They found that when multiracial youth were compared with monoracial majority (White) adolescents, multiracial adolescents appeared to be faring worse; however, when compared with monoracial minority adolescents, multiracial youth were faring as well. Further, clinical samples appeared to suffer from identity-related psychological concerns, such as rejection or confusion; however, there was little evidence of these psychological concerns in nonclinical samples. The authors also found differences based on the era in which the study was conducted. For example, in studies conducted prior to 1995, multiracials were more likely to report experiences of rejection only; after 1995, multiracials reported experiences of both rejection and acceptance in relationships with peers. These findings suggest that psychological outcomes for youth of mixed ancestry are more complex than can be captured by early models noting poorer psychological prognoses. These findings also contain implications for comparing people of mixed race to those of White majority background. Moreover, the similarities between multiracial youth and monoracial minority youth suggest there may be ways in which the effects of discrimination relate to differences in outcomes between multiracial adolescent, and monoracial Whites.

VALUES/ATTITUDES

An important component of developing multicultural competency lies in reflecting upon one's own experiences, backgrounds, beliefs, values, and attitudes. There has been an emphasis in the literature on the importance of mental health practitioners developing this awareness as it relates to race and multiracial people (Gillem & Thompson, 2004; Nishimura, 2004; Root, 1994). In considering clinical practice with people of mixed ancestry, it is recommended that clinicians engage in exploration of their own ethnic/racial backgrounds and how rules of hypodescent may have impacted their ethnic/racial identifications. Further, engaging in exploration of one's own intersecting identities, including race/ethnicity, sexuality, socioeconomic status, spirituality/religion, ability, language, education, size, and gender, is an important process in developing awareness of one's own perspectives, biases, and blind spots with regard to these dimensions of identity.

Another aspect of developing awareness in working with clients of mixed ancestry is for mental health practitioners to evaluate and challenge the attitudes they hold regarding this population. Such self-exploration includes gaining greater understanding of messages received through the media, parents, peers, and the community. It is particularly important for clinicians to consider the zeitgeist in which they were raised and how legal, sociocultural, and political factors contributed to notions about race, hypodescent, and the psychological well-being of mixed-race individuals.

It is also important for mental health practitioners to gain awareness of the attitudes and values that are essential in working toward developing multicultural competency with clients of mixed ancestry. Mental health practitioners should reject the myth that being biracial or multiracial causes psychological problems and should, rather, consider an ecological perspective acknowledging that any distress related to being mixed-race is the result of racism and internalized racist beliefs (Root, 1994). In working with multiracial clients it is important to understand and honor the fluidity of the process of ethnic identity development and to recognize multiple healthy statuses of resolution in this process (Root, 1999). Researchers and experts have, therefore, advocated for mental health practitioners to embrace and integrate into clinical practice an ecological, empowering, strengths-based perspective (Buchanan & Acevedo, 2004; Edwards & Pedrotti, 2004; Pedrotti, Edwards, & Lopez, 2008; Root, 1999).

Buchanan and Acevedo (2004) outlined several suggestions for working with racially ambiguous and nonvisible minority women, including helpful attitudes and values for mental health practitioners and effective intervention skills. These concepts may apply equally well to working clinically with multiracial men and women, and are listed below:

Guidelines for Therapists Working with Clients of Mixed Ancestry

1. Discuss issues of race and culture and foster a supportive environment for the client to explore related concerns.

2. Consider how phenotype, particularly ambiguity, may relate to unique issues in ethnic identity.

3. Understand the tendency for these clients to feel pessimism about others' intentions as a result of having been privy to racist discourse by others who may not have recognized their ethnic background.

4. Recognize that some multiracial clients may experience rejection by some of their social reference groups.

5. Have knowledge of community resources (such as organizations, support groups, and campus clubs and organizations for college students) that may be of interest to clients.

(continued)

(*continued*)

6. Embrace a worldview based on multicultural competency, considering the client's individual perspective and cultural context, and develop the ability to utilize culturally relevant interventions.

7. Employ a strengths-based perspective in which positive aspects of multiracial clients' multiple, intersecting identities are explored and integrated.

8. Explore additional concerns regarding clients' multiple, intersecting identities including sexual objectification for women of mixed ancestry.

Source: Buchanan & Acevedo (2004).

SKILLS

The APA outlines guidelines for cultural competency in practice, research, training, and education (APA, 2002). These guidelines advise psychologists to develop awareness of their own attitudes, values, and beliefs and the potential impact of these on their work. Researchers and practitioners are encouraged to recognize the importance of multicultural knowledge about ethnic and racial groups, and to incorporate multicultural competency into education, training, research, practice, and policy. In fact, therapists and counselors are obligated to seek information regarding the cultural variables of clients with whom they work (Nishimura, 2004). With multiracial clients in particular, mental health practitioners should be knowledgeable about identity development models, and must seek to understand cultural values, beliefs, and practices of each of their clients' ethnic heritages, as any given client may embrace one of these cultures or a combination thereof (Nishimura, 2004). Accordingly, psychologists are encouraged to develop skills in providing culturally competent research and services. These guidelines are relevant to developing multicultural competence in applying clinical skills and conducting research with people of mixed ancestry. Further, mental health practitioners should be knowledgeable about utilizing interventions that are culturally relevant and should establish a positive, empowering therapeutic relationship (Edwards & Pedrotti, 2004).

In providing therapy or counseling services for multiracial clients, various approaches have been recommended, including those which are strengths-based (Gillem & Thompson, 2004), empowering (Pedrotti et al., 2008), validating (Buchanan & Acevedo, 2004; Edwards & Pedrotti, 2004; Nishimura, 2004; Pedrotti et al., 2008), consciousness-raising (Buchanan & Acevedo, 2004), and ecologically informed (Root, 1999). It is recommended that practitioners consider ecological context, sociocultural factors, and identity development variables for each client. Given the propensity for traditional approaches to focus on pathology, and given the historical context of mixed-race people having been viewed through a pathological lens, Edwards and Pedrotti (2004) recommend a balanced approach that acknowledges coping strategies related to presenting problems, and draws on strengths as buffers to the challenges. Gillem and Thompson (2004) likewise discuss the importance of mental health practitioners understanding and addressing the role of relevant sociocultural factors and clients' strengths in coping with related experiences. Therefore, several therapeutic approaches that embody these values are presented next.

Narrative Therapy Approach

A narrative approach has been suggested as a therapeutic model that is empowering, validating, and strengths based (Edwards & Pedrotti, 2004; Pedrotti et al., 2008). Recommended avenues for exploration include: (a) the influence of environment and context, (b) multiracial development as a process that is not necessarily linear, (c) ascribed identity versus self-definition, and

(d) the richness of multiple heritages. These authors argue that a narrative approach may allow for exploration of the client's story as an aid to understanding cultural assumptions and influences. The authors suggest the strategy of supporting the client in telling her or his story as a multiracial person, with multiple sides. In telling their stories, clients can recognize influences of community demographics (whether homogeneous or more diverse), and acknowledge experiences of rejection and acceptance, isolation and inclusion, self-perception versus perception by others, and self-identification versus ascribed identification. This strategy allows clients to integrate a more comprehensive sense of self. Edwards and Pedrotti (2004), moreover, recommended an intervention based on the counselor or therapist supporting the client in reauthoring his or her story to integrate a more adaptive perspective. These authors also recommended utilizing the intervention of writing to consider contextual variables and thereby externalize, rather than internalize, experiences of racism and discrimination. This intervention also allows clients to reframe their perspectives on struggles with such negative external forces. Finally, the authors recommended validating the resilience of clients in response to their challenges and integrating interventions of hope therapy, which, through narratives and storytelling, allows clients to develop hope, a sense of agency, and means for navigating obstacles.

Feminist Therapy Approach

Nishimura (2004) recommended applying feminist therapy techniques and concepts in clinical work with biracial women. These concepts can also be adapted and applied when working with multiracial men as well. Nishimura encouraged supporting clients in consciousness-raising by addressing oppression, sex-role stereotyping, and institutionalized sexism as contributing to problems faced by multiracial women. Exploring these ecological factors validates clients' experiences of sociocultural and political realities and the influence these have on their lives and presenting concerns. In applying these concepts to multiracial men, mental health practitioners can use these corollary suggestions by supporting consciousness-raising in addressing the role of racial and ethnic oppression, stereotyping, and institutional racism.

Community Psychology, Ecological Approach

Community psychologists recognize and build on an individual's strengths (Dalton, Elias, & Wandersman, 2001). Within this ecological, strengths-based approach, dysfunctions are understood as resulting from social problems within the systems surrounding the person. Presenting problems are analyzed using multiple levels, thus reducing the likelihood of "blaming the victim" by assessing the victim outside of contributing contextual variables.

Bronfenbrenner (1977; 1979) provided an ecological systems model with the visual image of a nesting doll figure as a metaphor for the multiple layers of analyses. This is a multilevel relationship encompassing an individual's interactions with the *microsystem*, *exosystem*, and *macrosystem* that form an ecological web surrounding the individual, as well as the *mesosystems* that provide temporary linkages between systems.

The individual serves as the center of the web, the smallest doll in the analogy put forth by Bronfenbrenner (1977, 1979; Dalton et al., 2001). This level concerns the individual and his or her personal problems and adaptations to stressors. Interventions at this level, such as psychotherapy, are person focused. This level also involves individual characteristics that are influenced by the other levels within the system, including social group memberships such as ethnicity, gender, sexual orientation, religion/spirituality, class, size, ability, language, and immigration status, as well as personal variables such as personality type and phenotypic expression. At the individual level, mental health practitioners should consider multiple, intersecting identities, the ways in which clients hold social group memberships, and the manners in which each of these identities is influenced by multiple systems. A clinician may consider the following questions as useful in assessing self-identification and the saliency of ethnic identity in the context of the presenting concerns:

1. How would you describe your ethnicity? Has this been consistent throughout your life, or have there been times in which you identified differently?
2. How has gender been a factor for you?
3. Has religion/spirituality been a factor in your identification? If so, how?
4. Has your mixed ancestry allowed you to identify with multiple groups?
5. What strengths have you gleaned from your mixed ancestry?
6. What, if any, difficulties have you encountered because of your mixed ancestry?

For example, consider the role of gender in the experience of mixed-race individuals. Gender is a significant intersecting identity for multiracial individuals as multiracial women, in particular, have unique experiences that should be explored therapeutically. With regard to religion/spirituality, consider Case Vignette 8.2 of Sumaya, whose father is Muslim and mother is Protestant. The religious beliefs of Sumaya's parents converge on some points, while differing on others. Sumaya not only explored her identity as a mixed-race woman; she also explored beliefs about gender and identity as a woman of color while considering her own values in comparison to those of her parents.

The microsystem consists of the relationships surrounding the individual, such as family, peers, and residential settings (Bronfenbrenner, 1977, 1979; Dalton et al., 2001). In considering this ecological level, a mental health practitioner might examine the relationships a person of mixed ancestry has with peers, the presence of social support, and the multiple relationships among family members as well as the demographic characteristics of these relationships.

The role of parents can be a very important one for persons of mixed ancestry, particularly in childhood. Miville et al. (2005) discussed the significance of parents, who often play the most

important role in the identity development of multiracial children. Parents can facilitate adaptive identity development by helping children to connect with their ancestry and identities. The authors also found that connections with extended family played an important role, regardless of whether multiracial children had distant or close relationships with these family members, and impacted a sense of connection with the children's cultural origins. Parental influence includes such additional factors as parents' levels of comfort in addressing racial issues and parents' own ethnic identities and cultural beliefs. Interfamilial racism can also affect identity development. Multiracial children can internalize negative stereotypes or racist ideology or can feel a complex sense of distance from family members with racist ideology.

During intake or initial assessment with a multiracial client, a mental health practitioner might inquire about influential relationships, including friends and family. Asking some of the following questions during intake, and/or throughout the course of treatment, may help the clinician gain a clearer understanding of influences that contributed to the client's sense of self and self-identification. This process may also serve to validate the client's experience.

1. How have peer relationships contributed to your sense of self and self-identification?
2. With which peer groups have you identified most during childhood? During adolescence? During young adulthood? How has your identification with these groups been related to your self-identification and fluidity in identity?
3. Have there been times you felt accepted by peers from various ethnic groups? Have there been times you felt rejected by peers from various ethnic groups? What were those experiences like for you?
4. Describe the family with whom you were raised. How has your interaction with your family influenced your sense of self? Consider, for example, the case study of Julie, who identifies as "Blackipino" and has

greater knowledge of and familiarity with her Filipino culture as she was raised primarily by her mother, a Filipino woman, and her mother's family.

5. How have your interactions with extended family influenced your sense of self?
6. Who explained to you about your mixed ancestry? How did they explain this?
7. What did your parents tell you about your identity?

The exosystem is the next largest system of interaction, and includes the schools, neighborhoods, and communities within which an individual interacts (Bronfenbrenner, 1977, 1979; Dalton et al., 2001). Clinicians should assess clients' experiences with racism—both monoracial and multiracial—and any relevant coping strategies they have developed, such as use of support networks and reference groups, to buffer the effects of these stressors. Mental health practitioners should also work with clients to identify and validate strengths related to their multiracial identity—for example, how their mixed heritage can increase psychological functioning (Miville et al., 2005). In working with a client of mixed ancestry, a counselor may assess the significance of these influences on the person's identity by asking the following questions as part of the assessment process:

1. What was the demographic makeup of your neighborhood when growing up?
2. Were there other persons in your community who identify as you do (mixed-race, biracial, African American, Arab/Middle Eastern, Asian Pacific Islander, Latina/o, etc.)?
3. What was the demographic makeup of your school?
4. Were there cultural-specific organizations in your school (i.e., mixed-race student association, Black Students Association, Movimiento Estudiantil Chicano de Aztlán (MEChA), Latino Student Association, Asian/Pacific Islander Student Association, Middle Eastern Student Association, etc.)? Were you involved with any of these organizations? Which?

5. Were you able to have contact with role models who identify as you do (teachers, community members or leaders)?
6. In what ways have you experienced racism, discrimination, and stereotypes? How have you coped with these stressors?
7. What are your strengths related to the richness of your mixed ancestry? How have these contributed to your resilience? Your ability to relate to, and be open toward, others?

The macrosystem represents the largest social context within which individuals operate (Bronfenbrenner, 1977, 1979; Dalton et al., 2001). This ecological level includes such sociopolitical and sociocultural influences as the media, legal systems, educational systems, and government policies, which can influence problems at all levels. Consider the role of the 2000 Census in permitting respondents to check more than one box and how this influenced the mixed-race movement. Consider how laws, such as antimiscegenation statutes, influenced interracial families and multiracial individuals. Finally, consider the probability of oppression and discrimination influencing a multiracial individual's sense of self as well as both self-identification and perception of how others have identified him or her.

SUMMARY

This chapter is intended to serve as a resource to assist mental health practitioners in developing multicultural competency in working with people of mixed ancestry. As this population continues to grow, it is important that mental health practitioners develop awareness, knowledge, and skills relevant to the unique cultural context of multiracial individuals. Therefore, this chapter has focused on providing mental health practitioners with an overview of critical historical and ecological factors related to this population, ethnic identity development models, and applied case studies. With the intent of increasing mental health practitioners' awareness of attitudes and values, *Pause & Ponder* exercises were included throughout the chapter to encourage readers to reflect, think critically about the text and their own background, and consider how their values and attitudes may impact clinical work with clients of mixed ancestry. Guidelines were presented regarding attitudes and values that are critical in developing multicultural competency in clinical practice with clients of mixed ancestry. The author also recommended tools for mental health practitioners to utilize in developing their skills in clinical practice with clients of mixed ancestry. These included suggested assessment questions designed to determine the saliency and meaning of these issues for a client, as well as recommended therapeutic approaches. It is hoped that readers will have a greater understanding of the ways in which they may incorporate assessment questions, suggested therapeutic and conceptual approaches, and resources into clinical practice, research, training, and supervision.

RESOURCES

The following resources are provided as suggestions for further inquiry and as tools students, clinicians, trainees, and supervisors can utilize to help improve the quality of the services they provide.

JOURNAL ARTICLES AND BOOK CHAPTERS

AhnAllen, J. M., Suyemoto, K. L., & Carter, A. S. (2006). Relationship between physical appearance, sense of belonging and exclusion, and racial/ethnic self-identification among multiracial Japanese European Americans. *Cultural Diversity and Ethnic Minority Psychology*, 12(4), 673–686.

American Psychological Association (2002). Guidelines for multicultural education, training, research, practice, and organizational change for psychologists. Available at http://www.apa.org/pi/multiculturalguidelines/formats.html.

Bratter, J. (2007). Will "multiracial" survive to the next generation?: The racial classification of children of multiracial parents. *Social Forces*, 86(2), 821–849.

Brunsma, D. L., & Rockquemore, K. A. (2001). The new color complex: Appearances and biracial identity. *Identity*, 3, 225–246.

Buchanan, N. T., & Acevedo, C. A. (2004). When face and soul collide: Therapeutic concerns with racially ambiguous and nonvisible minority women. *Women & Therapy*, 27(1/2), 119–331.

Doyle, J. M., & Kao, G. (2007). Are racial identities of multiracials stable? Changing self-identification among single and multiple race individuals. *Social Psychology Quarterly*, 70(4), 405–423.

Edwards, L. M., & Pedrotti, J. T. (2004). Utilizing the strengths of our cultures: Therapy with biracial women and girls. *Women & Therapy*, 27(1/2), 33–43.

Esbach, K. (1995). The enduring and vanishing American Indian: Growth and intermarriage in the 1990. *Ethnic and Racial Studies*, 18(1), 89–108.

Fernandez, C. A. (1992). La Raza and the melting pot: A comparative look at multiethnicity. In M. P. P. Root (Ed.), *Racially mixed people in America* (pp. 126–143). Newbury Park, CA: Sage.

Fhagen-Smith, P. (2003). *Mixed ancestry racial/ethnic identity development model*. Wellesley, MA: Wellesley Centers for Women.

Gaskins, P. (1979). Eurasians: Strengths in coping. *Asian Directions*, 2, 1–8.

Gibbs, J. T. (1989). Biracial adolescents. In J. T. Gibbs, L. N. Huang, & Associates (Eds.), *Children of color: Psychological interventions with minority youth* (pp. 322–350). San Francisco: Jossey-Bass.

Gillem, A. R., & Thompson, C. A. (2004). Introduction: Biracial women in therapy: Between the rock of gender and the hard place of race. *Women & Therapy*, 27(1/2), 1–18.

Harris, D. R., & Sim, J. J. (2002). Who is multiracial? Assessing the complexity of lived race. *American Sociological Review*, 67, 614–627.

Herman, M. (2004). Forced to choose: Some determinants of racial identification in multiracial adolescents. *Child Development*, 75(3), 730–748.

Hitlin, S., Brown, J. S., & Elder, Jr., G. H. (2006). Racial self-categorization in adolescence: Multiracial development and social pathways. *Child Development*, 77(5), 1298–1308.

Kerwin, C., & Ponterotto, J. G. (1995). Biracial identity development: Theory and research. In J. D. Ponterotto, J. M. Casas, L. A. Suzuki, & C. M. Alexander (Eds.). *Handbook of multicultural counseling*. Thousand Oaks, CA: Sage. 199–217.

Kerwin, C., Ponterotto, J. G., Jackson, B. L., & Harris, A. (1993). Racial identity in biracial children: A qualitative investigation. *Journal of Counseling Psychology, 40*(2), 221–231.

Kich, G. K., (1992). The developmental process of asserting a biracial, bicultural identity. In M. P. P. Root (Ed.), *Racially mixed people in America* (pp. 305–320). Newbury Park, CA: Sage.

Krebs, N. B. (2000). For students with multicultural heritage: A refreshing, confrontative approach. *Multicultural Education, 8*(2), 25–27.

Miville, M. L., Constantine, M. G., Baysden, M. F., & So-Lloyd, G. (2005). Chameleon changes: An exploration of racial identity themes of multiracial people. *Journal of Counseling Psychology, 52*(4), 507–516.

Nishimura, N. (2004). Counseling biracial women: An intersection of multiculturalism and feminism. *Women & Therapy, 27*(1/2), 133–145.

Pedrotti, J. T., Edwards, L. M., & Lopez, S. J. (2008). Working with multiracial clients in therapy: Bridging theory, research, and practice. *Professional Psychology: Research and Practice, 39*(2), 192–201.

Poston, W. S. C. (1990). The biracial identity development model: A needed addition. *Journal of Counseling & Development, 69*, 152–155.

Renn, K. (2008). Research on biracial and multiracial identity development: Overview and synthesis. *New Directions for Student Services, 123*, 13–21.

Root, M. P. P. (1990). Resolving "other" status: Identity development of biracial individuals. *Women and Therapy, 9*, 185–205.

Root, M. P. P. (1994). Mixed race women. In L. Comas Diaz & B. Green (Eds.), *Women of color and mental health: The healing tapestry*. New York: Guilford.

Root, M. P. P. (1998). Experiences and processes affecting racial identity development: Preliminary results from the biracial sibling project. *Cultural Diversity and Mental Health, 4*(3), 237–247.

Root, M. P. P. (1999). The biracial baby boom: Understanding ecological constructions of racial identity in the twenty-first century. In R. H. Sheets and E. R. Hollins (Eds.), *Aspects of human development: Racial and ethnic identity in school practices*. Mahwah, NJ: Lawrence Erlbaum.

Root, M. P. P. (2001). Factors influencing the variation in racial and ethnic identity of mixed-heritage persons of Asian ancestry. In T. K. Williams-Leon and C. L. Nakashima (Eds.), *The sum of our parts: Mixed heritage Asian Americans* (pp. 61–70). Philadelphia: Temple University.

Root, M. P. P. (2001). Negotiating the margins. In J. G. Ponterotto, J. M. Casas, L. A. Suzuki, & C. M. Alexander (Eds.), *Handbook of multicultural counseling* (2nd ed., pp. 113–122). Thousand Oaks: Sage Publications.

Root, M. P. P. (2002). Methodological issues in multiracial research. In G. Nagayama-Hall & S. Okazaki (Eds.), *Asian American psychology: Scientific innovations for the 21st century*. Thousand Oaks, CA: Sage Publications.

Root, M. P. P. (2003). Multiracial families and children: Implications for educational research and practice. In J. A. Banks & C. A. McGee Banks (Eds.), *Handbook of research on multicultural education* (2nd ed., pp. 110–124). San Francisco: Jossey-Bass.

Root, M. P. P. (2003). Bill of rights for racially mixed people. In M. P. P. Root, & M. Kelly (Eds.), *The multiracial child resource book: Living complex identities* (p. 32). Seattle: Mavin Foundation.

Root, M. P. P. (2003). Give mixed race identities: From relic to revolution. In L. I. Winters & H. Debose (Eds.), *New faces in a changing America: Multiracial identity in the 21st century*. Thousand Oaks, CA: Sage.

Root, M. P. P. (2003). Issues specific to general multiracial heritage. In M. P. P. Root, & M. Kelly (Eds.), *The multiracial child resource book: Living complex identities* (pp. 132–134). Seattle: Mavin Foundation.

Root, M. P. P. (2003). Racial identity development and persons of mixed racial heritage. In M. P. P. and M. Kelly (Eds.), *The multiracial child resource book: Living complex identities* (pp. 34–41). Seattle: Mavin Foundation.

Root, M. P. P. (2003). Racial experiences questionnaire. In M. P. P. Root & M. Kelley (Eds.), *The multiracial child resource book*. Seattle: Mavin Foundation.

Root, M. P. P. (2004). From exotic to a dime a dozen. *Women and Therapy (special issue), 27*(1/2), 19–31.

Shih, M., Bonam, C., Sanchez, D., & Peck, C. (2007). The social construction of race: Biracial identity and vulnerability of stereotypes. *Cultural Diversity and Ethnic Minority Psychology, 13*(2), 125–133.

Shih, M., & Sanchez, D. T. (2005). Perspectives and research on the positive and negative implications of having multiple racial identities. *Psychological Bulletin, 131*(4), 569–591.

Spickard, P. R. (1992). The illogic of American racial categories. In M. P. P. Root (Ed.), *Racially mixed people in America* (pp. 12–23). Newbury Park, CA: Sage.

Stephan, C. W. (1992). Mixed-heritage individuals: Ethnic identity and trait characteristics. In M. P. P. Root (Ed.), *Racially mixed people in America* (pp. 50–63). Newbury Park, CA: Sage.

Sundstrom, R. R. (2001). Being and being mixed race. *Social Theory and Practice*, 27(2), 285–307.

Thornton, M. C., & Wason, S. (1995). Intermarriage. In D. Levinson (Ed.), *Encyclopedia of marriage and the family* (pp. 396–402). New York: Macmillan.

Wellesley Centers for Women (2008). Examining mixed-ancestry identity in adolescents. *Research and Action Report*, 30(1), 2–3.

BOOKS

Beltran, M., & Fojas, C. (Ed.). (2008). *Mixed race Hollywood*. New York: New York University Press.

Brown, U. (2001). *The interracial experience: Growing up black/white racially mixed in the United States*. Westport, CT: Praeger.

Chiong, J. A. (1998). *Racial categorization of multiracial children in schools*. Westport, CT: Bergin & Garvey.

Comas-Diaz, L., & Greene, B. (1994). *Women of color: Integrating ethnic and gender identities in psychotherapy*. New York: Guilford Press.

DaCosta, K. (2007). *Making multiracials: State, family, and market in the redrawing of the color line*. Stanford, CA: Stanford University Press.

Dalmage, H. M. (2000). *Tripping the color line: Black/white multiracial families in a racially divided world*. Piscataway, NJ: Rutgers University Press.

Davis, F. J. (1991). *Who is black: One nation's definition*. University Park, PA: Pennsylvania State University Press.

Fulbeck, K. (2006). *Part Asian, 100% Hapa*. San Francisco: Chronicle Books.

Funderburg, L. (1994). *Black, white, other: Biracial Americans talk about race and identity*. New York: William Morrow.

Gaskins, P. F. (1999). *What are you?: Voices of mixed-race young people*. New York: Henry Holt.

Gillem, A. R. & Thompson, C. A. (Eds.). (2004). *Biracial women in therapy: Between the rock of gender and the hard place of race*. New York: Haworth Press.

Holloway, J. E. (2006). *Neither black nor white. The saga of an American family: The complete story*. Northridge, CA: New World African Press.

Hunter, M. L. (2005). *Race, gender, and the politics of skin tone*. New York: Taylor & Francis Group.

Ifekwunigwe, J. (Ed.). (2004). *Mixed race studies: A reader*. New York: Routledge.

Jackson Nakazawa, D. (2003). *Does anybody else look like me?: A parent's guide to raising multiracial children*. Cambridge, MA: Perseus Books.

Kauanui, J. K. (2008). *Hawaiian blood: Colonialism and the politics of sovereignty and indigeneity (narrating native histories)*. Durham, NC: Duke University Press.

McCarthy, M. (2001). *My eyes only look out: Experiences of Irish people of mixed race parentage*. Kerry, Ireland: Brandon Books.

O'Hearn, C. (Ed.). (1998). *Half and half: Writers on growing up biracial and bicultural*. New York: Random House.

Ramirez, M., III. (1997). *Multicultural/multiracial: Mestizo perspectives in personality and mental health*. Lanham, MD: Jason Aronson.

Rockquemore, K. A., & Brunsma, D. L. (2002). *Beyond black: Biracial identity in America*. Thousand Oaks, CA: Sage.

Rondilla, J., & Spickard, P. (2007). *Is lighter better?: Skin-tone discrimination among Asian Americans*. Lanham, MD: Rowman & Littlefield.

Root, M. P. P. (Ed.). (1992). *Racially mixed people in America*. Thousand Oaks: Sage.

Root, M. P. P. (Ed.). (1996). *The multiracial experience: Racial borders as the new frontier*. Thousand Oaks: Sage.

Root, M. P. P. (2001). *Love's revolution: Racial intermarriage*. Philadelphia: Temple University Press.

Root, M. P. P., & Kelley, M. (Eds.). (2003). *The multiracial child resource book*. Seattle: Mavin Foundation.

Russell, K., Wilson, M., & Hall, R. (1992). *The color complex: The politics of skin color among African - Americans*. New York: Bantam Doubleday Dell.

Stonequist, E. (1937). *The marginal man: A study in personality and culture conflict*. New York: Russell & Russell.

Wallace, K. (2001). *Relative/outsider: The art and politics of identity among mixed heritage students*. Westport, CT: Ablex.

Williams, K. M. (2006). *Mark one or more: Civil rights in multiracial America. The politics of race and ethnicity*. Ann Arbor, MI: The University of Michigan Press.

Williams-Leon, T., Nakashima, C. L., & Omi, M. (2001). *The sum of our parts: Mixed-heritage Asian Americans (Asian American History and Culture)*. Philadelphia: Temple University Press.

Winters, L. I., & DeBose, H. L. (Eds.). (2003). *New faces in a changing America: Multiracial identity in the*

21st century (Sage masters in modern social thoughts). Thousand Oaks: Sage.

Zack, N. (1995). *American mixed race: The culture of micro-diversity*. Lanham, MD: Rowman and Littlefield.

Zack, N. (2005). *Thinking about race*. Belmont, CA: Wadsworth.

Zarembka, J. M. (2007). *The pigment of your imagination: Mixed race in a global society*. Washington, DC: Madera Press.

MEMOIRS, BIOGRAPHIES, AND NOVELS WITH BIRACIAL/MULTIRACIAL THEMES

Chai, M. L. (2007). *Hapa girl: A memoir*. Philadelphia: Temple University Press.

Cross, J. (2007). *Secret daughter: A mixed race daughter and the mother who gave her away*. New York: Penguin Group.

Haizlip, S. T. (1994). *The sweeter the juice: A family memoir in black and white*. New York: Touchstone.

Holmes, K. (2005). *Black, white and gold*. UK: Virgin Books.

Larsen, N. (2002). *Passing*. New York: Random House.

Martin, J. A. (2006). *When white is black*. Minnesota: Rivers Bend Press.

McBride, J. (2006). *The color of water: A black man's tribute to his white mother*. New York: Berkeley Publishing Group.

Obama, B. (2004). *Dreams of my father: A story of race and inheritance*. New York: Random House.

Oyeyumi, H. (2005). *The Icarus girl*. New York: Random House.

Senna, D. (1998). *Causcasia: A novel*. New York: Riverhead Books.

Senna, D. (2000). *From Caucasia with love*. New York: Bloomsbury.

Straight, S. (2006). *A million nightingales*. New York: Random House.

Walker, R. (2001). *Black, white, and Jewish: Autobiography of a shifting self*. New York: Riverhead Books.

NEWS ARTICLES

Coates, T. P. (2007, February 1). Is Obama black enough? *Time*. Retrieved July 28, 2009, from http://www.time.com/time/nation/article/0,8599,1584736,00.html

Fram, A. (2008, November 8). "Mutts like me" shows Obama's racial comfort. *Associated Press*. Retrieved July 28, 2009, from http://www.msnbc.msn.com/id/27606637/

Rhee, F. (2008, November 10). Chewing over Obama's "mutt" reference. *Political Intelligence*. Retrieved July 28, 2009, from http://www.boston.com/news/politics/politicalintelligence/2008/11/chewing_over_ob.html

CHILDREN'S BOOKS

Benjamin, F. (2008). *My two grannies*. Kentish Town, London: Frances Lincoln Children Books.

Davol, M. (1993). *Black, white, just right*. Park Ridge, Illinois: Albert Whitman.

Uff, C. (2001). *Happy birthday, Lulu*. London: Orchard Books.

Vance, K. R. (2007). *My rainbow family*. Bloomington, Indiana: Authorhouse.

Wayans, K., & Knotts, K. (2008). *All mixed up!: Amy Hodgepodge No. 1*. New York: Gimme Dap Productions.

MOVIES WITH BIRACIAL, MULTIRACIAL, AND/OR INTERRACIAL THEMES

Benton, R. (Director), & Roth, P. (Writer). (2003). *The human stain*. United States: Miramax Films.

Brady, E. (Writer/Director). (1998). *The nephew*. United States: Irish DreamTime.

Buhler, W-E. (1986). *Amerasia*. West Germany: Red Harvest Film.

Chadha, G. (2000). (Writer/Director). *What's cooking?* United States: Because Entertainment.

Haley, A., Stevens, D. (Writers), & Erman, J. (Director). (1993). *Queen*. [Motion picture]. United States: Elliot Friedgen.

Handler, M. (Writer/Director), & Larreta, A. (Writer). (1988). *Mestizo*. Cuba: Instituto Cubano del Arte e Industrias Cinematograficos (ICAIC).

Koppelman, C. (Writer/Director). (1999). *Dumbarton bridge*. United States: Bridge Partners.

Mahmood, J. (Writer/Director). (2008). *Shades of Ray*. Los Angeles: Cinetic.

Parker, A. (Writer/Director). (1990). *Come see the paradise*. United States: Twentieth Century-Fox Film Corporation.

Redroad, R. (Writer/Director). (2001). *The doe boy.* United States: Anthony J. Vozza Productions.

Shum, M. (Writer/Director). (1994). *Double happiness.* Canada: British Columbia Film Commission.

Swan, A. (Writer/Director). (1998). *Mixing Nia.* United States: Arrowhead Pictures.

Tennant, A. (Director). (1997). *Fools rush in.* United States: Columbia Pictures Corporation.

Walker-Pearlman, J. (Writer/Director). (2005). *Constellation.* United States: Constellation, LLC.

DOCUMENTARIES

Boerman, T., & Reiziger, S. (2004). *A knock out.*

Crenshaw, C., & Caffey, P. (Directors). (1999). *Black women on: The light, dark thang.*

Cross, J. (1996). *Secret daughter.*

Deer, T. (2008). *Club native.*

Onwurah, N. (1991). *The body beautiful.*

Onwurah, N. (1998). *Coffee colored children.*

Thakur, S. (1999). *Seven hours to burn.*

Valcin, N. (Director). (1999). *Black, bold and beautiful: Black women's hair.*

Zaman, N. (1994). *Beyond black and white.*

APA MULTICULTURAL COUNSELING PSYCHOTHERAPY VIDEO SERIES

Angus, L. (n.d.). Narrative therapy.

Brown, L. (n.d.). Feminist therapy.

Comas-Diaz, L. (n.d.). Ethnocultural psychotherapy.

Root, M.P.P. (n.d.). Mixed-race identities.

WEB SITES AND ORGANIZATIONS

Association of Multiethnic Americans (AMEA): http://www.ameasite.org

Dr. Maria P. Root: http://www.drmariaroot.com/

HalfKorean.com: http://www.halfkorean.com

Halvsie: For, by, and about half Japanese: http://www.halvsie.com/tags/halvsies

Intermix: http://www.intermix.org.uk

Mavin Foundation: http://www.mavinfoundation.org

Mixed Heritage Center: http://www.mixedheritage center.org

Mixed Student Resources: http://www.mixedstudent resources.com

Multiracial Americans of Southern California (M.A.S.C.): http://www.mascsite.org

My Shoes Online Community: For multiracial individuals who have white appearance: http://myshoes.com/myshoes.html

Of Many Colors: Portraits of Multiracial Families exhibit: http://www.familydiv.org/ofmanycolors.php

The Topaz Club: http://www.thetopazclub.com

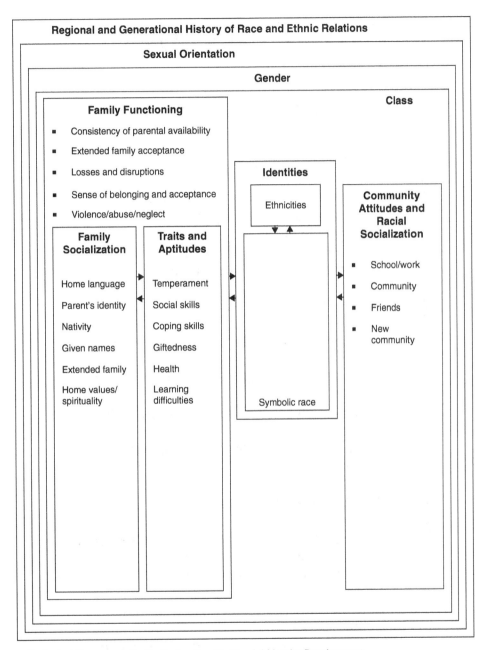

Figure 8.1 Ecological Framework for Understanding Multiracial Identity Development
Source: Maria P. P. Root, PhD (2002).

Bill of Rights

for

People of Mixed Heritage

I **HAVE THE RIGHT...**

Not to justify my existence in this world.
Not to keep the races separate within me.
Not to justify my ethnic legitimacy.
Not to be responsible for people's discomfort with
my physical or ethnic ambiguity.

I **HAVE THE RIGHT...**

To identify myself differently than strangers
expect me to identify.
To identify myself differently than how my parents
identify me.
To identify myself differently than my brothers and
sisters.
To identify myself differently in different
situations.

I **HAVE THE RIGHT...**

To create a vocabulary to communicate about
being multiracial or multiethnic.
To change my identity over my lifetime—and more
than once.
To have loyalties and identification with more
than one group of people.
To freely choose whom I befriend and love.

Figure 8.2 Bill of Rights for People of Mixed Heritage
Source: Maria P. P. Root, PhD (1993, 1994).

COMPETENCY BENCHMARK TABLES

The purpose of the Competency Benchmarks (Tables 8.1–8.4) is to create developmental models for defining and measuring competencies in professional psychology; each chapter in this *Handbook* applies the diversity competence for mental health practitioners in their work with a particular diverse population.

Table 8.1   Developmental-Level Competencies I

READINESS LEVEL—ENTRY TO PRACTICUM	
Competencies	Learning Process and Activities
Knowledge The student is gaining knowledge in: • Multiculturalism (inclusive of racial and ethnic groups and ethnic identity development models, as well as other identities) and is engaged in the process of learning that all individuals, including themselves, are cultural beings with worldviews that shape and influence their attitudes, emotions, perceptions, and experiences. • The importance of reflective practice and self-awareness. • Core counseling skills and theories. • Ethics code.	At this stage of development, the emphasis in psychotherapist education is on instilling knowledge of foundational domains as grounding for subsequent attainment of functional multicultural competencies. Students at this stage become aware of the principles and practices of the field, though they are not yet able to apply their knowledge to practice. The training curriculum is focused upon knowledge of core areas, including literature on multiculturalism (inclusive of racial and ethnic identities), ethics, foundational counseling skills, scientific knowledge, and the importance of reflective practice and self-awareness.
Skills The student is: • Developing his or her ability to demonstrate empathic listening skills, respect, and interest when talking with individuals expressing different values and belief systems. • Learning to critically examine the diversity literature.	It is important that, throughout the curriculum, trainers and teachers define individual and cultural differences broadly, including racial and ethnic differences and ethnic identity development. This should enable students to have a developing awareness of how to extrapolate their emerging multicultural competencies, including implications for racial and ethnic identity, on multiple systemic levels of individual and cultural differences.
Values and Attitudes The student demonstrates: • Willingness to engage in self-exploration—to consider own motives, attitudes, behaviors and effect on others. • Intellectual curiosity and flexibility. • Ability to value expressions of diverse viewpoints and belief systems.	While many students, through their life experiences, have an understanding of racial and ethnic dimensions of diversity, some students may have less developed knowledge with regard to persons of mixed ancestry or multiracial identities. Students would be expected to have fundamental knowledge of definitions of race and ethnicity, and personal awareness of their own ethnic identity.

Table 8.2   Developmental-Level Competencies II

READINESS LEVEL—ENTRY TO INTERNSHIP	
Competencies	**Learning Process and Activities**
Knowledge The student has: • Knowledge of multiple dimensions of diversity (e.g., race/ethnicity, class, age, ability, sexuality, religion/spirituality, etc.). • Knowledge of ethnic identity models. • Knowledge of an ecological model/framework. • Understanding of the terminology used to define mixed ancestry and multiracial identities. • Understanding of the impact of racism and other relevant *isms* (e.g., sexism, heterosexism, ableism, audism, classism, ageism, etc.) for people of mixed ancestry. • Knowledge of strength-based approaches and application. • General understanding of the importance of integrating relevant multicultural issues and cultural identities into therapeutic practice. • Understanding of the importance of consulting with supervisors and colleagues when presented with unfamiliar multiracial identities.	At this level of development, students are building on their education and applied experiences (such as supervised practicum experiences) to attain a core set of foundational multicultural competencies. They can then begin applying this knowledge to clinical practice. As a result of being exposed to didactic training and close supervision, students attain the multicultural values and attitudes appropriate to their level of development. Foundational knowledge and multicultural values and attitudes are becoming well established, but skills in working with people of mixed ancestry would be expected to be rudimentary at this level of development. Learning occurs through multiple modalities: • Didactic training in academic programs may occur in multicultural competency courses and culture-specific courses (e.g., women's issues, Multiracial, African American, Latino/a, religion/spirituality, and GLBTQ courses) and may be infused into the core curriculum (e.g., ethics, assessment, multicultural competency, career counseling, research, human growth and development, and clinical courses). • Providing therapy, under supervision, to clients representing a diversity of mixed-ancestry identities in practicum experiences. • Receiving supervision from psychotherapists knowledgeable and skilled in working with people of mixed ancestry. • Seeking additional study and professional development opportunities (e.g., multicultural conferences and trainings on clinical practice with people of mixed ancestry). Topics to be covered in didactic training include: • Definitions of *biracial, multiracial,* and colloquial terms used to describe or identify people of various mixed ancestries. • Ethnic identity development models. • Ecological models. • Strength-based approaches and relevant interventions. • Role of phenotype and physical ambiguity in self-identification. • Self-identification versus other-identification. • Fluidity in self-identification for people of mixed ancestry. • Basic research literature on psychological considerations for people of mixed ancestry.
Skills Skills in the following areas are beginning to develop: • Integrating inquiries about the client's culture and ethnic identity into the initial intake assessment. • Applying an ecological framework for assessing a client's experiences at multiple systemic levels. • Assessing and validating clients' strengths. • Discerning level of competence to provide psychotherapy to persons of mixed ancestry and providing appropriate referrals and adjunctive referrals to community resources. • Building therapeutic alliance to foster a trusting, safe, and open therapeutic climate to discuss issues of mixed-ancestry identity as well as other salient identities.	
Values and Attitudes Demonstrates self-awareness and appropriate cultural and multicultural attitudes as evidenced by the following: • Understands that ethnic identity is an aspect of worldview and multicultural diversity. • Displays awareness of own intersecting identities (gender, ethnicity, socioeconomic status [SES], sexual orientation, ability, spirituality/religion, etc.) and ability to discern clients' intersecting identities.	

READINESS LEVEL—ENTRY TO INTERNSHIP	
Competencies	Learning Process and Activities
• Demonstrates commitment to examine and challenge own attitudes and biases regarding people of mixed ancestry. • Shows openness and cognitive flexibility to allow space for the fluidity in self-identification for people of mixed-ancestry. • Evinces genuine respect for ethnic identity exploration and development.	Trainers and teachers could offer students enrolled in multicultural diversity courses an option to research people of mixed ancestry as a project for the class and could include focus on any of the abovementioned topics.

Table 8.3   Developmental-Level Competencies III

READINESS LEVEL—ENTRY TO PROFESSIONAL PRACTICE		
Competencies		Learning Process and Activities
Knowledge	Knowledge of: • Literature on ethnic identity development with people of mixed ancestry. • Various ethnic groups and relevant cultural considerations. • Beliefs and behaviors that are considered normative, healthy, and adaptive in the ethnic identity development process. • The psychological effects of experiences of racism at multiple systemic levels, as well as the impact of other relevant *isms* (e.g., sexism, heterosexism, classism, ableism, audism [discrimination against deaf or hard of hearing people], ageism, etc.) that clients may have experienced. • The relevance of phenotype, including skin color, hair texture, and definition of facial features, in the exploration of self-versus-other perception. • Community resources, including campus organizations, local and national organizations, leading researchers and theorists, and psychotherapists specializing in working with people of mixed ancestry. • Strengths-based approaches such as narrative therapy, feminist therapy, and community psychology. • Understanding that working with people of mixed ancestry is a unique aspect of ethnic identity within multicultural counseling competency.	In the earlier stages of training, students solidified their professional knowledge base and attained appropriate values and attitudes while developing increasingly sophisticated clinical skills. At the level of Entry to Professional Practice, psychotherapists have attained the full range of competencies in the domains expected of all independent practitioners. Preparation for this level of competency takes place through closely supervised clinical work, augmented by professional reading, personal exploration, and training opportunities such as professional development and training seminars. Clinical supervisors observe students' clinical work, provide training in assessment, case conceptualization, and treatment planning, and challenge supervisees to examine their countertransference reactions, biases, and values to develop their supervisees' clinical competency in working with people of mixed ancestry. Additional methods by which students can attain competency in working with persons of mixed ancestry include: • Seeking opportunities to provide therapy to clients of mixed ancestry. • Supervision provided by supervisors knowledgeable and skilled in working with people of mixed ancestry. • Self-directed study and professional development opportunities. • Internship and postdoctoral seminar training in multicultural competency and multiracial identities.
Skills	Skills are demonstrated by the ability to: • Assess saliency of ethnic identity and the relationship of cultural issues within the	

(continued)

Table 8.3 Developmental-Level Competencies III (continued)

READINESS LEVEL—ENTRY TO PROFESSIONAL PRACTICE	
Competencies	**Learning Process and Activities**
context of the presenting problems/concerns and symptoms. • Diagnose and formulate appropriate and culturally relevant treatment plans with consideration for ethnic identity and influence of multiple systems and individual differences. • Utilize strengths-based assessments, conceptualizations, and interventions. • Identify the limits of own competency in addressing ethnic identity and cultural issues with people of mixed ancestry. • Form a trusting therapeutic relationship with clients so that clients may express issues relevant to ethnic identity, familial-cultural dynamics, and unique cultural experiences as persons of mixed ancestry. • Use supervision to enhance clinical skills and multicultural competency in serving persons of mixed ancestry. • Establish effective consultation relationships with colleagues and supervisors with expertise in serving this population. • Foster an environment in which supervisees and trainees feel safe to talk, explore, and discuss issues related to culture and identity.	• Presenting and participating in clinical case conferences that include discussion of clients with mixed ancestry.
Values and Attitudes Awareness of own ethnic background and identity and associated biases; willingness to continually broaden self-knowledge; and commitment to expanding knowledge of persons of mixed ancestry as part of multicultural competency enhancement.	

Table 8.4 Developmental-Level Competencies IV

READINESS LEVEL—ADVANCED PRACTICE AND SPECIALIZATION	
Competencies	**Learning Process and Activities**
Knowledge Extensive knowledge of: • Mixed ancestry/multiracial literature. • Ethnic identity development models for singular and multiple ethnic identities. • Historical context and development of ethnic identity models and varying adaptive identity-resolution statuses for people of mixed ancestry. • Impact of mixed ancestries upon human development and identity development.	Psychotherapists who have a particular interest in clinical work with people of mixed ancestry may seek to attain advanced levels of competency. Learning activities will vary depending on the psychotherapist's unique background, established competencies, and interest areas. For example, psychotherapists working in college/university counseling centers may wish to focus on identity development along the developmental trajectory for people of mixed ancestry.

READINESS LEVEL—ADVANCED PRACTICE AND SPECIALIZATION

Competencies		Learning Process and Activities
	• Ecological and strengths-based approaches and interventions. • *Isms* (e.g., racism, sexism, heterosexism, classism, ableism, ageism, audism, and religious oppression, etc.) and the impact on multiple systemic levels. • Multiple identities and the saliency of identities for a given client.	Regardless of the focus area, learning activities can include: • Professional reading (information about diverse singular and multiple ethnic identities and cultural themes; empirical studies, and literature on theory and practice). • Teaching courses on people of mixed ancestry and multiracial identities. • Attending and leading educational workshops. • Peer consultation groups. • Consultation with knowledgeable mental health professionals with expertise in clinical applications with people of mixed ancestry.
Skills	Advanced skills in: • Providing a variety of relevant therapeutic assessments and interventions. • Integrating knowledge of key concepts into treatment (phenotype; experiences of racism at multiple systemic levels, including family, peer, social contexts, and institutional). • Differentiating between healthy and adaptive ethnic-identity-resolution statuses and the impact of racism (and other relevant *isms*) for clients of mixed ancestry. • Proactively and appropriately sharing knowledge of people of mixed ancestry within work setting and with members of other mental health professions. • Providing effective supervision to trainees working with clients of mixed ancestry.	
Values and Attitudes	Well-integrated values and attitudes demonstrated by the following: • Continually engages in broadening knowledge of resources and ongoing professional development with regard to persons of mixed ancestry. • Maintains involvement in relevant local and national groups and organizations. • Independently and proactively provides ethical and legal consultation and supervision to trainees and other professionals. • Independently monitors own relevant cultural values and beliefs in relation to working with people of mixed ancestry. • Works for social justice to enhance understanding among diverse individuals and advocate for systemic social change.	

REFERENCES

AhnAllen, J. M., Suyemoto, K. L., & Carter, A. S. (2006). Relationship between physical appearance, sense of belonging and exclusion, and racial/ethnic self-identification among multiracial Japanese European Americans. *Cultural Diversity and Ethnic Minority Psychology, 12*(4), 673–686.

American Psychological Association. (2002). Guidelines for multicultural education, training, research, practice, and organizational change for psychologists. Retrieved July 7, 2009, from http://www.apa.org/pi/multiculturalguidelines.pdf

Bratter, J. (2007). Will "multiracial" survive to the next generation?: The racial classification of children of multiracial parents. *Social Forces, 86*(2), 821–849.

Bronfenbrenner, U. (1977). Toward an experimental ecology of human development. *American Psychologist, 32,* 513–529.

Bronfenbrenner, U. (1979). *The ecology of human development: Experiments by nature and design.* Cambridge, MA: Harvard University Press.

Brunsma, D. L., & Rockquemore, K. A. (2001). The new color complex: Appearances and biracial identity. *Identity, 3,* 225–246.

Buchanan, N. T., & Acevedo, C. A. (2004). When face and soul collide: Therapeutic concerns with racially ambiguous and nonvisible minority women. *Women & Therapy, 27*(1/2), 119–331.

Coates, T. P. (2007, February 1). Is Obama black enough? *Time.* Retrieved July 28, 2009, from http://www.time.com/time/nation/article/0,8599,1584736,00.html

Cross, J. E., Jr. (1991). *Shades of black: Diversity in African-American identity.* Philadelphia: Temple.

Cross, W. E. (1987). A two-factor theory of black identity: Implications for the study of identity development in minority children. In J. S. Phinney & M. J. Rotheram (Eds.), *Children's ethnic socialization: Pluralism and development* (pp. 117–133). Newbury Park, CA: Sage.

Dalton, J. H., Elias, M. J., & Wandersman, A. (2001). *Community psychology: Linking individuals and communities.* Stamford: Wadsworth.

Davis, F. J. (1991). *Who is black: One nation's definition.* University Park, PA: Pennsylvania State University Press.

Doyle, J. M., & Kao, G. (2007). Are racial identities of multiracials stable? Changing self-identification among single and multiple race individuals. *Social Psychology Quarterly, 70*(4), 405–423.

Edwards, L. M., & Pedrotti, J. T. (2004). Utilizing the strengths of our cultures: Therapy with biracial women and girls. *Women & Therapy, 27*(1/2), 33–43.

Esbach, K. (1995). The enduring and vanishing American Indian: Growth and intermarriage in the 1990s. *Ethnic and Racial Studies, 18*(1), 89–108.

Fernandez, C. A. (1992). La Raza and the melting pot: A comparative look at multiethnicity. In M.P.P.

Root (Ed.), *Racially mixed people in America* (pp. 126–143). Newbury Park, CA: Sage.

Fhagen-Smith, P. (2003). *Mixed ancestry racial/ethnic identity development model.* Wellesley, MA: Wellesley Centers for Women.

Fram, A. (2008, November 8). "Mutts like me" shows Obama's racial comfort. *Associated Press.* Retrieved July 28, 2009, from http://www.msnbc.msn.com/id/27606637/

Fulbeck, K. (2006). *Part Asian, 100% Hapa.* San Francisco: Chronicle Books.

Gaskins, P. (1979). Eurasians: Strengths in coping. *Asian Directions, 2,* 1–8.

Gillem, A. R., & Thompson, C. A. (2004). Introduction: Biracial women in therapy: Between the rock of gender and the hard place of race. *Women & Therapy, 27*(1/2), 1–18.

Harris, D. R., & Sim, J. J. (2002). Who is multiracial? Assessing the complexity of lived race. *American Sociological Review, 67,* 614–627.

Helms, J. E., & Cook, D. A. (1999). *Using race and culture in counseling and psychotherapy: Theory and process.* Boston: Allyn & Bacon.

Helms, J. E., & Talleyrand, R. M. (1997). Race is not ethnicity. *American Psychologist, 52*(11), 1246–1247.

Herman, M. (2004). Forced to choose: Some determinants of racial identification in multiracial adolescents. *Child Development, 75*(3), 730–748.

Hitlin, S., Brown, J. S., & Elder, Jr., G. H. (2006). Racial self-categorization in adolescence: Multiracial development and social pathways. *Child Development, 77*(5), 1298–1308.

Hunter, M. L. (2005). *Race, gender, and the politics of skin tone.* New York: Taylor & Francis Group.

Jones, N. A., & Symens Smith, A. (2001). *The two or more races population: 2000.* Census 2000 Brief No. C2KBR/01-6. Washington, DC: U.S. Census Bureau.

Kerwin, C., & Ponterotto, J. G. (1995). Biracial identity development: Theory and research. In J. D. Ponterotto, J. M. Casas, L. A. Suzuki, & C. M. Alexander (Eds.), *Handbook of multicultural counseling* (pp. 199–217). Thousand Oaks, CA: Sage.

Kerwin, C., Ponterotto, J. G., Jackson, B. L., & Harris, A. (1993). Racial identity in biracial children: A qualitative investigation. *Journal of Counseling Psychology, 40*(2), 221–231.

Kich, G. K. (1992). The developmental process of asserting a biracial, bicultural identity. In M. P. P.

Root (Ed.), *Racially mixed people in America* (pp. 304–320). Newbury Park, CA: Sage.

Krebs, N. B. (2000). For students with multicultural heritage: A refreshing, confrontative approach. *Multicultural Education, 8*(2), 25–27.

Miville, M. L., Constantine, M. G., Baysden, M. F., & So-Lloyd, G. (2005). Chameleon changes: An exploration of racial identity themes of multiracial people. *Journal of Counseling Psychology, 52*(4), 507–516.

Morten, G., & Atkinson, D. R. (1983). Minority identity development and preference for counselor race. *Journal of Negro Education, 52*, 156–161.

Nishimura, N. (2004). Counseling biracial women: An intersection of multiculturalism and feminism. *Women & Therapy, 27*(1/2), 133–145.

Parham, T. A., & Helms, J. E. (1985). Relation of racial identity attitudes to self-actualization and affective states in Black students. *Journal of Counseling Psychology, 32*, 431–440.

Pedrotti, J. T., Edwards, L. M., & Lopez, S. J. (2008). Working with multiracial clients in therapy: Bridging theory, research, and practice. *Professional Psychology: Research and Practice, 39*(2), 192–201.

Poston, W. S. C. (1990). The biracial identity development model: A needed addition. *Journal of Counseling & Development, 69*, 152–155.

Renn, K. (2008). Research on biracial and multiracial identity development: Overview and synthesis. *New Directions for Student Services, 123*, 13–21.

Rhee, F. (2008, November 10). Chewing over Obama's "mutt" reference. *Political Intelligence*. Retrieved July 28, 2009, from http://www.boston.com/news/politics/politicalintelligence/2008/11/chewing_over_ob.html

Rockquemore, K. A., & Brunsma, D. L. (2002). *Beyond black: Biracial identity in America*. Thousand Oaks, CA: Sage.

Root, M. P. P. (1990). Resolving "other" status: Identity development of biracial individuals. *Women and Therapy, 9*, 185–205.

Root, M. P. P. (Ed.). (1992). *Racially mixed people in America*. Thousand Oaks: Sage.

Root, M. P. P. (1994). Mixed race women. In L. Comas Diaz & B. Green (Eds.), *Women of color and mental health: The healing tapestry*. New York: Guilford.

Root, M. P. P. (1996). *The multiracial experience: Racial borders as the new frontier*. Thousand Oaks, CA: Sage.

Root, M. P. P. (1998). Experiences and processes affecting racial identity development: Preliminary results from the biracial sibling project. *Cultural Diversity and Mental Health, 4*(3), 237–247.

Root, M. P. P. (1999). The biracial baby boom: Understanding ecological constructions of racial identity in the twenty-first century. In R. H. Sheets & E. R. Hollins (Eds.), *Aspects of human development: Racial and ethnic identity in school practices*. Mahwah, NJ: Lawrence Erlbaum.

Root, M. P. P. (2001). *Love's revolution: racial intermarriage*. Philadelphia: Temple University Press.

Root, M. P. P. (2003). Racial experiences questionnaire. In M. P. P. Root & M. Kelley (Eds.), *The Multiracial Child Resource Book*. Seattle: Mavin Foundation.

Root, M. P. P. (2004). From exotic to a dime a dozen. *Women and Therapy (special issue), 27*(1/2), 19–31.

Roysircar-Sodowski, G., & Kuo, P. Y. (2001). Determining cultural validity of personality assessment: Some guidelines. In D. B. Pope-Davis and H. L. K. Coleman (Eds.), *The intersection of race, class, and gender in multicultural counseling*. Thousand Oaks, CA: Sage Publications.

Russell, K., Wilson, M., & Hall, R. (1992). *The color complex: The politics of skin color among African - Americans*. New York: Bantam Doubleday Dell.

Shih, M., Bonam, C., Sanchez, D., & Peck, C. (2007). The social construction of race: Biracial identity and vulnerability of stereotypes. *Cultural Diversity and Ethnic Minority Psychology, 13*(2), 125–133.

Shih, M., & Sanchez, D. T. (2005). Perspectives and research on the positive and negative implications of having multiple racial identities. *Psychological Bulletin, 131*(4), 569–591.

Spickard, P. R. (1992). The illogic of American racial categories. In M. P. P. Root (Ed.), *Racially mixed people in America* (pp. 12–23). Newbury Park, CA: Sage.

Stephan, C. W. (1992). Mixed-heritage individuals: Ethnic identity and trait characteristics. In M. P. P. Root (Ed.), *Racially mixed people in America* (pp. 50–63). Newbury Park, CA: Sage.

Stonequist, E. (1937). *The marginal man: A study in personality and culture conflict*. New York: Russell & Russell.

Sundstrom, R. R. (2001). Being and being mixed race. *Social Theory and Practice, 27*(2), 285–307.

Thornton, M. C., & Wason, S. (1995). Intermarriage. In D. Levinson (Ed.), *Encyclopedia of marriage and the family* (pp. 396–402). New York: Macmillan.

Walters, R. (2007). Barack Obama and the politics of blackness. *Journal of Black Studies, 38*(1), 7–29.

CHAPTER 9

BECOMING A RACIALLY COMPETENT THERAPIST

DELIDA SANCHEZ and CLAYTIE DAVIS III

INTRODUCTION

November 4, 2008, marked one of the most significant dates in American history with the election of the first Black president of the United States, Barack Obama. Millions of Americans expressed myriad emotions ranging from exhilaration, joy, and pride to disbelief, fear, disdain, and intense anger. The impact and implications of Obama's election are enormous for race relations in the United States and beyond. His biracial identity played a large part in his campaign and public persona, and is seen by many as the key to "healing political and racial division" (DaCosta, 2007). Analyzing the impact of this historic event is beyond the scope of this chapter; however, the authors felt it necessary to acknowledge this as a backdrop to the changing face (and race) of leadership in our time and the possible implications for counseling and treatment.

This chapter provides an overview of the current empirical and theoretical literature on race and racial counseling competencies, highlights current barriers to effective multicultural training, and reviews knowledge, skills, and values/attitudes/awareness necessary for addressing race in education, training, and clinical practice. Additionally, resources, training tools, and developmental tables that illustrate multicultural counseling competency knowledge, skills, and values necessary for clinical work as identified in the Competency Benchmarks Document (APA, 2007) are also presented.

The Multicultural Counseling Competencies have been identified as the "centerpiece" of the multicultural movement in counselor education and counseling psychology (Ponterotto, Fuertes, & Chen, 2000). Much of the multicultural competency research and training is based on the seminal work of Sue et al. (1982). It has been over 25 years since the introduction of Sue et al.'s (1982) tripartite model of multicultural counseling competencies (MCCs), which originally addressed counselor-competency areas with issues involving four American racial minority groups: Native American/Alaskan Natives, African Americans, Asian Americans, and Hispanic Americans/Latinos. Since the introduction of the MCCs in 1982, competencies for working with multiracial (including biracial) individuals have also been developed. Given the unique needs of multiracial individuals—a racial minority group that differs from other racial minority groups—having coalesced around the notion of mixedness rather than sameness and lacking a similar within-racial-group language, history, or culture (DaCosta, 2007), a separate chapter has been devoted to their racial needs (see Chapter 8).

The multicultural competencies model consists of three broad areas: (1) attitudes and beliefs—awareness of one's own assumptions, values, and biases; (2) knowledge—understanding the worldview of culturally diverse clients; and (3) skills—developing appropriate intervention strategies and techniques (Sue et al., 1982). The adoption of the MCCs as guidelines for psychological practice by the American Psychological Association (APA, 2003) represents a major advance in multicultural counseling. Sanchez-Hucles & Jones (2005) identify the MCCs as an important tool for fighting oppression and monoculturalism in the field by informing counselors that they must be prepared to identify, understand, and discuss race, racism, and discrimination for racial minority clients.

KNOWLEDGE

Defining *Race*

Defining *race* has been one of the biggest challenges in psychology research and training and continues to be markedly controversial (Delgado-Romero, Galvan, Maschino, & Rowland, 2005). Definitions of race range from biological and genetic explanations—including skin pigmentation/color, hair texture, and physical features—to reflections of sociopolitically and economically constructed hierarchies (Lopez, 2000; Spickard, 1992) based on the relative superiority and inferiority of different races. For the most part, scholars now define race as a social construction, based on a biological derivative, with social hierarchies that can have psychological meaning comprised of emotions, thoughts, and attitudes about one's identification or lack thereof with their racial group (Carter, 1995). Within the United States, the following racial groups are officially recognized by the U.S. Census Bureau (2002): Asian/Pacific Islander, Black/African American, Native American, White, Latino/Hispanic (an ethnic racial group defined primarily by language), and multiracial.

The terms *race*, *ethnicity*, and *culture* are often used interchangeably in the multicultural literature (Carter & Pieterse, 2005). The overlap in definitions may lead to confusion in training when each is not clearly defined. There are important distinctions between race and ethnicity that should be noted and for this reason a separate chapter has been devoted to each of these reference groups, respectively. *Ethnicity* is defined as the connectedness groups share based on commonalities such as religion, nationality, region, and so forth, where specific aspects of cultural patterns are shared and where transmission over time creates a common history (Juby & Concepcion, 2005). Race can take on ethnic meaning when, and if, members of that biological group have evolved specific ways of living. For example, the term *Black* is often used to refer to African Americans as an ethnic group. One's

ethnic group can change over time; one's racial group membership does not.

Culture is defined as learned skills, attitudes, and behaviors that are transmitted from generation to generation, usually within the confines of a physical-social environment (Carter, 1995). Cultures or subcultures may be chosen or imposed. Within the United States, imposed racial group segregation and isolation from the dominant White culture led Blacks, Latinos, Native Americans and Asians to maintain distinct cultural patterns that identify them from each other as well as from White culture. However, each of these racial groups also endorses cultural patterns that might transgress race, particularly those needed to function in larger society. In this chapter, the term *racial-cultural* (values) will be used to connote the learned behaviors of racial groups in response to racial socialization. The complexity in definitions of race, ethnicity, and culture should be acknowledged in multicultural training as well as the fluidity within each of these reference groups.

Barriers to Competency in Multicultural Counseling

In the clinical setting, both counselor and client bring a vast network of attitudes, values, traditions, and worldviews that are informed and influenced by their respective racial group affiliations, which in turn may serve as both a barrier and a resource in treatment (Satcher, 2000; Zetzer & Shockley, 2005). In understanding the barriers to effective MCC training around issues of race, researchers have looked at systemic, institutional, and cultural factors that are insidious to American culture. Neville and colleagues (1996) identified the following barriers to effective multicultural training regarding racial competence: (a) continued silence about race and racism; (b) colorblindness; (c) the need to promote similarities and minimize differences; (d) low awareness of White racial identity and privilege; (e) the belief that racism hurts racial minorities and not White Americans, which creates little impetus to change; (f) faculty and supervisors who have not been trained in multiculturalism; (g) lack of empirically tested models that describe how to effectively develop multicultural counselors; (h) difficulty in knowing how to assess, evaluate, and establish accountability for cultural competency; (i) faculty, students, and supervisors who do not know how to talk about race and consequently have poor dialogues.

D. W. Sue and D. Sue (2003) proposed four major obstacles that block the path toward attaining racial-cultural competence: (1) difficulty acknowledging personal biases because such a realization is at odds with and threatens the self-image of those who consciously believe in justice and democracy; (2) people operating from a politeness protocol and disinclined to honestly examine, explore, and discuss in public unpleasant racial realities such as prejudice, stereotyping, and discrimination; (3) not accepting responsibility for any action or inaction that may directly or indirectly perpetuate injustice; and (4) resistance to dealing with "embedded emotions" (fear, guilt, anger, etc.) often associated with painful racial memories and images.

Race and Racism

Race and racism have powerful implications for personality development and mental health (Bruno, 2002; Carter, 1995, 2005; McCowan & Alston, 1998). Given the central role of race and racism in American history and sociopolitical life, the developmental processes and the life path of all Americans are affected by race (Carter, 1995, 2005; Carter & Cook, 1992). A system of racial meanings and stereotypes exists and seems to be a permanent feature of U.S. culture (Omi & Winant, 1986). Through racial socialization, individuals are infused with messages that determine the appropriateness or inappropriateness of their roles as racial beings (Carter, 1995, 2005). These messages are often developed by those racial groups who hold more

power and can exert more control over their own situations and the situations of lower-status groups, mainly through stereotypes. In the United States, Whites are the dominant racial group in terms of both population numbers and social, political, and economic influence. As a consequence, Whites have the ability to perpetuate racial power by denying race both as relevant to the lives of Whites and as an essential quality of those who are not White (Thompson, Shin, & Stephens, 2005). The professional dominance of White researchers and clinicians in psychology has also had significant implications for the perpetuation of racism and oppression and to the imposition of limited and dehumanizing racial categories on visibly racial (non-White) groups (Thompson et al., 2005; Trimble, Helms, & Root, 2003).

A primary identity issue for groups of color concerns the development of a positive sense of self as members of a racial group in a racist society (Helms, 1994, 2001). Knowing that one is a member of a stigmatized group has some predictable psychological, social, and behavioral consequences (Speight, 2007). Experiences with racial discrimination and harassment have been shown to cause stress, health-related problems, and psychological injury to persons of color (Carter, 2007). Specifically, racism-related stress places targets of racism at risk for depression and anxiety (Horowitz, Garber, Ciesla, Young, & Mufson, 2007) as well as high blood pressure, hypertension, stroke, and cardiovascular disease (Din-Dzietham, Nembhard, Collins, & Davis, 2004).

While personal identity development is also a central theme for Whites, they do not have to contend with society's generally negative evaluation of their group and do not have to defend against internalized racism, institutional or cultural racism, or racism-related stress. The focus on development may be more pronounced in other aspects of their lives (i.e., gender, sexual orientation, social class). Given the aforementioned, the psychological process of healthy racial identity development for Whites is that of acknowledging unearned privilege and internalizing an identity that is free of guilt, shame, and defensiveness for being White (Helms, 1990). A big component of the work of training White clinicians includes helping them confront colorblind racial attitudes—considered to be a more modern/contemporary form of racism (Spanierman & Poteat, 2005).

While overt forms of racism are not seen as much in the post–civil rights movement era and in the age of "political correctness," modern or contemporary forms of racism continue to exist and consist of the denial, distortion, and avoidance of the continued importance of race in American culture. According to Gushue & Constantine (2007):

> Color blind racial attitudes reflect aspects of contemporary racism. Unlike more overt forms of racism, the color-blind perspective does not make explicit claims about White superiority. Rather, these attitudes reflect the seemingly benign position that race should not and does not matter. Included in this stance, however, is a denial that racism continues to benefit White individuals. (p. 323)

For some, a colorblind approach to race may be viewed as a way of prevailing over overt racial prejudice. However, practitioners who adopt colorblind racial attitudes could seriously impair their ability to serve clients of color effectively and in a culturally sensitive manner (Gushue & Constantine, 2007).

Racial Identity

A first step in the process of better preparing to work with racially diverse populations is to ensure that Whites (and people of color) gain insight into their own racial identity and learn how to be more skilled in understanding and responding to issues of race (Sanchez-Hucles & Jones, 2005). Racial identity theory and racial identity measurement address the psychological consequences to individuals of being socialized in a society in which a person either does

(Whites) or does not (persons of color) have privilege based on his or her racial classification (Helms, 2005). Racial identity theories suggest that people's racial identities vary—that is, how and to what extent they identify with their respective racial groups—and that a person's race is more than his or her skin color or physical features. Additionally, racial identity theories postulate that a person's resolution of his or her identity is psychological. This is crucial because racial identity seems to guide an individual's feelings, thoughts, perceptions, and level of investment in his or her racial groups' cultural patterns (Helms, 1996) as well as other aspects of his or her identity (Carter, 1995; Carter & Pieterse, 2005). Racial identity functioning is said to unfold along a continuum from minimal awareness of race to an increasingly integrated understanding and appreciation of the similarities and differences between oneself and others.

The following tables (9.1 and 9.2, shown on the following page) highlight the racial identity statuses for persons of color as well as Whites. The racial identity statuses were originally based on a developmental stage model, proposed by Cross (1991) and other earlier proponents of racial identity theory (Helms, 1990), but have progressed to identity statuses of which an individual may express one or more levels, not necessarily in a sequential or developmental order.

Racial Identity Interaction Model

The psychological meaning that individuals attribute to their race and racial group affiliation is more important to determining the quality of a client-counselor relationship than simply matching clients and counselors based on race (Helms, 1990). Specifically, the clients' and counselors' racial identity resolutions directly affect the cognitive processing and interpersonal behaviors in therapy dyads, and group or family settings (Helms, 1995). The therapeutic relationship formation between culturally different clients and counselors may be significantly influenced when these individuals have similar value systems or worldviews (Burkard, Juarez-Huffaker, &

PEOPLE OF COLOR RACIAL IDENTITY

Conformity Status: This status is characterized by a deemphasis on or denigration of being a person of color.

Example: "I am not Asian American, I am an American."

Dissonance Status: This denotes the period where circumstances create confusion about what it means to be a person of color; the individual has the opportunity to reinterpret his or her worldview differently as a result of an experience, or to maintain the conformity status.

Example: "The security guard in the store wasn't really following me; he just happened to be in the area that I was in and might have been watching someone else."

Immersion/Emersion Status: For many at this point, there emerges an *us-versus-them* mentality where Whites are seen as the enemy and one's racial group is seen as good.

Example: "I don't want to attend that function; there isn't going to be anyone there who looks like me and I don't like being around White people."

Internalization Status: This status is characterized by an individual who has an identity that is not exclusionary; the person is able to see that all groups have positive attributes and that all groups have individuals that discriminate.

Example: "While I felt that I was stopped because of the color of my skin, I do know that not all White officers are racist and that some officers of color are not immune from stopping people of color."

Integrative Awareness Status: The individual is able to accept his or her multiple identities and has successfully managed the dissonance resulting from the previous statuses.

Example: "I love going to my church, where we all speak the same language and for the most part are of the same race; however, what I enjoy more is going to my daughter's school, where I get to interact with parents of all races. I feel I learn more in a multiracial group setting than when I am just with others from my own race."

Source: Helms (1994).

WHITE RACIAL IDENTITY STATUSES

Contact Status: This is characterized by limited involvement with individuals of color; the individual is likely to not see herself as a racial being and sees people "as people."

Example: "Why is the media focusing on Barack Obama's being Black? His grandmother is White and, more importantly, we are all part of the human race."

Disintegration Status: At some point the White individual experiences some event that calls into question his or her beliefs about race. This can lead to anxiety and confusion about the individual's position in his or her racial group, leaving the person with a difficult decision: Maintain the status quo (i.e., don't rock the boat), or begin to acknowledge that racism exists.

Example: "When I was with my friends on the golf course, and they joked about the way an Asian-American was speaking, I told them that was wrong; afterwards I felt like I was no longer part of the group . . . and I don't think my speaking up made a difference."

Reintegration Status: The individual accepts the reality that she is White and views those who are not White (or not conforming) as inferior. There is also a sense of privilege and entitlement present with this status.

(*continued*)

(*continued*)

Example: "Why should my child be punished for going to an elite prep school; if my child attended that inner-city school, he would be first in his class and could pick any college he wanted. Instead, he is just outside the top 10 percent and will likely be waitlisted."

Pseudo-independence Status: There is a move toward a positive White racial identity that does not denigrate other groups. There may be some level of discomfort in beginning to think about the role that Whites (and the individual) have played in oppressing other groups. In an effort to do good, the person may reach out to others groups but still view the world through mainstream society lenses.

Example: "I am working with my Latino coworker to help him get a raise; I have been showing him how to dress and what to talk about with our boss."

Immersion/Emersion Status: This status is characterized by a move to begin to understand one's own racial identity; what does it meant to be White? There is less of a focus on "not being a racist" and a shift to better understanding one's position in society without feeling guilty. An individual might choose to work against discrimination as a result of this new awareness.

Example: "I believe it is wrong to just put people in jail without understanding why individuals do what they do; the fact that there is a disproportionate number of Black men in prison suggests that something is not working in the educational system when individuals feel like they have no chance at life without turning to crime. I want to work with groups that are working with young children to see if I can be part of something different."

Autonomy Status: At this point the individual has an integrated identity that is at peace with being White and recognizes the privilege that comes with being White, perhaps even using it to help others. Individuals likely interact with people of many races and do not associate with groups that oppress others.

Example: "I believe that if my company is going to be successful it needs to reflect the diversity of our community and customers. I am committed to doing whatever is necessary to ensure that we bring in the best and brightest from all communities, even if it means spending more resources to do so."

Source: Helms (1995).

Ajmere, 2003). Because racial identity attitudes reflect distinct types of worldviews and values, a mismatch between therapist and client (of different races or of the same race) may lead to conflict, impasses, and early termination of treatment (Helms, 1995). Helms (1984) labeled three types of therapeutic dyads that were least ideal for treatment—*crossed* (client's and therapist's salient racial identity statuses represent affective opposites regarding race); *regressive* (the client's racial identity is more advanced than the therapist's); and *parallel* (the therapist and client express similar attitudes). Formation of a working alliance is facilitated when the therapist has a more integrated and flexible racial identity than

the client (*progressed*). To the extent that race is a recognized and valued aspect of a client's identity, a counselor who is cognizant of both the racial context and the impact of race on his or her own identity will have a better chance of creating a therapeutic alliance in which clients feel that their experiences are validated (Gushue & Constantine, 2007).

Research has documented a positive relationship between racial identity development and multicultural counseling competency (Neville et al., 1996; Vinson & Neimeyer, 2003). Neville, Spanierman, and Doan (2006) found that psychology students with lower levels of racial identity status—those who more strongly endorsed a colorblind racial ideology—demonstrated less multicultural counseling awareness and knowledge. Conversely, Vinson and Neimeyer (2003) found that Whites with higher racial identity statuses were reported to have higher levels of multicultural competency around race.

SKILLS

An essential component of racial counseling competency skills involves monitoring and applying knowledge of race in assessment, treatment, and consultation work with others. This includes self-awareness and self-regulation of one's thoughts, emotions, and feelings regarding racial dynamics that may occur in treatment, as well as acknowledgment of one's own racial identity level and that of one's client. One's racial competency skills can be demonstrated through one's ability to address race with clients as well as in supervision and considering the ethical issues involved in determining whether one is competent to work with individuals racially different from oneself.

The discussion of race early on in treatment is believed to increase the likelihood that clients will discuss racial issues that might adversely affect the therapeutic work (Thompson & Alexander, 2006). Mental health practitioners who demonstrate racial responsiveness are consistently perceived as being more credible and competent, particularly by clients of color (Knox, Burkard, Suzuki, & Ponterotto, 2003). Moreover, practitioners of color and White practitioners also perceive the discussion of race to have a positive effect on the therapy (Maxie, Arnold, & Stephenson, 2006). There is a need to be mindful of when and how race is discussed and managed as part of the therapeutic relationship (Cardemil & Battle, 2003). La Roche and Maxie (2003) argue that the practitioner must strive to understand the racial identity, level of consciousness, meaning of racial differences, experience of discrimination, and level of client distress when deciding when and whether race is to be discussed.

Broaching Race as a Multicultural Competence Skill

Day-Vines et al. (2007) proposed an empirically supported conceptual framework for addressing race (and ethnicity) in the counseling process. A detailed description of this technique is outlined in Sanchez, del Prado, and Davis III's chapter on ethnicity (in this *Handbook*). The five broaching styles (1) avoidant, (2) isolating, (3) continuing/incongruent, (4) integrated/congruent, and (5) infusing range from lower to more advanced levels of engaging clients in ethnic-related dialogues in counseling and are said to parallel the counselor's level of racial identity functioning (according to the White racial identity model). Thus, counselors who display advanced levels of broaching and possess heightened levels of racial identity functioning are likely to promote trusting and open relationships with their clients and accommodate a range of social and cultural experiences. On the other hand, counselors with low levels of broaching behavior and racial identity functioning have the potential to foster threatening and apprehensive relationships and perhaps refuse to acknowledge the significance of race in a client's life.

The Cultural Genogram

Integrating a racial-cultural genogram into treatment is another valuable skill mental health practitioners could develop to facilitate discussion of race with their clients. (See Experiential Activity 9.3 in this chapter.) It is also a training tool used for practitioners to gain self-awareness of the origins of their own values, beliefs, and biases as they relate to race (de las Fuentes, 2007). A derivative of the genogram used in therapy (McGoldrick, Gerson, & Shellenberger, 1999), the racial-cultural genogram is a map of three or more generations of family that illustrates racial-cultural relational patterns, demographic information, and history of its members, focusing specifically on biases, prejudices, pride, and shame issues that are passed down through the generations. One's family is the primary

CASE VIGNETTE 9.1

Chris is a 28-year-old White male working with an African American male mental health practitioner. In the session he discloses that he has never felt welcomed by his peers, both in high school and now at his current job. He adds that he believes that his coworkers are "discriminating against" him because he is not from the area. Chris currently lives in a predominantly Black and Latino neighborhood, the same neighborhood where he and his half-brother were raised by his stepmother after his father passed away when Chris was 5 years old. Chris attended mostly White schools with his brother via his mother's work as a cleaning staff member. He shared that he was often made fun of by his White peers because he "talked and acted Black." His brother has not had the same difficulty adjusting at school. What Chris has not shared with his therapist is that his stepmother is African American and that while his brother is biracial, he "looks Black." This is the only family that Chris has, and he feels very connected with Black culture and the Black experience.

Michael is currently the only person of color on the clinical staff and is often looked upon by his White colleagues as the "resident" expert on race. What his colleagues aren't aware of is that Michael was raised in a predominantly White neighborhood and "doesn't have much in common with many of the Black and Latino clients he works with." It often frustrates Michael that his colleagues assume that he and his clients are "the same" and feels he has more in common with his White colleagues given his similar class and educational background.

way in which one learns and develops an understanding about one's race (de las Fuentes, 2007) and how one's racial worldview is principally shaped.

There are multiple issues that could arise in this dynamic situation. Using Helms's Racial Identity Interaction Model as a guide (1990), one might best describe the relationship between Chris and Michael as parallel (see Case Vignette 9.1). Issues that might surface in the treatment are a difficulty empathizing with and understanding fully Chris's experience or helping Chris understand his feelings more openly as they relate to race. Supervision could be useful for Michael to discuss his feelings of frustration in working with Chris and for sharing his own feelings of not being treated fairly because of race. He may also be able to discuss how his own experiences of discrimination make it difficult to hear this particular client "complain." In an ideal supervisory relationship, this interaction could lead to an opportunity for the practitioner to learn more about his own biases, as well as about the

within-group differences of racial groups, including White Americans.

Using broaching techniques might also be helpful to address race in treatment. Inviting Chris to talk about his thoughts and feeling regarding working with an African-American male may help build trust and communication and allow Chris to share more of his racial family history. Using the racial-cultural genogram could also be helpful for Chris to look at racial cultural patterns in his family as well as his community and in helping to rectify conflicting feelings about being White and not "having access or acceptance" by his White peers.

VALUES/ATTITUDES/AWARENESS

It is crucial that practitioners at all levels—from practicum to senior mental health practitioner—examine their own values, attitudes, and biases resulting from their racial group membership. An important step in the process of better preparing mental health practitioners to work with racially diverse populations is to ensure that they gain insight into their own race, racial identity, experiences, or lack thereof, with privilege, racism, and racial discrimination, and learn how to be more skilled in understanding and responding to issues of race (Sanchez-Hucles & Jones, 2005). Fundamental to this is one's willingness to address internal issues related to one's personal belief systems, behaviors, and emotions when interacting with one's own and other racial groups.

Acknowledging one's biases and preconceived notions about race can be a daunting task. As previously stated, one barrier to multicultural competency around race is the need for people to perceive and experience themselves as moral, decent, and fair. In order to maintain this perception, they may be disinclined to honestly examine, explore, and discuss unpleasant racial realities such as prejudice, stereotyping, and discrimination (D. W. Sue & D. Sue, 2003). Additionally, because race is such an emotionally volatile and sensitive subject, engaging in difficult dialogues about race can be challenging (Spanierman & Poteat, 2005). Common fears among hites are: being seen as a racist; being isolated, ostracized, or rejected; and potential loss of privilege if they align themselves with those who are oppressed (Sanchez-Hucles & Jones, 2005). Common concerns for persons of color are the pressure to take a leadership role in discussions about race because of assumed expertise and fear that Whites are "not going to do the work." Racial minorities also fear vulnerability, being misunderstood, and feel anger and frustration. In order to develop racial competencies, one must overcome resistance to dialoguing about race. One must learn to distinguish between "uncomfortable" feelings and lack of safety, an important key to racial competency development, as these feelings will continue to surface at times throughout one's increasing awareness. Thus, an important value/attitude for practitioners to have around race is to be open to and acknowledge "embedded emotions"—feelings of anxiety, fear, anger, distrust,

and discomfort often associated with painful racial memories and images. One's racial awareness can be increased through participation in conferences and workshops, where one has an opportunity to begin engaging in racial self-exploration through group experiences and exercises such as journaling, cultural sharing, reaction papers, role-playing, videotaping, cross-cultural immersion experiences, cross-cultural simulation experiences, experiential exercises, fishbowl exercises, small-group processing, and focus groups.

For White practitioners, learning about and participating in workshops on privilege is one way of cultivating self-awareness. For example, McIntosh's (1988) work on White privilege, "Unpacking the Invisible Knapsack," allows White individuals to identify privileges that European Americans have in U.S. society and take for granted that non-Whites may not have. Some privileges are: (a) going into a store and not being automatically viewed as a potential shoplifter; (b) going to college and not being automatically thought of in terms of affirmative action; (c) going to school and finding role models of a similar background; (d) when applying for a job, the people in power will be of the same race; (e) when speaking up in a group, not assumed to be speaking on behalf of an entire racial group; (f) when studying history in school, learning about one's own heritage; and (g) when walking down a street at night, not being perceived as a threat.

For practitioners of color, becoming aware of internalized racism and psychological, physical, and emotional stressors associated with racism-related stress will also help in their work with racially diverse clients. If one is feeling angry at the "White man" and is working with a White client, one's biases may be extremely counter-therapeutic. Similarly, internalized racism and the idealization of White culture may also make a practitioner of color ineffective with clients of color who are talking about very painful and real experiences with discrimination. Regardless of race, racial cultural competence requires accepting responsibility for one's racial biases and any action or inaction that may directly or indirectly perpetuate racism/discrimination/injustice. Realizing how one's own biases and actions may contribute to inequities means that one can no longer escape personal responsibility for change. The eradication of bias is more than an intellectual exercise.

SUPERVISION AND TRAINING

Many training programs and agencies have attempted to incorporate the MCCs into their curriculum with mixed results. Only a few training programs have responded with well-conceived courses and practica that hold students and faculty accountable to an accepted level of professional cultural competence around race (Sanchez-Hucles & Jones, 2005). While it has been shown that multicultural education produces positive results related to MCCs (Smith, Constantine, Dunn, Dinehart, & Montoya, 2006), it has been argued that most multicultural training highlights the development of knowledge, skills, and sensitivity without deliberate focus on racial self-awareness (Carter, 2003; Utsey, Hammar, & Gernat, 2005).

An important factor in the successful facilitation of racial knowledge, skills, and awareness in supervision and training is the availability of time and resources allocated to racial competency training. Enlisting organizational support for diversity efforts around race from one's institution/school/department/organization/center is crucial. There must be time and funds allocated at the organizational level that reflect a larger overall commitment to multiculturalism. In addition, embedding racial cultural competencies into the structure of training and supervision is central to providing a safe space for trainees to have the opportunity to participate fully. Setting ground rules and clear goals for the training (e.g., develop better listening and critical thinking skills around race) so that all participants (trainees and supervisors) agree to commit to and be accountable for the duration of the training is also helpful in facilitating racial cultural competency training and supervision.

Some important goals for training and supervision around race are: (a) to cultivate the formation of trusting therapeutic relationships with clients so that clients may express racial concerns if relevant and provide basic therapeutic interventions; (b) to know how to perform an assessment of clients' racial identity and worldviews and to assess the relevance of racial issues to therapy; (c) to diagnose and formulate appropriate treatment plans that are sensitive to the client's racial worldview, including how multiple systems and individual differences impact clients; (d) to identify the limits of one's own competency with racial issues and refer appropriately; (e) to use supervision to enhance working with members of all racial groups; and (f) to establish effective consultation relationships with community resources.

Basic knowledge and sensitivity to the scientific, theoretical, and contextual issues related to race as they apply to professional psychology is obtained mainly through coursework. Included in this are learning definitions of *race*, *racism*, *prejudice*, and *oppression*, and learning about racism in psychology (and in the United States in particular), racial identity models, current inequities in the mental health system, as well as the impact of race on authority/lack of authority of psychologists. There are several models in the literature regarding racial identity, including but not limited to: Helms's (1995) People of Color Racial Identity model; the Racial/Cultural Identity Development model by D. W. Sue and D. Sue (1999); the Cross (1991) model of African American development; the Ruiz (1990) model for Latino identity development; and Neville, Lilly, Duran, Lee, and Brown's Color Blind Ideology (2000).

Creating Safe Spaces for Dialogue in Training and Supervision

Creating safe spaces to discuss race is essential for training and supervision. A safe space, however, is not synonymous with a comfortable space. Instructors must work to create an environment that is both challenging and supportive.

This includes countering socially desirable and politically correct environments and encouraging students and supervisees to be honest about their negative feelings regarding race (Spanierman & Poteat, 2005). Models of this are reflected at certain institutions, such as Columbia University Teachers College Racial-Cultural Counseling Laboratory (Carter, 2003). Young and Davis-Russell (2002) also developed a four-tiered training environment program that includes creating a climate for inquiry around race, focusing on cognitive inquiry, focusing on emotional inquiry, and developing skills for mindful listening.

By creating a safe environment for the discussion and exploration of race, training programs can encourage White trainees to examine the meaning of their Whiteness in relation to the self (i.e., ego), and increase their awareness regarding the insidious nature of racism. Understanding and acknowledging one's privilege is key to conducting diversity work (training, treatment, and supervision). Many White practitioners are only vaguely aware of the degree to which their own racial background influences their own beliefs, value systems, and behaviors. The increase of self-knowledge and awareness is integral to understanding how responses to racial-cultural diversity are likely to manifest. D'Andrea (2005) suggests that White students in particular be made aware of the ways in which they are likely to react to issues of race and ethnicity as they arise in the counseling and supervision dyad.

Studies and vignettes might serve as a model for facilitating discussions related to issues of race and racism that will encourage trainees to fearlessly confront their own racist socialization and White privilege expectations (D'Andrea, 2005). Vignettes can be used to explore the defensive reactions of White counselor trainees to race-related anxiety that counselors and supervisors experience in reaction to racially provocative counseling and supervision situations. This can be overwhelming to the extent that effective therapeutic interventions are hampered by defense mechanisms mobilized to protect the ego from a possible threat (Utsey & Gernat,

2002). Training activities such as questions and vignettes can also strive to help racial minority counselors explore their reactions to different racial groups. Multicultural training may be enhanced and perceived as more equitable if all participants, not just White Americans, challenged themselves to grow in new areas.

Racial identity models can also provide a relatively nonthreatening focus for discussing racial differences. The models examine individual differences rather than sweeping generalizations about racial groups, generalizations that can contribute to alienation and defensiveness when individuals discuss racial issues. Individuals can discuss their racial differences from a perspective of "growth and development" rather than "blame."

Multicultural Competency Training for People of Color

Satcher (2000) challenged the profession by stating, "therapists of all races should be expected to receive appropriate training to provide culturally competent services that reflect sensitivity to individual differences and validity to group identity" (p. 13). Thus, demonstrating multicultural competence in the area of race is not only incumbent upon White therapists. However, there is little research focusing on the dynamics of racial-minority individuals counseling White clients or other racial-minority clients (Carter, 1995; Maxie et al., 2006; Sanchez-Hucles & Jones, 2005). In regard to therapists of color, not much is known about how their own racial histories, racial identity, and possible experiences with discrimination might impact cross-cultural work (Maxie et al., 2006). Carter (1995) explored racial identity within racial dyads including therapists of color and White clients (and clients of color) and found that these dyads were strongly influenced by each participant's racial identity status, not racial group membership. In particular, lower levels of racial identity of the therapist (where one's sense of self is less tied to one's race and/or where one has negative beliefs about one's race)

CASE VIGNETTE 9.2

Rebecca is a 21-year-old White American woman seeking counseling following a semester studying abroad. Rebecca spent last year in Africa and reports she is having a "lack of faith." She does not understand why so many people are in poverty and feels guilty for what she has. In session, she shares with her mental health professional of color that she does not see the point of going to school when so many others don't have an opportunity to get an education and therefore are unlikely to have their situation change. She asks, "What's the point?"

were correlated with poorer outcomes of treatment. Higher levels of therapists' racial identity were associated with an increased focus on intrapsychic issues and better outcomes.

While there continues to be a dearth of empirical literature that explores the racial competencies of persons of color (Utsey et al., 2005), there are misleading assumptions about their "assumed expertise regarding race." In the first author's former work as a training director at a university counseling center, both White interns and interns of color often assumed that racial-minority members were racially competent by virtue of their racial-minority status and thus needed less training than White trainees. In the fortuitous year of an all-intern-of-color class, interns expressed feeling competition with each other around who was more racially aware, discriminated against, and ultimately culturally competent. Painful discussions were initially avoided and then engaged in as a result of the co-creation of a safe and nurturing environment. Through these experiences, interns acknowledged the self-and-other imposed pressure to be a spokesperson for their race, and varying degrees of distrust and dislike of Whites as well as toward their own and other racial minority groups. These shared experiences are consistent with those described by Sanchez-Hucles and Jones (2005), who proposed that strong anti-White feelings can have a significant impact in cross-cultural clinical work.

It might be helpful for supervisors/trainers to encourage trainees of color to explore their own reactions to working with White clients. Case Vignette 9.2 describes a scenario where a trainee has the opportunity to explore race in supervision.

Similar to their White trainee counterparts, trainees of color should be prepared to share their reactions to Rebecca. Perhaps they share her sense of helplessness and powerlessness over having any effect of change over poverty. Perhaps they feel anger toward her as a White person who feels the need to help "poor Africans." In order for training counselors to become culturally competent regarding race, it is important that they learn how to systematically consider the ways in which their own personal and professional experiences as a racial being influence their clinical work. Increasing one's awareness and knowledge of race is necessary for effective multicultural counseling relationships, working alliances, accurate formulation of case conceptualization, and the construction and implementation of a culturally responsive treatment plan (Constantine & Ladany, 2001; Sodowsky, 1996).

Critical Incident Analysis–Based Training: Developing Active Racial/Cultural Awareness

Many of the aforementioned approaches to training in the area of racial competencies address mainly the cognitive domain of multicultural awareness (Collins & Pieterse, 2007). These approaches when used alone have several limitations, including: the marginalization of salient racial events (e.g., cultural immersion experience) as either "isolated" and/or "superimposed" on "normal life," the simplification of others' racial experiences (via role-play simulation and fishbowl exercises), and distancing from the immediacy of racial experiences via journals and reaction papers. These limitations risk conveying the message that racial reality is something that happens only at certain times and in certain circumstances and can be explored only in specific classes or exercises. Important systemic issues are thus missed and ignored, including the communication that multiculturalism is a way of life—part of daily existence in this country—and not an issue marginalized to specific contexts (Collins & Pieterse, 2007).

Collins and Pieterse (2007) suggest incorporating a critical incident analysis as an approach to racial/cultural awareness. They argue that critical incident analysis can lead to increased attention to, understanding of, and insight about how race influences counseling and supervision. Critical incident analysis is described as "an observable human activity (or incident)—a snapshot, vignette, brief episode, situation or encounter which is of interest that is sufficiently complete in itself to permit racial inferences and predictions to be made about the person

performing the act" (p. 17). It incorporates four core elements: (1) acknowledgment of the significance of the incident; (2) confrontation or disclosure of one's internal processes in the interaction; (3) reflection—forming an understanding of the interaction, and using models such as racial identity theory to increase the understanding of patterns of behavior and interactions; and (4) commitment—to the process of trying to understand, and to developing an increased awareness of racial behavior.

The use of critical incident analysis in training for racial awareness focuses on the experience of racial reality that undergirds the demonstrable competencies. Whereas didactic instruction, practicum placements, and externships may focus on the demonstrable skills a trainee exhibits, critical incident analysis elicits an exploration of the thoughts, feelings, and defenses, that reside underneath and provide the basis for the demonstrable skills.

CASE VIGNETTE 9.3

During a case conference presentation with senior staff and interns, a White American female intern presents her client, Susan. Susan is a 20-year-old Asian American female in her second year of law school. She came to counseling for help in managing problems related to her family and her relationship with her partner. Susan states that for the past two years she has been in a relationship with a 25-year-old White man. She adds that she has had to keep the relationship a secret from her parents, to whom she is very close, because her parents are "traditional" and want her to marry someone of the same race. Susan respects her parents and is grateful for the sacrifices they have made for the family (e.g., immigrating to the United States). Susan becomes tearful as she shares that she feels trapped: "I love my boyfriend and I love my parents, and I feel like I cannot have both." While presenting about the client, the intern states that "she just doesn't understand why her client's family is so prejudiced."

Using the critical incident analysis model for Case Vignette 9.3, the critical incident may be considered the client's presenting concern, or the intern's response to her client's concerns during case conference. There is an opportunity for all those participating in the case conference to: (a) verbally acknowledge the significance of race both in the case as well as for the intern and

themselves, (b) to confront or disclose one's internal reaction/processes of the interaction through sharing and discussion of thoughts and feelings, (c) to reflect on one's racial understanding using racial identity models/tools that foster awareness (see tables presented earlier), and (d) a commitment to helping both the intern and her client understand and develop an awareness of racial behavior through continued discussion and supervision. Additionally, it would be important to include the exploration of the unique racial dynamics among the staff and how this may be impacting the intern's training and client case conceptualization.

A continuation of one's self-exploration around race is expected and strongly encouraged throughout all phases of training and supervision. As trainees progress through training, they have a chance to reevaluate their racial-cultural patterns from a more complex level given their internalization of earlier course material on race and begin to engage in exploration of the intersections of race with other reference groups such as gender, sexual orientation, social class, ability/disability, and so on.

IMPLICATIONS/CONCLUSION

Despite the change in racial landscape in the United States, as well as Obama's historic election to the presidency, race continues to be insidious to the infrastructure of U.S. culture. Open acknowledgment of race and racism and barriers to cultural competency need to kept front and center regarding competency development. This chapter has highlighted the importance of mental health practitioners doing more than just being accepting of individuals of all races. In order to provide quality care, counselors must be aware of how race impacts who they are as individuals as well as learn how race influences the lives of others. We posit that much of this work begins with mental health practitioners becoming aware of their racial identity status and how this does (and does not) influence their work with clients. Similarly, practitioners must continue having dialogues about race; the more this can happen in nonclinical settings (e.g., seminars, case conferences, classes, consultation with colleagues) the easier it will be for practitioners to confront race as a counseling competence. It is not enough to merely be aware of the multicultural counseling competencies. Mental health practitioners must do more self-exploration and skill building. It is our hope that counselors find the case vignettes and other resources presented here to be a step in that direction.

RESOURCES

The following resources are provided as suggestions for further inquiry and as tools students, clinicians, trainees, and supervisors can utilize to help improve the quality of the services they provide.

EXPERIENTIAL ACTIVITY 9.1: SELF–AWARENESS AND SELF–ASSESSMENT EXERCISES

Individuals should be encouraged to read an autobiography of an individual of another race as well as their own race. This exercise allows beginning therapists to distinguish their feelings of tuning into others' race as well as their own. Individuals would then write a brief report that highlights examples of the racial identity statues of each person using the People of Color Statuses or White Racial Identity Statuses (Helms, 1995). This obviously requires that instructors or facilitators be aware of and knowledgeable in using the statuses. Examples of books that individuals might consider include: *Crusade for Justice: The Autobiography of Ida B. Wells*, by Duster; *Up from Slavery*, by Booker T. Washington; *The Lakota Women*, by Mary Crow Dog; *Cesar Chavez: Autobiography of LA Causa*, by Jacques Levy and Cesar Chavez; *Among the White Moon Faces: An Asian-American Memoir*, by Shirley Geok-Lin Lim; *Falling Leaves: The Memoir of an Unwanted Chinese Daughter*, by Adeline Yen Mah; *My Life*, by Bill Clinton; and *Anne Frank: The Diary of a Young Girl*, by Anne Frank.

Alternatively, individuals could be asked to identify where they are in terms of their own racial identity status, providing examples of why they believe they are of a certain status(es). It is important for facilitators to remind individuals that no status is "better" than another but that each status represents a means of viewing the world, which has implications for the work they do. Participants might discuss how their status would interact with clients of differing and similar statuses across races. In addition, individuals can share how they might use knowledge of racial identity status(es) in clinical work.

Clinton, B. (2004). *My life.* New York: Alfred A. Knopf.

Dog, M. (1991). *The Lakota women.* New York: Harper Perennial.

Duster, A. (Ed.). (1970). *Crusade for justice: The autobiography of Ida B. Wells.* Chicago: University of Chicago Press.

Frank, A. (1952). *Anne Frank: The diary of a young girl.* New York: Doubleday.

Levy, J. E., & Chavez, C. (1975). *César Chávez: Autobiography of La Causa.* New York: Norton.

Lim, S. (1996). *Among the white moon faces: An Asian-American memoir of homelands.* New York: The Feminist Press.

Mah, A. (1997). *Falling leaves: The memoir of an unwanted Chinese daughter.*

Washington, Booker T. (1901). *Up from slavery: An autobiography.* New York: Doubleday.

EXPERIENTIAL ACTIVITY 9.2: STEP FORWARD IF . . .

This exercise allows participants to explore how much they think about their race and its influence on their day-to-day activities and life in general. Facilitators will need to provide a safe place that will foster honesty among group participants. This exercise is best when the group is fairly heterogeneous. Prior to beginning the exercise, individuals should be informed that they are going to be asked to respond to several statements regarding race, although they will not have to explain their answer. Relatedly, participants are encouraged to be as honest as they can, but ultimately only they know how they truly feel. Participants should be informed that at the end of the exercise there will be a debriefing where a discussion will take place. Facilitators can give an example such as, "I feel a little nervous about doing this exercise." If you agree with the statement you would take a step forward; if not, you would stay where you are. Individuals are then asked to line up on one side of the room and reminded that each time they respond to a statement in the affirmative they will take one step forward.

Sample Items

1. I think of myself as a racial being.
2. When people see me, I think they first see my race.
3. I believe it is probably safest to only date someone of the same race.
4. I believe some people think that my race indicates something about my intellectual capacity.
5. I am proud to be a member of my race.
6. I am able to watch several television shows that depict people of my race in a positive light.
7. In class, I am usually surrounded by people of my race.
8. There are times when I wish I was of a different race.

(continued)

(continued)

9. I tend to like what history says about what those of my race have accomplished.

10. I believe there is too much focus on race in society today.

11. I believe that the police generally treat individuals of my race fairly.

12. I live in a community that is made up of mostly individuals of my race.

13. In class, I sometimes wonder if I would be perceived as smarter if I was of a different race.

14. When someone of my race is in the news for doing something bad, I feel a sense of shame.

15. I believe the election of Barack Obama suggests that America now treats all races pretty much equal.

At the end of the exercise, participants should be debriefed regarding their experience. Facilitators might arrange the group in a circle to facilitate sharing. There are many ways to interpret several of the items and it is likely that some students will want to explain why they answered a certain way. Depending on the diversity of the group, the facilitator might comment on the courage it might have taken some individuals to be so honest. The facilitator should remind participants that the purpose of the exercise is to demonstrate how race impacts each of us individually and those with whom work (both our peers and clients)—and not to understand individuals' politics. And while it is important to keep the focus on race, the facilitator might point out that we have multiple identities and that if we replaced the word *race* with *gender* on several of the items many individuals might be in different places in the room.

Sample Debriefing Questions

1. What was it like for you to respond to these questions in this group?

2. Were you surprised by the range of responses in the class?

3. What surprised you most about your own responses?

4. What about this exercise caused you the most anxiety? And how might that be helpful to you as a therapist?

5. What did you learn about yourself?

EXPERIENTIAL ACTIVITY 9.3: RACIAL GENOGRAM

This activity allows participants to explore how much (or little) racial diversity exists within their family. In addition, this activity serves as a nice reminder to individuals that we are all racial beings. This activity can be done in a seminar or class setting (e.g., de las Fuentes, 2007), or individuals can be asked to do the genogram outside of class. It is helpful if the instructor/ facilitator shares his or her genogram first to model expectations and a certain level of disclosure. Finally, it is critical that instructors allow for group members to check in with them should they be uncomfortable with this exercise. For example, some individuals might not know much about their biological family (e.g., they were adopted, estranged relationship with family) or feel shame in being able to go back only two or three generations (e.g., due to slavery). In these situations, facilitators should encourage participants to share to the extent they are comfortable highlighting why there may be limitations in various genograms, which could serve as a teachable moment for all in the class.

At the most basic level the genogram could look like a family tree with the individual toward the top, bottom, or middle (i.e., individuals should be encouraged to be as creative as they like).

More traditional genograms typically place the trainee in the center, with two generations above (parents and grandparents) and one below if they have children or are partnered. It is up to the instructor to decide how much creativity to allow participants. Regardless of the output sought, we suggest instructors encourage their participants to interview family members, and others in their family, asking questions like, "What does it mean to you to be Native American?" "In what ways has your race impacted your life?" "How have things changed for our family over the generations?" "What are commonalities in our family (e.g., heavy church involvement, divorce rates, high school graduates, diabetes)?" These are just a few of the types of questions participants might use while interviewing elders and younger individuals in their family and community.

One option for the presentation of the genograms is to set the room up like an academic poster session, where individuals have their genograms taped to the wall. Prior to anyone presenting, the group should be allowed time to walk around and look at the various genograms and range of ways they were created. Once the presentations begin, the facilitator might need to model asking questions of the presenter as it can often be embarrassing or culturally incongruent to talk about one's family. The facilitator might begin by asking, "What was it like to do this genogram?" and allow others in the group to validate the range of experiences. It is critical that enough time be given to each participant to share his or her genogram with the class. We recommend that at least 15 minutes be given per participant. Thus, this exercise might need to take place over several meetings, depending on the length of the seminar or class.

Finally, at the conclusion of the sharing of the genograms, participants should be asked to reflect on what they learned about themselves and others as racial beings as a result of the exercise. How might this new awareness impact their interactions with those who shared in the group, as well as their work as therapists?

EXPERIENTIAL ACTIVITY 9.4

New professionals are encouraged to challenge themselves to be part of an ongoing work/process group specifically focused on race (as well as other identity groups). For individuals in an agency, they might work with the management team to inquire about working with an outside consultant to facilitate dialogues about race (and other identities) and how it impacts the work done in that setting. Or, individuals might take turns facilitating dialogues or discussions about articles, chapters, or books related to the race. Alternatively, individuals could engage in the critical incident analysis developed by Collins and Pieterse (2007), which is referenced in this chapter.

COMPETENCY BENCHMARK TABLES

Tables 9.1 through 9.4 describe the four developmental levels of education and training: Readiness for Practicum, Readiness for Internship, Readiness for Entry into Practice, and Readiness for Advanced Practice and Specialization. Each level reflects the requisite awareness, knowledge, and skills that are expected for training and development. One's advancement or lack thereof in each level is assessed via a variety of methods: supervisor/faculty feedback based on direct observation of professional activities (live or recorded observation, co-therapy); client satisfaction surveys; client no-show or dropout rates; self, peer, and supervisory evaluation of inclusion of race, and ethnic case conceptualization. This is outlined for each developmental level.

Table 9.1 Developmental-Level Competencies I

READINESS LEVEL—ENTRY TO PRACTICUM	
Competencies	Learning Process and Activities
Knowledge — The student is gaining knowledge in: • Multiculturalism—the student is engaged in the process of learning that all individuals, including themselves, are racial beings with worldviews that shape and influence their attitudes, emotions, perceptions, and experiences. • The importance of reflective practice and self-awareness. • Core counseling skills and theories. • Ethics code.	At this stage of development, the emphasis in psychotherapist education is instilling knowledge of foundational domains that provide the groundwork for subsequent attainment of functional competencies. Students at this stage become aware of the principles and practices of the field, but they are not yet able to apply their knowledge to practice. Therefore, the training curriculum is focused on knowledge of core areas, including literature on multiculturalism, ethics, basic counseling skills, scientific knowledge, and the importance of reflective practice and self-awareness.
Skills — The student is: • Beginning to develop the ability to demonstrate empathic listening skills, respect, and interest when talking with individuals expressing different values and belief systems. • Learning to critically examine the literature about race and racism.	It is important that throughout the curriculum, trainers and teachers define individual and cultural differences broadly, to include race. This should enable students to have a developing awareness of how to extrapolate their emerging multicultural competencies to include the race of individuals and racial differences.
Values and Attitudes — The student demonstrates: • Willingness to engage in self-exploration to consider own motives, attitudes, behaviors, and effect on others. • Intellectual curiosity and flexibility. • Ability to value expressions of diverse viewpoints and belief systems.	Most students, through their life experiences, would be expected to have basic knowledge of the different races and the ongoing debate regarding race as a biological or social construct.

Table 9.2 Developmental-Level Competencies II

READINESS LEVEL—ENTRY TO INTERNSHIP	
Competencies	Learning Process and Activities
Knowledge — The student has: • General understanding of the traditions and worldviews of the races. • Knowledge that working with racial issues in therapy may be contraindicated in certain circumstances, though not yet well understood. • Understanding of the importance of consulting with supervisors and others when presented with unfamiliar racial client issues.	At this level of development, students are building on their education and applied experiences (such as supervised practicum experiences) to attain a core set of foundational competencies. They can then begin applying this knowledge to professional practice. As a result of being exposed to didactic training and close supervision, students attain the multicultural values and attitudes appropriate to their level of development. Foundational knowledge and multicultural values and attitudes are becoming well established, but skills in working with racial issues would be expected to be rudimentary at this level of development.
Skills — Skills in the following areas are beginning to develop: • Discerning personal limits of openness to talking about race and, after consultation with supervisors, referring clients to appropriate resources if not able to work with them.	Learning occurs through multiple modalities: • Receiving racial didactic training in academic programs may occur in multicultural courses, or

READINESS LEVEL—ENTRY TO INTERNSHIP	
Competencies	Learning Process and Activities
Values and Attitudes	• Building therapeutic alliance to create a trusting, safe, and open therapeutic climate to discuss racial issues, if indicated. Demonstrates self-awareness and appropriate cultural and multicultural attitudes as evidenced by the following: • Understands that race may influence the worldview of the individual. • Awareness of own intersecting individual dimensions (gender, ethnicity, SES, sexual orientation, ability, etc.) and ability to discern clients' intersecting identities. • Commitment to examine and challenge own racial attitudes and biases. • Willingness to admit own limitations in ability to be open to talking about the influence race has on individuals' sense of self. • Demonstrates genuine respect for varying racial perspectives.	culture-specific courses (e.g., women's issues, Latino/a, and GLB courses), and it may be infused into the core curriculum (e.g., ethics, assessment, multicultural, career counseling, research, human growth and development, and clinical courses). • Providing therapy, under supervision, to clients representing racial diversity in practicum experiences. • Receiving supervision from psychotherapists knowledgeable and skilled in working with racial issues. • Seeking additional study and professional development opportunities (e.g., to attain knowledge of the history of the racial groups in America). Topics to be covered in didactic training include: • Relation of race competency to multicultural competency. • Relationship of racial worldviews to individual and cultural differences (e.g., including age, gender, sexual orientation, SES, and ethnicity). • Basic research literature describing the relevance of race to wellness and physical health, as well as mental health. • Definitions of *race*, *ethnicity*, and *culture*. Trainers and teachers could offer students enrolled in multicultural diversity courses an option to research race and racism.

Table 9.3 Developmental-Level Competencies III

READINESS LEVEL—ENTRY TO PROFESSIONAL PRACTICE	
Competencies	Learning Process and Activities
Knowledge	Knowledge of: • Literature on the relationship between race and mental and physical health; knowledge of the range of possible racial client issues. • Beliefs and behaviors that are considered normative and healthy within client's racial group. • Community resources, including leaders from the community. • Understanding that working with racial issues is an aspect of multicultural counseling competency.	In the earlier stages of training, students solidified their professional knowledge base and attained appropriate values and attitudes while developing increasingly sophisticated clinical skills. At the level of Entry to Professional Practice, psychotherapists have attained the full range of competencies in the domains expected of all independent practitioners. Preparation for this level of competency takes place through closely supervised clinical work, augmented by professional reading, personal exploration, and training opportunities such as professional development and training seminars.
Skills	Skills are demonstrated by the ability to: • Perform a basic assessment of clients' racial identity and worldviews to assess the relevance	Clinical supervisors observe students' clinical work, provide training in assessment, case

(continued)

Table 9.3   Developmental-Level Competencies III (*continued*)

READINESS LEVEL—ENTRY TO PROFESSIONAL PRACTICE	
Competencies	Learning Process and Activities
of racial issues to therapy; assess for contraindications. • Diagnose and formulate appropriate treatment plans that are sensitive to the client's spiritual worldview, including how multiple systems and individual differences impact client. • Identify the limits of one's own competency with racial issues and refer appropriately. • Form a trusting therapeutic relationship with clients so that clients may express racial concerns if relevant and provide basic therapeutic interventions. • Use supervision to enhance working with members of all racial groups. • Establish effective consultation relationships with community resources. • Create climate in which supervisees and trainees feel safe to talk about racial issues.	conceptualization, and treatment planning, and challenge supervisees to examine their countertransference reactions, biases, and values to develop their supervisees' clinical competency with race and racial issues. Additional methods by which students can attain competency at this level include: • Seeking opportunities to provide therapy to clients representing racial diversity. • Supervision provided by supervisors knowledgeable and skilled in working with racial issues. • Self-directed study and professional development opportunities. • Internship and postdoctoral seminar training in racial issues. • Presenting and participating in clinical case conferences that include discussion of racial aspects of cases.
Values and Attitudes Awareness of own racial identity and associated biases, willingness to continually broaden self-knowledge, and commitment to expanding knowledge of racial belief systems as part of multicultural competency enhancement.	

Table 9.4   Developmental-Level Competencies IV

READINESS LEVEL—ADVANCED PRACTICE AND SPECIALIZATION	
Competencies	Learning Process and Activities
Knowledge Extensive knowledge of: • Literature regarding the experiences of the races in America. • Racial identity development models. • Impact of racial experiences upon human development. • Racial traditions.	Psychotherapists who have a particular interest in racial aspects of diversity as they apply to clinical work may seek to attain advanced levels of competency. Learning activities will vary depending on the psychotherapist's unique background, established competencies, and interest areas. For example, psychotherapists working in college counseling center settings might explore a client's racial identity as it relates to his or her adjustment to the campus. Similarly, psychotherapists working with a client who has suffered the loss of a loved one might inquire about religion as a source of support. Regardless of the focus area, learning activities can include: • Professional reading (information about diverse racial beliefs; empirical studies, and literature on theory and practice).
Skills Advanced skills in: • Providing a variety of interventions taking into consideration the race of the client. • Integrating knowledge of race (racial identity, religion) into treatment. • Proactively sharing knowledge of racial issues in the work setting with members of other mental health professions. • Differentiating between healthy and unhealthy expressions with full knowledge of the wide range of multiculturally appropriate expressions.	

READINESS LEVEL—ADVANCED PRACTICE AND SPECIALIZATION

Competencies		Learning Process and Activities
Values and Attitudes	• Provide effective supervision to trainees working with client racial issues. Well-integrated values and attitudes demonstrated by the following: • Continually engages in broadening knowledge of resources and for continuing professional development. • Actively cultivates relationships with community leaders. • Involved in local and national groups and organizations relevant to racial issues (e.g., National Conference on Race and Ethnicity). • Independently and proactively provides ethical and legal consultation and supervision to trainees and other professionals. • Works for social justice to enhance understanding among individuals with different faith beliefs. • Independently monitors own racial identity in relation to work with others with awareness and sensitivity to varying racial worldviews.	• Teaching. • Attending and leading educational workshops. • Peer consultation groups. • Consultation with knowledgeable mental health professionals. • Participation in unfamiliar racial events (i.e., attending an event where you are likely to be in the racial minority). This could include attending a religious service, class, etc.

REFERENCES

American Psychological Association. (2003). Guidelines on multicultural education, training, research, practice, and organizational change for psychologists. *American Psychologist, 58,* 377–402.

American Psychological Association. (2007). Assessment of Competency Benchmarks Work Group: A developmental model for defining and measuring competence in professional psychology. Product of the Assessment of Competency Benchmarks Work Group convened by the APA Board of Educational Affairs in collaboration with the Council of Chairs of Training Councils (CCTC).

Bruno, D. E. (2002). Racial identity and psychological adjustment among African-American college students. [Unpublished thesis.] New Britain: Central Connecticut State University.

Burkard, A. W., Juarez-Huffaker M., & Ajmere, K. (2003). White racial identity attitudes as a predictor of client perceptions of cross-cultural working alliances. *Journal of Multicultural Counseling and Development, 31*(4), 226–244.

Cardemil, E. V., & Battle, C. L. (2003). Guess who's coming to therapy? Getting comfortable with conversations about race and ethnicity in psychotherapy. *Professional Psychology: Research and Practice, 34,* 278–286.

Carter, R. T. (1995). *The influence of race and racial identity in psychotherapy: Toward a racially inclusive model.* New York: Wiley.

Carter, R. T. (2003). Becoming racially and culturally competent: The racial-cultural counseling laboratory. *Journal of Multicultural Counseling and Development, 31*(1), 20–30.

Carter, R. T. (2005). Teaching racial-cultural counseling competence: A racially inclusive model. In R. T. Carter (Ed.), *Handbook of racial-cultural psychology and counseling: Training and practice* (Vol. 1, pp. 36–56). Hoboken, NJ: Wiley.

Carter, R. T. (2007). Racism and psychological and emotional injury: Recognizing and assessing race-based traumatic stress. *The Counseling Psychologist, 35,* 13–105.

Carter, R. T., & Cook, D. (1992). A culturally relevant perspective for understanding the career paths of visible racial/ethnic group people. In Z. Liebowitz & D. Lea (Eds.), *Adult career development* (2nd ed., pp. 192–217). Washington, DC: National Career Development Association.

Carter, R. T., & Pieterse, A. L. (2005). Race: A social and psychological analysis of the term and its meaning. In R. T. Carter (Ed.), *Handbook of Racial-Cultural Psychology and Counseling, Volume 1* (pp. 41–63). Hoboken, NJ: Wiley.

Collins, N. M., & Pieterse, A. L. (2007). Critical incident analysis based training: An approach for developing active racial/cultural awareness. *Journal of Counseling & Development, 85*(4), 14–23.

Constantine, M. G., & Ladany, N. (2001). New visions for defining and assessing multicultural counseling competence. In J. G. Ponterotto, J. M. Casas, L. A. Suzuki, & Alexander, C. M. (Eds.). *Handbook of multicultural counselling* (2nd ed., pp. 482–498). Thousand Oaks, CA: Sage.

Cross, W. E. (1991). *Shades of black: Diversity in African-American identity*. Philadelphia: Temple University Press.

D'Andrea, M. (2005). Continuing the cultural liberation and transformation of counseling psychology. *The Counseling Psychologist, 33*, 524–537.

DaCosta, K. M. (2007). *Making multiracials: State, family, and market in the redrawing of the color line*. Stanford, CA: Stanford University Press.

Day-Vines, N. L., Wood, S. M., Grothaus, T., Craigen, L., Holman, A., Dotson-Blake, K. et al. (2007). Broaching the subjects of race, ethnicity and culture during the counseling process. *Journal of Counseling & Development, 85*, 401–409.

de las Fuentes (2007). Applying the Multicultural Guidelines to Latina/o American populations. In M. G. Constantine (Ed.), *Clinical practice with people of color: A guide to becoming culturally competent*. New York: Teachers College Press.

Delgado-Romero, E. A., Galvan, N., Maschino, P. & Rowland, M. (2005). Race and ethnicity in empirical counseling and counseling psychology research: A 10-year review. *The Counseling Psychologist, 33*(4), 419–448.

Din-Dzietham, R., Nembhard, W. N., Collins, R., & Davis, S. K. (2004). Perceived stress following race-based discrimination at work is associated with hypertension in African-Americans: The Metro Atlanta Health Disease Study, 1999–2001. *Social Science and Medicine, 58*, 449–461.

Gushue, G. V., & Constantine, M. G. (2007). Color-blind racial attitudes and white racial identity attitudes in psychology trainees. *Professional Psychology: Research and Practice, 38*(3), 321–328.

Helms, J. E. (1984). Toward a theoretical explanation of the effects of race on counseling: A black and white model. *The Counseling Psychologist, 12*, 153–165.

Helms, J. E. (1990). *Black and white racial identity: Theory, research and practice*. Westport, CT: Greenwood.

Helms, J. E. (1994). The conceptualization of racial identity and other "racial" constructs. In E. J. Trickett, R. J. Watts, & D. Birmen (Eds.), *Human diversity: Perspectives on people in context* (pp. 285–311). San Francisco: Jossey-Bass.

Helms, J. E. (1995). An update of Helms's White and People of Color Racial Identity Models. In J. G. Ponterotto, J. M. Casas, L. A. Suzuki, & C. M. Alexander (Eds.), *Handbook of multicultural counseling* (pp. 181–198). Thousand Oaks, CA: Sage.

Helms, J. E. (1996). Toward a methodology for measuring and assessing racial as distinguished from ethnic identity. In G. R. Sodowsky, & J. Impara (Eds.). *Multicultural assessment in counseling and clinical Psychology*. Lincoln, NE: Buros Institute of Mental Measurement.

Helms, J. E. (2001). An update of Helms's white and people of color racial identity models. In J. G. Ponterotto, J. M. Casas, L. A. Suzuki, & C. M. Alexander (Eds.), *Handbook of multicultural counselling* (2nd ed., pp. 181–198). Thousand Oaks, CA: Sage.

Helms, J. E. (2005). Challenging issues of reliability as reflected in evaluation of the White Racial Identity Attitude Scale. In R. T. Carter (Ed.), *Handbook of racial-cultural psychology and counseling: Theory and research* (Vol. 1, 2nd ed., pp. 360–389). Hoboken, NJ: Wiley.

Horowitz, J. L., Garber, J., Ciesla, J. A., Young, J. F., & Mufson, L. (2007). Prevention of depressive symptoms in adolescents: A randomized trial of cognitive-behavior and interpersonal prevention programs. *Journal of Consulting and Clinical Psychology, 75*(5), 693–706.

Jones, J. M. (2003). Constructing race and deconstructing racism: A cultural psychology approach. In G. Bernal, J. E. Trimble, A. K. Burlew, & F. T. L. Leong (Eds.), *Handbook of racial and ethnic minority psychology* (pp. 276–0290). Thousand Oaks, CA: Sage.

Juby, H. L., & Concepcion, W. R. (2005). Ethnicity: The term and its meaning. In Carter, R. T. (Ed.), *Handbook of racial-cultural psychology and counseling, Volume 1* (pp. 26–40). Hoboken, NJ: Wiley.

Knox, S., Burkard, A. W., Suzuki, L. A., & Ponterotto, J. G. (2003). African-American and European

American therapists' experiences of addressing race in cross-racial psychotherapy dyads. *Journal of Counseling Psychology, 50,* 466–481.

LaRoche, M. J., & Maxie, A. (2003). Ten considerations in addressing cultural differences in psychotherapy. *Professional Psychology: Research and Practice, 34,* 180–186.

Lopez, H. I. (2000). The social construction of race. In R. Delgado & J. Stefancic (Eds.), *Critical race theory: The cutting edge* (2nd ed., pp. 163–175). Philadelphia: Temple University Press.

Maxie, A. C., Arnold, D. H., & Stephenson, M. (2006). Do therapists address ethnic and racial differences in cross-cultural psychotherapy? *Psychotherapy: Theory, Research, Practice, Training, 43*(1), 85–98.

McCowan, C. J., & Alston, R. J. (1998). Racial identity, African self-consciousness and career decision making in African-American college women. *Journal of Multicultural Counseling & Development, 26*(1), 216–235.

McGoldrick, M., Gerson, R., & Shellenberger, S. (1999). *Genograms: Assessment and intervention* (2nd ed.). New York: Guilford Press.

McIntosh, P. (1988). White privilege: Unpacking the invisible knapsack. Excerpted from Working Paper 189, *White privilege and male privilege: A personal account of coming to see correspondences through work in women's studies.* Wellesley College Center for Research on Women, Wellesley MA 02181.

National Council of Schools and Programs in Professional Psychology (2007, August 15). *Competency Developmental Achievement Levels (DALs) of the National Council of Schools and Programs in Professional Psychology (NCSPP).* Retrieved February 10, 2009, from http://www.ncspp.info/DALof%20NCSPP%209-21-07.pdf

Neville, H. A., Heppner, M., Louie, C., Thompson, C., Brooks, L., & Baker, C. (1996). The impact of multicultural training on white racial identity attitudes and therapy competencies. *Professional Psychology: Research and Practice, 27,* 83–89.

Neville, H. A., Lilly, R. L., Duran, G., Lee, R., & Browne, L. (2000). Construction and initial validation of the Color-Blind Racial Attitudes Scale (CoBRAS). *Journal of Counseling Psychology, 47,* 59–70.

Neville, H. A., Spanierman, L., & Doan, B-T. (2006). Exploring the association between color-blind racial ideology and multicultural counseling competencies. *Cultural Diversity and Ethnic Minority Psychologists, 12*(2), 275–290.

Omi, M., & Winant, H. (1986). *Racial formation in the U.S. from the 1960s to the 1980s.* New York: Routledge.

Ponterotto, J. G, Fuertes, J. N., & Chen, E. C. (2000). Models of multicultural counseling. In S. D. Brown & R. W. Lent (Eds.), *Handbook of counseling psychology* (3rd ed., p. 639). New York: Wiley.

Ruiz, A. S. (1990). Ethnic identity: Crisis and resolution. *Journal of Multicultural Counseling and Development, 18,* 29–40.

Sanchez-Hucles, J., & Jones, N. (2005). Breaking the silence around race in training, practice, and research. *The Counseling Psychologist, 33,* 547–558.

Satcher, D. (2000). Mental health: A report of the Surgeon General—executive summary. *Professional Psychology: Research and Practice, 31*(1), 5–13.

Smith, T. B., Constantine, M. G., Dunn, T. W., Dinehart, J. M., & Montoya, J. A. (2006). Multicultural education in the mental health professions: A meta-analytic review. *Journal of Counseling Psychology, 53,* 132–145.

Sodowsky, G. R. (1996). *Multicultural assessment in counseling and clinical psychology.* Lincoln, NE: Buros Institute of Mental Instruments.

Spanierman, L. B., & Poteat, V.P. (2005). Moving beyond complacency to commitment: Multicultural research in counseling psychology. *The Counseling Psychologist, 33,* 513–523.

Speight, S. L. (2007). Internalized racism: One more piece of the puzzle. *The Counseling Psychologist, 35* (1), 126–134.

Spickard, P. R. (1992). The illogic of American racial categories. In M. P. P. Root (Ed.), *Racially mixed people in America* (pp. 12–23). Newbury Park, CA: Sage.

Sue, D. W., Bernier, J. B., Durran, M., Feinberg, L., Pederson, P., & Smith, E., et al. (1982). Position paper: Cross-cultural counseling competencies. *The Counseling Psychologist, 10,* 45–52.

Sue, D. W., & Sue, D. (1999). *Counseling the culturally different: Theory and practice* (3rd ed.). New York: Wiley.

Sue, D. W., & Sue, D. (2003). *Counseling the culturally diverse: Theory and practice* (4th ed.). New York: Wiley.

Thompson, V. L. S., & Alexander, H. (2006). Therapists' race and African-American clients' reactions to therapy. *Psychotherapy: Theory, Research, Practice, Training, 43*(1), 99–110.

Thompson, C. E., Shin, C. E., & Stephens, J. (2005). Race and research evidence. In R. T. Carter (Ed.,)

Handbook of racial-cultural psychology and counseling: Theory and research (Vol. 1, pp. 277–294). Hoboken, NJ: Wiley.

Trimble, J. E., Helms, J. E., & Root, M. P. P. (2003). Social and psychological perspectives on ethnic and racial identity. In N. G. Bernal, J. E. Trimble, A. K., Burlew, Y. F. T. L. Leong (Eds.), *Handbook of racial and ethnic minority psychology* (pp. 239–275). Thousand Oaks, CA: Sage.

U. S. Census Bureau. (2002). Racial and ethnic segregation in the United States: 1980–2000. Census 2000 Special Report.

Utsey, S. O., & Gernat, C. A. (2002). White racial identity attitudes and the ego defense mechanisms used by white counselor trainees in racially provocative counseling situations. *Journal of Counseling and Development, 80,* 475–483.

Utsey, S. O., Hammar, L., & Gernat, C. A., (2005). Examining the reactions of white, black, and Latino/a counseling psychologists to a study of racial issues in counseling and supervision dyads. *The Counseling Psychologist, 33*(4), 565–573.

Vinson, T. S., & Neimeyer, G. J., (2003). The relationship between racial identity development and multicultural counseling competency: A second look. *Journal of Multicultural Counseling and Development, 31,* 262–277.

Young, G., & Davis-Russell, E. (2002). The vicissitudes of cultural competence: Dealing with difficulty classroom dialogue. In E. Davis-Russell (Ed.), *The California school of professional psychology handbook of multicultural education, research, and training* (pp. 37–53). San Francisco: Jossey-Bass.

Zetzer, H. A., & Shockley, M. E. (2005). *Build the field and they will come: Multicultural organizational development for mental health agencies.* Multicultural Access and Treatment Demonstration Project: Antioch University, Santa Barbara, Child Abuse Listening and Mediation, Family Service Agency of Santa Barbara, & University of California, Santa Barbara.

CHAPTER 10

COMPETENCIES FOR WORKING WITH SEXUAL ORIENTATION AND MULTIPLE CULTURAL IDENTITIES

BARRY A. SCHREIER and KIM DUDLEY LASSITER

INTRODUCTION

Gay, lesbian, bisexual, transgendered, queer, questioning, curious, interested, allied, and intersexed (GLBTQQCIAI) has become an alphabet soup that challenges mental health practitioners to stay current in order to remain competent with a rapidly changing population (American Psychological Association, 2000). GLBTQQCIAI has had an extended evolution from its initial term of *homosexuality* to its current, more encompassing term of *queer*. DeAngelis (2002) noted in the *Monitor on Psychology* that sexual orientation and sexual identity have become increasingly complex and ever-changing constructs. The newest generation of those once called LGB is now seeking self-definitions that transcend existing categories. As DeAngelis stated, "Many LGBT youth, for instance, now call themselves 'queer' as a blanket term for their community" and "it's more common for today's young LGBT people to express and accept fluid gender and sexual identities" (DeAngelis, 2002, p. 42).

It is an exciting time in the evolution of theory and research regarding the experiences, development, and self-definition of sexual orientation and sexual identity. The knowledge base is shifting rapidly in response to an increased awareness of ever-expanding constructions of sexual identities. Sexual orientation and sexual identity are therefore part of a continually changing field of study and practice for mental health practitioners (Minton, 1997). Garnets (2002) stated, "Failure to recognize the complexity of contemporary identities will seriously limit the effectiveness of psychologist's work" (p. 126). Articulating precise terminology to depict such rapidly changing phenomena is a challenge, and for those new to working with sexual orientation and sexual identity, the acronyms and distinctions can be confusing.

The transforming landscape associated with sexual orientation and sexual identity has led many to conclude that mental health practitioners are insufficiently trained to effectively and ethically work with sexual orientation and sexual identity (Anhalt, Morris, Scotti, & Cohen, 2003; Biaggio, Orchard, Larson, Petrino, & Mihara, 2003; Murphy, Rawlings, & Howe, 2002; Phillips, 2000; Schneider, Brown, & Glassgold, 2002). The purpose of this chapter, then, is to provide mental health practitioners, trainers, programmers, researchers, students, and supervisors with a base of knowledge, sensitivity, and skills for working ethically and effectively in this ever-developing domain of practice. This chapter includes: (a) terminology; (b) historical context of sexual orientation and sexual identity, including the development of treatment standards; (c) elements of competency, including knowledge, skills, and attitudes/values; (d) specific elements of clinical interventions, including assessment, treatment techniques, and treatment planning; (e) resources for clinicians, students, teachers, and supervisors; (f) and developmentally based competency guidelines. Case vignettes are used to illustrate theoretical and pragmatic discussions. Finally, resources (e.g., experiential activities and instructional plans) are provided both for the formal training of mental health practitioners and for self-directed lifelong learning.

TERMINOLOGY

There are a number of terms that have been used to describe sexuality, many of which have been used interchangeably (Worthington, 2004), including: *sexual orientation, sexuality, affectional identity, affectional preference, sexual identity, sexual preference, sexual orientation identity,* and so on (APA, 2001). There has also been a differentiation made between *sexual orientation* as something innately predispositional and *sexual identity* as awareness of and affiliation with one's innate sexual predisposition (Worthington, Savoy, Dillon, & Vernaglia, 2002). In essence, sexual identity is a function of adaptation while sexual orientation is an innate predisposition (Ellis & Mitchell, 2000).

The discrete relationship between sexual orientation and sexual identity are highlighted by *essentialist* and *constructivist* theories that underlie these two terms and guide current usage (Broido, 2000). Essentialist theory posits that sexual orientation is the fixed, unitary, inborn nature of an individual (LeVay, 1993) and is further defined by the innate sexual and affectional attraction to another of the same, opposite, and/or both sexes (Bell, Weinberg, & Hammersmith, 1981). Alternatively, constructivist theory characterizes sexual identity as fluid and constructed by complex configurations of societal, historical, intrapsychic, interpersonal, and other factors (Patterson, 1995; Stein, 1997). Definitions of *sexual orientation* and *sexual identity* in mainstream psychological literature are primarily based in essentialist theory and primarily reflect Western culture (Broido, 2000; Horowitz & Newcomb, 2001).

For the current chapter, the authors use the terms *sexual orientation* and *sexual identity (SO/SI)* in order to acknowledge the traditional distinction between the two constructs (Worthington, 2004) as well as to broadly represent the multiplicity of variables inherent in sexuality, which include: desire, identity, needs, values, expression, affiliation, identification, arousal, biological sex, behavior, attraction, gender-object choice, politics, and affection. SO/SI provides the broadest umbrella under which to refer to the

myriad constructs and will be used throughout this chapter unless referring to historically based models and theories, where the language of the time is referenced.

Any exploration of sexuality cannot be conducted without reference to gender, as the two are inextricably linked (E. Blackwood, personal communication, November 11, 2004). However, due to the complexity of the interface between gender and SO/SI and the space constraints of a single chapter, we highly recommend Chapters 7, 14, and 16, which discuss men, gender identity/expression, and women respectively. This can provide content concerning the overlap of gender with sexual orientation that is needed to competently provide service to clients with complex, multiple cultural identities.

HISTORICAL CONTEXT OF SEXUAL ORIENTATION AND SEXUAL IDENTITY

The term *SO/SI* developed out of a century of study of homosexuality and bisexuality starting in the later nineteenth century, including works by Sigmund Freud and other psychology pioneers (Trujillo, 1997). These studies were typically based on the perspective of homosexuality as deviant and used observation as the primary method of examination. More rigorous empirical studies began in the 1930s (Minton, 1997), one example being the work of Alfred Kinsey, who conducted what was the most empirically controlled research of the time to develop the "Kinsey Scale" (Kinsey, Pomeroy, & Martin, 1948). Kinsey presented sexual orientation on a six-point scale based on behaviors, psychological responses, and physical attractions ranging from exclusively heterosexual to exclusively homosexual. This conceptualization placed homosexuality and bisexuality on a continuum of naturally occurring phenomenon to be understood rather than pathologized (Kinsey et al., 1948). Through Kinsey's work, the complexities of SO were illuminated and the simplicity of a dichotomous model based merely on physiological arousal was challenged. Kinsey's work was followed by another landmark study by Hooker (1957), who found no differences between samples of heterosexual and homosexual men on projective tests of personality characteristics. Hooker's work was pivotal in de-pathologizing SO and bringing it into the realm of empirical study.

Research focused on SI developed in the late 1970s. The work of Cass (1979; 1984), Troiden (1989), and others (e.g., Shively & DeCecco, 1977) established stage models of SI formation suggesting a step-by-step developmental progression individuals take in developing their SI. As with other stage models in psychology, the model proposed that individuals could stagnate at any one stage or progress through all stages. Growth was thought to occur as the individual addressed discrepancies between personal and societal self-perceptions. These models represented a shift away from Kinsey's more fluid continuum of SO to more discrete categorical approaches to SI. At the same time that stage models were being developed, the American Psychiatric Association declassified homosexuality as a mental disorder (American Psychiatric Association, 1973) as did the APA (Conger, 1975, p. 633).

As the research and conceptualization of SO/SI became more sophisticated, stage models came under criticism as being: (a) too simple and linear; (b) based mostly on nonempirical observational methodology; (c) negligent of bisexuality; (d) confounding of individual with group identities; (e) too discrete in their categorizations of sexuality; and (f) noninclusive of multiracial, multiethnic, and gender identities (McCarn & Fassinger, 1996; Reynolds & Hanjorgiris, 2000). In response to these criticisms, models were developed that focused on the more complex nature of multiple identity development and were inclusive, for the first time, of bisexuality (Klein, Sepekoff, & Wolf, 1985).

The demand for additional sophistication and complexity deepened as SO/SI was conceptualized alongside other cultural identities, such as race, gender, ethnicity, and religion. Coleman (1987) expanded on Klein's work to include gender and gender identity when conceptualizing SO/SI. Morales (1989) and Arredondo (1999) developed identity models for racial-minority gay men and lesbians that acknowledged community belonging, identity negotiations, ethnicity, culture, gender, language, physical ability, and social class. Reynolds and Pope (1991) developed a model that took into account the effects and implications of broader sociological factors such as oppression as it related to multiple identity development. As Garnets (2002) stated, "No single element of identity, be it race, ethnicity, class, disability, gender, or sexual orientation can truly be understood except in relation to others" (p. 126).

The evolution of SO/SI models has more recently expanded to include the study of heterosexuality, which was previously assumed to be "normative" and thus not in need of empirical analysis (Greene, 2003). Worthington and Mohr (2002) put forth a theory of heterosexual identity development, adding it as an SO/SI appropriate for study.

To illustrate the complexity of multiple identity conceptualizations of SO/SI, consider the following case of Markesh, who is 31 years of age and works in the United States on a 5-year grant that provides him with experience he will eventually apply in his home country. Markesh's case provides an excellent example of multiple identities and the fluid, nonstatic nature of SI. Here he speaks of his experience of his SO/SI in his first session with his individual therapist (see Case Vignette 10.1).

Markesh's circumstances are complex and multifaceted. While expressing the presence of same-sex behavior, he also expresses a previous lack of having a sense of SI associated with his SO. While engaging in same-sex activity, he had not felt the need to define himself as gay or bi to others until he was introduced to the concept of SI. This vignette also demonstrates the influence of culture and how Markesh perceives a same-sex SI to be part of who he is in the United States, although a same-sex SI will not be practical or safe once he returns to his country of origin, even if same-sex SO is.

CASE VIGNETTE 10.1

I am not sure whether I am, you know, that way, and I want to see if it is the case or not. I am feeling confused and stressed-out about it. There is not even a word for this in my country and I do not know how I would even explain this at home. I was with a guy once, I mean, I kissed him, well, he kissed me and I didn't stop him. We had sex and it was very good. He is the one who told me I was gay as I would not have considered it otherwise. My father is very devout and would never approve; I would have to come home immediately. I am not sure why Americans call it "gay" as there is nothing gay about it. Being Muslim does not help. I am told I will go to Hell. I pray and am smart enough to know that Allah looks out for us. Allah does not allow anything to be that Allah does not want. White friends see me as brown since 9/11. And Moslem friends must never know as they would kill me. I am interested more in White guys, but they do not find me attractive. This is okay for me now, here, but I will need to change to go home.

ELEMENTS OF COMPETENCY

The recent literature on competencies in professional psychology (Hatcher & Lassiter, 2007; Kaslow, 2004; Rodolfa, Bent, Eisman, Nelson, Rehm, & Ritchie, 2005) describes competency in terms of its knowledge, skill, values, and attitude components. In terms of providing guidance for educators and self-directed learners, some offerings are level specific, such as the Practicum Competencies Outline (Hatcher & Lassiter, 2007), which is targeted at doctoral-level pre-internship training, whereas others cover the breadth of one's professional development and career, such as the Cube Model (Rodolfa et al., 2005) and the Competency Benchmarks document (APA, 2007). Because few graduate programs offer courses focused on SO/SI, practitioners aiming to be SO/SI competent may have to be self-directed learners intentionally seeking opportunities to build knowledge and skill in this domain.

Following the format of the Competency Benchmarks document, we provide suggestions for competence at four levels of professional training, each building upon the previous: (1) Entry to Practicum, (2) Entry to Internship, (3) Entry to Professional Practice, and (4) Advanced Practice and Specialization. Despite steady growth of SO/SI scholarship, competencies for counseling around SO/SI have not been empirically specified (Israel, Ketz, Detrie, Burke, & Shulman, 2003) but instead rely for the most part on the accumulated wisdom of seasoned educators and scholars (Hatcher & Lassiter, 2007). The reader is encouraged therefore to treat our allocations of competencies to specific readiness levels of practice as tentative pending empirical verification.

The allocation of SO/SI knowledge, skills, values, and attitudes to the four readiness levels described above was accomplished through review of professional guideline documents (APA 2000, 2003), the competencies and training literatures (e.g., the Association for Lesbian, Gay, Bisexual, and Transgender Issues in Counseling [ALGBTIC], 2008), and comparing skill acquisition with parallel domains, specifically multicultural counseling competencies (Firestein, 2007; Israel & Selvidge, 2003).

KNOWLEDGE

The knowledge element of SO/SI competence falls into three categories: cultural knowledge, theoretical and empirical knowledge, and knowledge regarding SO/SI treatment concerns, or frequent presenting problems.

Prior to beginning practicum, students are learning about multiculturalism, inclusive of SO/SI (Kocarek & Pelling, 2003). Specifically, they are learning that all people, themselves included, are cultural beings with multiple overlapping and intersecting identities, which include but are not limited to gender, SO/SI, race, ethnicity, nationality, age, ability status, spirituality/religion, socioeconomic status (SES), social class, and appearance (Beckstead & Israel, 2007). Therefore, no one is "just gay." Rather, an individual might be a lower-SES, young gay Latino Catholic, or an upper-SES, retired bisexual Jewish female. While this complexity may seem daunting for novice clinicians, it represents the rich diversity of human experience and the reason we must always consider our clients as people of complex identities.

As the student progresses through graduate training in preparation for internship, theoretical and empirical knowledge is introduced. SO/SI development models are a critical component of this content, including knowledge of essentialist and constructionist theories, human sexuality and development across the lifespan, and the discrete and shared variance between sex, sexuality, and SO/SI. Students acknowledge the diversity that always accompanies SO/SI (Garrett & Barret, 2003; Greene, 2007) and through assessment courses learn appropriate use of standard assessment instruments for SO/SI, paying particular attention to the potential for bias (ALGBTIC, 2008; Matthews, 2007). Through multicultural course content and infusion of SO/SI into other clinical courses and practicum experiences, students acquire general knowledge of the beliefs, practices, language, and traditions of specific SO/SI cultures as well as the availability of community resources and how to access them. It is also at the graduate level that students are introduced to the concepts of bi/homophobia, bi/homonegativity, internalized bi/homophobia, heterosexual bias, and heterosexual privilege (Biaggio, et al., 2003). As stated by Garrett and Barret (2003), "The question is not 'Are you prejudiced against gay people?' but 'How do your often unconscious prejudices and biases about gay and lesbian people influence your counseling?'" (p. 140). In this context, students understand myths and stereotypes

about SO/SI (i.e., misinformation) and recognize that, as a diverse community embedded in a heterosexist society, racism, sexism, and other forms of prejudice also exist within SO/SI communities (Mulick & Wright, 2002).

Upon completion of internship and entry to independent professional practice, the SO/SI-competent mental health practitioner acquires greater depth and breadth of both cultural and theoretical/empirical knowledge. There is greater familiarity with current research and scholarship on SO/SI issues, including the relationship between SO/SI and mental and physical health, and controversial "reorientation" or conversion therapies and the identity incongruence experienced by many between their spiritual/religious identity and SO/SI. Mental health practitioners at this level are knowledgeable concerning the ethical and methodological issues involved in conducting research with SO/SI and incorporate SO/SI variables in their research (ALGBTIC, 2008).

It is at this level that mental health practitioners are beginning to grasp the breadth of treatment concerns common to working with SO/SI (Garnets, Hancock, Cochran, Goodchilds, & Peplau, 1991). As many authors have noted, (Fassinger & Arseneau, 2007; Matthews, 2007; Murphy et al., 2002), some treatment foci are specific to SO/SI status, such as coming out and finding community, whereas others are not, such as substance-use disorders or relationship conflicts. However, even with treatment foci common across client populations (partner violence, parenting, medical issues), the mental health practitioner at this level of competence understands how the context of client SO/SI influences case conceptualization and treatment interventions (Biaggio, et al., 2003; Liddle, 2007). Treatment concerns common to SO/SI are outlined in the chart on the following page.

The mental health practitioner who engages in advanced practice and specialization in SO/SI has a correspondingly deeper and more sophisticated understanding of the knowledge base, including cultural (SO/SI histories and traditions), theoretical (SO/SI development models and case conceptualization), and empirical

TREATMENT CONCERNS

- Coming out and differences in the process, depending on when in life it occurs.
- Relationships, with limited templates for how healthy relationships work.
- Family, including family of choice, family of origin, parenting, and adoption issues.
- Social support/community building.
- Health-care interface, including health concerns of specific SO/SI populations (e.g., impact of HIV/AIDS on the gay community).
- Sexuality (including specific sexual practices such as BDSM) and safer sex practices.
- Developmental/lifespan issues: aging, estate management in the absence of supportive legislation.
- Minority stress: hate crimes, multiple oppression, discrimination, violence.
- Vocational/career/workplace issues (e.g., discrimination, the lavender ceiling, coming-out decisions and the impact on work life).
- Specific diagnostic issues:
    - Substance-use disorders and their higher prevalence among specific SO/SI communities.
    - Domestic-partner violence and the risks of coming out to health and safety systems when seeking assistance.
    - Increased risk of suicide due to impact of multiple oppressions, limited support networks, and depression.
- Spirituality/religion and potential incongruence or conflict with SO/SI.

literatures. Those specializing in SO/SI practice are also knowledgeable regarding social, legal, and political policies affecting SO/SI, that is, antidiscrimination laws in the workplace (Fassinger, 2008), as well as current events and their potential impact on clients and their families (i.e., state legislative actions affecting same-sex marriage options; Patterson, 2007; Stevenson, 2007).

SKILLS

In their recent review of research on psychotherapy, Bieschke, Paul, and Blasko (2007) "conclude that LGB individuals often enter into therapeutic situations uncertain of the reception they will receive" (p. 294). Among the most critical of skills, then, is creating a sufficiently safe therapeutic environment to permit an open discussion of SO/SI issues. In this context, safety is characterized

as a "supportive, validating, and nonjudgmental environment" (Potocznik, 2007; p. 139). Safety is communicated in a variety of ways, signaling that the organization and the practitioner operating within it are affirming and nurturing of a variety of SO/SIs. Examples include: inclusive language use throughout the therapeutic process from telephone pre-screenings to ongoing individual appointments, inclusive language on paperwork, magazines and literature in waiting areas, and the display of friendly symbols in waiting areas and therapy rooms (Biaggio et al., 2003; Matthews, 2007).

Clinicians in training are routinely encouraged not to make assumptions about clients, especially clients culturally different from themselves (Sue, 1998), as assumptions can preempt the gathering of accurate information about clients and their concerns. This unwritten rule is particularly true of competence with SO/SI: Clients of any age or life circumstance may be at any phase in their SO/SI when they enter treatment and their presenting problems may or may not be directly related to their SO/SI status (Liddle, 2007). Inaccurate clinician assumptions regarding SO/SI status can effectively shut down treatment.

The skills of self-reflection leading to self-awareness regarding one's SO/SI attitudes and beliefs is fundamental to communicating genuine respect for varying SO/SI groups. Mental health practitioners at all levels of competence need to be mindful of what they bring to the therapeutic encounter and recognize when they are unable to provide affirmation and nurturance to a client (metacompetence) or be cognizant of the limits of their competence (Hatcher & Lassiter, 2007).

Upon completion of internship and entry to independent professional practice, the SO/SI-competent mental health practitioner is expanding clinical competencies of SO/SI assessment, alliance building, diagnosis, and treatment planning. In particular, practitioners have an enhanced appreciation for and efficacy working with the complexity of multiple identities and their associated stresses and strengths (Bridges, Selvidge, & Matthews, 2003). It is at this stage of professional development that mental health practitioners begin to establish consultative relationships with leaders from various SO/SI communities, provide effective nurturance-based education and training, and engage in SO/SI-inclusive research (e.g., include SO/SI variables in addition to typical demographic variables).

The mental health practitioner who engages in advanced practice and specialization in SO/SI demonstrates culture-specific expertise (Sue, 1998) in providing a variety of interventions (individual, couples, family, and group therapy; community and political/legal advocacy); sophisticated case conceptualization, integrating fluid SO/SI with other cultural identities; proactive sharing of accurate knowledge of SO/SI issues with supervisees and colleagues; SO/SI-affirmative supervision, that is, where all SO/SIs are accepted as equally valid (Halpert, Reinhardt, & Toohey, 2007); and the formulation of research questions and methodologies inclusive of SO/SI (ALGBTIC, 2008; Arnett, 2008; Herek, Kimmel, Amaro, & Melton, 1991).

VALUES AND ATTITUDES

Reflective practice and self-assessment are competencies considered core to a number of domains of professional practice, to the extent they have been described as foundational competencies, "the building blocks of what psychologists do" (Rodolfa et al., 2005, p. 350). The recognition of the importance of reflective practice and the resulting awareness of one's own cultural identities represents the starting line for SO/SI competence (Biaggio, et al., 2003). However, in addition to this cognitive appreciation of reflection and self-awareness, SO/SI competence requires that it be practiced and become a skill and be valued as an ongoing professional activity. Hence, reflective practice and self-awareness is a competency that spans all three competency components: knowledge, skill, and values and attitudes.

At the outset of professional training, students are expected to be willing to engage in self-exploration, to have intellectual curiosity, and to value experiences, attitudes, and belief systems that differ from their own (Hatcher & Lassiter, 2007). Unlike other facets of cultural identity, many students will not have foundational knowledge of SO/SI through their own life experiences, attributable in part to the fact that sexuality is a sensitive topic in most cultures and open, non-defensive reflection on one's own SO/SI is rarely encouraged (Schneider et al., 2002). In addition, "as members of a heterosexist society, all of us, regardless of sexual orientation, bring our heterosexual biases into our work as counselors and therapists" (Bieschke, Perez, & DeBord, 2007, p. 5). As a result, students may be unaware of or misinformed about SO/SI cultural communities at best, defensive and homonegative at worst. This places an added burden on educators and supervisors to provide both accurate SO/SI information and an environment conducive to processing and personalizing it in order to enable students to progress from a position of SO/SI tolerance to one of nurturing SO/SI diversity (Biaggio, et al., 2003).

Additionally, it is important for students, early on, to develop their knowledge and self-awareness as to the variety of negative and positive attitudes when working with SO/SI. Negative attitudes typically associated with SO/SI come under the traditional term of *bi/homophobia*. This is defined as an intense, irrational fear of same-sex relations that becomes overwhelming to a person. In common usage, bi/homophobia is the fear of intimate relationships with persons of the same sex (Pellegrini, 1992). Below are listed four negative homophobic levels and four positive levels of attitudes toward lesbian and gay relationships/people (Riddle, 1985). The competency tables at the end of this chapter reference these attitudes and the growth expected in mental health practitioners as they develop through the competency levels.

Negative Levels of Attitude

1. **Repulsion:** Homosexuality is seen as a "crime against nature." Homosexuals are sick, crazy, immoral, sinful, wicked, and so on. Anything is justified to change them: prison, hospitalization, reorientation/conversion therapy, and electroshock therapy.

2. **Pity:** Heterosexuality is more mature and certainly to be preferred. Any possibility of "becoming straight" should be reinforced, and those who seem to be born "that way" should be pitied.

3. **Tolerance:** Homosexuality is just a phase of adolescent development that many go through and most people "grow out of." Thus, lesbians/gays are less mature than "straights" and should be treated with protectiveness and indulgence.

4. **Acceptance:** Still implies there is something to accept. Characterized by such statements as "You are not a lesbian to me, you are a person!" or "What you do in bed is your own business," or "That's fine with me as long as you don't flaunt it!"

Positive Levels of Attitude

1. **Support:** Work to safeguard the rights of LGBs. People at this level may be uncomfortable themselves, but they are aware of the homophobic climate and the irrational unfairness.

2. **Admiration:** Acknowledges that being LGB in our society takes strength. People at this level are willing to truly examine their homophobic attitudes, values, and behaviors.

3. **Appreciation:** Value the diversity of people and see LGBs as a valid part of that diversity. These people are willing to combat homophobia in themselves and others.

4. **Nurturance:** Assumes that LGBs are indispensable in our society. They view LGBs with genuine affection and delight, and are willing to be allies and advocates.

As training progresses to internship and independent practice, the SO/SI-competent mental health practitioner continues to self-monitor regarding SO/SI biases and expresses willingness "to reexamine a number of traditional notions about psychological health and maturity, love, committed partnership, monogamy, and marriage" (Firestein, 2007, p. 110). Practitioners at this stage of professional development seek opportunities to fill gaps in knowledge and skill, recognize the importance of challenging misinformation or bias about SO/SI (ALGBTIC, 2008; Garnets et al., 1991), acknowledge the role of heterosexual allies in social reform (Stone, 2003), and begin to explore avenues of SO/SI advocacy.

The mental health practitioner who engages in advanced practice and specialization in SO/SI continually broadens his or her knowledge of SO/SI resources and demonstrates commitment through maintaining relationships with SO/SI community leaders and involvement in SO/SI local and national groups and organizations, and engages in advocacy on SO/SI issues (Garnets, 2007; Patterson, 2007). Those engaged in advanced practice proactively provide SO/SI-informed consultation to supervisees and other professionals, modeling awareness of and sensitivity to the varying SO/SI status of others and "develop interventions to prevent and ameliorate the harmful effects of stigma and discrimination" (Fassinger & Arseneau, 2007, p. 43). For such individuals, SO/SI affirmation permeates all professional roles and activities (Bieschke, Perez, & DeBord, 2007).

Research Implications

As mental health practitioners develop their competency with SO/SI, they will have increasing ability to include SO/SI variables in research practices. The use of language and defining variables is a key component. Researchers make use of fundamental concepts (e.g., sexual orientation, sexual identity, homophobia, and so on) when conducting research. As researchers develop greater competency they will turn to more complex concepts as defined by essentialist or constructivist definitions, multiple identities (Arredondo, 1999; Reynolds & Pope, 1991), and analyzing the individual in relationship with social reference groups (Leck, 1994; McCarn & Fassinger, 1996). More complex issues in conducting research on SO/SI in women, as an example, have been addressed by Rothblum (2000) and Rust (2000) and , who noted that women might not define "sexual behavior" in terms of genital contact, and might not define "sexual orientation" based on sexual behavior.

Training Implications

A variety of resources are available for mental health practitioners interested in ongoing training and supervision that include SO/SI. The Guidelines for Psychotherapy with Lesbian, Gay, and Bisexual Clients (APA, 2000), which draws from the APA Code of Ethics (APA, 2002), are especially relevant to the fundamentals of training and supervision. Broad issues identified in the Guidelines encourage mental health practitioners to continually increase their knowledge and understanding of SO/SI issues as well as to explore personally held beliefs, values, attitudes, and biases. Furthermore, the Guidelines support

an understanding of more intermediate concepts such as multiple identities, including generational effects.

As mental health practitioners develop advanced competency, there will be greater focus on increasing complexities in training and supervision. The training issues and strategies cogently articulated by Phillips (2000) and Biaggio et al. (2003) include such complexities as how constructivist and essentialist perspectives on SO/SI can be incorporated into training and supervision. What follows are sample questions that could be used to address educating and training in these two belief systems:

- Does the system or institution hold an essentialist perspective of sexuality?
- Are supervisors knowledgeable about constructivist perspectives of sexuality, and are these perspectives taught in classes or seminars?
- Can constructivist perspectives be infused throughout the curriculum?
- If there is a separate sexuality seminar, are both essentialism and constructivism presented and discussed?
- Is language inclusive of both theories provided throughout training?
- Are the multiple variables subsumed within the terms *sexual orientation*, *sexual identity*, or *sexualities* identified and explored?
- Are models related to sexuality (e.g., of sexual identity) critiqued for the underlying assumptions?
- Are there supervisors who represent various SOs/SIs?
- Are various SOs/SIs affirmed by and connected to the institution or individual?
- Is every individual encouraged or expected to increase self-awareness, knowledge, and sensitivity (and decrease biases) about SO/SI?

Intervention

With the declassification of homosexuality as a mental disorder and the development of increasingly complex multiple-identity models, empirically based standards of clinical practice have been established for mental health practitioners working with people around SO/SI. Division 44 (Society for the Psychological Study of Lesbian, Gay, and Bisexual Issues) of the APA developed "Guidelines for Psychotherapy with Lesbian, Gay, & Bisexual Clients" (APA, 2000), which provided the first organized and comprehensive guidelines for working with SO/SI.

These Guidelines encourage mental health professionals to extend their personal and professional knowledge and understanding of SO/SI and to explore and challenge their associated attitudes and beliefs.

Furthermore, the Guidelines support an understanding of multiple identities, community and family relationships, training and education, the powerful impact of negative societal attitudes

---

Guidelines for Psychotherapy with Lesbian, Gay, and Bisexual Clients

Attitudes Toward Homosexuality and Bisexuality

- Guideline 1. Psychologists understand that homosexuality and bisexuality are not indicative of mental illness.

- Guideline 2. Psychologists are encouraged to recognize how their attitudes and knowledge about lesbian, gay, and bisexual issues may be relevant to assessment and treatment and seek consultation or make appropriate referrals when indicated.

- Guideline 3. Psychologists strive to understand the ways in which social stigmatization (i.e., prejudice, discrimination, and violence) poses risks to the mental health and wellbeing of lesbian, gay, and bisexual clients.

- Guideline 4. Psychologists strive to understand how inaccurate or prejudicial views of homosexuality or bisexuality may affect the client's presentation in treatment and the therapeutic process.

Relationships and Families

- Guideline 5. Psychologists strive to be knowledgeable about and respect the importance of lesbian, gay, and bisexual relationships.

- Guideline 6. Psychologists strive to understand the particular circumstances and challenges facing lesbian, gay, and bisexual parents.

- Guideline 7. Psychologists recognize that the families of lesbian, gay, and bisexual people may include people who are not legally or biologically related.

- Guideline 8. Psychologists strive to understand how a person's homosexual or bisexual orientation may have an impact on his or her family of origin and the relationship to that family of origin.

Issues of Diversity

- Guideline 9. Psychologists are encouraged to recognize the particular life issues or challenges experienced by lesbian, gay, and bisexual members of racial and ethnic minorities that are related to multiple and often conflicting cultural norms, values, and beliefs.

- Guideline 10. Psychologists are encouraged to recognize the particular challenges experienced by bisexual individuals.

- Guideline 11. Psychologists strive to understand the special problems and risks that exist for lesbian, gay, and bisexual youth.

- Guideline 12. Psychologists consider generational differences within lesbian, gay, and bisexual populations, and the particular challenges that may be experienced by lesbian, gay, and bisexual older adults.
- Guideline 13. Psychologists are encouraged to recognize the particular challenges experienced by lesbian, gay, and bisexual individuals with physical, sensory, and/or cognitive/emotional disabilities.

Education

- Guideline 14. Psychologists support the provision of professional education and training on lesbian, gay, and bisexual issues.
- Guideline 15. Psychologists are encouraged to increase their knowledge and understanding of homosexuality and bisexuality through continuing education, training, supervision, and consultation.
- Guideline 16. Psychologists make reasonable efforts to familiarize themselves with relevant mental health, educational, and community resources for lesbian, gay, and bisexual people.

and beliefs, and the importance of generational effects. The Guidelines, divided into four sections, including attitudes, relationships, diversity, and education, are "intended to facilitate the continued systematic development of the profession and to help insure a high level of professional practice by psychologists" (p. 1440).

While the APA has taken a stance in promoting standards of clinical practice for working with SO/SI, society at large lags behind with respect to acknowledging civil and legal rights for people around SO/SI issues and the impact of countervailing conservative religious beliefs about SO/SI (Haldeman, 1994; Miville & Ferguson, 2004). These sociocultural issues, especially concerning religious beliefs, influence mental health practitioners and clients alike and are a significant force affecting the broad practice of mental health.

Similarly, an additional issue pertaining to standards of treatment and spirituality/religion is reorientation therapies, also known as change, conversion, or reparative therapies (Morrow, Beckstead, Hayes, & Haldeman, 2004). Numerous mental health organizations, for example, the APA (1998), the American Psychiatric Association (1973), and the American Counseling Association (1998) have passed resolutions stating that reorientation therapies are based on faulty research methodologies and assumptions. Furthermore, it

is posited that reorientation therapies do not provide the positive outcomes they claim and are conversely the cause of deleterious outcomes (Tozer & McClanahan, 1999). Recently, attempts have been made to depolarize the debate between pro- and anti-reorientation therapists by assisting clients in addressing the conflicts between their spiritual/religious and SO/SI identities (Beckstead & Morrow, 2004). These authors found that instead of engaging in an "ex-gay or out-gay" dichotomy, it is of greater service to attend to clients experiencing distress due to conflict between spirituality and religious beliefs and their SO/SI by assisting them in self-acceptance and positive self-identity development. This can be done through numerous intervention approaches that emotionally "hold" a client and allow identity exploration using accurate information and unconditional support by a therapist and others (Beckstead & Morrow, 2004). This being stated, mainstream psychology remains firm that reorientation therapies do not achieve the outcomes that they purport (Schreier, 1998). Competent mental health practitioners are aware of reorientation therapies, but do not engage in them nor offer them as a viable option. Instead, mental health practitioners engage clients to find positive identity and acceptance that addresses both spirituality/religion and SO/SI identities

CASE VIGNETTE 10.2

"I'm queer and I like it. I have always been queer. It can be confusing at times, as everyone wants me to define myself. I don't mind it all that much; it's just such a big deal with so many others. I have a bunch of straight friends who know I'm queer, but they never mention it, as if it doesn't exist, or I'm no different from them. The butch dykes won't leave me alone and the femme girls treat me like a guy. Maybe I'm a LUG (lesbian until graduation)? I like kissing on girls, but girls don't lead. In fact, I don't like all girls, just some. Maybe I'm a guy? Okay, I do feel like the bottom line is I'm queer. I just don't want the labeling thing to be a major hangup, as it really should be no big woop! I dated a Malaysian guy last year. I told him I was queer and he didn't even know what I was talking about. I liked that he didn't know what I was talking about, he just liked me. But how could he not know anything about this? Does queer not happen in Malaysia?"

and assists in managing the difficulties that can come with identity incongruence (Haldeman, 2004).

INTERVENTION TECHNIQUES

A case example is provided to demonstrate the multiple intersects, fluidity, and complex relationships that SO/SI can present. Katrenia is 20 years of age and is a junior at a large Midwestern university. Katrenia speaks of her experience of her SO/SI in this first session with her individual therapist (see Case Vignette 10.2).

Treatment Plan

Generating treatment plans is often a challenge, particularly for novice mental health practitioners. Given the added complexity of cases involving multiple cultural identities, this task becomes significantly more difficult. What follows is a sample treatment plan, using the information from Case Vignette 10.2. This is offered to demonstrate the application of a range of possible knowledge, skills, and values one might select when conceptualizing a complex client situation, that is, one that involves multiple cultural identities in addition to SO/SI.

SAMPLE TREATMENT PLAN

- Explore the need for self-identification under one identity or self-identification under multiple identities:
  - Declaring a bimodal identity, such as gay or straight vs. the more fluid queer (i.e., Katrenia referring to herself as a LUG).
  - Identifying as queer (i.e., Katrenia's increased confusion when pressed to self-identify with an exclusive and discrete SO label, e.g., gay or lesbian).
- Assist client in understanding the typical struggles between:
  - Singular or multiple salient SIs.
  - Low or high need for SI coherence with other congruent or conflictual cultural identities.
  - Degree of fixed or fluid SI.
- Manage client feelings of invalidation by friends, family, social networks, cultural communities, and larger society (i.e., Katrenia feeling hurt that her friends never mention she is queer and feeling her SO/SI has no value to others).

- Instruct client in understanding the historical and political contributions of essentialism and constructivism on SO/SI (i.e., Katrenia feeling invalidated by her friends' singular construct of self-identification and not understanding the many possible frameworks of SO/SI).
- Assist client in developing empathy and patience for other perspectives (i.e., Katrenia being angry with others for not understanding her when she may not fully understand herself).
- Explore self-identity separate from her SO/SI (i.e., Katrenia's Malaysian friend not knowing what queer is and attraction to the content of Katrenia's personality).
- Explore the construction of SO/SI through distinct discussions of desire, arousal, biological sex, attraction, gender-object choice, and affection (i.e., Katrenia's attraction to girls who lead and to men who see her personality rather than her SO/SI).
- Explore gender identity (see Chapter 1) (i.e., the attribution that Katrenia is a guy [masculine] by femme and butch women).
- Use language to gauge a client's need to either self-identify SO/SI or leave it fluid:
  - Queer, gay, or lesbian, "someone who is attracted to women" or a "man having sex with men," and so on.
- Track client need to come out (i.e., Katrenia does not share her need to come out, but shares her desire for acknowledgment of her queerness as something that makes her different from her friends).
- Explore client need for group affiliation (i.e., Katrenia desires group affiliation with her straight friends).

RESOURCES FOR CLINICIANS, STUDENTS, TRAINERS, AND SUPERVISORS

There are many practical experiential activities and instructional plans designed to assist with the exploration of knowledge, attitudes and beliefs, and skill capacity building.

Schreier and Werden (2000) detail several exercises focused on coming out, identity development, stereotypes, and cultural community building. Hillman and Martin (2002) describe an experiential activity designed to assist individuals in self-reflecting, in a purposively created non-threatening environment, specifically targeted at challenging intolerant beliefs and attitudes. The American Medical Students Association developed a comprehensive package of lessons, film discussions, PowerPoint presentations, and exercises for education and training situations. The lessons range from relationship exploration, to discussions of sexuality, to medical issues specific to people who are gay, lesbian, and bisexual (American Medical Students Association, 2008). Ponterotto, Utsey, and Pedersen (2006) provide field-tested tools in the form of concrete and easy-to-implement experiential activities and assessment measures for working with prejudicial attitudes and beliefs against numerous minority identities including SO/SI. There are additional practical applications that have been designed to help challenge attitudes and beliefs and develop skills working within specific populations connected with SO/SI, including: substance abuse (Picucci, 1992; Tyler, Jackman-Wheitner, Strader, & Lenox, 1997), relationships (Alexander, 1997), sexuality and intimacy (Hall, 1987), and college students (Wall & Evans, 2000). *The Continuum Complete International Encyclopedia of Sexuality* (Francoeur & Noonan, 2004) provides information on SO/SI-based behaviors among children, adolescents, and adults in over 60 countries.

There are classroom lesson plans developed to teach and train students regarding the complexity of SO/SI either as a singular identity concept or in relationship to other cultural identities (Greene & Croom, 2000; Hillman & Martin, 2002; Litterdale, 2002; Madson, 2001; Pearson, 2003). Eichstedt (1996) developed a series of classroom experiences and accompanying instructional plans to assist students in exploring their attitudes and beliefs toward SO/SI as well as toward public displays of affection. These exercises provide experiential activities for teaching and training appropriate for a variety of developmental levels.

SUMMARY

The purpose of this chapter is to provide mental health practitioners, trainers, researchers, students, and supervisors with a base of knowledge, sensitivity, and skills for working with SO/SI. The authors outline content areas necessary to achieve developing levels of competence to practice broadly and generally as well as within specific areas of SO/SI expertise. It is hoped that through this information, case vignettes, and examples, readers not only have good knowledge and understanding, but also have a pragmatic sense of how to make use of this knowledge and understanding to develop a base of skill competencies. This would hold true not only for clinical practice, but also in the areas of training, research, and psychoeducational programming.

RESOURCES

The following resources are provided as suggestions for further inquiry and as tools students, clinicians, trainees, and supervisors can utilize to help improve the quality of the services they provide

SELF-AWARENESS AND SELF-ASSESSMENT EXERCISES

EXPERIENTIAL ACTIVITY 10.1

This experiential activity allows individuals to explore how much experience they have had with SO/SI cultural communities. Participants are asked to stand and then take a seat if they are not able to meet the criteria of each question, as it is asked. Questions are progressive in that each asks about increasing levels of experience with people and cultures based on SO/SI diversity. As participants sit, they can assess their level of experience in relationship to others standing longer. It is important to debrief with participants afterward for their experiences of the exercise and to give opportunity to reflect on themselves as a result of self-awareness that develops. This experiential activity is particularly useful at the *Entry to Practicum* level of development:

Last "LGBQ-Affirming Person" Standing

1. Stay standing if you have ever heard someone say any of the following words: lesbian, gay, bi, or queer.
2. Stay standing if you have ever seen the portrayal of a LGBQ person on TV.
3. Stay standing if you are aware of LGBQ-specific issues being discussed in state or federal governments.
4. Stay standing if the nondiscrimination policies of an employer would enter into your decision to work for that employer.
5. Stay standing if you've ever had someone come out to you.

6. Stay standing if you have an LGBQ friend or family member.

7. Stay standing if you've ever been to a gay and/or lesbian bar or LGBQ pride event.

8. Stay standing if you consider yourself to be an ally of the LGBQ communities.

9. Stay standing if you grew up in a church/temple/mosque or other religion that is openly welcoming/affirming of LGBQ people.

Source: Schreier (2009).

This experiential activity allows students to visualize basic assumptions that occur as a result of heterosexism. The reversal nature of this activity allows students the opportunity to experience what a day would be like if the world were LGBQ and being straight was the exception. This activity is best done as a guided visualization and should be set up as such by the facilitator. It is important to debrief with participants afterward concerning their experiences and for them to reflect on themselves as a result of the self-awareness that develops. This exercise is particularly useful at the *Entry to Internship* level of development:

You are sound asleep and the alarm goes off. You wake and look around, taking in everything in your room, just like every morning. You begin your morning ritual: shower, brush your teeth, dress, and head to the kitchen for breakfast. You sit down at your kitchen table just like you do every morning. As you have breakfast, you pick up yesterday's campus newspaper. The headlines read, "President to Consider Military Action," "Unemployment Improving Fed Says," and "Mayor Denounces Health Benefits for Opposite Sex Couples—Says Subversion of Marriage." Typical morning headlines. You toss the paper on the table, finish breakfast, and head to class. As you step outside, Fall is the air and it is just a little cooler than it has been. You take a deep breath and begin your usual walk to campus. You get no further than three doors and you encounter your neighbors, Phil and Mike. Phil is just saying goodbye to Mike as Mike goes off to work. They kiss goodbye, and Mike comes over and gives you a big hug hello. You have always admired Phil and Mike for the commitment they have with each other. Silently you remind yourself that you, too, one day, will have such a relationship with someone special, just like they do. As for now, you smile and greet Phil and Mike as usual. Phil kisses you on the cheek and warns you to dress warm, as Fall is on its way. You smile and head to class again.

You arrive on campus and make your way to your first class. As you cross in front of the Union, you see tables set up for the annual campus organization fair. You pass by tables for such organizations as Campus Baptist Fellowship, Sigma Alpha Mu—The Gay Men's Fraternity, The Communication Club, the Field Hockey Club, The Lesbian Avengers, and the Heterosexual Alliance. You notice the Heterosexual Alliance table does not have a lot of folks around like most other tables. Out of curiosity, you decide to check them out. You walk up and there sit two smiling people welcoming you. They offer you literature, which you take and quickly make your way down the sidewalk before they can talk any further. You read the brochure, which talks about being straight in a LGBQ world and the difficulties in acceptance. The brochure talks about heterophobia, straight bashing, and university discrimination, such as denial of tuition remission for staff and faculty opposite-sex partners. You note this, crumple the brochure up, and toss it. On the way to the Education Building, you see lots of guys lying together on the grass as usual. You walk further and see a guy and girl sitting together and you stop for a second to stare until they

(continued)

(continued)

stare back, at which point you move on, a little embarrassed. Not completely against it, but just rarely see it.

Class goes well and you head downtown to grab a snack before your next class. As you head downtown, your friend Lisa runs up. She seems happier than usual and is very excited about something. She shares that the girl she has been eyeing for the last 2 months finally asked her out. This appears to make Lisa very happy and you tell her so. You ask about their date and Lisa tells you that they are going out for dinner and then going dancing at the local lesbian bar. You both give each other that knowing sex glance. You tell her you want details next week, and say goodbye.

You meander past the Union and start to walk among all the poster tables set up. The first table has lots of inspirational posters. One talks about love and commitment featuring a faint image of two guys holding hands walking on a beach. You walk to movie posters and look at two, one for "In and Out" with Kevin Kline and another for "Queer as Folk" on Showtime. You decide to buy a small poster for your house that says "It's In to Be Out." You pocket your change and stick your new poster in your backpack and continue your walk. You arrive at the local drugstore. You walk in to get a Coke. As you wait in line, you notice the magazine shelf. *GQ* features an article called "Does the Man You Love Really Love You: Hints to See If Men Really Can Make It Together." You also notice *Elle* and an article called "Women Are from Mars and Venus: Women and Relationships and Making It Work." You buy your Coke and head to class.

You go to the Business School to sit in your usual tax class seat. The professor talks about taxes for married couples and says two men or two women are now able to save more money filing jointly than ever before because the current administration did away with marriage penalty taxes. He goes on to talk about how couples fare better than singles. He makes a disparaging remark about a man and woman in a relationship and how they want tax benefits. He notes this will not happen despite straight efforts to compare themselves to LGBQ people. You take notes, but are not paying attention because it's a great day and you'd rather be outside. Class ends and you go out to enjoy the day.

As you cross the street, a big truck comes barreling down and you notice it has the usual mud flaps of some big muscled guy silhouetted in silver on each flap. You look up at the guy driving the truck and chuckle quietly to yourself and head home. You arrive home and your roommate has already gotten the mail and left it on the kitchen table. You leaf through your mail and notice the University Alumni Association is hitting you up for money. You open the envelope and there is a big splashy, glossy sheet inside with a photo of two women sitting, looking dreamily at each other in front of a lit-up campus fountain. The caption reads, "Be a Part of the University Family." With eventual student loans needing your attention first, you toss the request in the recycle bin. You camp out in the living room and turn on the TV. The CNN news anchor announces that Tom Cruise and Peyton Manning were married yesterday in a private ceremony on the Isle of St. Croix. You are surprised because you didn't even know they were dating. You decide this is a typical Hollywood marriage that won't last 2 years, especially between a movie star and a football player. You shake your head and go into the kitchen to make lunch. As you are making a sandwich, the phone rings. It's your mom. She calls to ask if you heard the news that Mr. Grady, the high school history teacher, has been living with a woman for years. You say you hadn't heard, but are not surprised because he always acted so straight when you were in high school and there had been rumors. Your mom asks you what you mean by "acted straight." You say, "Well, all macho, dominant, bossy, and tough." Your mom reminds you it is just rumor and not to tell anyone else until she can find out for sure. You hang up laughing at your mom's need to tell you and her request you not tell anyone else, and go back to making lunch.

You finish lunch. You go into your bedroom and pack your gym clothes into your bag to go work out before studying. You walk to the rec center and head to the locker rooms. As you go into the locker rooms you notice a guy standing in the hall watching a woman go by and it is clear that he is eyeing her. You think to yourself once again that while you don't feel strongly one way or the other about heterosexuality, you do feel strongly they should keep that behavior to themselves. As you sit in the locker room changing, you notice the straight guy from the hallway comes in and sits down next to you. You finish changing and you head to the treadmills and continue to think about this. As you do your workout, you think of a bunch of questions you would want to ask someone who is heterosexual to find out what it is like: When and how do they realize they are hetero; is heterosexuality just a phase; do they just need to be with someone of the same sex to see what it is like to get over being hetero; why do they make their heterosexuality so public; why is divorce so prevalent; what exactly do they do in bed; can heteros be good parents when they are responsible for the majority of the child abuse; and a bunch more questions. All these thoughts jumble around as you work up a sweat and call it quits. You head back to the locker room, shower, and change. You grab your books and head to the library for the rest of the day.

Reflecting on the day so far, you decide there is a lot of heterosexuality all around, although you never realized it before. You decide it is something to think further about as you study.

Source: Schreier (2009).

SO/SI ISSUES SEMINAR

Topics and Activities

Trainers and clinicians may select activities from among the following suggestions:

A. Knowledge gained through didactic training and independent study on:

1. Relation of SO/SI competency to multicultural competency.
2. Individual and cultural identities (including age, gender, religion/spirituality, SES, ethnicity) relating to SO/SI issues.
3. SO/SI issues relevant to specific ethnic and racial cultures, for example, being on the down-low or MSMs (men having sex with men).
4. Essentialist and constructionist theories of SO/SI.
5. Generational shifts for SO/SI over the past 50 years.
6. Negative attitudes and belief sets: homophobia or homonegativity, biphobia or binegativity, heterosexism, sexism, and so on.
7. Literature describing the relevance of SO/SI to wellness, physical health, faith/spiritual, and communal, mental health.
8. Definitions of SO/SI nomenclature and its related terms: *lesbian, gay, bi, queer,* and so on.
9. SO/SI issues around the world, including cultures that have neither language nor constructs for understanding SO/SI (Western and Eastern cultural viewpoints).
10. SO/SI development models.
11. SO/SI assessment methods; diagnosis, case conceptualization, and treatment planning.
12. Healthy and unhealthy SO/SI expressions (e.g., "sexual addictions"); understanding of psychopathology as well as beliefs and behavior that are considered normative and healthy within client's SO/SI community (i.e., safe BDSM practices).
13. Legislative impact (i.e., feelings of disenfranchisement due to legislative action of civil rights for same-sex couples).
14. Therapy issues that have SO/SI components: medical decision making, grief, abuse recovery, aging, death and dying, addiction, career development.

15. Interpersonal process issues in psycho-therapy.

16. Ethical/legal standards: informed consent to provide SO/SI interventions, potential dual roles, one's own level of SO/SI integration and the impact on clients who may be at different or similar levels of integration.

17. Resource information: SO/SI leaders from various religions and faith traditions, Western and Eastern traditions, therapists specializing in SO/SI therapy.

B. Awareness of own attitudes and beliefs:

1. May use one or more of the following techniques to explore one's own beliefs, attitudes, and experiences: familial geno-gram, journaling, family member inter-view, and SO/SI lifeline. Some examples include: What are your first memories of learning about SO/SI? What were the SO/SI beliefs and attitudes in your family-of-origin? To what degree have you as-cribed to those same beliefs and attitudes? What factors have affected the degree to which you have ascribed to belief and attitude sets about SO/SI throughout the course of your life?

C. Activities to build knowledge, awareness, and skills:

1. Visit an unfamiliar service for SO/SI.
2. Write a paper describing the beliefs and practices of two unfamiliar SO/SI cultural traditions.
3. Invite SO/SI leaders to a seminar.

4. Participate in group discussions of SO/SI issues.

5. Participate in a civil rights actions group working on legal issues related to SO/SI.

6. Participate in pride events in your community.

7. Discuss therapy case examples and SO/SI issues scenarios. Identify possible therapeu-tic interventions, interpersonal process issues, and ethical/legal dilemmas.

8. Choose an SO/SI concept and research how it is addressed in several world reli-gions, race and ethnic cultures, or across generational lives.

9. Explore SO/SI concepts through reading historical texts (e.g., the development of sexual identity in America, the civil rights movement in America and elsewhere in the world, or the impact of the Internet on SO/SI development in the past 10 years).

10. Participate in SO/SI experiences (e.g., book readings, movie festivals, SO/SI speaker events, lobbying for SO/SI civil rights, and so on).

COMPETENCY BENCHMARK TABLES

The purpose of the Competency Benchmarks (Tables 10.1–10.4) is to create developmental models for defining and measuring competencies in professional psychology; each chapter in this *Handbook* applies the diversity competence for mental health practitioners in their work with a particular diverse population.

Table 10.1   Developmental-Level Competencies I

READINESS LEVEL—ENTRY TO PRACTICUM	
Competencies	Learning Process and Activities
Knowledge	The student is gaining knowledge in:	At this stage of development, the emphasis is on instilling knowledge of foundational domains that provide the groundwork for subsequent attainment of functional multicultural competencies. Students at this stage become aware of the principles and
	• Multiculturalism (inclusive of SO/SI)—the student is engaged in the process of learning that all individuals, including themselves, are cultural beings with worldviews that shape	

READINESS LEVEL—ENTRY TO PRACTICUM

Competencies		Learning Process and Activities
	and influence their beliefs, attitudes, emotions, perceptions, and experiences. • The importance of reflective practice and self-awareness of one's cultural identities and the cultural identities of others. • Core counseling skills and theories, particularly as they embrace and pertain to the value of multiculturalism. • Ethics code upholding professionals to develop knowledge, sensitivity, and skills in multicultural practice.	practices of the field, but they are not yet able to apply their knowledge to practice. Training curriculum is focused on knowledge of core areas, including literature on multiculturalism (inclusive of SO/SI), ethics, foundational counseling skills, scientific knowledge, and the importance of reflective practice and self-awareness. Throughout the curriculum, trainers and educators define individual and cultural differences broadly, inclusive of SO/SI. This should enable students to have a developing awareness of how to extrapolate their emerging multicultural competencies to include SO/SI.
Skills	The student is: • Developing the ability to demonstrate empathic listening skills, respect, and interest when talking with individuals expressing different values and belief systems. • Learning to critically examine the diversity literature.	Many students will not have foundational knowledge of SO/SI through their own life experiences, and therefore may not be aware of terminology and resources. As the overall topic of sexuality is sensitive in most cultures, students may not have been encouraged to reflect on their own SO/SI in an open, nondefensive manner and may inversely have heightened defensiveness to SO/SI.
Values and Attitudes	The student demonstrates: • Willingness to engage in self-exploration to consider own beliefs, attitudes, behaviors, and the implicit and explicit effect of these on others. • Intellectual curiosity and emotional flexibility. • Ability to value expressions of diverse attitude and belief systems.	

Table 10.2   Developmental-Level Competencies II

READINESS LEVEL—ENTRY TO INTERNSHIP

Competencies		Learning Process and Activities
Knowledge	The student has: • Knowledge of relevant professional guidelines: Guidelines for Psychotherapy with Lesbian, Gay, and Bisexual Clients; Guidelines on Multicultural Education, Training, Research, Practice, and Organizational Change for Psychologists. • Knowledge of human sexuality and models of SO/SI identity development. • General understanding of the beliefs, practices, and traditions of SO/SI cultures. • Understanding of bi/homophobia, bi/homonegativity, internalized bi/homophobia, heterosexual bias, heterosexism, sexism, and heterosexual privilege belief systems. • Understanding of the discrete and shared variance between sex, sexuality, and SO/SI.	At this level of development, students are building on their education and applied experiences (i.e., supervised practicum experiences) to attain a core set of foundational competencies. They can then begin applying these competencies in professional practice. Foundational knowledge and multicultural beliefs and attitudes are becoming well established, but skill in working with SO/SI issues is expected to be rudimentary at this level of development. Learning occurs through multiple modalities: • Receiving SO/SI didactic training in academic programs, which may occur in multicultural courses or culture-specific courses (e.g., women's issues, Latino/a, and SO/SI courses). It may also be infused into the core curriculum (e.g., ethics/law, assessment, multicultural,

(continued)

Table 10.2   Developmental-Level Competencies II (*continued*)

READINESS LEVEL—ENTRY TO INTERNSHIP	
Competencies	**Learning Process and Activities**
	• Understanding of the differences between tolerant, affirming, and nurturing attitudes toward SO/SI. • Knowledge of essentialist and constructionist theories of SO/SI. • Knowledge of reorientation therapies and identity incongruence between spirituality/religion and SO/SI identities.	career counseling, research, human growth and development, and clinical courses). • Providing therapy, under supervision, to clients representing SO/SI diversity in practicum experiences. • Receiving supervision from mental health practitioners knowledgeable and skilled in working with SO/SI issues. • Seeking additional study and professional development opportunities (i.e., to attain knowledge of various SOs/SIs).
Skills	Skills in the following areas are beginning to develop: • Use of gender-neutral or gender-inclusive language. • Alliance-building to create a trusting, safe, and open therapeutic climate to discuss SO/SI issues. • Recognition of client cues regarding communication of SO/SI concerns. • Discernment of personal limits of openness to SO/SI and, after consultation with supervisors, referring clients to appropriate resources if not able to work with SO/SI in no less than an affirming therapeutic manner. • Genuine respect for varying SO/SI groups.	• Exploring media, such as newspapers, magazines, film, music, cultural events (e.g., *The Advocate*, HRC, National Coming Out Month, LGBTQ Film Festivals, and so on). Topics to be covered in didactic training include: • Relationship of SO/SI competency to multicultural competency. • Relationship of SO/SI to individual and cultural differences (e.g., age, gender, spirituality/religion, SES, and ethnicity). • Basic research literature describing the relevance of SO/SI to wellness, physical health, and mental health. • Definitions, histories, and traditions of SO/SI.
Values and Attitudes	Demonstrates self-awareness and appropriate cultural and multicultural attitudes as evidenced by the following: • Knowledge of SO/SI as an aspect of multicultural diversity. • Awareness of own intersecting individual dimensions (gender, sex, ethnicity, SES, SO/SI, spirituality/religion, etc.) and ability to discern clients' intersecting identities. • Commitment to examine and challenge own SO/SI negative attitudes and beliefs. • Willingness to admit any limitations in ability to be no less than affirming to SO/SI. • Commitment to moving from a position of tolerance for SO/SI issues to one of nurturance of SO/SI issues.	Trainers and educators must offer students enrolled in multicultural diversity courses an option to research SO/SI as a project for the class and provide resources through which students can be exposed to/experience SO/SI culture, politics, history, language, symbols, and customs.

COMPETENCY BENCHMARK TABLES

Table 10.3 Developmental-Level Competencies III

READINESS LEVEL—ENTRY TO PROFESSIONAL PRACTICE

Competencies		Learning Process and Activities
Knowledge	Knowledge of: • Relationship between SO/SI and mental and physical health. • Treatment concerns common to SO/SI (coming out, relationships, family, social support, health care, law, sexuality and safer sex). • Beliefs and behaviors that are considered normative and healthy within client's SO/SI. • SO/SI as always being a part of a more complex identity matrix, including race, ethnicity, age, spirituality/religion, SES, and others. • Community resources, including leaders from various SO/SI communities, and mental health practitioners specializing in SO/SI nurturing therapy. • The effect of SO/SI in the supervisory relationship. • Using SO/SI variables in research practices. • Using SO/SI variables in psychoeducational programming.	In the earlier stages of training, students solidified their professional knowledge base and attained appropriate values, beliefs, and attitudes while developing increasingly sophisticated clinical skills. At the level of Entry to Professional Practice, mental health practitioners have attained the full range of competencies in the domains expected of all independent practitioners. Preparation for this level of competency takes place through closely supervised clinical work, augmented by professional reading, personal exploration, and training opportunities such as professional development and training seminars. Clinical supervisors observe students' clinical work, provide training in assessment, case conceptualization, and treatment planning, and challenge supervisees to examine their process-based relational reactions with clients, biases, and beliefs to develop their supervisees' clinical competency with SO/SI issues.
Skills	Skills are demonstrated by the ability to: • Perform a basic assessment of clients' SO/SI and to assess the relevance of SO/SI issues to therapy. • Diagnose and formulate appropriate treatment plans that are sensitive to the client's SO/SI, including how multiple identities and individual strengths, stress level, support systems, and coping skills impact client. • Form trusting therapeutic relationships (inclusive of the therapist's own SO/SI) with clients to provide basic SO/SI therapeutic interventions so clients may express SO/SI concerns when relevant. • Establish effective consultation relationships with leaders from various SO/SI communities. • Create climate in which supervisees and trainees feel safe to talk about SO/SI issues. • Readily use SO/SI variables in research along with other usual demographic variables when sampling, and so on. • Provide effective instruction, with an emphasis on nurturance-based programming. • Provide a supportive environment for engaging clients with identity incongruence due to SO/SI conflict with other salient identities (e.g., spirituality/religion, race/ethnicity, age, SES, etc.).	Additional methods by which students can attain SO/SI competency at this level include: • Seeking opportunities to provide therapy to clients representing SO/SI diversity. • Supervision provided by supervisors knowledgeable and skilled in working with SO/SI. • Self-directed study and professional development opportunities through cultural immersion experiences. • Internship and postdoctoral seminar training in SO/SI issues • Presenting and participating in clinical case conferences that include discussion of SO/SI aspects of cases.
Values and Attitudes	Awareness of own SO/SI and associated biases, willingness to continually broaden self-knowledge, and commitment to expanding knowledge of SO/SI as part of multicultural competency enhancement.	

Table 10.4   Developmental-Level Competencies IV

READINESS LEVEL—ADVANCED PRACTICE AND SPECIALIZATION	
Competencies	**Learning Process and Activities**
Knowledge Extensive knowledge of: • SO/SI literature and resources. • SO/SI development models and case conceptualization. • Impact of sexuality on human development. • SO/SI histories and traditions. • Specific issues within the SO/SI communities that are a frequent focus of therapy. • Current events relevant to SO/SI and their potential negative and positive impact on clients (e.g., state legislative actions affecting same-sex marriage options, tax and medical decision-making issues etc.).	Mental health practitioners who have a particular interest in SO/SI as it applies to clinical work may seek to attain advanced levels of competency. Learning activities will vary depending on the mental health practitioner's unique background, established competencies, SO/SI, and interest areas. For example, mental health practitioners working in substance-abuse treatment settings may wish to focus on SO/SI within this broader clinical population. Similarly, mental health practitioners working in a hospice setting may choose to focus on the difficulties faced by SO/SI around death and dying (HIV/AIDS issues, privileging of partners as "family" by medical staff).
Skills Advanced skills in: • Providing a variety of SO/SI interventions (individual, couples, group therapy, community, political/legal advocacy). • Case conceptualization, integrating SO/SI within a framework of other cultural identities. • Proactively sharing knowledge of SO/SI issues in the work setting with members of various health and mental health professions. • Differentiating between healthy and unhealthy sexual behaviors with full knowledge of the wide range of SO/SI expression. • Providing effective supervision to supervisees working with SO/SI.	Regardless of the focus area, learning activities include: • Professional reading (information about sexual minority groups; empirical studies, and literature on theory and practice). • Teaching self through the teaching of others. • Attending and leading continuing-education workshops. • Peer-consultation groups. • Consultation with knowledgeable mental health professionals and leaders in SO/SI communities. • Participation in unfamiliar SO/SI experiences (e.g., attendance at PFLAG meetings, political and social events).
Values and Attitudes Well-integrated values and attitudes demonstrated by the following: • Continually engages in broadening knowledge of SO/SI resources. • Actively cultivates relationships with SO/SI community leaders. • Involvement in local and national groups and organizations relevant to SO/SI issues. • Independently and proactively provides consultation and supervision to trainees and other professionals. • Values advocacy for social justice to enhance understanding among individuals on SO/SI issues (i.e., being an ally). • Independently monitors own SO/SI status in relation to work with others with awareness and sensitivity to varying SO/SI statuses of others.	

REFERENCES

Alexander, C. J. (1997). *Growth and intimacy for gay men: A workbook.* Binghamton, NY: Harrington Park Press/Haworth Press.

American Counseling Association. (1998). *ACA code of ethics and standards of practice.* Alexandria, VA.

American Medical Students Association. (2008). LGBT local projects in a box. Retrieved October 12, 2008, from http://www.amsa.org/lgbt/projects.cfm

American Psychiatric Association. (1973). Position statement on homosexuality and civil rights. *American Journal of Psychiatry*, *131*(4), 497.

American Psychological Association. (1998). *Resolution on the therapeutic responses to sexual orientation*. Washington, DC.

American Psychological Association. (2000). Guidelines for psychotherapy with lesbian, gay, and bisexual clients. *The American Psychologist*, *55*(12), 1140–1451.

American Psychological Association. (2001). *Publication manual of the American Psychological Association* (5th ed.). Washington, DC: American Psychological Association.

American Psychological Association. (2002). Ethical principles of psychologists and the code of conduct. Retrieved October 12, 2008, from http://www.apa .org/ethics/code2002.html

American Psychological Association. (2003). Guidelines on multicultural education, training, research, practice, and organizational change for psychologists. *American Psychologist*, *58*, 377–402.

American Psychological Association. (2007). Assessment of competencies benchmarks workgroup: A developmental model for the defining and measuring competence in professional psychology. Retrieved on October 27, 2008, from http://www.apa .org/ed/graduate/comp_benchmark.pdf

Anhalt, K., Morris, T. L., Scotti, J. R., & Cohen, S. H. (2003). Students perspectives on training in gay, lesbian, and bisexual issues: A survey of behavioral clinical psychology programs. *Cognitive & Behavioral Practice*, *10*(3), 255–263.

Arnett, J. J. (2008). The neglected 95%: Why American psychology needs to become less American. *American Psychologist*, *63*, 602–614.

Arredondo, P. (1999). Multicultural counseling competencies as tools to address racism and oppression. *Journal of Counseling and Development*, *77*(1), 102–108.

Association for Lesbian, Gay, Bisexual & Transgender Issues in Counseling (2008). Competencies for counseling gay, lesbian, bisexual and transgendered [GLBT] Clients. Retrieved on October 3, 2008, from www.algbtic.org./resources/competencies.html.

Beckstead, A. L., & Morrow, S. L. (2004). Mormon clients' experiences of conversion therapy: The need for a new treatment approach. *The Counseling Psychologist*, *32*(5), 651–690.

Beckstead, L., & Israel, T. (2007). Affirmative counseling and psychotherapy focused on issues related to sexual orientation conflicts. In K. J. Bieschke, R. M. Perez, & K. A. DeBord (Eds.), *Handbook of counseling and psychotherapy with lesbian, gay, bisexual, and transgender clients* (pp. 221–244). Washington, DC: American Psychological Association.

Bell, A. P., Weinberg, M. S., & Hammersmith, S. K. (1981). *Sexual preference: Its development in men and women*. Bloomington, IN: Indiana University Press.

Biaggio, M., Orchard, S., Larson, J., Petrino, K., & Mihara, R. (2003). Guidelines for gay/lesbian/bisexual-affirmative educational practices in graduate psychology programs. *Professional Psychology: Research and Practice*, *34*, 548–554.

Bieschke, K. J., Paul, P. L., & Blasko, K. A. (2007). Review of empirical research focused on the experience of lesbian, gay, and bisexual clients in counseling and psychotherapy. In K. J. Bieschke, R. M. Perez, & K. A. DeBord (Eds.), *Handbook of counseling and psychotherapy with lesbian, gay, bisexual, and transgender clients* (pp. 293–315). Washington, DC: American Psychological Association.

Bieschke, K. J., Perez, R. M., & DeBord, K. A. (2007). Introduction: The challenge of providing affirmative psychotherapy while honoring diverse contexts. In K. J. Bieschke, R. M. Perez, & K. A. DeBord (Eds.), *Handbook of counseling and psychotherapy with lesbian, gay, bisexual, and transgender clients* (pp. 3–11). Washington, DC: American Psychological Association.

Bridges, S. K., Selvidge, M. D., & Matthews, C. R. (2003). Lesbian women of color: Therapeutic issues and challenges. *Journal of Multicultural Counseling and Development*, *31*, 113–130.

Broido, E. M. (2000). Constructing identity: The nature and meaning of lesbian, gay, and bisexual identities. In R. M. Perez, K. A. Debord, and K. J. Bieschke (Eds.), *The handbook of counseling and psychotherapy with lesbian, gay, and bisexual clients* (pp. 13–34). Washington, DC: American Psychological Association.

Cass, V. (1979). Homosexual identity formation: A theoretical model. *Journal of Homosexuality*, *4*(3), 219–235.

Cass, V. (1984). Homosexual identity: A concept in need of a definition. *Journal of Homosexuality*, *9*, 105–126.

Coleman, E. (1987). Assessment of sexual orientation. *Journal of Homosexuality*, *14*, 9–24.

Conger, J. J. (1975). Proceedings of the American Psychological Association, Inc., for the year 1974: Minutes of the Annual Meeting of the Council of Representatives. *American Psychologist*, *30*, 620–651.

DeAngelis, T. (2002). A new generation of issues for LGBT clients. *APA Monitor, 33*(2), 42–44.

Eichstedt, J. L. (1996). Heterosexism and gay/lesbian/bisexual experiences: Teaching strategies and exercises. *Teaching Sociology, 24*(4), 384–388.

Ellis, A. L., & Mitchell, R. W. (2000). Sexual orientation. In L. T. Szuchman & F. Muscarella (Eds.), *Psychological perspectives on human sexuality* (pp. 196–231). New York: Wiley.

Fassinger, R. E. (2008). Workplace diversity and public policy. *American Psychologist, 63,* 252–268.

Fassinger, R. E., & Arseneau, J. R. (2007). "I'd rather get wet than be under that umbrella": Differentiating the experiences and identities of lesbian, gay, bisexual, and transgendered people. In K. J. Bieschke, R. M. Perez, & K. A. DeBord (Eds.), *Handbook of counseling and psychotherapy with lesbian, gay, bisexual, and transgender clients* (pp. 19–49). Washington, DC: American Psychological Association.

Firestein, B. A. (2007). Cultural and relational contexts of bisexual women: Implications for therapy. In K. J. Bieschke, R. M. Perez, & K. A. DeBord (Eds.), *Handbook of counseling and psychotherapy with lesbian, gay, bisexual, and transgender clients* (pp. 91–117). Washington, DC: American Psychological Association.

Francoeur, R. T., & Noonan, R. J. (2004). *The continuum complete international encyclopedia of sexuality.* New York: Continuum Complete Publishing Group.

Garnets, L. (2007). Foreword: The "coming of age" of lesbian, gay, bisexual, and transgendered-affirmative psychology. In K. J. Bieschke, R. M. Perez, & K. A. DeBord (Eds.), *Handbook of counseling and psychotherapy with lesbian, gay, bisexual, and transgender clients* (pp. xi–xvi). Washington, DC: American Psychological Association.

Garnets, L. D. (2002). Sexual orientations in perspective. *Cultural Diversity and Ethnic Minority Psychology 8*(2), 115–129.

Garnets, L., Hancock, K. A., Cochran, S. D., Goodchilds, J., & Peplau, L. A. (1991). Issues in psychotherapy with lesbians and gay men: A survey of psychologists. *American Psychologist, 46,* 964–972.

Garrett, M. T., & Barret, B. (2003). Two spirit: Counseling Native American gay, lesbian, and bisexual people. *Journal of Multicultural Counseling and Development, 31,* 131–142.

Greene, B. (2003). Beyond heterosexism and across the cultural divide: Developing an inclusive lesbian, gay, bisexual psychology: A look into the future. In L. Garnets & D. C. Kimmel (Eds.), *Psychological perspectives on lesbian, gay, and bisexual experiences.* New York: Columbia University Press.

Greene, B. (2007). Delivering ethical psychological services to lesbian, gay, and bisexual clients. In K. J. Bieschke, R. M. Perez, & K. A. DeBord (Eds.), *Handbook of counseling and psychotherapy with lesbian, gay, bisexual, and transgender clients* (pp. 181–199). Washington, DC: American Psychological Association.

Greene, B., & Croom, G. L. (2000). Lesbian, gay, and bisexual people of color: A challenge to representative sampling in empirical research. In B. Greene, & G. L. Croom (Eds.), *Education, research, and practice in lesbian, gay, bisexual, and transgendered psychology: A resource manual,* Vol. 5 (pp. 263–281). Thousand Oaks, CA: Sage.

Haldeman, D. C. (1994). The practice and ethics of sexual orientation conversion therapies. *Journal of Consulting and Clinical Psychology, 62,* 221–227.

Haldeman, D. C. (2004). When sexual and religious orientation collide: Considerations in working with conflicted same-sex attracted male clients. *The Counseling Psychologist, 32*(5), 691–715.

Hall, M. (1987). Sex therapy with lesbian couples: A four stage approach. *Journal of Homosexuality, 14*(1–2), 137–156.

Halpert, S. C., Reinhardt, B., & Toohey, M. J. (2007). Affirmative clinical supervision. In K. J. Bieschke, R. M. Perez, & K. A. DeBord (Eds.), *Handbook of counseling and psychotherapy with lesbian, gay, bisexual, and transgender clients* (pp. 341–358). Washington, DC: American Psychological Association.

Hatcher, R. L., & Lassiter, K. D. (2007). Initial training in professional psychology: The Practicum Competencies Outline. *Training and Education in Professional Psychology, 1,* 49–63.

Herek, G. M., Kimmel, D. C., Amaro, H., & Melton, G. B. (1991). Avoiding heterosexist bias in psychological research. *American Psychologist, 46,* 957–963.

Hillman, J., & Martin, R. A. (2002). Lessons about gay and lesbian lives: A spaceship exercise. *Teaching Psychology, 29*(4), 308–311.

Hooker, E. (1957). The adjustment of the male overt homosexual. *Journal of Projective Techniques, 21,* 18–31.

Horowitz, J. L., & Newcomb, M. D. (2001). A multidimensional approach to homosexual identity. *Journal of Homosexuality, 42,* 1–19.

Israel, T., Ketz, K., Detrie, P., Burke, M., & Shulman, J. (2003). Identifying counselor competencies for working with lesbian, gay, and bisexual clients. *Journal of Gay & Lesbian Psychotherapy, 7*, 3–21.

Israel, T., & Selvidge, M. (2003). Contributions of multicultural counseling to counselor competence with lesbian, gay, and bisexual clients. *Journal of Multicultural Counseling and Development, 31*, 84–98.

Kaslow, N. (2004). Competencies in professional psychology. *American Psychologist, 59*, 774–781.

Kinsey, A. C., Pomeroy, W. B., & Martin, C. E. (1948). *Sexual behavior in the human male.* Philadelphia: W. B. Saunders.

Klein, F., Sepekoff, B., & Wolf, T. J. (1985). Sexual orientation: A multi-variable dynamic process. *Journal of Homosexuality, 11*, 35–50.

Kocarek, C. E., & Pelling, N. J. (2003). Beyond knowledge and awareness: Enhancing counselor skills for work with gay, lesbian, and bisexual clients. *Journal of Multicultural Counseling and Development, 31*, 99–112.

Leck, G. M. (1994). Politics of adolescent sexual identity and queer responses. *The High School Journal, 77*(1–2), 186–192.

LeVay, S. (1993). *The sexual brain.* Cambridge, MA: MIT Press.

Liddle, B. J. (2007). Mutual bonds: Lesbian women's lives and communities. In K. J. Bieschke, R. M. Perez, & K. A. DeBord (Eds.), *Handbook of counseling and psychotherapy with lesbian, gay, bisexual, and transgender clients* (pp. 51–69). Washington, DC: American Psychological Association.

Litterdale, M. A. (2002). Practitioner training for counseling lesbian, gay, and bisexual clients. *Journal of Lesbian Studies, 6*(3/4), 111–120.

Madson, L. (2001). Inferences regarding the personality traits and sexual orientation of physically androgynous people. *Psychology of Women Quarterly, 24*(2), 148–160.

Matthews, C. R. (2007). Affirmative lesbian, gay, and bisexual counseling with all clients. In K. J. Bieschke, R. M. Perez, & K. A. DeBord (Eds.), *Handbook of counseling and psychotherapy with lesbian, gay, bisexual, and transgender clients* (pp. 201–219). Washington, DC: American Psychological Association.

McCarn, S. R., & Fassinger, R. E. (1996). Revisioning sexual minority identity formation: A new model of lesbian identity and its implications for counseling and research. *The Counseling Psychologist, 24*, 508–534.

Minton, H. L. (1997). Queer theory: Historical roots and implications for psychology. *Theory and Psychology, 7*(3), 337–353.

Miville, M. L., & Ferguson, A. D. (2004). Impossible choices: Identity and values at a crossroad. *The Counseling Psychologist, 32*(5), 760–770.

Morales, E. S. (1989). Ethnic minority families and minority gays and lesbians. *Marriage and Family Review, 6*(1–2), 217–223.

Morrow, S. L., Beckstead, A. L., Hayes, J. A., & Haldeman, D. C. (2004). Impossible dreams, impossible choices, and thoughts about depolarizing the debate. *The Counseling Psychologist, 32*(5), 778–785.

Mulick, P. S., & Wright, L. W. (2002). Examining the existence of biphobia in the heterosexual and homosexual populations. *Journal of Bisexuality,* 46–64.

Murphy, J. A., Rawlings, E. I., & Howe, S. R. (2002). A survey of clinical psychologists on treating lesbian, gay and bisexual clients. *Professional Psychology: Research and Practice, 33*, 183–189.

Patterson, C. J. (2007). Lesbian and gay family issues in the context of changing legal and social policy environments. In K. J. Bieschke, R. M. Perez, & K. A. DeBord (Eds.), *Handbook of counseling and psychotherapy with lesbian, gay, bisexual, and transgender clients* (pp. 359–377). Washington, DC: American Psychological Association.

Patterson, C. P. (1995). Special issue: Overview. *Developmental Psychology, 31*(1), 3–11.

Pearson, Q. M. (2003). Breaking the silence in the counselor education classroom: A training seminar on counseling sexual minority clients. *Journal of Counseling and Development, 81*, 292–300.

Pellegrini, A. (1992). Shifting the terms of hetero/sexism: Gender, power, homophobias. In W. J. Bluefield (Ed.), *Homophobia: How we all pay the price.* New York: Beacon Press.

Phillips, J. (2000). Training issues and considerations. In R. M. Perez, K. A. DeBord, & K. J. Bieschke (Eds.), *Handbook of counseling and psychotherapy with lesbian, gay, and bisexual clients* (pp. 337–358.). Washington, DC: American Psychological Association.

Picucci, M. (1992). Planning an experiential weekend workshop for lesbians and gay males in recovery. *Journal of Chemical Dependency Treatment, 5*(1), 119–139.

Ponterotto, J. G., Utsey, S. O., & Pedersen, P. B. (2006). *Preventing prejudice: A guide for counselors, educators, and parents* (2nd ed.). Thousand Oaks, CA: Sage.

Potocznik, D. J. (2007). Development of bisexual men's identities and relationships. In K. J. Bieschke, R. M. Perez, & K. A. DeBord (Eds.), *Handbook of counseling and psychotherapy with lesbian, gay, bisexual, and transgender clients* (pp. 119–145). Washington, DC: American Psychological Association.

Reynolds, A. L., & Hanjorgiris, W. F. (2000). Coming out: Lesbian, gay, and bisexual identity development. In R. M. Perez, K. A. Debord, & K. J. Bieschke (Eds.), *The handbook of counseling and psychotherapy with lesbian, gay, and bisexual clients* (pp. 35–55). Washington, DC: American Psychological Association.

Reynolds, A. L., & Pope, R. L. (1991). The complexities of diversity: Exploring multiple oppressions. *Journal of Counseling & Development, 70,* 174–180.

Riddle, D. (1985). Opening doors of understanding and acceptance: A facilitator's guide for presenting workshops on lesbian and gay issues. [Organized by Kathy Bear and Amy Reynolds.]

Rodolfa, E., Bent, R., Eisman, E., Nelson, P., Rehm, L., & Ritchie, P. (2005). A cube model for competency development: Implications for psychology educators and regulators. *Professional Psychology: Research and Practice, 36,* 347–354.

Rothblum, E. D. (2000). Sexual orientation and sex in women's lives: Conceptual and methodological issues. *Journal of Social Issues, 56,* 193–204.

Rust, O. K. (2000). Bisexuality: A contemporary paradox for women. *Journal of Social Issues, 56,* 205–221.

Schneider, M. S., Brown, L. S., & Glassgold, J. M. (2002). Implementing the resolution on appropriate therapeutic responses to sexual orientation: A guide for the perplexed. *Professional Psychology: Research and Practice, 33*(3), 265–276.

Schreier, B.A. (2009). Last LGBQ affirming person standing. Unpublished manuscript.

Schreier, B. A. (1998). Of shoes, and ships, and sealing wax: The faulty and specious assumptions of sexual reorientation therapy. *Journal of Mental Health Counseling, 20*(4), 305–314.

Schreier, B. A., & Werden, D. L. (2000). Psychoeducational programming: Creating a context of mental health for people who are lesbian, gay, or bisexual In R. M. Perez, K. A. Debord, & K. J. Bieschke (Eds.), *The handbook of counseling and psychotherapy with lesbian, gay, and bisexual clients* (pp. 359–382). Washington, DC: American Psychological Association.

Shively, M., & DeCecco, J. (1977). Components of sexual identity. *Journal of Homosexuality, 3,* 41–48.

Stein, T. S. (1997). Deconstructing sexual orientation: Understanding the phenomenon of sexual orientation. *Journal of Homosexuality, 34*(1), 81–86.

Stevenson, M. R. (2007). Public policy, mental health, and lesbian, gay, bisexual, and transgendered clients. In K. J. Bieschke, R. M. Perez, & K. A. DeBord (Eds.), *Handbook of counseling and psychotherapy with lesbian, gay, bisexual, and transgender clients* (pp. 379–397). Washington, DC: American Psychological Association.

Stone, C. B. (2003). Counselors as advocates for gay, lesbian, and bisexual youth: A call for equity and action. *Journal of Multicultural Counseling and Development, 31,* 143–155.

Sue, S. (1998). In search of cultural competence in psychotherapy and counseling. *American Psychologist, 53,* 440–448.

Tozer, E. E., & McClanahan, M. K. (1999). Treating the purple menace: Ethical considerations of conversion therapy and affirmative alternatives. *The Counseling Psychologist, 27*(5), 722–742.

Troiden, R. R. (1989). The formation of homosexual identities. *Journal of Homosexuality, 17*(1/2), 43–73.

Trujillo, C. M. (1997). Sexual identity and the discontents of difference. In B. Greene (Ed.), *Ethnic and cultural diversity among lesbians and gay men* (pp. 266–278). Thousand Oaks, CA: Sage.

Tyler, J. M., Jackman-Wheitner, L., Strader, S., & Lenox, R. (1997). A change-model approach to raising awareness of gay, lesbian, and bisexual issues among graduate students in counseling. *Journal of Sex Education & Therapy, 22*(2), 37–43.

Wall, V. A., & Evans, N. J. (2000). *Toward acceptance: Sexual orientation issues on campus.* Alexandria, VA: American Association of Counseling and Development.

Worthington, R. L. (2004). Sexual identity, sexual orientation, religious identity, and change: Is it possible to depolarize the debate? *The Counseling Psychologist, 32*(5), 741–749.

Worthington, R. L., & Mohr, J. J. (2002). Theorizing heterosexual identity development. *Counseling Psychologist, 30*(4), 491–495.

Worthington, R. L., Savoy, H., Dillon, F. R., & Vernaglia, E. R. (2002). Heterosexual identity development: A multidimensional model of individual and group identity. [Monograph]. *The Counseling Psychologist, 30,* 496–531.

CHAPTER 11

SIZEISM: AN UNRECOGNIZED PREJUDICE

ROKI ABAKOUI and ROSEMARY E. SIMMONS

INTRODUCTION

Much concern has been expressed over the last few decades regarding the rise in rates of "overweight" and "obese" individuals in society at large. Many researchers have touted the vast increase in obesity and expressed concerns that the United States is in the midst of an epidemic (Boero, 2007; Oliver 2005; U.S. Department of Health and Human Services, 2001). A "War on Obesity" was declared by former Surgeon General C. Everett Koop in the mid-1990s. Unfortunately, this declaration often has been used to fight a war against fat people, resulting in increased stigmatization rather than increased health for large individuals. This unfortunate by-product increases the difficulty for people of size finding physical and mental health professionals who are knowledgeable about health at any size. And, as will be discussed later in the chapter, a close look at the data contradicts the assertions that there is in fact an epidemic regarding "obesity."

The field of psychology has not been immune to this "war." Psychologists see many people with concerns about their size, weight, and/or body image. For clients with size concerns, the stigmatization of fat has led to symptoms of depression and anxiety, body image disturbances, and other psychological distress (Ashmore, Friedman, Reichmann, & Musante, 2008; Friedman et al., 2005). Anti-fat attitudes also lead to chronic dieting and weight cycling with its negative effects on psychological health (Marchesini et al., 2004). The fear of fat also contributes to the development of disturbed eating and eating disorders (Garner, Garfinkel, Rockert & Olmsted, 1987; Laliberte, Newton, McCabe, & Mills, 2007; Striegel-Moore, Silberstein, Frensch, & Rodin, 1989).

This chapter will provide information and methods for mental health practitioners to work with clients who are concerned about their size. First, barriers to competent treatment will be discussed. A framework for competent treatment, Health at Every Size (Robison, 2005), will then be provided. Next, information will be introduced that identifies knowledge that is basic for competency, including the areas of ethics and individual and cultural diversity. Developing competencies in assessment, conceptualization, and treatment will lead to better treatment outcomes for clients. Therefore, relevant skills in assessment, intervention, and training will be included. The authors will then discuss the attitudes and values necessary to provide culturally sensitive services. The chapter concludes with case examples, sample assessment questions, exercises for increasing self-awareness, and activities for a size acceptance seminar.

DEFINITION OF TERMS

The word *fat* will be used throughout the chapter instead of the commonly used terms *overweight* and *obese*. *Fat* describes the size of a person as an objective statement of size. Though it is used pejoratively by many in society, the size acceptance community uses it to simply describe one's body size and to destigmatize the word *fat* (Bacon, 2008). This usage is similar to that of those in the LGBT community who embrace *queer* versus using the more clinical term of *homosexual* (Brontsema, 2004). The word *overweight* implies that there is a correct weight that a person exceeds and *obese* denotes a medical condition. Both terms are typically used to indicate that a person's body size is a problem.

BARRIERS TO COMPETENCY IN COUNSELING PEOPLE OF SIZE

What images does the word *fat* bring to your mind? Pictures of torsos with big bellies and massive thighs with a shopping cart piled high? Pictures of fat people taken from behind as they waddle down the street? These images, along with many others, are common depictions of fat people. Fat people are thought to be gluttons who cannot or will not control their appetite. They are reviled in the news media, blamed for runaway health-care costs, and considered anathema by the dominant cultural ideal.

Many studies over the past 30 years have demonstrated the prejudice held within American society toward fat people. The biases against fat people are present in employment settings (Larkin & Pines, 1979; Rothblum, Brand, Miller, & Oetjen, 1990), in the health professions (Adams, Smith, Wilbur, & Grady, 1993; Crandall, 1994), and among the general public (e.g., Hiller, 1981; Tiggeman & Rothblum, 1988). Even mental health professionals who work with fat clients hold these biases. Psychologists' diagnosis and treatment planning has been found to vary dependent on client weight (Abakoui, 1998; K. Davis-Coelho, Waltz, & B. Davis-Coelho, 2000). In one study, using vignettes that varied client weight (a self-description of being either 10 lb or 80 lb overweight) and gender, the fat client had a worse prognosis and was more likely to receive an Axis II diagnosis than the average-weight client (Abakoui, 1998). In another study that used a photograph of a woman that varied in appearance (fat versus non-fat, created by using theatrical makeup and padding), the fat client again was given a worse prognosis and was more likely to receive an eating disorder diagnosis while the non-fat client was diagnosed with an adjustment disorder (Davis-Coelho et al., 2000). Young and Powell (1985) found that mental health

practitioners rated a "moderately obese" woman as more dysfunctional and impaired than they did the average-weight woman or the "mildly obese" woman. Schwartz, O'Neal Chambliss, Brownell, Blair, and Billington (2003) surveyed medical and mental health professionals at a conference on "obesity" about their attitudes toward fat people. They found that health professionals who specialized in working with fat people held very strong implicit pro-thin/anti-fat biases. Teachman and Brownell (2001) found similar results in a sample of general medical professionals at a continuing-education meeting. The evidence is clear that as a group, mental health practitioners hold the same biases and prejudices as society at large.

Where do these prejudices come from? Body-size standards have been part of appearance, health, social norms, and socioeconomic status throughout history. These norms regarding standards of beauty have changed as industrialization and economic status continually change within a country, culture, or, at times, even within families. When food is scarce, being larger in size has been a sign of health and economic comfort and security. Conversely, as countries become more industrialized and wealth increases for a portion of the population, thinness is associated with wealth (Ball & Crawford, 2005). The body size considered attractive and healthy at one point in history (e.g., Rubenesque women in paintings of the seventeenth century, or Marilyn Monroe in the 1950s), would be considered "overweight," if not "obese," in our current climate. What was once considered an ideal form or preference in the past has now become reified into stringent standards for body size and shape that all are told to emulate—not only to be considered attractive, but also for their health.

In the 1940s, the Metropolitan Life Insurance Company published for the first time "ideal weights" for men and women (Seid, 1989). These weights were set lower than the average weights for men and women and were promoted as optimum for health and longevity. However, there was little solid data to support this notion (Gaesser, 2002). Nevertheless, the idea that one must modify his or her weight for health purposes became enshrined in American culture. Since the weights promoted for health were under the average for most people, a need was created for ways to lose weight. The weight-loss industry was born. (For a thorough and interesting history of American cultural norms related to size, see Seid, 1989.) This development injected a profit motive into the debate about size and health that is rarely addressed in media reports and even research studies (Bacon, 2008; Boero, 2007).

Concurrently, theoretical beliefs in the mental health community supported the ideas that large size represented maladjustment and ill health. Psychological treatment has been primarily aimed at facilitating adherence to a diet and exercise plan with the goal of weight loss (Brownell, 1998; Cogan & Rothblum, 1992). It is assumed that weight loss will result in better health (physically and psychologically) and increase attractiveness. Though awareness is increasing of the negative effect stigmatization has on fat people, the prescription is still to get rid of the fat rather than addressing the prejudices that lead to stigmatization.

Case Vignette 11.1 demonstrates the use of the traditional paradigm for treating a person of size. The mental health practitioner is not aware of the problematic effects of a weight-loss focus.

In accepting Evelyn's focus on weight-loss as the solution and treatment goal, the mental health practitioner misses the impact that Evelyn's dieting history, her failed attempts at permanent weight loss, and her husband's criticism has had on her self-esteem and mood. By attempting to empower Evelyn yet again through exerting control over her weight, the stage is set for another failed weight-loss attempt and continued feelings of guilt, lack of agency within her life, and low self-worth. A more effective approach would seek to empower Evelyn independent of her weight by helping her to increase health-promoting behaviors, reinforcing behavior change (not weight-loss), and addressing her fears about the marital relationship.

It is not surprising that Evelyn would view weight-loss as a solution to her distress. There are many reasons for this: (a) there is a strong cultural focus on thinness that is associated with beauty and happiness, (b) weight is viewed as within a person's control and thus it is a moral failing if one is not thin, (c) a focus on weight-loss (internal locus of control) is viewed as more easily achieved than a focus on societal oppression and learning how to have self-worth when one is a target of oppression, (d) weight is easier to focus on than the painful reality of having a partner who criticizes you and finds you wanting, and (e) a focus on the difficulties of her marital situation may expose deeper concerns about the viability of the relationship.

CASE VIGNETTE 11.1

Evelyn is a 50-year-old married White woman. She presents with concerns about her marital relationship and dissatisfaction with her weight. She has an extensive dieting history, typically losing 20 or more pounds and then regaining the lost weight within a year or two. This has occurred multiple times. She is highly critical of her inability to lose weight and keep it off. She reports feeling down, low self-esteem, feelings of guilt, and fear her husband will leave if she doesn't improve her appearance. She states that he regularly comments on her weight and compares her unfavorably to thinner women of their acquaintance. The clinician accepts Evelyn's conceptualization of the problem and develops a treatment plan including exercise and a weight-loss diet as well as a focus on increasing her self-esteem. Evelyn is referred to a nutritionist to help her learn proper nutrition and a physician for medication for her mood and weight-loss. She is also encouraged to consider marital counseling for her relationship concerns.

ELEMENTS OF COMPETENCY

Body size is distributed along a continuum, and fat is a naturally occurring state for humans. The old paradigm when working with a fat client, even when the client was not concerned about his or her size, was focused on behavior modification with a weight-loss plan and a target "ideal" weight (Brownell, 1998; Cogan & Rothblum, 1992). There is an ongoing search for interventions that will have greater efficacy than the oft-cited 90 to 95 percent failure rate for weight-loss efforts (Brownell & Rodin, 1994; Mark, 2006; Rosenbaum, Leibel, & Hirsch, 1997; Stunkard, 1958; Wilson, 1994).

Professionals in mental health and medical fields started questioning the dominant paradigm (fat is unhealthy; dieting is the solution) in the 1950s (Bruch, 1957). However, strong questioning of the efficacy of dieting and our traditional way of managing people's weight dissatisfaction did not take hold until the 1980s. Though these voices continue to be in the minority in mental health and medicine, the paradigm is shifting and research is being conducted to ascertain the efficacy of non-dieting approaches for weight dissatisfaction, body-image disturbances, and related low self-esteem and medical conditions.

The non-diet approach has evolved into interventions with a Health at Every Size (HAES) focus. HAES approaches typically involve improving health, both psychological and physical, through a focus on empowerment and health behavior change rather than weight-loss.

KNOWLEDGE

For competency in the treatment of people of size, there are many areas with which to familiarize oneself. This includes the literature on ethical standards, individual and cultural diversity, assessment, diagnosis, case conceptualization, intervention, and training pertaining to size issues (see the table at the bottom of the page).

Ethical Standards

As psychologists and psychologists-in-training, we must adhere to ethical principles and standards when working with any client (American Psychological Association, 2002). When working with anyone, including people of size, the preeminent ethic to uphold is to do no harm (Connors & Melcher, 1993). The old paradigm

---

COMPETENCIES FOR COUNSELORS WORKING WITH SIZE CONCERNS

The Tenets of HAES (Kratina & Shuman, 2003)

- Health enhancement—attention to emotional, physical, and spiritual wellbeing, without focus on weight-loss or achieving a specific "ideal weight."
- Size and self-acceptance—respect and appreciation for the wonderful diversity of body shapes and sizes (including one's own!), rather than the pursuit of an idealized weight or shape.
- The pleasure of eating well—eating based on internal cues of hunger, satiety, and appetite and individual nutritional needs rather than on external food plans or diets.
- The joy of movement—encouraging all physical activities for the associated pleasure and health benefits, rather than following a specific routine of regimented exercise for the primary purpose of weight-loss.
- An end to weight bias—recognition that body shape, size, and/or weight are not evidence of any particular way of eating, level of physical activity, personality, psychological issue, or moral character; confirmation that there is beauty and worth in every body.

of diet and exercise does not have the empirical support or efficacy we would demand for any treatment plan we would use with a client. The *New England Journal of Medicine*, in an editorial (Kassirer & Angell, 1998), noted that the cure may be worse than the condition and cautioned against using weight-loss as a treatment with overweight patients. The most common outcome of dieting is weight-gain and there is "a mountain of scientific evidence about the health hazards of chronic dieting and weight fluctuation" (Gaesser, 2002).

Another important ethical principle is to respect the rights and dignity of all people, including diverse populations. Treatment approaches with the goal of thinness reflect how the acceptance of weight diversity lags behind that of other aspects of diversity, and violate this ethical principle (Connors & Melcher, 1993). The focus of changing fat people so that they will be less stigmatized is akin to practices prevalent in the past of changing sexual orientation in order to help gay people avoid prejudice.

The non-diet approach, HAES, has empirical support for improving both psychological well-being and physical health (Bacon, Van Loan, Stern, & Keim, 2005; Bacon et al., 2002; Robinson & Bacon, 1996; Tenzer, 1989) and acknowledges the diversity of body size and weight in human beings.

Individual and Cultural Diversity

The National Association to Advance Fat Acceptance (NAAFA, http://www.naafaonline.com) was founded in 1969 to improve the quality of life for fat people. In 1973, a more radical group, the Fat Underground, was founded by women who had been influenced by radical therapy and radical feminism (Mayer, 1983). They subscribed to the belief that psychological problems were caused by oppressive societal institutions and practices. Oppression of fat people, especially women, then would be the cause of distress rather than being fat itself (see Schoenfielder & Wieser, 1983 for a collection of writings by Fat Underground members). Fat oppression and its effects on people of size became the subject matter of many books within feminist and larger sociological contexts (Goodman, 1995; Louderbeck, 1970; Millman, 1980; Schwartz, 1986).

Size Acceptance Identity Development Model

The Spiral of Acceptance (Erdman, 1995) is, to our knowledge, the only identity development model of size acceptance. It was developed for women; further research would be needed to determine how applicable it is to men and whether something new needs to be created that is inclusive of all people of size. Erdman posits that coming to accept your size is a process and a personal decision one needs to make. Further, she states that there is no one way to be size accepting and that it can be defined individually.

Through qualitative research, Erdman (1995) identified six indicators that mark the various behaviors and attitudes that women hold as they move through the Spiral of Acceptance. The first indicator is a woman's attitude toward and relationship with food. Is that relationship compulsive and diet focused or more relaxed and basically a nonissue in life? The second indicator relates to body image. Does she hold a "creative" body image, seeing herself as smaller than in reality? Or, has she moved toward perceiving her body as it is and no longer stigmatizes herself for being "fat"? A woman's time orientation is the third indicator. Is she living in the present, doing the things she wants now rather than waiting until she is thin enough to do them? Living a lifestyle that is inner-determined is the fourth indicator. The fifth indicator is the ability and willingness to seek out size-accepting support while the sixth is becoming involved in something larger than oneself. These indicators are mapped out within a four-stage model that proceeds from Pre-Acceptance to Decisive Acceptance. Erdman also provides ideas for moving along the process of size acceptance.

Research on Weight and Health

Studies have shown that as a group, fat people eat no more than their thinner counterparts (Garner & Wooley, 1991). As to unhappiness, a recent study found that fat men commit suicide at a significantly lower rate than thin men and their mental-health-related quality of life improved as body mass index (BMI) increased (Mukamal, Kawachi, Miller, & Rimm, 2007). Many studies conducted at the Cooper Institute for Aerobic Fitness have demonstrated that healthy bodies come in all sizes and that fitness is related to activity level rather than body size. In fact, obese, fit men had the same death rate as lean, fit men and half the death rate of thin, unfit men (Blair, Kohl III, Paffenbarger, Clark, Cooper, & Gibbons, 1989). In addition, for the fat people who do have health problems, such as high blood pressure, high cholesterol, or insulin resistance, they can improve their health through lifestyle changes independent of weight loss (Gaesser, 2002). As to premature mortality due to being "overweight" and "obese," data indicate more premature deaths occur for those with a BMI less than 25 than for those with a BMI greater than or equal to 25. In fact, the lowest mortality was found to be in the BMI range of 25 to 29.9, weights that are currently classified as "overweight" (Flegal, Graubard, Williamson, & Gail, 2005).

"Obesity" as a disease is so accepted, that to argue that maybe it is not weight that causes the diseases associated with it is seen as heresy by many. However, the vast majority of the studies connecting weight to disease are correlational in nature. Since correlation does not equal causation, disease states such as type II diabetes may be caused by an unknown third process, which also causes weight gain. It is possible that in many of the diseases, for which weight is a risk factor, weight may be a symptom of the disease rather than a cause. Another factor to consider is the fact that many fat people have a history of losing and regaining weight, or weight cycling. Research has identified the harmful effects of even one loss/regain cycle such as increased levels of cholesterol,

blood pressure, and insulin-resistance (Blair, Shaten, Brownell, Collins, & Lissner, 1993; Ernsberger, Koletsky, Baskin, & Collins, 1996; Holbrook, Barrett-Connor, & Wingard, 1989; Kajioka, Tsuzuku, Shimokata, & Sato, 2002; Pfohl, Luft, Blomberg, & Schmulling, 1994). The more obese an individual, the more likely they have experienced multiple loss/regain cycles and repeated damage to their bodies (Ikeda, Lyons, Schwartzman, & Mitchell, 2004). This could account for the correlation between many of the diseases attributed to "obesity" and be a third factor driving both increased weight and disease development.

The stereotypes of fat people attribute their large size to overeating and sedentary living. Though this way of living is true for many people of size, it also true of many thin people as well. Much research has looked for causes of fatness and there is strong evidence for primarily genetic causes. In fact, weight is as heritable as height, in the 0.7 to 0.8 range (Friedman, 2004). Studies of adoptees and studies of twins reared apart versus twins reared together provide good data when examining genetic versus environmental influences. Stunkard, Foch, and Hrubec (1986) looked at over 500 adults who had been adopted in their first year of life. In fact, 55 percent were adopted within the first month of life. The study found that adoptees' size was similar to their biological parents, and had no relation to their adoptive parents. In another study, the BMI of twins reared apart versus twins reared together had similar findings. The identical twins in the study had nearly identical BMIs regardless if they were brought up together or reared apart. Fraternal twins had a bit more variation regarding their BMI, which would make sense since they share some of the same genes, but not all (Stunkard, Harris, Pederson, & McClearn, 1990). Other studies of twins support the same conclusion, leading the researchers to conclude that 70 percent of weight variation is accounted for by genetics (Allison et al., 1996, Stunkard et al., 1986).

The belief that Americans are becoming dramatically more "obese" is questionable on close examination of the research (Campos, Saguy, Ernsberger, Oliver, & Gaesser, 2006). In fact, people at the lower end of the weight distribution curve have gained little or no weight, whereas those in the vast majority are about 3 to 5 kg heavier than those in the previous generation (Flegal, Carroll, Kuczmarski, & Johnson, 1998). There has been a significant increase of weight in the heaviest individuals (Freedman, Khan, Serdula, Galuska, & Dietz, 2002). It is likely that one must have a predisposition to a large size in order for lifestyle choices to have a dramatic effect on size. Also, the effect of chronic dieting probably has contributed to the increase in weight of the largest people in American society. With each episode of restricted eating, the body's metabolism slows down and the set-point is raised, meaning fewer calories are needed to maintain a larger size (Coakley, Rimm, Colditz, Kawachi, & Willett, 1998; Stice, Presnell, & Shaw, 2005). A study of adolescent girls found that those who pursue weight-control efforts were more likely to gain weight and become obese than girls who did not (Stice, Cameron, Killeen, Hayward, & Taylor, 1999).

This is not to say that lifestyle factors are not important for health. However, the cultural context needs to be taken into account rather than solely attributing the use of health-related behaviors to individual choice. In a culture where exercise as a daily part of life is discouraged due to developments favoring cars for transportation, rather than walking or public transport, people get less exercise than they have in the past (Hill & Peters, 1998; Poston & Foreyt, 1999). For children, it is especially striking that access to play and movement has been restricted due to perceptions of danger and the elimination of physical education in schools (Hill & Peters, 1998; Poston & Foreyt, 1999; Srinivasan, O'Fallon, & Dearry, 2003). Another factor for rising rates of obesity may be the tendency for mothers to restrict calories while pregnant. This is a likely consequence of the cultural emphasis on thinness and fear of fat. In animal studies, the offspring of mothers who restricted food intake while pregnant were more likely to have low birthweights and have a higher risk of developing diabetes later in life unless they maintained a very low caloric intake lifelong (Krechowec, Vickers, Gertler, & Breier, 2006; Vickers, Breier, Cutfield, Hofman, & Gluckman, 2000).

Even if the hypothesis that increased weight is a major issue that needs to be addressed is accepted, the research does not provide for any effective long-term solutions (Cogan & Ernsberger, 1999; Mann et al., 2007). As mentioned earlier, the standard treatment of caloric restriction and increased physical activity has not been proven to work for the vast majority of individuals who undertake a diet-and-exercise program, and weight cycling is the most likely result of a diet. Bariatric surgery is now being used for those who have not succeeded at dieting for weight-loss. Long-term follow-up data is missing for this intervention as well. Reports of weight-regain and complications increase the longer one follows patients after surgery (Suter, Calmes, Paroz, & Giusti, 2006). It appears that everyone has a biologically predetermined "healthy weight" that is rigorously defended by their metabolism unless extreme measures are taken. This would make size similar to sexual orientation in that both are aspects of diversity that society has disapproved of and stigmatized, attributing the fat person's size and the gay person's same-sex desires to choice rather than biological predisposition.

This very brief overview of the research related to fat and health is a starting point for gathering the information a multiculturally competent mental health practitioner needs to work with people of size. Further exposure to the research as well as fat culture is necessary to understand both the experience of oppression of this population as well as the celebratory aspects of accepting and embracing one's size as a naturally occurring aspect of diversity. In addition to the various articles and books cited so far, a bibliography of selected readings and experiential exercises is listed in the Resources section of the chapter.

SKILLS

Assessment Skills

As with any client, accurate assessment is important. Given the lack of size acceptance in the dominant cultures and the emphasis on thinness, weight-neutral language is important when assessing clients' level of comfort with their body. Use of terms such as *obesity* and *overweight* are better avoided. The first indicates that the person's size is a medical problem that needs to be fixed. The latter indicates that there is some predetermined size that is the "correct" weight for this particular person. From the beginning, as a culturally competent clinician, it is important to distinguish your approach from that of the prejudicial majority and possibly the other health providers your client has seen. What is the relationship (if any) of the client's presenting concerns to his or her size? As with any minority group member, the client's diversity characteristics may have nothing to do with the presenting concerns

for which she or he comes to treatment. In addition, how do other diversity factors (e.g., race, ethnicity, sexual orientation, socioeconomic status, gender) interact with size? Some subcultures are more size-accepting, others less so than the majority culture.

When forming a conceptualization, as with any other client, the core issues must be identified. An additional consideration to incorporate is how the client's minority status as a person of size influences and/or compounds the problems he or she is bringing to therapy. Even if the presenting concerns are not related to the client's status as a person of size, as a clinician it is important to maintain an awareness of the minority status(es) of the client and how it (they) may affect treatment at any point.

Intervention Skills

In treatment planning, assessment and conceptualization will guide the choice of interventions. Crucial to effective size-accepting treatment is

SAMPLE HAES ASSESSMENT QUESTIONS

- How do you feel about your body/weight/size?
- Does your body/weight/size impact you? What are the positive effects? What are the negative?
- How do your concerns about your body/weight/size impact the issues you came into therapy to discuss?
- How long have your body/weight/size struggles been of concern?
- What is your dieting history?
  - What was your highest weight?
  - What was your lowest adult weight?
  - How many times have you gained and lost more than 10 pounds?
  - How old were you when you first dieted?
  - Have you taken medication (prescribed or over the counter) to aid with weight loss?
- What do other family members look like? Are their bodies and weight similar to yours? Different from yours? Do other family members diet?
- Have others criticized you and/or teased you about your body/size/weight?
- What kinds of exercise and/or physical activity do you engage in? Do you like it?
- What kinds of foods do you eat? What percentage of the time do you eat out? At home? Have you had any education about healthy nutrition?

- How do you decide when and what to eat?
  - Do you eat when hungry? Stop when you are full?
  - What do you base your food choices on? Internal cues? External rules?
  - Do you avoid certain foods? Why?
- How do you feel after eating?
- Do you weigh yourself? How often? What effect does seeing your weight have on your mood?

the use of the HAES tenets listed earlier in this chapter. They provide a framework for approaching the client and his or her presenting concerns that relate to size. The reader is directed to the Resources section of this chapter for sample interventions listed by HAES tenet. Another important skill is weight neutrality. The size of clients and people in general is not good or bad, or necessarily indicative of health status. Whether any client gains, loses, or maintains a particular weight should not affect the quality of the care provided or be part of the evaluation of the effectiveness of treatment (an exception to this would be in cases of anorexia, where weight gain is necessary for sustaining life). With other interventions, the focus should be on behavior change and reinforcing behavior change. It should be no different when working on healthy behaviors with clients of size. Thus, commenting on weight-loss or gain with either approval or disapproval would be counterproductive. Rather, the focus should remain on the behavior of the client and examining whether it is effective and health-promoting.

It is not surprising that many clients will hold fat-phobic attitudes and consequently be highly critical of themselves due to their perceived failure at achieving and maintaining a societally acceptable weight. It will not be an easy task for clients to move toward size acceptance given the messages they are bombarded with in the media and from family and friends. The mental health practitioner may be the first person in their lives to suggest that there is an alternative to conventional prescriptions to lose weight and that their size is a facet of diversity.

To facilitate this process, helping the client to develop an "emotional immune system"

(Burgard, 1998) will be essential. Just as a person can decrease his or her vulnerability to colds and flu through taking care to maintain his or her immune system by eating well, reducing stress, and so on, a person can also decrease his or her vulnerability to prejudicial statements and the bigotry of others by augmenting his or her emotional immune system. Providing clients with education about HAES is important. This alternative viewpoint gives the client another lens through which he or she can view size. It also provides a way out of the dilemma of accepting a larger size when he or she is barraged with the perceived health threats of larger size. Clients need education about the myths related to fat and health. Explain how news reports may sensationalize or oversimplify research studies and discuss how the media is embedded in the larger fat-phobic culture. Mindfulness skills (Linehan, 1993) such as "observe" and "describe" will also aid the client in using less loaded language and facilitate a nonjudgmental stance regarding his or her size. Mindfulness skills provide a useful frame for increasing the client's knowledge of effective and ineffective coping skills and mindful eating.

As is crucial when working with individuals from any marginalized group, empowerment is key. Bibliotherapy may be used to expose clients to other perspectives and increase their awareness of others like them. It is important to increase clients' exposure to positive images of people of size. Clients should be introduced to movies, books, and art with people of size and/or a diversity of sizes (see the Resources section later in the chapter for suggestions). It is helpful to reduce exposure to the negative images of fat people in the popular media and culture and instead a size-supporting system outside of therapy should be located. There may be local NAAFA groups or other organized groups available. There are many fat-accepting listserves on the Internet and clients can explore these with as much participation as they find comfortable.

The process of becoming more size- and self-accepting is a slow one. Clients must be encouraged to consider what they have tried in the past to change their body/size/weight and the results they have achieved with those efforts. Clients may compare their own experiences with what they are learning from the research, readings, and other resources. Mental health practitioners should explore the meaning of being fat for their clients, identifying expectations and fantasies about the results of achieving thinness. Recognizing the loss of the dream of being thin will require ongoing empathy. Often, there is a grieving process that accompanies the acceptance of being larger than wanted. General body-image work will be helpful as well. There are many good resources to draw from listed in the Resources section at the end of the chapter.

When it comes to health concerns and eating behavior, the focus should be on gradual, incremental change toward healthier behaviors. Dramatic changes rarely are maintained over the long term. For clients to truly benefit, it is most useful to suggest slowing down and changing one or two behaviors at a time. Helping clients find a way to incorporate regular movement into their life is an excellent first step to improve health. Development of attuned eating is also important; being mindful of internal cues will help clients learn how to eat in ways that are beneficial for them and decrease bingeing and feelings of being out of control with food (Munter & Hirschman, 1988; Tribole, 1995).

Contraindications to the Use of HAES

Using a HAES approach seems counterintuitive when there are health concerns such as anorexia. However, HAES promotes eating based on nutritional needs and overall health. In cases of

anorexia, eating to gain weight is necessary for proper body functioning and to sustain life. HAES can also be used even when there are limitations on diet or exercise due to health problems such as diabetes and other conditions that are negatively affected by certain foods. HAES does not promote eating whatever you want regardless of the health consequences. Rather, HAES encourages people to become aware of how foods they eat affect them and to eat based on what positively affects their sense of overall wellbeing and their nutritional needs. Thus, someone with diabetes may choose to limit carbohydrates, due to the deleterious effects eating them in an unrestrained manner would have on their blood sugar, not because they need to lose weight. The treatment goal in a HAES approach is improved health. Weight and size may change as a side effect of improved health but is not a stated, observed, or measured goal of HAES treatment.

Collaboration and Referral Skills

It is important to be aware of the stance professionals take regarding weight before referring to them. Any positive work with a client can be compromised by another health provider suggesting yet another diet or focusing on weight-loss. Consulting a nutritionist may be helpful for dietary information. There are many nutritionists who use a HAES approach.

Clients need mental health practitioners to advocate for their needs with physicians. Many fat people, especially women, avoid seeing a medical doctor due to past negative experiences with health-care providers (Olson, Schumaker, & Yawn, 1994). Some health concerns can be ameliorated with medication and it is better to have them treated sooner rather than waiting to lose weight, which may or may not help the condition. Clients need education about the research related to health and weight and encouragement to inform their physicians as well. Though the physician may not be open to the information, empowering clients to assert their needs is important. Asking the physician to treat the presenting problem as he or she would if the patient were thin is a helpful way to know what treatment is needed. At times, the client may need to change physicians in order to receive appropriate care.

Supervision and Training Skills

Effective training involves multiple levels for supervisees. Didactic presentations in seminars, coursework, experiential activities, and clinical supervision all play a role. During training, it is vital that trainees receive weekly supervision of their treatment of the client. Clinical sessions should be videotaped, audiotaped, or live-observed by a supervisor who has knowledge and experience in working with this population.

Increasing trainee openness in this area is crucial. We all have been raised in a fat-phobic culture with the related misinformation, and where prejudice may be masked as concern for the fat person. Few trainees will begin their training knowing that the genetic and behavioral components that are a part of health apply to weight and size as well. We must help trainees increase their awareness of their own biases while being careful not to overwhelm them so much that they shut down and cannot take in new information. Trainees will have their own weight and body-size struggles. Some will have significant dieting histories. It can be very difficult to accept that promoting dieting reflects a lack of size acceptance. Of course, people have a right to make their own decisions regarding their bodies. However, when working with clients it is an ethical duty to work with techniques that the research demonstrates are efficacious and non-harming. Dieting does not meet this standard, whereas HAES does.

An interesting model has been developed for professionals who are developing an identity as a HAES clinician (P. Lyons, personal communication, 2008). Lyons has identified beliefs and actions associated with specific stages (Never, Someday, Soon, Now, Forever) as individuals

transition from the dominant paradigm (i.e., a weight-loss focus) to HAES. These stages correspond to the Precontemplation, Contemplation, Preparation, Action, and Maintenance stages that are from the Stages of Change Model developed by Prochaska and DiClemente (1983). Similar to how one uses clients' stages when conceptualizing therapeutic approach and interventions, clinicians can use Lyons' model to assess where they are in their process of becoming a HAES practitioner and activities in which they can participate to foster their growth. For example, the key beliefs and actions of the current paradigm, that is, the need to "reduce obesity," are represented in the Never column. As one moves to the right through Lyons' stages, questions are raised about those beliefs to promote reflection, and suggestions for action are offered to facilitate clinicians' shift to a HAES stance.

Case Vignette 11.2 (on the following page) demonstrates the use of Lyons' model in providing clinical supervision. The clinician is not aware of the problematic effects of a weight-loss focus for her new client.

As Andrea's supervisor, in which stage of change would you place Andrea using Lyons' model? Would you support these treatment goals? If you want to make changes in Andrea's treatment plan, how do you do so in an educational and personally respectful manner? Can the treatment plan be changed using the HAES treatment approach and still meet the client's goals?

Andrea's thinking appears to be reflective of the precontemplation stage with some movement into the contemplation stage. She is aware that "fad diets" aren't healthy but believes "lifestyle changes" that focus on decreasing fat and caloric intake and pairing that diet with an exercise routine is a healthy approach to weight-loss. It is important to guide Andrea to factual information regarding the ineffectiveness of diets and weight-loss methods. The supervisor can validate that Andrea's treatment approach is a highly used and recognized approach to a client's goal for weight-loss. In supervision, the supervisor can provide a quick overview of the research regarding the ineffectiveness of weight-loss

CASE VIGNETTE 11.2

Andrea is a doctoral student in a counseling psychology program and is completing her practicum at the University Counseling Center. Andrea recently completed an intake with a 20-year-old European American female student. She is using time in supervision to acquaint you, her clinical supervisor, with the client and share her treatment recommendations in response to the client's goals for therapy.

The client is a sophomore and her presenting problem is that she is unhappy with her life. She reports a history of being uncomfortable in social settings and this semester finds her social discomfort interfering with a core class, speech communication. The client reports a history of always being a "chubby kid" who was teased in elementary school. The client has meaningful relationships with her peers, but has never dated. When she is among people she does not know well, "especially guys my age," she reports feeling self-conscious about her appearance and knows the guys aren't attracted to her because she is so fat. These feelings of discomfort have increased in her speech communication class, where she is required to present a 2-to-5-minute speech every other week. Her class is 60 percent male. The client reports, "I'm tired of being fat, tired of being told 'you have such a pretty face,' and I'm finally ready to do something about it. I want to lose twenty pounds and finally get a boyfriend. I want counseling to help me stick to a diet once and for all."

Andrea reviewed the Personality Assessment Inventory report, which reported no clinical elevations. She used the clinical interview to confirm the client did not meet criteria for social anxiety, generalized anxiety, or depression. Andrea concludes that the client is struggling with developmental issues that are being exacerbated by her weight and the negative social consequences of being fat. Her treatment plan includes referring the client to the nutritionist to learn about making healthy food choices so the client can reduce her fat and caloric intake, create a workout routine, and set a goal of losing two pounds per week. Andrea states she is aware that weight-loss that occurs quickly is not healthy and is more likely to be regained. She wants her client to learn how to lose weight the healthy way by making lifestyle changes, not by going on a crazy fad diet.

methods and supplement the discussion with assigned readings from the "Weight and Health" section of the Resources section of this chapter. The supervisor and Andrea can agree that the first session will be used to gather a weight and diet history and the client's current food intake and physical activity—all physical movement, not just "exercise." This plan meets both the non-HAES and HAES approach to treatment.

The second supervision session can be spent listening to Andrea's reactions to the readings, addressing concerns, and introducing the HAES approach. The two tenets to pay attention to initially would be the pleasure of eating well and the joy of movement. This will aid Andrea in creating treatment goals that reflect the HAES model and still are addressing the client's presenting concerns of weight. Sessions could focus on mindfulness to teach the client about mindful eating (i.e., cues of hunger, fullness, satiety, the influence different foods have your sense of overall wellbeing) and assisting the client in identifying which types of movement are playful and enjoyable versus those that are regimented or punitive.

The proposed strategies reflect the initial steps in introducing Andrea and her client to HAES while giving Andrea time to begin making the paradigm shift. The information shared in supervision, and the additional readings, increase Andrea's knowledge base, while at the same time increasing her awareness of the myths she has learned and biases she holds. Supervision can be used as a forum for Andrea to challenge the readings that confront her myths and biases, and receive validation that this research and literature counters popular press and popular medical opinion, and to allow an environment to be created in supervision that is nonjudgmental, safe, and yet uncomfortable at times as long-held beliefs are viewed in a different light.

Stages of Change

How Professionals Can Move Away from "Reducing Obesity" to a Health-at-Every-Size Model

Never/ Precontemplation	Someday/ Contemplation	Soon/ Preparation	Now/Action	Forever/ Maintenance
Obesity is a very serious disease; I'm right—there's no problem.	There is controversy. Maybe I'm not right— maybe there is a problem.	Weight research is mixed; gather new info/read across disciplines.	Be open to alternatives; begin to try new approaches; small steps.	Focus on health for all. Get support from colleagues.
Weight-loss is essential to improve health.	How? Treatments don't last for 95% of people.	Read about HAES alternatives; discuss.	Evaluate benefits and barriers to new approach.	Keep up with standard research; do your own.
Dieting/caloric restraint is necessary. Goal of exercise is weight-loss.	But dieting can increase problems/ eating disorders. Many benefits of activity.	Talk with people who've stopped dieting/weight obsession. How?	Stop dieting yourself. Try practicing what you are recommending.	Keep returning to self-trust/ body acceptance/ whole-person focus.
Only a BMI below 25 is a "healthy weight."	But there are healthy fat people/unhealthy thin?	Whole-person focus vs. weight per se.	Listen to patients/clients trying new approach.	Talk more publicly/"come out" more often.
The medical model works; drugs/ surgery when diet and exercise fail.	Health is more than physical appearance. What about psychosocial issues?	Learn more about multicultural bias, issues, & alternative views.	Get skills/ training to work with different models & populations.	Keep up with size acceptance, multicultural/ mind-body literature.
Tell people what to do: lose weight; keep trying.	How do I feel when told what to do by "experts"?	Question authority; listen more, talk less.	Learn to use empowerment models.	Remember, there is no one answer for all.
Keep the pressure on: "thin is best" for all.	How has pressuring helped people?	Isn't weight bias & discrimination wrong?	Increase awareness of your own & cultural attitudes.	Ensure weight neutrality. Oppose weight bias.

Source: Lyons (2008), used by permission.

Providing a safe environment for addressing multicultural issues is never easy. For a thorough guide to incorporating multicultural issues into discussions with trainees, the reader should see Fouad and Arredondo (2007). In addition, training recommendations and resources are provided in Tables 11.1 through 11.4 and in the Resources section of this chapter for HAES-informed clinical work.

VALUES AND ATTITUDES

There are many myths and stereotypes about fat people as well as misinformation about what it means to be fat. It is "common knowledge" that fat people are unhealthy, unhappy, and gluttonous. Rarely is it noted that many people live long and happy lives in large bodies. "Obesity" is classified as a disease and is thought to cause other diseases. Losing weight, we are told, is just a matter of discipline. Fat people only need to have enough willpower and the thin person within will emerge. And given that willpower is all it takes, life will improve greatly once the weight is lost and one is thin. After all, thin people are always happy, healthy, and never overeat. As we have seen, the truth is much more complex and the damage these myths cause is real. The Resources section of this chapter includes a self-awareness exercise devoted to the myths commonly held about size and weight.

Though dietary restriction and exercise with a goal of weight-loss is typically ineffectual and not maintained long-term, improving one's nutritional intake and increasing movement are beneficial for all. When identifying behavioral changes in these two areas, it is important to remember that the goal is improved health and wellbeing. Weight-loss and change in size may be a side effect of increasing healthful behaviors. However, weight-gain (e.g., increasing muscle mass) and lack of weight change may also be outcomes. Improving one's health is a worthy goal, nonetheless.

As in any therapy, alertness to transference reactions from clients is necessary. Mental health practitioners who are on the thin side may find clients doubting their ability to understand concerns related to size. On the other hand, clients may find it especially meaningful to have someone thin validate their reality and accept them just as they are. Heavier mental health practitioners may be perceived by clients as having "given up." Alternatively, clients may perceive heavier clinicians as a role model for size acceptance. They may ask questions about how the mental health practitioner feels about his or her body and whether she or he has ever struggled with size acceptance.

When working with clients of size, it is important to remain aware of reactions to them and to the therapy. When size is an aspect of the work, it often triggers countertransference in the therapist around his or her own size acceptance (see Matz & Frankel, 2004 for a thorough discussion of transference and countertransference phenomena when working with large clients). It is easy to communicate fat-phobic attitudes, even when it is unintended. Chairs that aren't big enough for clients to be comfortable replicate their experience outside of therapy of being too big to fit. Congratulating clients on weight-loss sets up a no-win situation. Do they then need to continue with weight-loss and/or keep it off to receive continued approval? If they regain weight, how will the mental health practitioner feel about them then? If clinicians are too expressive of attitudes about fat acceptance, clients may feel pushed to accept themselves faster than they are able, therefore not experiencing respect for their identity and pacing for change. They may feel they cannot discuss their desire to lose weight and their struggles around accepting themselves because the mental health practitioner wants them to quickly accept being fat and won't indicate approval in the absence of such acceptance.

Case Example

Case Vignette 11.3 demonstrates how to use HAES in assessment and intervention. The

CASE VIGNETTE 11.3

The client is a 28-year-old partnered Latina lesbian. She is distressed by her size and her mother's insistence that she lose weight because it is so unhealthy to be fat. She feels hopeless about resolving this issue because she has tried diets in the past and can never stick with one long enough to be successful. She explains that she eats too much and that is why she is fat. She adds that she often eats in secret because she is so ashamed of eating and her lack of control. She describes her partner as supportive but at a loss about how to help her.

HAES approach is always to be used in conjunction with typical assessment and interventions strategies.

Issues to Consider

- What HAES assessment questions do you need to ask?
- What countertransference reactions do you have (if any)?
- What are the potential ethical issues in this case? How might you resolve them?
- What issues do you feel able to address and what do you think is outside your competence?
- Should you consult with other health-care professionals?
- How will you address the impact of this client's multiple identities on her presenting concern?
- Is it appropriate for you to provide counseling to this client? If not, what is your treatment plan?

Therapy Goals

- Aid the client in exploring and establishing her goals for treatment versus the goals others have established for her.
- Help her define what is distressing to her:

  ○ Distressed about her weight and/or size?
  ○ Distressed about her mother's criticism of her weight?
  ○ Distressed about her health?
  ○ Distressed because she feels hopeless and shamed, and has a sense of failure due to previous diets not working?
  ○ Distressed about her eating habits?

- How would her life change if she did weigh x amount or was x size?

Exploring the answers to these questions will facilitate the client's and counselor's establishment of collaborative goals for treatment.

HAES Treatment Plan

- Educate client about research addressing the ineffectiveness of dieting and benefits of health-promoting behaviors.
- Obtain informed consent for a HAES focus in therapy.
- Assess client's eating behaviors (see questions that follow).
- Assess client's nutritional knowledge (see questions that follow) and refer to a nutritionist if appropriate.
- Assess health status (see questions that follow) and refer to physician if appropriate.
- Teach cognitive-behavioral strategies to facilitate health-promoting behavior.
- Empower client to accept herself as she is and to engage in health-related behaviors out of self-love rather than as a reaction to her negative self-perception. (Behavior change will be more effective and lasting if done from a place of self-care versus self-loathing.)
- Connect client with a size-acceptance community for additional support.
- Improve client's ability to be in relationship with her mother even if her mother does not understand the client's choices.

- Improve client's ability to identify her needs and communicate them to her partner.

HAES Assessment Questions

- Assess the client's body weight and dieting history. What was her highest weight? Lowest adult weight? Number of loss/gain cycles?
- Assess the client's attitude about her weight and health. How does she feel about her body, size, and weight? Does the client have any health concerns?
- Assess the family's weight and health history. What is her familial weight and health history? Is her body build and weight similar to others in the family?
- Assess her eating patterns and for possible disordered eating. What kinds of foods does she eat and in what amounts? Is she bingeing? How often does she binge eat? Purge? Restrict her intake? How does she choose what she eats? What cues does she use to decide when to eat?
- Assess current nutritional intake and attitudes concerning food. A three-day recall will help assess current nutritional intake. Does client enjoy food? Does she label foods "good" and "bad"? Are there foods she refuses to eat? Does she eat as a means of self-soothing or coping with emotions?
- What kinds of exercise does she engage in? Does she enjoy it?
- Assess for familial attitudes about weight and size. What is her family's attitude about weight? Does it differ for men and women? Does anyone else pressure her about her weight besides her mother? Is anyone else in the family pressured about their weight?
- Assess for cultural attitudes about weight and size. What is the attitude in the Latino community about body weight and size? Does it differ for men and women? Was she ever teased or treated as "less than" by peers due to her weight?
- Assess for possible interactions with weight and sexual orientation. Is she out to her family? Do attitudes about weight differ for lesbians, her family, and in the larger Latino

culture? Does her size imply anything about her sexual orientation to her family or to the community?
- Assess for possible misunderstandings related to her mother's pressure to lose weight. Does her mother's concern for her weight fit within the context of familial and community attitudes about weight? Are there other concerns about her daughter that the mother may not be discussing and using weight as a proxy for those concerns?
- How does her partner feel about her (the client's) weight and body?
- Does the client have friends and family members who are supportive of her and who are accepting of her weight and size?

Intervention Techniques

The interventions that follow can be categorized primarily within the interpersonal, cognitive-behavioral, and feminist theoretical schools of thought. They can be incorporated by clinicians who work from other perspectives and are not meant to be exclusive of other approaches.

An interpersonal focus would include discussion of the client's relationship history with her family, friends, partner, and co-workers in order to identify patterns in interpersonal relationships. These patterns may explicate how her weight has come to be an issue in her relationship with her mother and to determine if it is an issue in other areas of her life. Further exploration of difficulties in those relationship(s) will help determine when these difficulties arose and the foci of the conflict (e.g., size and weight, eating habits, health, career choice, contact with family of origin, sexual orientation, spirituality, etc.), broaden the relational context, and remove some of the focus on the client's weight as the "problem."

Additionally, from an interpersonal frame, the client could come to understand the role she plays in various relationships, which would allow her the freedom to evaluate whether the roles she has taken are effective and satisfying for her. This might lead to her changing some of her interactional patterns and feeling better about herself and her relationships. Increasing her sense of empowerment in relationships, regardless of her weight, would help her to see that her weight is not necessarily a barrier to satisfaction and self-efficacy.

Identifying the role that eating plays in her interpersonal interactions would be beneficial. Are her food choices and amounts eaten based on internal cues informing her of what she needs? Or, are her choices based on reactions to others and their expectations? Is she complying with or rejecting the expectations of others?

Cognitive-behavioral strategies could include an exploration of the client's thoughts related to her body and weight and then a discussion of the evidence she has for her beliefs. Psychoeducation about weight and health including the topics of the binge-deprivation cycle as well as weight cycling and its deleterious effects on health would be beneficial. Homework assignments, such as assigned readings from the General Size Acceptance reading list from page 334, can challenge common societal myths about weight and health and give the client tools to begin identifying and challenging the myths that have become "facts" in her mind. Mindfulness skills (Linehan, 1993) will allow the client to observe and describe her thoughts, feelings, and behaviors, relationships, and her body from a nonjudgmental stance and increase her ability to engage in effective coping skills. Working on wanted behavior change would involve her identifying one or two behaviors to start with, for example, increasing the movement in her life by going for a walk three times a week for a half-hour, and then developing strategies to implement the plan, identifying possible barriers to the new behavior and strategies to address the barriers, monitoring her behavior, and then highlighting reinforcements for making the changes.

From a feminist perspective, introducing the concept of size-acceptance and the larger society's fat prejudice would be crucial. Putting size in the context of diversity similar to sexual orientation and race would help her connect her experiences around her weight with those she has related to being a Latina and a lesbian. Encouraging her to explore size-accepting communities would be useful to help her develop a support system, hopefully adding to those she already has in place for her sexual orientation and her race. Empowerment will be key and sets the stage for the client to improve her relationships with others, her overall sense of well-being, and self-acceptance.

SUMMARY

The purpose of this chapter was to provide information and ideas for working with fat clients as well as resources for the practitioner, trainee, and supervisor. Working with weight-dissatisfied large clients is challenging at best. They experience such distress and see the goal of weight-loss as the magical solution that will free them of their discomfort. These issues are typically not addressed outside of an eating disorder and weight-loss focused frame. It is incumbent upon us to educate ourselves and our clients about what is real and what is possible. Empowerment and acceptance will make lasting changes in how our clients feel and how they treat themselves. Working in an ethical and empathic way with our large-size clients requires nothing less.

RESOURCES

The following resources are provided as suggestions for further inquiry and as tools students, clinicians, trainees, and supervisors can utilize to help improve the quality of the services they provide.

ASSESSMENT OF ATTITUDES AND VALUES

Harvard University, Project Implicit Web site. Implicit Association Test (Weight Version). https://implicit.harvard.edu/implicit/

Kano, S. (1989). Fat Acceptance Behavior Assessment. *Making peace with food* (rev. ed.). New York: Harper & Row.

GENERAL SIZE ACCEPTANCE

Bernell, B. (2000). *Bountiful women: Large women's secrets for living the life they desire.* Berkeley, CA: Wildcat Canyon Press.

Bliss, K. (2002). *Don't weight: Eat healthy and get moving now!* Haverford, PA: Infinity.

Bovey, S. (1994). *The forbidden body: Why being fat is not a sin.* London: Harper Pandora.

Braziel, J., & Lebesco, K. (2001). *Bodies out of bounds: Fatness and transgression.* University of California Berkeley Press.

Brown, L., & Rothblum, E. (1989). *Overcoming fear of fat.* New York: Harrington Park Press.

Bruno, B. (1996). *Worth your weight: What you can do about a weight problem.* Bethel, CT: Rutledge Books.

Cooper, C. (1998). *Fat and proud: The politics of size.* London: Women's Press, Ltd.

Edut, O. (2003). *Body outlaws: Rewriting the rules of beauty and body image.* Emeryville, CA: Seal Press.

Erdman, C. (1995). *Nothing to lose: A guide to sane living in a larger body.* San Francisco: Harper.

Erdman, C. (1997). *Live large!* San Francisco: Harper.

Garrison, T., & Levitsky, D. (1993). *Fed up! A woman's guide to freedom from the diet/weight prison.* New York: Carroll & Graf.

Goodman, C. (1995). *The invisible woman: Confronting weight prejudice in America.* Carlsbad, CA: Gurze.

Johnson, C. (2001). *Self-esteem comes in all sizes: How to be happy and healthy at your natural weight* (rev. ed.). Carlsbad, CA: Gurze Books.

Koppelman, S. (2003). *The strange history of Suzanne LaFleshe: And other stories of women and weight.* New York: Feminist Press at CUNY.

Munter, C., & Hirschman, J. (1995). *When women stop hating their bodies.* New York: Ballantine.

Schoenfielder, L., & Wieser, B. (Eds.). (1983). *Shadow on a tightrope: Writings by women on fat oppression.* Iowa City: Aunt Lute Press.

Schroeder, C. R. (1992). *Fat is not a four-letter word.* Minneapolis, MN: Chronimed.

Schwartz, H. (1986). *Never satisfied: A cultural history of diets, fantasies, and fat.* New York: Free Press.

Seid, R. P. (1989). *Never too thin: Why women are at war with their bodies.* New York: Prentice Hall.

Shanker, W. (2004). *The fat girl's guide to life.* New York: Bloomsbury.

Sobal, J., & Maurer, D. (1999). *Interpreting weight: The social management of fatness and thinness.* New York: Aldine de Gruyter.

Thomas, P., & Wilkerson, C. (2005). *Taking up space: How eating well & exercising regularly changed my life.* Nashville: Pearlsong Press.

Wann, M. (1998). *Fat! So?* Berkeley: Ten Speed Press.

Wiley, C. (1994). *Journeys to self-acceptance: Fat women speak.* Freedom, CA: Crossing Press.

TREATMENT FROM A HAES PERSPECTIVE

Berg, F. (2001). *Children and teens afraid to eat: Helping youth in today's weight-obsessed world.* Hettinger, ND: Healthy Weight Publishing Network.

Ciliska, D. (1990). *Beyond dieting: Psychoeducational interventions for chronically obese women.* New York: Brunner-Mazel.

Erdman, C. (1995). *Nothing to lose: A guide to sane living in a larger body.* San Francisco: Harper.

Fallon, P., Katzman, M., & Wooley, S. (1993). *Feminist perspectives on eating disorders.* New York: Guilford Press.

Hutchinson, M. (1985). *Transforming body image.* Trumansburg, NY: Crossing Press.

Hutchinson, M. (1999). *200 ways to love the body you have.* Freedom, CA: Crossing Press.

Kratina, K., King, N., & Hayes, D. (2002). *Moving away from diets.* Lake Dallas, TX: Helm.

Matz, J., & Frankel, E. (2004). *Beyond the shadow of a diet: The therapist's guide to treating compulsive eating.* New York: Brunner-Routledge.

Munter, C., & Hirschman, J. (1988). *Overcoming overeating.* New York: Fawcett Columbine.

Robison, J., & Carrier, K. (2004). *The spirit and science of holistic health: More than broccoli, jogging, and bottled water . . . more than yoga, herbs, and meditation.* Bloomington, IN: AuthorHouse.

Tribole, E. (1995). *Intuitive eating: A recovery book for the chronic dieter.* New York: St. Martin's Press.

WEIGHT AND HEALTH

Bacon, L. (2008). *Health at every size: The surprising truth about your weight.* Dallas, TX: BenBella Books.

Bennett, W., & Gurin, J. (1982). *Dieter's dilemma.* New York: Basic Books.

Campos, P. (2004). *The diet myth: Why America's obsession with weight is hazardous to your health.* New York: Gotham Books.

Fraser, L. (1997). *Losing it: America's obsession with weight and the industry that feeds on it.* New York: Dutton.

Gaesser, G. (2002). *Big fat lies: The truth about your weight and your health.* New York: Ballantine.

Gard, M., & Wright, J. (2005). *The obesity epidemic: Science, morality and ideology.* Oxon, UK: Routledge.

Jonas, S., & Konner, L. (1997). *Just the weigh you are: How to be fit and healthy, whatever your size.* Shelbourne, VT: Chapters.

Lyons, P., & Burgard, D. (1988). *Great shape: The first fitness guide for large women.* New York: Morrow.

Mundy, A. (2001). *Dispensing with the truth: The victims, the drug companies, and the dramatic story behind the battle over Fen-Phen.* New York: St. Martin's Press.

Oliver, J. E. (2006). *Fat politics: The Real story behind America's obesity epidemic.* New York: Oxford University Press.

Big Fat Blog—http://www.bigfatblog.com/

Body Positive—http://www.bodypositive.com

Council on Size and Weight Discrimination—http://www.cswd.org/

Dr. Jon Robison, HAES practitioner of holistic health—http://www.jonrobison.net/

Dr. Linda Bacon, HAES nutritional researcher—http://www.Lindabacon.org/HAESCommunity

Fat Acceptance Art & Resources—http://www.casagordita.com/fatacc.htm

Fat Diabetics Support List—http://ww3.telerama.com/~moose/fa-diab.html

Fat Friendly Health Professionals List—http://cat-and-dragon.com/stef/fat/ffp.html

Largesse, the Network for Size Esteem—http://largesse.net/

National Association to Advance Fat Acceptance (NAAFA)—http://www.naafa.org

Plus Size Yellow Pages—http://www.plussizeyellowpages.com/Books.htm

Show-Me-the-Data mailing list (for professionals and activists)—send your request to: show methedata-subscribe@yahoogroups.com

VoluptuArt—http://www.voluptuart.com

ONLINE RESOURCES

Abundia—http://www.abundia.org/

Association for Size Diversity and Health—http://www.sizediversityandhealth.org/

SAMPLE HAES INTERVENTIONS BY TENET

INTERVENTIONS RELATED TO THE HAES TENETS

Health Enhancement

- Is size hindering movement or activities? If so, how? Develop an action plan to work toward desired activity (break it down into small achievable steps).
- Which activities bring positive emotions? Which activities bring negative emotions or critical thoughts?
- Cognitive-behavioral strategies to facilitate health-promoting behavior.
- Behavior changes engaged in as act of self-love vs. self-loathing.
- Journal behavioral changes toward increased health; reward self for behavior.
- Focus on all therapy goals (not just those related to size, weight, and body image) to enhance emotional and spiritual wellbeing.

Size and Self-Acceptance

- Education about diversity in body shapes.

(continued)

(*continued*)

- Explore dream of how life would change if person were at "ideal weight"; explore how person can achieve those goals without losing weight.
- Assess size-acceptance identity and focus on indicators of interest to client.
- Empower client to accept self as she or he is.
- Body image–enhancement activities (see Resources listings).
- Grieve loss of dream of the "ideal weight."

The Pleasure of Eating Well

- Mindfulness skills—to recognize internal cues of hunger and satiety, to increase pleasure in tasting food, to incorporate all senses in eating food (taste, smell, texture, visual appeal, sounds during food preparation), to recognize effects of food on body and mood.
- Nutritional education—education regarding risks of weight cycling, set-point theory, and eating for nutritional and health benefits; if medical condition requires nutritional intervention (e.g., high cholesterol and need to increase fiber; diabetic and need to decrease carbohydrates), recipe modification of individual's 20 favorite meals.
- Experimenting with foods—trying new foods, trying new methods of food preparation, eating foods in season, eating foods from different ethnic cultures.

The Joy of Movement

- Shift focus from "working out" to "playing" and "body movement."
- Review what body movement activities individual participated in when a child/adolescent.
- Fantasize about what movement activities the person would like to engage in; therapist may need to supply list of possibilities.
- Pair body movement with social interactions (walking buddy, joining a team or class that is size accepting).
- Pair body movement with daily needs (taking steps instead of elevator, parking car farther from building, bicycling or walking to local stores, etc.).

An End to Weight Bias

- Education about sociocultural bias and diversity in body size.
- Bibliotherapy affirming size acceptance.
- Positive affirmations concerning body and self.
- Connecting with size-accepting community for additional support.

SELF-AWARENESS AND
SELF-ASSESSMENT EXERCISES

EXERCISE 11.1

Title: 10 Percent
Audience: Counselors, counselors in training, or general population. Use scenarios 1, 2, and 3 for counselors and counselors in training. Use scenarios 1, 4, and 5 for the general population.

Time: 15–30 minutes

Activity: Guided visualization; experiential

Instructions: Ask participants to get comfortable in their chairs, take a few cleansing breaths, and focus on the moment for full participation. The task at hand is to listen to the following three scenarios and then share with the group what action you will take in each scenario.

Scenario 1: You are in need of a new *computer.* Your current computer is old, does not have enough memory or fast enough processing speed. You have enough money to buy a computer and you begin shopping for your new purchase. You speak to a salesperson about Computer ABC. The salesperson tells you the numerous merits of the ABC model; it has all of the capability and functions you desire, you hear how consumers have been very happy with its performance during a 6-month follow-up, and the price is within your budget.

Do you want to purchase the computer?	Yes	No
Do you have any additional questions for the salesperson prior to purchasing the computer?	Yes	No

(If a participant asks about performance of the computer after 6 months, you need to disclose that the research indicates that computer ABC has only a 10% successful performance rate after one year. The other 90% of ABC computers are no longer performing after one year.)

If no participant asks the previous question, have them make their final decision regarding the purchase of the ABC computer. After you have a show of hands regarding purchasing the computer, you disclose the research regarding the computer performance as written above.

Ask Participants the Following Questions:

1. Has anyone changed their mind regarding the purchase of the computer after hearing the research regarding the computer's performance after one year?

2. How do you feel about your purchase?

3. What thoughts, feelings, and reactions do you want to share with the ABC Computer Company?

4. Do you have any feelings about yourself regarding this purchase?

Scenario 2: Treatment Effectiveness: You have been researching a new therapy model for the treatment of anxiety for adults in outpatient therapy. The model sounds very promising and fellow clinicians have reported using the model in the past few months with some very positive outcomes. You are given an opportunity to attend a day-long training regarding this new treatment model and you jump at the chance. The morning session focuses on the principles of the treatment model and techniques used. During the afternoon session a clinician in the room states he has been using the therapy model for the past year and shares his experience. He states that initially his clients do quite well. They are committed to the model and their anxiety decreases a significant amount. As treatment progressed clients hit a plateau and he thought they would stabilize at this new baseline of anxiety, which was an improvement. However, several months later he found his clients' anxiety symptoms increasing again. He asks the presenter to respond to these observations. The presenter states that they have now completed two years of longitudinal research. The research indicates that although clients have initial success with the treatment, after one year 90 percent of the clients return to baseline level of anxiety or actually have higher levels of anxiety than they did when they entered treatment. The presenter quickly adds to keep in mind that 10 percent of the clients continued with their successfully lowered anxiety level after one year. The presenter goes on to

(continued)

(*continued*)

reiterate that during the first few months of treatment almost all participants did have lower anxiety for some time period.

Ask Participants the Following Questions:

1. What are your current thoughts about this treatment?
2. Do you have any concerns (ethical, client satisfaction, effectiveness, etc.)?
3. Who would choose to use this new treatment approach? Why?
4. Who has chosen not to use this new treatment approach? Why?
5. Is a 10 percent treatment effectiveness rate satisfactory for clinical use?

Scenario 3: Ask participants to think of the following question and respond silently to themselves rather than to the larger group:

Have any of you created a treatment plan for a client where the goal for treatment was weight-loss and the technique/method for that goal was dieting?

Have participants answer this question for themselves. Then provide them the research regarding diets being 10 percent effective after one year follow-up. Ninety percent of people who lose weight have gained all the lost weight back or even more after one year.

Ask the Following Questions and Have Them Think about Their Responses:

1. What are your current thoughts about using dieting as a treatment intervention?
2. Do you have any concerns (ethical, client satisfaction, effectiveness, etc.)?
3. Who would choose to use dieting as a treatment approach in the future with your clients? Why or why not?
4. Is a 10 percent treatment effectiveness rate satisfactory for clinical use?

The facilitator can choose to stop this activity at this point, or open up the floor for discussion and response from participants.

Scenario 4: You are in need of a new *car*. Your current car absolutely does not run anymore and the mechanic is saying it would cost three times the value of the car to repair it. You have enough money to buy a car and you begin shopping for your new purchase. You speak to a salesperson about the Super Car. The salesperson tells you the numerous merits of the Super Car; it is attractive, gets good gas mileage, you hear how consumers have been very happy with its performance during a 6-month follow-up, and the price is within your budget.

Do you want to purchase the car?	Yes	No
Do you have any additional questions for the salesperson prior to purchasing the car?	Yes	No

(If a participant asks about performance of the car after 6 months, you need to disclose that *Consumer Reports* indicates that Super Car has only a 10% successful performance rate after one year. The other 90% of Super Cars are no longer running after one year.)

If no participant asks the previous question, have them make their final decision regarding the purchase of the Super Car. After you have a show of hands regarding purchasing the car, you disclose the research regarding the car performance as written above.

Ask Participants the Following Questions:

1. Has anyone changed their mind regarding the purchase of the car after hearing the research regarding the car's performance after one year?

2. How do you feel about your purchase?

3. What thoughts, feelings, and reactions do you want to share with the Super Car Company?

4. Do you have any feelings about yourself regarding this purchase?

Scenario 5: Ask participants to think of the following question and respond silently to themselves rather than to the larger group:

Have you ever been on a diet or encouraged a dating partner, friend, or family member to go on a diet?

Have participants answer this question for themselves. Then provide them the research regarding diets being 10 percent effective after one year follow-up. Ninety percent of people who lose weight have gained all the lost weight back or even more after one year.

Ask the Following Questions and Have Them Think About Their Responses:

1. What are your current thoughts about going on a diet or encouraging others to do so?

2. Do you have any concerns about going on a diet?

3. Who would choose to go on a diet now after hearing this information? Why or why not?

4. Is a 10 percent effectiveness rate satisfactory for a diet?

Facilitator can choose to stop this activity at this point, or open up the floor for discussion and response from participants.

EXERCISE 11.2

Task: HAES treatment planning
Audience: Counselors and counselors in training
Activity: Clinical treatment planning; skill building
Instructions: Counselors may initially struggle on how to work with a client who has weight-loss as a goal and/or is dissatisfied with his or her weight. The initial response may be to suggest diets. Here are alternative treatment goals and methods to achieve them.

A. Ask client about initial goal and then explore what that would mean to the client.

Example Goal: I Want to Lose 20 Pounds

Questions to Ask:

1. What physical activities would you engage in if you lost 20 pounds?

2. What type of movement, activities, and events would you do/participate in, if you lost 20 pounds?

3. Would your clothes, fashion sense, or appearance change if you lost 20 pounds?

4. What health factors or health issues would change if you lost 20 pounds?

5. How else would your life change if you lost 20 pounds?

B. Examine the client's response to each of these questions and explore which of these outcomes could be achieved without weight loss.

Example for Question #1 about Physical Activities Client Wants to Engage In

1. Get up and down easier from floor to play with my small children.

2. Play outside with my children for 30 minutes.

(continued)

(*continued*)

3. Bicycle with my friends.

4. Walk three flights of stairs without being winded.

C. Assess how much they can currently do toward each of these physical activity goals.

D. Create hierarchy of importance on these four physical activity goals.

E. Create action plan for each of these four physical activity goals.

F. Create charting system for tracking progress toward goals.

Typically, a separate reward/reinforcement system does not need to be established because the progress toward the goal itself is rewarding, unlike diets, which often represent deprivation to clients.

EXERCISE 11.3

Myths, Misinformation, and Stereotypes Regarding Weight and Fat

Task: Assessment of attitudes and values
Audience: Counselors, counselors in training, or general population
Activity: Challenge myths held by participants
Instructions: Provide a paper copy of the myths to each participant. Read each statement out loud and have participant mark true or false to reflect his/her belief. After all statements have been answered, re-read each statement and have participants raise hand if they marked true. Discuss their beliefs and have audience members help write challenges to each myth.

Fat People Are Unhealthy:

- When I see a fat person, do I assume the person is "out of shape"?
- Am I surprised when a fat person performs a physical activity with grace, strength, and/or agility?
- Do I assume a fat person has health problems?
- When I see both a fat person and a thin person, do I assume one of them will be able to dance, swim, and/or play basketball better than the other one?
- When I see both a fat person and a thin person, do I assume the thin person has a lower cholesterol level than the fat person?

Fat People Are Unhappy:

- When I see a fat person at a movie alone, do I assume the person has no friends?
- When a fat person enters therapy to decrease depressive symptoms, do I assume the depression is caused by being fat? If so, do I assume weight-loss is the treatment of choice?

Fat People Are Gluttonous:

- Do I have an emotional reaction when I see a fat person at an "all-you-can-eat" restaurant? What emotions and thoughts do I experience?
- Do I have an emotional reaction when I see a fat person eating fast food, junk food, or dessert? What emotions and thoughts do I experience?

Fat People Use Food to Meet Unmet Emotional Needs:

- Do I think fat people are psychologically impaired in their intrapersonal or interpersonal functioning?
- Do I assume fat people binge eat?

Fat People Are Lonely:

- Am I surprised or think the person lucky when a fat person is partnered to an "attractive, normal-weight" person?
- When I see a fat person at a movie alone, do I assume the person has no friends?

Obesity Is a Disease and the "Cure" Is to Lose Weight:

- Do I assume that all information presented by popular media is correct?
- Do I assume that all information or educational campaigns promoted by the federal government is based on sound scientific evidence?
- Have I ever questioned the integrity or accuracy of a research article published in a professional journal?
- Have I ever questioned the accuracy of statements regarding fat as an epidemic or unhealthy state of being?

Losing Weight Is a Matter of Self-Discipline and Willpower:

- Do I assume fat people just don't "try hard enough"?
- Do I assume that if a fat person changed eating habits and activity level significantly and kept engaged in those activities at the same level for the rest of the person's life that she or he would achieve significant weight loss and keep it off?

Fat People Promote HAES So They Can Justify Their Fatness and Give Up on Goals for Increased Health:

- Do I find myself wondering about the size of the author when I read an article challenging society's views of fat people?
- Do I find myself wondering about the size of the author when I read a professional article that promotes health at every size?

Fat People Are Discriminated Against, So to Prevent Discrimination, It Is in Their Best Interest to Lose Weight:

- Have I ever thought people of color need to change their skin tone to avoid bias?
- Have I ever thought women need to change their gender to avoid bias?
- If I answered no to the above questions, why do I think of fat differently?

SIZE DIVERSITY SEMINAR

Topics and Activities

The following represent activities from which trainers and clinicians may select as part of a size diversity seminar.

A. Activities for increasing knowledge of size acceptance and HAES:

1. Relate competence in size issues to multicultural competency in general.
2. Contextualize individual and cultural differences (including age, gender, sexual orientation, socioeconomic status [SES], ethnicity) as they relate to size.
3. Literature and research describing the relationship of size and weight to wellness, physical health, and mental health.

4. Familiarize yourself with non-diet approaches to weight concerns.
5. Define attuned/intuitive eating.
6. Behaviors that improve health regardless of weight loss.
7. Spiral of Acceptance identity development model.
8. Size dissatisfaction assessment methods; diagnosis, case conceptualization, and treatment planning.
9. Healthy and unhealthy eating and weight attitudes; understanding of psychopathology as well as behavior that is considered normative in the larger culture but is deleterious to health.
10. Body shame and experiences of stigma and oppression.
11. Therapy concerns that may have a size component: relationship problems, sexual concerns, eating disorders, abuse recovery, addictions, social anxiety, exercise avoidance.
12. Collaboration with other health professionals and importance of advocacy for clients.
13. Theoretical orientation(s) and model(s) of psychotherapy—view of fatness.
14. HAES intervention techniques; risks and benefits; differentiating eating a specific diet for health reasons versus for weight loss.
15. Therapy issues that are frequently associated with size/weight: grief, abuse recovery, sexual identity development, aging, death and dying, addiction, career development.
16. Transference and countertransference issues.
17. Ethical/legal standards: informed consent to provide HAES interventions, obligation to do no harm, and use of interventions that have research support for efficacy.

B. Awareness of own attitudes and values—may use one or more of the following techniques to explore one's own beliefs, attitudes, and experiences: family weight and size history, journaling, family member interview, and personal dieting history. Some topics to reflect upon include: What are your first memories of learning about your body size? What were the beliefs and values about weight and size in your household? To what degree have you subscribed to those same beliefs? What factors have affected the degree to which you have subscribed to the dominant cultural beliefs throughout the course of your life? (Also see the self-assessment questionnaires earlier in this Resources section).

C. Activities to build knowledge, awareness, and skills:

1. Visit Web sites devoted to size acceptance and HAES.
2. Write a paper describing the tenets of HAES and contrast with the diet-as-usual approach.
3. Invite experts in HAES to the seminar.
4. Participate in group discussions of size issues.
5. Read personal accounts of the discrimination experiences of people of size.
6. Explore HAES treatment approaches through readings for therapists (see Resources listings).
7. Discuss therapy case examples and size-concern vignettes. Identify possible therapeutic interventions from a HAES perspective, transference and countertransference issues, and ethical dilemmas.
8. Gain exposure to images of people of size through artwork and movies.

COMPETENCY BENCHMARK TABLES

The purpose of the Competency Benchmarks (Tables 11.1–11.4) is to create developmental models for defining and measuring competencies in professional psychology; each chapter in this *Handbook* applies the diversity competence for mental health practitioners in their work with a particular diverse population.

Table 11.1   Developmental-Level Competencies I

READINESS LEVEL—ENTRY TO PRACTICUM	
Competencies	**Learning Process and Activities**
Knowledge	The student is gaining knowledge in: • Multiculturalism—the student is engaged in the process of learning that all individuals, including themselves, are cultural beings with worldviews that shape and influence their attitudes, emotions, perceptions, and experiences. • Learning that size is an aspect of diversity. • The importance of reflective practice and self-awareness. • Core counseling skills and theories. • Ethics code.	At this stage of development, the emphasis in psychotherapist education is on instilling knowledge of foundational domains that provide the groundwork for subsequent attainment of functional competencies. Students at this stage become aware of the principles and practices of the field, but they are not yet able to apply their knowledge to practice. Therefore, the training curriculum is focused on knowledge of core areas, including literature on multiculturalism, ethics, basic counseling skills, scientific knowledge, and the importance of reflective practice and self-awareness.
Skills	The student is: • Beginning to develop the ability to demonstrate empathic listening skills, respect, and interest when talking with individuals expressing different values and belief systems. • Learning to critically examine the diversity literature and implications for treatment interventions.	It is important that throughout the curriculum, trainers and teachers define individual and cultural differences broadly, to include body size and weight differences. This should enable students to have a developing awareness of how to extrapolate their emerging multicultural competencies to include the size and weight realm of individual and cultural differences.
Values and Attitudes	The student demonstrates: • Willingness to engage in self-exploration—to consider own motives, attitudes, behaviors, and effect on others. • Intellectual curiosity and flexibility. • Ability to value expressions of diverse viewpoints and belief systems.	Most students, through their life experiences, would be expected to have the basic knowledge that people come in a variety of sizes and shapes, awareness of the lack of effectiveness of dieting for lasting weight change, and personal awareness of their cultural identity including personal size acceptance or lack thereof.

Table 11.2   Developmental-Level Competencies II

READINESS LEVEL—ENTRY TO INTERNSHIP	
Competencies	**Learning Process and Activities**
Knowledge	The student has: • General understanding of the research data on health and size. • Knowledge that working with a weight-loss focus in therapy may be contraindicated in most circumstances, though not yet well understood. • Knowledge of non-diet approaches to health. • Understanding of the importance of consulting with supervisors and others when presented with client issues related to weight dissatisfaction.	At this level of development, students are building on their education and applied experiences (such as supervised practicum experiences) to attain a core set of foundational competencies. They can then begin applying this knowledge to professional practice. As a result of being exposed to didactic training and close supervision, students attain the multicultural values and attitudes appropriate to their level of development. Foundational knowledge and multicultural values and attitudes are becoming well established, but skills in working with weight and size issues would be expected to be rudimentary at this level of development.
Skills	Skills in the following areas are beginning to develop: • Discerning personal limits of openness to size-positive beliefs and attitudes and, after	

(continued)

Table 11.2   Developmental-Level Competencies II (*continued*)

READINESS LEVEL—ENTRY TO INTERNSHIP	
Competencies	Learning Process and Activities
	consultation with supervisors, referring clients to appropriate resources if not able to work with them. • Building therapeutic alliance to create a trusting, safe, and open therapeutic climate to discuss size issues, if indicated. • Facilitating an accepting body image with average-weight clients.	Learning occurs through multiple modalities: • Receiving size-positive and non-diet didactic training in academic programs may occur in multicultural courses or culture-specific courses (e.g., women's issues and GLB courses). It is not likely to be infused into the core curriculum (e.g., ethics, assessment, multicultural, career counseling, research, human growth and development, and clinical courses). See an example of curriculum infusion in the Resources section of this chapter.
Values and Attitudes	Demonstrates self-awareness and appropriate cultural and multicultural attitudes as evidenced by the following: • Understands that size is an aspect of diversity. • Awareness of own intersecting individual dimensions (gender, ethnicity, SES, sexual orientation, ability, etc.) and ability to discern clients' intersecting identities. • Commitment to examine and challenge own attitudes and biases about weight and size. • Willingness to admit own limitations in ability to be open to some expressions of size-positive beliefs. • Demonstrates genuine respect for people of varying body sizes and shapes.	• Providing therapy, under supervision, to clients representing diversity of body shapes and sizes in practicum experiences. • Receiving supervision from psychotherapists knowledgeable and skilled in working with size issues from a non-diet perspective. • Seeking additional study and professional development opportunities (e.g., to attain knowledge of HAES). Topics to be covered in didactic training include: • Relation of size competency to multicultural competency. • Relationship of a size-positive worldview to individual and cultural differences (e.g., including age, gender, sexual orientation, SES, and ethnicity). • Basic research literature describing the relevance of size and weight to wellness, physical health, mental health. Trainers and teachers could offer students enrolled in multicultural diversity courses an option to research size-related issues as a project for the class. Possible topics are cited in the Size Diversity Seminar outline in the Resources section of this chapter.

Table 11.3   Developmental-Level Competencies III

READINESS LEVEL—ENTRY TO PROFESSIONAL PRACTICE	
Competencies	Learning Process and Activities
Knowledge	Knowledge of: • Literature on the relationship between weight/size and mental and physical health; knowledge of the range of possible weight/size client issues. • Literature on non-diet approaches including HAES.	In the earlier stages of training, students solidified their professional knowledge base and attained appropriate values and attitudes while developing increasingly sophisticated clinical skills. At the level of Entry to Professional Practice, psychotherapists have attained the full range of

READINESS LEVEL—ENTRY TO PROFESSIONAL PRACTICE

Competencies		Learning Process and Activities
	• Beliefs and behaviors that are considered normative and healthy within a size-positive perspective. • Community resources, including nutritionists, physicians, and psychotherapists who work from a HAES perspective. • Understanding that working with fat clients is an aspect of multicultural counseling competency.	competencies in the domains expected of all independent practitioners. Preparation for this level of competency takes place through closely supervised clinical work, augmented by professional reading, personal exploration, and training opportunities such as professional development and training seminars. Clinical supervisors observe students' clinical work, provide training in assessment, case conceptualization, and treatment planning, and challenge supervisees to examine their countertransference reactions, biases, and values to develop their supervisees' clinical competency with weight/size issues.
Skills	Skills are demonstrated by the ability to: • Perform a basic assessment of clients' comfort with and acceptance of their size and to assess the relevance of size issues to therapy. • Diagnose and formulate appropriate treatment plans that are sensitive to the client's level of size-acceptance, including how multiple systems and individual differences impact client. • Identify the limits of one's own competency with size/weight issues and refer appropriately. • Form a trusting therapeutic relationship with clients so that clients may express size/weight concerns if relevant and provide basic HAES therapeutic interventions. • Facilitating body-image improvement with clients who are larger than societally accepted norms. • Use supervision to enhance HAES and other size-positive skills. • Establish effective consultation relationships with HAES providers in the community. • Create climate in which supervisees and trainees feel safe to talk about size/weight issues.	Additional methods by which students can attain HAES competency at this level include: • Seeking opportunities to provide therapy to clients representing size diversity. • Supervision provided by supervisors knowledgeable and skilled in working with weight/size issues. • Self-directed study and professional development opportunities. • Internship and postdoctoral seminar training in weight/size issues and HAES. • Presenting and participating in clinical case conferences that include discussion of size diversity and HAES as aspects of cases.
Values and Attitudes	Awareness of own size-acceptance and associated biases, willingness to continually broaden self-knowledge, and commitment to expanding knowledge of systemic size oppression and HAES treatment as part of multicultural competency enhancement.	

Table 11.4 Developmental-Level Competencies IV

READINESS LEVEL—ADVANCED PRACTICE AND SPECIALIZATION

Competencies		Learning Process and Activities
Knowledge	Extensive knowledge of: • HAES and weight/size-related literature. • The Spiral of Acceptance identity development model.	Psychotherapists who have a particular interest in size aspects of diversity as they apply to clinical work may seek to attain advanced levels of competency. *(continued)*

Table 11.4 Developmental-Level Competencies IV (*continued*)

READINESS LEVEL—ADVANCED PRACTICE AND SPECIALIZATION	
Competencies	**Learning Process and Activities**
Skills • Impact of weight-related oppression and size-acceptance experiences on health and human development. Advanced skills in: • Providing a variety of HAES interventions. • Integrating knowledge of HAES concepts (health enhancement, size and self-acceptance, eating according to internal cues, joyful movement, and an end to weight bias) into treatment. • Proactively sharing knowledge of size issues and HAES in the work setting with other mental health professionals. • Differentiating between healthy and unhealthy behaviors related to eating and exercise. • Advocating for clients to receive equitable and quality medical and psychological care regardless of size. • Providing effective supervision to trainees working with client weight/size issues.	Learning activities will vary depending on the psychotherapist's unique background, established competencies, and interest areas. For example, psychotherapists working in eating disorder treatment settings may wish to concentrate on HAES interventions focused on this population. Regardless of the focus area, learning activities can include: • Professional reading (information about size/weight and HAES; empirical studies and literature on theory and practice). • Teaching. • Research. • Attending and leading educational workshops. • Peer consultation groups. • Consultation with knowledgeable mental health professionals, HAES researchers, and other experts. • Participation in size-positive and HAES advocacy groups such as NAAFA and ASDAH (see Resources section).
Values and Attitudes Well-integrated values and attitudes demonstrated by the following: • Continually engages in broadening knowledge of HAES and size-acceptance resources and for continuing professional development. • Actively cultivates relationships with HAES providers in the community. • Involved in local and national groups and organizations relevant to weight/size issues. • Independently and proactively provides ethical and legal consultation and supervision to trainees and other professionals. • Works for social justice to enhance understanding among professionals and communities about the benefits of HAES for everyone. • Independently monitors own size acceptance in relation to work with others with awareness and sensitivity to varying levels of size acceptance.	

REFERENCES

Abakoui, R. A. (1998). Effects of weight status and gender on psychologists' diagnosis and treatment planning. [Doctoral dissertation, University of North Texas, 1998]. *Dissertation Abstracts International, 59,* 3677.

Adams, C. H., Smith, N. J., Wilbur, D. C., & Grady, K. (1993). The relationship of obesity to the frequency of pelvic examination: Do physician and patient attitudes make a difference? *Women & Health, 20*(2), 45–57.

Allison, D. B., Kaprio, J., Korkeila, M., Koskenvuo, M., Neale, M. C., & Hayakawa, K. (1996). The heritability of body mass index among an international sample of monozygotic twins reared apart. *International Journal of Obesity, 20*(6), 501–506.

American Psychological Association (2002). Ethical principles of psychologists and code of conduct. *American Psychologist, 57*(12), 1060–1073.

Ashmore, J. A., Friedman, K. E., Reichmann, S. K., & Musante, G. J. (2008). Weight-based stigmatization, psychological distress, and binge eating behavior among obese treatment-seeking adults. *Eating Behaviors, 9,* 203–209.

Bacon, L. (2008). *Health at every size: The surprising truth about your weight.* Dallas, TX: BenBella Books.

Bacon, L., Keim, N. L., Van Loan, M. D., Derricote, M., Gale, B., Kazaks, A., et al. (2002). Evaluating a "non-diet" wellness intervention for improvement of metabolic fitness, psychological well-being and eating and activity behaviors. *International Journal of Obesity, 26,* 854–865.

Bacon, L., Van Loan, M., Stern, J. S., & Keim, N. (2005). Size acceptance and intuitive eating improve health for obese female chronic dieters. *Journal of American Dietetic Association, 105,* 929–936.

Ball, K., & Crawford, D. (2005). Socioeconomic status and weight change in adults: A review. *Social Sciences & Medicine, 60,* 1987–2010.

Blair, S. N., Kohl, III, H. W., Paffenbarger, Jr., R. S., Clark, D. G., Cooper, K. H., & Gibbons, L. W. (1989). Physical fitness and all-cause mortality: A prospective study of healthy men and women. *Journal of the American Medical Association, 262* (17), 2395–2401.

Blair, S. N., Shaten, J., Brownell, K., Collins, G., & Lissner, L. (1993). Body weight change, all-cause mortality, and cause-specific mortality in the Multiple Risk Factor Intervention Trial. *Annals of Internal Medicine, 119,* 749–757.

Boero, N. (2007). All the news that's fat to print: The American "obesity epidemic" and the media. *Qualitative Sociology, 30,* 41–60.

Brontsema, R. (2004). A queer revolution: Reconceptualizing the debate over linguistic reclamation. *Colorado Research in Linguistics, 17*(1), 1–17.

Brownell, K. D. (1998). *The LEARN program for weight control.* Dallas, TX: American Health Publishing.

Brownell, K. D., & Rodin, J. (1994). The dieting maelstrom: Is it possible and advisable to lose weight? *American Psychologist, 49,* 781–791.

Bruch, H. (1957). *The Importance of Overweight.* New York: W. W. Norton.

Burgard, D. (1998). The emotional immune system. Retrieved May 5, 2007, from http://www.bodypositive.com/emotimmu.htm.

Campos, P., Saguy, A., Ernsberger, P., Oliver, E., & Gaesser, G. (2006). The epidemiology of overweight and obesity: Public health crisis or moral panic? *International Journal of Epidemiology, 35*(1), 55–60.

Coakley, E. H., Rimm, E. B., Colditz, G., Kawachi, I., & Willett, W. (1998). Predictors of weight change in men: Results from the health professionals follow-up study. *International Journal of Obesity and Related Metabolic Disorders, 22*(2), 89–96.

Cogan, J. C., & Ernsberger, P. (1999). Dieting, weight, and health: Reconceptualizing research and policy. *Journal of Social Issues, 55*(2), 187–205.

Cogan, J. C., & Rothblum, E. D. (1992). Outcomes of weight-loss programs. *Genetic, Social, and General Psychology Monographs, 118,* 385–415.

Connors, M. E., & Melcher, S. A. (1993). Ethical issues in the treatment of weight-dissatisfied clients. *Professional Psychology: Research and Practice, 24* (4), 404–408.

Crandall, C. (1994). Prejudice against fat people: Ideology and self-interest. *Journal of Personality and Social Psychology, 66,* 882–894.

Davis-Coelho, K., Waltz, J., & Davis-Coelho, B. (2000). Awareness and prevention of bias against fat clients in psychotherapy. *Professional Psychology: Research and Practice, 31*(6), 682–684.

Erdman, C. (1995). *Nothing to lose: A guide to sane living in a larger body.* San Francisco: Harper.

Ernsberger, P., Koletsky, R. J., Baskin, J. S., & Collins, L. A. (1996). Consequences of weight cycling in obese spontaneously hypertensive rats. *American Journal of Physiology, 270*(4, pt. 2), 864–872.

Flegal, K. M., Carroll, M. D., Kuczmarski, R. J., & Johnson, C. L. (1998). Overweight and obesity in the United States: Prevalence and trends, 1960–1994. *International Journal of Obesity, 22,* 39–47.

Flegal, K. M., Graubard, B. I., Williamson, D. F., & Gail, M. H. (2005). Excess deaths associated with underweight, overweight, and obesity. *Journal of the American Medical Association, 293,* 1861–1867.

Fouad, N. A., & Arredondo, P. (2007). *Becoming culturally oriented: Practical advice for psychologists and educators.* Washington, DC: American Psychological Association.

Freedman, D. S., Khan, L. K., Serdula, M. K., Galuska, D. A., & Dietz, W. H. (2002). Trends and correlates of class 3 obesity in the United States from 1990 through 2000. *Journal of the American Medical Association, 288,* 1758–1761.

Friedman, J. (2004). Modern science versus the stigma of obesity. *Nature Medicine, 10*(6), 563–569.

Friedman, K. E., Reichmann, S. K., Costanzo, P. R., Zelli, A., Ashmore, J. A., & Musante, G. J. (2005). Weight stigmatization and ideological beliefs: Relation of psychological functioning in obese adults. *Obesity Research, 13*(5), 907–916.

Gaesser, G. (2002). *Big fat lies: The truth about your weight and your health.* New York: Ballantine.

Garner, D., Garfinkel, P. E., Rockert, W., & Olmsted, M. P. (1987). A prospective study of eating disturbances in the ballet. *Psychotherapy and Psychosomatics, 48,* 170–175.

Garner, D., & Wooley, S. (1991). Confronting the failure of behavioral and dietary treatments for obesity. *Clinical Psychology Review, 11,* 729–780.

Goodman, C. (1995). *The invisible woman: Confronting weight prejudice in America.* CA: Gurze.

Hill, J. O., & Peters, J. C. (1998). Environmental contributions to the obesity epidemic. *Science, 280,* 1371–1374.

Hiller, D. V. (1981). The salience of overweight in personality characterization. *The Journal of Psychology, 108,* 233–240.

Holbrook, T. L., Barrett-Connor, E., & Wingard, D. L. (1989). The association of lifetime weight and weight control patterns with diabetes among men and women in an adult community. *International Journal of Obesity and Related Metabolic Disorders, 13,* 723–729.

Ikeda, J. P., Lyons, P., Schwartzman, F., & Mitchell, R. A. (2004). Self-reported dieting experiences of women with body mass indexes of 30 or more. *Journal of the American Dietetic Association, 104,* 972–974.

Kajioka, T., Tsuzuku, S., Shimokata, H., & Sato, Y. (2002). Effects of intentional weight cycling on non-obese young women. *Metabolism, 51*(2), 149–154.

Kassirer, J. P., & Angell, M. (1998). Losing weight: An ill-fated New Year's resolution. *New England Journal of Medicine, 338*(1), 52–54.

Kratina, K., & Shuman, E. (2003). Health at every size. Retrieved May 5, 2007, from http://www.aweighout.com

Krechowec, S. O., Vickers, M., Gertler, A., & Breier, B. H. (2006). Prenatal influences on leptin sensitivity and susceptibility to diet-induced obesity. *Journal of Endocrinology, 189*(2), 355–363.

Laliberte, M., Newton, M., McCabe, R. & Mills, J. S. (2007). Controlling your weight versus controlling your lifestyle: How beliefs about weight control affect risk for disordered eating, body dissatisfaction and self-esteem. *Cognitive Therapy and Research, 31,* 853–869.

Larkin, J. C., & Pines, H. A. (1979). No fat persons need apply: Experimental studies of the overweight stereotype and hiring preference. *Sociology of Work and Occupations, 6,* 312–327.

Linehan, M. (1993). *Skills training manual for treating borderline personality disorder.* New York: Guilford Press.

Louderbeck, L. (1970). *Fat power: Whatever you weigh is right.* Stroud, Gloucestershire, UK: Hawthorn Books.

Mann, T., Tomiyama, A. J., Westling, E., Lew, A., Samuels, B., & Chatman, J. (2007). Medicare's search for effective obesity treatments: Diets are not the answer. *American Psychologist, 62*(3), 220–233.

Marchesini, G., Cuzzolaro, M., Mannucci, E., Dalle-Grave, R., Gennaro, M., Tomasi, F., et al. (2004). Weight cycling in treatment-seeking obese persons: Data from the QUOVADIS study. *International Journal of Obesity, 28,* 1456–1462.

Mark, A. L. (2006). Dietary therapy for obesity is a failure and pharmacotherapy is the future: A point of view. *Clinical and Experimental Pharmacology and Physiology, 33,* 857–862.

Matz, J., & Frankel, E. (2004). *Beyond a shadow of a diet: The therapist's guide to treating compulsive eating.* New York: Brunner-Routledge.

Mayer, V. (1983). Foreword. In L. Schoenfielder & B. Wieser (Eds.), *Shadow on a tightrope: Writings by women on fat oppression* (pp. ix-xvii). Iowa City: Aunt Lute Press.

Millman, M. (1980). *Such a pretty face: Being fat in America.* New York: Norton.

Mukamal, K. J., Kawachi, I., Miller, M., & Rimm, E. B. (2007). Body mass index and risk of suicide among men. *Archives of Internal Medicine, 167,* 468–475.

Munter, C., & Hirschman, J. (1988). *Overcoming overeating.* New York: Fawcett Columbine.

Oliver, J. E. (2005). *Fat Politics: The real story behind America's obesity epidemic.* New York: Oxford University Press.

Olson, C. L., Schumaker, H. D., & Yawn, B. P. (1994). Overweight women delay medical care. *Archives of Family Medicine, 3,* 888–892.

Pfohl, M., Luft, D., Blomberg, I., & Schmulling, R. M. (1994). Long-term changes of body weight and cardiovascular risk factors after weight reduction with group therapy and dexfenfluramine.

International Journal of Obesity Related Metabolic Disorders, 18(6), 391–395.

Poston, W. S. C., & Foreyt, J. P. (1999). Obesity is an environmental issue. *Atherosclerosis, 146*, 201–209.

Prochaska, J. O., & DiClemente, C. C. (1983). Stages and processes of self-change in smoking: Toward an integrative model of change. *Journal of Consulting and Clinical Psychology, 5*, 390–395.

Robinson, B. E., & Bacon, J. G. (1996). The "If only I were thin . . . " treatment program: Decreasing the stigmatizing effects of fatness. *Professional Psychology: Research and Practice, (27)*2, 175–183.

Robison, J. (2005). Health at every size: Toward a new paradigm of weight and health. *Medscape General Medicine, 7*(3), 13.

Rosenbaum, M., Leibel, R. I., & Hirsch, J. (1997). Obesity. *New England Journal of Medicine 337*(6), 396–407.

Rothblum, E. D., Brand, P. A., Miller, C. T., & Oetjen, H. A. (1990). The relationship between obesity, employment discrimination, and employment-related victimization. *Journal of Vocational Behavior, 37*, 251–266.

Schoenfielder, L., & Wieser, B. (Eds.). (1983). *Shadow on a tightrope: Writings by women on fat oppression.* Iowa City: Aunt Lute Press.

Schwartz, H. (1986). *Never satisfied: A cultural history of diets, fantasies, and fat.* New York: Free Press.

Schwartz, M., O'Neal Chambliss, H., Brownell, K., Blair, S., & Billington, C. (2003). Weight bias among health professionals specializing in obesity. *Obesity Research, 11*(9), 1033–1039.

Seid, R. P. (1989). *Never too thin: Why women are at war with their bodies.* New York: Prentice Hall Press.

Srinivasan, S., O'Fallon, L. R., & Dearry, A. (2003). Creating healthy communities, healthy homes, healthy people: Initiating a research agenda on the built environment and public health. *American Journal of Public Health, 93*(9), 1446–1450.

Stice, E., Cameron, R., Killeen, J. D., Hayward, C., & Taylor, C. B. (1999). Naturalistic weight reduction efforts prospectively predict growth in relative weight and onset of obesity among female adolescents. *Journal of Consulting and Clinical Psychology, 67*(6), 967–974.

Stice, E., Presnall, K., & Shaw, H. (2005). Psychological and behavioral risk factors for obesity onset in adolescent girls: A prospective study. *Journal of Consulting and Clinical Psychology, 73*(2), 195–202.

Striegel-Moore, R. H., Silberstein, L. R., Frensch, P., & Rodin, J. (1989). A prospective study of disordered eating among college students. *International Journal of Eating Disorders, 8*, 499–509.

Stunkard, A. J. (1958). The management of obesity. *New York State Journal of Medicine, 58*, 79–87.

Stunkard, A. J., Foch, T. T., & Hrubec, Z. (1986). A twin study of human obesity. *Journal of the American Medical Association, 256*, 51–54.

Stunkard, A. J., Harris, J. R., Pederson, N. L., & McClearn, G. E. (1990). The body mass index of twins who have been reared apart. *New England Journal of Medicine, 322*, 1483–1487.

Stunkard, A. J., Sorensen, T. L., Hanis, C., Teasdale, T. W., Chakraborty, R., Schull, W. J., et al. (1986). An adoption study of human obesity. *New England Journal of Medicine, 314*, 193–198.

Suter, M., Calmes, J. M., Paroz, A., & Giusti, V. (2006). A 10-year experience with laparoscopic gastric banding for morbid obesity: High long-term complication and failure rates. *Obesity Surgery, 16*, 829–835.

Teachman, B. A., & Brownell, K. D. (2001). Implicit anti-fat bias among health professionals: Is anyone immune? *International Journal of Obesity, 25*, 1525–1531.

Tenzer, S. (1989). Fat acceptance therapy (FAT): A non-dieting group approach to physical wellness, insight and self-acceptance. *Women & Therapy, 8* (3), 39–47.

Tiggeman, M., & Rothblum, E. D. (1988). Gender differences in social consequences of perceived overweight in the United States and Australia. *Sex Roles, 18*(1/2), 75–86.

Tribole, E. (1995). *Intuitive eating: A recovery book for the chronic dieter.* New York: St. Martin's Press.

U.S. Department of Health and Human Services. (2001). *The Surgeon General's call to action to prevent and decrease overweight and obesity.* Washington, DC: U.S. Government Printing Office.

Vickers, M. H., Breier, B. H., Cutfield, W. S., Hofman, P. L., & Gluckman, P. D. (2000). Fetal origins of hyperphagia, obesity, and hypertension and postnatal amplification by hypercaloric nutrition. *American Journal of Physiology-Endocrinology and Metabolism, 279*(1), 83–87.

Wilson, G. T. (1994). Behavioral treatment of obesity: Thirty years and counting. *Advances in Behaviour Research and Therapy, 16*, 31–75.

Young, L. M., & Powell, B. (1985). The effects of obesity on the clinical judgments of mental health professionals. *Journal of Health and Social Behavior, 26*, 233–246.

CHAPTER 12

DEVELOPING COMPETENCY IN SOCIAL CLASS AND CLASSISM IN COUNSELING AND PSYCHOTHERAPY

WILLIAM MING LIU, JULIE CORKERY, and JENNI THOME

CASE VIGNETTE 12.1

"The client just comes in and complains. He seems to blame everything going wrong for him on everyone else but doesn't seem to want to change." The doctoral student counseling this male client at the Veterans Administration hospital was exhausted working with him. In a practicum class, the trainee described the client as depressing and frustrating and that it did not seem the client wanted to make any substantial changes in his life to escape his presenting issue of depression. The client, a Vietnam combat veteran who lived on Social Security disability assistance and traveled two hours for treatment, was in psychotherapy for the first time in his life. The doctoral student, an advanced practicum male student using a cognitive-behavioral approach, described his reluctance to continue working with this client. "Why continue working with him if he's not interested in doing anything in therapy?" The ensuing discussion by the students in the practicum class focused mostly on supporting the doctoral student and helping him confront the client and the client's lack of initiative and motivation for change. The intent was to push the client to confront his own depression and to make some choices.

INTRODUCTION

Given this client information, how would a social class and classism–competent mental health practitioner approach this client and work with him? And what does it mean to inform one's therapeutic approach with a social class and classism consciousness? One way to use social class to inform counseling is to simply understand that the client may come from a poor or working-class background and perhaps he does not understand the role of therapy and he needs additional education. Or perhaps the client is gaining something from psychotherapy and "venting" is a positive experience even though no change occurs. But how could the trainee better conceptualize the client and his experiences in psychotherapy?

One suggestion to the student was that even though the client and trainee had worked together for three sessions, they were still in the roles of establishing trustworthiness and credibility (Sue & Zane, 1987). The clinical intention still was to strengthen rapport and the working alliance. One way the trainee could further strengthen their working alliance would be to develop his capacity to "hold" the client's frustration and depression. It was suggested that instead of immediately moving to interventions to alleviate and treat the client's depression, and attributing the client's venting to his lack of motivation and interest in changing, the trainee should consider his presentation in session as a reflection of his experience as a lower and working-class individual within a health-care setting (Hopps & Liu, 2006).

To help the trainee further empathize with the client, it was suggested that the trainee consider the research on lower- and working-class individuals that indicated that they tend to have poor experiences in health-care environments (Hopps & Liu, 2006); that they may anticipate poor and aggressive interactions with those in different social class groups (usually in higher social class groups) because of previous negative experiences (Gallo, Smith, & Cox, 2006); and that these individuals generally have depleted their psychological resources and usually have less psychological resources from which to draw (Gallo, Bogart, Vranceanu, & Matthews, 2005). The terse interactions in session were reframed as an opportunity for the client to finally interact with his health-care setting and to potentially feel some empowerment and ownership over his health care. It was posited that the trainee was likely the first person to engage the client about his well-being and give the client an opportunity to respond. With this new conceptualization, the trainee felt better able to decipher the client's actions in session and better able to contain and hold the client's distress.

This clinical example illustrates the potential ubiquity of social class, classism, and socioeconomic status (SES) in the lives of clients and clinicians. It is simple enough to say that social class, classism, and SES permeate every aspect of our lives, yet mental health practitioners have had difficulty understanding and integrating these economic concepts into counseling, psychotherapy, assessment, and training (Liu, 2001, 2006; Liu & Ali, 2008; Liu & Arguello, 2006; Liu, Ali, Soleck, Hopps, Dunston, & Pickett, 2004; Liu, Soleck, Hopps, Dunston, & Pickett, 2004). Therefore, this chapter is intended to help mental-health professionals and trainees expand their social class and classism competencies. The chapter authors will operationalize social class and classism and discuss a subjective approach to understanding social class, the Social Class Worldview Model-Revised (SCWM-R) (Liu, in press).

Presenting a subjective or phenomenological approach to social class is important since it allows for mental health practitioners to discuss social class as a personal experience and link affect and cognitions to these experiences. The model allows for a different dialogue around social class that does not center on objective indices such as income, education, or occupation, and does not focus on discussing individuals and groups of people within social class categories such as middle-, lower-, or upper-class. The SCWM-R also connects the exploration of social class with classism, a co-construct much like race and racism or gender and sexism. Linking the constructs of social class and classism allows mental-health providers and trainees an opportunity to explore and develop competencies that require understanding the client but more importantly to understand their own social class and classism history and worldview.

Following the SCWM-R, a review of literature will be followed with sections about knowledge, skills, and values important for social class and classism–informed research and practice. To illustrate some of the points made throughout the chapter, two case vignettes will highlight how mental health practitioners may use the SCWM-R to understand and work with their clients. Finally, we include a description of resources and activities to assist in training about social class and classism issue.

DEFINITION OF TERMS

When mental health practitioners describe a client as *middle-class*, what do they mean? What are the criteria that make up "middle-class" to any particular person, and more importantly, how does the mental health practitioner respond to a "middle-class" client? To other mental health practitioners, when a client is described as "middle-class," what comes to mind? What criteria are attended to and how is the "middle-class" client conceptualized? It would seem to be a simple issue of delineating and articulating what *middle-class* means; but for each mental health practitioner, these descriptors may elicit an array of characteristics that may be related to the clinician's history, experiences, and socialization about social class and SES.

Turning to the extant literature on SES and social class in psychology offers very little help. The research and theoretical literature have been complicated by definitional problems, with little agreement among researchers about the operational definitions of SES or social class (Liu, et al., 2004; Oakes & Rossi, 2003). Liu (2001) found in his initial review of the multicultural competency literature that much of the discussion on SES and social class and classism was parenthetical; that is, many authors would suggest additional focus on clients' cultural background such as race, gender, and social class. Contributing to the clinical confusion was the fact that *SES* and *social class* were constructs conceptualized and imported from sociology, and both terms refer to macro-level affects and effects. Traditional sociological measures of SES and social class included such indicators as income, occupational status, and educational level (Grusky, 2001). mental health practitioners have largely adopted this sociological approach of using various levels of income, education, and occupation to indicate a particular social class standing or SES position. But the problems with this approach are twofold: (1) there is no evidence that these three indicators affect a particular social class position consistently, and (2) the approach assumes that everyone within a social class group (e.g., middle-class) experiences and perceives of the world similarly (Liu, in press; Liu & Ali, 2008; Liu & Hernandez, in press).

Although mental health practitioners have attempted to refine these sociological conceptualizations of social class and SES, invariably these assumptions permeate psychological approaches. Liu (2001, 2002, 2006) critiqued these psychological approaches as still focused on the macro effects of social class and SES and only intimating psychological experiences, affect, and behaviors. These new stratification approaches succeeded in merely creating additional striations in the already existing stratification paradigm (e.g., upper-middle-class, lower-working-class). Unfortunately, these newer approaches were akin to developing finer ways to grade skin color as a way to understand race and racism; these approaches focused on the objective indicators and attributed meaning without exploring how people made meaning of their social class and experiences with classism.

To move away from these indicator-based social class theories (e.g., Ostrove, Adler, Kuppermann, & Washington, 2000), Liu et al. (2004) offered a conceptualization of social class in the context of modern classism theory and focused on a subjective/phenomenological approach. They advocated for the use of the term *social class*, rather than *SES*, to highlight its relationship to classism and reinforce the conceptualization of social class and classism as meaningful only through their interdependency, much like race and racism. Therefore, throughout the remainder of the chapter, *social class* will be used as the term that captures the operational characteristics that are important for the discussion of competencies. Additionally, they posited their approach to social class through the theory of worldviews. The premise is that, as mental health practitioners, we study psychological phenomena and intrapsychic processes. For instance, mental health practitioners explore racial identity, internalized racialism, racist attitudes and beliefs, or racism-related psychological stress, not race or racism specifically. Thus, social class should also describe a particular psychological phenomenon such as worldview, identity, or acculturation.

THE SOCIAL CLASS WORLDVIEW MODEL—REVISED

Burgeoning research on SES and social class in psychology has suggested the utility of a phenomenological or subjective approach (Adler, Boyce, Chesney, Folkman, & Syme, 1993; Cohen, et al., 2008; Ostrove et al., 2000; Sapolsky, 2005). From this standpoint, Liu (2001) developed the first iteration of the Social Class Worldview Model (SCWM). The SCWM in the original and revised form (Liu, in press) is a heuristic that describes theoretically the interrelationships between the individual's context, psychological experiences, and classism. The SCWM posits a feedback circuit that explains an individual's motivations, affect, and behaviors with respect to maintaining the individual's social class position. With respect to an individual's context, the SCWM assumes that people live within economic cultures that place demands and expectations on individuals. That is, an economic culture such as one's neighborhood or working environment is the group within which social class is meaningful. There are not necessarily permanent or identifiable delineators of one's economic culture; instead, these boundaries are subjectively interpreted and employed by the individual. The significance of an economic culture (EC) is that the SCWM assumes a multiplicity of ECs. Liu (in press) posits that there is not one unitary "middle-class," but multiple "middle-class" ECs with their own norms, values, and expectations. For instance, two people with similar incomes, occupations, and educational levels may experience different pressures and expectations of being "middle-class" if one lives in Manhattan, New York, and the other in Manhattan, Kansas. These expectations and demands within the EC are conceptualized to represent resources (capital) the individual is to accumulate and use. The three types of capital are *social* capital (i.e., relationships and networks), *human* capital (i.e., physical and other inherent abilities and gifts), and *cultural* capital (i.e., aesthetics and cultural tastes).

To make sense of these capital demands, the individual makes interpretations from his or her worldview. The worldview, or the psychological experience and the way in which the individual perceives, interprets, and acts on his or her world/environment, is comprised of the person's socialization messages from important family members and peers, and is also influenced by the individual's awareness and consciousness about being a social classed person (Liu, in press). Liu suggested that the more aware and integrated the individual is about being a social classed person, the more likely he or she is able to understand, decipher, and discriminate among all the expectations placed on the individual. In the SCWM—Revised, Liu describes individuals moving through a process of developing a Social Class and Classism Consciousness (SCCC). In the SCCC, there are three levels (No Social Class Consciousness, Social Class Self-Consciousness, and Social Class Consciousness) that represent increasing levels of cognitive sophistication in understanding social class and classism but also different ways in which the person understands social class and

classism. In the No Social Class Consciousness level, the individual is unaware of how social class and classism operates and does not see him- or herself as a social-classed person. In the Social Class Self-Consciousness level, the individual is primarily focused on self-interest and how he or she understands and impacts the social class and classism system. In the final level of Social Class Consciousness, the individual sees him- or herself in relationship to others and looks for ways to impact the immediate context.

Distributed throughout each of the three levels are ten different statuses that further describe different ways in which the individual conceptualizes him- or herself as a social classed person. The ten statuses are listed under the respective levels of consciousness:

No Social Class Consciousness

1. Unawareness (i.e., no real awareness of oneself as a social classed person)
2. Status Position Saliency (i.e., developing sense of different social class groups)
3. Questioning (i.e., exploring what it means to be a social classed person)

Social Class Self-Consciousness

4. Exploration and Justification (i.e., seeking support for previously held beliefs)
5. Despair (i.e., feeling that economic injustice is unchangeable)
6. The World Is Just (i.e., the world is overwhelmingly just and people get what they deserve)
7. Intellectualized Anger and Frustration (i.e., identifying and focusing on large macro-level issues of injustice)

Social Class Consciousness

8. Reinvestment (i.e., the individual explores the personal meaningfulness of social class and classism)
9. Engagement (i.e., the individual looks for ways to address issues of inequality in his or her life and environment)

10. Equilibration (i.e., the individual is able to understand and negotiate between power, privilege, and marginalization and is able to see positive aspects and consequences to the current economic system)

The other aspects comprising the worldview are the social class–based behaviors (e.g., etiquette), relationship to materialism, and the lifestyle considerations (e.g., the ways in which time is spent and valued). Depending on the EC, the facets of behaviors, materialism, and lifestyle are differently meaningful. That is, not all of these three aspects are equally dominant, but the individual uses one of these facets as the primary way in which he or she experiences social class and classism. For instance, for some individuals, having material possessions is the most important feature of being in a particular social class group, and he or she will experience classism as materialistic pressure and will likely view and evaluate others based on material possessions.

Classism, the last part of the SCWM, is conceptualized as negative attitudes and behaviors directed toward individuals perceived to be in a different social class. Liu (2001) posited three types of classism that are directed and experienced in relationship to other people:

- Downward classism (or prejudice and discrimination directed at those who are perceived to be in a lower social class group).
- Upward classism (or prejudice and discrimination directed at those who are perceived to be in a higher social class group, such as labeling someone "elitist" or a "snob").
- Lateral classism (or prejudice and discrimination directed at those perceived to be in a similar social class group, which may be experienced as pressure to "keep up with the Joneses" because the Joneses keep reminding you how you measure up).

In a revision of the SCWM, Liu (in press) theorizes that Internalized Classism is always triggered   from experiences of classism. Liu

suggested in the SCWM-Revised that internalized classism (or feelings of inadequacy, anxiety, frustration, and depression resulting from not being able to maintain one's social class position) is always triggered when one experiences any form of classism (i.e., downward, upward, or lateral). Internalized classism is evoked and motivates the person to find ways of accommodating and adjusting to these new demands and expectations. For example, an individual's EC may believe that taking a Caribbean cruise is fashionable and a hallmark of being in a particular social class. The expectation of taking a cruise is experienced as a lifestyle consideration (i.e., how one spends time and the value of leisure); this expectation may be promulgated through lateral classism (e.g., everyone else is taking a cruise; you should also). If the individual has not had that cruise experience, he or she may feel internalized classism (inadequate) and thus be motivated to find a means to accommodate this new expectation. If he or she is able to fulfill this demand, then the individual is able to maintain homeostasis and remain within his or her perceived social class group, but if he or she is not able to, the individual would experience disequilibrium.

BARRIERS TO COMPETENCY IN SOCIAL CLASS AND CLASSISM CONSCIOUS COUNSELING

There may be myriad reasons why social class and classism have been only recently identified within psychology and other mental health practice as critical areas of multicultural competence. First, as noted earlier, the literature has been plagued with lack of consistency in the definitions and use of basic terms, which include *SES*, *social class*, and *classism* (Liu et al., 2004; Oakes & Rossi, 2003). Additionally, mental health practitioners attempting to understand the effect of disparate indicators such as income, education, and occupation on the individual or how these indictors are relevant to the individual, find a near-impossible task (Liu et al., 2004). The difficulty of this task is related to the relative lack of research that supports any significant or meaningful aggregation of these variables, in any combination, and the dearth of theory to guide research and clinical practice. Second, explicit discussion of social class violates the myth that the United States constitutes a "classless society" (Baker, 1996), and the topic tends to arouse conflicted emotional responses (e.g., Fussell, 1983).

One way this myth of a classless society might be perpetuated is through the myth of meritocracy, or the widely held notion that social mobility is always possible and related to one's internal disposition toward working hard and persistence. Rags-to-riches stories (e.g., *Rocky*, *Cinderella*, Horatio Alger's nineteenth-century novels, today's reality television program, *American Idol*) reflect an enduring theme of upward class mobility in our cultural mythology. This upward mobility bias denigrates individuals who do not seek social class mobility and prizes those who subscribe to the myth of meritocracy (Liu & Ali, 2008). A recently convened taskforce to investigate the psychological impact of social class and SES in psychology developed a Task Force Report on Socioeconomic Status, and the authors of the report note that evidence that contradicts the deeply held belief in social mobility does little to displace it (Saegert et al., 2006). They note that a *New York Times* poll found that 40 percent of respondents believed that the likelihood of upward mobility had increased over the past 30 years, even though objective measures suggest otherwise (Scott & Leonhardt, 2005). Providing further support that a pervasive belief in meritocracy exists within the middle class, the Cozzarelli, Wilkinson, and Tagler (2001) sample of middle-class college students were more likely to attribute poverty to internal attributes of impoverished people rather than to external or cultural factors. Several other indicators suggest that upward class mobility is decreasing, rather than increasing. Income disparity and inequality (Liu & Ali, 2008) has only increased in recent decades. In 1982, the top 5 percent of income earners took about 16 percent of the total aggregated income, contrasted with the bottom 40 percent of income earners, who earned approximately 14 percent of the total aggregated income at that time. In 2002, the top 5 percent of income earners received more than 21 percent of the total aggregated income in the United States, while the bottom 40 percent of income earners shared only about 13 percent of the aggregated income (Center for Popular Economics, 2004).

Finally, a particularly delicate source of resistance within the multicultural movement may stem from a sense of competition for limited resources. The process of shedding light on economic inequality may be perceived as detracting attention and resources that may otherwise be used to address other aspects of social injustice with which economic inequality intersects. But just as race, as a singular construct, is ineffective in explaining injustice, inequity, and marginalization, so is the truncated focus on social class and classism as the only important factor. Social class and classism and race and racism, along with other forms of minority statuses and identities, have to be explored as intersectionalities. In any of these intersections, individuals must recognize they live in contexts and situations that require them to negotiate between tenuous privileges and potential marginalization (Liu & Pope-Davis, 2003a). Thus, a poor White man, depending on the context, may be able to exert privileges associated with being racially White and a man, but still suffer as a result of his poor social class background.

These barriers are examples of ways in which cultures, institutions, and individuals may be resistant to exploring and understanding the impact of social class in mental health practice. Institutions certainly may be unyielding in dismantling power and social structures that privilege some individuals and groups over others and consequently create inequality and marginalization. Individuals as well may be reticent to understand or explore the socialization messages they received from family and friends about social class, mobility, success, and privilege. Moreover, for some others, it may be difficult to disentangle the complex interconnections and interdependencies of race, social class, and gender. As a result, some may give up and avoid these difficult dialogues altogether.

SOCIAL CLASS AND CLASSISM COMPETENCY TRAINING IN PSYCHOLOGY

Professional organizations representing many counseling-related fields include social class or SES in their nondiscrimination statements within their ethical codes (American Association for Marriage and Family Therapists, 2001; American Counseling Association, 2005; American Psychological Association (APA), 2002; National Association of Social Workers, 1996). The National Association of Social Workers (NASW) Code (1996) specifically charges social workers with the obligation to value social justice: "Social workers' social change efforts are focused primarily on issues of poverty, unemployment, discrimination, and other forms of social injustice." More recently, the NASW (2007) published Indicators for the Achievement of the NASW Standards for Cultural Competence in Social Work Practice. The authors stated that "[c]ulturally competent social workers will . . . possess specific knowledge about U.S., global, social, cultural, and political systems—how they operate and how they serve or fail to serve client groups; [and] include knowledge about institutional, class, cultural, and language barriers to service" (p. 24). Many of the counseling-related professions have alluded to poverty, SES, and social class in their ethical codes, and social work, in particular, has long challenged its professionals to engage in efforts to address the ill-effects of poverty. The focus of the historical efforts has been to understand and address poverty at the institutional level.

For psychologists, the Assessment of Competency Benchmarks Work Group (APA Work Group on Assessment of Competency Benchmarks, 2007) was convened recently by the APA Board of Educational Affairs in collaboration with the Council of Chairs of Training Councils (CCTC) (see Table 12.1). The work group identified competencies, including knowledge, values,

and skills, expected for trainees in their work with regard to individual-cultural diversity expected at three levels of training. While these competency benchmarks were written by the CCTC, they are applicable to other health-care practitioners and training. In the next sections, we will identify knowledge, skills, and values needed for social class and classism–conscious mental health practice.

KNOWLEDGE

One place to start might be the APA Guidelines on Multicultural Education, Training, Research, Practice, and Organizational Change for Psychologists (APA, 2003), which states the following: "Psychologists are encouraged to recognize the impor-tance of multicultural sensitivity/responsiveness to, knowledge of, and understanding about ethnically and racially different individuals" (p. 385). We are advocating for mental health professionals to acquire knowledge of social class and classism as an aspect of human diversity, and learn ways to understand and respond well to individuals who identify with social classes different from their own class identities. In addition, mental health professionals must recognize some of the ways that social class experiences have shaped worldviews.

Mental health practitioners should also know that much of our research has been derived from convenience samples, often college students. An analysis of the empirical articles published in the *Journal of Counseling Psychology* between 1973 and 1998 indicated that 56 percent of the samples were comprised of college student participants (Buboltz, Miller, & Williams, 1999). In contrast, only 24.4 percent of citizens aged 25 and older in the year 2000 had a college degree (Census Bureau, 2001). What we know about counseling may apply most directly only to college students, in which middle-class mind-set and wealthier young adults may often be overrepresented.

The Competency Benchmark Work Group (APA Work Group on Assessment of Competency Benchmarks, 2007) indicated that trainees should have knowledge and awareness of their cultural identities as they enter practicum. We believe that beginning practicum students should have developed, at a minimum, rudimentary awareness and consciousness of themselves as social classed individuals and have some consciousness of a social class system (Liu, in press; Liu & Hernandez, 2010). The important feature of being competent around social class and classism is understanding oneself as a social classed person and exploring one's previous experiences and socialization around social class and classism. Liu (in press) speculates that these unexplored socialization messages from parents and peers, along with traumatic experiences around classism, may potentially manifest themselves as negative bias, collusion, or overidentification with clients when social class or classism is triggered in session.

Further, practicum students should gain familiarity with some of the social class and classism literature. For example, the SES Task Force Report (Saegert et al., 2006) would provide an overview of issues, and the APA homepage focusing on SES provides additional resources (http://www .apa.org/pi/ses/homepage.html). Consistent with the Benchmarks Work Group model's guidelines (APA Work Group on Assessment of Competency Benchmarks, 2007), we would expect that upon entry to internship, predoctoral interns would be able to apply knowledge regarding intersecting and complex dimensions of diversity, especially as it pertains to how social class and classism may inform other dimensions of the client's background, such as race or gender.

SKILLS

The Competency Benchmark Work Group (American Psychological Association Work Group on Assessment of Competency Benchmarks, 2007) built on Rodolfa and colleagues' (2005) *cube model* for competency development. Rodolfa and colleagues classified cultural diversity as a foundational competency, which undergirds multiple roles and functions that mental

health professionals fill. The Competency Benchmark Work Group (APA Work Group on Assessment of Competency Benchmarks, 2007) elaborated on the multiple functional competencies, including assessment–diagnosis–case conceptualization, intervention, consultation, research-evaluation, supervision-teaching, and management-administration. Mental-health professionals need to integrate class consciousness across these functional roles.

Assessment and Case Conceptualization

Social class and classism–conscious mental-health professionals should consider sociopolitical (e.g., unequal distribution of power), socio-historical (e.g., biased and inaccurate histories of peoples), and socio-structural (e.g., legal, education, and economic systems) forces that marginalize and oppress individuals (Liu & Ali, 2005). Also, just as important is an understanding of the individual and personal explanations for problems in living. Attributing problems in living to structural causes suggests that professionals may best intervene in the context of their roles as organizational consultants or administrators. If mental-health practitioners fail to consider the structural explanations as they conceptualize cases, they are at high risk to make errors by encouraging the clients to accept responsibility for circumstances over which they have limited or no influence. In so doing, they are at risk of straining their therapeutic relationships and of missing opportunities to challenge self-denigrating beliefs (Liu & Pope-Davis, 2005).

Although tolerance for ambiguity is a valuable capacity in any counseling endeavor, it is particularly necessary when exploring structural versus personal attributions for human problems. Humility about the problems that poor people face is especially appropriate, given the limits of our research base. Because of the risk for errors, it is essential that mental-health-care practitioners use transparent and collaborative processes to assess personal and structural contributions to client problems and to develop interventions accordingly.

Liu and Ali (2008) developed a framework from which the SCWM-R may be used in counseling, and they recommend that practitioners explore the client's experiences with classism and its effects on the client's life. They recommend four steps in the exploration and action process: (1) help clients identify and understand their economic culture; (2) help clients identify social messages they receive(d); (3) identify clients' experiences with classism and move them toward developing adaptive, realistic, and healthy expectations about themselves; and (4) integration and action. In the following chart, Liu and Ali (2008) included sample queries for helping clinicians to explore their clients' social class and classism experiences.

Social Class Interventions Using the Social Class Worldview Model

The social class interventions are targeted toward the client's experiences of classism. Upward, downward, lateral, and internalized classisms are the focus of the therapist. Through collaboration, clients are helped in the following ways:

- Clients gain insight about their experiences of classism, their worldview, and the pressures they experience as a part of an economic culture.
- Empathy by the therapist toward the client's classism experiences is important.
- The therapist challenges the client's irrational cognitions about his or her social status and what he or she needs to do to maintain or achieve a social status. And the therapist helps clients integrate their history with their current situation.
- Clients are encouraged to develop self-efficacy in coping with and managing their situation.
- Clients are helped to identify situations in which certain feelings are tied to classism experiences.

Step 1—Help the client identify and understand his or her economic culture.

Sample Query:
- Tell me what kind of pressure you feel/experience as you try to keep up with your friends.

    Identify answers that touch on cultural, social, and human capital pressures/expectations.

Step 2—Help the client identify the social class messages he or she receive(d).

Sample Queries:
- What would your parent(s)/peers say about your current situation?
- How would your parent(s)/peers help you resolve your current situation?
- List the ways you are acting to live out messages given to you by your parent(s)/peers.
- Tell me about your peer group and/or your support network.

    Identify answers that focus on strong/salient cultural socialization messages still running in the client's mind, which drive the client's behavior and attitudes.

Step 2a—Help the client identify social class behaviors, lifestyles, and material possessions that are salient to the client in his or her current situation.

Sample Queries:
- Tell me how you imagine your life.
- How would you ideally be spending your time?

(continued)

(*continued*)

- What do others have that you want?
- What do you notice about how other people act/behave that you like?

Identify answers that pinpoint the client's materialism values; how he has changed his lifestyle to fit into a new group, and how he has changed his behavior to belong in a new group.

Step 3—Identify the client's experiences with classism and move toward developing an adaptive, realistic, and healthy expectation about him- or herself.

Sample Queries:

- Do people look down on you?
- Do you look down on others who are not like you?
- What do your peers expect from you to maintain your status with them?
- What does it feel like for you when you can't keep up with your peers? What do you do?

Identify answers that express high social class expectations and the negative consequences related to not meeting specific demands. Additionally, in what ways is the client participating in classism to maintain her social class standing?

Step 4—Help the client integrate his or her experiences of classism.

Sample query:

- Now that we've started talking about all these aspects of your social class experience, can you tell me what it means to you?
- What are you aware of about yourself that you didn't know before we started?

Identify an ability to understand and integrate the social class discussions into other aspects of the client's life.

Step 4a—Help the client take action and make changes in his or her life.

Sample query:

- *Sample query:* What is the one thing you could do to change your awareness, situation, or perception?

Identify an ability to make personal changes in the client's life.

The first three steps in Liu and Ali's process inform assessment and case conceptualization, helping the mental health practitioner and the client to develop a shared understanding of the client's problems in living. Entry-level professionals should have the competencies to facilitate a discussion and exploration of the social class and classism–related experiences and identities of their psychotherapy clients. To illustrate some of these concepts identified so far, case examples are provided (See Case Vignette 12.2 on the following page.)

Using some of Liu and Ali's (2008) sample queries, the mental health practitioner could explore and incorporate the following information into the case conceptualization. In their model, the mental health practitioner's first task is to help clients identify and understand their economic culture:

CASE VIGNETTE 12.2

Sally, a 24-year-old single White European American heterosexual woman, presents with symptoms of major depressive disorder. She reports that for approximately the past year, she has experienced lack of joy, difficulty with concentration, low motivation, crying spells, and morbid thinking. She reports vague, passive suicidal ideation. She denies any plan or intention to self-harm. She earned a bachelor's degree in Anthropology at age 22, and she reports that her academic progress had gone smoothly. Since graduation, she has worked as a legal secretary. During the first interview, she indicated that she has been "so fortunate," with parents who are described as supportive, both emotionally and financially. She clarified that she is currently financially self-supporting. She expressed annoyance with herself for the experience of distress, questioning whether her issues warrant attention.

COUNSELOR: Tell me what kind of pressure you feel/experience as you try to keep up with your friends.

SALLY: They have always accepted me, no matter what. We met when we prepared for a study-abroad semester, before several of us went to Germany. My friends moved away after college to attend graduate school. They are very nice, but they're really busy. They have gotten together three times since college, but the only way I can go is if my parents pay for me to travel. I don't want to ask them for money. My friends are in graduate programs and seem to have enough money to buy good food, and they travel easily. They don't care much about brands and fancy clothes, but they assume that we all can provide easily for ourselves and can afford to travel to maintain our relationships.

Liu and Ali (2008) suggested that the mental health practitioner identify answers that touch on cultural, social, and human capital pressures/expectations. In Sally's case, the mental health practitioner might note the valuing of academic achievement, learning, autonomy, and travel. Her friends invest in travel to maintain their relationships. Materialism for its own sake does not appear to be central.

The mental health practitioner's second step in Liu and Ali's (2008) suggested process is to help clients identify the social class messages they receive(d):

COUNSELOR: How would your parent(s) help you resolve your current situation?

SALLY: My parents just want me to be happy. I know they will support whatever I want to do. My family is great; I admire them so much. My parents worked their way through college and have set good examples for us. Dad is a high school superintendent; mom is an audiologist. Since my siblings and I moved out of the house, my mom volunteers at the free medical clinic. My sister is a physician; she works for Doctors without Borders. Jared, my brother, is a district attorney. He works long hours and has too many cases, but he wants to make a difference.

COUNSELOR: How would your friends help you resolve your current situation?

SALLY: I don't talk to my friends very much anymore, not about my struggles. I haven't made new close friendships since college.

COUNSELOR: In what ways are you acting to live out messages given to you by your parents?

SALLY: I'm not living out messages given to me by my parents at all. They have always wanted us to do well in school and work to make the world a better place. I tried pretty hard in school, but I didn't do that well. I wanted to go to law school, but I would never be accepted to a strong school. My parents say that they don't care how we do in school or in our careers, as long as we do our best. They never say they are disappointed in me, but I know they are. I think they are. Maybe it's just me who believes that I am such a failure. I'm not sure.

Liu and Ali (2008) suggest that the mental-health provider identify answers that focus on strong/salient cultural socialization messages still running in the client's mind that drive the client's behavior and attitudes. Additionally, the mental health practitioner might note Sally's social class identification group's salient valuing of academic and career status and achievement. There is also a clear valuing of social service. The mental health practitioner might also note an implicit expectation that family members, as individuals, have a relatively wide sphere of influence.

The third step in Liu and Ali's (2008) recommended process is to identify clients' experiences with classism and move them toward developing an adaptive, realistic, and healthy expectation about themselves. One way to conceptualize Sally's case is to examine her experience of lateral classism (e.g., "keeping up with the Joneses"), related to her conclusion that she is not able to develop and maintain human capital (i.e., admittance to high-status graduate program, professional helping skills), social capital (e.g., maintenance of long-distance relationships), and cultural capital (e.g., travel, perhaps more expensive foods and gym memberships). She has not yet adjusted her expectations or integrated values from her friends and family to match her current situation. The transition is likely to require acceptance

of grief and loss, so that she has more energy to invest in making her current circumstances more satisfying. Sally might be looking down on others who hold positions similar to hers in her workplace, based on classist assumptions.

Case Vignette 12.3 is the next clinical example. This case is about Juan, and similar to the first case example, the mental health practitioner's first task is to help clients identify and understand their economic culture (Liu & Ali, 2008):

COUNSELOR: Tell me what kind of pressure you feel/experience as you try to keep up with your friends.

JUAN: My friends like to play soccer and hang out. We go to the local bar after games and have a few beers. I have a lot of friends; they regard me as an easy-going guy who is a good soccer player. They count on me to be funny and happy. Since I got injured, though, I just don't feel like seeing them.

Liu and Ali (2008) suggest that the mental-health-care practitioner identify answers that touch on cultural, social, and human capital pressures/expectations. So far, it appears that athletic prowess and social ease and availability are valued. The mental health practitioner's second step in Liu and Ali's (2008) suggested process is to help clients identify the social class messages they receive(d):

COUNSELOR: How would your parent(s) help you resolve your current situation?

JUAN: They tell me not to worry; I have always been healthy, and I'm recovering quickly from

CASE VIGNETTE 12.3

Juan is a 19-year-old Mexican American part-time factory worker. He is taking a course at the local community college in preparation to take the GED exam. He was referred to a community college mental health practitioner by a physician who had treated Juan for a job-related injury. Juan reports that he has been plagued by panic attacks that began a week or two after his injury. His injury prevents him from attending work, but he expects to recover fully. During the panic attacks, Juan is most distressed by fears that he will die of a heart attack. He denies previous experience of panic or undue anxiety. Although Juan does not mind missing his work, he misses playing soccer in his men's soccer league.

my injury. They said they can provide for me in the meantime.

COUNSELOR: How would your friends help you resolve your current situation?

JUAN: They ask me to come to games, or at least meet them at the local bar. I don't talk with them about the panic. They would think that I'm just being silly. They'd remind me that my leg is getting better.

COUNSELOR: In what ways are you acting to live out messages given to you by your parents?

JUAN: My parents are grateful that I have helped them and my younger brother and sister. They respect me and my choices. They tell me not to worry; I have always been healthy, and I'm recovering quickly from my injury. They were disappointed when I stopped going to high school, but they knew they needed me to do other things. I started working a few hours in the factory, and I was earning good money and was able to pay for my car. My mother is always tired; her job is really hard. She needs for us not to complain. My dad lost his zest and energy after he was disabled, and he probably drinks too much. Complaining about that doesn't change it, so we do the best we can.

COUNSELOR: What do others have that you want?

JUAN: I want my father to be the way he was before he got hurt. Everything changed after that. He is undocumented, so he sure didn't have disability insurance. He was just so beaten down, and my mom was always worried about how she would pay bills and feed us. I want a safer job, and I want disability insurance. I know I'm going to be fine this time, but what about the next time? I don't mind working hard; I actually like working up a sweat, but I am scared about what's going to happen to me and anyone who depends on me, if my body doesn't hold up.

Liu and Ali (2008) recommend that the mental-health-care practitioner identify answers that focus on strong/salient cultural socialization messages still running in the client's mind that drive the client's behavior and attitudes. Exploration

reveals that Juan is expected (and expects) to contribute to his family-of-origin in a range of ways, providing assistance with errands, transportation, and child care. Financial contributions are expected occasionally, but not necessarily consistently. He also reveals an expectation that he endure difficult circumstances without complaint or acknowledgment. This coping style may have been adaptive, but it may have blocked Juan's awareness of his emotional responses to his earlier losses, as well as his insight about the source of his recent panic attacks.

The third step in Liu and Ali's (2008) recommended process is to identify clients' experiences with classism and move them toward developing an adaptive, realistic, and healthy expectation about themselves. The identification of the client's experiences with classism continues to inform the conceptualization, while beginning to also provide an environment for self-reflection and reevaluation, which also serves as an intervention.

Again, Liu and Ali's (2008) sample suggested sample queries could be utilized.

COUNSELOR: Do people look down on you?

JUAN: I suppose some of the White guys who went to high school with me think I am a low-life because I didn't graduate. They might think I'm stupid, but I used to write really great stories in elementary school. I had to write in English. My stories are always better in Spanish. They weren't too bad. I haven't thought about that for a long time. I feel kind of stupid at this point.

COUNSELOR: Do you look down on others who are not like you?

JUAN: I don't know. I know a few guys who are all talk and no action. They are always afraid to get their hands dirty. If someone was disrespecting me or one of my friends on the soccer field, we would act.

Juan has met many of the demands of his economic culture. He has developed human capital of physical ability and ability to respond to the needs of others through emotional attunement and storytelling. He has maintained a strong social support network of friends and has earned a place of respect in his family. Although we do not know a lot about his material values, we know that he purchased a car at an early age and is able to contribute to his family financially. However, a temporary interruption in his physical ability elicited panic about revisiting past losses and anxiety about an ongoing source of vulnerability. Juan's vulnerability to suffering greatly should he lose physical ability stems in part from structural inequalities. Because the process of acknowledging vulnerability has not been adaptive or well-developed, Juan has not yet fully incorporated full awareness of its implications. Further, he may also have internalized beliefs that his intellectual capacity is limited, based in part on how others respond to his educational level. He may have developed a social class-based disdain for intellectual approaches, rather than physical approaches, which might also affect his current dilemmas.

Intervention

Liu and Ali (2008) indicate that after identifying the client's experiences of classism, the next step is to help the client "move toward developing an adaptive, realistic, and healthy expectation" about him- or herself. They list several types of interventions toward that end, and toward the client's goal of integration and action.

One way to achieve this is through culturally congruent interventions that are also informed by social class. As illustrated in the example cases, social class and classism worldview and consciousness are embedded in the case conceptualizations.

Depending on the mental health practitioner's theoretical orientation, the mental health practitioner may approach the intervention process in varying ways. For example, psychodynamic therapists might seek to identify a Core Maladaptive Pattern and work to help the client gain insight and provide a corrective emotional experience. In Sally's case, the mental health practitioner might note Sally's global hesitancy and shame about not being as autonomous and capable as she expects herself to be. The therapist might also notice that Sally questions whether her issues warrant the

therapist's time and empathy. The therapist observes that Sally is not reaching out to established friends, nor is she developing new friendships. Sally's therapist might choose to use the here-and-now relationships to explore how Sally got the idea that the therapist might not be interested in Sally's painful experiences, in an attempt to help Sally gain insight about her transferential response to the help-seeking process. From an object-relations perspective in which a new and corrective experience is emphasized, the therapist may focus heavily on helping create a feeling of safety and acceptance of Sally's need for support. The core fear, if not maladaptive pattern, in Juan's case may be that although he is proud of his competency and resiliency, he fears rejection/ destitution if he slips in his ability to take care of himself and others. The mental health practitioner might note that Juan initially focuses heavily on his competence and place of respect within his social network, with little initial tolerance for exploring the triggers for anxiety. From this framework, the mental health practitioner would work to gently support awareness and acceptance of his vulnerability, in part to enable Juan to gain flexibility in planning for how to manage it.

A humanistic mental health practitioner might focus on clients' awareness of strengths, as a counter to negative social class–related self-perceptions. Although Sally feels incapable of autonomy and achievement, she has completed a bachelor's degree and adapted to a new culture during a study-abroad year. She is viewed as competent by others in her office. She has been covering her own expenses and has been reliable as a worker. Juan is fluent in English and Spanish. He is physically capable and can generally sustain physical labor. He is a good nurturer and fun for others to be around. The focus on strengths may serve to correct irrational beliefs.

Cognitive behavioral mental health practitioners should note potential cognitive errors and encourage the clients to review evidence for the erroneous conclusions. They might note types of errors. Sally engages in all-or-nothing thinking. "If I don't have wide influence to provide service or affect social policies, then my service efforts are worthless. I must be very highly achieving in relation to others close to me for me to feel proud of my own accomplishments." Juan's anxiety-provoking belief, "if my competence slips, my well-being is in immediate jeopardy," is not fully founded, though it has some basis in reality. He may want to use the crisis and opportunity to address his desire for greater security, perhaps by seeking a factory job that carries benefits. Alternatively, he may want to pursue additional education. He may be affected by another irrational belief, if he has internalized stereotypes about less educated people: "Because I did not persist in high school, I am not capable of being successful beyond the GED."

Liu and Ali's (2008) fourth intervention is to help the client integrate the client's history with his or her current situation. In both case examples, they are struggling to do so. Sally is likely to maintain her values of hard work, social support, and achievement, but she may need to identify new ways to implement those values that are consistent with her personality and abilities. She may need to similarly reevaluate her criteria for acceptable friends. Juan is likely to maintain his valuing of his interpersonal responsiveness, physical ability, and maintenance of social networks, but he may wish to take steps toward increasing his financial security, to the extent that he is able. Because he has enjoyed academic pursuits, he may wish to challenge his negative perceptions about the use of intellectual strategies to address issues.

Some research suggests that individuals from poor and working-class backgrounds, because of their job and work experiences, are often lacking decision authority and skill discretion, that these jobs are often authoritarian (i.e., unidirectional power structures) (Karasek & Theorell, 1990), and that individuals from these environments may also expect and prefer directive counseling approaches. In these situations, it may be necessary to embrace these expectations at the beginning as a means of developing trustworthiness and credibility with the client (Sue & Zane, 1987). Clinicians also have to be sensitive to the client's real access to resources and be aware

of the clinician's assumptions and expectations. For instance, for some clients from impoverished contexts, there are real concerns for safety, access to money, food, and safe shelter. It is important to be aware that, along with these possible material deficiencies, the client's history of hostile and aggressed experiences may aggravate his or her interpersonal interactions.

Clinicians need to able to address the entire array of social class issues clients may be reluctant to discuss. For instance, openly discussing income and money is often regarded as a social taboo (Krueger, 1986). Not only is income incredibly difficult to accurately report (since people often do not discuss spending on credit, other aspects of wealth and assets, and how savings are used), but in fact, Croizet and Claire (1998) found that for some people in lower social classes, a query about one's income elicits a form of stereotype threat (i.e., a poor person's internalized stereotypes that poor people are deficient or bad). Therefore, clinicians need to evolve their comfort and develop ways in which social class and classism may be discussed and explored. mental health practitioners also need to be conscious that social class and classism are relevant issues regardless of where the individual is on the economic spectrum. Thus, the poor and the affluent may have salient social class and classism issues that may have similar psychological effects but vary by type and magnitude. And both the poor and the affluent person may be experiencing lateral classism because they do not possess the "right" material objects for their social class group, but the types and magnitude of their materialism may vary. Regardless of how the mental health practitioner discusses social class and classism, clients generally appreciate a clinician's awareness, sensitivity, and willingness to address all aspects of the client's experiences and identities (Thompson & Jenal, 1994).

Consultation

Vera and Speight (2003) suggested that if mental health practitioners are to be truly multiculturally competent, they must expand their roles beyond that of counseling and psychotherapy. They suggest that psychology model social workers' commitment to address needs broadly. They quote Mather and Lager (2000): "In order to offset the negative and reinforce the positive effects of societal issues, it important for social workers to gain greater knowledge of societal issues and develop skills in advocacy, negotiation, organization, and policy implementation" (p. 19). Further, Vera and Speight (2003) indicate that the "ability to design, implement, and evaluate community interventions that promote community empowerment [is] a critical element in multicultural competence" (p. 265).

Consistent with the Benchmarks Work Group model (APA Work Group on Assessment of Competency Benchmarks, 2007) we would expect that upon entry to internship, predoctoral interns would be able to apply knowledge, skills, and attitudes regarding intersecting and complex dimensions of diversity. Professionals who choose to specialize and engage in advanced social class–related practice could involve themselves on policymaking boards for organizations designed to address class-related needs. They might also oversee projects designed to meet class-based needs of particular groups of people.

Research

Additional research efforts that involve people who do not attend college as subjects and collaborators are needed to expand our knowledge base. Simply attending to and reporting about subjects' social class and classism worldview and experiences and related circumstances would help consumers of research have more knowledge about the generalizability of findings. Vera and Speight (2003) similarly advocate for the use of methods that involve stakeholders as participants. They also suggest that research would focus on the assessment of needs or impact of public policies within particular communities or populations.

Furthermore, scholars should examine the values that underlie their terminology and their selection of outcome measures. Belle and Doucet (2003) referred to studies of "welfare-dependent"

mothers, rather than "welfare-reliant" or "job-reliant" people. Liu (2006) also noted that researchers should speak of people and individuals from poor situations rather than "poor people." The authors also note the importance of careful selection of outcome measures and consider measures which will provide the researchers with a comprehensive profile of the people being studied.

Supervision

As trainers and clinicians, we need to self-monitor to avoid enactments of classism, either upwardly, downwardly, or laterally. In our role as trainers, we are often helping our trainees move into or maintain middle-class lifestyles, and perhaps middle-class identities. Trainers have the potential to enact classism in each direction.

Trainees who come from wealthy backgrounds may be subject to being targets of upward classism, although becoming a mental health professional may entail downward social class mobility for these trainees. This upward classism may come from clients, but it may also be bias from classmates and instructors. Some of these individuals may retain some support from family wealth. And trainers should empathize with trainees who may experience downward mobility rather than regarding the experience of downward mobility as simply a "learning experience." Highly privileged trainees may encounter emerging awareness of their history of unearned privilege, a process that often elicits significant discomfort and distress, particularly if the trainee has not yet developed skills to cope with such awareness. Trainers need to respect the learning process and needs of the trainee, and to continually assess whether they are providing a safe, respectful environment in which all of their trainees can explore their developing professional identities.

As one avenue toward increasing empathy for trainees who come from working-class backgrounds, trainers could acquaint themselves with some qualitative reports about the experience of people from the working class who move to professional roles. Lubrano (2004) provides biographical and autobiographical examples of "class straddlers" who struggle to maintain dual social class identities. His book poignantly illustrates his interviewees' internal conflicts and their desire to maintain connections to their working-class roots.

Trainers should also be vigilant about reviewing their own social class–based assumptions. They should avoid enactments of classism that could occur if trainers act on judgments that are unrelated to professional achievement and success. The kind of vacations, leisure activities, food preferences, and selection of clothing brands and styles has social-class relevance. Trainers should guard against making classist judgments about activities or expressions differing from their own aesthetic values. In a clinical practice environment, although exploration and examination of appropriate professional demeanor and clothing are essential, particularly as trainees are challenged to consider what their self-presentation may communicate to their clients, trainers should be mindful of the possible internal conflicts that may arise as trainees work to integrate personal identities, including class identities with professional identities.

The examination of social class and classism is often sensitive. Trainers must have patience for the developmental process. Increasing social class and classism consciousness may elicit internal inconsistencies within an individual's values, a process that typically provokes anxiety. Ideally, mental health professionals and trainees are committed to social justice values and willingly engage in exploration of their class privileges as well as class disadvantages, despite discomfort.

VALUES AND ATTITUDES

With regard to attitudes, the APA Guidelines on Multicultural Education, Training, Research, Practice, and Organizational Change for Psychologists (APA, 2003) state the following: "Psychologists are encouraged to recognize that as cultural beings, they may hold attitudes and beliefs that can detrimentally influence their perceptions of and interactions with individuals who are

ethnically and racially different from themselves" (p. 377). The same statement applies to mental-health professionals' perceptions of and interactions with individuals who identify with different social classes than themselves.

As trainees begin to provide supervised services, their awareness of themselves as social classed persons may be quite rudimentary. But because the concern for the welfare of others and commitment to provide ethical services are expected, the process of self-reflection is highly prized. Therefore, supervised practice and didactic training must provide opportunities for trainees to examine their social class–related biases.

Research already shows that mental health practitioners hold a negative bias against those from lower- and working-class backgrounds (Garb, 1997; Wang et al., 2005). These biases often appear as poorer prognoses, more severe diagnoses, and shorter and poorer psychological treatment for the poor. Lott and Bullock (2007) identify several mechanisms through which U.S. citizens are exposed to inaccurate representations of poor people. These mechanisms include a wide variety of media outlets, but also electoral candidates often target middle-class voters, framing issues in a manner that is perceived to be attractive to and protective of that politically active group's interests (Lott & Bullock, 2007). Additionally, college students tend to hold less positive views of poor people than they do of middle-class people (Cozzarelli et al., 2001).

One way in which mental health providers may also evidence a bias is through an *upward mobility bias* (Liu & Ali, 2008; Liu et al., 2007). The upward mobility bias posits that, living in the United States with its prominent focus on the myth of meritocracy, mental health providers may also assume that individuals are always motivated toward upward social mobility. In part, the upward mobility bias is a socialized belief, especially among people in the middle class (Liu et al., 2007). Thus, for some clinicians, it may be possible that when confronted with clients who are not interested in social class upward mobility, the clinician may attribute negative dispositional characteristics such as lack of motivation, poor work ethic, or lack of direction in life. But as Liu has argued, there are potentially many individuals who are satisfied with their current life situation (e.g., their current job and responsibilities) and are not interested in constant social mobility but are primarily concerned with maintaining their current social status.

While social class and classism bias is often focused on those from poor backgrounds for current situations, clinicians also need to be aware of their bias against people in affluence or who are in and from wealthy backgrounds. Others have already discussed the psychological distress associated with affluence such as anxiety and depression, as well as the resultant substance abuse, poor subjective wellbeing, and interpersonal conflict (Levine, 2006; Luthar & D'Avanzo, 1999; Luthar & Latendresse, 2005; Twenge, 2006). The psychological distress and other socio-emotional problems may be minimized or dismissed by clinicians if they focus only on the objective research suggesting a mental health gradient wherein those in upper-social classes are better off than those in the lower economic brackets (Gallo & Matthews, 2003). But, as Liu has posited, this is where a focus on objective indices fails the clinician. It is accurate that the affluent and wealthy have more access to health care and other resources that allow them to be far better off than those who are poor. Yet the subjective experience of affluence may be much different from what the objective indicators show and this subjective experience may be related to psychological distress and problem behavioral sequelae. Liu also suggests that clinicians may operate from the position of "upward" classism and may harbor perceptions of those in affluence as being "elitists" and "snobs" and act in accordance with these underlying values and beliefs. Failing to explore and understand this bias may be as detrimental to the affluent client as downward classism (i.e., prejudice and discrimination against those perceived to be in a lower social class) is to the client from a poor background. Thus, upward mobility bias, much like upward, downward, and lateral classism, are forms of bias and prejudice of which mental health providers need to be aware.

By the time that trainees complete internships and enter their professions, they should be conscious of the intersectionalities between social class and classism and many other aspects of identity, including race, ethnicity, gender, ability/disability, and sexual orientation (Saegert et al., 2006). Entering professionals are expected to be sensitive to the complex and shifting salience of differing aspects of an individual's identity. Professionals will maintain awareness that individuals may identify with more than one oppressed group, and most individuals will identify with some privileged group(s).

Although no mental-health professional will be completely knowledgeable about the entire range of economic cultures in which their clients function, it is incumbent upon the professionals to remain curious about the social class–related expectations and experiences of their clients. Understanding the demands within a client's economic culture may provide a means to help the clinician maintain empathy for the clients' experiences of events, even if the meaning of the events would be completely different within the clinician's frame of reference.

Although all professionals should commit themselves to provide social class–conscious service and to address classism through their professional roles, some commit themselves to advanced practice and specialization. These professionals may conduct class-related research, serve on policymaking boards, and maintain active relationships with agencies that hold missions to address classism at the local level.

SUMMARY

The purpose of this chapter was to outline a social class and classism–informed approach to working with clients and to provide clinicians in training, at the different entry through internship and professional levels, a roadmap of the hallmarks that mark competent practice. We have outlined the important areas of knowledge, skills, and attitudes and values necessary to work with clients around issues of social class and classism. Because of the limited space, this chapter implicitly focuses on work with lower- and working-class individuals; these competencies also apply to working with middle- and affluent-class individuals. But regardless of the social class of the individual, it is critical to remember that social class and classism–conscious work with clients first starts with an exploration, understanding, and integration of the ways in which social class and classism have impacted the lives of the clinician and supervisor. It is simple to develop the factual knowledge and requisite skills to work competently with clients from various social class backgrounds, but to work competently and effectively, clinicians need to understand how their social class and classism experiences may positively affect therapy as well as distort and bias their approaches. Through the case study illustrations, the authors have attempted to show how the Social Class Worldview Model—Revised (SCWM-R) may be used to illuminate the client's experiences with social class and classism.

RESOURCES

The following resources are provided as suggestions for further inquiry and as tools students, clinicians, trainees, and supervisors can utilize to help improve the quality of the services they provide.

Training activities that increase awareness and knowledge about social class issues will help individuals explore beliefs about meritocracy and the perceived fluidity of class boundaries in the United States. They may help remove social class blinders and raise awareness of interpersonal and institutional classism, ensuring that budding and seasoned clinicians practice with sensitivity to social class variables.

Experiential exercises provide opportunities for self-reflection and knowledge acquisition. The current ethics code in psychology (APA, 2002) requires that training programs identify in their admission and program materials if they "require students or supervisees to disclose personal information in course- or program-related activities, either orally or in writing, regarding . . . relationships with parents, peers, and spouses or significant others" (p. 1068). Because social class–related values are transmitted in the context of our relationships with others, generally first within our families and later within our peer networks, some self-disclosure about those relationships may be inherent in the exploration and clarification of our own values and attitudes. Although we may communicate about social class identity in nuanced ways such as clothing choices, discussion of leisure activities, and manner of expression, it remains unusual to discuss social class identification openly. We encourage trainers to provide information in their admissions materials about the types of self-disclosure that are encouraged in their programs.

The following are some exercises that may also increase knowledge and initiate dialogue about social class as a diversity issue. The list is not exhaustive, but it offers some exercises that may be useful in exploring diversity issues in general, and may be applied to social class in particular. When possible, a source is cited for each of these activities; however, many of them have been passed down, and thus the originator is not known.

EXERCISE 12.1: CULTURAL COAT-OF-ARMS

Trainers ask participants to create a *cultural coat-of-arms* or *cultural wheel*, with education, occupation, and income, among other identity components. This activity may be used to raise awareness of the economic culture in which each grew up, the ways in which the economic culture may have changed, and how it has affected one's worldview. Trainees can use the activity as a stimulus to explore what it would be like to work with a client or supervisee whose cultural coat-of-arms or wheel looks very different from the trainees'. The discussion can also be used to encourage trainees how to sensitively inquire about and address various aspects of identity, including social class.

EXERCISE 12.2: CONTAINER EXERCISE

J. Powell and J. Lines (personal communication, April 20, 2007) developed the *container exercise*. Each participant prepares a container that holds objects of symbolic importance to him or her. The shape of the container and items attached to the exterior (e.g., words, drawings, photos) may be symbolic of the public aspects of the creator's identity. Inside the container each individual places some things that represent his or her private self, those things that are not so obvious or that people discover only when they get to know the individual much better. These may be objects, mementos, or other things that symbolize the individual's private self (e.g., personal or family history, values, allegiances, important moments). Using time limits, participants take turns sharing stories about their containers to the extent they feel comfortable. General processing is done after each individual shares, and aspects of social class may be one area that trainees and facilitators explore.

EXERCISE 12.3: WHEEL OF LIFE

Roffman (1996) described a classroom exercise in which she asks students to construct a *wheel of life*, a pie chart with influences including gender, sexual orientation, race ethnicity, social class, schooling, and family structure. Her students engage in telling stories of their identity development. She noted that most often the aspects that are consonant with the dominant culture take less space on their charts than the aspects that are marginalized. Her students often report that they have never articulated differences in identity before. Roffman reported that her students comment that social class, in particular, has rarely been discussed before, and that students are often unsure about their social class membership. Further she notes that "students need to know that they are not alone, that there is little in our society that encourages a critical analysis of class" (p. 176).

EXERCISE 12.4: FILMS

People Like Us

Participants watch the PBS documentary, *People Like Us* (Kolker & Alvarez, 2001), and use their supporting Web site: http://www.pbs.org/peoplelikeus/index.html. This engaging film, coupled with the Web site, provides a great opportunity to learn about social class and to increase identity awareness. The Web site describes itself as "a place to learn how social class works in America and to test your own preconceptions about who belongs where on the social scale." There are games, resources, personal stories, provocative links, and posting areas to help raise awareness of social class.

Breaking Away (Yates, 1979) is an Oscar-winning film about a high school graduate who dreams of becoming a champion bicyclist, and who poses as an exchange student to mask his working-class (mining family) roots, much to the frustration of his parents. The movie can serve as a stimulus piece to explore the tension, cultural conflict, and range of feelings experienced by a low-income, first-generation college student who is attempting to straddle cultures.

Social Class, Economic Privilege and Counseling (Liu, Greenfeld, & Turesky, 2008) is a training video discussing aspects of social class and classism as a subjective and phenomenological experience. Using the Social Class Worldview Model (SCWM), the video demonstrates how the model may be used to explore and explain social class and classism to clients. The video also presents a number of provocative issues and may be used to generate class discussion along with illustrating social class and classism–conscious counseling.

EXERCISE 12.5: DIVERSITY-EXCHANGE

Trainees participate in a *diversity-exchange* activity or event that brings them out of their own cultural comfort zones. They describe the activity and discuss their reactions with the group of trainees. Examples of activities could include volunteering at a homeless shelter, soup kitchen, or community mental health center. The activities provide trainees the opportunity to see the consequences of poverty, work with agencies that seek to reduce class inequality, and experience the shortage of services available to poor people.

COMPETENCY BENCHMARK TABLES

The purpose of the Competency Benchmarks (Tables 12.1–12.4) is to create developmental models for defining and measuring competencies in professional psychology; each chapter in this *Handbook* applies the diversity competence for mental health practitioners in their work with a particular diverse population.

Table 12.1   Developmental-Level Competencies I

READINESS LEVEL—ENTRY TO PRACTICUM	
Competencies	Learning Process and Activities
Knowledge	• Knowledge of and familiarity with ethics code expected. • Some knowledge of the social class demographics of the population the student is serving is important. • Knowledge that inequality exists and that this inequality is perpetuated by institutions, the culture, and the individual.	At this stage of development, the emphasis in psychotherapist education is on instilling knowledge of foundational domains that provide the groundwork for subsequent attainment of functional competencies. Students at this stage become aware of the principles and practices of the field, but they are not yet able to apply their knowledge to practice.
Skills	• Self-reflective and engaged in early exploration of professional identity. At this level, student's awareness of self as a social classed person may be minimally developed. • Awareness of some of the limits in the research base, with few studies specifying social class identities of subject. • Tolerance for ambiguity and uncertainty. • Consideration for how financial resources affect accessibility of services when making referrals. • Integration of his or her social class worldview. • Ability to articulate and discuss social class and classism issues at a macro level (e.g., societal and environmental).	Therefore, the training curriculum is focused on knowledge of core areas, including literature on multiculturalism, ethics, basic counseling skills, scientific knowledge, and the importance of reflective practice and self- awareness. It is important that throughout the curriculum, trainers and teachers define individual and cultural differences broadly to include social class differences. This should enable students to have a developing awareness of how to extrapolate their emerging multicultural competencies to include social class differences. Because of the implicitness of social class and its influence on our lives, many students may be just starting to examine their identities and experiences through a social class lens.
Values and Attitudes	• Concern with the welfare of others. • Awareness of social class as one aspect of identity that intersects with multiple aspects of identity. Student may be minimally aware of ways that uneven distribution of privilege and	Students may experience a wide range of reactions to social class and classism issues in the classroom and in counseling. For many students, this may be the first opportunity for them to explore these issues, and much like race and racism, they are expected to

(continued)

Table 12.1   Developmental-Level Competencies I (*continued*)

READINESS LEVEL—ENTRY TO PRACTICUM	
Competencies	Learning Process and Activities
oppression affect human experience and is open to further considering these ways. • Openness to examining stereotypes she or he may hold about people who identify with a range of social classes. • Awareness of his or her own social class–related biases. • Valuation of social class as an identity, culture, and personal and group experience.	reflect on their own social class history, family socialization messages, and classism experiences. Students need to be sensitive to and aware of their own hidden social class and classism injuries and trauma and how these experiences may affect counseling.

Table 12.2   Developmental-Level Competencies II

READINESS LEVEL—ENTRY TO INTERNSHIP		
Competencies		Learning Process and Activities
Knowledge	Trainee has basic foundational competency in: • Multiculturalism—the trainee is aware of social class as one aspect of identity that intersects with multiple aspects of identity. Trainee can identify multiple aspects of identity (e.g., ability/disability, sexual orientation, gender, race, ethnicity) with which social class intersects. • Awareness of the social class gradient's relationship with mental health. Trainee is aware of social causation and social drift theories as explanations for the SES gradient. • Awareness of the health-care and treatment disparities among those with varying levels of insurance coverage. • Awareness of some of the limits in the research base, with few studies specifying social class identities of subjects.	At this level of development, students are building on their education and applied experiences (such as supervised practicum experiences) to attain a core set of foundational competencies. They can then begin to apply this knowledge to professional practice. As a result of being exposed to didactic training and close supervision, students attain the multicultural values and attitudes appropriate to their level of development. Foundational knowledge and multicultural values and attitudes are becoming well established, but skills in working with social class–related issues could be expected to be somewhat rudimentary at this level of development. Because of structural influences that may lead people to socially distance themselves from people who are impoverished (Lott, 2002), trainees would benefit from specific training about poverty. Learning occurs through multiple modalities:
Skills	• Articulates ways that classism in enacted in multiple directions (i.e., upward, downward, lateral, internalized). • Examines stereotypes s/he may hold about people who identify with a range of social classes. • Consults appropriately and manages affective responses effectively.	• Receiving didactic training in academic programs may occur in multicultural courses and it should be infused into the core curriculum (e.g., ethics, assessment, multicultural, career counseling, research, human growth and development, and clinical courses). • Providing therapy, under supervision, to clients representing diversity of social classes in practicum experiences.

Table 12.2 Developmental-Level Competencies II (*continued*)

READINESS LEVEL—ENTRY TO INTERNSHIP

Competencies		Learning Process and Activities
	• Maintains acceptance of ambiguity and uncertainty. • Skills to facilitate exploration of ways that class-related experiences have influenced identity. • Considers how the values and experiences of researchers influence foci and methods of research. The trainee can analyze empirical literature and identify assumptions on which the inquiries and findings are based. • Considers how financial resources affect accessibility of services and is becoming active in identifying accessible services.	• Receiving supervision from psychotherapists knowledgeable and skilled in working from social class–conscious stance. • Seeking additional study and professional development opportunities. Topics to be covered in didactic training include: • Relationship of social class competency to multicultural competency. • Relationship of social class to other individual differences (e.g., gender, sexual orientation, ability/disability, race, ethnicity). • Basic research literature describing the relationships between social class and physical health/mental health. Trainers and teachers could offer students enrolled in multicultural diversity courses an option to research social class as a project for the class.
Values and Attitudes	• Self-reflective and engaged in exploration of professional contexts and identities; trainee is engaging with exploration of how his or her emerging professional identity interacts with other aspects of his or her identity, including social class and classism. • Considers and consults with supervisors about how professional expressions of social-class identities (e.g., clothing) may affect consumers of service. Trainee makes intentional decisions about self-presentation. • Appreciates and tolerates ambiguity. The trainee has moved beyond a dichotomous perspective of inequality that valorizes the poor and demonizes the affluent and values the complex intersections of individuals throughout the economic spectrum.	

Table 12.3 Developmental-Level Competencies III

READINESS LEVEL—ENTRY TO PROFESSIONAL PRACTICE

Competencies		Learning Process and Activities
Knowledge	Professional has basic foundational competency in: • Multiculturalism—the professional is aware of social class as one aspect of identity that intersects with multiple aspects of identity. Professional can identify multiple aspects of identity (e.g., ability/disability, sexual orientation, gender, race, ethnicity) with which social class intersects. • Awareness of the social class gradient's relationship with mental health. Professional is aware of social causation and social drift	At the level of Entry to Professional Practice, psychotherapists have attained the full range of competencies in the domains expected of all independent practitioners. The foundational competencies are not so new, but rather, the expectation is that the foundational competencies are integrated and deepened. Preparation for this level of competency takes place through closely supervised clinical work, augmented by professional reading, personal exploration, and training opportunities such as professional development and training seminars.

(*continued*)

Table 12.3 Developmental-Level Competencies III (*continued*)

READINESS LEVEL—ENTRY TO PROFESSIONAL PRACTICE	
Competencies	**Learning Process and Activities**
	theories as explanations for the social class gradient.	Clinical supervisors observe students' clinical work, provide training in assessment, case conceptualization and treatment planning, and challenge supervisees to examine their countertransference reactions, biases, and values to develop their supervisees' clinical competency with social class issues.
Skills	• Articulates ways that classism is enacted in multiple directions (i.e., upward, downward, lateral, internalized). • Consults appropriately about class-related issues. • Accepts uncertainty about the range of influence individuals have over their circumstances, given structural barriers and resources. • Possesses skills to facilitate exploration of ways that social class experiences have affected others. • Considers how the values and experiences of researchers influence foci and methods of research. The professional can analyze empirical literature and identify assumptions on which the inquiries and findings are based. • Considers how financial resources affect accessibility of services when making referrals and is active in identifying accessible services.	Additional methods by which students can attain social class competency at this level include: • Seeking opportunities to provide therapy to clients representing social class diversity. • Supervision provided by supervisors knowledgeable and skilled in working with social class issues. • Self-directed study and professional development opportunities. • Internship and postdoctoral seminar training in social class issues. • Presenting and participating in clinical case conferences that include discussion of social class aspects of cases.
Values and Attitudes	• Self-reflective and engaged in exploration of professional contexts and identities. Professional may be integrating changes in own class identity. • Considers social class–related messages in professional presentation of self. • Conceptualizes him- or herself as someone who is constantly negotiating between his or her privileges.	

Table 12.4 Developmental-Level Competencies

READINESS LEVEL—ADVANCED PRACTICE AND SPECIALIZATION	
Competencies	**Learning Process and Activities**
Knowledge	Professional has competency in: • Multiculturalism—the professional is aware of social class as one aspect of identity that intersects with multiple aspects of identity. Professional can identify multiple aspects of identity (e.g., ability/disability, sexual orientation, gender, race, ethnicity) with which social class intersects.	Psychotherapists who have a particular interest in social class identities may seek to attain advanced levels of competency and specialization. Learning activities will vary depending on the mental health practitioners' unique background, established competencies, and interest areas. For example, psychotherapists may serve on local policymaking boards. Researchers may seek to investigate class-related experiences of individuals.

Table 12.4   Developmental-Level Competencies (*continued*)

READINESS LEVEL—ADVANCED PRACTICE AND SPECIALIZATION

Competencies		Learning Process and Activities
	• Awareness of professional contexts and identities; social class and other aspects of personal identity are integrated into professional identity.	Regardless of the focus area, learning activities can include:
Skills	• Provides consultation and training about class-related issues. • Assumes leadership roles, perhaps serving on policymaking boards for agencies designed to serve less advantaged populations. • Educates others about class-related issues and provides education to others. • Demonstrates awareness of ways that social class experiences have influenced the professional's identity. • May conduct research that uses "methodologies that include research participants as active agents in the research process, the development and evaluation of interventions, and the development of theories" (Blustein, McWhirter, & Perry, 2005). Professional works to maintain relationships with agencies that serve less advantaged populations.	• Professional reading (information about diverse social class identities; empirical studies, and literature on theory and practice). • Teaching. • Attending and leading educational workshops. • Peer consultation groups. • Conducting research.
Values and Attitudes	Commitment to productively address issues of classism, taking concrete measures to do so.	

REFERENCES

Adler, N. E., Boyce, W. T., Chesney, M., Folkman, S., & Syme, L. (1993). Socioeconomic inequalities in health: No easy solution. *Journal of the American Medical Association, 269,* 3140–3145.

American Association for Marriage and Family Therapists. (2001). *Code of ethics.* American Association for Marriage and Family Therapists.

American Counseling Association. (2005). *Code of ethics.* American Counseling Association.

American Psychological Association. (2002). Ethical principles of psychologists and code of conduct. *American Psychologist, 57,* 1060–1073.

American Psychological Association. (2003). Guidelines on multicultural education, training, research, practice, and organizational change for psychologists. *American Psychologist, 58,* 377–402.

American Psychological Association, Work Group on Assessment of Competency Benchmarks. (2007). *A developmental model for the defining and measuring competence in professional psychology.* Washington, DC: American Psychological Association.

Baker, N. L. (1996). Confusions and silences on the topic of class. *Women and Therapy, 18*(3/4), 13–23.

Belle, D., & Doucet, J. (2003). Poverty, inequality, and discrimination as sources of depression among U.S. women. *Psychology of Women Quarterly, 27,* 101–113.

Blustein, D. L., McWhirter, E. H., & Perry, J. C. (2005). An emancipatory communitarian approach to vocational development theory, research, and practice. *The Counseling Psychologist, 33,* 141–179.

Buboltz, W. C., Miller, M., & Williams, D. J. (1999). Content analysis of research in the Journal of Counseling Psychology (1973–1998). *Journal of Counseling Psychology, 46,* 496–503.

Bullock, H. E. (1995). Class acts: Middle-class responses to the poor. In B. Lott & D. Maluso (Eds.), *The social psychology of interpersonal discrimination* (pp. 118–159). New York: Guildford Press.

Center for Popular Economics. (2004). The ultimate field guide to the U.S. economy. Retrieved April 23, 2007, from fguilde.org.

Cohen, S., Alper, C. M., Doyle, W. J., Adler, N., Treanor, J. J., & Turner, R. B. (2008). Objective and subjective socioeconomic status and susceptibility to the common cold. *Health Psychology, 27,* 269–274.

Cozzarelli, C., Wilkinson, A. V., & Tagler, M. J. (2001). Attitudes toward the poor and attributions for poverty. *Journal of Social Issues, 57,* 207–227.

Croizet, J. C., & Claire, T. (1998). Extending the concept of stereotype threat to social class: The intellectual underperformance of students for low socioeconomic backgrounds. *Personality and Social Psychology Bulletin, 24,* 588–594.

Fussell, P. (1983). *Class: A guide through the American status system.* New York: Touchstone.

Gallo, L. C., Bogart, L. M., Vranceanu, A. M., & Matthews, K. A. (2005). Socioeconomic status, resources, psychological experiences, and emotional responses: A test of the reserve capacity model. *Journal of Personality and Social Psychology, 88,* 386–399.

Gallo, L. C., & Matthews, K. A. (2003). Understanding the association between socioeconomic status and physical health: Do negative emotions play a role? *Psychological Bulletin, 129,* 10–51.

Gallo, L. C., Smith, T. W., & Cox, C. M. (2006). Socioeconomic status, psychosocial processes, and perceived health: An interpersonal perspective. *Annals of Behavioral Medicine, 31,* 109–119.

Garb, H. N. (1997). Race, bias, social class bias, and gender bias in clinical judgement. *Clinical Psychology Scientific Practice, 4,* 99–120.

Grusky, D. (Ed.). (2001). *Social Stratification: Class, race, and gender in sociological perspective.* Boulder, CO: Westview Press.

Hopps, J., & Liu, W. M. (2006). Working for social justice from within the health care system: The role of social class in psychology. In R. L. Toporek, L. H. Gerstein, N. A. Fouad, G. Roysircar, & T. Israel (Eds.), *Handbook for social justice in counseling psychology: Leadership, vision, and action* (pp. 318–337). Thousand Oaks, CA: Sage.

Karasek, R., & Theorell, T. (1990). *Healthy work: Stress productivity and the reconstruction of working life.* New York: Basic Books.

Kolker, A. & Alvarez, L. (Producers/Directors). (2001). *People like us: Social class in America. A documentary special for public television.* [Motion Picture]. Center for American Media, http://www.pbs.org/peoplelikeus/about/index.html. Available through CAM Film Library, P.O. Box 1084, Harriman, NY 10926.

Krueger, D. W. (Ed.). (1986). *The last taboo: Money as a symbol and reality in psychotherapy and psychoanalysis.* New York: Brunner/Mazel.

Levine, M. (2006). *The price of privilege: How parental pressure and material advantage are creating a generation of disconnected and unhappy kids.* New York: Harper Collins.

Liu, W. M. (2001). Expanding our understanding of multiculturalism: Developing a social class worldview model. In D. B. Pope-Davis & H. L. K. Coleman (Eds.), *The intersection of race, class, and gender in counseling psychology* (pp. 127–170). Thousand Oaks, CA: Sage.

Liu, W. M. (2002). The social class-related experiences of men: Integrating theory and practice. *Professional Psychology: Research and Practice, 33,* 355–360.

Liu, W. M. (2006). Classism is much more complex. *American Psychologist, 61,* 337–338.

Liu, W. M. (In press). Developing a social class and classism consciousness: Implications for research and practice. In E. Altmaier & J. I. Hansen (Eds.). *Handbook of counseling psychology.* New York: Oxford Press.

Liu, W. M., & Ali, S. R. (2005). Addressing social class and classism in vocational theory and practice: Extending the emancipatory communitarian approach. *The Counseling Psychologist, 33,* 189–196.

Liu, W. M., & Ali, S. R. (2008). Social class and classism: Understanding the impact of poverty and inequality. In S. D. Brown & R. W. Lent (Eds.), *Handbook of counseling psychology* (4th ed.). Hoboken, NJ: Wiley.

Liu, W. M., Ali, S. R., Soleck, G., Hopps, J., Dunston, K., & Pickett, T., Jr. (2004). Using social class in counseling psychology research. *Journal of Counseling Psychology, 51,* 3–18.

Liu, W. M., & Arguello, J. (2006). Social class and classism in counseling. *Counseling and Human Development, 39*(3), 1–12.

Liu, W. M., Greenfeld, J., & Turesky, D. (Producer/Director). (2008). *Social class, economic privilege and counseling.* [Training video]. Available from Micro-training Associates, 141 Walnut Street, Hanover, MA 02339.

Liu, W. M., & Hernandez, N. (2010). Counseling those in poverty. In M. J. Ratts, J. A. Lewis, & R. L. Toporek (Eds.). *American Counseling Association Advocacy Competencies: An Advocacy Framework for Counselors* (pp. 43–54) Alexandria, VA: American Counseling Association.

Liu, W. M., Pickett, T., Jr., & Ivey, A. E. (2007). White middle-class privilege: Social class bias and implications for training and practice. *Journal of Multicultural Counseling and Development, 35,* 194–207.

Liu, W. M., & Pope-Davis, D. B. (2003a). Moving from diversity to multiculturalism: Exploring power and the implications for psychology. In D. B. Pope-Davis, H. L. K. Coleman, W. M. Liu, & R. L. Toporek (Eds.), *Handbook of multicultural competencies in counseling and psychology* (pp. 90–102). Thousand Oaks, CA: Sage.

Liu, W. M., & Pope-Davis, D. B. (2003b). Understanding classism to effect personal change. In T. B. Smith (Ed.), *Practicing multiculturalism: Internalizing and affirming diversity in counseling and psychology* (pp. 294–310). New York: Allyn & Bacon.

Liu, W. M., & Pope-Davis, D. B. (2005). The Working alliance, therapy ruptures and impasses, and counseling competencies: Implications for counselor training and education. In R. T. Carter (Ed.), *Handbook of racial-cultural psychology and counseling, Vol. 2* (pp. 148–167). New York: Wiley.

Liu, W. M., Soleck, G., Hopps, J., Dunston, K., & Pickett, T. (2004). A new framework to understand social class in counseling: The social class worldview and modern classism theory. *Journal of Multicultural Counseling and Development, 32,* 95–122.

Lott, B. (2002). Cognitive and behavioral distancing from the poor. *American Psychologist, 57,* 100–110.

Lott, B., & Bullock, H. (2007). The psychology and politics of class warfare. Chapter in *Psychology and economic injustice* (pp. 77–98). Washington, DC: American Psychological Association.

Lubrano, A. (2004). *Limbo: Blue-collar roots, White-collar dreams.* Hoboken, NJ: Wiley.

Luthar, S. S., & D'Avanzo, K. (1999). Contextual factors in substance use: A study of suburban and inner-city adolescents. *Development and Psychopathology, 11,* 845–867.

Luthar, S. S., & Latendresse, S. J. (2005). Children of the affluent: Challenges to well-being. *Current Directions in Psychological Science, 14,* 49–53.

Mather, J. H., & Lager, P. B. (2000). *Child welfare: A unifying model of practice.* Belmont, CA: Brooks/Cole.

National Association of Social Workers. (1996). *Code of ethics.* National Association of Social Workers.

National Association of Social Workers. (2007). Indicators for the achievement of the NASW standards for cultural competence in social work. Retrieved on March 1, 2009, from http://www.socialworkers.org/sections/credentials/cultural_comp.asp

Oakes, J. M., & Rossi, P. H. (2003). The measurement of SES in health research: Current practice and steps toward a new approach. *Social Science and Medicine, 56,* 769–784.

Ostrove, J. M., Adler, N. E., Kuppermann, M., & Washington, A. E. (2000). Objective and subjective assessments of socioeconomic status and their relationship to self-rated health in an ethnically diverse sample of pregnant women. *Health Psychology, 19,* 613–618.

Rodolfa, E. R., Bent, R. J., Eisman, E., Nelson, P. D., Rehn, L. & Ritchie, P. (2005). A cube model for competency development: Implications for educators and regulators. *Professional Psychology: Research and Practice, 36,* 347–354.

Roffman, E. (1996). A class conscious perspective on the use of self as instrument in graduate clinical training. *Women and Therapy, 18,* 165–179.

Saegert, S. C., Adler, N. E., Bullock, H. E., Cauce, A. M., Liu, W. M., & Wyche, K. F. (2006). *Report on the APA Task Force on Socioeconomic Status.* Washington, DC: American Psychological Association.

Sapolsky, R. (2005, December). Sick of poverty. *Scientific American, 293*(6), 92–99.

Scott, J., & Leonhardt, D. (2005, May 15). Class in America: Shadowy lines that still divide. *The New York Times,* pp. YT *1,* 16–18.

Smith, L. (2005). Psychotherapy, classism, and the poor: Conspicuous by their absence. *American Psychologist, 60,* 687–696.

Sue, S., & Zane, N. (1987). The role of culture and cultural techniques in psychotherapy: A critique and reformulation. *American Psychologist, 2*(1), 37–45.

Thompson, C. E., & Jenal, S. L. (1994). Interracial and intraracial quasi-counseling interactions when counselors avoid discussing racial issues. *Journal of Counseling Psychology, 41,* 484–491.

Twenge, J. M. (2006). *Generation me: Why today's young Americans are more confident, assertive, entitled—and more miserable than ever before.* New York: Free Press.

U.S. Census Bureau. (2001). Census 2000 supplementary survey profile for the United States. Retrieved April 21, 2007, from http://quickfacts.census .gov/qfd/states/19000.html.

Vera, E. M., & Speight, S. L. (2003). Multicultural competence, social justice, and counseling psychology: Expanding our roles. *The Counseling Psychologist, 31,* 253–272.

Wang, P. S., Lane, M., Olfson, M., Pincus, H.A., Wells, K. B., & Kessler, R. C. (2005). Twelve-month use of mental-health services in the United States: Results from a National Comorbidity Survey replication. *Archives of General Psychiatry, 62,* 629–640.

Yates, P. (Producer/Director). (1979). *Breaking Away.* [Motion Picture]. Twentieth Century-Fox.

CHAPTER 13

DEVELOPING COMPETENCY IN SPIRITUAL AND RELIGIOUS ASPECTS OF COUNSELING

JULIE SAVAGE and SARAH ARMSTRONG

INTRODUCTION

As mental health professionals have continued to learn about the diversity of spiritual and religious worldviews held by the clients they serve, greater attention has been focused on attaining competency in knowledge, personal awareness, and therapeutic skills to improve client lives. For an increasingly diverse U.S. population, and therefore for many psychotherapy clients, religion and spirituality are central aspects of their identity and worldview (Arredondo & Glauner, 1992; Bartoli, 2007; Constantine, 1999; Richards & Bergin, 2000; D. W. Sue & D. Sue, 2007). In many cultures, spirituality and religion are inseparable from physical, mental, or health concerns (Fukuyama & Sevig, 1999). Frequently cited research indicates that the overwhelming majority of Americans believe that faith is an important part of their lives and feel a need to experience spiritual growth (Gallup, 1998; Gallup, 2008; Gallup & Johnson, 2003), and that many therapy clients wish their psychotherapists would address religious and spiritual issues during therapy (Rose, Westefeld, & Ansley, 2001). Addressing these concerns can be especially important when working with ethnic/racial minority groups, women, and members of the working class, who are more likely to report that spirituality plays an important role in their lives (Cervantes & Parham, 2005; Gall et al., 2005; Hodge, 2004; Richards & Bergin, 2000).

The purpose of this chapter is to provide mental health practitioners, students, educators, trainers, and supervisors with guidelines and resources for expanding their competencies in assessing and working with spiritual and religious issues. We will first provide definitions of spirituality and religion, explore barriers to competency in religious and spiritual issues, and discuss requisite areas of knowledge (individual and cultural diversity, assessment, diagnosis and case conceptualization, and ethical and legal standards). Next, we will describe important skills (relationship, assessment, intervention, referral, and supervision and training) as well as the attitudes and values necessary to provide multiculturally sensitive services to individuals with a wide range of spiritual and religious worldviews. Throughout the chapter, we will provide case vignettes and examples, spiritual and religious assessment questions, an example of a religiously adapted therapy, information about incorporating spiritual and religious issues into supervision, exercises for increasing self-awareness and knowledge of spiritual and religious belief systems and issues, outlines for spiritual and religious issues seminars, and methods for integrating spiritual and religious information into a training curriculum.

We believe this information will assist mental health practitioners, students, educators, trainers, and supervisors in furthering their religious and spiritual competency development.

DEFINITIONS OF SPIRITUALITY AND RELIGION

Many definitions of *spirituality* and *religion* have been advanced throughout the literature. *Spirituality* is defined as a state of being attuned with God or the Divine Intelligence that governs or harmonizes the universe (Richards & Bergin, 2005). It is a "search for the sacred" (Pargament, 1999, p. 12), and includes thoughts and feelings of enlightenment, vision, harmony with truth, transcendence, and oneness with God (James, 1936). It is a part of the human essence (Maslow, 1968) and a complex, multifaceted construct that manifests in the process of an individual's behavior, beliefs, and experience (Miller & Thoresen, 1999). Native American spirituality encompasses a sense of the sacred in all of creation, including sky, water, mountains, and animals (Frame, 2003). Although spirituality is often equated with belief in God or a higher power, for many individuals, their sense of spirituality is experienced as a transcendent "oneness" with the universe or with nature. Therefore, even individuals who identify as atheist or agnostic may experience their own unique form of spirituality that provides them with a sense of self-transcendence.

Religion is frequently defined as an organized system of faith, worship, cumulative traditions, and prescribed rituals (Worthington, 1989). Religious beliefs, practices, and feelings are often expressed institutionally and denominationally through participating in public religious rituals and reading sacred writings (Richards & Bergin, 2005). There are six primary components of religions (Fukuyama & Sevig, 1999, p. 6): (1) ritual: private and/or public ceremonial behavior; (2) doctrine: affirmations about the relationship of the individual to the ultimate; (3) emotion: the presence of feelings (awe, love, fear, etc.); (4) knowledge: intellectual familiarity with sacred writings and principles; (5) ethics: rules for the guidance of interpersonal behavior, connoting right and wrong, good and bad; and (6) community: involvement in a community of the faithful

According to Frame (2003), religion is one form of spirituality and the concepts of religion and spirituality are not mutually exclusive. In a study exploring how individuals identify themselves on the spiritual and religious dimensions, Zinnbauer et al., (1997) found that most respondents to their study identified themselves as both spiritual and religious (74%), whereas 19 percent identified themselves as spiritual but not religious and 4 percent labeled themselves as religious but not spiritual. Therefore, it is important for psychotherapists to explore each client's individual definition of his or her personal religion or spiritual belief system to avoid making inaccurate assumptions. It is also important for psychotherapists to understand their own beliefs and perspectives. For the purposes of this chapter, we will use the terms *spirituality* and *religion* together (S/R), except when citing research or beliefs specific to one domain or the other.

BARRIERS TO COMPETENCY IN SPIRITUAL/RELIGIOUS COUNSELING

Charged by ethical codes and practice guidelines to practice in a multiculturally sensitive manner, psychotherapists may find it difficult to incorporate S/R factors into treatment for a number of reasons. First, many mental health practitioners feel unprepared to address S/R issues in counseling (Brawer, Handal, Fabricatore, & Wajda-Johnston, 2002; Golston, Savage, & Cohen, 1998; Hage, 2006; Miller, 1999; Myers & Williard, 2003; Pate & High, 1995; Schulte, Skinner, & Claiborn, 2002). Frazier and Hansen (2009) found that even those psychotherapists who believe that it is important to incorporate S/R issues into counseling engage in these behaviors less frequently than one would expect.

Psychotherapists may also feel uncomfortable with the topic because they may not have explored it for themselves. When compared to the general population, smaller percentages of psychotherapists indicate that religion is an important factor in their lives; hence, they may not recognize it as important for their clients (Bergin, 1991; Bergin & Jensen, 1990; Delaney, Miller & Bisono, 2007; Russell & Yarhouse, 2006; Shafranske, 2000). Personal S/R beliefs influence psychotherapists' attitudes about addressing S/R issues in therapy. According to Gonsiorek (2009), any negative biases held by nonreligious and by religious therapists could result in negative evaluations of clients' beliefs. Psychotherapists holding belief systems that differ from their clients' belief systems may find it challenging to support certain S/R views or they may avoid addressing aspects of religious and spiritual identity out of a desire to respect the individual's belief system.

As a result, psychotherapists may overlook S/R issues by failing to recognize their importance when conducting assessments or by underestimating the importance of these factors when formulating treatment interventions. Because they may not have learned how to incorporate S/R issues into clinical work, psychotherapists may communicate discomfort discussing these topics with clients, thereby curtailing communication in an area that could be of primary importance and also a resource for therapy success.

Case Vignette 13.1 illustrates an example in which a psychotherapist who is unaware of the importance of assessing S/R issues may miss important clinical issues, since the client is not identifying S/R issues as a focus of therapy.

CASE VIGNETTE 13.1

Robert, who is a 30-year-old, single, heterosexual European-American male client, presents with issues of loneliness and lack of direction in life. He finds it difficult to make friends and he feels that others do not understand or relate to him—he feels very "different." He is estranged from his family, compounding his loneliness. He has depressive symptoms, including lack of energy, difficulty concentrating, early insomnia, and weight gain. He says that he "doesn't know who he is" and feels he is drifting in life. He asks you for guidance in how to get his life back on track. He mentions that he recently left the Seventh-day Adventist religion because he felt that his beliefs had changed and were no longer compatible with the beliefs held by other members of the religion. He has no regrets about leaving the religion, and he does not see it as related to his current problems. The psychotherapist accepts Robert's statement of the problem and creates a treatment plan consisting of social skills training and self-esteem building. He recommends that Robert join several clubs to make friends, and he refers Robert to a psychiatrist for medication of his depression.

By accepting Robert's statement that leaving his religion has no relationship to his current concerns, the psychotherapist may miss key factors in case conceptualization and treatment planning, thereby rendering the therapy less effective. If the psychotherapist had conducted a brief S/R assessment, she or he may have determined that Robert's depression, loneliness, and identity confusion may be directly related to S/R issues. Because Robert was raised in the

Seventh-day Adventist religion, it is likely that his family, friends, and community were all members of the religion and that he derived his sense of identity from his religious affiliation. In this tradition, beliefs and role expectations are clearly defined. When Robert found himself questioning the doctrine, he may have felt increasingly "different" and isolated from everyone who was important to him. When he revealed his doubts and began behaving in ways counter to religious expectations (such as drinking alcohol), family and friends made well-meaning efforts to persuade him to return to his religious practices, which likely left him feeling unsupported, misunderstood, and possibly ashamed of his "deviant" thoughts. His decision to leave the religion most likely alienated him from his family and community. In addition, it is possible that he felt alienated from God, leaving him potentially feeling guilty, angry, and without purpose.

Robert may have found it difficult to make new friends because most people he encountered have little understanding of his background, and/or he may have felt out of step with others in his age group. Many members of the majority religious culture may have little knowledge of, or they may have negative perceptions of, his religion. Although Robert left the religion, it cannot be assumed that his attitudes toward it are entirely critical. As the religion no doubt formed major aspects of his identity, it is entirely likely that he could find positive meaning in aspects of his experience growing up in the religion.

There can be a number of reasons that Robert may have denied that S/R issues were related to his current concerns: (a) it may be too painful or threatening to acknowledge the impact his decision has had on his life; (b) he may be quite concrete in his thinking and unaccustomed to

thinking in psychological terms; (c) he may consciously or unconsciously want to feel that the religion no longer has power or influence in his life; and (d) he may still feel a sense of loyalty toward his previous religion, which might make him reluctant to expose his past to others.

ELEMENTS OF COMPETENCY

The S/R competencies literature derives from the medical, psychiatric, social work, counseling, nursing, and psychology literature. The Association of Spiritual, Ethical and Religious Values in Counseling (ASERVIC) developed a list of spiritual and religious competencies for psychotherapists, which is widely used by helping professionals (2009). Drawing upon this literature, we will outline knowledge, skills, attitudes, and values essential to competent therapy practice. We have defined four levels of S/R competencies using the levels described in the Assessment of Competency Benchmark document (2007): Entry to Practicum, Entry to Internship, Entry to Professional Practice, and Advanced Practice and Specialization levels, which are Tables 13.1 through 13.4 in the Resources section of this chapter. Also in the Resources section are listings of the literature on curricula and competencies for S/R training.

RELIGIOUS AND SPIRITUAL COMPETENCIES FOR COUNSELORS

Culture and Worldview

- Describe the similarities and differences between spirituality and religion, including the basic beliefs of various spiritual systems, major world religions, agnosticism, and atheism.
- Recognize that the client's beliefs (or absence of beliefs) about S/R are central to his or her worldview and can influence psychosocial functioning.

Counselor Self-Awareness

- Explore his or her attitudes, beliefs, and values about spirituality and/or religion.
- Evaluate the influence of his or her own S/R beliefs and values on the client and the counseling process.
- Identify the limits of his or her understanding of the client's S/R perspective and have knowledge of religious and spiritual resources for consultation and referral.

Human and Spiritual Development

- Describe and apply various models of S/R development and their relationship to human development.

Communication

- Respond to client communications about S/R with acceptance and sensitivity.
- Use S/R concepts that are consistent with the client's S/R perspectives and that are acceptable to the client.
- Recognize S/R themes in client communication and address these with the client when therapeutically relevant.

Assessment

- Gather information about the client's S/R perspective from the client and/or other sources during intake and assessment.

Diagnosis and Treatment

- When making a diagnosis, recognize that the client's S/R perspectives can a) enhance well-being; b) contribute to client problems; and/or c) exacerbate symptoms.
- Set goals with the client consistent with the client's S/R perspectives.
- Be able to a) modify therapeutic techniques to include a client's S/R perspectives, and b) utilize S/R practices as techniques when appropriate and acceptable to a client's viewpoint.
- Therapeutically apply theory and current research supporting the inclusion of a client's S/R perspectives and practices.

Source: Association of Spiritual, Ethical, and Religious Values in Counseling (ASERVIC, 2009).

KNOWLEDGE

There are numerous areas of knowledge required for competency in S/R issues, including the S/R literature pertaining to individual and cultural diversity, assessment, diagnosis, case conceptualization, intervention, ethical and legal standards, and supervision and teaching.

S/R interventions have proven to be of benefit to a variety of presenting client concerns, such as depression, anxiety, grief and loss, trauma, death and dying, abuse recovery, addiction (particularly 12-step spirituality), marital issues, and eating disorders. In our Resources section later in this chapter, we refer the reader to a variety of articles and Web sites that synthesize these research findings. There are also important applications for individuals representing diversity of ethnicity, ability, age, gender, culture, and sexual orientation.

Individual and Cultural Diversity

Numerous authors (e.g., Allport, 1952; Fowler, 1995; Koenig, 1994; Poll & Smith, 2003) have proposed models of identity development that include elements of spiritual or religious development (see the Resources section on Spiritual and Religious Developmental Theories later in this chapter for additional references). In the majority of these models, individuals move from a stage of not being aware of the self in S/R terms, to a period of unquestioned acceptance of others' faith (e.g., parents), to learning about and questioning specific aspects of S/R, to an ultimate stage of integration of spiritual identity.

In their Dimensions of Personal Identity model, Arredondo and Glauner (1992) describe the myriad factors that create an individual's identity, including S/R beliefs, values, biases, assumptions, and privileges. The authors emphasize that psychotherapists need to engage in a process of understanding the extent to which they, and their clients, value each dimension of personal identity. This knowledge is required to understand each client, and to avoid imposing their biases upon their clients. In their model, Arredondo and Glauner place spirituality and religious beliefs in their "B" dimension, which is conceptualized as including aspects of identity that are changeable by the individual. In a personal communication, Schulte noted that "with no other aspect of identity is the presumption of personal choice as prevalent as with religion and spirituality . . . (making) it particularly pernicious to address . . . because (the therapist) may then be in the position of disagreeing with an aspect of the client's identity" (D. Schulte, personal communication, June 14, 2007). We discuss the importance of psychotherapist self-awareness of personal values and attitudes in greater detail later in this chapter.

It is important for psychotherapists to have knowledge of the beliefs and practices of the major Western and Eastern religious traditions as well as an understanding of the normative elements within those belief systems. They also need an understanding of S/R concepts (e.g., views of deity, human nature, morality, and life after death) and vocabulary (e.g., faith, sin, guilt, reincarnation, karma, forgiveness, mindfulness, and meditation) used in these traditions (Aten & Hernandez, 2004; Cervantes & Parham, 2005; McMinn, Ruiz, Marx, Wright, & Gilbert, 2006). The Spiritual and Religious Traditions section of the Resources section includes a listing of resources on spiritual practices and world religions. Table 13.5 provides a brief outline of S/R traditions and issues relevant to therapy.

Sue, Arredondo, and McDavis (1992) and D. W. Sue and S. Sue (2007) stress the importance of the integration of spirituality into multicultural counseling and therapeutic competence, and the latter article provides extensive

discussions of non-Western forms of indigenous healing. As approximately 80 percent of the world's population depends on alternative and complementary therapies for health and healing (Fukuyama & Sevig, 1999), psychotherapists should be mindful of the need to respect indigenous cultural belief systems (D. Y. Ho & R. T. Ho, 2007; D. W. Sue & S. Sue, 2007). For example, if one believes that mental illness is due to psychological factors, counseling or therapy may be indicated, and if one believes that abnormal behavior is a function of other forces (e.g., supernatural), the client would benefit from accessing a spiritual leader or healer in the client's faith tradition (D. W. Sue & S. Sue, 2007).

S/R issues can be salient for individuals with disabilities. Burke, Chauvin, and Miranti (2005) note that disabilities are sometimes construed as having religious or moral implications. Some faith or spiritual traditions may consider that individuals become disabled as a result of having committed a sin or through a failure of faith; conversely, disabilities may be seen as having been created as a test of faith (Burke, Chauvin, & Miranti, 2005). The individual with a disability might hold those beliefs, or the source of these beliefs might be members of the individual's community. Such beliefs may cause the individual to struggle with the S/R implications of his or her disability and therefore may be relevant to the therapy process.

It is important for psychotherapists to assess gay, lesbian, bisexual, and transgender (GLBT) clients' access to supportive S/R communities. Some may have a difficult time reconciling their sexuality or gender expression with views of their religion, which may lead them to detach from organized religion and thus experience feelings of isolation and/or alienation (Atkinson & Hackett, 1998). Other GLBT clients may already have religious communities that are affirming of their sexual and gender identities. If clients are encountering or anticipating rejection by their existing faith communities, psychotherapists can be helpful in providing GLBT clients information about affirming spiritual communities (Bartoli & Gillem, 2008; Lease, Horne, & Noffsinger-Frazier, 2005).

Some individuals may experience "double ostracism" (or multiple oppressions) due to multiple identities. For example, a Latino gay male who was raised in the Catholic religion may encounter rejection by his church and by members of his family and cultural community because of his sexual orientation. Even if the man does not identify currently as a Catholic, he may still feel great loss over the separation from his family and cultural community if the primary means in which his family and community interact is through mutually shared faith and religious rituals.

Even individuals who share a common culture, religion, or spiritual tradition may have widely differing S/R beliefs, practices, and worldviews (Fukuyama & Sevig, 1999; Gonsiorek, 2009). For example, individuals who identify with a particular religion may have widely varying degrees of religious beliefs and expressions. They may differ in their degree of *orthodoxy*,

which Frame (2003) defines as the extent to which the individual's belief system and behaviors are aligned with the traditions and doctrines of their religion. Religiously orthodox clients are more likely to believe that their psychological concerns are related to their spirituality (Richards & Bergin, 1997) and those who are less orthodox could be less receptive to psychotherapists' exploration of the S/R realm (Frame, 2003). As noted by Dwairy (2006), individuals may also differ in their religious orientation (degrees of collectivism, individualism, conservatism, or liberalism). If an individual was born in another country or is the descendent of immigrants, factors relating to the country of origin, degree of assimilation, socioeconomic status, and level of cultural identity development are salient (Dwairy, 2006). The following case vignette describes challenges relating to these factors.

CASE VIGNETTE 13.2

A 19-year-old Arab American Muslim female undergraduate student presents at her university counseling center experiencing significant family distress that is negatively impacting her academic work. Her parents, both professionals, met in the United States while each was attending graduate school. The client, who lives at home, has one younger brother, who is a senior in high school. The client says that since she began college her parents have become mistrustful and controlling of her. They fear she is being "corrupted" by American values because she has expressed an interest in dating a Christian man and she wants to dress in clothing that they consider to be "immodest." They fear that her actions will make her unmarriageable (they expect her to marry an Arab/Muslim man). She has started lying to her parents about her activities to conceal the fact that she is dating the Christian man. She feels angry at her parents because they don't respect her decisions and feels guilty about disappointing them. She views their interpretation of their religion as "old-fashioned" and she believes that she is practicing her faith appropriately, citing the fact that many other female Muslim college students dress in a similar manner. She says, "Don't they understand that we live in America now!"

To create a culturally appropriate treatment plan, the psychotherapist must gain an understanding of the client's cultural background, religious beliefs (level of religious orthodoxy, religious practices, and image of Allah) and

psychocultural factors (client's level of individuation, strictness of the family, and the client's ego strength). In assessing the client's culture, the psychotherapist would inquire about cultural attitudes toward obedience, the role of women, interfaith marriage, parental and family roles and expectations, and what implications these have for the client. Also, the psychotherapist would assess the client's level of acculturation, her parents' level of acculturation, and how the parents and extended family members deal with American cultural values.

Some things to be mindful of in working with this client within her culture include exploring the intersection of cultural issues with family issues (e.g., the client might be breaking family cultural expectations by talking about struggles within the family with an outsider), and the intersection of religious issues with gender-role expectations. Understanding family patterns of communication and conflict resolution would facilitate the formulation of intervention strategies. For example, if hers is a traditional family system in which women do not have an equal voice in decision making, the client may feel powerless to effect change in the system and the psychotherapist would then assist the client in reducing her distress using culturally appropriate techniques. On the other hand, if the family is less traditional, the client may choose to and also have more opportunity to individuate.

Dwairy (2006) provides an extensive discussion of parenting styles and individuation of Arab/Muslim youth. He states that in their collectivist sociocultural system, children are raised to maintain cohesion, harmony, and connectedness. The psychotherapist cannot assume that it is in the client's best interests to achieve independence and autonomy. Applying pressure to the client to "stand up for herself" could lead to devastating losses. The culturally sensitive psychotherapist, therefore, would respect the interdependency of the Arab/Muslim family system and assist the client in creating therapy goals that she is fully prepared for (if the goal includes confronting cultural expectations, then the client needs to be fully cognizant of potential repercussions). These principles apply to working with most individuals from non-Western, interdependent cultures such as Native American and Eastern S/R traditions.

Collaboration with the client as to what interventions to adopt would be critical and would begin with the establishment of trust in the psychotherapist and prioritizing her goals for treatment. Specific treatment strategies could include anxiety reduction/stress management, clarification of the client's cultural and religious values, determining the extent to which she wishes to work within or to confront culturally sanctioned behavior, and identifying positive female role models on which the client could model her attitudes and behavior.

The psychotherapist should be mindful of both beneficence (i.e., making sure that consideration is given to the reduction of physical symptoms of anxiety and stress) and nonmalfeasance (i.e., not erring on the side of over-aligning with any of the client's maladaptive behaviors because of the psychotherapist's rejection of the parental values and control). The psychotherapist should also explore any possible countertransference responses (e.g., strong feminist or religious values that may be similar to or different from the client's).

IMPLICATIONS FOR CLINICAL PRACTICE

- Recognize that S/R or lack thereof is an important aspect of an individual's identity and that clients may identify to greater or lesser degrees as S/R persons.
- Explore each client's individual definition of his or her S/R.
- Explore how the client's S/R has impacted or been impacted by other aspects of the individual's identity, such as gender, ability, ethnicity, sexual orientation, and culture.

Assessment, Diagnosis, and Case Conceptualization

To perform competent clinical assessment, diagnosis, and case conceptualization, psychotherapists must have knowledge of the range of possible S/R issues. Clients may be experiencing a loss or questioning of faith, anger at God, stresses relating to conversion to a new faith, or S/R identity development. Serious trauma, physical illness, death of a loved one, relationship or family problems, spiritual experiences, or near-death experiences may create a spiritual crisis or emergency. According to Fukuyama and Sevig (1999), "religious wounding" can occur when religious belief systems directly hurt or restrict people's authentic selves. The degree of wounding may be influenced by both family and community structures. For example, child abuse may be even more traumatic if the child's religious community supports the unquestioned parental authority under which the abuse occurs, or if clergy members inflict the abuse (Fukuyama & Sevig, 1999).

Arriving at accurate diagnoses can be confounded by a person's spiritual experiences. For example, "speaking in tongues," viewed by some religions as a spiritual gift, may be interpreted by psychotherapists as a frank indicator of psychosis. Guilt, a common symptom of depressive disorders, is also a natural part of certain religious traditions. For more extensive discussion of this topic and for resources for diagnostic assessment, see the Resources and Assessment sections of this chapter.

Ethical and Legal Standards

The ethical standards of all mental health professions require that practitioners become competent in working with multiculturally diverse clients. Many ethical standards specifically include religion or spirituality as aspects of diversity (e.g., the ethical guidelines for the American Association of Marriage and Family Therapists (2001), American Counseling Association (2005), American Psychiatric Association

(2001), American Psychological Association: Ethical Principles of Psychologists and Code of Ethics (2002b), and Guidelines for Providers of Psychological Services to Ethnic, Linguistic, and Culturally Diverse Populations (2002), Association for Counselor Education and Supervision 2005), and National Association of Social Workers, (2008). In addition, the American Psychological Association (2007) developed the Resolution on Religious, Religion-Based and/or Religion-Derived Prejudice, condemning prejudice relating to religious or spiritual beliefs, promoting tolerance and respect, and requiring that ethical psychologists appropriately address S/R issues in their professional work (Resolution on Religious, Religion-Based and/or Religion-Derived Prejudice.)

Gonsiorek (2009), Richards and Bergin (2005), Steen, Engels and Thweatt (2006), and Yarhouse and Van Orman, (1999) discuss a number of ethical considerations involved in S/R therapy work.

Kelly (1995) and Hage (2006) suggest that psychotherapists may ethically introduce spirituality or religion as a potential source of ideas, beliefs, and values under the following circumstances:

- The client is cognitively and affectively prepared to consider alternative ideas and values with free awareness.
- An S/R perspective is raised as one of several potential interventions.
- The psychotherapist does not advance a specific expression of spirituality or religion but facilitates consideration based on the client's beliefs.
- The psychotherapist does not move beyond her or his competence with respect to specific aspects of religion or spirituality.
- The psychotherapist focuses on the therapeutic relevance of the S/R ideas or beliefs.

In all cases, it is unethical for psychotherapists working in nonreligious settings "to promote, proselytize, or attempt to persuade clients, covertly or overtly, to their religious viewpoint or tradition" (Richards & Bergin, 2005, p. 201).

IMPLICATIONS FOR CLINICAL PRACTICE

- Avoid dual roles.
- Avoid usurping religious/spiritual authority.
- Communicate respect for religious and spiritual leaders and belief systems.
- Do not impose own S/R values.
- Secure informed consent for S/R interventions.
- Practice within the boundaries of own competency.
- Respect church–state boundaries in your work setting.

SKILLS

Relationship Skills

Competent psychotherapists are able to form positive therapeutic relationships with clients of widely varying S/R belief systems. Hodge (2004) proposed four ways in which psychotherapists may build spiritually sensitive relationships with clients: (a) demonstrating respect for clients' spiritual autonomy (which may be operationalized through the use of language that is consistent with the client's worldview); (b) assuming a position of "cultural anthropologist" by demonstrating an open, curious, nonjudgmental stance, with the goal of creating a safe therapeutic environment; (c) exhibiting sensitivity to the biases clients may have encountered in the larger secular culture; and (d) monitoring religious countertransference.

Assessment Skills

Assessment of S/R beliefs and attitudes (including the recognition of when S/R beliefs, attitudes, and practices are supportive or harmful in the client's life) is essential, as is the ability to incorporate assessment findings into the diagnosis, case conceptualization, and treatment planning. Psychotherapists should assess client beliefs and motivations, spiritual behaviors, and spiritual experiences (Gorusch & Miller, 1999), metaphysical worldview (e.g., Western, Eastern, atheistic, agnostic), religious affiliation if any, and degree of orthodoxy if the client is religious. Additional issues for assessment are the client's image of God (if relevant), value-lifestyle congruence, S/R identity, and S/R maturity (Richards & Bergin, 2000). The assessment process needs to continue throughout therapy, since (as is true with other sensitive clinical issues) clients may not be aware, or may not reveal, that their presenting concerns have S/R aspects until there is a trusting therapeutic relationship.

Assessment may uncover strengths and resources that can be utilized to enhance the client's progress. Focusing on strengths, capabilities, resilience, and resources can engender hope for the future and may assist in the client assuming personal responsibility (Hodge, 2004). By asking such questions, psychotherapists convey that they are open to discussing S/R concerns and that they value this aspect of their client's worldview.

Spirituality and religious beliefs can be pathways to actualizing human potential but they may also be sources of pain. Pathological forms of religious experience have been described in the literature, and can include scrupulosity (obsessive overconcern for one's sinfulness), repetitive denominational shifting, and ritualistic child abuse (Meadow & Kahoe, 1984). When conducting assessments of clients' S/R beliefs, psychotherapists need to be aware of/differentiate beliefs that represent "healthy" spirituality (promoting personal growth and increasing love of self and others) from "unhealthy" (hedonistic or guilt-driven practices) spirituality (Pargament, 1997). Richards and Bergin (2005) define healthy spirituality as including acceptance of responsibility, self-regulation, moral responsibility, integrity, warmth, empathy, forgiveness, benevolent power, tolerance, and growth orientation. In contrast, characteristics of unhealthy spirituality include preoccupation with self, denial of responsibility, addictions, poor reality testing, immoral behavior, role-playing, manipulation, and lack of forgiveness, self-aggrandizement, intolerance, prejudice, perfectionism, and rigidity (Richards & Bergin, 2005). Fukuyama and Sevig (1999) caution that what may appear to some psychotherapists as "unhealthy S/R practices" may be viewed as positive by others, depending on their individual perspective. For example, some individuals may view fundamentalist religions as too restrictive, yet these religions may provide a positive structure and lifestyle for many individuals (Fukuyama & Sevig, 1999). In addition, many non-Western S/R traditions embody beliefs that psychotherapists from a Western perspective might view as "passive" or "a denial of responsibility," among other negative attributions. For example, an appropriate expression of fatalism, the belief that one cannot change fate because certain things are preordained (Burke et al., 2005), could be interpreted by a psychotherapist as representing an "unhealthy" passivity. Therefore, it is important that psychotherapists be very cautious about making judgments about particular faith expressions.

Knowledge of cultural expressions of S/R is required for accurate assessment to avoid pathologizing experiences such as auditory or visual hallucinations, belief in witchcraft or the evil eye, and visions, which may be normative within the client's S/R traditions (Das, 1987; McNeill & Cervantes, 2008). Psychotherapists should also be skilled in the use of the diagnostic code "Religious or Spiritual Problem," used when the focus of clinical attention relates to spiritual issues (APA, 2000).

Josephson and Peteet (2004) describe two levels of assessment, a brief screening, and an in-depth interview. They recommend that psychotherapists provide a brief screening with all clients, to include questions about the client's current and past religious affiliation and beliefs, worldview, and presence or absence of current S/R concerns. By completing a brief screening, psychotherapists may then be in a position to determine whether the client has S/R issues relevant to the presenting concern and whether the psychotherapist has the requisite competency to proceed with further assessment and treatment of S/R issues. If psychotherapists determine that client issues are outside his or her scope of competency, they should provide a referral to appropriate resources.

SAMPLE SPIRITUAL/RELIGIOUS ASSESSMENT QUESTIONS

- What things do you believe in or have faith in? Do you currently feel connected to (God/higher power/the universe)?
- Are spiritual issues important to you in your life? How important were spiritual beliefs to you as a child? Are there any religious or spiritual issues you would like to talk about in counseling?
- Does the problem you are presenting with impact your spirituality? If so, how?
- Do you have S/R doubts or concerns?
- Describe your spiritual journey. What have been the high points? The lows?
- Have you ever had a transcendent S/R experience? What impact did the experience have upon you?
- What spiritual practices do you find most beneficial to you?
- What are your personal beliefs and practices regarding:
  - Individual responsibility, free will, personal relationship with (God/higher power), submitting to (God's) will, living life according to (higher power's/God's) plan, obedience?

(continued)

(*continued*)

- ○ Shame, faith, worthiness, guilt, sin, meaning/purpose of suffering, evil, concepts of sin, forgiveness, redemption, atonement, moral code, purpose of life?
- ○ Beliefs about death and an afterlife, reincarnation, karma, spirit possession, ancestor worship?
- ○ Beliefs about the role of S/R authority, gender-role issues (roles of men and women within the S/R tradition), attitudes toward sexuality, attitudes toward sexual orientation?
- ○ Expressions and practices (prayer, meditation, contemplation, mystical experiences, healing rituals, transition rituals, spiritual direction)?
- What is the extent of your knowledge of the doctrine of your S/R beliefs?
- Is there a relationship between your S/R beliefs and your cultural background? How would you describe it?
- Have you, or has your faith community experienced discrimination or oppression relating to S/R beliefs? How have you coped with it?
- Are you aware of any S/R resources that might help you deal with your current problems? Would you be willing to talk with (spiritual healer/shaman/spiritual director/clergy) about your problems?

Intervention Skills

There are many excellent resources for information about S/R interventions. In their book *Spiritually Oriented Psychotherapy*, Sperry and Shafranske (2005) devote individual chapters to theories and techniques for spiritually oriented therapy, including psychoanalytic, Jungian, cognitive-behavioral, humanistic, interpersonal, and transpersonal approaches. Richards and Bergin (2000) and Eck (2002) have provided comprehensive summaries of the most common religious and spiritual interventions used by psychotherapists

and Helmeke and Sori (2006) provide numerous exercises, handouts, and homework assignments incorporating a variety of theoretical approaches and techniques. *Spirituality and the Therapeutic Process: A Comprehensive Resource from Intake to Termination* (Aten & Leach, 2009) outlines numerous considerations and suggestions for each step of the therapeutic process and includes a comprehensive case discussion to illustrate various interventional techniques.

Below is an example of an S/R intervention from the perspective of rational-emotive and cognitive-behavioral therapy.

EXAMPLES OF RELIGIOUSLY ADAPTED RATIONAL-EMOTIVE AND COGNITIVE-BEHAVIORAL THERAPIES

Secular version: "I can always choose to give myself unconditional self-acceptance and see myself as a 'good person' just because I am alive and human—whether or not I act well and whether or not I am lovable."

Religious or spiritual version: "My God is merciful and will always accept me as a sinner while urging me to go and sin no more. Because God accepts the sinner, though not his or her sins, I can accept myself no matter how badly I behave."

Source: Ellis (2000), p. 32.

In addition to using spiritually oriented therapies, psychotherapists may recommend that clients engage in their own S/R practices outside of therapy, such as meditation and prayer, reading religious/spiritual texts, and working with spiritual healers such as a folk healer, curandero(a), shaman, or spiritual leader.

Johnson, Ridley, and Nielsen (2000) recommend that while psychotherapists should respect clients' beliefs, they should not "accept destructive religious beliefs for the sake of embracing diversity" (p. 16). The authors recommend two courses of action. The first is to consult (with the client's permission and informed consent) with the client's spiritual leader for "clarification of doctrine and pastoral support in the therapy process, which can be effective when clients hold idiosyncratic or inaccurate religious beliefs" that can be "appropriately corrected from within his or her faith community" (Johnson et al., 2000, p. 16). Psychotherapists should first ascertain whether clergy can contribute this perspective, and they must "exercise discretion in the selection of clergy with whom they collaborate."

Second, if clinicians share or understand the client's S/R beliefs, they can attempt to modify the "demanding and evaluative nature "of these beliefs. Psychotherapists can accomplish this by first helping clients recollect the teachings of their S/R tradition, then assisting clients in evaluating whether they are truly implementing those teachings (Johnson et al., p. 16). For example, if a client feels consumed by guilt over having had an abortion, she might believe that her sin is so great that she is damned. Although the doctrines of her religion include belief in God's mercy, understanding, and forgiveness of sins, she may be unable to access those positive and supportive religious beliefs. In this situation, it may be advantageous for both a psychotherapist and a religious leader to work with the client's psychological and religious issues. The psychotherapist can assist the client in processing her grief and loss. The religious leader can assist her in understanding the relevant religious doctrine and perform any appropriate religious rituals for healing, such as confession or atonement.

Contraindications for S/R Therapy

Prior to implementing any S/R intervention, it is necessary to assess for S/R contraindications. Several authors (Richards & Bergin, 2005; Sperry, 2000) provide contraindications for using S/R interventions: clients who are delusional, psychotic, or severely obsessive-compulsive; the presenting issues are not relevant to the S/R domain; clients who are underage and whose parents have not provided permission; clients who are spiritually immature (e.g., in the earliest stages of S/R identity development); and clients who perceive God as distant and condemning. Also, spiritual interventions are more risky and less likely to be effective if the therapeutic alliance is weak; there is low psychotherapist–client S/R values similarity; and the psychotherapist lacks multicultural and religious sensitivity (Richards & Bergin, 2005).

IMPLICATIONS FOR CLINICAL PRACTICE

- Gain informed consent.
- Conduct a thorough assessment.
- Ascertain whether there are any contraindications to S/R-focused therapy.
- Build a strong therapeutic relationship.
- Understand and work within the client's S/R belief system.
- Apply psychotherapy interventions tailored to the client's S/R belief system and adapted to S/R issues.
- Consult with S/R leaders and/or knowledgeable colleagues as needed.
- Refer client to S/R leaders when S/R rituals or practices are indicated.

Collaboration and Referral Skills

Effective S/R interventions use multiple resources, and psychotherapists can enhance client care by understanding that religious leaders and spiritual directors can complement their work. As noted in the Guidelines on Multicultural Education, Training, Research, Practice, and Organizational Change for Psychologists (American Psychological Association, 2002a), psychologists are encouraged to access interdisciplinary resources to coordinate and complement client care. Competent psychotherapists are able to discern when other professionals may be helpful in assisting clients with S/R issues and they are able to consult and/or refer to clergy, spiritual leaders, and spiritual directors when indicated (Richards, 2009). For example, ministers and healers can perform rituals such as giving blessings or forgiving sins and Native American shamans may perform spiritual rituals for healing. They can also assist with assessment and intervention plans and they may be able to provide information to enhance the psychotherapist's ability to assist the client. In addition, they can collaborate with the psychotherapist to determine when a referral to the S/R leaders would be appropriate. Helmeke and Sori (2006) outline strategies for networking with clergy and religious leaders.

Supervision and Training Skills

Bishop, Avila-Juarbe, and Thumme (2003) ask, ". . . how is it possible to educate counselors to competently and effectively address spiritual issues in the counseling process if spiritual issues are not addressed in the counselor supervision process?" (p. 39). Hatcher and Dudley Lassiter (2007) emphasize that the cornerstone of clinical training is direct observation of clinical activities by trained and competent supervisors. Quality training in S/R issues cannot occur without competent supervision of the learning process (Hatcher & Dudley Lassiter, 2007; Young, Cashwell, Wiggins-Frame, & Belaire, 2002). Polanski (2003) and Aten & Hernandez (2004)

have provided excellent guidelines for addressing religious and spiritual issues in supervision using the discrimination model of supervision (Bernard, 1997), and the integrated developmental model (Stoltenberg & Delworth, 1987), respectively.

Enhancing trainee openness to the development of S/R skills requires that trainers and supervisors be sensitive to concerns that trainees may have regarding discussions of their S/R beliefs. For example, individuals who identify as atheist or agnostic are in the minority in the United States, representing an estimated 7 to 12 percent of the population. Therefore, trainees who identify as atheist or agnostic may be reluctant to disclose their personal beliefs to supervisors and trainers because they may fear that their beliefs would engender disapproval. For example, trainees working in a religiously affiliated institution might assume they would be viewed negatively were they to disclose differing or contrasting faith perceptions. It is essential to acknowledge the importance of the immediate environment in which either the therapy or the supervision occurs. In contrast, trainees belonging to a religion or a spiritual tradition may have experienced discrimination in their personal and professional lives, and they may feel the need to protect that aspect of their identity by avoiding S/R topics in supervision and in professional discussions. Since supervision is essential to skill development, supervisors must attend to building open and trusting relationships while being inclusive of multiple S/R perspectives. Frazier and Hansen (2009) postulate that frank and open professional discussions of perceived barriers would increase psychotherapists' willingness to incorporate S/R interventions.

Trainers can develop students' S/R sensitivity, awareness, knowledge, and skills through coursework, seminars, and workshops. Miller (1999) stresses the importance of incorporating the teaching of S/R issues into all curriculum domains. Trainers and faculty are urged to integrate multiple perspectives when formulating the learning activities, syllabus, case examples, and readings. Fouad and Arredondo (2007) provide extensive information about instructional methods designed to promote learning and to provide a safe and inclusive environment when addressing multicultural issues in the classroom and other settings. We have incorporated training resources into Tables 13.1 through 13.4 and into the Resources section at the end of this chapter.

IMPLICATIONS FOR SUPERVISORS

- *Assessment approaches*: Encourage supervisees to ask open-ended questions about whether S/R beliefs are a salient feature in the client's experience and beliefs.
- *Individual and cultural differences*: Encourage supervisees to examine their own beliefs and values, reflect on their own experiences, explore different S/R traditions, and recognize the epistemological assumptions of their client's S/R system.
- *Interpersonal assessment*: Help supervisees work through their potential countertransference issues. Suggest use of spiritual genogram to help supervisees make sense of their own S/R heritage and explore ways in which their experiences may affect their work.
- *Theoretical orientation*: Encourage supervisees to know what their chosen theoretical orientation assumes and teaches about S/R and assist supervisees in constructing effective interventions that are consistent with their chosen orientation.
- *Problem conceptualization*: Address strengths of S/R orientation and bring attention to how S/R concern may actually be a metaphor for a larger therapeutic issue.
- *Selecting treatment goals and plans*: Help supervisees develop treatment goals and plans that are compatible with their client's S/R beliefs, values, and practices. Refer supervisees to professional publications, clergy, and S/R writings to enhance supervisee's range of understanding.
- *Ethics*: Train supervisees to work with S/R clients in an ethical manner by informing them of the ethical guidelines and codes that pertain to S/R clients and issues.
- *Intervention skills*: Incorporate discussions of S/R techniques to help supervisees examine their own understanding of S/R and the usefulness of S/R interventions.

See the Resources section for specific questions that may be used to increase self-awareness.

Source: Adapted from Aten and Hernandez (2004).

VALUES AND ATTITUDES

Psychotherapists are responsible for first knowing themselves, then extending this learning to build knowledge about other cultural beings (Fouad & Arredondo, 2007). In their Dimensions of Personal Identity model, Arredondo and Glauner (1992) describe the aspects of personal identity (including religion and spirituality) that influence beliefs, values, biases, assumptions, and privileges. They emphasize the need for self-reflection so that psychotherapists can be aware of their values and biases. The need for self-knowledge is particularly true in the area of S/R issues because the spiritual and religious worldviews and values of mainstream psychotherapists often conflict with those of their religious clients (Bergin, 1980; Bergin & Jensen, 1990; Jones, 1994). Since individuals typically attend to what they find personally important, psychotherapists who do not hold strong S/R beliefs may overlook or underestimate the importance of their clients' S/R beliefs. By examining their beliefs in the context of multicultural competency development, psychotherapists can become more aware of the cross-cultural aspects of working with clients who have differing S/R beliefs.

Richards and Bergin (2005) state that psychotherapists should not overtly or subtly pursue religious, spiritual, or moral goals that are contrary to their client's values and choices. Instead, they should work within their client's value framework and guard against imposing their own S/R values and beliefs on clients. Value imposition may take the form of active attempts to change clients' beliefs or choices, or it may take the form of overlooking important client issues. Some examples of inappropriate value imposition could include:

- A psychotherapist is seeing a client who is questioning her sexual orientation. The psychotherapist may subtly influence the client to deny and suppress her attraction to women because she has an S/R belief system that condemns homosexual behavior (Richards & Bergin, 2005).
- A religious client is entering therapy due to grief over the death of his best friend in a car accident. The client is wondering why he was not killed also. If the psychotherapist identifies as an atheist, she might overlook the spiritual aspects central to this client's issues, which

could include feeling angry with God for allowing his friend to die and wondering if he was saved because God has a plan for his life.

In these examples, the client and the psychotherapist did not share the same S/R beliefs. Having similar beliefs to the client's can be problematic if there are shared blind spots. According to Josephson and Peteet (2004), "in the same way that a religious therapist and religious patient might collude to avoid facing a fear of dying, an atheistic therapist might collude with an atheistic patient to assume that the patient's rejection of his or her family's faith is simply rational and without psychological significance" (p. 149).

As these examples illustrate, it is imperative for psychotherapists to become self-aware concerning their S/R beliefs, biases, and attitudes, as well as cultivating an attitude of openness and acceptance of others' belief systems. It is also crucial for clinicians to become aware of insurmountable countertransference reactions that would necessitate referral to another psychotherapist. To assist in the development of self-awareness, we have provided examples of self-awareness activities and exercises that can be used in classes, workshops, and in self-study in the Resources section of this chapter.

IMPLICATIONS FOR CLINICAL PRACTICE

- Examine own religious and spiritual attitudes, beliefs, biases, and blind spots.
- Challenge self to confront S/R biases, become more open, and attain greater respect for other S/R worldviews.
- Do not pursue religious, spiritual, or moral goals that are contrary to client's values and beliefs.
- Assess for insurmountable values conflicts and countertransference reactions that would require referral to another psychotherapist.

  See the Resources section for specific questions that may be used to increase self-awareness.

CASE EXAMPLE

In Case Vignette 13.3, we will describe assessment and intervention strategies specifically addressing S/R issues. These strategies are in

addition to the usual assessment process (e.g., assessing suicide risk factors, degree and history of depression, etc.) and intervention strategies (e.g., psychoeducation about the grief process, psychiatric treatment if indicated, and encouraging the client to seek a grief support group).

CASE VIGNETTE 13.3

The client is a 42-year-old divorced African American woman whose only child, an 11-year-old son, died one year ago of leukemia. She is deeply depressed and unable to find a reason for living. She reveals that while she has thought of suicide, she would never do it because it is a sin. She confesses that she cannot understand why God allowed her son to die. During her son's illness, she devoted herself to prayer and fasting and put her faith in the Lord to save him. She has been unable to pray since the funeral, and she feels angry and abandoned by God. When you ask if she has spoken with her minister, she says that she cannot talk about these feelings with him because she is afraid he would condemn her for her lack of faith.

Issues to Consider

- Do you have any countertransference reactions, either positive or negative?
- What spiritual assessment questions will you ask?
- What are the potential ethical issues (e.g., informed consent) in this case? How might you resolve them?
- Should you consult with her spiritual leader or another spiritual leader within her faith tradition?
- What issues do you feel competent to address and what issues do you not feel you are able to address?
- Do you feel that it is appropriate for you to provide her with counseling? If not, what is your treatment plan?

Therapy Goal

- Assist the client in working through her grief and, if this is her goal, helping her feel reconnected with her spirituality as a positive resource in her life and as a crucial aspect of her identity.

S/R Treatment Plan

- Gain informed consent from client for an S/R focus in therapy.
- Assess her spiritual beliefs (see questions below).
- Consult with knowledgeable colleagues and spiritual leaders as needed.
- Refer client to her S/R leader (if appropriate) to discuss her religious concerns and to engage in helpful religious practices and rituals.
- Draw upon client's S/R strengths, including beliefs, which provide comfort and hope.
- Work through grief process, including guilt and self-blame.
- Work through anger at God.
- Assist client in reconnecting with her S/R beliefs.

S/R Assessment Questions

- S/R history: Has it been positive up until now? Were there wounding experiences? Have her beliefs changed? Is there an intersection with her cultural heritage?
- What are her faith tradition's teachings about death, an afterlife, salvation and/or redemption, sin, forgiveness, the meaning of suffering, the purpose of life? To what degree does she subscribe to these beliefs? In other words, what is her degree of religious orthodoxy?
- What are the gender roles in her faith tradition? Are attitudes toward the role of women a factor? Does her faith tradition promote traditional gender roles? Does it marginalize or discriminate against women? Has she experienced sexism or felt devalued by men in positions of authority within her faith tradition?
- What is her image of God (loving and accepting, or demanding and harsh)? Has her image of God changed since the death of her son?

- Assessment of her faith community: What role does it play in her life? Has she experienced changes in her connection to her faith community (e.g., has she withdrawn from church members?). If she has experienced a change in her connection, what is the impact on her?
- Assess for possible misunderstandings relating to her religion. Does her perception of her minister's reaction seem accurate or inaccurate? Do her beliefs accurately reflect her faith tradition's teachings or are there misperceptions that could be corrected by consulting with clergy (by client and/or by psychotherapist), through reading sacred writings or other S/R writings, or through other means such as talking with trusted friends?
- Is there a need for atonement if she feels to blame in some way? If so, what is the atonement process in her S/R tradition?
- Are there are other S/R rituals within her faith tradition that might assist in her healing process?

Intervention Techniques

In this section, we have listed interventions from the perspective of a variety of theoretical orientations. They are not necessarily mutually exclusive, in that psychotherapists may choose to draw upon techniques from a variety of theoretical perspectives. See Richards and Bergin (2005) and Sperry and Shafranske (2005) for extensive discussions of intervention techniques from various theoretical perspectives.

- The *interpersonal* therapeutic approach might focus on exploration of how she has learned to deal with conflicts in relationships as an inroad to discussion about how (or if) she sees resolution of her anger at God. The psychotherapist can provide psychoeducation about anger as a normal human expression and could draw upon examples from the woman's faith tradition about how historical religious figures have expressed and worked through anger issues. It may also be useful to explore whether she believes it is possible to have an ongoing relationship with her son in death, or whether it may be possible for her to understand that a relationship with her deceased son may carry meaning and purpose for her in her life.
- The *humanistic* approach can include addressing the client's feelings of anger, loss, and separation from God, from her son, from her minister, and from herself. If her psychotherapist could create a foundation for self-acceptance by providing her with the experience of unconditional positive regard, empathy, and acceptance, her self-acceptance could improve. The psychotherapist could assist her in exploring her positive S/R beliefs and reflecting on how she could make meaning of the loss of her son according to the tenets of her religion. This approach would identify and build on the client's strengths and positive coping strategies.
- *Cognitive* strategies might include exploration of automatic thoughts (e.g., "I am a sinner, I am being punished, there is no happiness possible for me, I will never be forgiven by God or by my minister") and exploring evidence for or against these beliefs. Cognitive Behavioral Therapy (CBT) homework assignments might include reading stories from her faith tradition about forgiveness, spiritual perspectives on suffering, and existential questions about meaning in life. Identifying pleasurable events and making these part of a treatment plan would also be important, as would basic psychoeducation about stages of grief and its resolution.
- *Psychodynamic* approaches to this case would include a deeper exploration of past relationships (e.g., other significant relationship losses such as her husband/marriage; prior negative, harsh, and blaming experiences with males, which may lead her to expect such responses from her minister and from God). She may have experienced prior

abandonment issues. The psychotherapist could explore defensive strategies (e.g., bargaining with God through fasting and prayer) that have served to protect her ego from accepting the reality of death and its accompanying emotions.

- *Narrative* approaches may include helping the woman explore creative "stories" and alternative "endings" to this chapter in her life, focusing on possibilities, new meanings, and new opportunities. Using stories from her faith tradition may assist in this process.
- *Additional therapy techniques* can include guided imagery, mindfulness, gestalt work, and empty-chair exercises.
- Community grief support resource referrals: Compassionate Friends, Hospice.

For further examples, see Frame (2003) and Richards and Bergin (2003) for numerous case studies integrating a variety of theoretical approaches in working with S/R issues in therapy.

SUMMARY

The purpose of this chapter has been to provide mental health practitioners, students, trainers, educators, and supervisors with guidelines and resources for expanding their competencies in assessing and working with spiritual and religious issues. We have outlined requisite areas of knowledge (individual and cultural diversity, assessment, diagnosis and case conceptualization, and ethical and legal standards); skills (relationship, assessment, intervention, referral, and supervision and training); and the attitudes and values necessary to provide multiculturally sensitive services to individuals with a wide range of spiritual and religious worldviews. Through the case vignettes, examples, and resources provided, we hope that the reader has deepened his or her repertoire of religious and spiritual knowledge, skills,

and methods for integrating spiritual and religious information into competent training and practice.

RESOURCES FOR CLINICIANS, STUDENTS, TRAINERS, AND SUPERVISORS

In this section, we will provide suggestions and resources for building S/R competencies through self-assessment, training activities, academic curricula, and sources for additional information. These approaches may be used at a variety of levels of professional development (masters- and doctoral-level coursework, supervised practice, internship, postdoctoral residency, professional specialization, and independent professional development).

The section begins with a list of resources that includes books, journals, videos, and Web links. A series of experiential exercises is then followed by the tables.

Tables 13.1 through 13.4 describe foundational and functional competencies in S/R knowledge, skills, values, and attitudes at each level of practitioner skill development (Entry to Practicum, Entry to Internship, Entry to Professional Practice, and Advanced Practice and Specialization). Learning occurs as a developmental process in which earlier levels represent broad and general competencies, and higher-level competencies are increasingly specific and specialized (Rodolfa et al., 2005). For example, the Entry to Internship-level competencies described in Table 13.2 incorporate and build on the competencies attained at the Entry to Practicum level (Table 13.1).

Table 13.5 is a summary of major world religions (Islam, Buddhism, Hinduism, Christianity, Judaism) and Native American beliefs, including: views of deity, life after death, marriage, divorce, roles in the family and sexuality; tenets of the religion; and religious practices.

SPIRITUAL/RELIGIOUS COMPETENCIES RESOURCE GUIDE

Assessment

Aten, J. D. & Leach, M. M. (Eds.) (2009). *Spirituality and the therapeutic process: A comprehensive resource from intake to termination.* Washington, D.C. American Psychological Association.

Clarke, I. (Ed.) (2001). *Psychosis and spirituality.* Philadelphia, Whurr.

Gorusch, R. L., & Miller, W. R. (1999). Assessing spirituality. In W. R. Miller (Ed.), *Integrating spirituality into treatment* (pp. 47–64). Washington, DC: American Psychological Association.

Hathaway, W. L., Scott, S. Y., & Garver, S. A. (2004). Assessing religious/spiritual functioning: A neglected domain in clinical practice? *Professional Psychology: Research and Practice, 35*(1), 97–104.

Ho, D. Y. F. & Ho, R. T. H. (2007). Measuring spirituality and spiritual emptiness; toward ecumenicity and transcultural applicability. *Review of General Psychology, 11*(3), 62–74.

Hodge, D. R. (2005). *Spiritual assessment: Handbook for helping professionals.* Botsford, CT: North American Association of Christians in Social Work.

Kehoe, N. (2002). Spiritual assessment. Spirituality as a resource for psychological health and wellbeing [Special Issue]: Religion and psychology. *Psychological Inquiry, 13*(3).

Moberg, D. O. (2002). Assessing and measuring spirituality: Confronting dilemmas of universal and particular evaluative criteria. [Special issue]: Spirituality and adult development. *Journal of Adult Development, 9*(1), 41–60.

Stanard, R. P., Sandhu, D. S., & Painter, L. C. (2000) Assessment of spirituality in counseling. *Journal of Counseling and Development, 78,* 204–210.

Ethical Issues

American Psychological Association. (2008). Resolution on religious, religion-based and/or religion-derived prejudice. *American Psychologist (63),* 431–434.

Gonsiorek, J. C. (2009). Ethical challenges incorporating spirituality and religion into psychotherapy. *Professional Psychology: Research and Practice, 40*(4), 385–389.

McMinn, M. R. (2009). Ethical considerations with spiritually oriented interventions. *Professional Psychology: Research and Practice, 40*(4), 393–395.

Plante, T. G. (2007). Integrating spirituality and psychotherapy: Ethical issues and principles to consider. *Journal of Clinical Psychology, 63*(9) 891–902.

Steen, R. L., Engels, D., & Thweatt, W. T. III (2006). Ethical aspects of spirituality in counseling. *Counseling and Values, 50*(2), 108–118.

Tan, S.-Y. (2003). Integrating spiritual direction into psychotherapy: Ethical issues and guidelines. *Journal of Psychology and Theology, 31*(1), 14–23.

Yarhouse, M., & Van Orman, B. (1999). When psychologists work with religious clients: Applications of the general principles of ethical conduct. *Professional Psychology: Research and Practice, 30*(6), 557–562.

Multicultural and Diverse Populations

American Psychological Association. (2003). Guidelines on multicultural education, training, research, practice and organizational change for psychologists. *American Psychologist, 58*(5), 377–402.

Burke, M. T., Chauvin, J. C., & Miranti, J. G. (2005). *Religious and spiritual issues in counseling: Implications across diverse populations.* New York: Brunner-Routledge.

Burr, K. A. (2009). *Coming out, coming home: Making room for gay spirituality in therapy.* New York: Routledge/Taylor and Francis.

Cervantes, J. M., & Parham, T. A. (2005). Toward a meaningful spirituality for people of color: Lessons for the counseling practitioner. *Cultural Diversity and Ethnic Minority Psychology, 11*(1), 69–81.

Constantine, M. G. (1999). Spiritual and religious issues in counseling racial and ethnic minority populations: An introduction to the special issue. *Journal of Multicultural Counseling and Development, 27*(4), 179181.

Constantine, M. G., & Sue, D. W. (2006). Factors contributing to optimal human functioning in people of color in the United States. *Counseling Psychologist, 34*(2), 228–244.

Das, A. K. (1987). Indigenous models of therapy in traditional Asian societies. *Journal of Multicultural Counseling and Development. 15*(1), 25–37.

D'Andrea, L. M., & Sprenger, J. (2007). Atheism and nonspirituality as diversity issues in counseling. *Counseling and Values, 51*(1), 149–158.

Dwairy, M. (2006). *Counseling and psychotherapy with Arabs and Muslims: a culturally sensitive approach.* New York: Teachers College Press.

Fouad, N. A., & Arredondo, P. (2007). *Becoming culturally oriented: Practical advice for psychologists and educators.* Washington, DC: American Psychological Association.

Fukuyama, M. A., & Ferguson, A. D. (2000). Lesbian, gay, and bisexual people of color: Understanding cultural complexity and managing multiple oppressions. In R. M. Perez, K. A. DeBord, & K. J. Bieschke (Eds.), *Handbook of counseling and psychotherapy with lesbian, gay, and bisexual clients* (pps. 81–105). Washington, D.C.: American Psychological Association.

Fukuyama, M. A., Siahpoush, F., & Sevig, T. D. (2005). Religion and spirituality in a cultural context. In C. S. Cashwell, & J. S. Young (Eds.), *Integrating spirituality and religion into counseling: A guide to competent practice* (pp. 123–142). Alexandria, VA.: American Counseling Association.

Fukuyama, M., & Sevig, T. (1999). *Integrating spirituality into multicultural counseling*. Thousand Oaks, CA: Sage.

Josephson, A. M., & Peteet, J. R. (2004). *Handbook of spirituality and worldview in clinical practice*. Arlington, VA: American Psychiatric Publishing.

Kelly, E. W. (1995). *Spirituality and religion in counseling and psychotherapy: Diversity in theory and practice*. Alexandria, VA: American Counseling Association.

Lee, C. C. (Ed.). (2006). *Multicultural issues in counseling: New approaches to diversity* (3rd ed.). Alexandria, VA: American Counseling Association.

Mattis, J. S., Ahluwalia, M. K., Cowie, S. E., & Kirkland-Harris, A. M. (2006). Ethnicity, culture and spiritual development. In E. C. Roehlkepartain, P. E. King, L. Wagener, & P. L. Benson (Eds.), *The handbook of spiritual development in childhood and adolescence* (pp. 283–296). Thousand Oaks, CA: Sage.

McNeill, B. W. (Ed.) & Cervantes, J. M. (Ed.) (2008). *Latina/o healing practices: Mestizo and indigenous perspectives*. New York, Routledge/Taylor & Francis.

Pedersen, P., Draguns, J., Lonner, W., & Trimble, J. (Eds.). (2008). *Counseling across cultures* (6th ed.). Thousand Oaks, CA: Sage.

Singaravelu, H. D. & Pope, M. (2007). *A handbook for counseling international students in the United States*. Alexandria, VA: American Counseling Association.

Sue, D. W., & Sue, S. (2007). *Counseling the culturally diverse: Theory and practice* (5th ed.). Hoboken, NJ: Wiley.

Spiritual and Religious Developmental Theories

Dowling, E. M. & Scarlett, W. G. (Eds.) (2006). *Encyclopedia of religious and spiritual development*. Thousand Oaks, CA: Sage.

Fowler, J. W. (1995). *Stages of faith: The psychology of human development and the quest for meaning*. New York: Harper Collins.

Ingersoll, R. E. (1998). *Refining dimensions of spiritual wellness: A cross-traditional approach. Counseling and Values, 42*(3), 156–165.

Koenig, H. G. (1994). *Aging and God: Spiritual pathways to mental health in midlife and later years*. New York: Haworth Pastoral Press.

Poll, J. B., & Smith, T. B. (2003). The spiritual self: Toward a conceptualization of spiritual identity development. *Journal of Psychology and Theology, 31*(2), 129–142.

Roehlkepartain, E. C., King, P. E., Wagener, L., & Benson, P. L. (Eds.), (2006). *The handbook of spiritual development in childhood and adolescence*. Thousand Oaks, CA: Sage.

Spiritual and Religious Interventions

Aten, J. D., & Leach, M. M. (Eds.). (2009). *Spirituality and the therapeutic process: a comprehensive resource from intake to termination*. Washington, DC: American Psychological Association.

Briggs, M. K., & Rayle, A. D. (2005). Incorporating spirituality into core counseling courses: Ideas for classroom application. *Counseling and Values, 50*(1), 63–75.

Cashwell, C. S., & Young, J. S. (2004). *Integrating spirituality and religion into counseling: A guide to competent practice*. Alexandria, VA: American Counseling Association.

Eck, B. E. (2002). An exploration of the therapeutic use of spiritual disciplines in clinical practice. *Journal of Psychology and Christianity, 21*, 266–280.

Harris, A. H., Standard, S. D., & Thoresen, C. E. (2006). Integrating spiritual and religious factors into psychological treatment: Why and how. In E. O'Leary and M. Murphy (Eds.), *New approaches to integration in psychotherapy* (pp. 179–191). New York: Routledge/Taylor & Francis Group.

Helmeke, K. B., & Sori, C. (2006). *The therapist's notebook for integrating spirituality into counseling: Homework, handouts and activities for use in psychotherapy, Vols. 1 and 2*. Birmingham, NY: Haworth Press.

Miller, W. R. (Ed.) (1999). *Integrating spirituality into treatment: Resources for practitioners*. Washington, DC: American Psychological Association.

Pargament, K. J. (2007). *Spiritually integrated psychotherapy: Understanding and addressing the sacred*. New York: Guilford.

Plante, T. G. (2009). *Spiritual practices in psychotherapy: Thirteen tools for enhancing psychological health.* Washington, DC: American Psychological Association.

Puchalski, C. M. (Ed.) (2006). *A time for listening and caring: Spirituality and the care of the chronically ill and dying.* New York: Oxford University Press.

Richards, P. S., & Bergin, A. E. (2004). *Casebook for a spiritual strategy in counseling and psychotherapy.* Washington, DC: American Psychological Association.

Richards, P. S., & Bergin, A. E. (2005) *A spiritual strategy for counseling and psychotherapy* (2nd ed.). Washington, DC: American Psychological Association.

Sperry, L., & Shafranske, E. (Eds.), (2005). *Spiritually-oriented psychotherapy.* Washington, DC: American Psychological Association.

Taylor, E. J. (2007). *What do I say? Talking with patients about spirituality.* West Conshohocken, PA: Templeton Foundation.

Zinnbauer, B. J., & Pargament, K. I. (2000). Working with the sacred: Four approaches to religious and spiritual issues in counseling. *Journal of Counseling & Development, 78*(2), 162–171.

Spiritual and Religious Traditions

Dowd, E. T., & Nielson, S. (2006). *The psychologies in religion: Working with the religious client.* New York: Springer.

Fukuyama, M., & Sevig, T. (1999). *Integrating spirituality into multicultural counseling.* Thousand Oaks, CA: Sage.

Josephson, A. M., & Peteet, J. R. (2004). *Handbook of spirituality and worldview in clinical practice.* Arlington, VA: American Psychiatric Publishing.

Levitt, D. H. & Balkin, R. S. (2003). *Religious diversity from a Jewish perspective. Counseling and Values, 48*(1), 57–66.

Miller, G. (2003). *Incorporating spirituality in counseling and psychotherapy: Theory and technique.* Hoboken, NJ: Wiley.

Molloy, M. (2008). *Experiencing the world's religions: tradition, challenge, and change* (4th Ed.). Boston: McGraw Hill.

Olson, R. P. (Ed.). (2002). *Religious theories of personality and psychotherapy: East meets West.* New York: Haworth Press.

Richards, P. S., & Bergin, A. E. (Eds.). (2000). *Handbook of psychotherapy and religious diversity.* Washington, DC: American Psychological Association.

Supervision

Aten, J. D., & Hernandez, B. C. (2004). Addressing religion in clinical supervision: A model. *Psychotherapy: Theory, Research, Practice, Training, 41*(2), 152–160.

Berkel, L. A., Constantine, M. G., & Olson, E. A. (2007) Supervisor multicultural competence: Addressing religious and spiritual issues with counseling students in supervision. *The Clinical Supervisor, 26*(1/2), 3–15.

Bishop, D. R., Avila-Juarbe, E., & Thumme, B. (2003). Recognizing spirituality as an important factor in counselor supervision: Issues and insights. *Counseling and Values, 48*(1), 34–46.

Miller, M. M., Korinek, A. W., & Ivey, D. C. (2006). Integrating spirituality into training: The spiritual issues supervision scale. *American Journal of Family Therapy, 34*(4), 355–372.

Polanski, P. J. (2003). Spirituality in supervision. *Counseling and Values, 47*(131–141).

Training in Spiritual and Religious Competencies

Association for Counselor Education and Supervision (ACES). (2005). Ethical guidelines for counseling supervisors. Retrieved January 11, 2010, from http://www.acesonline.net/ethical_guidelines.asp

Bartoli, E. (2007) Religious and spiritual issues in psychotherapy practice: Training the trainer. *Psychotherapy: Theory, Research, Practice, Training, 44*(1), 54–65.

Cashwell, C. S., & Young, J. S. (2004). Spirituality in counselor training: A content analysis of syllabi from introductory spirituality courses. Appendix A: Compilation of reading lists from the 14 syllabi reviewed by the authors. Appendix B: Bibliography compiled by the authors to orient readers to each of the nine competencies. *Counseling and Values, 48*(2), 96–109.

Council for Accreditation of Counseling and Related Educational Programs (CACREP). (2001). Standards for counselor preparation. *Accreditation Manual.* Alexandria, VA: Author.

Hage, S. M. (2006). A closer look at the role of spirituality in psychology training programs. *Professional Psychology: Research and Practice, 37*(3), 303–310.

Miller, W. R. (1999). Diversity training in spiritual and religious issues. In W. R. Miller (Ed.), *Integrating spirituality into treatment: Resources for practitioners* (pp. 253–264). Washington, DC: American Psychological Association.

Myers, J. E., & Williard, K. (2003). Integrating spirituality into counselor preparation: A developmental wellness approach. *Counseling and Values*, *47*(2), 142–155.

Russell, S. R., & Yarhouse, M. A. (2006). Training in religion/spirituality within APA-accredited psychology predoctoral internships. *Professional Psychology: Research and Practice*, *37*(4), 430–436.

Yarhouse, M. A., & Fisher, W. (2002) Levels of training to address religion in clinical practice. *Psychotherapy: Theory, Research, Practice, Training*, *39*(2), 171–176.

TRAINING RESOURCES: MEDIA

The American Psychological Association Video Series *Spirituality* has videotaped distinguished psychologists illustrating how to work with patients using approaches grounded in an awareness of spiritual perspectives. Topics include: addressing issues of spirituality and religion in psychotherapy; Christian counseling; mindfulness therapy; mindfulness-based cognitive therapy for depression; mindfulness for addiction problems; spiritual awareness therapy; and theistic integrative psychology.

The American Psychological Association Division 36 (Psychology of Religion) journal, *Psychology of Religion and Spirituality*, publishes scholarly articles on spiritual and religious issues in psychology and related fields.

Web Resources

Your Guide to Religions of the World. http://www.bbc.co.uk/religion/religions

The Pew Forum on Religion and Public Life. http://www.religions.pewforum.org

Duke University Center for Spirituality, Theology and Health. http://www.spiritualityandhealth.duke.edu/index.html

The Center for Spiritual Development in Childhood and Adolescence. http://www.spiritualdevelopmentcenter.org

University of Pennsylvania Center for Spirituality and the Mind. http://www.uphs.upenn.edu/

John Templeton Foundation Web site. This organization is devoted to the scientific study of religion. http://www.templeton.org

University of Minnesota Center for Spirituality and Healing. http://www.csh.umn.edu

EXERCISE 13.1: SELF-AWARENESS AND SELF-ASSESSMENT EXERCISES

A. What is your comfort level in discussing S/R issues with clients? What concerns or fears do you have about addressing S/R issues in therapy?

B. Does a psychotherapist need to have S/R beliefs in God/higher power to be qualified to work with clients who have S/R issues? Why or why not?

C. With which S/R beliefs do you experience comfort and discomfort? Why?

D. Define *religion*. Define *spirituality*.

E. What ethical dilemmas could arise in doing S/R therapy? How can you best confront these dilemmas in an ethical manner?

F. Under what circumstances would you refer to a spiritual leader? What is the process for referring to a spiritual leader?

G. Under what circumstances would you not want to refer to a spiritual leader?

H. In the geographic area and population in which you live, what are the most frequent S/R traditions you can expect to encounter? How familiar are you with those traditions?

I. What is your knowledge of world religions? Which ones are most familiar to you? Which are least familiar?

J. What information is contained in a spiritual assessment?

K. Give some examples of possible client "multiple identities" relating to diversity issues, including spirituality.

(continued)

(*continued*)

L. What are some of the positive aspects of working with a client whose S/R beliefs are similar to yours? What are some of the negative aspects?

M. What are some of the positive aspects of working with a client whose S/R beliefs are different from yours? What are some of the challenges?

N. Circle the S/R attitude that best describes you (adapted from Kelly, 1990):

  1. *Religiously committed:* deep personal religious commitment that permeates all aspects of my life.

  2. *Religiously loyal:* have received the expectations of family and community, impacting the way I think and act, but not as deeply integrated as the religiously committed.

  3. *Spiritually committed:* not identified with a specific religion but committed to spirituality.

  4. *Religiously and spiritually open:* not identified with religion or spirituality but able to become open to exploration.

  5. *Superficially religious:* I ascribe to religious beliefs or affiliations but do not have inner commitment.

  6. *Religiously tolerant and indifferent:* I do not feel a need for S/R in my life.

  7. *Nonreligious:* I do not view religion or spirituality as necessary and I reject them.

  8. I identify as an agnostic.

  9. I identify as an atheist (I do not believe in God or a higher power).

  10. I am hostile to religion.

O. How does your S/R attitude potentially affect your work with clients?

EXERCISE 13.2

This exercise may be conducted as a group discussion or as an individual self-awareness exercise. When done in a group setting, it is essential to set ground rules incorporating mutual respect for all viewpoints, openness to learning from each other, and confidentiality.

A. List names of world religions.

B. Rate each religion on these dimensions:

  1. Level of knowledge you have about the religion

  2. Degree of similarity to your own belief system (e.g., ranging from very similar to very dissimilar)

  3. Your attitude toward the religion (positive, negative, neutral) and any experiences you have had that influence your attitude toward this religion

C. Choose two religions that are different from your own, and toward which you have a *negative* attitude. Research the chosen religions on the following dimensions and describe the S/R belief system, religious/spiritual practices (if applicable), similarity in value system to your own, and aspects that you admire about the chosen religions.

D. What you have learned about these S/R beliefs systems? Have your attitudes toward the religions remained the same? Changed? Reflect on the relative impact of this experience on your view of S/R issues.

SPIRITUAL/RELIGIOUS ISSUES SEMINAR

Topics and Activities

Trainers and clinicians may select activities from among the following suggestions.

A. Knowledge gained through didactic training and independent study:

1. Relation of S/R competency to multicultural competency.
2. Individual and cultural differences: (including age, gender, sexual orientation, socioeconomic status [SES], ethnicity) relating to S/R issues.
3. Literature describing the relevance of S/R to wellness, physical health, mental health.
4. Definitions of religion, spirituality, agnosticism, and atheism.
5. World religions and spiritual traditions (Western, non-Western, and indigenous).
6. Spiritual practices, including different forms of prayer, meditation, healing rituals, and spiritual direction.
7. S/R development models.
8. S/R assessment methods; diagnosis, case conceptualization, and treatment planning.
9. Healthy and unhealthy S/R expressions (e.g., "religious addiction"); understanding of psychopathology as well as religious beliefs and behavior that are considered normative and healthy within client's religious tradition.
10. Spiritual wounding.
11. "Dark Night of the Soul" (e.g., loss of faith, feeling distant from God, and/or being unable to pray).
12. Positive religious coping styles and S/R problem-solving style (self-directing, deferring, collaborative).
13. Theoretical orientation(s) and model(s) of psychotherapy—view of S/R beliefs.
14. S/R intervention techniques; risks and benefits; contraindications to using S/R interventions.

15. Therapy issues that frequently have an S/R component: grief, abuse recovery, sexual identity development, aging, death and dying, addiction, career development.
16. Transference and countertransference issues.
17. Ethical/legal standards: informed consent to provide S/R interventions, potential dual roles, and separation of church and state.
18. Roles of psychotherapists, ministers/religious or spiritual leaders, and spiritual directors.
19. Resource information: S/R leaders from various religions and faith traditions, spiritual healers, psychotherapists specializing in S/R therapy.

B. Awareness of own attitudes and values—may use one or more of the following techniques to explore one's own beliefs, attitudes, and experiences: spiritual genogram, journaling, family member interview, and S/R lifeline. Some examples include: What are your first memories of learning about S/R? What were the S/R beliefs and values in your household? To what degree have you ascribed to those same beliefs? What factors have affected the degree to which you have ascribed to S/R beliefs throughout the course of your life? (Also see the self-assessment questions in Exercise 13.1.)

C. Activities to build knowledge, awareness, and skills:

1. Visit an unfamiliar S/R service.
2. Write a paper describing the beliefs and practices of two unfamiliar S/R traditions.
3. Invite S/R leaders to the seminar.
4. Participate in group discussions of S/R issues.
5. Visit a 12-step program and read 12-step literature.
6. Participate in hospital grand rounds relating to death and dying.
7. Discuss therapy case examples and S/R issues scenarios. Identify possible therapeutic interventions, transference and

countertransference issues, and ethical dilemmas.

8. Choose an S/R concept and research how it is addressed in several world religions (e.g., sin, forgiveness, afterlife).

9. Explore S/R concepts through reading sacred texts (e.g., read the Bible's book of Job and discuss the meaning of suffering, read excerpts from the Koran and the Book of Mormon).

10. Participate in S/R experiences (e.g., meditation, yoga, contemplative exercises, guided imagery, expressive artwork and dance).

Integration of S/R Issues Into the Training Curriculum

The Council for Accreditation of Counseling and Related Educational Programs (CACREP) Standards (2001) suggests ways to integrate S/R into counselor preparation in the following curriculum domains:

1. Human growth and development courses (connection of cognitive, social, and moral development with the development of S/R beliefs, attitudes, and practices)

2. Social and cultural foundations (multicultural coursework)

3. Helping relationships courses (interviewing skills, counseling skills)

4. Group therapy (create an environment of mutual respect; demonstrate and use role-play techniques to use with S/R dilemmas)

5. Career and lifestyle development (examine influence of S/R issues on career decision making, starting with one's own exploration of personal values)

6. Appraisal (assess S/R issues during intake process, then use more specific S/R assessment if appropriate)

7. Research and program development (study of S/R literature)

8. Ethics (understanding of ethical issues relevant to S/R issues)

COMPETENCY BENCHMARK TABLES

The purpose of the Competency Benchmarks (Tables 13.1–13.4) is to create developmental models for defining and measuring competencies in professional psychology; each chapter in this *Handbook* applies the diversity competence for mental health practitioners in their work with a particular diverse population.

Table 13.1   Developmental-Level Competencies I

READINESS LEVEL—ENTRY TO PRACTICUM	
Competencies	Learning Process and Activities
Knowledge	The student is gaining knowledge in:	At this stage of development, the emphasis in psychotherapist education is on instilling knowledge of foundational domains that provide the groundwork for subsequent attainment of functional competencies. Students at this stage become aware of the principles and practices of the field, but they are not yet able to apply their knowledge to practice.
	• Multiculturalism—the student is engaged in the process of learning that all individuals, including themselves, are cultural beings with worldviews that shape and influence their attitudes, emotions, perceptions, and experiences.	
	• The importance of reflective practice and self-awareness.	Therefore, the training curriculum is focused on knowledge of core areas, including literature on multiculturalism, ethics, basic counseling skills, scientific knowledge, and the importance of reflective practice and self-awareness.
	• Core counseling skills and theories.	
	• Ethics code.	
Skills	The student is:	It is important that throughout the curriculum, trainers and teachers define individual and cultural differences broadly to include S/R differences. This should enable students to have a developing
	• Beginning to develop the ability to demonstrate empathic listening skills, respect, and interest when talking with individuals expressing different values and belief systems.	

READINESS LEVEL—ENTRY TO PRACTICUM	
Competencies	**Learning Process and Activities**
Values and Attitudes	• Learning to critically examine the diversity literature. The student demonstrates: • Willingness to engage in self-exploration—to consider own motives, attitudes, behaviors, and effect on others. • Intellectual curiosity and flexibility. • Ability to value expressions of diverse viewpoints and belief systems.	awareness of how to extrapolate their emerging multicultural competencies to include the S/R realm of individual and cultural differences. Most students, through their life experiences, would be expected to have basic knowledge of at least one S/R tradition, awareness of the definitions of *spirituality* and *religion*, and personal awareness of their cultural identity.

Table 13.2   Developmental-Level Competencies II

READINESS LEVEL—ENTRY TO INTERNSHIP	
Competencies	**Learning Process and Activities**
Knowledge	The student has: • General understanding of the traditions, beliefs, and practices of several of the world's major religions. • Understanding of potential ethical dual roles possible in S/R counseling. • Knowledge that working with S/R issues in therapy may be contraindicated in certain circumstances, though not yet well understood. • Understanding of the importance of consulting with supervisors and others when presented with unfamiliar S/R client issues.	At this level of development, students are building on their education and applied experiences (such as supervised practicum experiences) to attain a core set of foundational competencies. They can then begin applying this knowledge to professional practice. As a result of being exposed to didactic training and close supervision, students attain the multicultural values and attitudes appropriate to their level of development. Foundational knowledge and multicultural values and attitudes are becoming well established, but skills in working with S/R issues would be expected to be rudimentary at this level of development.
Skills	Skills in the following areas are beginning to develop: • Discerning personal limits of openness to S/R beliefs and attitudes and, after consultation with supervisors, referring clients to appropriate resources if not able to work with them. • Building therapeutic alliance to create a trusting, safe, and open therapeutic climate to discuss S/R issues, if indicated. • Learning to use the *DSM-IV-TR* diagnostic category "Religious or Spiritual Problem."	Learning occurs through multiple modalities: • Receiving S/R didactic training in academic programs may occur in multicultural courses or culture-specific courses (e.g., women's issues, Latino/a, and GLBT courses) and it may be infused into the core curriculum (e.g., ethics, assessment, multicultural, career counseling, research, human growth and development, and clinical courses. See an example of curriculum infusion in the Resources section of this chapter.
Values and Attitudes	Demonstrates self-awareness and appropriate cultural and multicultural attitudes as evidenced by the following: • Understands that spirituality is an aspect of worldview and multicultural diversity. • Awareness of own intersecting individual dimensions (gender, ethnicity, SES, sexual orientation, ability, etc.) and ability to discern clients' intersecting identities. • Commitment to examine and challenge own S/R attitudes and biases. • Willingness to admit own limitations in ability to be open to some expressions of S/R beliefs. • Demonstrates genuine respect for varying spiritual and religious perspectives.	• Providing therapy, under supervision, to clients representing diversity of S/R beliefs in practicum experiences. • Receiving supervision from psychotherapists knowledgeable and skilled in working with S/R issues. • Seeking additional study and professional development opportunities (e.g., to attain knowledge of several world religions). Topics to be covered in didactic training include: • Relation of S/R competency to multicultural competency. • Relationship of S/R worldviews to individual and cultural differences (e.g., including age, gender, sexual orientation, SES, and ethnicity).

(continued)

Table 13.2   Developmental-Level Competencies II (*continued*)

READINESS LEVEL—ENTRY TO INTERNSHIP	
Competencies	Learning Process and Activities
	• Basic research literature describing the relevance of S/R to wellness, physical health, mental health. • Definitions of *religion*, *spirituality*, *agnosticism*, and *atheism*. Trainers and teachers could offer students enrolled in multicultural diversity courses an option to research spirituality and religion as a project for the class. Possible topics are cited in the Spiritual/Religious Issues Seminar outline in the Resources section of this chapter.

Table 13.3   Developmental-Level Competencies III

READINESS LEVEL—ENTRY TO PROFESSIONAL PRACTICE		
Competencies		Learning Process and Activities
Knowledge	Knowledge of: • Literature on the relationship between S/R beliefs and mental and physical health; knowledge of the range of possible S/R client issues. • Major Western and Eastern religions and spiritual expressions, concepts, and vocabulary pertaining to the populations with which one works. • Beliefs and behaviors that are considered normative and healthy within client's religious tradition. • Community resources, including S/R leaders from various religions and faith traditions, spiritual healers, and psychotherapists specializing in S/R therapy. • Understanding that working with S/R beliefs is an aspect of multicultural counseling competency.	In the earlier stages of training, students solidified their professional knowledge base and attained appropriate values and attitudes while developing increasingly sophisticated clinical skills. At the level of Entry to Professional Practice, psychotherapists have attained the full range of competencies in the domains expected of all independent practitioners. Preparation for this level of competency takes place through closely supervised clinical work, augmented by professional reading, personal exploration, and training opportunities such as professional development and training seminars. Clinical supervisors observe students' clinical work, provide training in assessment, case conceptualization, and treatment planning, and challenge supervisees to examine their countertransference reactions, biases, and values to develop their supervisees' clinical competency with S/R issues.
Skills	Skills are demonstrated by the ability to: • Perform a basic assessment of clients' S/R beliefs and worldviews and to assess the relevance of S/R issues to therapy; assess for contraindications. • Diagnose and formulate appropriate treatment plans that are sensitive to the client's spiritual worldview, including how multiple systems and individual differences impact client. • Identify the limits of one's own competency with S/R issues and refer appropriately. • Form a trusting therapeutic relationship with clients so that clients may express S/R concerns if relevant and provide basic S/R therapeutic interventions. • Use supervision to enhance S/R skills. • Avoid S/R dual roles and boundary violations. • Establish effective consultation relationships with S/R leaders. • Create climate in which supervisees and trainees feel safe to talk about S/R issues.	Additional methods by which students can attain S/R competency at this level include: • Seeking opportunities to provide therapy to clients representing S/R diversity. • Supervision provided by supervisors knowledgeable and skilled in working with S/R issues. • Self-directed study and professional development opportunities. • Internship and postdoctoral seminar training in S/R issues. • Presenting and participating in clinical case conferences that include discussion of S/R aspects of cases.

READINESS LEVEL—ENTRY TO PROFESSIONAL PRACTICE	
Competencies	Learning Process and Activities
Values and Attitudes	Awareness of own spiritual worldview and associated biases, willingness to continually broaden self-knowledge, and commitment to expanding knowledge of S/R belief systems as part of multicultural competency enhancement.	

Table 13.4 Developmental-Level Competencies IV

READINESS LEVEL—ADVANCED PRACTICE AND SPECIALIZATION	
Competencies	Learning Process and Activities
Knowledge	Extensive knowledge of: • S/R literature. • Religious/spiritual faith development models. • Impact of S/R experiences upon human development. • Spiritual and religious belief traditions.	Psychotherapists who have a particular interest in S/R aspects of diversity as they apply to clinical work may seek to attain advanced levels of competency. Learning activities will vary depending on the psychotherapist's unique background, established competencies, and interest areas. For example, psychotherapists working in substance abuse treatment settings may wish to concentrate on spiritual interventions focused on this population. Similarly, psychotherapists working in a hospice setting may choose to focus on the S/R aspects of death and dying.
Skills	Advanced skills in: • Providing a variety of S/R interventions. • Integrating knowledge of S/R concepts (forgiveness, surrender, compassion, meaning and acceptance from both psychological and spiritual perspectives) into treatment. • Proactively sharing knowledge of S/R issues in the work setting with members of other mental health professions. • Performing differential diagnosis of mystical/religious experiences versus psychosis. • Differentiating between healthy and unhealthy spiritual expressions with full knowledge of the wide range of multiculturally appropriate expressions of S/R. • Addressing growth-restricting beliefs, cults, mind control, subjugation of members to a leader, and "religious addiction." • Providing effective supervision to trainees working with client S/R issues.	Regardless of the focus area, learning activities can include: • Professional reading (information about diverse S/R beliefs; empirical studies, and literature on theory and practice). • Teaching. • Attending and leading educational workshops. • Peer consultation groups. • Consultation with knowledgeable mental health professionals, S/R leaders, clergy, and spiritual directors. • Participation in unfamiliar S/R experiences (e.g., meditation, yoga, contemplative exercises, guided imagery, New Age practices, body work, chanting, expressive artwork and dance).
Values and Attitudes	Well-integrated values and attitudes demonstrated by the following: • Continually engages in broadening knowledge of S/R resources and for continuing professional development. • Actively cultivates relationships with S/R community leaders. • Involved in local and national groups and organizations relevant to S/R issues. • Independently and proactively provides ethical and legal consultation and supervision to trainees and other professionals. • Works for social justice to enhance understanding among individuals with different faith beliefs. • Independently monitors own S/R identity in relation to work with others with awareness and sensitivity to varying S/R belief systems.	

Table 13.5 Major World Religions

Beliefs	Islam	Buddhism	Hinduism	Christianity	Judaism	Native American Spirituality
View of Deity	One God, Allah, creator of all things in the universe. All powerful, all seeing, and all knowing. Each person is individually responsible to Allah.	Buddhists do not worship a God. Siddhartha Gautama became the Buddha ("the Enlightened One" in Sanskrit). People pray to good and evil deities.	There is One Supreme God with many forms (male and female, such as Vishnu and Shiva). Dharma is the cosmic law that directs all processes in the universe.	Holy Trinity: Father, Son, and Holy Spirit. God: All knowing, loving, Creator. Jesus is the messiah who died to atone for human sins and offer salvation.	One Supreme God, also called Jehovah or Yahweh, Creator, all knowing, all seeing, and all powerful.	The Sacred is an entity of infinite design and simplicity. It includes the natural elements, creatures, unseen powers, and source of life.
Beliefs and Tenets of the Religion	People are inherently good. Humans have free will to choose good or evil. Belief in predestination: Much is preordained by Allah. All are to follow the Five Pillars of Islam: profession of faith, ritual prayer five times/day with ritual cleansing, Ramadan fast, palmsgiving, and pilgrimage to Mecca.	Each person creates his or her own happiness and is the product of his or her own actions. Karma is created by positive and negative actions that determine the next life, or incarnation. Belief in the "middle way" or "all things in moderation," so asceticism is rejected. Follow the Eightfold Path.	Humans are divine and only need to uncover their illusions. All things are holy because they come from a single sacred source and are one. The world is full of change, struggle, and suffering. Belief in Karma, the law of cause and effect. Strong tradition in asceticism.	Only God's grace can free people from sin. Humans have free will and must choose good over evil. Christians are to follow the Ten Commandments and the teachings of the Gospels. God will provide for those who believe.	Jews were chosen by God to receive he divine law. There is a Covenant between God and the Jews: He would reward them if they kept His law, and would punish those who did not. Humans have free will to choose good over evil. Three forms of Judaism: Orthodox, Conservative, and Reform. Some see themselves as cultural Jews rather than religious Jews.	Each tribe has different traditions and practices regarding spirituality. Both tribal and Christian beliefs may be present. All believe in the importance of living in harmony with all things. Everything is created with a purpose to fulfill; none should interfere. Illness, distress, and problematic behaviors are caused by lack of harmony. Mind, body, spirit, and nature are a single unified entity.
View of Life after Death	Good and bad deeds will be reviewed by Allah on Judgment Day, and individuals are consigned to Paradise or to Hell.	Belief in reincarnation. Based upon accumulated Karma, assigned to a better new life or a worse one.	Belief in reincarnation. Based upon accumulated Karma, assigned to a better new life or a worse one.	Eternal life after death. After God's judgment, will be consigned to Heaven or Hell. Christians focus on life after death as the ultimate goal.	Souls of humans will be judged. Concept of an afterlife has many interpretations. Emphasis on living this life rather than focusing on the afterlife.	Some groups believe in reincarnation. Others believe that humans return as ghosts or that there is an afterworld.
Religious Practices	Prayer, meditation, and reading Holy writings. Restrictions: alcohol and products of swine and carrion. The Immam	Meditation, prayer offerings, working with guru, daily worship, participating in festivals and rituals.	Meditation, daily prayers, recital of mantras, chanting, charity, asceticism, pilgrimages, yoga	Living as a moral life, accepting Jesus and prayer brings one closer to God. Most denominations have two	Obeying God's commandments, living a worthy life, adhering to religious duties, doing good deeds, respecting	Use of rituals, ceremonies, and prayers to maintain and restore harmony. Shamans have *(continued)*

is the prayer leader in the mosque.	Prayer at shrines, temples, and family altars. Buddhists are vegetarians and do not kill any form of life.	practice, offerings (flowers, fruits, etc.,) and worship of deities. Devout Hindus do not kill any form of life as it may be a reincarnated soul.	sacraments: baptism and communion. Others (e.g. Catholic) include reconciliation ("confession"), confirmation, and marriage.	others, Orthodox Jews and some Conservatives keep Kosher (ritual slaughter, separation of meat and dairy, and not eating shellfish and pork products).	the knowledge and skills to access the Sacred. Vision Quest is a rite of passage for young men. Dancing, drumming, and chanting. Sweat lodges provide purification and religious renewal.
Views of Marriage, Divorce, Roles in Family, Sexuality Strongly interdependent, extended family structures. Collectivist. Premarital sex prohibited; birth control accepted. No abortion permitted after the fetus is at 120 days gestation (when the soul enters the fetus). Divorce is undesirable. Homosexuality is prohibited. Situational homosexual behavior may have occurred due to separation of the sexes. Polygamy permitted conditionally for men but is less common in modern life.	Civil marriage, not religious. Divorce not prohibited. Premarital sex not explicitly banned but beliefs may vary by culture. As there is a strong prohibition against causing any type of harm or suffering, abortion is not accepted. Individuals make their own choices and accept the accompanying Karma. View on homosexuality is unclear. If divorce occurs, individuals should accept suffering, avoid anger, and feel compassion for the partner.	Marriage is a sacrament and a religious duty—alliance between families. Marriage arranged. Traditional Hindu families are patriarchal. In India, selective abortion may be performed. Premarital sex not condoned. Caste system determines suitable marriage partners, social roles, and type of work. Ancient Hindu texts refer to homosexuality as acceptable; in current culture, there is a negative attitude towards homosexuality.	Fundamentalist Christians, Evangelicals, and Catholics do not condone divorce, abortion, or premarital sex, and they believe that homosexual acts are sinful. They may also have more traditional gender-role beliefs. Many liberal Protestant churches are more accepting of premarital sex, birth control, abortion, homosexuality, and divorce.	Views about gender roles, sexuality, and GLB issues depend on the level of orthodoxy. Jewish law prohibits abortion except when the mother's life is endangered. Divorce can be accepted. Orthodox and Conservative movements require a divorce according to Jewish law in addition to civil divorce. Some Reform congregations support outreach to gays and lesbians, including ordination and commitment ceremonies.	Strong extended family with fluid boundaries. Children may live with extended family members at different times. Discipline of children a shared responsibility of family members. Divorce and remarriage are accepted. Varying gender roles; some groups are patriarchal, others are matriarchal.

Sources:

Dwairy, M. (2006). *Counseling and psychotherapy with Arabs and Muslims; A culturally sensitive approach.* New York: Teachers College Press.

Frame, M. W. (2003). *Integrating Religion and Spirituality Into Counseling: A comprehensive approach.* Pacific Grove, CA: Brooks/Cole.

Levinson, D., (Ed.) (1996). *Religion: A Cross-Cultural Encyclopedia.* Santa Barbara: ABC-CLIO, Inc.

Molloy, M. (2008). *Experiencing the World's Religions; Tradition, Challenge, and Change.* (4th ed.). Boston: McGraw Hill.

Onedera, J. D., (Ed.). (2008). *The Role of Religion in Marriage and Family Counseling.* New York: Routledge.

Richards, P. S., & Bergin, A. E. (Eds.). (2000). *Handbook of psychotherapy and religious diversity.* Washington, DC: American Psychological Association.

Richards, P. S., & Bergin, A. E. (2005). *A spiritual strategy for counseling and psychotherapy.* (2nd ed.). Washington, D.C.: American Psychological Association.

Rye, M. S., Pargament, K. I., Ali, M. A., Beck, G. L., Dorff, E. N., Hallisey, C., et al. (2000). Religious perspectives on forgiveness. In M. E. McCullough, K. I. Pargament, & C. E. Thoresen (Eds.), *Forgiveness: Theory, research & practice.* New York: Guilford Press.

REFERENCES

Allport, G. W. (1952). *The individual and his religion*. New York: Macmillan.

American Association of Marriage and Family Therapists. (2001). *Code of ethics*. Retrieved October 24, 2008, from http://www.aamft.org/resources/lrm_plan/Ethics/ethicscode2001.asp

American Counseling Association. (2005). *ACA code of ethics*. Alexandria, VA: Author.

American Psychiatric Association. (2000). *Diagnostic and statistical manual of mental disorders*, Fourth Edition, [text revision]. Washington, DC: Author.

American Psychiatric Association. (2001). *Code of medical ethics*. Arlington, VA: Author.

American Psychological Association. (2002). *Guidelines for providers of psychological services to ethnic, linguistic, and culturally diverse populations*. Retrieved December 14, 2009, from http://www.apa.org/pi/oema/guide.html

American Psychological Association. (2002a). Guidelines on multicultural education, training, research, practice and organizational change for psychologists. *American Psychologist, 58*(5), 377–402.

American Psychological Association. (2002b). *Ethical principles of psychologists and code of ethics*. Retrieved October 24, 2008, from http://www.apa.org/ethics/.

American Psychological Association Council of Representatives. (2007, August). Resolution on religious, religion-based and/or religion-derived prejudice. Retrieved March 12, 2010, from http://www.apa.org/about/governance/council/policy/religiousdiscrimination.pdf

Arredondo, P., & Glauner, T. (1992). *Personal dimensions of identity model*. Boston: Empowerment Workshops.

Assessment of Competency Benchmarks Work Group: Competencies Benchmark Document. (2007). *American Psychological Association Board of Educational Affairs in collaboration with the Council of Chairs of Training Councils*. Retrieved October 28, 2008, from http://www.apa.org/ed/graduate/comp_bench mark.pdf

Association for Counselor Education and Supervision. (2005). *Ethical guidelines for counseling supervisors*. Retrieved January 11, 2010 from http://www.acesonline.net/ethical_guidelines.asp

Association of Spiritual, Ethical and Religious Values in Counseling (ASERVIC). (Revised 2009). Competencies for addressing spiritual and religious issues in counseling. Retrieved May 26, 2010, from http://aservic.org/?pageid=133

Aten, J. D., & Hernandez, B. C. (2004). Addressing religion in clinical supervision: A model. *Psychotherapy: Theory, Research, Practice, Training, 41*(2), 152–160.

Aten, J. D., & Leach, M. M. (Eds.). (2009). *Spirituality and the therapeutic process: a comprehensive resource from intake to termination*. Washington, DC: American Psychological Association.

Atkinson, D. R., & Hackett, G. (1998). *Counseling diverse populations* (2nd ed.). Boston: McGraw Hill.

Bartoli, E. (2007). Religious and spiritual issues in psychotherapy practice: Training the trainer. *Psychotherapy: Theory, Research, Practice, Training, 44* (1), 54–65.

Bartoli, E., & Gillem, A. R. (2008). Continuing to depolarize the debate on sexual orientation and religion: Identity and the therapeutic process. *Professional Psychology: Research and Practice, 39*(2), 202–209.

Bergin, A. E. (1980). Psychotherapy and religious values. *Journal of Consulting and Clinical Psychology, 48*, 75–105.

Bergin, A. E. (1991). Values and religious issues in psychotherapy and mental health. *American Psychologist, 46*, 394–403.

Bergin, A. E., & Jensen, J. P. (1990). Religiosity of psychotherapists: A national survey. *Psychotherapy: Theory, Research, Practice, Training [Special Issue]: Psychotherapy and Religion, 27*(1), 3–7.

Bernard, J. M. (1997). The discrimination model. In C. E. Watkins, Jr. (Ed.), *Handbook of psychotherapy supervision* (pp. 310–327).

Bishop, D. R., Avila-Juarbe, E., & Thumme, B. (2003). Recognizing spirituality as an important factor in counselor supervision: Issues and insights. *Counseling and Values, 48*(1), 34–46.

Brawer, P. A., Handal, P. J., Fabricatore, R. R., & Wajda-Johnston, V. A. (2002). Training and education in religion/spirituality within APA-accredited clinical psychology programs. *Professional Psychology: Research and Practice, 33*(2), 203–206.

Burke, M. T., Chauvin, J. C., & Miranti, J. G. (2005). *Religious and spiritual issues in counseling: Applications across diverse populations*. New York: Brunner-Routledge.

Cervantes, J. M., & Parham, T. A. (2005). Toward a meaningful spirituality for people of color: Lessons for the counseling practitioner. *Cultural Diversity and Ethnic Minority Psychology, 11*(1), 69–81.

Constantine, M. G. (1999). Spiritual and religious issues in counseling racial and ethnic minority populations: An introduction to the special issue. *Journal of Multicultural Counseling and Development, 27*(4), 179–181.

Council for Accreditation of Counseling and Related Educational Programs (CACREP). (2001). *Standards for counselor preparation*. [Accreditation manual]. Alexandria, VA: Author.

Das, A. K. (1987). Indigenous models of therapy in traditional Asian societies. *Journal of Multicultural Counseling and Development. 15*(1), 25–37.

Delaney, H. D., Miller, W. R., & Bisono, A. M. (2007). Religiosity and spirituality among psychologists: A survey of clinician members of the American Psychological Association. *Professional Psychology: Research and Practice, 38*, 538–546.

Dwairy, M. (2006). *Counseling and psychotherapy with Arabs and Muslims: A culturally sensitive approach*. New York: Teachers College Press.

Eck, B. E. (2002). An exploration of the therapeutic use of spiritual disciplines in clinical practice. *Journal of Psychology and Christianity, 21*, 266–280.

Ellis, A. (2000). Can rational emotive behavior therapy (REBT) be effectively used with people who have devout beliefs in God and religion? *Professional Psychology: Research and Practice, 31*, 29–33.

Fouad, N. A., & Arredondo, P. (2007). *Becoming culturally oriented: Practical advice for psychologists and educators*. Washington, DC: American Psychological Association.

Fowler, J. W. (1995). *Stages of faith: The psychology of human development and the quest for meaning*. New York: Harper Collins.

Frame, M. W. (2003). *Integrating religion and spirituality into counseling: A comprehensive approach*. Pacific Grove, CA: Brooks/Cole.

Frazier, R. E., & Hansen, N. D. (2009). Religious/spiritual psychotherapy behaviors: Do we do what we believe to be important? *Professional Psychology: Research and Practice, 40*(1), 81–87.

Fukuyama, M., & Sevig, T. (1999). *Integrating spirituality into multicultural counseling*. Thousand Oaks, CA: Sage.

Gall, T., Charbonneau, C., Clark, N., Grant, K., Joseph, A. & Shouldice, L. (2005). Understanding the nature and role of spirituality in relation to coping and health: A conceptual framework. *Canadian Psychology, 46*(2), 88–104.

Gallup, G., Jr. (1998). *Religion in America*. Princeton, NJ: Princeton Religious Research Center.

Gallup, G. Jr. (2008). *Religion and social trends*. [The Gallup Organization.] Wilmington, DC. Retrieved October 24, 2008, from http://www.gallup.com/poll/1690/Religion.aspx

Gallup, G., Jr., & Johnson, B. R. (2003, January 28). *New index tracks "Spiritual State of the Union."* [The Gallup Organization.] Wilmington, DC: Scholarly Resources. Retrieved April 12, 2007, from http://www.gallup.com/poll/tb/religValue/20030128.asp#rm

Gladding, S. T. (1995). Creativity in counseling. *Counseling and Human Development, 28*, 1–12.

Golston, S. S., Savage, J. S., & Cohen, M. C. (1998). Internship training practices regarding religious and spiritual issues. Paper presented at the 106th Annual Convention of the American Psychological Association.

Gonsiorek, J. C. (2009). Ethical challenges incorporating spirituality and religion into psychotherapy. *Professional Psychology: Research and Practice, 40*(4), 385–389.

Gorusch, R. L., & Miller, W. R. (1999). Assessing spirituality. In W. R. Miller (Ed.), *Integrating spirituality into treatment* (pp. 47–64). Washington, DC: American Psychological Association.

Hage, S. M. (2006). A closer look at the role of spirituality in psychology training programs. *Professional Psychology: Research and Practice, 37*(3), 303–310.

Hatcher, R. L., & Dudley Lassiter, K. (2007). Initial training in professional psychology: The practicum competencies outline. *Training and Education in Professional Psychology, 1*(1), 49–63.

Helmeke, K. B., & Sori, C. (2006). *The therapist's notebook for integrating spirituality into counseling: Homework, handouts and activities for use in psychotherapy, Vols. 1 and 2*. Birmingham, NY: Haworth Press.

Hodge, D. R. (2004). Spirituality and people with mental illness: Developing spiritual competency in assessment and intervention. *Families in Society, 85*(1), 36–44.

Ho, D. Y., & Ho, R. T. (2007). Measuring spirituality and spiritual emptiness; toward ecumenicity and transcultural applicability. *Review of General Psychology, 11*(3), 62–74.

James, W. (1936). *The varieties of religious experience*. New York: Modern Library.

Johnson, W. B., Ridley, C. R., & Nielsen, S. R. (2000). Religiously sensitive rational emotive behavior therapy: Elegant solutions and ethical risks. *Professional Psychology: Research and Practice, 31*, 14–20.

Jones, S. L. (1994). A constructive relationship for religion with the science and profession of psychology: Perhaps the boldest model yet. *American Psychologist, 49,* 184–199.

Josephson, A. M., & Peteet, J. R. (2004). *Handbook of spirituality and worldview in clinical practice.* Arlington, VA: American Psychiatric Publishing.

Kelly, E. W. (1990). Counselor responsiveness to client religiousness. *Counseling and Values, 35,* 69–72.

Kelly, E. W. (1995). *Spirituality and religion in counseling and psychotherapy: Diversity in theory and practice.* Alexandria, VA: American Counseling Association.

Koenig, H. G. (1994). *Aging and God: Spiritual pathways to mental health in midlife and later years.* New York: Haworth Pastoral Press.

Lease, S. H., Horne, S. G., & Noffsinger-Frazier, N. (2005). Affirming faith experiences and psychological health for Caucasian lesbian, gay and bisexual individuals. *Journal of Counseling Psychology, 52*(3), 378–388.

Levinson, D. (Ed.). (1996). *Religion: A cross-cultural encyclopedia.* Santa Barbara: ABC-CLIO.

Maslow, A. H. (1968). *Toward a psychology of being.* New York: Van Nostrand.

McMinn, M. R., Ruiz, J. N., Marx, D., Wright, J. B., & Gilbert, N. B. (2006). Professional psychology and the doctrines of sin and grace: Christian leaders' perspectives. *Professional Psychology: Research and Practice, 37*(3), 295–302.

McNeill, B. W. & Cervantes, J. M. (Eds.). (2008). *Latina/o healing practices: Mestizo and indigenous perspectives.* New York, Routledge/Taylor & Francis.

Meadow, M. J., & Kahoe, R. D. (1984). *Psychology of religion: Religion in individual lives.* New York: Harper & Row.

Miller, W. R. (Ed.). (1999). *Integrating spirituality into treatment.* Washington DC: American Psychological Association.

Miller, W. R., & Thoresen, C. E. (1999). Spirituality and health. In W. R. Miller (Ed.), *Integrating spirituality into treatment* (p. 318). Washington DC: American Psychological Association.

Molloy, M. (2008). *Experiencing the world's religions: Tradition, challenge, and change* (4th ed.). Boston: McGraw Hill.

Myers, J. E., & Williard, K. (2003). Integrating spirituality into counselor preparation: A developmental wellness approach. *Counseling and Values, 47*(2), 142–155.

National Association of Social Workers. (2008). Code of Ethics. *National Association of Social Workers.* Retrieved on January 11, 2010 from http://www.socialworkers.org/pubs/code/code.asp

Onedera, J. D. (Ed.). (2008). *The role of religion in marriage and family counseling.* New York: Routledge.

Pargament, K. I. (1997). *The psychology of religion and coping.* New York: Guilford Press.

Pargament, K. I. (1999). The psychology of religion and spirituality? Yes and no. *International Journal for the Psychology of Religion, 9,* 3–16.

Pargament, K. I. (2002). The bitter and the sweet: An evaluation of the costs and benefits of religiousness. *Psychological Inquiry, 13*(3), 168–181.

Pate, R. H., & High, H. J. (1995). The importance of client religious beliefs and practices in the education of counselors in CACREP-accredited programs. *Counseling and Values, 40,* 2–5.

Pew Forum on Religion and Public Life. (2008). *U.S. religious landscape survey: Final reports.* Retrieved January 4, 2010 from http://religions.pewforum.org/reports

Polanski, P. J. (2003). Spirituality in supervision. *Counseling and Values, 47*(2), 131–141.

Poll, J. B., & Smith, T. B. (2003). The spiritual self: toward a conceptualization of spiritual identity development. *Journal of Psychology and Theology, 31*(2), 129–142.

Richards, P. S. (2009). Toward religious and spiritual competence for psychologists: Some reflections and recommendations. *Professional Psychology: Research and Practice, 40*(4), 389–391.

Richards, P. S., & Bergin, A. E. (1997). *A spiritual strategy for counseling and psychotherapy.* Washington, DC: American Psychological Association.

Richards, P. S., & Bergin, A. E. (2000). *Handbook of psychotherapy and religious diversity.* Washington, DC: American Psychological Association.

Richards, P. S., & Bergin, A. E. (2003). *Casebook for a spiritual strategy in counseling and psychotherapy.* Washington, DC: American Psychological Association.

Richards, P. S., & Bergin, A. E. (2005). *A spiritual strategy for counseling and psychotherapy* (2nd ed.). Washington, DC: American Psychological Association.

Rodolfa, E. R., Bent, R., Eisman, E., Nelson, P., Rehm, L., & Ritchie, P. (2005). A cube model for competency development: Implications for psychology educators and regulators. *Professional Psychology: Research and Practice, 36*(4), 347–354.

Rose, E. M., Westefeld, J. S., & Ansley, T. N. (2001). Spiritual issues in counseling: Clients' beliefs and preferences. *Journal of Counseling Psychology, 48*(1), 61–71.

Russell, S. R., & Yarhouse, M. A. (2006). Training in religion/spirituality within APA-accredited psychology predoctoral internships. *Professional Psychology: Research and Practice, 37*(4), 430–436.

Rye, M. S., Pargament, K. I., Ali, M. A., Beck, G. L., Dorff, E. N., Hallisey, C., et al. (2000). Religious perspectives on forgiveness. In M. E. McCullough, K. I. Pargament, & C. E. Thoresen (Eds.), *Forgiveness: Theory, research & practice*. New York: Guilford Press.

Schulte, D. L., Skinner, T. A., & Claiborn, C. D. (2002). Religious and spiritual issues in counseling psychology training. *The Counseling Psychologist, 30*(1), 118–134.

Shafranske, E. (2000). Religious involvement and professional practices of psychiatrists and other mental health professionals. *Psychiatric Annals, 30*, 525–532.

Sperry, L. (2000). Spirituality and psychiatry: Incorporating the spiritual dimension into clinical practice. *Psychiatric Annals, 30*(8), 518–523.

Sperry, L., & Shafranske, E. (Eds.) (2005). *Spirituality-oriented psychotherapy*. Washington, DC: American Psychological Association.

Steen, R. L., Engels, D., & Thweatt, W. T. III. (2006). Ethical aspects of spirituality in counseling. *Counseling and Values, 50*(2), 108–118.

Stoltenberg, C. D., & Delworth, U. (1987) *Supervising counselors and therapists*. San Francisco: Jossey-Bass.

Sue, D. W., Arredondo, P., & McDavis, R. J. (1992). Multicultural counseling competencies and standards: A call to the profession. *Journal of Counseling and Development, 70*, 477–483.

Sue, D. W., & Sue, S. (2007). *Counseling the culturally diverse: Theory and practice* (5th ed.). Hoboken, NJ: Wiley.

Worthington, E. L., Jr. (1989). Religious faith across the life span: Implications for counseling and research. *The Counseling Psychologist, 17*, 515–612.

Yarhouse, M., & Van Orman, B. (1999). When psychologists work with religious clients: Applications of the general principles of ethical conduct. *Professional Psychology: Research and Practice, 30*(6), 557–562.

Young, J. S., Cashwell, C., Wiggins-Frame, M., & Belaire, C. (2002). Spiritual and religious competencies: A national survey of CACREP-accredited programs. *Counseling and Values, 47*(1), 22–33.

Zinnbauer, B. J., Pargament, K. I., Cole, B., Rye, M. S., Butter, E. M., Blavich, T. G., et al. (1997). Religion and spirituality: Unfuzzying the fuzzy. *Journal for the Scientific Study of Religion, 36*, 549.

CHAPTER 14

COUNSELING COMPETENCY WITH TRANSGENDER AND INTERSEX PERSONS

ANNELIESE A. SINGH, CYNTHIA J. BOYD, and JOY S. WHITMAN

INTRODUCTION

> "I just want a therapist who 'gets' me. I don't want to have to explain gender, sex, and all that other stuff. I have been to so many therapists where I have to educate them.
> I have to tell them first that I am not a 'freak.' Then, I have to make sure they feel comfortable. And then we get down to my real issues."
>
> —LUKE, 21-YEAR-OLD TRANSGENDER MAN

As this quote illustrates, there remains a lack of mental health practitioner competency with transgender and intersex issues. More often than not, transgender and intersex clients find themselves in the position of educating their mental health practitioners about their identity in order to feel safe and understood in counseling environments (Pickering, 2005). Indeed, mental health practitioners who are adequately trained to work with transgender and intersex issues are few and far between (Chen-Hayes, 2001; Singh, Hays, & Watson, in press). As the numbers of transgender and intersex people seeking treatment continues to rise across school, community, and university counseling settings (Zucker, Bradley, Owen-Anderson, Kibblewhite, & Cantor, 2008), the absence of well-trained mental health practitioners on these issues becomes an increasingly serious training concern for the field of counseling and psychology. Because transgender and intersex people commonly face societal discrimination and misunderstanding of their gender identity and expression (Carroll, Gilroy, & Ryan, 2002; Clements-Nolle, Marx, & Katz, 2006; Patton, 2007), it is important that mental health practitioners are aware of the impact of this prejudice on their mental wellbeing. In addition, there is a wide range of body modifications (e.g., hormonal treatment, surgical options) transgender and intersex people may (or may not) need, desire, or select to bring their internal and external sense of gender into alignment. In these situations, there are standards (Meyer et al., 2001) that require transgender and intersex clients to work with a mental health practitioner before engaging in desired treatments, making the need for practitioners well-versed in transgender and intersex issues critical.

This chapter addresses identities located along both the biologically influenced continuum of sex identity and the more socially constructed continuum of gender identity and expression. Previously understood to be dichotomous and fixed, research and experience have informed current thinking by elucidating the more fluid nature of sex and gender (Berenbaum, 2006; Fausto-Sterling, 2000). These constructs together are reflective of a broad range of human experiences, identities, and expressions. The importance of understanding the issues salient to these particular identities cannot be understated, as every individual who presents for therapy either explicitly or implicitly holds sex and gender identities that are located along these continua and has internalized related societal messages (Sausa, 2005; Singh et al., in press).

The purpose of this chapter is to provide mental health practitioners, students, educators, and supervisors with guidelines and resources to work toward developing practice and training competency with transgender and intersex concerns in counseling. The chapter opens with an overview of the knowledge mental health practitioners should have when working with transgender and intersex clients, including: important terminology and history; potential challenges to providing affirmative treatment; and existing professional guidelines. Next, the chapter provides an overview of the skills necessary when working with transgender and intersex people in counseling practice (e.g., individual, family counseling) in order to provide affirmative and ethical treatment. Then, the critical values and attitudes mental health practitioners should develop in working with transgender people are reviewed, in addition to advocacy efforts mental health practitioners may engage in to improve counseling practice and societal environments for transgender and intersex people. Case vignettes are provided to bring alive the complexity involved in working with transgender and intersex clients. Finally, there are both significant similarities and differences in the issues transgender and intersex people face, and they are noted throughout the chapter.

TRANSGENDER AND INTERSEX 101: DEFINING IMPORTANT TERMS AND USING APPROPRIATE LANGUAGE

Developing competency in working with issues of sex and gender identity may feel overwhelming at first, as there are many concepts to define and understand. While several of these definitions are discussed in this section, the reader is also referred to the charts for summaries of important terms.

With both transgender and intersex people, mental health practitioners should first be aware of the difference between the terms *sex* and *gender* (Carroll et al., 2002). While one's sex refers to the physiological determinants of "male" and "female," gender refers to one's understanding of being masculine or feminine and/or aspects of both masculinity and femininity. Separate from but related to sex and sex identity, *gender* is defined by society and reflects the social norms of what is considered to be feminine and masculine. Often confused with biological sex, gender is not tied to anatomy. Gender identity is the interplay of the internalization of society's instructions and an innate sense of one's location along the gender continuum (Mallon, 1999). This perception of self may or may not be consistent with the gender role that society has assigned to one's biological sex.

Though gender identity is an internal psychological construct, there is a social aspect to gender as well (Korrell & Lorah, 2007). It is expressed outwardly in a variety of ways, including through clothing, hairstyles, mannerisms, ways of speaking, chosen jobs or careers, hobbies, and interpersonal styles. This communication may be purposeful or accidental, may transform over time or depend on situational variables, and may or may not be congruent with one's internal sense of gender identity.

There has been a longstanding emphasis in the field on viewing gender and sex as central organizing principles for identity development (Davidson, 2007). Therefore, practitioners and theorists have developed theories and interventions that are based substantially on the sex and gender of the individual, but often narrowly, with regard only to the binary sex and gender identities of male/masculine and female/feminine (Sanchez & Vilain, 2009). This focus has highlighted that gender and sex influence how individuals experience the world both intrapersonally and interpersonally, but the binary conceptualization of gender is insufficient to describe the full range of human experience (Davidson, 2007). Gender identities and expressions are complex and can be described in myriad ways, including feminine, masculine, androgynous, transgender, gender queer, gender nonconforming, and gender bending. For transgender and intersex people in particular, the societal assignment of gender to one's sex, which typically occurs at birth, may be problematic, as these individuals may have gender-variant expression and/or physiology that does not conform to the rigid binary conceptions of sex and gender (Dreger, 1999; Sausa, 2005).

Transgender

Transgender is an umbrella term that refers to individuals whose gender identity transgresses traditional definitions of "male" and "female." Many of these individuals experience themselves as a gender other than the one to which they have been assigned. The word *assigned* is used to recognize that medical professionals and society at large typically assume a gender identity based on chromosomes and secondary sex characteristics. The individual is then referred to as having a certain gender, even though the assignment may not match the person's internal gender identity.

Mental health practitioners should also be aware that transgender people may choose to use words such as *tranny* in their community as a word of empowerment, but it is not appropriate for those outside the transgender community to use this term (due to its use often as a derogatory term by the lesbian, gay, bisexual, transgender, queer (LGBTQ) and heterosexual communities), unless they are given specific permission. No matter how a transgender person expresses gender, it is the mental health practitioner's role to normalize the wide range of gender expression as a natural variation of humankind. In addition, mental health practitioners should be aware of and able to communicate to the client the recognition that the language and terms underneath the transgender umbrella continue to evolve and grow in order to support clients in finding terms that best fit their own conceptions of their gender.

Especially when working with youth, mental health practitioners may find that clients identify primarily with the term *transgender*, but do not desire or choose to have hormonal or surgical body modifications. Increasingly, mental health practitioners may work with college-aged students who identify as *genderqueer*—meaning that they reject the very idea of gender itself and the societal accoutrements that are assigned through the gender binary. There are also transgender clients who prefer the use of pronouns such as *hir* and *ze*, as opposed to *her* and *he*, to refer to themselves in recognition that traditional gender binary pronouns do not fit their gender identity. Other transgender people have reclaimed the word *boy*, and self-identify as a *boi* or *tranny-boi* to acknowledge gender fluidity and their transgender identity, in addition to their reclaiming of the word *boy* (Carroll, 2010).

To better describe the development of a transgender identity, Bockting and Coleman (2007) identified a transgender identity development model that includes the following stages: (a) Pre-coming Out, (b) Coming Out, (c) Exploration, (d) Intimacy, and (e) Identity Integration. In the first stage, individuals experience cross-gender feelings but have not yet named it as such. As a result, it might be characterized by a sense of social isolation and fear that is exacerbated by the social stigma associated with gender nonconformity. In the second stage, individuals come out to themselves and others, risking rejection and allowing for possible acceptance and connection. In the third stage, individuals invest in exploring the community, self, and resources, which is followed by the fourth stage of intimacy that is achieved when authentic connections with the community and allies are formed. The pride that is generated in the fourth stage leads to the final stage of integrating public and private identities into a positive self-image.

Transsexual

Underneath the transgender umbrella is transsexuality. The term *transsexual* refers to individuals who may seek hormones and/or surgery to bring their bodies into closer conformity with their self-identified gender (Mallon, 1999). Persons assigned "male" at birth, but who identify as women, may define themselves as *male-to-female* (or *MtF*). Similarly, *female-to-males* (or *FtMs*) are assigned "female" at birth, but identify as men. Whereas transgender individuals may not choose to alter their appearance or anatomy in anyway, the defining characteristic of transsexuality is a felt imperative to alter one's body and/or gender expression (Diamond, 2002). Many individuals who can be categorized as transsexual according to the above definition never use the term for themselves because, instead, they identify simply according to their internal experience of themselves as male or female. Especially following the use of hormones or surgery, since one's body is then a congruent representation of the individual's gender identity, the term *transsexual* can feel inaccurate, disrespectful, or diminishing (Lev, 2004).

Sex-reassignment surgery and hormone therapy are substantiated in the literature as effective interventions for transsexuals who want to pursue body modification (Smith, Van Goozen, Kuiper, & Cohen-Kettenis, 2005). For many transsexuals, hormone therapy is the first step toward body modification; for some, it is the only major medical intervention. Hormone therapy can serve many purposes for a transsexual, resulting in both physical and psychological reduction of tension. It does so by diminishing secondary sex characteristics of the original sex and augments the development of secondary sex characteristics of the preferred sex (Brown & Rounsley, 1996). For example, administration of synthetic testosterone may induce growth of facial hair and deepening of the voice for FtM transsexuals, whereas the administration of estrogen may induce breast development and increased fat deposits around the hips and thighs for MtF transsexuals (deVries, Cohen-Kettenis, & Delemarre-van de Waal, 2006). As a result, the person's sense of self and well-being may be increased as the person's internal and external experience of his or her gender becomes more aligned (Sobralske, 2005).

Additionally, in a study of 325 participants by Smith et al. (2005), sex-reassignment surgery resulted in an absence of gender dysphoria for the entire after-treatment group. There have been major advancements in the techniques used for both MtF and FtM surgeries, with very positive outcomes and few complications (Krueger, Yekani, Hundt, & Daverio, 2007; Spehr, 2007).

Devor (2004) proposed a model of transsexual identity development to elucidate the possible experiences of exploration, understanding, and acceptance. Underlying the model are the two concepts of *witnessing* and *mirroring*. The desire to be witnessed by others in the manner in which the individual wishes to be seen, is a core need in this process. Having an unacknowledged component of identity makes it difficult to integrate and so this external and objective validation is understood to be critical to identity development. Mirroring is the experience of relating to someone with a similar identity, and therefore seeing oneself in another. Mental health practitioners can be instrumental both in witnessing the authentic identity of the client and in assisting the client in identifying and connecting with the transgender community. The importance of obtaining balanced information and finding a supportive community is paramount in the process of healthy identity formation. Holding negative views of the transsexual community and beliefs that a transsexual identity will necessarily result in a negative outcome has been shown to be correlated with higher levels of psychological distress in male-to-female transsexuals (Sanchez & Vilain, 2009).

The stages posited are the following: (a) abiding anxiety regarding a pervasive sense of feeling different, (b) identity confusion about originally assigned gender and sex, (c) identity comparisons about originally assigned gender and sex, (d) discovery of transsexualism, (e) identity confusion about transsexualism, (f) identity comparisons about transsexualism, (g) tolerance of transsexual identity, (h) delay before acceptance of transsexual identity, (i) acceptance of transsexualism identity, (j) delay before transition, (k) transition, (l) acceptance of post-transition gender and sex identities, (m) integration, and (n) pride.

TRANSGENDER: DEFINITIONS AND TERMS

Cis-Gender   A "match" between one's sex assigned at birth and one's gender identity, behavior, and expression. A "non-transgender" person; a useful term to help explore non-transgender privilege.

Cross-Dresser   A person who occasionally wears clothing considered typical for another gender, but who does not necessarily desire to change gender. Reasons for cross-dressing can range from a need to express a feminine or masculine side to attainment of erotic gratification. Cross-dressers can be of any sexual orientation. Many cross-dressers identify as heterosexual.

Drag King/Drag Queen   Wearing the clothing of another gender, often involving the presentation of exaggerated, stereotypical gender characteristics. Individuals may identify as drag kings (female in drag) or drag queens (male in drag) when performing gender as parody, art, or entertainment.

Female   A term assigned to a person at birth whose sex produces ova and has traditionally defined anatomy (e.g., vagina, uterus) and chromosomal (XX) makeup of a girl.

FTM (Female to Male)   A term used to identify a person assigned a female gender at birth (or who is female-bodied) and who identifies as a male, lives as a man, or identifies as masculine.

Gender   A social construct based on a group of emotional and psychological characteristics that classify an individual as feminine, masculine, androgynous, or other. Gender can be understood to have several components, including gender identity, gender expression, and gender role.

Gender Identity   The inner sense of being a man, a male, a woman, a female, both, neither, butch, femme, two-spirit, bi-gender, or another configuration of gender. Gender identity usually matches with one's physical anatomy but sometimes does not. Gender identity includes one's sense of self and the image that one presents to the world.

Genderqueer/Fluid Gender   A term used by some people who may or may not fit on the spectrum of trans, or be labeled as trans, but who identify their gender and sexual orientation to be somewhere on the continuum in between or outside the binary gender system altogether.

Male   A term assigned to a person at birth whose sex produces spermatozoa and refers to traditionally defined anatomy (e.g., penis, scrotum) and chromosomal makeup (XY) of a boy.

MTF (Male to Female)   A term used to identify a person assigned a male gender at birth (or who is male-bodied) and who identifies as a female, lives as a woman, or identifies as feminine.

Passing   A term used to refer to describe the process by which transgender persons' gender identity is perceived in a way that is consistent with their experience of their gender identity.

Transgender or Trans   A term used to describe those who transgress social gender norms; often used as an umbrella term to include transsexual, genderqueer, gender nonconforming, cross-dressers, and so on. People must self-identify as transgender in order for the term to be appropriately used to describe them.

Transsexuals   Persons who experience intense, persistent, long-term discomfort with their body and self-image due to the belief that their assigned gender is inappropriate. They may then take steps to adapt or change their body, gender role, and gender expression to achieve what they know their true gender to be.

Source: Lambda Legal (2008). *Bending the mold: An action kit for transgender students.*

Intersex

The Intersex Society of North America (2008) defines *intersex* as "a general term used for a variety of conditions in which a person is born with a reproductive or sexual anatomy that doesn't seem to fit the typical definitions of female or male" (p. 1). Broadly speaking, intersexuality constitutes a range of anatomical conditions in which an individual's anatomy or chromosomes are some combination of male and female (Diamond, 2002). Individuals are often described as intersex if they cannot be easily categorized as male or female, so there is no one common set of biological traits used to distinguish the intersex community. Instead, the central experience shared by this population is the medicalization or pathologizing of their anatomy (Fausto-Sterling, 2000). Most individuals whose anatomy fits this description identify themselves as male, female, or transgender, not as intersex.

The physiological manifestations of intersexuality are varied. For instance, it could be that the individual's genitals are male, but the reproductive organs include ovaries. It is also possible that the external genitalia appear to be somewhere in between what is commonly viewed to be male or female, as in a large clitoris, small penis, or a scrotum that is divided so that it looks like labia. There is little consensus, however, on what constitutes "key" or "essential" female and male anatomy, and so the decision to label an individual as intersex, male, or female is always socially and culturally influenced (Fausto-Sterling, 2000). The incidence is therefore difficult to determine, because it depends on the definition used. It is estimated that 1 in 2000 individuals are born with sex chromosomes, external genitalia, or an internal reproductive system that is not considered to be standard for either males or females (Preeves, 2003).

The practice of surgically altering the genitalia of intersex infants was endorsed in a news release by the American Academy of Pediatrics in 1996. It is consistent with the work of John Money (1973), who held that gender identity is taught and arises primarily from psychosocial rearing (nurture), and not directly from biology (nature). Money asserted that all children must have their gender identity fixed very early in life for a consistent, "successful" gender identity to form. He also argued that from very early in life a child's anatomy must match the "standard" anatomy for her or his gender. In his view, for gender identity to form psychosocially, boys primarily require adequate penises with no vagina, and girls primarily require a vagina with no easily noticeable phallus. This approach necessitates secrecy on the part of parents and medical personnel in order to successfully convince the patient and community of the assigned gender role, as it is assumed that any anatomical variation expressed will yield poor results.

Though medical professionals disagree about whether early surgery is justified and warranted, many current medical approaches advocate for surgery in newborns only in cases where functionality is impaired. It has been noted that performing surgery for cosmetic rather than functional reasons, in order to relieve parental distress or enhance parent–child attachment, has not proven to be effective (Hughes, Houk, Ahmed, & Lee, 2006). Moreover, to focus on and engage in the exterior alteration of the sex of an intersex individual is ethically questionable when the interior emotional life of this individual is neglected (Morland, 2008). It should also be noted that in 2004, the American Counseling Association (ACA) passed a resolution to protect intersex children from unwanted surgery, secrecy, and shame.

An antiquated—and currently incorrect—term that was historically used to describe intersex people is *hermaphrodite*. Similarly, language referring to genitalia as "ambiguous" has lost favor (due to its pathologizing of intersex people); rather, best practice is to use words such as *atypical* (Rosario, 2006, p. 94). Feder and Karkazis (2008) question the more recent use of nomenclature such as *disorders of sex development (DSD)* to refer to intersex conditions, questioning whether "it reinforces the tendency to view gender-atypical bodies as pathological, or could it mark an important advance in the treatment of the underlying conditions so frequently associated with gender-atypical bodies?" (p. 33). Because many intersex people may not be aware of their intersex status due to medical information being withheld from them, atypical development of sex organs as one approaches puberty, and/or discovery of infertility as an adult, mental health practitioners will more likely work with intersex people who are unaware of their intersex condition than with those who have this information (Hird, 2008). Mental health practitioners should be aware of the general differences between transgender and intersex people. Whereas transgender people may have an *internal* sense of sex and gender as incongruent, intersex people typically come to an awareness of their atypicality when doctors or parents notice something unusual about their *bodies* (Preeves, 2003). See below for other terminology used with intersex people.

KNOWLEDGE

Historical Perspectives

The historical context of sexual orientation includes the mislabeling of homosexuality as *transgenderism* (Lev, 2007). As a means to categorize individuals attracted to others of the same sex, sexologists in the 19th century often used the term *inversion*. However, the term *inverts* was also used to define those who experienced their gender as members of the opposite biological sex (Hekma, 1994). Lev notes that "inverts were identified as the 'third sex,' and all homosexuality was assumed to be inverted" (p. 150). She continues to describe the conflation of gender identity with sexual orientation by discussing how society has historically viewed heterosexual couples as normative and therefore assumed that within a same-sex relationship, one member

---

INTERSEX: SOME IMPORTANT DEFINITIONS AND TERMS

Androgen Insensitivity Syndrome (AIS)   A genetic condition, inherited (except for occasional spontaneous mutations), occurring in approximately 1 in 20,000 individuals. In an individual with complete AIS, the body's cells are unable to respond to androgen, or "male" hormones. (*Male* hormones is an unfortunate term, since these hormones are ordinarily present and active in both males and females.) Some individuals have partial androgen insensitivity.

Congenital Adrenal Hyperplasia (CAH)   The most prevalent cause of intersex among people with XX chromosomes. About 1 in 10,000 to 18,000 are born with CAH, but it does not cause intersex in those with XY chromosomes, so the prevalence of CAH-related intersex is about 1 in 20,000 to 1 in 36,000.

Intersex   A general term used for a variety of conditions in which a person is born with a reproductive or sexual anatomy that doesn't seem to fit the typical definitions of female or male.

Klinefelter Syndrome   Men with Klinefelter syndrome inherit an extra X chromosome from either father or mother; their karyotype is 47,XXY. Klinefelter is quite common, occurring in 1 in 500 to 1 in 1,000 male births.

Turner Syndrome   People with Turner syndrome have only one X chromosome present and fully functional. This is sometimes referred to as 45,XO or 45,X karyotype. In a person with Turner syndrome, female sex characteristics are usually present, but underdeveloped compared to the typical female.

Source: From Intersex Society of North America (www.isna.org).

behaves as the "opposite" sex. All cross-gendered behavior was assumed to occur within the context of a same-sex relationship and, with little known about homosexuality, "gender transposition" became intimately connected to same-sex relationships (Lev, 2004, p. 150). Therefore, there often exists the erroneous assumption that one's sex or gender identity determines or is synonymous with one's sexual orientation. In fact, there is no causal or consistent relationship among any combination of the three identity continua. In this chapter, we endeavor to clarify the complex nature of sex and gender as separate but related constructs and sexual orientation will not be covered in any depth. For further information on sexual orientation, please see Chapter 10.

Barriers to Counseling Competency with Transgender and Intersex People

A significant barrier to counseling competency with transgender and intersex clients is the current sociopolitical climate in the United States, which maintains a toxic environment of misunderstanding, fear, discrimination—and sometimes violence—toward individuals who do not fit into the binary gender system (Bockting & Coleman, 2007). Mental health practitioners should be aware that the International Transgender Day of Remembrance (2008) organization reported an increase in violent hate crimes resulting in death against transgender people from 36 people in 2007 to 54 people in 2008. Practitioners should also know that very few states have hate crime legislation that recognizes crimes against transgender and intersex people on the basis of sex and gender, and when these crimes are tracked they are typically underreported. To be better prepared to address potential concerns of safety and trauma when working with transgender and intersex people, mental health practitioners should be aware of the high rates of violent hate crimes these groups face. In addition, there is limited hate crime legislation that protects persons whose gender identity, expression, and behaviors are nonconforming.

An obvious, but notable, barrier to counseling competency with transgender and intersex people is that few professionals have expertise in responding to their presenting needs as clients (Chen-Hayes, 2001; Singh et al., in review). Indeed, for those who have not received adequate training with these transgender and intersex people, working with individuals who present with identities that fall outside of the traditional dichotomous framework of gender and sex can be intimidating and/or confusing. Many mental health practitioners continue to conflate sex and gender with one another, as well as with sexual orientation. Though these components of identity may be interrelated, they constitute distinctly different aspects of identity. Therefore, it can be tempting to refer transgender and intersex clients to other providers. However, because of the very limited mental health resources available to transgender and intersex people, it is important for mental health practitioners to educate themselves and gain competence in working with these groups.

Transgender People in Counseling

Mental health practitioners should have knowledge of competencies existing within professional organizations for transgender and intersex people (Korell & Lorah, 2007). The Task Force on Gender Identity and Gender Variance of Division 44 (Society for the Study of Lesbian, Gay, and Bisexual Issues) of the American Psychological Association (APA) released a report on transgender people that was made a resolution by APA in 2008 (APA, 2008). This document provides an in-depth review of the scientific research with transgender people and makes recommendations for psychotherapy assessment, diagnosis, and practice. The report is an important document for mental health practitioners to review carefully for general guidelines, although the report lacks sufficient attention to the lives of transgender people of color. A strength of the report, however, is its focus on transgender youth, medical care and insurance concerns, and research recommendations, which mental health practitioners may use as a resource to increase their own knowledge and to share this information with clients. The report does not cover intersex concerns; yet, it does call on the field to similarly make recommendations for counseling competency with intersex people.

The Association of Lesbian, Gay, Bisexual, and Transgender Issues in Counseling (ALGBTIC), a division of the American Counseling Association (ACA), developed counseling competencies with transgender clients that are grounded in a feminist, wellness, and strength-based framework (ALGBTIC, 2009). Whereas the APA Task Force on Gender Identity and Gender Variance focuses on recommendations for practice, the ALGBTIC transgender competencies focus on training standards and attend specifically to multicultural and social justice issues counselors should consider when working with transgender clients. Ultimately, mental health practitioners should be familiar with both the ALGBTIC Transgender Competencies and the APA resolution when working with transgender people in counseling.

In addition to obtaining knowledge of these guidelines, it is important that mental health practitioners be aware of the current debate on the classification of *gender identity disorder (GID)* as a mental disorder. The APA Task Force on Gender Identity and Gender Variance report does not specifically challenge the labeling of GID as a mental health disorder. As we go to press with this chapter, the American Psychiatric Association has organized a Sexual and Gender Identity Disorders Work Group that will work on the next revision of this section in the *Diagnostic and Statistical Manual of Mental Disorders-IV-TR* (2000). Brill and Pepper (2008) stated that there are many transgender people and mental health practitioners who do not believe GID is a psychiatric disorder, but rather a medical disorder that is biologically (and not mentally) based. There are yet others who agree with this view but who also assert that until adequate medical care and insurance coverage exists for transgender people (a diagnosis of GID *sometimes* allows transgender clients to have their medical care—such as hormonal as surgical procedures—covered under insurance), a diagnosis of GID is necessary. Ultimately, mental health practitioners should be aware of the range of researchers, practitioners, and advocates in the transgender field of psychology and psychiatry (ALGBTIC, 2009), and be able to communicate where their approach to practice with transgender people falls with regard to this issue.

Transsexual People in Counseling

In 1979, the World Professional Association for Transgender Health, Inc. (WPATH), which was formally known as the Harry Benjamin International Gender Dysphoria Association (HBIGDA), created the WPATH Standards of Care (SOC) for Gender Identity Disorders (Meyer et al., 2001). The standards state that sex reassignment for transsexuals is medically necessary to resolve gender dysphoria. The process by which gender dysphoria is substantiated is complex, however. Transsexuals are often in the position of relying on mental health practitioners to provide a formal diagnosis of gender identity disorder in order to be considered as candidates for medical intervention. Therefore, mental health practitioners are given the role of gatekeepers. Individuals are required to present one recommendation letter from a mental health professional for hormone therapy, and two additional letters from other medical providers are required for genital reconstruction. It is important to note that many individuals are insulted by the need for professional documentation and permission to modify their bodies (Preeves, 2003). Carroll and colleagues (2002) noted that in 1993, at the Conference on Transgender Law and Employment Policy, the International Bill of Gender Rights argued for the right not to conform to a medically enforced regimen that includes a psychiatric diagnosis.

According to the WPATH Standards of Care (SOC), sex reassignment consists of Real-Life Experience, which entails living for 24 hours per day in the gender identity of the congruent gender for a minimum of one year. It also includes legal name and sex change on identity documents, hormone treatment, relevant medical procedures, and psychotherapy is strongly recommended. Practitioners should know that these surgeries are (often referred to as "bottom surgery"), breast enhancement, and/or mastectomy ("top surgery") is not always considered to be a prerequisite for legal or social recognition of sex reassignment so that they can appropriately support individuals through the legal process of identity reconstruction. Especially because these surgeries are expensive and often not covered by insurance, clients may have inaccurate information that they must have surgeries in order to have a legal name change; mental health practitioners can help them clarify this (which often varies from state to state).

In order for an individual to be eligible for hormone treatment under the SOC, the person must be at least 18 years of age, must demonstrate knowledge of hormone medical limitations and social benefits and risks, and must provide either documentation of Real-Life Experience of at least three months prior to the administration of hormones or a period of psychotherapy of a duration specified by the mental health professional after the initial evaluation (usually a minimum of three months).

The guidelines do provide for exceptions to the age minimum and duration of psychotherapy following evaluation. This is especially significant for prepubescent adolescents and adolescents, and the SOC outlines the use of fully reversible and partially reversible interventions for these adolescents. Fully reversible hormone treatment involves the use of puberty-delaying hormones when puberty begins to forestall the advent of full pubertal changes, providing more time for the child and family to explore gender identity and to ease the child into adolescence if the child later decides to pursue sex changes. Partially reversible interventions may begin for adolescents at age 16 and include masculinizing and feminizing hormone therapy. See the listing of WPATH Standards of Care (SOC).

WPATH STANDARDS OF CARE (SOC)

With regard to the counseling recommendation, WPATH Standards of Care suggests 10 tasks for the mental health professional:

1. Accurately diagnose the person's gender identity disorder (GID), since an official diagnosis is often required by the medical establishment to justify treatment as well as for insurance reimbursement, in the rare cases that sex-reassignment surgery is a covered treatment.

2. Accurately diagnose any co-morbid psychiatric conditions and ensure treatment.

3. Counsel the individual about the range of treatment options and their implications.

4. Engage in psychotherapy in order to fully explore identity, address the effects of societal stigma and discrimination, and treat any co-morbid disorders.

5. Ascertain eligibility and psychological readiness for hormone and surgical therapy.

6. Make formal recommendations to medical and surgical colleagues about psychological readiness to transition.

7. Document the client's relevant history in a letter of recommendation.

8. Serve as a colleague on a team of professionals with interest in GID in order to provide a multidisciplinary approach to treatment.

9. Educate family members, employers, and institutions about gender identity disorders.

10. Be available for client follow-up. The SOC are minimum standards and state that some established medical programs may require longer time periods and/or more documentation.

Source: Meyer et al., (2001).

If the individual chooses to have surgery for body modification, it is in no way considered to be elective or cosmetic (which would not be covered by insurance policies), according to WPATH, because it is necessary for the resolution of the diagnosis of gender identity disorder. Surgeries for a male-to-female individual may include facial feminization, breast augmentation, and genital reconstruction. For female-to-male individuals, surgery may include a complete hysterectomy, mastectomy, and genital reconstruction (e.g., penile and testicular prostheses). Though insurance coverage for such surgeries can be difficult, some carriers are beginning to offer such benefits, as are some large corporations and universities.

Intersex People in Counseling

There is scant literature in the field of psychology on working with intersex individuals. As a result, their unique psychological experiences are largely unexplored. The medical and psychological communities have thus far responded to this issue as a primarily medical problem that necessitates surgical resolution. This is akin to suggesting that a person, who may experience discrimination based on his or her race or other physical characteristic that is otherwise benign, should undergo medical treatment to appear more like the majority.

In fact, the medical intervention itself is often the very cause of distress in intersex individuals (Preeves, 2003). The underlying psychosocial concerns, including the damaging experiences of discrimination and marginalization, warrant serious consideration and intervention from the psychological community (Fausto-Sterling, 2000).

Many current theories and practices are based on presumptions that there is an anatomically correct way to be a male or a female, and that infants born with ambiguous genitalia, who challenge these assumptions, should be reconstructed to fit into (and thereby reinforce) them. In fact, Coogan (2006) suggests that biological sex is as complex as gender and that to agree to the dichotomy of biological sex negates the existence of intersex individuals.

The strict conception of "normal" sexual anatomy and "normal" sex behavior underlying prevailing treatment protocols may also influence the ways in which clinicians might view and therefore treat intersex clients (Preeves, 2003). These individuals are often treated as though their genitalia are abnormal and therefore inferior, rendering their identity as intersex invisible or invalid. Through recognizing the validity of intersex individuals' experiences, bodies, and identities, therapy can be a powerful experience (Hird, 2008). See Case Vignette 14.1 for a case study of an intersex person.

CASE VIGNETTE 14.1

The Case of Marena

Marena is a 30-year-old Latina who moved to the United States from Venezuela. Though she possesses male external genitalia, Marena's voice never deepened at puberty, she doesn't have facial hair, and her physical frame is more typically feminine. She believed herself to be female since she was a young child. Peers taunted her as a child for being too feminine and she described a childhood of social isolation and shame.

Marena's parents wouldn't allow her to identify openly as female in any way, so she decided to relocate for college so that she could pursue hormone treatment and live her life freely as a woman. She presents for counseling because she is pursuing sex-reassignment surgery and counseling is required prior to surgical intervention. She explained that it has

(continued)

(*continued*)

been discovered, during a routine medical exam in preparation for her surgery, that she possesses internal female reproductive anatomy. Marena reports feeling elated at the validation of her internal sense of herself as female, but also great distress and anger toward her family of origin who she realizes must have concealed her genital surgery when she was an infant and who have constantly invalidated her felt identity throughout her life.

You help Marena process her anger and resentment toward the medical establishment and her family. You work to understand and process the cultural expectations regarding gender roles placed on her by her family and community in Venezuela. You provide her with relevant information and resources for support and medical concerns. You process strategies for Marena to disclose about her full identity, experiences, and surgery to important people in her life. You work collaboratively to construct a new, cohesive narrative of her life story that includes this recent information and enables her to embrace her identity as an intersex individual who identifies as female.

SKILLS

Counseling Transgender Individuals and Their Families

The interventions and skills necessary to effectively address concerns unique to the transgender, transsexual, and intersex communities must be discussed with the implicit understanding that no identity is one-dimensional. The particular intersection of race and ethnicity, social class, gender identity, sex identity, disability, religion/spirituality, sexual orientation, age, and educational attainment within any one individual impacts the salience of the specific identities held, available emotional and practical resources, and general well-being. Using this lens to conceptualize clients' presenting concerns will greatly enhance the effectiveness of the counseling provided (APA, 2002). Also essential to working with the trans community is adopting the perspective of affirming identity and the right of individuals to identify themselves, rather than a focus on "treating" gender dysphoria (Bockting, 1997). Understanding the client's "cultural context" and improving coping strategies should be the focus of counseling; this approach avoids helping the client to adapt to societal norms (Carroll et al., 2002, p. 133). Another important guideline is that whether a client's outward gender presentation appears traditional or unconventional, mental health

practitioners should seek to understand the client's own internal experience and definition of his or her gender.

Members of the transgender community present with the same wide range of concerns seen in the general population, in addition to societal marginalization, identity confusion, internalized stigma, shame, isolation, body-image issues, and abuse/violence (deVries et al., 2006). Since many clients may not feel comfortable disclosing sex and gender concerns during an initial session, routinely assessing for related concerns is an essential skill (White & Goldberg, 2006). If a client responds affirmatively to a general inquiry, it is important to explore further. Before proceeding, it is respectful and necessary to ask the client which, if any, pronoun and name is appropriate to use in reference to the client. Asking these types of questions early on allows the mental health practitioner to convey awareness of transgender issues early in treatment and avoids potential stressors in building a strong therapeutic relationship.

As a guide to a thorough assessment, White and Goldberg (2006) suggest the following: discussing the nature of the concerns (e.g., discrepant body and gender, gender roles, age of onset, intensity of concern); looking at the impact of such concerns on every aspect of the client's life and functionality (e.g., family, peers, school, activities, employment); asking about coping strategies and noting resiliency/strengths; talking about internalized messages regarding gender variance; and considering the full range of psychosocial and cultural factors relevant to the client.

Carroll (2000) adds that it is important to ascertain the options the client has considered with regard to gender expression and body modification as part of a thorough assessment. If the client chooses to transition, it is recommended that the mental health practitioner ensure client awareness and full consideration of all available possibilities. In addition to envisioning the positive outcomes of transitioning, it is essential that there is a frank discussion about the potential challenges. For example, male-to-female transsexuals should be aware of the effects of sexism on their lives, such as lower pay and objectification (Carroll, 2000) and medical complications associated with taking estrogen, such as thrombosis and altered liver function (Levy, Crown, & Reid, 2003). Female-to-male transsexuals should consider the medical side-effects of male hormones, such as male pattern baldness, overproduction of red blood cells, and temperament changes (Carroll, 2000; Levy et al., 2003). There remain unresolved questions (Lawrence, 2007) about whether transsexuals are at increased risk for cancer due to hormonal treatments; therefore, it is likely that mental health practitioners will need to be prepared to understand this research (which is beyond the scope of this chapter) in order to have relevant discussions with their clients.

When clients have decided to make a medical transition through gender expression, hormones, and possibly body modification, the counselor can play an important role in assisting in processing critical, related decisions. Carroll (2000) suggests the following concerns receive explicit attention in therapy: (a) the timing and process by which the client will make a full transition to another gender role; (b) how this will be navigated at work or school; (c) when, how, and to whom to disclose about the process; and (d) when and where to obtain hormone and surgical treatment.

The literature has shown that social class and economic status are central to mental health, in that those with lower economic means experience more social injustice and stress (Albee, 2000). Unfortunately, transsexual individuals report higher rates of unemployment and poverty than are found in other populations (APA, 2007), which is even further compounded by the fact that racial minorities, too, are disproportionately economically disadvantaged (Ridley, 2005). As a result, transsexual individuals of color, especially those in the male-to-female spectrum, who may also experience sexism, are likely to suffer from extremely high levels of distress as the result of multiple oppressions (Currah & Minter, 2000).

Related to this vulnerability is the fact that safety is a paramount concern for transsexual clients, as they can be particularly vulnerable to violence (Currah & Minter, 2000). This is especially true for individuals who are financially dependent upon another, have a cognitive impairment or physical disability, work in the sex trade, or are homeless (White & Goldberg, 2006). Therefore, a thorough assessment of a client's environment must be conducted immediately, safe resources identified, and safety plans created. Mental health practitioners should explore the financial resources clients have if they are interested in pursuing a legal name change and medical procedures. Those clients without insurance coverage and/or financial resources may experience distress because they may never anticipate having the necessary means to do so. In these situations, mental health practitioners should explore the psychological distress related to financial and insurance decisions, combined with advocacy connecting clients with potential community resources for low-cost medical providers.

Transgender people may have several "coming-out" processes. Without the language, support, or resources to define themselves as transgender, they may have initially come out as lesbian, gay, or bisexual (dickey, Burnes, & Singh, in review). Therefore, when embracing their gender identity, there may be a second coming-out process about being transgender. Following that, the individual may then reconsider the initial label chosen for sexual orientation and come out once more with a different orientation that takes into account the more accurate gender identity. Recent studies (dickey et al., in review; Veale, Clarke, & Lomax, 2008) have examined the sexual orientation of transgender people who identify as gay, lesbian, bisexual, and/or queer, but the literature is still nascent.

Families often reject and abandon transgender adolescents, and transgender adults can be subject to employment discrimination, both of which can lead to homelessness (Bockting, 1997; Carroll, 2010). This, combined with the reality of the high costs of hormones and sex-reassignment surgeries (especially without medical insurance), is one reason why so many transsexuals become involved in the sex work trade (Klein, 1999). Therefore, a focus on case management with regard to finding affordable housing and shelters that are safe for transgender guests can be an important component to a competent counseling approach (White & Goldberg, 2006).

Career concerns for transgender individuals must be attended to as well. Transgender people are often worried about losing their jobs if they transition; being discriminated against and harassed at work; negotiating which bathroom to use; and losing their job experience and work history under their prior name (Pepper & Lorah, 2008). There will be different career concerns mental health practitioners should assess depending on whether a transgender client has already transitioned at their workplace, is seeking work as someone who has newly made a social and/or medical transition, or is visually perceived as gender-ambiguous. To address these concerns, Pepper and Lorah recommend four career counseling components for clinicians working with transgender individuals. They include: (1) familiarization with which businesses and organizations include a gender identity nondiscrimination policy; (2) knowledge about the process of transitioning and how to live this process in the workplace; (3) use of nonbiased career assessments as most are heterosexist; and (4) knowledge and use of sexual identity management models to assist transgender individuals

in the management of their identities, such as Lev's (2004) Transgender Emergence Model.

The Transgender Emergence Model can offer specific interventions with transgender individuals; the first stage begins with normalizing clients' experiences and gender identity. It is also important at this stage to provide a safe space for these individuals to discuss their thoughts and feelings with no agenda for change. In the second stage, clients begin to seek information and support, and it is therefore imperative that the clinician help clients gain accurate and current information, find supportive trans networks, help "pace their emergence process," and help them examine their choices and the effects (p. 247). As they enter the third stage of emergence, clients come out to significant others, such as partners and families. In the fourth stage, as clients engage in exploration of their trans identity and begin to self-label, providing the safe space, once again, for them to try on various behaviors and to examine their feelings will be the bulk of the clinical work. Advocacy in work environments or school at these junctures may be necessary as clients engage in more public-lived experiences as transsexual. During the fifth stage, clients may move into deeper transition concerns, involving body modification. In the final stage of emergence, integration and pride, mental health practitioners' on-going support is necessary as clients may experience post-transition depression or the need to educate family members.

It is important to note that because body image concerns may be prevalent in this community (deVries et al., 2006) it can become a theme in therapy in a variety of ways. Male-to-female transsexuals for example, often fall prey to strict cultural norms for women of thinness (White & Goldberg, 2006). Discomfort with one's anatomy and dystonic secondary sex characteristics may also be very emotionally painful. In addition, this dissonance can make an important discussion about safe sex practices uncomfortable, leading to an avoidance of such discussions in therapy and with sexual partners (deVries et al., 2006). Body dysmorphia and disordered eating behaviors should be evaluated

CASE VIGNETTE 14.2

The Case of Eliza

Background

Eliza is a 21-year-old, European-American transgender woman (assigned male at birth, but identifies as a woman) who is a college student and presents with concerns of stress regarding family conflict and misunderstanding about her gender identity. She saw a previous mental health practitioner for three years in another state who supported her in accessing hormones and breast augmentation. She reports using her financial aid checks to access necessary hormonal and surgical treatments because her insurance did not cover these procedures. Eliza has been disconnected from her family throughout her transition because of their refusal to accept her as their daughter or to use correct female pronouns. Eliza states she would like to reconnect with her family, who are now open to discussing her gender with her.

Skills

- Affirm Eliza's gender identity and recognize her resilience.
- Explore Eliza's family history, cultural background, resources, issues around safety, and the degree of support she has in the transgender community.
- Provide Eliza with paper and Internet resources to share with her family.
- Ensure that she is well educated about medical issues and options available.
- Explore expectations for family counseling and identify coping resources she has for the best- and worst-case scenarios.

and treated as part of a comprehensive therapy approach. Lev (2004) also proposes a family emergence model to describe the developmental process of the family when someone transitions. The stages include discovery and disclosure, turmoil, negotiation, and finding balance. At each stage, a clinician's support for the client and family is imperative, as is creating a safe place for disclosure. See Case Vignette 14.2 for an example of skillful work with a transgender client.

Counseling Intersex Individuals and Their Families

Though intersex individuals will present in therapy for the entire range of concerns salient to any population, examples of scenarios where intersex-related people might be at the forefront include providing consultation, support, and/or therapy to the families of newborns or young children who are intersex, to adolescent and adult intersex individuals who have just learned/discovered that they are intersex, or to intersex adults and adolescents who are (re)defining their gender identity when the assigned gender is experienced as incongruent (Preeves, 2003). In all cases, paramount to building a strong working alliance is the ability to operate from the understanding that psychological distress is not caused by gender or sex ambiguity, but rather it is the direct result of societal stigma, subsequent trauma, and lack of validation from family and medical practitioners of the individual's felt sense of being different or atypical. It is important to remember that the medical treatment and resulting interference with body image and sexual dysfunction also is a significant cause of distress, shame, and stigma (Chase, 1998; Diamond & Sigmundson, 1997).

Providing services to the family of intersex newborns can be pivotal (Harmon-Smith, 1999). The family members are typically shocked, confused, and frightened. They are in need of support and validation of their feelings. It is important that they are provided with accurate information about the relevant psychological concerns so that they can make appropriate medical decisions. Specifically, a distinction between the needs of the child and those of the parents must be made, since surgery is a viable option only to treat a true medical condition, not as a strategy to reduce the distress of the parents over the child's anatomy (Marut Schober, 1999).

There is evidence to suggest that the least psychologically damaging course of action is to delay surgical intervention until the individual is in the position to make an informed, independent decision (Dreger, 1999). An American Counseling Association (ACA) resolution to protect intersex children from unwanted surgery, secrecy, and shame states that the ACA "supports the rights of people old enough to make an informed choice to elect or refuse medical procedures including surgical and hormonal interventions which influence the sexual appearance and/or functioning of their bodies" (2004, para. 10). It is also important that parents understand that there is no empirical evidence to demonstrate that there is a causal relationship between growing up with atypical genitalia and significant psychological distress (Berenbaum, 2006). Therefore, it is not psychologically or medically necessary to alter the genitalia to be consistent with the assigned gender of the child.

Frequently, knowledge of intersexuality has been concealed from intersex individuals (Dreger, 1999). Preeves (2003) noted that adults who learned about the medical procedures performed without their permission or knowledge, reported feeling degraded and shamed. Furthermore, the concealment of medical information about intersex people can be harmful, and suggests a need for silence (Dreger, 2003). Therefore, a central component of healing from the

trauma includes validation of any sense of betrayal individuals may feel if they learn only later in life that they were the recipients of reconstructive surgeries and/or hormone treatment. The implicit message conveyed was that they were not acceptable as they were born, which can be enormously damaging to self-esteem (Preeves, 2003). Parents and the child can also benefit from understanding that concealment of intersexuality and surgical interventions can result in myriad psychological concerns for the child (Preeves, 2003).

The process of exploring a gender identity may also be salient for intersex individuals if their assigned gender is incongruent with their internal experience. Providing a safe space in which to process their feelings and create a cohesive and authentic narrative through which to describe their experience can be a powerful intervention for clients who have not before been encouraged to define and embrace their own identities. Clients can experience a great deal of empowerment through reclaiming their own stories (Coventry, 1999).

Additionally, intersex individuals may have experienced events in their lives where they have been shamed, marginalized, and oppressed as the result of living in a society with little factual knowledge about variations in sex and gender (Preeves, 2003). Naming these experiences as social injustices and processing the impact on their self-esteem and functioning can facilitate healing. Finally, inviting intersex clients to explore common aspects of life that make people happy, such as the creation of a successful career or good social relationships, can help balance the focus on adjustment to their medical condition with experiences that connect them to larger communities and the human condition (Berenbaum, 2006).

VALUES AND ATTITUDES

Little training exists for clinicians working with transgender and intersex clients. Given this reality, how ready therapists are to adopt a trans- and intersex-positive and affirming approach is unknown, but imperative (Carroll & Gilroy, 2002). Mental health practitioners must identify and confront potential internalized negative attitudes they may have toward transgender (termed *transphobia*) (Carroll & Gilroy, 2002) and intersex people in order to work toward competency with these client concerns. This stance requires clinicians to confront the binary categorization of gender and to examine how they may be contributing to the propagation of this system. A thoughtful and honest exploration of one's beliefs about gender identity and one's sexism is central to this process. Perhaps questions such as "Do I believe in a binary categorization of sex and gender?" and "What are my values about gender and gender roles?" can facilitate the exploration. A useful resource to explore the concept of gender and one's beliefs about gender is *My Gender Workbook* (Bornstein, 1998). The various exercises ask questions about gender behavior, attitudes, and aptitudes.

This can lead to an assessment of one's transphobia. Raj (2002) suggests there are many ways by which mental health practitioners may inadvertently manifest this stance. They include but are not limited to: (a) pathologizing transsexual and intersex clients as mentally ill, (b) withholding recommendations for medical intervention, and (c) denying the existence of transsexual individuals. Clinicians must evaluate their beliefs that individuals can be transgender, transsexual, or intersex and the varied ways that can be lived. Raj created a transpositive therapeutic model that outlines a variety of necessary values and attitudes. Overall, it is important to express an "attitude that is respectful, sensitive, accepting, validating, affirming, empathic, caring, compassionate, encouraging, supportive, and mutually trusting and trustworthy. In brief, the therapist is expected to affirm/validate any form of gender or sexual variance expressed by the client, and to appropriately support the client's right to self-determination wherever possible" (2002, para. 2). Using language that is transpositive,

culturally sensitive, and devoid of pathologizing terminology is crucial.

Carroll and Gilroy (2002) suggest that mental health practitioners may turn to bibliotherapy for themselves to develop positive attitudes and values toward transgender people. The authors suggest using transgender biographies, novels, and films. Bibliotherapy is also a helpful approach to learning about intersex people (see the Resources section for a list of transgender- and intersex-positive media). We suggest that mental health practitioners consider forming discussion groups around these media resources, with a leader who has experience with the topic and who can facilitate a structured exploration of how these media shift attitudes/values and approaches to treatment. These discussions should also include reflection on knowledge and skills mental health practitioners want to work on in further developing their competency with transgender and intersex clients.

Advocacy

Because one of the primary causes of psychological distress for transgender, transsexual, and intersex individuals is discrimination and oppression, effective advocacy is essential and should include a focus on institutional, political, and social change. Vera and Speight (2003) note that if sociohistorical context is not considered in the conceptualization of presenting concerns, and oppression is not directly addressed, then the treatment of individuals will perpetuate the injustices they have already experienced. Advocating for social change is part of our professional responsibility as mental health practitioners to act as role models in both our behavior and our communicated values (APA, 2002; Lewis, Arnold, House, & Toporek, 2003; NASW, 2001). A critical piece of advocacy and counseling competency with those who fall under the umbrella of transgender is to be able to ask and explore with transgender and intersex clients what terms best fit their experience of sex and gender in their lives in a way that

ADVOCACY IN WORKING WITH TRANSGENDER AND INTERSEX PEOPLE

1. Assess organizational paperwork to remove gender- and sex-binary terms such as *male* and *female*. Provide space for clients to write in their own gender and sex identities.

2. Identify gaps in transgender and intersex mental health care in your community. For instance, if there are no support groups and a lack of adequately trained psychiatrists in your area, consider partnering with local transgender and intersex community organizers, activists, and other practitioners to develop resources and education opportunities.

3. Ask your agency director to organize training for *all* staff on providing affirmative treatment for transgender and intersex people.

4. Collaborate with university, community, school, and other organizations on local, national, and international initiatives designed to improve the quality of life for transgender and intersex people.

5. Provide lectures and workshops for medical, educational, and mental health personnel to help reduce stigma.

6. Learn about the antidiscrimination policies in places of employment, at educational institutions, and at the state and local levels, and identify ways to work toward the inclusion of gender identity where it has been omitted.

7. Organize a letter-writing campaign urging insurance companies and employers to cover medical benefits for sex-reassignment surgeries and to eliminate transsexual exclusions on their policies. Letters to medical organizations that outline the importance of delaying unnecessary genital reconstruction in intersex infants is another potentially powerful intervention.

supports a connection between mental health practitioner and client in therapy. Above, we list several advocacy strategies mental health practitioners can initiate both within and outside of their clinical settings.

with transgender and intersex clients. The Resources section (books, videos, and Web sites) provides information not only for the practitioner but for the clients for whom they will provide treatment.

SUMMARY

This chapter provided an overview of the important components mental health practitioners must address when counseling transgender and intersex individuals. It reviewed the necessary knowledge and skills and the values and attitudes in need of exploration and change in order to provide competent care to these clients. Advocacy efforts as a means to change systems that cause psychological distress for transgender and intersex were offered to help mental health practitioners enhance their multicultural competency. Finally, case vignettes were provided for mental health practitioners who plan to work

RESOURCES

The following resources are provided as suggestions for further inquiry and as tools students, clinicians, trainees, and supervisors can utilize in improving the quality of the services they provide to transgender and intersex individuals.

BOOKS

Brill, S., & Pepper, R. (2008). *The transgender child: A handbook for families and professionals*. San Francisco: Cleis Press.

Feinberg, L. (1998). *Trans liberation: Beyond pink or blue*. Boston, MA: Beacon Press.

Lev, A. (2004). *Transgender emergence: Therapeutic guidelines for working with gender-variant people and their families*. New York: The Haworth Clinical Practice Press.

EXPERIENTIAL EXERCISES

Bornstein, K. (1998) *My gender workbook*. New York City: Taylor & Francis.

Cedar. (2007, February 23). *The cis-gender checklist*. Retrieved on April 22, 2009, from http://www.takesupspace.wordpress.com

Whitman, J. S., & Boyd, C. J. (Eds.). (2003). *The therapist's notebook for lesbian, gay, and bisexual clients: Homework, handouts, and activities for use in psychotherapy*. Binghamton, NY: Haworth Press.

FILMS

Normal (2003).	Transgender woman (adult and family).
Ma Vie en Rose (1997).	Transgender youth (child and adolescent).
Southern Comfort (2001).	Transgender man (documentary, community support).
TransAmerica (2005).	Transgender woman (adult and family).
TransGeneration (2005).	Trangender youth (traditional college-age and community support).

WEB SITES AND WEB RESOURCES

Association of LGBT Issues in Counseling	http://www.algbtic.org
Center of Excellence for Transgender HIV Prevention	http://www.transhealth.ucsf.edu
FTM International	http://www.ftmi.org
Intersex Society of North America	http://www.isna.org
Lambda Legal's "toolkit" for transgender youth	http://www.lambdalegal.org
National Coalition for LGBT Health	http://www.lgbthealth.net.org
National Transgender Equality	http://www.ncte.org
Parents, Friends, and Family of LGBT Youth	http://www.pflag.org
Transgender Law Center	http://www.transgenderlawcenter.org
OutProud's Web site for transgender youth	http://www.transproud.com
World Professional Association of Transgender Health	http://www.wpath.org

COMPETENCY BENCHMARK TABLES

The purpose of the Competency Benchmarks (Tables 14.1–14.4) is to create developmental models for defining and measuring competencies in professional psychology; each chapter in this *Handbook* applies the diversity competence for mental health practitioners in their work with a particular diverse population.

Table 14.1   Developmental-Level Competencies I

READINESS LEVEL—ENTRY TO PRACTICUM	
Competencies	Learning Process and Activities
Knowledge The student is gaining knowledge in: • Multiculturalism—the student is engaged in the process of learning that all individuals, including themselves, are cultural beings with worldviews that shape and influence their attitudes, emotions, perceptions, and experiences.	At this stage of development, the emphasis in mental health practitioner education is instilling knowledge of foundational domains that provide the groundwork for subsequent attainment of functional competencies. Students at this stage become aware of the principles and practices ofthe field, but

(continued)

Table 14.1   Developmental-Level Competencies I (*continued*)

READINESS LEVEL—ENTRY TO PRACTICUM	
Competencies	Learning Process and Activities
	<ul><li>The importance of reflective practice and self-awareness when working with transgender and intersex clients.</li><li>Core counseling skills and theories helpful to building a strong therapeutic alliance with transgender and intersex clients.</li><li>APA Ethics code, WPATH Standards of Care, APA Resolution, ALGBTIC Transgender Competencies.</li></ul>	they are not yet able to apply their knowledge to practice. Therefore, the training curriculum is focused on knowledge of core areas, including literature on multiculturalism, ethics, basic counseling skills, scientific knowledge, and the importance of reflective practice and self-awareness.
Skills	The student is: <ul><li>Beginning to develop the ability to demonstrate empathic listening skills, respect, and interest when talking with individuals expressing gender identities that may be outside of the traditional, binary assumptions of gender.</li><li>Learning to critically examine the diversity literature with regard to transgender and intersex people.</li></ul>	It is important that throughout the curriculum, trainers and teachers define individual and cultural differences broadly, to include gender identity differences. This should enable students to have a developing awareness of how to extrapolate their emerging multicultural competencies to include the gender identity realm of individual and cultural differences.
Values and Attitudes	The student demonstrates: <ul><li>Willingness to engage in self-exploration—to consider own motives, attitudes, behaviors, and effect on others with regard to one's own gender identity.</li><li>Intellectual curiosity and flexibility about the social construction of gender and the ways society defines gender.</li><li>Ability to value expressions of diverse viewpoints and belief systems about gender identity.</li></ul>	Most students, through their life experiences, would be expected to have basic knowledge of the important terms and definitions used when discussing transgender and intersex people, awareness of the impact of discrimination on transgender and intersex people's lives, and personal awareness of how multiple identities may intersect with gender identity and expression.

Table 14.2   Developmental-Level Competencies II

READINESS LEVEL—ENTRY TO INTERNSHIP	
Competencies	Learning Process and Activities
Knowledge	The student has: <ul><li>General understanding of the key definitions and terms for working with transgender and intersex clients.</li><li>Understanding of the differences and similarities between transgender and intersex people (e.g., assessment, diagnosis).</li><li>Knowledge of the family, social support, and other factors influencing the mental health of transgender and intersex people.</li><li>Understanding of the ethical guidelines and standards of care in the field pertaining to work with transgender and intersex people.</li></ul>	At this level of development, students are building on their education and applied experiences (such as supervised practicum experiences) to attain a core set of foundational competencies. They can then begin applying this knowledge to professional practice. As a result of being exposed to didactic training and close supervision, students attain the multicultural values and attitudes appropriate to their level of development. Foundational knowledge and multicultural values and attitudes are becoming well established, but skills in working with gender identity issues would be expected to be rudimentary at this level of development.

READINESS LEVEL—ENTRY TO INTERNSHIP	
Competencies	Learning Process and Activities
Skills Skills in the following areas are beginning to develop: • Using the pronouns and language that transgender and intersex clients say is important to them. Recognizing and correcting mistakes in using these pronouns and language. • Building therapeutic alliance by using basic counseling skills, as well as the ability to empathize with clients who may be dealing with societal discrimination and prejudice. • Learning to use the *DSM-IV-TR* diagnostic categories of Gender Identity Disorder and Sex Development Disorders and understand the ways these diagnoses can be pathologizing of clients' experience.	Learning occurs through multiple modalities: • Receiving transgender and intersex didactic training in academic programs may occur in multicultural courses or culture-specific courses (e.g., women's issues, Latino/a, and LGBTQQ [lesbian, gay, bisexual, transgender, queer, questioning] courses) and it may be infused into the core curriculum (e.g., ethics, assessment, multicultural, career counseling, research, human growth and development, and clinical courses). • Providing therapy, under supervision, to clients representing diversity of identity expressions in practicum experiences. • Receiving supervision from psychotherapists knowledgeable and skilled in working with transgender and intersex people.
Values and Attitudes Demonstrates self-awareness and appropriate cultural and multicultural attitudes as evidenced by the following: • Understands that gender identity and expression is an important dimension of cultural identity. • Identifies stereotypes and biases toward transgender and intersex people and is committed to exploring and challenging these assumptions. • Awareness of own intersecting individual dimensions (gender, ethnicity, socioeconomic status (SES), sexual orientation, ability, etc.) and ability to discern clients' intersecting identities. • Willingness to admit own limitations in ability to be open to some expressions of gender identity. • Demonstrates genuine respect for varying gender identities and expression.	• Seeking additional study and professional development opportunities (e.g., to attain knowledge of common counseling issues when working with transgender and intersex people). Topics to be covered in didactic training include: • Relation of gender identity competency to multicultural competency. • Relationship of gender identity to individual and cultural differences (e.g., including age, gender, sexual orientation, SES, and ethnicity). • Basic research literature describing the relevance of gender identity to wellness, physical health, mental health. • Definitions of sex and gender and how other related terms are used when working with transgender and intersex people. Trainers and teachers could offer students enrolled in multicultural diversity courses an option to research gender identity as a class project. Possible topics could use the media resources listed in this chapter to supplement learning and structure discussions.

Table 14.3   Developmental-Level Competencies III

READINESS LEVEL—ENTRY TO PROFESSIONAL PRACTICE	
Competencies	Learning Process and Activities
Knowledge Knowledge of the following: • Literature on the relationship between gender identity and physical health; knowledge of the range of possible gender identities clients may have.	In the earlier stages of training, students solidified their professional knowledge base and attained appropriate values and attitudes while developing increasingly sophisticated clinical skills with *(continued)*

Table 14.3 Developmental-Level Competencies III (*continued*)

	READINESS LEVEL—ENTRY TO PROFESSIONAL PRACTICE	
Competencies		Learning Process and Activities

	• Understanding the current debate on the inclusion of Gender Identity Disorder (GID) in the *DSM-IV-TR* and familiarity with the WPATH Standards of Care. • Familiarity with the APA Resolution and ALGBTIC Competencies. • Understanding the current debate on early and late surgical and hormonal interventions with intersex people. • Knowing and being able to access the community resources, including support groups and activist organizations, transgender and intersex people use. • Understanding that working with gender identity and expression is an aspect of multicultural counseling competency.	transgender and intersex people. At the level of Entry to Professional Practice, psychotherapists have attained the full range of competencies in the domains expected of all independent practitioners with regard to gender identity and its intersection with other dimensions of culture (e.g., race/ethnicity). Preparation for this level of competency takes place through closely supervised clinical work, augmented by professional reading, personal exploration, and training opportunities such as professional development and training seminars. Clinical supervisors observe students' clinical work, provide training in assessment, case conceptualization, and treatment planning, and challenge supervisees to examine their countertransference reactions, biases, and values to develop their supervisees' clinical competency with gender identity and expression.
Skills	Skills are demonstrated by the ability to: • Perform a basic assessment of clients' gender identity issues related to therapy; assess for contraindications. • Diagnose and formulate appropriate treatment plans that are sensitive to the client's worldview and understanding of the client's own gender identity, including how multiple systems and individual differences impact client. • Identify the limits of one's own competency with gender identity issues and refer appropriately. • Form a trusting therapeutic relationship with clients so that clients may express gender identity concerns if relevant and provide basic affirmative explorations of gender identity. • Use supervision to enhance skills with transgender and intersex clients. • Assess the client's environment to determine safety concerns and sources of oppression and discrimination. • Work to address such concerns by creating safety plans, identifying more inclusive work and community environments, and building upon internal and external resources. • Create climate in which supervisees and trainees feel safe to talk about gender identity issues. • Be able to communicate about the role mental health practitioners have in counseling (e.g., gatekeepers).	Additional methods by which students can attain competency at with transgender and intersex people at this level include: • Seeking opportunities to provide therapy to clients representing gender identity diversity. • Supervision provided by supervisors knowledgeable and skilled in working with transgender and intersex people. • Self-directed study and professional development opportunities. • Internship and postdoctoral seminar training in gender identity issues. • Presenting and participating in clinical case conferences that include discussion of gender identity aspects of cases.
Values and Attitudes	Be reflective and aware of assumptions made about clients based on sex and gender, understand the practice implications of these assumptions, and commit to expanding knowledge of gender identity as part of multicultural competency enhancement.	

Table 14.4   **Developmental-Level Competencies IV**

READINESS LEVEL—ADVANCED PRACTICE AND SPECIALIZATION

Competencies		Learning Process and Activities
Knowledge	Extensive knowledge of: • Transgender and intersex literature. • Models of practice with transgender and intersex people. • Impact of gender identity upon human development. • Local, national, and Internet transgender and intersex community resources and current sociopolitical climate and the impact on the transgender and intersex communities. • Advocacy initiatives on transgender and intersex concerns (e.g., employment discrimination). • Information and resources to educate colleagues and trainees to increase their knowledge base with transgender and intersex people.	Psychotherapists who have a particular interest in transgender and intersex issues as they apply to clinical work may seek to attain advanced levels of competency. Learning activities will vary depending on the mental health practitioner's unique background, established competencies, and interest areas. For example, practitioners working in college counseling settings may wish to ensure transgender and intersex issues are not included in lesbian, gay, and bisexual training without specifically attending to issues important to transgender and intersex people (i.e., a "coming-out" group should attend to gender identity as well as sexual orientation). Similarly, mental health practitioners working with youth should use their knowledge of gender identity diversity to seek to understand, support, and affirm a wide expression of gender identity in youth.
Skills	Advanced skills in the following: • Assess whether gender concerns are primary or secondary concerns in counseling. If there are co-morbid mental health concerns (e.g., depression), be able to collaboratively work. • Actively advocate for change in social, economic, educational, and political structures within which clients live. • Assist colleagues and trainees in identifying salient treatment concerns and interventions with transgender and intersex clients. • Respond to and integrate the interpersonal, intrapersonal, social, and cultural identities of clients, and address experiences of oppression and discrimination. • Knowledge of the wide range of multiculturally appropriate expressions of gender identity and expression. • Advocate for clients to their families and communities. • Provide effective supervision to trainees working with client gender identity issues.	Regardless of the focus area, learning activities can include: • Professional reading (information about diverse gender identities; empirical studies, and literature on theory and practice). • Teaching. • Attending and leading educational workshops. • Peer consultation groups. • Consultation with knowledgeable mental health professionals, and transgender and intersex leaders. • Participation in community events related to supporting the transgender and intersex community (i.e., Transgender Day of Remembrance and Intersex Awareness).
Values and Attitudes	Well-integrated values and attitudes demonstrated by the following: • Continually engages in broadening knowledge of gender identity resources and for continuing professional development. • Actively cultivates relationships with transgender and intersex community leaders. • Involved in local and national groups and organiza-tions relevant to spiritual/religious (S/R) issues. • Independently and proactively provides ethical and legal consultation and supervision to trainees and other professionals on gender identity. • Works for social justice to enhance understanding among individuals with different gender identities. • Independently monitors own gender identity in relation to work with others with awareness and sensitivity to varying gender identities and expression.	

REFERENCES

Albee, G. W. (2000). Commentary on prevention and counseling psychology. *The Counseling Psychologist, 28*, 845–853.

Alderson, J., Madill, A., & Balen, A. (2004). Fear of devaluation: Understanding the experience of intersexed women with androgen insensitivity syndrome. *British Journal of Health Psychology, 9*(1), 81–101.

Association of Lesbian, Gay, Bisexual, and Transgender Issues in Counseling. (2009). *Competencies for counseling transgender clients.* Alexandria, VA: Author.

American Academy of Pediatrics. (1996). Timing of elective surgery on the genitalia of male children with particular reference to the risks, benefits, and psychological effects of surgery and anesthesia. *Pediatrics, 97*(4), 590–594.

American Counseling Association. (2004, March). Resolutions adopted by governing council. Retrieved November 11, 2008, from http://www.counseling.org/PressRoom/NewsReleases.aspx?AGuid=244405dc-044e-46ae-aeac-60ca1c8bd6dc.

American Psychiatric Association. (2000). *Diagnostic and statistical manual of mental disorders* (4th ed.). Washington, DC: Author.

American Psychological Association. (2002). *Multicultural guidelines on education and training, research, practice and organizational change for psychologists.* Washington, DC: Author.

American Psychological Association. (2007). *Report of the APA taskforce on socioeconomic status.* Washington, DC: Author.

American Psychological Association. (2008, August). Resolution on transgender, gender identity, and gender expression non-discrimination. Retrieved February 16, 2009, from http://www.apa.org/pi/lgbc/policy/transgender.html

Association of Lesbian, Gay, Bisexual, and Transgender Issues in Counseling. (2009). Transgender competencies. Retrieved May 15, 2009, from http://algbtic.org/resources

Berenbaum, S. A. (2006). Psychological outcome in children with disorders of sex development: Implications for treatment and understanding typical development. *Annual Review of Sex Research, 17*, 1–38.

Bockting, W. O. (1997). Transgender coming out: Implications for the clinical management of gender dysphoria. In B. Bullough, V. L. Bullough, &

J. Elias (Eds.), *Gender blending* (pp. 48–52). Amherst, NY: Prometheus Books.

Bockting, W., & Coleman, E. (2007). Developmental stages of the transgender coming out process: Toward an integrated identity. In R. Ettner, E. Eyler, & S. Monstrey (Eds.), *Principles of Transgender Medicine and Surgery* (pp. 185-205). Binghamton, NY: Haworth Press.

Bockting, W. O., Robinson, B. E., Benner, A., & Scheltema, K. (2004). Patient satisfaction with transgender health services. *Journal of Sex & Marital Therapy, 30*, 277–294.

Bornstein, K. (1998). *My gender workbook: How to become a real man, a real woman, the real you, or something else entirely.* New York: Routledge.

Brill, S., & Pepper, R. (2008). *The transgender child: A handbook for families and professionals.* San Francisco: Cleis Press.

Brown, M. L., & Rounsley, C. A. (1996). *True selves: Understanding transsexualism: For families, friends, coworkers, and helping professions.* New York: Wiley.

Carroll, L. C. (2010). *Counseling sexual and gender minorities.* Upper Saddle River, NJ: Merrill/Pearson.

Carroll, L. C., & Gilroy, P. J. (2002). Transgender issues in counselor preparation. *Counselor Education and Supervision, 41*(4), 233–244.

Carroll, L. C., Gilroy, P. J., & Ryan, J. (2002). Counseling transgendered, transsexual, and gender-variant clients. *Journal of Counseling & Development, 80* (2), 131–139.

Carroll, R. A. (2000). Assessment and treatment of gender dysphoria. In S. R. Leiblum & R. C. Rosen (Eds.), *Principles and practice of sex therapy* (3rd ed.). New York: Guilford.

Chase, C. (1998). Surgical progress is not the answer to intersexuality. *Journal of Clinical Ethics, 9*, 385–392.

Chavez, S. C., & Lorah, P. (2007). An overview of affirmative psychotherapy and counseling with transgender clients. In K. J. Bieschke, R. M. Perez, & K. A. DeBord (Eds.), *Handbook of counseling and psychotherapy with lesbian, gay, bisexual, and transgender clients.* Washington, DC: American Psychological Association.

Chen-Hayes, S. F. (2001). Counseling and advocacy with transgender and gender-variant persons in schools and families. *Journal of Humanistic Counseling, Education, & Development, 40*(1), 34–49.

Clements-Nolle, K., Marx, R., & Katz, M. (2006). Attempted suicide among transgender persons: The influence of gender-based discrimination and victimization. *Journal of Homosexuality*, *51*, 53–69.

Coogan, K. (2006). Fleshy specificity: (Re)considering transsexual subjects in lesbian communities. In A.P. Aragón (Ed.), *Challenging lesbian norms: Intersex, transgender, intersectional, and queer perspectives* (pp. 17–41). Binghamton, NY: Harrington Park Press.

Cooper, K. (1999). Practice with transgendered youth and their families. *Journal of Gay & Lesbian Social Services*, *10*, 111–129.

Coventry, M. (1999). Finding the words. In A. D. Dreger (Ed.), *Intersex in the age of ethics*. Hagerstown, MD: UniversityPublishing Group.

Currah, P., & Minter, S. (2000). *Transgender equality: A handbook for activists and policymakers*. New York: National Gay and Lesbian Task Force and National Center for Lesbian Rights.

Davidson, M. (2007). Seeking refuge under the umbrella: Inclusion, exclusion, and organizing within the category transgender. *Sexuality Research & Social Policy*, *4*(4), 60–80.

Denny, D. (2004). Changing Models of Transsexualism. *Journal of Gay and Lesbian Psychotherapy*, *8*(1/2), 25–40.

Devor, A. H. (2004). Witnessing and mirroring: A fourteen stage model of transsexual identity. *Journal of Gay and Lesbian Psychotherapy*, *8*(1/2), 41–67.

deVries, A. L. C., Cohen-Kettenis, P. T., & Delemarre-van de Waal, H. (2006). Clinical management of gender dysphoria in adolescents. *International Journal of Transgenderism*, *9*(3/4), 83–94.

Diamond, M. (2002). Sex and gender are different: Sexual identity and gender identity are different. *Clinical Child Psychology and Psychiatry*, *7*, 320–334.

Diamond, M., & Sigmundson, H. K. (1997). Management of intersexuality. *Archives of Pediatric and Adolescent Medicine*, *151*, 1046–1050.

dickey, L. M., Burnes, T. D., & Singh, A. A. (in progress). Sexual orientation identity development of female-to-male transsexuals: A qualitative exploration.

Dreger, A. D. (1998). *Hermaphrodites and the medical intervention of sex*. Cambridge, MA: Harvard University Press.

Dreger, A. D. (Ed.). (1999). *Intersex in the age of ethics*. Hagerstown, MD: University Publishing Group.

Dreger, A. D. (2003). *Shifting the paradigm of intersex treatment*. Retrieved November 7, 2008, from http://www.isna.org/compare.html

Fausto-Sterling, A. (1997). How to build a man. In V.A. Rosario (Ed.), *Science and homosexualities* (pp. 219–225). New York: Routledge.

Fausto-Sterling, A. (2000). *Sexing the body*. New York: Basic Books.

Feder, E. K., & Karkazis, K. (2008). What's in a name?: The controversy over "disorders of sex development." *Hastings Center Report*, *38*(5), 33–36.

Harmon-Smith, H. (1999). A. mother's 10 commandments to medical professionals: Treating intersex in the newborn. In Dreger, A. D. (Ed.), *Intersex in the age of ethics*. Hagerstown, MD: University Publishing Group.

Hekma, G. (1994). A female soul in a male body: Sexual inversion as gender inversion in nineteenth-century sexology. In G. Herdt (Ed.), *Third sex third gender: Beyond sexual dimorphism in culture and history* (pp. 213–240). New York: Zone Books.

Hird, M. J. (2008). Queer(y)ing intersex: Reflections on counseling people with intersex conditions. In L. Moon (Ed.), *Feeling queer or queer feelings? Radical approaches to counseling sex, sexualities, and genders*. New York: Routledge/Taylor & Francis Group.

Hughes, I. A., Houk, C., Ahmed, S. F., & Lee, P. A. (2006). Consensus statement on the management of intersex disorders. *Journal of Pediatric Urology*, *2*(3), 148–162.

Intersex Society of North America. (2008). *What is intersex?* Retrieved March 15, 2009, from http://www.isna.org

Klein, R. (1999). Group work practice with transgendered male to female sex workers. *Journal of Gay and Lesbian Social Services*, *10*(3/4), 95–109.

Korell, S. C., & Lorah, P. (2007). An overview of affirmative psychotherapy and counseling with transgender clients. In K. J. Bieschke, R. M. Perez, & K. A. DeBord (Eds.), *Handbook of counseling and psychotherapy with lesbian, gay, bisexual, and transgender clients* (pp. 271–288). Washington, DC: American Psychological Association.

Kosciw, J. G., & Diaz, E. M. (2006). *The 2005 national school climate survey: The experiences of lesbian, gay, bisexual and transgender youth in our nation's schools*. New York: GLSEN.

Krueger, M., Yekani, S. A. H., Hundt, G. V., & Daverio, P. J. (2007). One-stage sex reassignment surgery from female to male. *International Journal of Transgenderism*, *10*(1), 15–18.

Lambda Legal. (2008). *Bending the mold: An action kit for transgender youth*. Retrieved October 31, 2008, from www.lambdalegal.org

Lawrence, A. (2007). Transgender health concerns. In I. H. Meyer & M. E. Northridge (Eds.), *The health of sexual minorities: Public health perspectives on lesbian, gay, bisexual, and transgender populations* (pp. 473–505). New York: Springer Science & Business Media.

Lev, A. I. (2004). *Transgender emergence: Therapeutic guidelines for working with gender-variant people and their families.* New York: Haworth Press.

Lev, A. (2007). Transgender communities: Developing identity through connection. In K. Bieschke, R. Perez, & K. DeBord (Eds.), *Handbook of counseling and psychotherapy with lesbian, gay, bisexual, and transgender clients* (2nd ed., pp. 147–175). Washington, DC: American Psychological Association.

Levy, A., Crown, A., & Reid, R. (2003). Endocrine intervention for transsexuals. *Clinical Endocrinology, 59,* 409–418.

Lewis, J., Arnold, M., House, R., & Toporek, R. (2003). *Advocacy competencies.* [Electronic version]. Retrieved February 15, 2009, from http://www.counseling.org/Publications

Mallon, G. P. (1999). Appendix A: A glossary of transgendered definitions. In G. P. Mallon (Ed.), *Social services with transgendered youth* (pp. 143–145). Binghamton, NY: Harrington Park Press.

Marut Schober, J. (1999). A. surgeon's response to the intersex controversy. In Dreger, A. D. (Ed.), *Intersex in the age of ethics.* Hagerstown, MD: University Publishing Group.

Meyer, W., Bockting, W., Cohen-Kettenis, P., Coleman, E., Diceglie, D., Devor, H., et al. (2001, January-March). Harry Benjamin International Gender Dysphoria Association's standards of care for gender identity disorders (6th version). *International Journal of Transgenderism, 5*(1). [Online]. Available at: http://www.symposium.com/ijt/soc.2001/index.htm

Money, J. (1973). *Man and woman, boy and girl: Differentiation and dimorphism of gender identity from conception to maturity.* Baltimore MD: Johns Hopkins University Press.

Morland, I. (2008). Intimate violations: Intersex and the ethics of bodily integrity. *Feminism Psychology, 18,* 425–430.

National Association of Social Workers. (2001). *NASW standards for cultural competence in social work practice.* Retrieved February 20, 2009, from http://www.socialworkers.org/sections/credentials/cultural_comp.asp

Patton, C. (2007). *Anti-lesbian, gay, bisexual, and transgender violence in 2006.* New York: National Coalition of Anti-Violence Programs.

Pepper, S. M., & Lorah, P. (2008). Career issues and workplace considerations for the transsexual community: Bridging a gap of knowledge for career counselors and mental health care providers. *The Career Development Quarterly, 56*(4), 330–343.

Pfafflin, F. (1992). Regrets after sex reassignment surgery. In W.O. Bockting & E. Coleman (Eds.), *Gender dysphoria: Interdisciplinary approaches in clinical management.* Binghamton, NY: Haworth Press.

Pickering, D. L. (2005). Counselor self-efficacy with transgendered clients: Implications for training. *Dissertation Abstracts International,* DAI-A 66/10, 3577.

Preeves, S. E. (2003). *Intersex and identity: The contested self.* Rutgers, NJ: Rutgers University Press.

Raj, R. (2002). Towards a transpositive therapeutic model: Developing clinical sensitivity and cultural competence in the effective support of transsexual and transgendered clients. *International Journal of Transgenderism, 6*(2). Retrieved March 15, 2009, from http://www.symposion.com/ijt/ijtvo06no02_04.html

Ridley, C. R. (2005). *Overcoming unintentional racism in counseling and therapy: A practitioner's guide to intentional intervention* (2nd ed.). Thousand Oaks, CA: Sage.

Rosario, V. A. (2006). An interview with Cheryl Chase. *Journal of Gay & Lesbian Psychotherapy, 10* (2), 93–104.

Sanchez, F. J., & Vilain, E. (2009). Collective self-esteem as a coping resource for male-to-female transsexuals. *Journal of Counseling Psychology, 56* (1), 202–209.

Sausa, L. A. (2005). Translating research into practice: Trans youth recommendations for improving school systems. *The Journal of Gay and Lesbian Issues in Education, 3*(1), 15–28.

Singh, A. A., Hays, D. G., & Watson, L. (in review). The resilience experiences of transgender individuals. *Journal of Counseling and Development.*

Smith, Y. L. S., Van Goozen, S. H. M., Kuiper, A. J., & Cohen-Kettenis, P. T. (2005). Sex reassignment: Outcomes and predictors of treatment for adolescent and adult transsexuals. *Psychological Medicine, 35,* 89–99.

Sobralske, M. (2005). Primary care needs of patients who have undergone gender reassignment. *Journal of the American Academy of Nurse Practitioners*, *17*(4), 133–138.

Spehr, C. (2007). Male to female sex reassignment surgery in transsexuals. *International Journal of Transgenderism*, *10*(1), 25–37.

Veale., J. F., Clarke, D. E., & Lomax, T. C. (2008). Sexuality of male-to-female transsexuals. *Archives of Sexual Behavior*, *37*(4), 586–597.

Vera, E. M., & Speight, S. L. (2003). Multicultural competence, social justice, and counseling psychology:

Expanding our roles. *The Counseling Psychologist*, *31*, 253–272.

White, C. H., & Goldberg, J. M. (2006). Social and medical transgender case advocacy. *International Journal of Transgenderism*, *9*(3/4), 197–217.

Zucker, K. J., Bradley, S. J., Owen-Anderson, A., Kibblewhite, S. J., & Cantor, J. M. (2008). Is gender identity disorder in adolescents coming out of the closet? *Journal of Sex & Marital Therapy*, *34*, 287–290.

CHAPTER 15

WHITE IDENTITY AND PRIVILEGE

JEANA L. DRESSEL, SHELLY KERR, and HAROLD B. STEVENS

INTRODUCTION

Frances Kendall (2006), a prominent writer in the area of White privilege, states that White individuals must actively examine how their own race affects their lives. She maintains that the failure to understand how White people individually and as a group perpetuate White superiority is likely to result in superficial relationships with people of color, limited effectiveness in diverse workplaces, and inequality and injustice in society at large. The pervasiveness of White privilege, ethnocentrism, and unintentional racism impedes progress toward developing multicultural competencies (Ancis & Szymanski, 2001). Manglitz (2003) asserts that the examination of the problems of racism has focused on those harmed by racism, rather than those who benefit from it. The author also notes that the topics of White identity, power, and privilege have typically been left out of the examination of racism.

It is important to address White privilege and White racial identity in mental health professional settings and training programs (Abrams & Gibson, 2007; Ancis & Szymanski, 2001; Pack-Brown, 1999). The majority of counseling and psychology students and mental health professionals are White (Ancis & Szymanski, 2001; Pack-Brown, 1999). The American Psychological Association has identified self-awareness as a fundamental component of cultural competence. However, multicultural psychology literature has focused on knowledge and information pertaining to culturally diverse groups and has paid limited attention to fostering trainees' own ethnic and cultural awareness (Ancis & Szymanski, 2001; Richardson & Molinaro, 1996). The Council on Social Work Education's *Educational Policy and Accreditation Standards* (2008) sets the expectation that social workers "understand how diversity characterizes and shapes the human experience and is critical to the formation of identity" (p. 4). Abrams and Gibson (2007) cite these standards as a basis for their recommendation that social work curricula include content on White identity and White privilege, and note that this content is consistent with models of social work that focus on creating change at the systemic level.

This chapter will follow the format of other chapters in this book by addressing the audience of mental health practitioners, students, educators, trainers, and supervisors with suggestions, guidelines, and resources for working, teaching, and training in the area of White privilege and White identity. In contrast to other chapters, however, this topic focuses on knowledge, self-awareness, and skills gained by White students or mental health workers about themselves, rather than focusing more directly on the experience of the client. Mental health trainees and professionals of color or international colleagues and trainees may find this chapter helpful in their experiences as trainers, supervisors, and colleagues of White mental health trainees and professionals. As mental health professionals increase their own knowledge and self-awareness, they can translate this learning into better multicultural skills with diverse clients and trainees. Suggested competencies for practicum, internship, entry into professional practice, and advanced/specialization levels in terms of the essential components of knowledge, skills, and values and attitudes are provided in Tables 15.1 through 15.4 at the end of this chapter. This can be a very difficult area for educators, trainers, or supervisors to tackle in class or other training arenas and key issues that make this true will be reviewed in detail. Vignettes will be provided for discussion purposes.

DEFINITIONS OF *PRIVILEGE* AND *WHITE PRIVILEGE*

Privilege can be defined as "a right, immunity, or benefit granted as a particular benefit, advantage, or favor" (Merriam-Webster, n.d.). Wildman and Davis (2002) identify two key elements of privilege. First, the characteristics and attributes of the privileged group are the societal norm and benefit members of the privileged group. Second, privileged group members can rely on their privilege to avoid speaking out against oppression. Cullinan (1999) articulates three presumptions about a dominant cultural group that perpetuate privilege for that group: innocence, worthiness, and competence. Innocence means that dominant-culture members are generally considered to be without blame, whereas others are viewed suspiciously. The presumption of worthiness means that those in the dominant culture are believed to deserve attention, service, and respect. Competence refers to dominant-culture individuals being treated as competent and given autonomy and encouragement.

White privilege, specifically, is an institutional set of unearned benefits granted to White people (Kendall, 2001, 2006; McIntosh, 1989; Sue, 2003). Sue (2003) defines White privilege as "unearned advantages and benefits" given to White individuals based on a system that was "normed on the experiences, values, and perceptions" of White individuals (p. 7). McIntosh (1989) characterizes White privilege as "an invisible package of unearned assets which I can count on cashing in each day, but about which I was 'meant' to remain oblivious" (p. 10). She likens it to "an invisible weightless knapsack of special provisions, maps, passports, codebooks, visas, clothes, tools, and blank checks" (p. 10). Kendall (2006) describes White privilege as "an institutional, rather than personal, set of benefits granted to" (p. 63) people whose race resembles that of the people who are in power.

White privilege is a concept that is systemically embedded in Western society. It is based on the premise that White people are superior to others (Sue, 2003; Wildman & Davis, 2002), and it confers dominance on them (Sue, 2003). White privilege is an unspoken and protected secret (Sue, 2003, 2004). Sue (2004) suggests that White people must maintain a façade of colorblindness in order to deny to themselves that they benefit from being White and how their Whiteness affects individuals of color. Those possessing the privilege may be more resistant to examining White privilege than racism. White people can see the problem of racism as belonging to others, while White privilege involves more personal responsibility (Frankenberg, 1993). White privilege's invisibility strengthens and maintains it. Keeping silent about privilege maintains the status quo and superiority of White individuals (Sue, 2004; Wildman & Davis, 2002).

Several authors identify privileges enjoyed by White people (Cullinan, 1999; Kendall, 2001, 2006; McIntosh, 1989; Sue, 2003). These individuals have greater access to power and resources than do people of color (Kendall, 2001). All White individuals have White privilege, but to differing extents based on other aspects of identity such as gender, sexual orientation, socioeconomic status, physical ability, and so on (Kendall, 2006). Over the past two decades, Peggy McIntosh (2002) has enumerated numerous specific conditions that White people enjoy, including being able to choose to be around people of their own race most of the time, being able to shop without being followed or harassed, knowing that their children will be given educational materials in which their race is reflected, not having their behavior perceived as socially inappropriate attributed to their race, and being able to succeed without being viewed as a credit to their race. More recently, McIntosh (2008) has developed a more complete autobiographical list of forty-six privileges with respect to her African American female colleagues and published in a Knapsack of White Privilege. It is highly recommended as a compelling document for other Whites to consider in their own personal explorations.

Kendall (2006) also identifies a number of privileges enjoyed by White people. They have the privilege of expecting to be educated about race by the people most affected by racism, people of color. They are often not expected to know how to deal with racial situations and are given more leniency to deal ineffectively with those situations without being perceived as incompetent. White people also have the privilege of being able to distance themselves from other White individuals whom they perceive to be the ones who do not get it and to see themselves as liberal and progressive exceptions. Kendall also describes the ability of those who are not people of color to discount those who are, including discounting the comments or behaviors of people of color, and to make assessments that alter their future. She provides examples such as deciding that a potential employee is "not a good fit for our organization," not appearing rude when rephrasing or translating for others as if they cannot speak for themselves, implying that they know how a person of color feels based on of one of their own negative experiences, shaping appropriate language for others, defining parameters of conversation and communication, and keeping White culture, manners, and language central (Kendall, 2006). McIntyre (1997) referred to the process by which White people control discussion and avoid critical communication to keep themselves from examining their own role in perpetuating racism as "White talk" (p. 45).

However, Kendall (2006) indicates that White privilege also has a negative impact on those who benefit from it. White individuals may avoid examining these costs (see, e.g., Spanierman, Todd, & Anderson, 2009). Many White people do not perceive themselves as being powerful or having privilege. If White individuals are aware of their privilege, they are often only aware of the benefits of privilege and not the costs. Understanding the benefits and costs of White privilege means facing the fact that White privilege was constructed and maintained by people just like oneself. By living in a system that views Whiteness as the standard by which normalcy is measured, White people lose the opportunity for authentic relationships in or outside their group. They lose trust from those outside their group and they live by standards imposed on them by their own group, which may not be a matter of personal choice. They also lose their ability to

view the world from other perspectives. Kendall notes that "those of us who are White can't choose to not get the privileges we are granted, but we can choose how to use them" (p. 38).

DEVELOPMENTAL MODELS

White racial identity development models describe movement from White people's lack of awareness of themselves as racial beings toward increased racial consciousness and a capacity for abandoning privileges of racism. Helms' (1995) White Racial Identity Model offers one understanding of White identity development. Helms describes developmental statuses that are not strictly linear and may overlap or be revisited. Movement between statuses occurs when White people have racially based experiences and are faced with the necessity of coping with those experiences. Helms contends that White individuals come to view themselves as entitled to certain privileges and they learn to protect those privileges by denying and distorting racial events. Healthy White identity development results in individuals recognizing and relinquishing their usual strategies for responding to racial experiences.

White people in the *Contact* status are satisfied with the racial status quo and are oblivious to racism and their own role in it. In the *Disintegration* status, they experience anxiety in facing racial moral dilemmas that force them to choose between loyalty to their own group and doing what is right. White individuals in the *Reintegration* status idealize their own group and express denigration and intolerance for other groups. The *Pseudo-independence* status involves an intellectualized commitment to their own group and deceptive tolerance of other groups. The *Immersion/Emersion* status refers to the search for an understanding of the personal meaning of racism and how one benefits from being White. Individuals in the *Autonomy* status use internal standards to define themselves and are able to relinquish the privileges of racism. Sue et al.'s (1998) summary of each status is provided here.

HELMS' WHITE RACIAL IDENTITY STATUSES

1. *Contact:* People in this status are oblivious to racism, lack an understanding of racism, have minimal experiences with Black people, and may profess to be color blind. Societal influence in perpetuating stereotypes and the superior/inferior dichotomy associated between Blacks and Whites are not noticed, but accepted unconsciously or consciously without critical thought or analysis. Racial and cultural differences are considered unimportant and these individuals seldom perceive themselves as dominant group members, or as having biases and prejudices.

2. *Disintegration:* In this stage, the person becomes conflicted over unresolvable racial moral dilemmas that are frequently perceived as polar opposites: believing one is nonracist, yet not wanting one's son or daughter to marry a minority group member; believing that "all men are created equal," yet society treating Blacks as second-class citizens; and not acknowledging that oppression exists while witnessing it (à la the beating of Rodney King in Los Angeles). The person becomes increasingly conscious of his or her Whiteness and may experience dissonance and conflict between choosing between own-group loyalty and humanism.

3. *Reintegration:* Because of the tremendous influence that societal ideology exerts, initial resolution of dissonance often moves in the direction of the dominant ideology associated with race and one's own socioracial group identity. This stage may be characterized as a regression, for the tendency is to idealize one's socioracial group and to be intolerant of other minority groups. There is a firmer and more conscious belief in White racial superiority and racial/ethnic minorities are blamed for their own problems.

4. *Pseudo-Independence:* A person is likely to move into this phase due to a painful or insightful encounter or event, which jars the person from Reintegration status. The person begins to attempt an understanding of racial, cultural, and sexual orientation differences and may reach out to interact with minority group members. The choice of minority individuals, however, is based on how "similar" they are to him or her, and the primary mechanism used to understand racial issues is intellectual and conceptual. An attempt to understand has not reached the experiential and affective domains. In other words, understanding European American White privilege, the sociopolitical aspects of race, and issues of bias, prejudice, and discrimination tend to be more an intellectual exercise.

5. *Immersion/Emersion:* If the person is reinforced to continue a personal exploration of himself or herself as a racial being, questions become focused on what it means to be White. Helms states that the person searches for an understanding of the personal meaning of racism and the ways by which one benefits from White privilege. There is an increasing willingness to truly confront one's own biases, to redefine Whiteness, and to become more activist in directly combating racism and oppression. This stage is marked with the increasing experiential and affective understanding that were lacking in the previous status.

6. *Autonomy:* Increasing awareness of one's own Whiteness, reduced feelings of guilt, acceptance of one's own role in perpetuating racism, and renewed determination to abandon White entitlement leads to an autonomy status. The person is knowledgeable about racial, ethnic, and cultural differences, values the diversity, and is no longer fearful, intimidated, or uncomfortable with the experiential reality of race. Development of a nonracist White identity becomes increasingly strong.

Source: Sue et al., (1998, pp. 52–53). Adapted from Helms (1995, pp. 181–191).

Scott and Robinson (2001) address the convergence of race and gender attitudes that White men may exhibit as a result of societally constructed attitudes. This is a nonlinear model using types. They propose that a *type* suggests the ability to change with education and experience, and that counseling can facilitate this change. They identify five types that seem to parallel the Helms (1995) and D. W. Sue and D Sue (1990) models but include the impact of male identity as well. Scott and Robinson (2001) suggest that the "entrenchment of individualism and perceived threats to the American dream could be a contributing factor to racism and restricted racial identity development in the White male" (p. 417). They believe that self-interrogation and reflection lead to knowledge, and that it is then that White men can "challenge the debilitating socialized notion that they are superior to others" (p. 418). Working toward a less racist view thus entails events that create dissonance between existing belief systems and real-life experiences with those who are *not* White men. At that point, White males have the potential to reevaluate their culture, both as it exists around them and to the extent that they have internalized it, and may recognize the degree to which both racism and sexism are inherent in each. This, in Scott and Robinson's view, is when a White male chooses either to go back to an earlier identity type or to begin to acknowledge the role that power and privilege play in his life. Although Scott and Robinson use these identities to develop strategies for males as clients, we would contend that this level of awareness may be equally helpful for mental health practitioners and trainees.

INDIVIDUAL RESPONSIBILITY

Being conscious of one's role in perpetuating racism or the ways in which one benefits from White privilege is an important step in achieving a nonracist White identity (Ancis & Szymanski, 2001). Individuals must be willing to confront the historical, systemic nature of racism and oppression and to recognize how Whiteness and White privilege

are invisible norms in society and systems (Manglitz, 2003). Kendall (2006) talks about keeping Whiteness explicit through awareness of how being White affects daily experience and how White superiority is maintained. She encourages White people to consider their personal access to institutional power, resources, and influence in education, employment, medical care, social opportunities, housing based on race, and socioeconomic status. McIntyre (1997) refers to "making Whiteness public" (p. 41) or the importance of White individuals acknowledging their own collusion with systems that perpetuate racism.

Responding to shame and guilt is an important aspect of addressing White privilege (Arminio, 2001; Kendall, 2006: Manglitz, 2003; Parker & Schwartz, 2002). Manglitz (2003) indicates that White individuals need to sit with their Whiteness long enough to endure and understand the pain and confusion associated with awareness of their own privilege. Even though White individuals may collaborate with colleagues of color, they must do the hard work themselves and not depend on these colleagues to alleviate their own discomfort.

KNOWLEDGE

Challenging the perceived universality of Whiteness and examining White racial identity leads to a deeper understanding of culture and privilege (Ortiz & Rhoads, 2000). In order to address issues of White privilege, professionals and trainees must be familiar with the literature on Whiteness and White privilege, as well as the literature that describes the process of developing an antiracist White identity (Abrams & Gibson, 2007; Manglitz, 2003).

Understanding of the concept of privilege is a basic tenet of knowledge. Becoming aware of how some groups or people have privilege and profit from better access to resources—schools, food, medicine, transport, and so forth—means learning how others do not. Intentionally learning about the hidden aspects of one's own economic and social benefits requires uncovering what other groups experience differently. The shock of truly comprehending this discrepancy can feel overwhelming to sensitive, well-meaning mental health practitioners who begin to realize how much they may take for granted and how pervasive their privilege can be. This is a time when they need support to remain open and continually learning, and to recognize that this task is more important than avoiding the experience of guilt or shame. Obviously, if mental health practitioners cannot work through their own shame experiences in facing their privilege, they are not going to be effective in working with multicultural clients when this is triggered.

Barriers to Competency in White Privilege

Kendall (2006) has identified what she calls barriers to clarity. She notes that White people have little awareness of social structures as being separate from individuals and that hence it is hard for White people to see themselves as part of a larger entity or system. Therefore everything about Whiteness becomes very personal. A second barrier is the common belief that racism is an interpersonal problem. This leads White people to believe that "if we could just be friends, everything would be fine." This becomes an even more inviting stance if there is extreme pain in looking at what has been done to others by one's ancestors. Often White people do not know what to do with all of this information. Kendall also suggests that White people tend to measure their privilege by looking at what others have received that they have not. She suggests that this allows White people to disavow privilege and access to power and influence because of concurrent membership in a nonprivileged group. Kendall also points out that a barrier that keeps White people from acknowledging their privilege is the desire to believe that what *they* have accomplished or achieved is based on personal merit. Finally, Kendall notes that White people, in seeing themselves as well meaning and good people, find it difficult to accept that they might have some responsibility or role in hurting others and benefiting from Whiteness.

Overcoming Barriers and Gaining Knowledge

How does one gain knowledge about White privilege and White identity? Miller and Garan (2008), in their book, *Racism in the United States: Implications for the Helping Profession*, suggest that people of color are more likely to be aware of racism and their roles as "racial actors" than White people. The authors believe that, in learning about Whiteness and privilege, it may be helpful to gain a historical perspective. Knowing the context in which these terms came about may give people of privilege and others a way to understand that which is outside of themselves as a prerequisite to understanding how it relates to them. Writers such as Zinn (2003), Williams (2005), and Malcomson (2000) offer readers a glimpse into how the institution of racism came about and how it is perpetuated today, sometimes without thought. As Helms' (1995) model acknowledges, there is a developmental piece to learning about privilege, and those with privilege appear to learn at an intellectual level first. For many, recognizing their own privilege becomes more difficult. Literature and film, including works of fiction, autobiographies, memoirs, short stories, and documentaries portraying the lives of those traditionally disempowered by dominant American culture, can be avenues for additional growth.[1] Janet Helms' (1992) book, *A Race Is a Nice Thing to Have: A Guide to Being a White Person or Understanding the White Person in Your Life*, is an excellent source for exercises. One helpful starting exercise is called "What Is White?" (Helms, 1992). Brown,

---

[1] A few brief examples might include: *Makes Me Wanna Holler* (Nathan McCall, New York: Vintage Books, 1995); *How the Garcia Girls Lost Their Accents* (Julia Alvarez, Chapel Hill, NC: Algonquin Books of Chapel Hill, 1991); the short story, *This Is What It Means to Say, Phoenix, Arizona* (Sherman Alexie, in *The Best American Short Stories, 1994*, Tobias Wolff & Katrina Kenison, Eds., Boston: Houghton Mifflin, 1994); and the film, *The Color of Fear* (Lee Mun Wah, Oakland, CA: Stir-Fry Productions, 1994). The Resources section at the end of this chapter provides additional information and suggestions.

Parham and Yonker (1996) similarly pose three questions in focusing on training positive attitudes around Whiteness: How do you define Whiteness? How does it feel to be White? What are the advantages (disadvantages) of being White? Please see the Resources section at the end of this chapter for a list of these and other suggested readings.

A second step is to seek out experiences by attending workshops and conferences to learn more. There are national conferences on White privilege, including the White Privilege Conference (http://www.uccs.edu/~wpc/) and the Pedagogy of Privilege Conference (https://portfolio.du.edu/pc/port?portfolio=pedagogy_of_privilege). But a mental health practitioner could also take the risk of engaging others in talking about privilege, instead of remaining silent. This important step could begin with something as simple as asking a series of questions, such as

- What privileges are you aware of, or do you even think about it?
- Do you think about who has or does not have privilege, or what privilege is?
- Are your friends all from the same ethnic group? All able bodied? All Christian? All heterosexual? If so, what meaning do you attribute to those facts?

Many variations of these questions exist and can be tailored to specific circumstances.

SKILLS

The skills involved in combating White privilege may be more difficult to develop than many other skills related to cultural competency. Individuals who can acknowledge their privilege may still have trouble understanding how it impacts themselves and others. Miller and Garan (2008) have gone so far as to entitle one of their chapters, "Why is it so difficult for people with privilege to see racism?" (pp. 87–102). For mental health practitioners, and probably more so for White therapists, this has many implications. Because mental health practitioners value self-reflection and awareness of self, their inability to look at their privilege can impede this process. Often guilt and shame create a defensiveness that prevents further exploration. The result may be an unwillingness to acknowledge or work through these issues. It seems axiomatic, therefore, that a foundational skill in the arena of privilege is the ability to recognize defensiveness as it relates to privilege. By honestly grappling with these issues, we become more culturally competent professionals, and are better able to understand our clients, colleagues, other professionals, and ourselves.

Basic Skills Acquisition

In Case Vignette 15.1, Paul valiantly tries to take his appropriate role as a trainee (despite the

CASE VIGNETTE 15.1

Paul is a 44-year-old White graduate student completing his pre-doctoral internship at a college counseling center. He is returning to his office following a staff meeting when the parents of a student meet him in the waiting room asking to talk with Paul about some concerns regarding their son. Paul apologizes and identifies himself as a psychology intern and then turns to the director of the center, Carina, who also is returning from the staff meeting. She is a 50-year-old Latina, who has been director for five years. He introduces her as the director and suggests that she might be the person with whom the parents would like to speak. The parents appear bewildered and continue to engage Paul about the issue, occasionally looking at the director but for the most part looking at Paul.

privileges granted to him by his gender and race) by informing the parents about his role and introducing his director. Yet the parents appear to continue to treat the director as secondary. How do Carina and Paul handle this situation? Do they respond to the implied cultural comfort of the parents and let Paul be the one to handle their concern? Does Carina assert her authority, speak up, and take control? Will this help the parents, or should they both continue to listen and try to further assess what might be going on? Is the bewilderment related to the gender/race/authority expectations of the parents or something else? Both Paul and Carina might struggle with their own discomfort with the situation in addition to awareness of their obligations to the parents. The director–trainee hierarchy within the center can make that more or less difficult depending on Carina's security in her role as director and Paul's in his role as intern. The stressful nature of the situation may be exacerbated by tension, not only regarding the parents in their confusion, but also between the trainee and director in terms of how this moment will be resolved. In this case the White intern has demonstrated an awareness of how his Whiteness and gender became associated with status. Is there a further step Paul might take to support the director? Or should he step back and let Carina take over? What we do not know is the previous relationship between Carina and Paul. Has there been a comfortable relationship between them such that they are both able to let the priority be what seems most comfortable for the parents? Is there any prior history that makes it especially

important that Paul support Carina in her role as the authority figure? These are some of the contextual issues that are also of concern. Given all of these issues, Paul needs to be particularly mindful of his nonverbal and verbal communication. His ethnicity, gender, age, and size (although the last is unspecified) may automatically state to the parents, "I'm in charge." Carina may also need to step forward and take the role of Director as her own by graciously welcoming them in that capacity.

Another important skill is the willingness to engage with the question, "How do race and privilege play a role in what I am doing?" and to actively address issues raised by the answer. We have found that asking this question (to a person of privilege) in even the most seemingly transparent circumstances can shed new light on a supervisory or therapeutic situation. The ability to consider how one may be perceived in a cross-cultural dyad is crucial. Denial or lack of awareness of one's privilege can have a devastatingly negative impact on the relationship. See Ramos-Sánchez et al. (2002) for examples characterizing supervisory problems involving legal, ethical, and multicultural issues that were "strikingly severe in nature." These examples were noted for being "particularly pernicious and harmful" to trainees despite their relatively low reported frequency in the sample (p. 201). If the dyad is not cross-cultural (e.g., involving a White supervisor and a White practicum student), the pair can inadvertently collude in ways that may be oppressive and destructive for the client or supervisee.

CASE VIGNETTE 15.2

Xuan is a graduate student in counseling doing a practicum at a mental health center. He is an international student from Taiwan. You will be his supervisor for the next semester. Two previous supervisors agree that he seems to lack connection with his clients, and he has a history of clients either "no showing" or not returning to therapy after one or two visits. Prior reports state that he does not have the necessary basic communication skills and lacks empathy with clients. Concern has been expressed as to the appropriateness of his being a therapist. He has been limited to seeing one or two clients with the hopes that intense supervision on these cases will help. In supervision, although his accent is "heavy," he has an excellent vocabulary, knows his theory, and conceptualizes clients well. When watching him on videotape he seems nervous, presumably in part due to his recognition that he is under scrutiny. At the same time, you notice that his reflections are generally accurate and empathic. However, when the client uses a metaphor to describe something, Xuan sometimes seems mystified as to what the client meant or parrots back what the client said. Other times, he interprets the metaphor literally, and then the client seems confused.

Here is a situation in which the two previous supervisors have to some degree colluded to believe that Xuan needs at the minimum remediation and possibly even expulsion from the program. As a mental health practitioner, the White supervisor could have used privilege to collude and agree that Xuan is not an effective therapist. By explicitly acknowledging issues of privilege in this situation, however, the supervisor and Xuan might be able to define the difficulty here as primarily a linguistic issue (i.e., Xuan's unfamiliarity with metaphorical expression in English). This cultural element inhibited Xuan's success as a trainee and represented a multicultural language issue for both the counseling and supervision dyads. Viewed in this light, remediation takes on a different tone and becomes much more hopeful in terms of helping Xuan to become a successful mental health practitioner.

Advanced Skills Acquisition

In Case Vignette 15.2, with the recognition and knowledge of privilege, a different response is possible. The opportunity to understand how any formalized program can sometimes become oppressive and how privilege plays a role in this can then be appreciated. Hence, another skill is the ability to recognize these dynamics and, in some cases, look beyond typical expectations. In Case Vignette 15.2 an international student was working in his second language and missed nuances that native speakers take for granted.

CASE VIGNETTE 15.3

Latisha is a licensed psychologist working at a student counseling center at a predominately White university. She is an African American female. Part of her role at the center is Coordinator of the Drug and Alcohol Program. The program as it exists provides services primarily to students being referred by the student judicial committee and by law enforcement establishments throughout the state. Recently, campus fraternities expressed concern about how they were viewed on campus related to alcohol consumption. They were also concerned about some particular members and their personal consumption habits. The fraternities requested that a program be developed to which they could refer their members for evaluation, recommendations, and, if necessary, treatment. This was a concern for Latisha as she saw this as creating an avenue of resources available to a specific group that circumvented the traditional judicial system. Because the fraternities were largely White, this seemed to create a special privilege in terms of race and socioeconomics. When Latisha hinted at this as a possibility to higher-level administrators, they minimized her concern by noting that alcohol consumption was a serious issue in the fraternities and that plans were ultimately to expand this program to include all students.

As a supervisor to a White intern, Latisha pointed out this incident as an example of privilege. The intern, already defensive about aspects of his own privilege, saw the program in the same light as the administration. He spent time talking with the other two interns about this. They concluded that this was not an example of privilege but rather a true attempt to deal with the drinking problem on campus and that Latisha was biased in her appraisal of the situation.

Why would the services and program being developed be considered a source of privilege for the fraternities? While the intention may be to extend this program to other groups, it starts with a specific population, fraternity members. Considerable personnel time and monies will now be given to develop a program that is targeted for a select group of these students, problem drinkers. Further, these individuals might be able to avoid judicial consequences for their potentially disruptive and/or destructive behavior by being referred directly to treatment options. Other students on campus still have to pay consequences for their drinking behavior—but if you are White and have the money and qualities it takes to be accepted into a fraternity, you can also qualify for this program that may get you out of a problematic situation. For example, if a student gets drunk and breaks some furniture, he would be identified for this program. Although the behavior is identified as significant enough for treatment, there would be no judicial consequences because that step would be avoided. Is that privilege?

Obviously, the administration wants to be supportive of fraternities taking proactive steps on behalf of their members, but is there an alternative that does not provide a specialized privilege for an already privileged group? Also,

has Latisha been set up in her position with few allies (e.g., others who would support her view) surrounding her? Is she one of a few persons of color in the Student Affairs Division or with the sensitivity to recognize issues of diversity and privilege? For Latisha, how might she begin to challenge the thinking of the three interns? Even if she does not convince them that this is an example of privilege, how does she begin to get them to question their acceptance that it is *not*?

In consideration of the same vignette, are the interns using their privilege to determine that their supervisor may be off the mark? Does this lead them to think she might be "overdoing it on the multicultural end"? Will their feedback describe their supervision as being biased and too narrow minded? The circumstances described in this vignette might represent an ideal opportunity for another professional who has privilege to identify this action as an exercise of privilege and to empower Latisha. This could be done by recognizing, with Latisha, what has happened and determining how best to be of support, be it through advocacy, listening and understanding, and so on. It may also include learning to sit with the discomfort in recognizing how one's own privilege may have contributed to the system.

VALUES AND ATTITUDES

One of the most challenging issues for those who possess White privilege is its invisibility. White individuals may not be able to see their own privilege, and may not all share the same openness to considering the possibility of discovering it. The differing values of the White working and middle classes, for instance, can impact how members of

Comparison of Working- and Middle-Class Values

Working Class	Middle Class
• Make as much money as you can to pay for as good a life as you can get.	• Possesses "cultural capital"—knowing about networking, cultural information, and using contracts; identifies with brands of clothing, cars, watches, etc.
• Whatever-it-takes work ethic; forthright manner—open, honest; fatalism, resignation about life.	• Sense of belonging—speaks language of proud majority

Working Class	Middle Class
• Blue-collar roots.	culture and supervisors, etc. (jargon, customs, nonverbals).
• Respect for parents, close contact with extended family, loyalty and sense of solidarity with family and community.	• Privilege of education, expects extras.
	• Individuality.
• Physicality; understanding what it takes in a hard world; belief that it's a struggle to make it.	• Kids have, say, choices.
	• Intellectual challenge and choices.
• Kids to do what they're told, strict, authoritarian obedience over curiosity.	• Relates to images in popular culture.
	• Analytical, cultivated, logical.
• Limited images in the media.	• Emotional restraint of anger; surface appearance of getting along.
• Mistrust of eggheads—trust common sense, luck, and intuition.	• Understands the language and how to question doctors/ lawyers.
• Emotionally expressive—tougher, flashier, louder.	
• Desire to see that all have a good job.	• Pressure to out-achieve parents and expects a good job.
• Bowling, basketball, NASCAR, baseball.	• Racquetball, tennis, golf, football.
• My country, right or wrong.	• Questioning of politics or apathy more prominent.
• Acquiescence to expert authority; don't tell me what to do in my own territory.	• Protesting/questioning authority.
	• I have to do this . . .
• I am what I am.	• Subtle expression of prejudice.
• Overt prejudices.	• Indoors, desk work.
• Outdoors, manual, physical work.	• Upscale restaurant chains or privately owned restaurants.
• Fast-food restaurants.	• Delayed child bearing until after completing college.
• Age of pregnancy more common in high school.	• Expects to be a manager or upper-level/career worker.
• Expects to be a worker.	

Source: Adapted from Lubrano (2004, pp. 7–29).

each class view their own opportunities for advancement and success. See the table for a contrast between traditional working- and middle-class values.

That their Whiteness gives them privilege may be harder for some working-class members to recognize than middle-class members who experience less economic stress and have more access to higher-end jobs and advancement. Also, referencing some of the dynamics described above, middle-class individuals might be less awed by doctors/lawyers, hoping eventually to enter the financial upper class themselves; working-class individuals may perceive themselves as disenfranchised relative to both of these groups and thus find it difficult to view themselves as privileged. They may see themselves scrambling as hard as any other worker and may feel that minorities in fact get advantages due to affirmative action. These same workers are unlikely to believe employment and hiring statistics over the "truth" of what they see. They see persons of color doing as well as they are doing—so how could there be a problem? That the White individual may be less likely to be stopped by police (see, e.g., Clark, 2006), more likely to be given favorable treatment for loans or a raise (see, e.g., Zito, 2003), and so forth, might never have occurred to them. Yet, those details can mean a significant quality-of-life difference between two people from ostensibly comparable socioeconomic circumstances. This is a hidden reality of privilege that those who possess it may not have encountered or considered.

However, some White working-class individuals and persons of color may share a number of similar values described earlier, such as maintaining close ties with family and community, openness of expression, and so on. Some working-class members may, in fact, be more comfortable with diversity than their more educated peers because they have more experience living and working alongside individuals from other cultures. This level of comparative acceptance varies with the extent of isolation from other groups and the degree of tension that exists between the diverse communities. The middle-class value of being subtle in expressing prejudice noted previously makes it harder for these individuals to broach their personal biases, as it is considered unacceptable to do so. This speaks to the issue of shame discussed earlier in the chapter: If you have been taught that you should not be prejudiced, it is difficult to face that you are. This is one way in which the working-class value of "not trusting the eggheads" might have evolved, in that people may have sensed that some more highly educated individuals were not being totally honest with themselves.

While class may correlate with one subset of an individual's values, religion, or ethnicity (i.e., identification as Italian, Polish, etc.), exposure to persons of color may also be influential. A recent qualitative study of White students at a Midwestern university presents a unique picture of attitudes of students coming from predominantly White hometowns with minimal exposure to diversity (Spanierman et al., 2008). The interview technique allowed the investigators to discover the personal reactions of White college students who had limited contact with persons of color and the dissonance that they encountered when thinking about affirmative action versus outright discrimination. They frequently expressed anger at perceived advantage for those receiving affirmative action and frequently expressed empathy for those being discriminated against. This study noted that the two students who demonstrated the highest levels of racial awareness and sensitivity reported painful experiences that isolated them from White peers for their beliefs or actions.

Case Vignette 15.4 provides an example of interactions between two White people from

CASE VIGNETTE 15.4

David, a White social work intern from a working-class background, has been assigned to work with Randall, a White undergraduate first-year student who has advanced placement and is unhappy at his university. Randall presents as intellectualized and is very critical of the school and the immaturity of the students in his residence hall. He questions David about his credentials and how far along he is in his program. Randall also uses jargon during the interview to let it be known that he knows psychological theory and that a well-known psychologist is a family friend. David takes this in stride externally, without getting defensive. David is also aware of the class difference, for example, that this student is wearing clothes David could not have afforded as a student and makes reference to his car, which David never would have owned as an undergraduate. David is aware that he is becoming irritated with Randall, and recognizes that it is due to the client's attitude of superiority. He tries to monitor any negative reactions and returns his focus to what might be going on for the client. He allows Randall to continue to talk and learns how Randall is unsuccessfully trying to find friends and start relationships. The client is unable to say that he is not fitting in. He can say that he isn't challenged in his classes and that he is bored with the drinking and the parties. He can say what's wrong, but he can't say what he feels vulnerable about. David is struggling with being direct with Randall—partially due to his lack of connection with him and partially due to his discomfort with his own internal dislike of Randall. He is aware of this and is considering an extended intake option, which would allow him to seek supervision and meet with the student again after he has openly explored his reaction with his supervisor. He suspects that how he is reacting to Randall may also be how others are reacting to him, and that, if he can get a handle on this, he could be especially helpful to Randall.

different class backgrounds. David is demonstrating an awareness of his interpersonal reaction to the client within the session and also some psychotherapeutic conceptualization of how he might use his reaction clinically. At this point, however, his level of awareness of possible class differences is unknown and remains something to be explored. Is he aware of why he is irritated by the client, Randall? He appears to have an awareness at some level of greater privilege and an attitude of superiority on the client's part. As a supervisor, what would you do with this? If David were a practicum-level student who did not demonstrate the same insight and were aware only of feeling irritated by and disconnected from Randall, how would you proceed as a supervisor? For a taped session, the best teaching tool might be to stop the tape and note the interaction, including what each person said, how the therapist felt at that time, and so on, then continue to slowly move through the tape in a similar fashion. David in this vignette reflects the expected developmental level of an intern who can recognize some dissonance in the session, monitor it to some extent, and then set a goal for an extended intake and supervision.

What values and underlying factors facilitate individuals being open to owning their privilege? One answer might be found in Helms' (1995) White Racial Identity Model, which states that it is important to reach the Immersion/Emersion developmental stage in which the individual is searching for an understanding of racism and his or her own part and privilege within that system. It has been previously noted that mental health practitioners have the responsibility for first knowing themselves (Fouad & Arredondo, 2006), but for those White people wanting to work in a field that is becoming increasingly multicultural, it is imperative that this self-knowledge include an appreciation and understanding of their White privilege and their Whiteness. As noted earlier, this is not easy when there are few White role models comfortable in the teaching of White privilege and where the educational system remains predominantly tailored to meet the perceived needs of White students—often in settings still largely segregated by economics.

Pragmatically, what do those who value learning in this area and who have an attitude of openness *do* in light of the realities of privilege? The challenge of White privilege and being White is that as long as White people are in the majority and/or retain the majority of assets (i.e., finances, institutional power) they will have to be continually vigilant about their own privilege. Privilege is both invisible and built into the social fabric of American culture. Unless they choose to work in a multicultural environment, White people may not see their own privilege. For mental health workers it is imperative that they seek out ways to continually challenge themselves to learn and stay aware. The individual who does not understand her or his privilege can believe in equality but can unintentionally communicate a lack of understanding about *in*equality in interactions with others. This naiveté can injure others in the way career counselors were known to have done for many years by steering women and persons of color to work below their abilities.[2]

Exercise Suggestions

By acknowledging and working through their personal values and attitudes, White students and practitioners can more fully prepare themselves to work ethically and effectively with multicultural clients. Individuals who cannot face their own racism and biases cannot know in what ways they are failing their clients. Writings on White privilege reflect the dilemma that arises for many White people when they realize that they cannot promote equality and justice and retain privilege (see, e.g., McIntyre, 1997, p. 57). An exercise that can challenge an individual either personally or in the classroom is the Personal Racial Moral Dilemma from Helms (1992). This

---

[2] Kenneth B. Clark, for example, was famously counseled to attend vocational school (see, e.g., Jones & Pettigrew, 2005).

challenges individuals to identify two racial moral dilemmas and then answer six questions concerning their responses to the situations with respect to the dimensions of justice, compassion, and so forth. This is not a simple exercise but one requiring deep thought and reflection on one's own personal values and actions. Another suggestion is to use the motivational list that follows (developed by one of the authors with doctoral trainees during their internship) or to develop other personal goals. Those individuals who are ready to move beyond exercises to more active involvement might follow the recommendations of Brown and colleagues (1996) and take a cross-cultural course, immersing themselves in cultural experiences that provide challenges to their beliefs and worldviews.

Expectations for White students working with culturally different clients include familiarity with the definition of *White privilege* and basic application of this concept to their own experiences. The student should be able to apply readings in the area to understand, at a preliminary level, how this

---

WHAT YOU CAN DO ABOUT WHITE PRIVILEGE

1. Accept the discomfort of confronting racism and discrimination rather than trying to keep things "nice."

2. Meet the anger of persons of color rather than denying the cause or deflecting it with guilty submission.

3. Critically look for how you perpetuate and accept White privilege today.

4. Do not distance yourself from the active (and uncomfortable, maybe upsetting/disturbing) process of self-reflection through distancing, silence, withdrawal, being nice, keeping it safe, or derailing.

5. Speak and learn about your racial identity; that you don't have one is not an acceptable answer for the dialogue. Learn how you can discover it without using people of color as your guides or experts.

6. Speak up and acknowledge when White privilege is present.

7. Acknowledge that you have privileges.

8. Don't get stuck in guilt (which is self-focused) and fail to move into the challenge of facing yourself and confronting changing.

9. Acknowledge the way that European American/able-bodied/heterosexual values permeate everyday standards of interpersonal interaction.

10. Suspend judgment about how someone dresses, talks, eats, etc.

11. Accept that you can't always succeed at all these goals, but don't quit or give up.

12. Be an ally for others who are in the minority and take responsibility for learning how to be a *good* ally.

13. Take responsibility for your privilege and do not expect gratitude from others when:
    - You seek to challenge the status quo.
    - You act as an ally.
    - You use your privilege to help or support another.

14. Understand that the journey never ends.

Source: Developed by Jeana L. Dressel, PhD, Kristen Kelly, PhD, and Joseph Severino, MA (2002–2003).

might be impacting clients. While students' lack of experience may limit their ability to predict how their privilege might be anticipated by clients, students may be able to establish an empathic bond for the stresses of limited finances of clients, and so on. Their honest desire to help and develop a positive relationship may overcome some of the lack of understanding of their own privilege.

CASE VIGNETTE 15.5

Ruth is a White practicum student, interpersonally very warm and caring but with limited experience with diverse clients. She is excited to begin working with Jeanette, a first-generation Chicana student, who works 30 hours per week, sends part of her monies home to the family, and is taking 17 credits. Jeanette is complaining about anxiety and stress and doesn't know what to do. She is looking to Ruth for help and does not want to take any psychotropic medications for the anxiety. Ruth has advised her to cut back on her work hours and has also worked out a plan to help her with some anxiety-reduction techniques. Jeanette is too polite to mention to Ruth that cutting back on the work is not possible, although she does like the idea of the anxiety-reduction techniques.

In Case Vignette 15.5 the client will most likely return to treatment because she is getting part of what she wants; however, she may not experience herself as being understood by her therapist. Ruth has failed to appreciate that first-generation students and students of color may have financial obligations requiring them to work during school, and that they may experience pressure to finish school as quickly as they can. The failure of skill highlighted in this vignette might be Ruth's lack of in-depth exploration of these stresses. Had she inquired further, she might have learned that it would not be possible for Jeanette to cut back on her work hours. Ruth's values and attitudes will be tested in supervision as to whether she is open to learning about what she missed in meeting with her client. Does she demonstrate willingness to learn and appreciation for new insights when what she has missed is pointed out to her? It is expected at this level that practicum students will have limited abilities to understand some of their clients, and that supervision will be an important place for this learning. The value that beginning students place on supervision as a place to learn—their attitude for openness, learning, and taking that learning back to the client—is an essential component of growth in this area.

TRAINING

Individuals in roles as educators and trainers must first engage in dialogues about racism, power, and White privilege before they can effectively engage students and trainees in these types of dialogues (Henze, Lucas, & Scott, 1998). Talking about these issues in a meaningful way often generates powerful emotions in participants (Abrams & Gibson, 2007; Arminio, 2001; Hays, Chang, & Dean, 2004; Tatum, 1992) ranging from guilt and shame to anger and despair (Tatum, 1992). Poorly facilitated discussions can dissolve into name-calling and stereotyping, leaving participants feeling guilty or angry (Henze et al., 1998). These discussions can raise issues of which participants were previously unaware without bringing any resolution or closure (Henze et al., 1998).

White counselor trainees often experience shame as they examine their own biases and stereotypes, as well as societal prejudice and oppression. Parker and Schwartz (2002) differentiate shame (perceiving one's core self to be bad) from guilt (feeling regret for acts or behaviors). They describe shame as more overwhelming and immobilizing than guilt, and, therefore, more of an impediment to increasing multicultural competence. These authors recommend addressing explicitly the experience of shame in multicultural training with counselor trainees. They believe that a more positive learning environment is created when trainees are prepared in advance for the situation they might encounter. Finally, they recommend that trainers explain the purpose of multicultural activities or exercises, describe the common emotions (including shame) that might be elicited by participation, role-play training activities that could be shame provoking before expecting trainees to engage in those activities on their own, and allow participants to withdraw from uncomfortable activities. They emphasize that these activities should be conducted within a structured, clearly communicated and supportive environment, and they provide questions for trainers to guide the self-disclosure process.

Arminio's (2001) qualitative study of six graduate students in a college student personnel graduate program focused on race-related guilt. The researcher conceptualized guilt as grief related to the loss of a positive sense of self. He found that guilt was exacerbated by interactions with individuals of color. Arminio indicates that individuals can choose what to do with their guilt; they may deny it, label it as pathological, or learn from it. Kendall (2006) suggests that guilt often keeps White people from taking action or causes responding out of obligation rather than genuine desire. Participants in the Arminio (2001) study indicated that their feelings of guilt stimulated growth and learning.

Trainees' abilities to become more aware of their emotional reactions and to understand and express their feelings may result in increased multicultural competence (Parker & Schwartz, 2002). Arminio's study indicates that graduate students' feelings of guilt actually stimulated their growth and learning. However, the context within which White people express their feelings about their identities and privilege may be important as well. McIntyre (1997) uses the term *privileged affect* to refer to affective strategies that minimize the consequences of racism for people of color and focus on the feelings of White

people. An overemphasis on White people's feelings of powerless, defensiveness, and fear can allow them to give up responsibility for their privilege. As noted previously, Manglitz (2003) emphasizes the importance of privileged individuals working through these challenging feelings themselves, without looking to colleagues of color for protection and absolution.

Addressing White Privilege in Mental Health Training Settings

A few authors have discussed the relevance of White privilege to general and adult education. A paucity of literature, however, exists related to White privilege in the mental health profession.[3] Niehuis (2005) finds only five articles in her review of 20 years of social science and psychology literature on teaching students about White privilege.

Manglitz (2003) posits that adult educators are often unaware of the extent to which theories and research in the field of adult education reinforce White racist attitudes and assumptions. The author explains that Whiteness is considered to be the norm against which all others are taught and evaluated. The norm is consistent with common educational values of meritocracy, individualism, and rational, linear thinking.

A discussion about racism, power, and White privilege among 60 elementary and secondary teachers in California during a staff development institute led Henze and colleagues (1998) to conclude that teachers were hesitant to engage in dialogue about power, racism, and White privilege with colleagues. They found that teachers tended to avoid direct discussions about racism. Instead, the teachers seemed to prefer to dilute the issue and focus on discussions such

---

[3] For a historical perspective, see Robert V. Guthrie's classic excoriation of the mental health field and academia, *Even the Rat Was White.* Guthrie, R. (1976). *Even the rat was White: A historical view of psychology.* New York: Harper & Row.

as "dealing with diversity," "respecting differences," "celebrating diversity," and "promoting multiculturalism" (p. 191). Sue (2004) also notes the tendency for White people to perceive acknowledging differences as creating divisiveness and discomfort and to prefer to focus on commonalities.

Ancis and Szymanski's (2001) study involved 34 White masters-level counseling students enrolled in a *Social and Cultural Issues in Counseling* course. Participants read the McIntosh (1989) paper on White privilege, identified one or more of the conditions described by McIntosh, and provided reactions to the condition(s). Using a qualitative methodology to analyze data, the researchers identified three themes representing increasing levels of awareness. The first theme, Lack of Awareness and Denial of White Privilege, includes the following subthemes: (a) anger and defensiveness; (b) attribution of differential treatment to nonracial factors such as gender, manners, and socioeconomic status (SES); (c) focusing on incidents that are exceptions to the rule or isolated experiences to delegitimize the existence of White privilege; (d) lack of connection between one's own marginalized status and other *isms* and resentment that others do not recognize this marginalization; and (e) denying the existence of White privilege, but acknowledging feeling prompted to think about the personal benefits of being White. The second theme, Demonstrated Awareness of White Privilege and Discrimination, includes the following subthemes: (a) sadness and disgust about privilege and moving beyond feelings of guilt to more critical analysis of one's own privilege; and (b) awareness of White privilege, but without accepting responsibility for one's position or clearly indicating unwillingness to challenge or relinquish privilege. The third theme, Higher Order Awareness and Commitment to Action, includes these subthemes: (a) understanding of the pervasiveness of privilege and possibility of oppression due to aspects of one's identity without minimizing the privileges enjoyed from being White, (b) understanding of the majority's resistance to change, (c) understanding the effects of privilege on people of color, and (d) being moved to act or initiate action.

Hays and colleagues' (2004) qualitative analysis of interviews conducted with counselors working at university counseling centers and in private practice found that many participants had some awareness of their own privilege. However, those same participants had difficulty identifying ways in which privilege was manifested in daily life. Participants who were unaware of their own privilege expressed beliefs that they and others had succeeded because of their own hard work (meritocracy) and that White people experience reverse discrimination because they are required to include everyone. These participants tended to focus on the exceptions that minimized their own personal privilege. They denied their own privilege, while expressing the awareness that others might perceive them to have privilege.

White Identity and Supervision

Further complications within this area are worthy of consideration. The differing developmental levels of supervisors and supervisees are of concern. Potentially, a supervisee of color might be more knowledgeable, skillful, and aware of privilege and identity than his or her supervisor (Cook, 1994) and this can significantly impact the safety and openness of the supervision experience. Cook proposes a progressive supervisory dyad based on Helms' (1990) White Racial Identity Model in which the supervisor is at a more advanced level than the supervisee. In the Regressive supervisory dyad, supervisees would be at a more advanced level than supervisors and would most likely suppress their identities. The dialog between supervisor and supervisee on this dimension would be minimal. Ladany, Brittan-Powell, and Pannu (1997) add to this conceptual model by including a Progressive dyad in which both the supervisor and supervisee are at advanced levels of racial identity development. This Parallel Progressive dyad proved most successful among the various pairings in terms of supervisory agreements on goals and tasks of supervision, as well as emotional bonds between supervisor and supervisee. Parallel Low (supervisor/supervisee are both low in racial identity development) and Regressive (supervisor is lower in racial identity development than the

supervisee) were least influential in multicultural development of the supervisee.

Chang, Hays, and Shoffner (2003) combine the work of several authors, including Cook (1994), in a useful overview of multiple combinations of supervisor–supervisee developmental stages, reproduced here.

Supervisor's Racial Identity Status	Conformity	Dissonance	Resistance and Immersion	Introspection	Integrative Awareness
Contact	Parallel: Unawareness of racial/cultural issues; neither the supervisor nor supervisee increase multicultural competence; myth of sameness	Regressive: Supervisor unaware of racial/cultural issues; supervisor could unconsciously push supervisee into self-depreciating attitudes and beliefs	Regressive: Supervisor unaware of racial/cultural issues; supervisee may attempt to reform supervisor; short, conflictual relationship	Regressive: Supervisor unaware of racial/cultural issues; supervisee frustrated with supervisor's obliviousness to race; supervisory relationship ends in frustration	Regressive: Supervisor unaware of racial/cultural issues; premature termination because supervisee views supervisor as inexpert
Disintegration	Parallel: Supervisor attempts to protect and nurture supervisee; supervisee idealizes supervisor	Parallel: Supervisee attempts to protect and nurture supervisee; supervisee has conflictual feelings	Regressive: Supervisee mistrusts supervisor and views supervisor as part of the oppressive group	Regressive: Unproductive relationship; supervisee may become frustrated with supervisor and view supervisor as patronizing	Regressive: Unproductive; supervisee may attempt to reform supervisor; premature termination with supervisee perceiving supervisor as inexpert
Reintegration	Parallel: Belief in White supremacy; supervisor maintains supervisee at the conformity stage	Regressive: Conflictual relationship; growing mistrust in supervisory relationship	Parallel: Mutual anxiety and dislike because they do not empathize with one another's racial/cultural attitudes	Regressive: Supervisor imposes dominant values; supervisee may either accept or reject; confusing relationship for supervisee	Regressive: Unproductive; supervisee may become frustrated with supervisor; terminate supervisory relationship
Pseudo-independence	Progressive: Supervisor recognizes racial/cultural issues; may discuss	Progressive: Supervisor recognizes racial/cultural issues; open discussion	Progressive: Supervisor recognizes racial/cultural issues; supervisee may	Progressive: Open discussion of racial/cultural issues; supervisor still lacks	Regressive: Supervisee may become frustrated with supervisor's

Supervisor's Racial Identity Status	Conformity	Dissonance	Resistance and Immersion	Introspection	Integrative Awareness
	racial differences; supervisee will find racial/cultural issues anxiety provoking	of racial differences	mistrust supervisor	working knowledge of how to adapt skills and knowledge to supervisee of color	inability to adapt skills and knowledge to supervisee of color; supervisor may improve multicultural competence while working with this supervisee
Immersion/ Emersion	Progressive: Supervisor willing to confront racial/cultural issues; supervisee may find this very threatening	Progressive: Supervisor can assist supervisee in resolving racial/cultural conflict	Progressive: Supervisor can dispel supervisee's view of dominant culture; supervisee may be distrusting of supervisor	Parallel: Mutually enhancing relationship; awareness of racial/cultural issues in supervisor	Parallel: Cultural issues are openly recognized and discussed
Autonomy	Progressive: Supervisor recognizes racial/cultural issues; provides a culturally sensitive approach to supervision	Progressive: Supervisor recognizes racial/cultural issues; provides a culturally sensitive approach	Progressive: Supervisor recognizes racial/cultural issues; supervisee may be resistant to working with a White supervisor	Progressive: Supervisor recognizes racial/cultural issues; can assist supervisee in resolving ethnic identity conflict	Parallel: Both recognize race/ethnicity as an important part of each person's identity; culturally sensitive approach to supervision; movement by both toward advocacy

Thus, the basic supervisory structures adapted by Chang and colleagues (2003) include:

- *Parallel Relationship*—the supervisor and the supervisee exhibit similar racial identity status.
- *Crossed–Regressive*—the supervisor and supervisee exhibit opposite racial identity status where the supervisee is more advanced than the supervisor.
- *Crossed–Progressive*—the supervisor and supervisee exhibit opposite racial identity status where the supervisor is more advanced than the supervisee.

Conceptualizing supervisory relationships in these terms assists supervisors and supervisees alike in understanding potential dynamics around multicultural issues. It is important to note that,

CASE VIGNETTE 15.6

Steve is a 55-year-old White male psychologist. He has been licensed and practicing psychology for over 20 years. He is supervising Juan, a 28-year-old Latino male pre-doctoral intern. Steve has felt successful most of his career. He attends several conferences a year and is particularly interested in trauma. He occasionally attends a seminar or presentation about multicultural counseling at these conferences but generally finds other more "pertinent" presentations to attend. He has never attended a conference that focused expressly on multicultural competency. Steve, however, believes that he is culturally competent and is aware of several diverse clients whom he has helped. Juan is in the second month of his internship. He came from a competitive training program and has learned to do things the "right way" in order to survive graduate school. He has been taught cultural competency "by the book" and is aware that several of his professors know this information at a "politically correct" level. The result is that Juan often recognizes privilege and oppression but also realizes that articulating it can affect his success in the program. Juan is currently working with an African American veteran suffering from post traumatic stress disorder (PTSD). Juan understands that his client is struggling with trust issues about the mental health system and is quite skeptical about treatment. Juan has become desperate because the client's symptoms are worsening. Steve knows interventions for PTSD that would help and is expecting Juan to implement them. Juan is aware of how his client's mistrust may sabotage the treatment but feels unable to address this with his supervisor because his supervisor knows the "right' treatment for PTSD and believes that the client "must trust him by now."

when the teaching/training role combines with that of evaluator, another level of complication is introduced. The need to self-disclose in order to learn and grow requires safety and trust. This makes the knowledge, skill, and value awareness level of the supervisor crucial for competent and quality supervision of a White supervisor with a supervisee of color. These ideas have been incorporated into Case Vignette 15.6.

Steve, being unaware of his privilege as a White male supervisor, has either failed to recognize or has minimized its impact on his supervisee's level of comfort and safety in supervision with him. Additionally, Steve has not been able to consider the client's experience of mistrust with the mental health system. Juan, having had previous experiences with his academic program and probably in life in general, has learned not to challenge the supervisor's expertise. Juan is in a position where he may try to address the mistrust of his client and allow trust to grow. However, he also feels the pressure to administer treatment prematurely. If this happens, the treatment has

the potential to be ineffective, thus reinforcing the client's mistrust of the system. This outcome might be circumvented if Steve were able to discuss his own privilege with Juan in a way that allowed them both to acknowledge its impact on the situation while validating Juan's knowledge of the circumstances and clinical insights as vital treatment components. As it stands, however, this vignette would be an example of a Regressive Supervisory dyad, discussed previously (Cook, 1994).

Why, in Case Vignette 15.6, did Steve not acknowledge his privilege? Possible explanations include: (a) his training about privilege was probably limited, which in turn impeded his awareness of the extent and impact of privilege; (b) consciously or unconsciously, he may not have wanted to admit his privilege; (c) his sense of himself as a competent and culturally sensitive psychotherapist might have been challenged, and it would be uncomfortable to admit this; and (d) admitting his privilege in a university program or environment might lead to isolation or pressure to ignore it. This vignette points out an uncomfortable reality: namely, that trainers and supervisors may be significantly challenged in this area and may have the need for further training.

A number of factors may hinder the recognition of privilege and interfere with it being addressed effectively in therapy and supervision contexts. First, the concept of multicultural counseling is a relatively young part of the mental health field; within that, privilege is one of the newest components. As Ladany et al. (2005) point out, it is not uncommon for trainees to be better versed in concepts of multiculturalism than supervisors who have been in the field for some time. With respect to privilege, members of such dyads could inadvertently collude to overlook or oversimplify the impact of privilege in their work. In addition, while many aspects of multiculturalism emphasize new ways of looking at various cultures and achieving insights as to different lifestyles—learning that can generally be viewed as positive and educational—work around privilege requires recognition of the unfairness of the world and how those with privilege benefit from this. Owning one's role in this can be very uncomfortable. Becoming aware of privilege can generate guilt, defensiveness, and minimization of its impact, and mental health practitioners may intentionally or inadvertently use privilege to ignore these realities.

Finally, the literature about privilege focuses on individual awareness of privilege and how it is used. Relatively little research highlights application of theory to practice. Other than acknowledging that privilege exists and having the insight to recognize when one is using it, practitioners may be left with few practical techniques or strategies for combating privilege. Steve and Juan's vignette illustrates the risk of missing important clinical issues when the dynamics of privilege are not addressed in a supervisory relationship. Ancis and Ladany's (2001) work highlights several of these potential red flags; their analysis of Developmental Stages and Supervision Dyads is summarized in the following. What is particularly valuable in their model is the recognition that individuals can become aware and knowledgeable of privilege and have progressed through stages of interpersonal self-awareness and understanding of one oppressed group (i.e., ethnic/disabled/working-class/gay-lesbian-bisexual-transgender/female) but lack this development with other groups. This model provides some detail about what to expect from the various combinations of supervisory dyads of differing developmental levels of the supervisor and supervisee and therefore is furthering the work of the previous authors (Helms, 1990; Cook, 1994; Chang et al., 2003).

DEVELOPMENTAL STAGES AND SUPERVISION DYADS

Ancis and Ladany (2001) offer a heuristic model of nonoppressive interpersonal development that presumes supervisors and supervisees in the United States come from (a) socially oppressed groups (*SOG*) that encompass females, persons of color, gay/lesbian/bisexual/transgender, disabled, and working-class persons; or (b) socially privileged groups (*SPG*) that include male, White, heterosexual, European-American, physically abled, and middle- to upper-class persons. As individuals progress through developmental phases that the authors term *means of interpersonal functioning (MIF)*, they demonstrate common features designated by four stages: Adaptation, Incongruence, Exploration, and Integration. The authors note that a person can be more advanced in his or her MIF on one demographic variable (i.e., a White woman as a feminist who is aware of her lack of privilege/status but is less aware of her White privilege), and that the progress in supervision can be predicted by the levels of each member's MIF for the differing demographic variables.

(*continued*)

(continued)

At the *Adaptation* stage, members of the SOG and the SPG demonstrate a superficial understanding of differences, minimal awareness of oppression, and limited emotional awareness. Supervisors in this stage are predicted to:

1. Minimize and dismiss their trainees' expression of multicultural competence.
2. Refer to clients based on inaccurate stereotypes.
3. Become anxious if oppression issues emerge in supervision.
4. Inaccurately perceive [themselves] as quite multiculturally competent.
5. Exhibit oppressive beliefs in the presence of SPG trainees.
6. Demonstrate limited integrative complexity when it comes to conceptualizing trainees and clients in a multicultural framework (p. 69).

Supervisees at this stage are unlikely to be multiculturally aware.

At the *Incongruence* stage, persons in either the oppressed (SOG) or privileged (SPG) groups, in terms of their MIF, are experiencing conflict, confusion, and dissonance. The previous defense of denial of oppression no longer works, and persons at this stage are more apt to minimize and rationalize oppression. As supervisors, they are going to pay minimal attention to multicultural issues in the demographic area(s) in which they are not developed. This is a stage in which collusion with the supervisee to not explore multicultural issues is apt to occur. For the supervisee, they are less likely to bring up multicultural issues in order to keep things safe in supervision.

The third stage of MIF is *Exploration*. At this stage, members of either the SOG or the SPG have begun to explore what it means to be a part of these groups. Emotions of anger and shame can arise from this. This stage results in more insightful consideration and active searching. For those in the SOG, it is more likely to lead to cultural immersion and exploration, while those in the SPG may begin to question their role in the oppression. As supervisors, individuals are proactive on multicultural issues and the self-exploration process. The danger at this stage is that this process may be overemphasized for the level of the supervisee or not always integrated into the larger context of supervision.

In the final stage, *Integration*, persons have integrated their awareness, behaviors, and interactions into a commitment to a nonoppressive environment. Persons who have privilege use it to benefit equality and promote change. Supervisors at this stage are able to discuss and process multicultural issues between themselves and their supervisees, facilitate their supervisees' development from the different stages (Adaptation–Exploration), and address clients' multicultural issues. Supervisees at this stage can empathize with their clients and openly face new biases they might encounter.

Supervisors and supervisees at different combinations of stages can lead to dynamically different outcomes. Using the terms noted earlier, a *Progressive* match is where the supervisor is more advanced than the supervisee (i.e., supervisor-Integration/supervisee-Adaptation). In this type of dyad the supervisor will be able to guide and develop the trainee's growth, although there may be resistance on the part of the supervisee. Supervision involving a *Parallel-Advanced* dyad, in which the supervisor and supervisee are at comparable levels of MIF, representing either the Exploration or Integration stages, is apt to be mutually satisfying, collaborative, and possibly creative. Rather than being complacent, both persons place high importance on multicultural understanding and meaning. Another dyad possibility, the *Parallel Delayed*, would involve a supervisor and

> supervisee either at the Adaptation or Incongruence stage. This would be an uncomfortable supervisory dyad; the relationship is likely to be weak, and multicultural issues are likely to be overlooked or minimized. This might be a supervision structure in which the supervisor is too busy for anything but brief sessions or professes a case management style. On the part of the supervisee, tardiness and technical compliance without open and personal disclosure may characterize the supervisory situation.

Recommendations for Training

A few recommendations have been made regarding training in the area of White privilege. Henze and colleagues' (1998) study illustrates the importance of considering the power and ethnicity of facilitators and trainers. Participants may be reluctant to disclose thoughts and feelings openly if they fear being negatively evaluated or faced with retaliation. Highly charged terms (e.g., *power*, *privilege*, and *racism*) should be defined, clarified, and examined as individuals may perceive a concept such as *power* to have positive and negative implications (Henze et al., 1998). It is important to engage in trust-building exercises with groups before beginning dialogues about White privilege in order to create safety. Ground rules that assure safety should be established before engaging in these dialogues (Henze et al., 1998). Ancis and Szymanski (2001) recommend that training in White privilege include readings and exercises that explore how White privilege limits White mental health professionals' own interpersonal functioning. They also recommend the use of exercises that challenge students to relate their own experiences of being treated unfairly to racial discrimination and White privilege. They suggest using exercises that identify situations in which group members' race, ethnicity, gender, sexual orientation, and social class were advantageous and disadvantageous as a means of gaining understanding of privilege. For example, they suggest that students could participate in small group discussions in which they identify similarities and differences between their experiences. They also recommend case studies that examine the intersection of race, gender, sexual orientation, and socioeconomic class. Because defensiveness, anger, guilt, and shame may interfere with honest

self-examination, journaling may be another way to describe affective reactions to the exploration of White privilege.

Complications and Cautions for Training

Merely summarizing the cautions noted in the literature above shows what a daunting responsibility it is to train or educate in this area. These issues make it difficult for discussions and training:

- Avoidance of discussion because it causes discomfort and is seen as divisive
- Lack of awareness of privilege
- Denial of privilege or attribution to nonracial factors
- Anger/defensiveness about privilege
- Focusing on exceptions
- Experiencing shame and the overpowering nature of feeling bad and being unable to sit with this
- White individuals having to do the hard work themselves (as in facing shame) without comfort from their colleagues of color
- Training, power, and ethnicity of the facilitators
- Need for ground rules
- Use of exercises

Furthermore, awareness of these considerations is not enough. Even discussions involving trained facilitators and groups of professionals can go awry, and the more open and unguided the discussion, the more likely it is to veer in an unexpected direction. Many of us carry past wounds that may be unintentionally invoked. This is a very difficult area in which to train, and, once shame has been triggered for someone, he or she may become increasingly sensitive to the charged nature of the topic. It is a moment with great potential for change for those involved, but it may be perceived as a positive or negative crisis depending on whether they interpret a sense of violation or containment and facilitation. Whereas this chapter provides information geared toward generating ideas about starting a discussion in this area, it should not be used to immediately implement training for others. Learning and doing one's own work must come first.

SUMMARY

The work on White privilege highlighted in this chapter is a step that White people must take in meeting the criteria for true Multicultural Counseling Competency. According to the Multicultural Counseling Competencies articulated by Sue, Arredondo, and McDavis (1992), the process of becoming culturally self-aware includes the awareness of one's own biases and limitations. In addition, this awareness includes being comfortable with one's racial, ethnic, and cultural differences. We have discussed how White people need to become aware of their racial identity and understand their privilege. This self-awareness should then be utilized to understand how they are different from their clients interpersonally, culturally, and along many other dimensions, rather than continuing to view their clients as being different from the perceived White "norm." Gaining self-knowledge requires an ongoing process of learning, reflection, and skills acquisition. There is always the need to seek further training, consultation, educational, or enriching cultural experiences. As in the Multicultural Counseling Competencies, the goal would be to continually actively seek further opportunities for development of a more mature, informed identity as a White person, and to take an increasingly active role in promoting and enhancing the growth of others. This might mean taking risks to speak up more as one's career advances, thus becoming a leader or role model for others.

RESOURCES

Facilitating the development of White identity might be a tall order and goes beyond the classroom training. In coming to grips with their own developmental processes, White people face a daunting task: Can they choose to consider what makes them who they are? Willingness to explore and analyze assumptions around identity and self-perception is a crucial component of the struggle to gain the knowledge/awareness, skills, values, and attitudes that can lead to competency in this area. The training exercises and resources provided in this section are designed to aid mental health practitioners and their supervisors in these endeavors.

SUGGESTED TRAINING ACTIVITIES

Holladay (2000) suggests keeping a journal to track the encounters that one has with White privilege (or another privilege), and then imagining what would be different if you did not hold the privilege. Again, dialoguing and processing the experience improves the potential for learning. This is the case, too, with reading and viewing materials to further enlighten and challenge one's perceptions around privilege (see the Resources for Exercises in White Privilege). Holladay reminds us we must remember two things: First, an ability to see racism and privilege with our minds is merely a part of the assignment. This knowledge should manifest itself in our behaviors. Second, our awareness of race and racism is something that we do by choice (privilege)—and because of this our homework never ends (p. 4).

As mental health workers, we have to be aware of the impact that we have on others. Miller and Garran (2008) suggest that strong emotional reactions are likely to be engendered when broaching racism and other topics of diversity, and that these in turn are likely to influence and moderate one's sense of social identity. They recommend pairing and identifying one's identities, identifying which are apparent and which are not, and identifying which are satisfying and pride evoking and which are confusing and cause ambivalence or shame. They also suggest that we recognize how we monitor identities and whether we chose to present or hide certain parts of ourselves. Other suggestions include encouraging exploration of what "triggers" individuals in regard to race and racism (or other *isms*). They suggest asking questions such as, "What responses are most typical for you when you are triggered?" and "What do you find helps you or works for you when you are triggered?" (p. 13). Finally, they suggest that you answer questions related to racial identity formation such as:

- "When did you first become aware of your race or ethnicity?"
- "Did any critical events shape your awareness of your identity?"
- "How has racial identity affected your life?"
- "In what ways are you targeted?"
- "In what ways are you privileged?" (p. 12)

One useful exercise in facilitating participants' understanding of these concepts is completion of a "Sociocultural Identity Wheel" (see Miller & Garran, 2008, Chapter 1) for an explanation and example).

There are many other activities designed to bring about awareness of diversity issues. Most of these can be used, but the emphasis should be placed on recognizing that reactions can be processed through the lens of privilege. In the past, activities tended to focus on the experience of those oppressed and not the oppressors. Shifting the filter, as it were, has the potential of bringing new energy to these activities. Also, in light of the context of this training (i.e., its focus on preparing mental health professionals for practice), it would be important to address questions such as, "How would you apply what you have learned to what you do?" and more process-oriented themes. When interviewing applicants, faculty and potential employers can give clinical vignettes with multicultural implications. We suggest having a secondary question asking the respondents about the impact that privilege may have on the case. Similarly, in case seminars, presenters can be asked about the role that privilege may have in the clinical situation.

RESOURCES FOR EXERCISES IN WHITE PRIVILEGE

Butler, S. (2006). *Mirrors of privilege: Making Whiteness visible*. [DVD]. Oakland, CA: World Trust Educational Services.

Cassidy, L. M., & Mikulich A. (Eds.). (2002). *Interrupting White privilege: Catholic theologians break the silence*. Maryknoll, NY: Orbis Books.

Diller, A., Houston, B., Morgan, K. P., & Ayim, M. (1996). *The gender question in education: Theory, pedagogy, and politics*. Boulder, CO: Westview Press.

Helms, J. E. (1992). *A race is a nice thing to have: A guide to being a White person or understanding the White persons in your life*. Topeka, KS: Content Communications.

Malcomson, S. L. (2000). *One drop of blood: The American misadventure of race*. New York: Farrar Straus Giroux.

McIntosh, P. (2001). White privilege and male privilege. In M. L. Anderson & P. Hill Collins (Eds.), *Race, class and gender* (4th ed., pp. 95–105.). Belmont, CA: Wadsworth/Thomson Learning.

McIntosh, P. (1990, winter). Male privilege: A personal account of coming to see correspondences through work in women's studies. [Issue of Independent School.] Wellesley College Center for Research on Women. Wellesley, MA.

Miller, J., & Garran, A. M. (2008). *Racism in the United States: Implications for the helping profession*. Belmont, CA: Thomson Brooks/Cole. [Chapter 5, "Why is it so difficult for people with privilege to see racism?" (pp. 87–102); Chapter 3, "A brief history of racism in the United States and implications for the helping profession" (pp. 34-60)].

Pedagogy of Privilege Conference. (2009) Available at: https://portfolio.du.edu/pc/port?portfolio=pedagogy_of_privilege

Rothenberg, P. S. (Ed.). (2002) *White privilege: Essential readings on the other side of racism*. New York: Worth.

Wah, L. M. (1997). *Color of fear two: Walking each other home*. Berkeley, CA: Stirfry Productions.

White Privilege Conference, (Web site). http://www.uccs.edu/~wpc/

Wildman, S. M. (1996). *Privilege revealed: How invisible preference undermines America* (pp. 85–102). New York: New York University Press.

Williams, D. (2005). *A people's history of the Civil War: Struggles for the meaning of freedom.* New York: New Press.

Wise, T. (2008). *Tim Wise on white privilege: Racism, white denial and the cost of inequality.* [DVD]. Media Education Foundation.

Yancy, G. (Ed.). (2004). *What White looks like: African American philosophers on the Whiteness question.* New York: Routledge.

Zinn, H. (1980). *A. people's history of the United States.* New York: Harper & Row.

COMPETENCY BENCHMARK TABLES

The purpose of the Competency Benchmarks (Tables 15.1–15.4) is to create developmental models for defining and measuring competencies in professional psychology; each chapter in this *Handbook* applies the diversity competence for mental health practitioners in their work with a particular diverse population.

Table 15.1   Developmental-Level Competencies I

READINESS LEVEL—ENTRY TO PRACTICUM	
Competencies	Learning Process and Activities
Knowledge The student is gaining knowledge in: • Multiculturalism—the student is engaged in the process of learning that all individuals, including themselves, are cultural beings with worldviews that shape and influence their attitudes, emotions, perceptions, and experiences. (This includes exposure to concepts of racial identity and privilege.) • The importance of reflective practice and self-awareness (including issues of privilege). • Core counseling skills and theories. • Ethics code (including provisions related directly and indirectly to culturally competent practice). **Skills** The student is: • Beginning to develop the ability to demonstrate empathic listening skills, respect, and interest when talking with individuals expressing different values and belief systems. • Learning to critically examine the diversity literature. **Values and Attitudes** The student demonstrates: • Willingness to engage in self-exploration—to consider own motives, attitudes, behaviors, and effect on others (as well as areas of privilege/lack of privilege). • Intellectual curiosity and flexibility. • Ability to value expressions of diverse viewpoints and belief systems.	The task of this developmental stage is acquiring a basic understanding of the foundational domains that lay the groundwork for subsequent attainment of the functional multicultural competencies. Students at this stage become increasingly aware of the principles and practices of the field, but are not yet able to effectively apply their knowledge to practice. The training curriculum is focused on knowledge of core areas, including literature on multiculturalism, ethics, basic counseling skills, scientific knowledge, and the importance of reflective practice and self-awareness. (Through these materials, the student is introduced to introductory identity development and privilege dynamics theory.) It is important that throughout the curriculum, trainers and teachers define individual and cultural differences broadly and acknowledge differences in privileged and nonprivileged status. This should enable students to have a developing awareness of how to extrapolate their emerging multicultural competencies to include recognition of privilege and identity in relation to individual and cultural differences. All students, through their life experiences, will have benefited from and/or paid the costs of privilege along various dimensions. However, many students, particularly those who are privileged in multiple areas, may be unaware of the existence of the privilege from which they have benefited. For example, awareness of racial privilege may be minimal among White students. Students of color and students who lack privilege in other areas may be more aware of the realities of privilege dynamics on a day-to-day basis.

Table 15.2   Developmental-Level Competencies II

READINESS LEVEL—ENTRY TO INTERNSHIP	
Competencies	**Learning Process and Activities**
Knowledge The student has: • Clear understanding of the professional, legal, and ethical guidelines relevant to diversity and multicultural awareness in his or her field of practice (e.g., APA Ethical Guidelines, Ethical Guidelines for Social Work Professionals). • Basic familiarity with identity development theory, including person of color and White identity development models. • Working understanding of key concepts in privilege literature (e.g., privilege, White privilege, sociocultural identity). • General awareness (at the intellectual level) of potential clinical and supervisory implications of privilege dynamics. • Appreciation for the importance of supervision, consultation, personal therapy, etc., around emotionally charged and difficult issues related to privilege in general and White privilege in particular.	At this level of development, students are building on their education and applied experiences (supervised practica, etc.) to attain a core set of foundational competencies. They can then begin applying this knowledge to professional practice. Through didactic and experiential learning, students have begun to internalize developmentally appropriate multicultural values and attitudes. This foundational knowledge and awareness is becoming well established, but skills in working with issues of privilege and identity likely remain rudimentary at this point. Learning occurs through multiple modalities: • Didactic training in academic programs through course-specific assignments, experiential exercises, and readings (see this chapter's Resources section for specific tools and suggestions). Ideally, this training constitutes an integral part of the core curriculum and issues of privilege, identity development, etc., are explicitly incorporated into each class.
Skills Skills in the following areas are beginning to develop: • Ability to recognize and articulate issues of privilege in therapeutic, supervisory, and other interpersonal professional situations. • Capacity to perceive broader context of institutionalized and systemic privilege; growing awareness and ownership of privilege on personal level. • Acknowledgment of personal struggles, defensiveness, and blindspots regarding issues of privilege and identity. • Understanding theoretical risks of over- or under-identifying with similar/dissimilar others (if not always how to avoid doing so). • Recognizing strengths and limitations of categorical classification (e.g., current *DSM* diagnosis) in capturing salient variables around self-identification and power and privilege differentials.	• Content-specific coursework focusing directly on topics of privilege and oppression, disenfranchisement and empowerment, multiple role identity, etc. • Supervision around identifying and addressing privilege dynamics in clinical situations; overt acknowledgment of privilege issues in supervision as well as within the broader training context. • Experiential exercises developed to increase awareness of privilege and take the student out of his or her comfort zone in this area. • Professional development opportunities (such as workshops, conferences, colloquia). Topics to be covered in didactic training include: • Necessity of understanding privilege dynamics as a prerequisite to multicultural competency. • Relationship between privilege and multiple cultural identities (e.g., intersection between SES and race; gender and SES, and so forth).
Values and Attitudes Demonstrates self-awareness and appropriate cultural and multicultural attitudes as evidenced by the following: • Understanding of privilege as an important factor in multicultural diversity and all interpersonal interactions. • Conceptualization of self and others to include some awareness of intersecting individual dimensions (gender, ethnicity, SES, sexual orientation, ability, spirituality, etc.); recognizing link between these identities and privilege (or the lack thereof).	• Historical and current scholarship related to identity development theory and privilege. • Core definitions within the topic (including those related specifically to White privilege and sociocultural identity development). Trainers and supervisors could offer students/ trainees the opportunity to research particular issues in White privilege (e.g., challenges faced by first-generation White college students in seeing *(continued)*

Table 15.2 Developmental-Level Competencies II (*continued*)

READINESS LEVEL—ENTRY TO INTERNSHIP	
Competencies	Learning Process and Activities
• Commitment to examine and challenge own attitudes, assumptions, and biases around issues of privilege and identity. • Willingness to admit own limitations and blindspots in these areas. • Engagement in learning process; maintaining attitude of open-minded, respectful inquiry.	themselves as privileged) or to track examples of privilege in the media over the course of a specified time period.

Table 15.3 Developmental-Level Competencies III

READINESS LEVEL—ENTRY TO PROFESSIONAL PRACTICE		
Competencies		Learning Process and Activities
Knowledge	Knowledge of: • Literature on the relationship between mental health, identity development, and privilege dynamics; recognizing issues related to privilege in a broad range of clinical, supervisory, and interpersonal settings, as well as in institutional and systemic contexts. • Conceptual and definitional underpinnings of identity development theory and privilege literature, especially in the area of White privilege. • Identity- and privilege-specific skills, attitudes, and values associated with effective multicultural counseling and supervision. • Community resources, including ongoing training opportunities, individuals working as allies for traditionally disenfranchised groups, and role models for the development of a culturally astute, affirming, and positive White identity. • Potential for application of identity and privilege concepts to any professional activity (advocacy, research, training, program development and evaluation, school counseling, forensic assessment, group work, individual therapy, etc.).	In the earlier stages of training, students solidified their professional knowledge base and attained appropriate values and attitudes while developing increasingly sophisticated clinical skills. At the level of Entry to Professional Practice, psychotherapists have attained the full range of competencies in the domains expected of all independent practitioners. Preparation for this level of competency takes place through closely supervised clinical work, augmented by professional reading, personal exploration, and training opportunities such as professional development and training seminars. Clinical supervisors observe beginning practitioners' clinical work; provide training in assessment, diagnosis, case conceptualization, and treatment planning; challenge supervisees to examine their own perspectives on identity and personal privilege; and model appropriate and positive identity role integration. Additional methods by which beginning professionals can attain identity development and privilege competency at this level include:
Skills	Skills are demonstrated by the ability to: • Perform a basic assessment of clients' level of awareness around issues related to identity and privilege and identify potential privilege dynamics within the therapeutic or supervisory relationship. • Provide a thoughtful and thorough conceptualization of the client that includes diagnostic considerations as appropriate and is sensitive to the client's multiple sociocultural identities, level of acculturation along various dimensions, and developmental stage.	• Seeking opportunities to provide therapy to clients with sociocultural identities dissimilar from that of the clinician and/or who come from different positions of privilege; utilizing therapy with clients similar to the clinician along these domains to look critically at areas of over-identification, collusion, and minimization. • Locating supervisors who are culturally sensitive and developmentally advanced to serve as role models and mentors around White identity formation and privilege. • Taking advantage of professional development opportunities such as self-directed study and

READINESS LEVEL—ENTRY TO PROFESSIONAL PRACTICE	
Competencies	Learning Process and Activities
	• Identify the limits of his or her own competency, awareness, and/or willingness to engage around privilege and identity issues; seek supervision, consultation, additional training, and/or refer out as appropriate in a way that does not pathologize the client. • Form a trusting therapeutic (or supervisory) relationship with clients (supervisees) to create a safe space in which these issues can be explored; avoid imposing a personal agenda or values on clients or trainees. • Use supervision as a tool for self-reflection and skill development; challenge assumptions, check perspectives, evaluate for collusion, avoidance, or disengagement, and question "givens" in the room on a routine basis. • Apply identity development and privilege concepts effectively and ethically to a particular area of practice (e.g., teaching, research, assessment, consultation, etc.).	research focusing on one or more aspects of identity development and/or privilege. • Addressing these issues in internship and postdoctoral seminar training. • Presenting and participating in clinical case conferences that include discussions of privilege and personal identity (see text of this chapter for more information).
Values and Attitudes	Awareness of self-identity and personal privilege as well as associated biases and blindspots, willingness to continually broaden self-knowledge, and commitment to expanding theoretical and experiential knowledge of identity and privilege dynamics as part of growth toward multicultural competency.	

Table 15.4   Developmental-Level Competencies IV

READINESS LEVEL—ADVANCED PRACTICE AND SPECIALIZATION	
Competencies	Learning Process and Activities
Knowledge	Extensive knowledge of: • Literature, research, resources, definitional and conceptual bases, and best practice standards related to a broad cross-section of diversity topics. • Various identity formation models, including those related to general identity development for persons of color and various formulations of White identity development; some expertise around specific issues facing particular racial, ethnic, or other subgroups (e.g., African American identity development; Asian American identity development). • Privilege dynamics, including a substantive understanding of race privilege, gender privilege, etc., and how multiple identities intersect and inform one another.	Those who have a particular interest in the privilege and identity dynamics of diversity as they apply to clinical work may seek to attain advanced levels of competency. Learning activities will vary depending on the unique background, established competencies, and interest areas of the practitioner. For example, therapists working in correctional settings may wish to focus on identity development and privilege-related issues within the context of the criminal justice system. Those working with differently abled populations might highlight dynamics related to multiple privileged/nonprivileged identities, and so on. Regardless of the focus area, learning activities can include:

(continued)

Table 15.4 **Developmental-Level Competencies IV** (*continued*)

READINESS LEVEL—ADVANCED PRACTICE AND SPECIALIZATION	
Competencies	Learning Process and Activities

		Learning Process and Activities
	• Range of issues related to identity formation and privilege that typically arise in therapy and supervision situations.	• Professional reading (information drawn from the growing body of literature offering increasingly nuanced understandings of privilege, identity expression, etc.).
Skills	Advanced skills in:	• Teaching and scholarship.
	• Identifying and addressing issues around identity and privilege in thoughtful, validating, and effective ways that take into account the developmental level/stage of the client or supervisee.	• Continuing education (as either a participant or a presenter). • Coordinating peer consultation and workgroups (why not create an online newsletter or blog?).
	• Developing case conceptualizations that are holistic, clinically relevant, diagnostically useful, and empirically informed ways of understanding clients within each of their multiple identities and contexts. Issues of privilege are explicitly addressed and worked through, both at the client–therapist and therapist–supervisor levels.	• Consultation with knowledgeable mental health professionals, researchers, scholars, and activists in the field. • Challenging oneself through participation in exercises geared toward increasing identity awareness, deconstructing privilege, etc. See the Resources section of this chapter for suggestions.
	• Advocacy, mentorship, modeling, supervision, and outreach.	
Values and Attitudes	Well-integrated values and attitudes are demonstrated by the following:	
	• Ongoing professional development and active pursuit of opportunities for growth in this area; sophisticated understanding of self, others, and broader dynamics at work in the system—however, never stops learning, questioning, testing, and refining ideas.	
	• Emphasis on forming relationships with experts in the field, potential role models and mentors, etc.; seeks out new experiences, resources, tools, and skills to enhance professional practice and personal awareness (may include affiliation with local/state/regional/national agencies and organizations active in promoting social justice issues).	
	• Serves in turn as a resource for students, early career professionals, peers, and others through supervision, consultation, guest lecturing, mentorship; may take leadership role in professional and service organizations.	
	• Vigilantly self-monitors around privilege and identity issues; recognizes that ally status is not a "coat" that can be metaphorically taken off at the door of the therapy room; acts with sensitivity, respect, and cultural awareness in both professional and personal roles.	

REFERENCES

Abrams, L. S., & Gibson, P. (2007). Reframing multicultural education: Teaching White privilege in social work curriculum. *Journal of Social Work Education, 43*(1), 147–160.

Ancis, J. R., & Ladany, N. (2001). A multicultural framework for counselor supervision. In L. J. Bradley, & N. Ladany (Eds.), *Counselor supervision principles, process and practice* (pp. 63–90). Philadelphia: Brunner-Routledge.

Ancis, J. R., & Szymanski, D. M. (2001). Awareness of White privilege among White counseling trainees. *The Counseling Psychologist, 29*(4), 548–569.

Arminio, J. (2001). Exploring the nature of race-related guilt. *Journal of Multicultural Counseling and Development, 29,* 239–252.

Brown, S. P., Parham, T. A., & Yonker, R. (1996). Influence of a cross-cultural training course on racial identity attitudes of White women and men: Preliminary perspectives. *Journal of Counseling and Development, 74,* 510–516.

Chang, C., Hays, D., & Shoffner, M. (2003). Cross-racial supervision: A development approach for White supervisors working with supervisees of color. *The Clinical Supervisor, 22*(2), 121–138.

Clark, M. (2006). Testimony of Melanca Clark, NAACP Legal Defense and Educational Fund, Inc., before the Committee on the Judiciary Council of the District of Columbia, concerning Bill 16-746, "Criminal Record Expungement Act of 2006," July 13, 2006.

Cook, D. A. (1994). Racial identity in supervision. *Counselor Education and Supervision, 34,* 132–141.

Council on Social Work Education. (2008). Educational policy and accreditation standards. Retrieved from http://www.cswe.org/accreditation/EPAS/epas.pdf

Cullinan, C. (1999). Vision, privilege, and the limits of tolerance. *Electronic Magazine of Multicultural Education, 1*(2). Retrieved May 2010 from: http://www.eastern.edu/publications/emme/1999spring/cullinan.html

Fouad, N. & Arredondo, P. (2006). *Becoming culturally oriented: Practical advice for psychologists and educators.* Washington D. C.: American Psychological Association.

Frankenberg, R. (1993). *White women, race matters: The social construction of Whiteness.* Minneapolis: University of Minnesota.

Hays, D. G., Chang, C. Y., & Dean, J. K. (2004). White counselors' conceptualization of privilege and oppression: Implications for counselor training. *Counselor Education and Supervision, 43,* 242–257.

Helms, J. E. (1990). *Black and White racial identity.* Westport, CT: Praeger.

Helms, J. E. (1992). *A. race is a nice thing to have: A guide to being a white person or understanding the white persons in your life* (pp. 7, 46, 51). Topeka, KS: Content Communications.

Helms, J. E. (1995). An update of Helms' White and people of color racial identity models. In J. G. Ponterotto, J. M. Casas, L. A. Suzuki, C. M. Alexander (Eds.), *Handbook of multicultural counseling* (pp. 181–198). Thousand Oaks, CA: Sage.

Henze, R., Lucas, T., & Scott, B. (1998). Dancing with the monster: Teachers discuss racism, power, and White privilege in education. *Urban Review, 30* (3), 187–210.

Holladay, J. (2000). *White antiracist activism: A personal roadmap.* Roselle, NJ: Crandall, Dostie & Douglas Books.

Jones, J. M., & Pettigrew, T. F. (2005). Obituary, Kenneth B. Clark [1914–2005]. *American Psychologist, 60*(6), 649–651.

Kendall, F. E. (2001). Understanding White privilege. California Alumni Association. Retrieved from http://www.alumni.berkeley.edu/Students/Leadership/Online_LRC/Diversity_Center/Unde.

Kendall, F. E. (2006). *Understanding White privilege: Creating pathways to authentic relationships across race.* New York: Routledge.

Ladany, N., Brittan-Powell, C. S., & Pannu, R. K. (1997). The influence of supervisory racial identity interaction and racial matching on the supervisory working alliance and supervisee multicultural competence. *Counselor Education and Supervision, 36,* 284–304.

Ladany, N., Friedlander, M. L., & Nelson, M. L. (2005). *Critical events in psychotherapy supervision: An interpersonal approach.* Washington, DC: American Psychological Association.

Lubrano, A. (2004). *Limbo, blue collar roots, White collar dreams.* Hoboken, NJ: Wiley.

Malcomson, S. L. (2000). *One drop of blood: The American misadventure of race.* New York: Farrar, Straus, & Giroux.

Manglitz, E. (2003). Challenging White privilege in adult education: A critical review of the literature. *Adult Education Quarterly, 53*(2), 119–134.

McIntosh, P. (1989). White privilege: Unpacking the invisible knapsack. *Peace and Freedom.* (July/

August) 10–12. Philadelphia, PA: Women's International League for Peace and Freedom.

McIntosh, P. (2002). White privilege: Unpacking the invisible knapsack. In P. S. Rothenberg (Ed.), *White privilege: Essential readings on the other side of racism* (pp. 97–102). New York: Worth.

McIntosh, P. (2008). White privilege and male privilege: A personal account of coming to see correspondences through work in women's studies. In M. McGoldrick & K. Hardy (Eds.), *Re-visioning family therapy* (2nd ed., pp. 238–249). New York: Guilford. [Reprinted from McIntosh, P. (1998). White privilege and male privilege: A personal account of coming to see correspondences through work in women's studies. Wellesley College Center for Research on Women (Working Paper No. 189)].

McIntyre, A. (1997). *Making meaning of Whiteness; Exploring racial identity with White teachers.* New York: State University of New York at Albany.

Merriam-Webster. (n.d.). Definition of *privilege*. Merriam-Webster's online dictionary. Retrieved May 2010 from http://www.merriam-webster.com/dictionary/privilege

Miller, J., & Garran, A. M. (2008). *Racism in the United States: Implications for the helping profession.* Belmont, CA: Thomson Brooks/Cole.

Niehuis, S. (2005). Helping White students explore White privilege outside the classroom. *North American Journal of Psychology, 7*(3), 481–492.

Ortiz, A. M., & Rhoads, R. A. (2000). Deconstructing Whiteness as part of a multicultural educational framework: From theory to practice. *Journal of College Student Development, 41*(1), 81–93.

Pack-Brown, S. P. (1999). Racism and White counselor training: Influence of White racial identity theory and research. *Journal of Counseling and Development, 77,* 87–92.

Parker, W. M., & Schwartz, R. C. (2002). On the experience of shame in multicultural counselling: Implications for White counsellors. *British Journal of Guidance and Counseling, 30*(3), 311–318.

Ramos-Sánchez, L., Esnil, E., Goodwin, A., Riggs, S., Touster, L. O., Wright, L. K., et al. (2002). Negative supervisory events: Effects on supervision satisfaction and supervisory alliances. *Professional Psychology: Research and Practice, 33*(2), 197–202.

Random House Webster's Unabridged Dictionary. (1997). New York: Random House.

Richardson, T. Q., & Molinaro, K. L. (1996). White counselor self-awareness: A prerequisite for developing multicultural competence. *Journal of Counseling and Development, 74,* 238–242.

Rothenberg, P. S. (2002). *White privilege: Essential readings on the other side of racism.* New York: Worth.

Scott, D. A., & Robinson, T. L. (2001). White male identity development: The key model. *Journal of Counseling and Development, 79*(4), 415–421.

Spanierman, L. B., Oh, E., Poteat, V. P., Hund, A. R., McClair, V. L., Beer, A. M., et al. (2008). White university students' responses to societal racism. *The Counseling Psychologist, 36*(6), 839–870.

Spanierman, L. B., Todd, N. R., & Anderson, C. J. (2009). Psychosocial costs of racism to Whites: Understanding patterns among university students. *Journal of Counseling Psychology, 56*(2), 239–252.

Sue, D. W. (2003). *Overcoming our racism: The journey to liberation.* San Francisco: Jossey-Bass.

Sue, D. W. (2004). Whiteness and ethnocentric monoculturalism: Making the invisible visible. *American Psychologist, 59*(8), 761–769.

Sue, D. W., Arredondo, P., & McDavis, R. (1992). Multicultural counseling competencies standards: A call to the profession. *Journal of Counseling and Development. 70,* 477–486.

Sue, D. W., Carter, R. T., Casas, J. M., Fouad, N. A., Ivey, A. E., Jensen, M., et al. (1998). *Multicultural counseling competencies: Individual and organizational development.* Thousand Oaks, CA: Sage.

Sue, D. W., & Sue, D. (1990). *Counseling the culturally different: Theory and practice.* New York: Wiley.

Tatum, B. D. (1992). Talking about race, learning about racism: The application of racial identity development theory in the classroom. *Harvard Educational Review, 62*(1), 1–24.

Wildman, S. M., & Davis, A. D. (2002). Making systems of privilege visible. In P. S. Rothenberg (Ed.), *White privilege: Essential readings on the other side of racism* (pp. 89–95). New York: Worth.

Williams, D. (2005). *A people's history of the Civil War: Struggles for the meaning of freedom.* New York: The New Press.

Zinn, H. (2003). *A Peoples history of the United States: 1492 to present.* New York: Perennial Classics.

Zito, K. (2003). Bay area's thin red line: Study says Blacks, Latinos face loan discrimination. *San Francisco Chronicle,* Oct. 26, 2003, G-1.

CHAPTER 16

COUNSELING COMPETENCIES WITH WOMEN: UNDERSTANDING GENDER IN THE CONTEXT OF MULTIPLE DIMENSIONS OF IDENTITY

Rebekah Smart

INTRODUCTION

What does it mean to work competently with women? Why focus on *women* as a group, particularly when they are so diverse? Mental health practitioners and the public may even consider many issues to be resolved as a result of gains women have made in recent decades (American Psychological Association; APA, 2007). However, after an extensive review of the literature, a joint task force within the American Psychological Association published the *Guidelines for Psychological Practice with Girls and Women* (APA, 2007) and concluded that the wellbeing of women remains adversely impacted by sexism, racism, classism, homophobia, and ableism. Women are more likely than men to experience a number of factors hazardous to their mental health: poverty, less pay for the same work, compounded responsibilities as income providers and caregivers, interpersonal violence (sexual abuse as children, rape, domestic violence), and media images that repeatedly devalue them. Of the sexes, it is women who have the higher rates of depression, anxiety, and eating disorders, and women who seek help more often. Yet, it is not only that many women are struggling and require help, it is also that the mental health professions need to be aware of the *context* of women's struggles, as well as acknowledge and work with women's resiliencies and strengths (APA, 2007). This has not always been the case; in fact, biases remain in psychological theories, conceptualizations, diagnostic categories, and treatment planning (APA, 2007).

A central task of developing multicultural competencies in working with women is being able to simultaneously understand issues important to them as a group (and within their multiple and intersecting identities), while not losing sight of the uniqueness of each woman's experience (APA, 2007). Women across cultures share common biological experiences, such as menstruation and menopause, and many experience similar role expectations, such as nurturing others (Goodwin & Fiske, 2001) and having children (Woollett & Marshall, 2001). However, an individual's experience is affected by unique personal factors and circumstances and intersects with her other affiliations and identities, such as culture, religion, ethnicity, sexual identity and orientation, and economic status (APA, 2007). The meaning of such varied experiences as menstruation, partnering, and work may differ according to these affiliations and contexts. Gendered experience is further affected by the degree to which an individual woman adheres to the norms and rules she is encouraged to follow. Which parts does she accept? What does she resist? How tolerant and supportive are her networks? Given the increasingly multicultural and global influences in society, what has she adopted from other cultural contexts?

The task force (APA, 2007) stated emphatically that mental health practitioners need to know how to help women navigate gender roles within complex identities and experiences. The guidelines draw on a biopsychosociocultural view of human problems, with particularly strong consideration of sociocultural context, which is consistent with ecological and systems perspectives (Kirst-Ashman & Hull, 2002) and feminist practice (Black & Joiner, 2008) in social work.

The purpose of this chapter is to provide practitioners, educators, supervisors, students, and trainees with guidelines and resources for enhancing multicultural competencies in working with women. It begins with a section on terms and concepts, followed by a brief account of some of the historical processes that have influenced the psychology of women. Then three sections illustrate essential capacities of the multiculturally competent mental health practitioner: (a) knowledge, (b) skills, and (c) attitudes and values. Throughout the chapter, case examples and a variety of resources are provided. The hope is that this information will not only assist readers in increasing their competency with women clients, but also inspire self-reflection and a commitment to further learning.

TERMS AND CONCEPTS

Good, Gilbert, and Scher (1990) state that *gender* "refers to the psychological, social, and cultural features and characteristics frequently associated with the biological categories of male and female" (p. 376). Every society constructs rules for how men and women should behave, and socializes their children accordingly (Bem, 1981). The process of how *gender role socialization* occurs is described in gender development theories such as social cognitive theory (Bussey & Bandura, 1999) and gender schema theory (Bem, 1981). They help explain the mechanisms by which males and females of a given culture understand and internalize the roles, attitudes, and behaviors expected of them (Bussey & Bandura, 1999). (For a review of the internalization of gender roles in children, see Powlishta, Sen, Serbin, Poulin-Dubois, & Eichstedt, 2001.)

Historically, most cultures have been *patriarchal*, meaning that men have had more access to and control of resources than have women, leading to more *power* (Goodwin & Fiske, 2001). People with more power are also able to *define* those with less power and set social norms and standards (Hare-Mustin, 1997). *Sexism* includes individual and institutional actions that support the power differential between men and women (Goodwin & Fiske, 2001). For example, women are still paid less for equal work in mid-management jobs, and women still do the majority of home and child care even when they work equally outside the home (Goodwin & Fiske, 2001).

Patriarchal views tend to promote the notion that men and women are very different (Hare-Mustin, 1997). Women in Western culture have

consistently been associated with the body (sexuality, giving birth, emotionality) and men with the mind (intellect and rationality) (Bordo, 1993; Wooley, 1994). This has contributed to *stereotypes* of women as overly emotional, more intuitive, less rational, and dangerously seductive (purity is then promoted in order to save women from their desires and men from succumbing to women's sexuality). In spite of a large body of research that suggests that differences in the qualities and aptitudes of men and women are minimal and similarities are more the norm, fascination with differences persists (Gilbert & Rader, 2001). The issues are exceedingly complex and reflect a source of strain and disagreement among feminist scholars and researchers (Kimball, 2001). The popular media also tend to focus more on differences and less on similarities (Hare-Mustin, 1997). This can lead to distorted perceptions that ultimately harm both men and women (Tavris, 1992) and contribute to rigid *gender roles* (e.g., "If women are better nurturers, they should stay in the home"). In addition, comparisons of women to men often rest on the notion that male qualities are the *norm*, which means that "maleness sets the standard for whatever is considered normal, average, or representative" (J. Sommers-Flanagan & R. Sommers-Flanagan, 2004, p. 337), and this is problematic in its own right, as those who do not meet that standard can be considered deficient. For a discussion of how beliefs about difference affect the practice of therapy, see Hare-Mustin and Marecek (1988).

Although the term *psychology of women* generally refers to the content issues faced by women, whereas *feminist psychology* identifies more with a value base and activism (Greene, 2003), the two have influenced each other, and both are reflected in this chapter. Many feminist psychologists have worked to challenge the prevalent stereotypes of differences between the genders and to eliminate the biases that serve to oppress women (Davis & Gergen, 1997); similarly, feminist social work practice has long addressed issues critically linked to women's historical lack of power, such as poverty and violence (Black & Joiner, 2008).

A BRIEF HISTORICAL BACKGROUND

The social work field has placed great emphasis on the "person-in-environment," and has sought to bring about social, structural, and economic changes in the society at large (Kirst-Ashman & Hull, 2002, p. 13), goals consistent with multicultural and feminist psychology. However, prior to the 1960s women's movement in the United States, few examined gender as an important dimension in human experience. Typically, White men were simply the *norm*, women were the *other* (de Beauvoir, 1989), and women's problems (and alleged inferiority) were thought to be determined by their biology and personality (Unger, 2001). The 1960s ushered in significant role changes, particularly for middle-class women, and inspired the examination of gender role bias and stereotyping in the culture at large as well as in the helping fields. Much of traditional psychotherapy not only had viewed women as inferior, weak, and masochistic (Unger, 2001), but had placed almost exclusive emphasis on the power of the individual, a model that stressed independence and autonomy (Constantine, Greer, & Kindaichi, 2003). Feminists noted that these very traits were consistently associated with men. One study was emblematic: I. K. Broverman, D. M. Broverman, Clarkson, Rosenkrantz, and Vogel (1970) found that therapists conceptualized *healthy adults* and *healthy men* similarly (i.e., independent, autonomous, and self-reliant), but conceptualized *healthy women* as less independent and more submissive. "Healthy" women did not meet the standard of healthy

adults. The blatant but unchallenged wrongness began, finally, to attract attention. Consciousness-raising groups and the rape-crisis and battered women's movements were critical to exposing how women's subordinate position in society was harming them (Evans, Kincade, Marbley, & Seem, 2005; Worell & Johnson, 2001). Critiques of the field of psychology began pointing out that it privileged stereotypically masculine traits, ignored the social context of mental illness, blamed victims of abuse, idealized motherhood but blamed mothers for their children's ills, and ignored women's strengths (Enns, 2003; Marecek, 2001).

An example of such critiques was the reexamination of developmental theories, which looked at how humans evolve through the lifespan. Most of those theories (e.g., Piaget, Erickson, Kohlberg) were found to view *male* development as *human* development (Greene, 2003). These theories rarely accounted for the socialization of women and, by extension, pathologized them. Gilligan's influential work (1982) challenged an established theory of moral development, and other collaborative work explored ideas of autonomy and independence in girls' development (Gilligan, Lyons, & Hanmer, 1990; Gilligan, Rogers, & Tolman, 1991). Girls, she and her colleagues asserted, developed in connection to others, and their values derived from attempts to maintain relationships, resulting in an emphasis on *interdependence* rather than the stereotypical version of male independence. They were different perhaps, but not deficient. A central conflict for girls and women, as they saw it, was how to negotiate increased opportunity and pressure to achieve while maintaining connectedness with others.

While exciting new research and ideas were emerging, a serious flaw in the feminist endeavor was taking place. Some White, middle-class feminists purposefully excluded women of color and ignored issues of poverty and class; others naively assumed that all women would join the cause against patriarchy, failing to understand that many women of color would not view being female as the worst of their oppressions (Comaz-Díaz & Greene, 1994; Evans et al.,

2005). In addition, many of their concerns were distinctly different: While middle-class women felt trapped at home by the traditional roles of housewife and mother, women of color and/or lower economic status often found it necessary to work outside the home, not having the choice to be full-time caregivers to their own children. To further complicate things, some women of color were in a double bind: In addition to a racist society, they suffered from sexism and violence in their own homes and communities (Comaz-Díaz & Greene, 1994; hooks, 1981).

In 1975, the American Psychological Association acknowledged that diagnoses of women were influenced by gender and race bias and stereotyping (Worell & Johnson, 2001). By the 1980s and 1990s, therapists and researchers of color, as well as lesbian and bisexual women, had expanded the critique of the field's nearly exclusive reliance on White, middle-class, heterosexual experience to the neglect of so many others (Worell & Johnson, 2001). As a result of the multicultural and feminist movements in psychology, a number of racial, ethnic, and cultural identity models were created, as were lesbian and gay identity models, acculturation and worldview models, and feminist and womanist identity models (see Constantine et al., 2003).

ELEMENTS OF COMPETENCY

Mental health professionals across disciplines are ethically required to be cognizant of diversity issues, including gender, and provide services that are non-sexist (American Counseling Association; ACA, 2005; APA, 2002; National Association of Social Workers; NASW, 1996). A number of practice guidelines relevant to women have been created, including those on older adults (APA, 2004), lesbian, gay, and bisexual clients (APA, 2000), and most recently, the *Guidelines for Psychological Practice with Girls and Women* (APA, 2007). In addition, practitioners and the public can find numerous resources through the *Women's Programs Office* (APA; see the Resources section later in the chapter), such as the Report of the APA Task Force on Mental Health and Abortion (APA, 2008), Report of the APA Task Force on the Sexualization of Girls (APA, Task Force, 2007) and information on topics such as poverty, depression, postpartum depression, and violence.

The *Guidelines for Psychological Practice with Girls and Women* (APA, 2007) is written by and for psychologists, but the document is also intended for practitioners across disciplines. Using these guidelines (11 in total, and stated in abbreviated form here), as well as other works, the knowledge, skills, and attitudes and values important to competent therapeutic practice with women will be discussed throughout this chapter. The competencies will then be placed in the context of four levels of counselor development: Entry to Practicum, Entry to Internship, Entry to Professional Practice, and Advanced Practice and Specialization (Assessment of Competency Benchmarks document, 2007) and can be found in Tables 16.1 to 16.4 at the end of this chapter.

Guidelines for Psychological Practice with Girls and Women

1. Psychologists strive to be aware of the effects of socialization, stereotyping, and unique life events on the development of girls and women across diverse cultural groups.

2. Psychologists are encouraged to recognize and utilize information about oppression, privilege, and identity development as they may affect girls and women.

3. Psychologists strive to understand the impact of bias and discrimination on the physical and mental health of those with whom they work.

4. Psychologists strive to use gender sensitive and culturally sensitive, affirming practices in providing services to girls and women.

5. Psychologists are encouraged to recognize how their socialization, attitudes, and knowledge about gender may affect their practice with girls and women.

6. Psychologists are encouraged to employ interventions and approaches that have been found to be effective in the treatment of issues of concern to girls and women.

7. Psychologists strive to foster therapeutic relationships and practices that promote initiative, empowerment, and expanded alternatives and choices for girls and women.

8. Psychologists strive to provide appropriate, unbiased assessments and diagnoses in their work with girls and women.

9. Psychologists strive to consider the problems of girls and women in their sociopolitical context.

10. Psychologists strive to acquaint themselves with and utilize relevant mental health, education, and community resources for girls and women.

11. Psychologists are encouraged to understand and work to change institutional and systemic bias that may impact girls and women.

Source: Adapted with permission, American Psychological Association (2007).

KNOWLEDGE

In order to be competent with respect to therapeutic practice with women, mental health practitioners require knowledge across the following areas: individual and cultural diversity; assessment and diagnosis; intervention; and ethical and legal standards. The *Guidelines for Psychological Practice with Girls and Women* (APA, 2007), noted in the previous chart, will be used to anchor the reader to needed aspects of practitioner knowledge, and will be referred to hereafter as *Guidelines 1–11* (with a page number from the publication provided for further exploration).

Individual and Cultural Diversity

Practitioners are encouraged to seek an understanding of gender role socializations and stereotypes across cultures (*Guideline 1*, APA 2007, p. 960), be aware of how oppressions and privileges may affect women' identities and health (*Guidelines 2 and 3*, pp. 961–962), and know

about the sociopolitical contexts of women's problems (*Guideline 9*, p. 968). Brown (1990b) contends there is no single form of women's socialization, but rather a variety of *socializations*, very dependent on culture, race, age, economic status, sexual orientation, and more. Just as men were treated as the norm in the mental health fields for so long, White, middle-class, heterosexual women are often treated as the norm when women's socialization is discussed, to the detriment of many. This is one reason why is it so important to consider women within multiple dimensions of identity.

Gilbert (1994) asserts that gender does not "reside within the person" so much as it is part of an interpersonal process, and views ". . . individuals' behavior as emerging from a web of interactions between their biological being and their social environment" (p. 541). Gilbert illustrates this concept with the example of women's stress with multiple roles (e.g., work, caregiving): The individual is impacted not only by her own socialization and abilities, but by circumstances, such as her partner's willingness to do childcare and the policies at her workplace. In this way, gender is *socially constructed* and part of an interactive process with forces both internal and external to the person.

Sexist discrimination places a woman at risk for stress and mental illness (Fischer & Holz, 2007), and research shows that women experiencing multiple oppressions (i.e., racism, homophobia, ageism, ableism) are even more at risk (APA, 2007). Many women of color have had to contend with oppressive factors within their own communities in addition to those of the society at large, such as sexist resentment from male partners at their accomplishments (Comaz-Díaz & Greene, 1994), or the "triple jeopardy" of being a woman, a person of color, and a lesbian, as described by Kanuha (1990) in the context of domestic violence. (Kanuha illustrates how the abused woman is then faced with potentially sexist attitudes, racism, and homophobia, not only from her own support systems, but from helping agencies as well.) In addition, some women of color struggle to negotiate conflicting gender norms (i.e., those of the dominant culture and those of their culture of origin) (Bradshaw, 1994; Vasquez, 1994).

Gender *stereotypes* have been described as "inferences about the personal characteristics and behaviors concerning males and females" (Durik et al., 2006, p. 429), but more specifically their effect is to reduce the complexity of human beings with less power and maintain the status of those with more power (Merskin, 2007). One way stereotypes come to be seen as real is through constant and repeated media depictions of the alleged characteristics of a group (Merskin, 2007). Research across many cultures has shown that women are stereotyped as "communal, caring, emotionally expressive, and responsive to others, but also passive, submissive, and weak" (Goodwin & Fiske, 2001, p. 362). This is also called the *warmth-expressiveness cluster* (as opposed to the *competence cluster* for men) (Kite, 2001). When women do not conform to the warmth-expressiveness cluster, they can be stereotyped as the opposite of warm and nurturing: They can be "sirens and shrews—manipulative, deceitful, and cold" (Goodwin & Fiske, 2001, p. 358). Women

of color, and those outside the mainstream (e.g., lesbian, disabled, older, immigrant), contend with the mainstream stereotypes as well as those laced with racism, homophobia, and other prejudices (Comaz-Díaz & Greene, 1994).

Gender role socializations and stereotypes can affect women's sense of identity. Identity "involves the way one views oneself in regard to qualities, characteristics, and values" (Vasquez, 1994, p.120), and its development is influenced by how an individual is treated by people close to her and how her group is perceived by the broader society. An example of how gender role socialization and stereotypes may impact women's sense of identity and increase their risk of mental health problems is seen in Fredrickson and Roberts' (1997) objectification theory. They propose that girls and women, more than boys and men, are excessively identified as *bodies*—freely looked at, commented upon, sexualized, referenced in terms of body parts—in numerous circumstances (interpersonal communication, harassment, media images, threats of rape and violence). These issues cause stress for many women, but even greater distress for those who feel they must respond to pressure to conform to mainstream ideals of femininity and beauty. Objectification theory holds that some women will come to treat *themselves* as objects, and subsequently be at risk for experiencing issues of shame, depression, anxiety, eating disorders, sexual problems, and emotional difficulties with the aging process or disabilities. Bordo (1993) points out that individuals respond to pressures differently depending on their ethnicity, class, race, and personal variables. For women of color, objectification mixes with racial stereotypes (e.g., Asian women as sexually subservient and exotic), potentially creating even greater levels of distress. On the other hand, some research indicates that African American women, for example, may be better at separating how they are perceived from their own self-concepts, possibly as a result of learning to cope with racial discrimination (Fredrickson & Roberts, 1997). In these ways, it can be seen how dominant culture norms about femininity are imposed on all women, but individual women respond to them depending on a host of factors.

The reader is referred to Table 16.5 at the end of this chapter for a chart on stereotypes and gender role socializations across broad cultural groups, but is encouraged to understand how individuals uniquely relate to the elements listed in the chart. For example, Vasquez (1994) states that traditional Latino cultures have had historically restrictive roles for women, leading many women to sacrifice their own happiness in favor of the family; however, she cautions against making assumptions: Social class, acculturation level, and the overall health and functioning of family members will influence how a young woman's identity develops. Thus, even though some cultures have tended to severely restrict gender roles for women, it is crucial to recognize there can be heterogeneity within the cultures and variability within families (Comaz-Díaz & Greene, 1994). Readers are encouraged to expand on the chart by seeking out research on other groups. In addition, questions to use with the chart are provided here. These are based in part on work by Brown (1990a) and Kress, Eriksen, Rayle, and Ford (2005), as well as on the broad concepts outlined in the guidelines for practice (APA, 2007).

The reader is encouraged to explore the racial and ethnic identity, acculturation, and gay and lesbian identity models discussed elsewhere in this text. In addition, Downing and Roush's (1985) *Feminist Identity Model* contends that women's identity progresses in stages from adherence to traditional norms to the development of a feminist identity and activist stance; Helms' *Womanist Identity Development Model* (Ossana, Helms, & Leonard, 1992), also a stage process, focuses on the shift from an *external* definition of womanhood to an *internal* one. The identity models have helped counselors understand some of the variability within groups, but also cannot easily convey the complexities of intersecting and multiple identities (Deaux & Stewart, 2001). For example, ethnic and feminist identity processes may conflict, particularly for immigrant women from cultures with more restrictive roles that are attracted to the relative freedoms offered by the new mainstream culture (Bradshaw, 1994).

Knowledge about gender roles, stereotypes, oppression, privilege, identity, and sociopolitical context provides important foundational information for mental health practitioners, and this is explored in a preliminary way in Case Vignette 16.1.

QUESTIONS FOR USING THE STEREOTYPES AND GENDER ROLE SOCIALIZATIONS CHART (TABLE 16.5)

- With what cultural group or groups does my client most closely identify?
- What sociopolitical factors (oppression, privilege) have influenced this group?
- Is my client a member of a subgroup that differs in important ways from the broad cultural group (e.g., Asian American, but more specifically Vietnamese American)?
- What other identities are salient for my client, and how do those intersect with her experience as a woman (e.g., sexual orientation, economic status, immigration and acculturation, religion)?
- What stereotypes have been asserted about women from this group?
- What are the dominant gender role norms of this group?
- To what degree do my client's family and social network adhere to these norms?
- To what degree does my client accept, question, or resist these norms?
- To what degree is my client influenced by the dominant culture's norms?
- Are there ways in which my client has dealt with these norms that have made her vulnerable and/or stronger?

CASE VIGNETTE 16.1

Lucy, a 23-year-old second-generation Korean American woman, presents with extreme worry about her weight. She lives with her parents and works in retail. In spite of knowing that she is not fat, she is concerned about a small amount of weight gain. She takes a triple dose of laxatives regularly and occasionally vomits her food. She has also been taking herbs her mother got for her to help her lose weight, in preparation for an upcoming trip to visit relatives in South Korea. She dislikes what she calls her "celery stalk legs." She says her mother has always criticized her weight, eating habits, academics, and friends, and is concerned about Lucy finding a husband. Lucy reports a lack of energy and has no "enthusiasm for life."

Utilizing Knowledge about Diversity for Clinical Practice with Lucy

Recognize that gender intersects with multiple dimensions of identity:

- Look at the Stereotypes and Gender Role Socializations Chart (Table 16.5) at the end of the chapter: Notice aspects of the mainstream European-American culture and family structure, gender norms, and intersecting factors that Lucy may contend with. Be aware of the Asian norms. Learn what norms are more specific to her particular culture and family.
- Look back at the Questions for Using the Stereotypes and Gender Role Socializations Chart:
  - What are the salient dimensions of identity for her? How does her acculturation level, ethnic/racial identity, and sexual orientation/identity impact her?
  - What gender role norms have impacted her most? Is she torn between different values? Is there intergenerational conflict about this? Does she resist certain norms and/or conform to others? Does she benefit and/or suffer from how she manages these norms?
  - What strengths and vulnerabilities seem to result from Lucy's dimensions of identity?

Recognize that external circumstances, such as sexism, racism, and homophobia, contribute to emotional distress.

- Has Lucy experienced discrimination, harassment, or teasing as a result of her gender, culture, appearance, or sexual orientation? Has she experienced privileges as a result?
- Know common stereotypes (see Table 16.5). Has Lucy internalized any of these stereotypes?
- What messages has Lucy internalized regarding beauty, control, and success?

Assessment and Diagnosis

Guideline 8 of the *Guidelines for Psychological Practice with Girls and Women* states that practitioners must ". . . strive to provide appropriate, unbiased assessments and diagnoses" (APA, 2007, p. 967). This necessarily involves practitioners engaging in a continual evaluation of their own values and biases (Brown, 1990a), as well as having knowledge about historical and current biases that affect women. Gender bias occurs in assessment and diagnosis for both men and women, and practitioners who use standardized assessment measures and tests should know on whom those measures were normed (APA, 2007). A good deal of criticism has focused on the use (or misuse) of the *Diagnostic and Statistical Manual of Mental Disorders* (4th ed., *DSM-IV*; American Psychiatric Association, 1994). Eriksen and Kress (2008) reviewed literature noting that even some experienced therapists provide different diagnoses for men and women who have the same symptoms. Women are harmed by over- and underdiagnosis. Eriksen and Kress report, for example, that girls are often socialized to internalize symptoms and therefore may go undiagnosed for Attention-Deficit/ Hyperactivity Disorder (ADHD). On the other hand, women may be labeled as personality disordered through overcompliance with gender norms ("dependent," "histrionic"), or because they exhibit coping behaviors resulting from trauma (Eriksen & Kress, 2008). Most diagnostic labels imply that the problem is with the individual, without acknowledgment of external realities, and this can create barriers with regard to conceptualization and treatment. Some feminist therapists are particularly attentive to issues of diagnosis, and take pains to arrive at diagnoses collaboratively with clients and explain symptoms less as pathology and more as *coping strategies* (Enns, 2004).

Brown (1990a) asserts that in addition to knowing their own biases and assumptions, practitioners should know what issues most affect women and assess for those accordingly, and know about women's development. Knowledge about assessment is considered in the work with Lucy (see Vignette 16.1). (See more about conducting assessment in the Skills section of this chapter.)

Utilizing Knowledge about Assessment for Clinical Practice with Lucy

- Know that bias (within the practitioner personally and/or within diagnostic systems like the *DSM*) exists and can affect assessment:

  ○ Do you assume that Asian American women do not struggle with weight and eating disorders?
  ○ Do you minimize her distress because she is slim?
  ○ Do you blame her mother for all of her distress?

- Know what issues are most common among women:

  ○ Assess Lucy for depression, eating disorders, past and current trauma.
  ○ Know that most people with eating disorders fit the "not otherwise specified" category.
  ○ Know that eating disorder symptoms appear to be increasing among women in Asian societies worldwide (Cummins, Simmons, & Zane, 2005; Gordon, 2001).

- Consider environmental influences on Lucy's emotional state:

  ○ What is expected of Lucy in terms of marriage, and is she accepting of this? For example, does she want to please her parents? Do you consider the possibility that Lucy is lesbian, bisexual, or otherwise identified?
  ○ What diversity factors (noted in the previous section) have influenced Lucy?

- Know about norms in girls' and women's development, biologically and psychologically (return to the Stereotypes and Gender Role Socializations chart in Table 16.5 and the corresponding Questions earlier in the chapter for a start).

- Consider Lucy's symptoms as an attempt to cope:

  ○ In what ways has her ability to express emotions and endure and resolve conflict been impacted by her gender, culture, family dynamics, and personal events and circumstances?
  ○ Do her symptoms provide a means of expressing distress? What are the biological, psychological, and sociocultural factors that influence her expression?

INTERVENTIONS

Practitioners should have knowledge of effective interventions for women (*Guideline 6*, APA, 2007, pp. 965–966). There are numerous sources of clinical expertise regarding work with women. Two excellent texts were edited by Comaz-Díaz and Greene (1994) and Brown and Root (1990), and more recent texts include edited works by Kopala and Keitel (2003) and Mirkin, Suyemoto, and Okun (2005) (see the Texts for Teaching and Practice section in the Resources guide later in the chapter). In these texts and others, practitioners can also find a great deal of material describing treatment for specific issues that affect women disproportionately, such as domestic violence, survivors of child sexual abuse, self-esteem, body image, and eating disorders. Practitioners should understand that many well-regarded treatment approaches and theoretical orientations are based on a European American male value system and may need to be adapted. (See Enns, 2003, for how adjustments can be made to a number of traditional therapies for a nonsexist approach; and Constantine et al., 2003, for a discussion of traditional therapies with women of color.) Returning to Lucy, knowledge about treatment is considered.

Utilizing Knowledge about Intervention for Clinical Practice with Lucy

- Know that empirically supported treatments for bulimia include cognitive behavioral therapy and interpersonal therapy, although they do not overtly consider diverse aspects of identity.
- Know that psychodynamic, feminist, integrative, and constructivist approaches are also used, but those too may require adaptations.
- Increase your knowledge by seeking out research and clinical expertise regarding the dimensions of Lucy's identity and how these may impact her symptoms and response to treatment.

Ethical and Legal Standards

Each major mental health profession provides its members with standards for ethical practice (ACA, 2005; APA, 2002; NASW, 1996). Members are obligated to follow their organization's ethical guidelines, as well as the legal mandates set by the state in which they practice (e.g., reporting child abuse); and informed consent

and confidentiality, within legal limits, are critical to ethical practice. The reader will also find *A Code of Ethics for Feminists* by the Feminist Therapy Institute (1999) in the Resources section, along with the other ethical standards.

Vasquez (2003), drawing on the work of Kitchener, examines some of the ethical principles underlying mental health laws and standards from a feminist perspective. For example, she states that therapists must gain an understanding of a woman client's cultural contexts in order to know how to perform *nonmaleficence* (otherwise known as "do no harm"). Without the willingness to explore a client's experience in the world, which is affected by her gender and other identities, it would be difficult indeed to honor the other principles of *beneficence, justice, autonomy*, and *fidelity*. Practitioners should avoid unduly influencing clients with their own views (Enns, 2004). Good et al. (1990) emphasize that individuals are helped by having *choices* regarding gendered behavior, beliefs, and values, regardless of whether these fit the practitioner's ideas, political correctness, or anyone else's ideas of what the person should be.

Vasquez (2003) explores how common ethics violations can harm women in particular. Sexual contact with a client is prohibited across the mental health professions, and yet it is the most common violation. By far, it is male therapists who exploit female clients; Vasquez points out the parallel with women's experience in society at large. She also discusses boundary, self-disclosure, and multiple relationship issues, stating on the one hand how important it is to have solid therapeutic boundaries, particularly with clients whose boundaries were historically violated, and on the other hand how ethics around these issues may not benefit some women and people of color. The White male model, from which most of the laws and ethics derive, value "separation, isolation, and strict boundaries" (p. 565), which do not easily allow for situations in which dual or multiple relationships might be helpful. She adds that the newest APA standards (2002) reflect a shift toward this understanding by acknowledging that multiple relationships are not

CASE VIGNETTE 16.2

Erin, a 27-year-old African American woman, a graduate student in her first month of an International Studies program, presents at her university counseling center. Two weeks ago, she began having panic attacks in class and has not attended since. She does not feel like she belongs in the program; her discomfort intensified when they began to focus on sociopolitical events in Africa. Her classmates (mostly male and none African American) and professor seemed to single her out for discussion on the topic. Erin also states that she had slept with one of her classmates, a guy who seems "very sweet." He is the only White guy she has been interested in but she feels uncomfortable about the possibility of a relationship with him, and cannot tell her grandmother, who raised her and with whom she is very close. At the end of the appointment, Erin asks if she might be able to see a therapist who is a woman of color. The practitioner exclaims, "But I'm Latina!"

automatically unethical, given that certain protections are in place. Similarly, self-disclosure, when done appropriately, is often helpful with people who may experience therapy as another situation in which they are required to expose their vulnerabilities to someone in a position of power (Vasquez, 2003).

Implications for Clinical Practice

- Provide clients with enough information to make a truly informed consent to therapy, including your theoretical orientation and ways of working, and the limits of confidentiality.
- Provide clients with information about other available forms of treatment.
- Practice within the boundaries of your own competency.
- Establish and maintain appropriate boundaries.
- Avoid imposing your own gender role values on clients.

SKILLS

In this section, skills in working with women are explored in the following areas: the therapeutic relationship, assessment, intervention, collaboration and referral, and supervision and training.

Case Vignette 16.2 is utilized in order to illustrate the major concepts.

Relationship Skills

The *Guidelines for Psychological Practice with Girls and Women* encourages practitioners to "foster therapeutic relationships and practices that promote initiative, empowerment, and expanded alternatives and choices" (*Guideline* 7, APA 2007, p. 966). Enns (2004) outlines four principles of the therapy relationship from a feminist perspective that are helpful regardless of one's theoretical orientation: (1) *The Therapist's Values*, (2) *Clients as Competent*, (3) *The Egalitarian Relationship*, and (4) *The Counseling Contract and Informed/Empowered Consent* (pp. 19–24). According to these principles, the practitioner's awareness of his or her own values is of utmost importance because therapy can never be entirely value-free, and pretending that it can is potentially damaging to clients. Clients are competent *experts* on themselves; they can collaborate on how their problems are defined and how solutions are sought. Furthermore, the coping strategies and strengths of even very distressed clients can be recognized. The emphasis on the egalitarian relationship is an attempt to reduce the unnecessary and exploitative elements of the power differential historically common between mental health practitioner and client. Practitioners acknowledge their professional expertise in order to help clients;

however, through collaboration, self-disclosure, genuineness, and role modeling they can create a more equal alliance. Finally, the mental health practitioner makes a commitment to initial and ongoing informed consent about the therapeutic process. Relationship skills are necessary during the entire process of therapy, but some ways in which these principles can be enacted in the beginning follow (see Vignette 16.2), utilizing the principles by Enns (2004).

Utilization of Relationship Skills with Erin

- The mental health practitioner considers her own values:

  - She reflects on her impact on Erin, and considers whether she signaled any biases or assumptions that may have influenced Erin's desire to see another therapist (e.g., she recalls some feelings of identification with Erin and saying, "I know just how you feel").
  - She reflects on her own ideas about women's roles and choices (e.g., she was very supportive about Erin's "right" to date the guy from class and not tell her grandmother, and realizes that was influenced by her struggle to assert her rights within her own family).
  - She reflects on her own identity as a Latina and what assumptions she made about how another woman of color might see her.

- The mental health practitioner views Erin as a competent collaborator:

  - She notices Erin's strengths, particularly in being able to ask for a different therapist.
  - She recognizes that many of Erin's actions and symptoms are an attempt to cope with a highly stressful environment.

- The mental health practitioner establishes an egalitarian relationship when possible:

  - She treats Erin with respect and invites her to collaborate on defining her problems and sorting out solutions.

  - She draws from skills in appropriate self-disclosure, role modeling, and genuineness to recover from her exclamation at the end and assists Erin in explaining her request for a different (perhaps African American) therapist.

- The mental health practitioner provides clear informed consent about the process of therapy:

  - She explains how she works.
  - She invites Erin to ask questions about the process.
  - She describes her commitment to confidentiality and the limitations of it.
  - She offers to help Erin obtain a different therapist if that is what she would like.

Assessment Skills

Brown (1990a) asserts that considering gender in the assessment process (both male and female) is necessary to basic, ethical assessment skills. In the Knowledge section of this chapter, it was emphasized that mental health practitioners know about their own and the field's biases, the common issues affecting women, and developmental factors common to women (Brown, 1990a). In this section, putting that knowledge into action through assessment skills is explored. Brown (1990a) recommends incorporating a *gender role analysis* into the process, which " . . . takes a phenomenological and cooperative perspective on assessment" (p. 14), and states that to use this well, practitioners need "a high degree of cultural literacy" (p. 13). This means that practitioners must try to understand the client's problems from her worldview. They need to ask the client what meaning her gender has for her within her family, social, and cultural contexts, and the stage of life she is in. The practitioner needs to assess ways in which the client has been *gender-role compliant* or *noncompliant*, and whether she has made gains or paid a price for her way of being. Gender-compliant ways of being (e.g., accommodating of others) may be viewed as functional in a woman's social context, even when they seem to harm the client. The practitioner may underdiagnose problems in this case because the woman's behavior is thought of as "normal." Similarly, noncompliant ways of being (e.g., highly sexual) could be a sign of real strength in the client (but pathologized for being outside the norm) or indicative of a serious problem. Practitioners need to keep all possibilities in mind as they assess. Finally, as they are incorporating other elements of assessment needed (regardless of gender), they need to consider whether the diagnosis they have determined is gender-biased or influenced by stereotypes; they can do this through self-reflection, consultation, and supervision (Brown, 1990a).

Although assessment would include many factors, a small sample of gender-role questions with Erin follows:

- What aspects of your culture or identity are particularly important for you?

- What sorts of messages about being a woman have you received?
- Are there ways that you try to live up to those messages or ways that you fight against them?
- Who or what has been your biggest influence in terms of how you see yourself and who you want to be?
- What is it like to be an African-American woman in an environment that is nearly all male and all White?

Other gender-related assessment questions, drawing on work from Brown (1990a) and also derived in part from Table 16.5 and the questions for that chart (earlier in the chapter) are provided here. Practitioners must use the range of clinical knowledge and awareness to determine which questions are appropriate and at what time they can be asked.

SAMPLE OF GENDER-RELATED ASSESSMENT QUESTIONS FOR WOMEN

- What groups or cultures do you identify with? Which ones are most important to you?
- How do you view your role as a woman?
- What other aspects of your life or identity inform how you view your role?
- What did you learn about being a woman as you grew up?
- What messages do you get from your family, peers, and media about how you should be or behave as a woman, and as a woman within the other contexts of your life (e.g., your religion, sexual orientation, culture)?
- Do you feel like you get "mixed messages" about being a woman? If so, what are they and how are you sorting those out?
- Are there ways in which you have followed the "rules" of being a woman in your culture? What is that like? Are there benefits to that? Are there drawbacks?
- Are there ways in which you have not followed the "rules"? What is that like? Are there benefits to that? Are there drawbacks?
- What expectations do you have of yourself? Are any of these related to being a woman?
- What expectations do others have of you? Are any of these related to being a woman?
- In what ways have your ideas about being a woman changed over time?
- How do you feel about other women?
- How do you feel about men?

(continued)

(continued)
- In what ways does your gender impact how you are in relationships?
- In what ways does your gender impact your choices about work or career?
- In what ways does your gender expand the possibilities in your life?
- In what ways does your gender limit the possibilities in your life?
- How do you feel about your abilities, intellectually, interpersonally, practically?
- How do you feel about your body and appearance?
- How do you feel about aging?

Intervention Skills

Intervention skills are shaped by practitioners' theoretical orientations, what populations they work with, clinical and supervision experiences, and knowledge of evidence-based practice for specific problems. In addition to knowing what sorts of treatment have been shown to work with specific issues common to women, the guidelines (APA, 2007) encourage practitioners to "use gender and culturally sensitive, affirming practices" (*Guideline 4*, p. 963) and to "promote initiative, empowerment, and expanded alternatives and choices" (*Guideline 7*, p. 966). Helping women clients understand how external barriers (e.g., poverty, rape, working outside the home while still managing the majority of childcare duties) have shaped their sense of what is possible is part of this process (Worell & Johnson, 2001). Enns (2004) writes that practitioners who focus on empowerment from a feminist perspective can help women find ways to express emotion, particularly emotion that goes against many women's socialization (e.g., anger); this ultimately can help with assertiveness, esteem, and effectiveness in communication. They can help clients sort through what barriers have been externally imposed on the client in order to free up some of the shame and guilt that many women experience; the idea is that when women understand their histories, choices, and coping in the context of their socialization and events often beyond their control, they will then have the energy to take charge of what they can. From there they may begin to develop different coping strategies and different relational dynamics. Practitioners will also draw attention to

strengths the client may have come to not see or value, something that helps clients have more energy and commitment to feeling well.

Worell and Johnson (2001), building on earlier work by the first author, provide an empowerment model of therapy that derives from principles across feminist theories and can be integrated with other approaches, such as cognitive-behavioral therapy. They identify ten possible goals or outcomes for clients:

1. Positive self-evaluation
2. Positive comfort–distress ratio
3. Gender- and culture-role awareness
4. Personal control and self-efficacy
5. Self-nurturance and self-care
6. Effective problem-solving skills
7. Competent use of assertiveness skills
8. Access to facilitative social, economic, and community resources
9. Gender and culture flexibility
10. Socially constructive activism (p. 324)

A few ways to approach intervention with Erin (see Vignette 16.2) are considered with these goals in mind. These are not in lieu of standard practices (such as making a medical referral or using empirically supported treatment for panic), but rather focus on ways in which a practitioner of any theoretical orientation can integrate a gender awareness into his or her work.

Implications for Clinical Practice with Erin

- Help Erin to differentiate external sources of her distress (e.g., a new program, a nearly all-White, all male environment, a new sexual experience, the disconnection from her grand-mother) from internal ones (to be explored).

- Help Erin to articulate the many aspects of her identity and process the impact of role expect-ations. This can lead to greater self-awareness and acceptance.
- Model flexibility in one's own identities and roles (e.g., the practitioner can portray com-petence and strength *and* be given to brief tearfulness in a touching moment; the practi-tioner may self-disclose something about his or her own identity negotiations). This can help expand Erin's notions of gender and culture identity.
- Help Erin recognize, express, and tolerate un-comfortable feelings and thoughts in the safe environment of therapy. This can help with managing affect and increasing a sense of efficacy.
- Help Erin explore how aspects of her social-ization may be contributing to how she inter-nalizes experiences, asserts herself, responds to stress, and interacts with others. This can lead to greater awareness and motivation for mak-ing changes.
- Help Erin view her current symptoms as cop-ing strategies and collaboratively identify her strengths. This can aid in problem solving, self-evaluation, assertiveness, and efficacy.
- Collaboratively devise ways in which Erin can take care of herself physically and emotionally (e.g., refer to a women's group, discuss spiri-tual resources if relevant).

Collaboration and Referral Skills

Appropriate referral to other resources is an important part of work with women (*Guideline 10*, APA, 2007, pp. 968–969). It is helpful when practitioners know about community resources that are specific to women. These include but are not limited to: low-cost counseling services, bat-tered women's shelters, substance abuse pro-grams for women, eating disorders clinics, rape crisis centers, and assistance for older, immigrant,

and refugee women. Job training, legal aid, food, and childcare services are often necessary before women who are poor and/or battered, for exam-ple, can truly engage in therapy. Practitioners need to be aware of how these same issues may affect specific populations in different ways (e.g., undocumented women in abusive re-lationships may have fears of deportation if they report abuse and require legal advice). In addi-tion, it is important for practitioners to know medical and support services for women who are experiencing postpartum depression, and diffi-culties with fertility, menopause, and issues like chronic fatigue syndrome, fibromyalgia, and irri-table bowel syndrome. See the Resources section later in the chapter.

Supervision and Training Skills

The mental health professions all stipulate train-ing guidelines specific to their disciplines (see Council on Social Work Education, CSWE, 2008; Council for Accreditation of Counseling and Related Educational Programs, CACREP, 2009; APA, 2002), and in accordance with multicultural competency, supervisors need to be cognizant of gender. Because common gender dynamics seen elsewhere also occur in the supervisory relationship, Barnes and Bernard (2003) state, "A first and essential strategy for supervisors is to understand that they must be vigilant about gender role assumptions and behaviors" (p. 542). Within the supervisory re-lationship, the power differential can be a source of strain, particularly if there is confusion about roles and expectations (Nelson & Friedlander, 2001). Supervisors also need to be cognizant of racial, gender, and class issues in the triad (supervisor, trainee, client), and be open to explo-ration with the supervisee (Owens-Patterson, 2000). Supervisors must pay attention to how they discuss and conceptualize clients and how they interact with supervisees.

Barnes and Bernard (2003), using work by Prouty, outline a number of *gender-sensitive* strat-egies that supervisors can utilize with the super-visee: (a) create a safe environment so that issues of gender and power are openly discussed; (b) model the importance of gender in clinical work by discussing assumptions, biases, and gender roles; and (c) observe how the supervisee reacts to discussions around gender and be willing to process that in light of the supervisee's work with clients. When the supervisor observes the trainee's work, he or she can call attention to gender and the intersection of multiple identities in a consistent way, and challenge the trainee to incorporate this awareness at every level. If the supervisor can be open about his or her own willingness to grow and learn, as Barnes and Bernard (2003) point out, "Such candor will help the supervisee to appreciate that cultural identity development is as rich and dimensional as individual identity development and is therefore a lifelong task" (p. 543).

VALUES AND ATTITUDES

The need for mental health practitioners to examine their own values and attitudes has become a cornerstone of feminist and multicultural practice, and practitioners are encouraged to "recognize how their socialization, attitudes, and knowledge about gender may affect their practice with girls and women" (see *Guideline* 5, APA 2007, p. 965). Some research has suggested that mental health practitioners can be biased with regard to women's competency as compared to men's (Danzinger & Welfel, 2000), or biased against women who reject particular gender role norms (Seem & Johnson, 1998). It is not necessarily easy to recognize one's own attitudes or to notice how one's gender socialization impacts the process of therapy. How do practitioners "promote initiative, empowerment, and expanded alternatives and choices" (*Guideline* 7, APA 2007, p. 966) or respect diverse gendered roles, behaviors, and values (e.g., Good et al., 1990) if they have not examined their own values? With the assumption that the vast majority of practitioners intend only to do good, it is important to highlight the necessity of becoming aware of unconscious or unexamined values.

IMPLICATIONS FOR SUPERVISORS

- Encourage supervisees to examine their own gender identities.
- Model ways to discuss gender and other identities by addressing the issues in supervision, by self-disclosing as appropriate, by being willing to process dynamics that occur between you and the supervisee.
- Encourage supervisees to notice their own biases and countertransference reactions in relation to their clients' genders.
- Consider working with one of the identity measures (e.g., Downing & Roush's [1985] *Feminist Identity Model* or Ossana et al.'s [1992] *Womanist Identity Development Model*) to help women supervisees understand their own processes more.
- Assist supervisees in attending to issues of gender in the assessment processes, paying particular attention to factors that lead to over- and underdiagnosis.
- Help supervisees to incorporate gender and other identities into case conceptualizations. Assist supervisees in attending to issues of gender in the treatment process, including interpersonal process between them and their clients, and how to conduct non-sexist therapy.
- Help supervisees work on collaborative goal-setting with clients that honors the various dimensions of clients' identities.

Source: Derived in part from Barnes and Bernard (2003).

Mental health practitioners who are not cognizant of the role of gender in their own lives or in society may simply fail to recognize its place in an individual's problems, and thereby inadvertently maintain the status quo, alienate the client, or unnecessarily perpetuate her sense of pathology (Good et al., 1990). They may also run the risk of imposing their own, unexamined, expectations of gender on their clients. They may struggle with not understanding where gender fits within women's multiple identities and impose a one-size-fits-all notion of women that is based on their own cultural values. This has led to profound misunderstandings about women of color in particular (Comaz-Díaz & Greene, 1994). Women have been misdiagnosed and offered treatment that tends to emphasize internal processes without an understanding of context (Eriksen & Kress, 2008). These issues are further impacted by managed care and the increased emphasis on symptom relief alone and medication (Wyche, 2001). What begins as a seemingly minor bias or attitude can translate into barriers to competency at all levels of care: assessment, diagnosis, treatment, and public policy.

A theme throughout this chapter has been the concept of power, particularly as women have experienced oppression due to a historical lack of power, rigid gender role socializations, conflicting and changing values in the larger society, and stereotyping. It is extremely important for practitioners to understand that women's mental health is directly affected by these issues (APA, 2007; Fischer & Holz, 2007; Fredrickson & Roberts, 1997; Jones, 2003). In addition, however, Jones (2003) proposes that given the multiple dimensions of a person's identity, it may be helpful to consider power in a multidimensional manner. This may be particularly relevant for how mental health practitioners understand issues of their own privilege, oppression, and values, as well as those of their clients.

Power can be thought of as a *process*, one that takes into account both more firmly rooted power structures and the shifting nature of power depending on circumstance. Jones (2003) notes that a woman lacking institutional power (a) needs to be understood within that context; (b) does not need to be viewed as *entirely* powerless; (c) may have particular personal strengths or exercise "subversive or creative power" in opposition to the mainstream (p. 32); (d) may experience multiple oppressions; (e) may experience oppression in one circumstance and be an oppressor herself in another; and (f) may have privilege and power in one circumstance, yet not in another. Mental health practitioners can monitor their own points of power and oppression to increase self-awareness, and understand that their clients may experience diverse kinds of power and oppression.

The relationship between client and mental health practitioner is one area where power is exhibited (Jones, 2003). Traditionally, practitioners hold the power to define clients; however, as has been noted already, practitioners can choose to examine their own dimensions of identity, values, and attitudes, and so better equip themselves to recognize their own power in the relationship and strive for a more egalitarian process to the extent possible (Enns, 2004). This includes both acknowledging that there *is* a power differential *and* minimizing it to the degree it is helpful to the client.

See the Resources section of this chapter for examples of self-awareness activities and exercises.

In the case vignette that follows, Melissa is a woman with racial privilege and economic and social power, but her struggle is connected to oppressive notions in her gender role socialization. A mental health practitioner would want to notice the mix of privilege and oppression, and notice his or her own countertransference to the client.

CASE EXAMPLE

A number of the issues discussed thus far in the chapter are illustrated in Case Vignette 16.3 and focus on gender-related aspects of assessment and intervention. Mental health practitioners

CASE VIGNETTE 16.3

Melissa, a 38-year-old European American, married, heterosexual woman is referred by her gynecologist to you, a mental health practitioner. Melissa works as an attorney and hopes to be pregnant soon, although she is undergoing fertility tests. A month ago she was informed that she has human papillomavirus (HPV) and told that a majority of people who have been sexually active carry the virus and that it can emerge at any time, sometimes years after contracting it. Melissa tells you that she has not slept or eaten much since receiving the news, has not been able to focus on work, and has not told her husband. "He won't understand. We used to joke about how stupid people are to have unprotected sex. He thinks we have no secrets . . . I never told him about this one guy or what happened with him. It was before we met . . . I've tried to forget it, really. What if I get cancer? What if I can't have a baby?"

must also be aware of the other aspects of general competent practice (e.g., crisis assessment and intervention, couples counseling, treatment for anxiety and depression).

Issues to Consider

- What are your countertransference reactions to Melissa?
- How do your preconceptions of her gender, culture, and presentation affect your ability to assess her accurately?
- What roles do your own gender, culture, economic and social status, and values play in your ability to work with the client?
- In what way are biological and psychological issues intertwined, and do you need to consult with other professionals or research fertility and sexually transmitted disease (STD) issues?

Therapy Goals

Possible goals (in collaboration with Melissa) include helping her to: identify, understand, and manage her feelings and anxieties; increase flexibility in her self-concept (in her gender role and other identities); increase a sense of self-worth; and increase interpersonal and self-care skills.

Gender-Related Treatment Plan

- Provide informed consent about your therapeutic orientation and the multicultural/gendered lens though which you work.
- Assess for past trauma and process accordingly.
- Consult with health professionals and/or refer as needed.
- Help Melissa to articulate important aspects of her identity, and what meanings her sexuality, the HPV, and having a baby hold for her.
- Help Melissa to view her current state as an attempt to cope with difficult circumstances.
- Help Melissa to connect aspects of her experience to her socialization as a woman.
- Help Melissa to differentiate external sources of distress (e.g., shame and guilt from gender-related expectations and experiences) from internal ones, and to see how they intersect.
- Help her work through feelings and, if appropriate, to reframe the meanings she has attributed to her sexuality, the HPV, and having a baby in light of new understandings.
- Assess the dynamics of Melissa's marriage, including possible power differentials and the level of support within the relationship.
- Identify strengths that Melissa can use to empower herself, and support her efforts to alter interpersonal patterns and coping strategies when helpful, and to take care of herself in

ways she has identified as important (e.g., physically, spiritually, relationally).

Gender-Related Assessment Questions

- How does Melissa see her role as a woman? What does she believe is expected of her and to what degree does she conform to these ideas or resist them? How has she been impacted by conforming or resisting?
- To what degree does her family of origin, culture, social class, educational level, and occupation influence her ideas about her identity? Where do these provide strengths and where do they inhibit her?
- How do role socializations influence Melissa's ideas about the HPV, fertility problems, and communication with her husband?
- To what degree has Melissa been impacted by negative media portrayals of women or portrayals that emphasize the "superwoman"? Who are her role models?
- What impact has Melissa's relationship and sexual history had upon her?
- Has she experienced abuse, assault, or other trauma?
- Has she experienced less overtly traumatic but sometimes powerfully cumulative effects of discrimination, harassment, judgment, or sexist treatment by medical professionals, partners, or colleagues?
- What roles do Melissa's husband and marriage play in her current distress and/or in her ability to feel better? Do the partners' gender role socializations interact in a way that affects Melissa's distress?

Gender-Related Interventions

This chapter has drawn heavily from feminist and multicultural perspectives because they shed light on specific aspects of women's experience. *Feminist therapy* is technically eclectic and varied, and is thought of as an "approach to therapy rather than a system of therapy in itself" (Worell

& Johnson, 2001, p. 320). This section explores some of the issues that would likely be a focus of feminist therapy with Melissa, and ends with a brief discussion of other modalities and their relationship to feminist ideas.

In connection with the treatment plan already addressed, a feminist practitioner might attend to three areas in particular: (a) how the biological issues also have sociocultural components to them; (b) how gender role norms and other identities affect the meanings Melissa has attributed to these circumstances; and (c) how past and present gendered experiences and power dynamics may have contributed to Melissa's symptoms, coping strategies, and interpersonal patterns.

Melissa's possible infertility and HPV are biological issues that have complex sociocultural implications for women. Motherhood is arguably the most dominant gender role for women; and in some women infertility can threaten their sense of identity and diminish their self-worth (Woollett & Marshall, 2001). Women contract STDs more easily than do men, and suffer more severe medical consequences from them, simply because of their anatomy (Hoffman & Baker, 2003). The meanings that Melissa attributes to these issues are likely dependent on her personality style, personal vulnerabilities and resilience, and relational experiences, but all of these are influenced by her gender, class, educational level, and cultural background. Attributing Melissa's distress exclusively to her as an individual who is somehow separate from these other forces would be a mistake from a feminist point of view. If Melissa is encouraged to examine her gender and culture norms, she may decide she can tolerate more flexibility within them, capitalize on her many strengths, and thereby relinquish some of her pain.

Technically, as stated earlier, the practitioner may use eclectic methods but could, for example, ask questions, reflect, or self-disclose on the influences of gender and culture. People of middle-class, Anglo-descended cultural backgrounds tend to have a worldview that individuals are in control (or should be) and that things should go well in their lives (McGill & Pearce,

2005), a view which is supported by historical positions of power and privilege. If things do not go well, it is often perceived as a personal failure. A gender role expectation of many middle-class women is the "superwoman": Obtain a good education; succeed professionally, marry, and become a mother; and remain attractive and physically fit (Chrisler, 2008). Furthermore, educated, assertive women still receive the message that their true worth depends on their ability to marry and have children, and they often receive the dual message to be successful, but still be pleasing to men and relatively passive about sex (Hoffman & Baker, 2003). Although changes have occurred in society, successful women are still required to be "nice," lest they violate the norm of *communality* (Rudman & Glick, 2001). Some women have internalized the notion that because they have freedoms (e.g., sexually), they are responsible for whatever results from exercising those freedoms, even if someone exploited or abused them (see the video of Laura Brown conducting feminist therapy in the Resources section later in the chapter). Melissa seems to assume that she contracted the virus from a former partner (when she could in fact have contracted it from her husband) and that, whatever happened between them, it was entirely her fault. Given the high rates of sexual abuse and assault (a power dynamic) that girls and women report, as well as coercion around sex, it must at least be considered that the HPV occurrence has triggered an earlier wound. Another potential power dynamic relates to Melissa's marriage. There is the possibility that she lacks a sense of equal power in the partnership, at least in some respects. For example, she may consider her husband to be more "moral" than she is, and someone who can and will judge her, perhaps harshly.

If notions stemming from gender and culture have been internalized so that Melissa recognizes them simply as *the truth* or as originating exclusively from within her, the likelihood of distress seems great; on the other hand, if she comes to see herself, not as a victim of circumstance and gender, but as an individual influenced by contexts, guilt and shame can be reduced and new ideas for how to be can emerge. A "positive comfort–distress ratio" and "positive self-evaluation" are important aspects of therapeutic outcome with women (Worell & Johnson, 2001, p. 324). Helping Melissa recognize the influence of mixed messages that many women receive may help her acknowledge her feelings and regulate them. Helping Melissa to identify power dynamics and how they contribute to internalized blame and shame may help release some of those feelings, and ultimately help her to take responsibility for her own actions and interpersonal behavior without devaluing herself.

For the sake of brevity, the example of Melissa has focused mostly on the importance of helping clients view themselves and their problems in context. However, as is probably clear to many readers, there is good reason to consider *psychodynamic therapy* with Melissa (e.g., How did early attachment to caregivers affect her ability to regulate affect, cope with adversity, and relate to others?), *interpersonal therapy* (What role transitions and disputes are happening?), *cognitive-behavioral therapy* (How do her cognitive schemas affect her current state?), *narrative therapy* (What stories does she tell about herself?), to name a few. In addition, many approaches can be integrated with feminist concepts and awareness (Enns, 2003; Worell & Johnson, 2001), and at this point, the reader can likely identify how gender socializations might impact attachment styles, role transitions, cognitive schemas, and self-stories. For a summary of traditional therapies and how they have been adapted to be more compatible with feminist principles, see Enns (2003).

SUMMARY

The purpose of this chapter has been to provide information, guidelines, resources, and references regarding therapeutic work with women. The focus of the chapter has largely been on the sociocultural context of women's lives, although it acknowledges the importance of a biopsychosociocultural framework. Although the subject has been women, both men and women are harmed by rigid gender socializations and stereotypes. It is hoped that students, practitioners, educators, and supervisors will continue to expand their notions of gender, and gender within multiple contexts.

RESOURCES

In this section, resources and ideas for increasing knowledge, skills, and self-awareness in working with women are provided. This section begins with a resource guide that includes journals, articles, books, videos, organizations, and Web resources, and then provides various exercises for trainers. Tables 16.1 through 16.4 describe the basic competencies (knowledge, skills, and values and attitudes) recommended at four different levels of development (Entry to Practicum, Entry to Internship, Entry to Professional Practice, and Advanced Practice and Specialization). Table 16.5 is a summary of the stereotypes and gender role socializations associated with four major groups in the United States. Please remember to utilize the questions for using this chart (earlier in the chapter).

AWARENESS OF GENDER IN ASSESSMENT

Brown, L. S. (1990). Taking account of gender in the clinical assessment interview. *Professional Psychology: Research and Practice, 21,* 12–17.

Eriksen, K., & Kress, V. E. (2005). *Beyond the DSM story: Ethical quandaries, challenges, and best practices.* New York: Sage.

Eriksen, K., & Kress, V. E. (2008). Gender and diagnosis: Struggles and suggestions for counselors. *Journal of Counseling and Development, 86,* 152–162.

Klonoff, E. A., Landrine, H., & Campbell, R. (2000). Sexist discrimination may account for well-known gender differences in psychiatric symptoms. *Psychology of Women Quarterly, 24,* 93–99.

Kress, V. E.W., Eriksen, K. P., Rayle, A. D., & Ford, S.J.W. (2005). The DSM-IV-TR and culture: Considerations for counselors. *Journal of Counseling and Development, 83,* 97–104.

TEXTS FOR TEACHING AND PRACTICE

Brown, L. S., & Root, M. P. P. (Eds.). (1990). *Diversity and complexity in feminist therapy.* New York: Harrington Park Press.

Chin, J. L. (Ed.) (2004). *The psychology of prejudice and discrimination (Vol. 3): Bias based on gender and sexual orientation.* Westport, CT: Praeger.

Choate, L. H. (2008). *Girls' and women's wellness: Contemporary counseling issues and interventions.* Alexandria, VA: American Counseling Association.

Comaz-Díaz, L., & Greene, B. (Eds.) (1994). *Women of color: Integrating ethnic and gender identities in psychotherapy.* New York: Guilford Press.

Enns, C. Z. (2004). *Feminist theories and feminist psychotherapies: Origins, themes, and diversity* (2nd Ed.). New York: Hayworth Press.

Gergen, M. M., & Davis, S. N. (Eds.). (1997). *Toward a new psychology of gender: A reader.* New York: Routledge.

Jackson, L. C., & Greene, B. (Eds.). (2000). *Psychotherapy with African American women: Innovations in psychodynamic perspectives and practice.* New York: Guilford Press.

Kopala, M., & Keitel, M. A. (Eds.). (2003). *Handbook of counseling women.* Thousand Oaks, CA: Sage.

McGoldrick, M., Giordano, J., & Garcia-Preto, N. (Eds.). (2005). *Ethnicity and family therapy* (3rd Ed.). New York: Guilford Press.

Mirkin, M. P., Suyemoto, K. L., & Okun, B. F. (Eds.). (2005). *Psychotherapy with women: Exploring diverse contexts and identities.* New York: Guilford Press.

Paludi, M. A. (Ed.). (2004). *Praeger guide to the psychology of gender.* Westport, CT: Praeger.

Tavris, C. (1992). *The mismeasure of woman.* New York: Simon & Schuster.

Unger, R. K. (2001). (Ed.). *Handbook of the psychology of women and gender.* New York: Wiley.

Worell, J., & Goodheart, C. D. (Eds.). (2006). *Handbook of girls' and women's psychological health.* Oxford: Oxford University Press.

WOMEN AND DEPRESSION

American Psychological Association. (2002). Summit on women and depression: Proceedings and recommendations. Available at: www.apa.org/pi/wpo/women&depression. [Pdf].

DOMESTIC VIOLENCE AND PARTNER ABUSE

http://www.domesticviolence.org

American Psychological Association: Intimate Partner Abuse and Relationship Violence: http://www.apa.org/about/division/abuse.html. Booklet available online at: http://www.apa.org/pi/parv.pdf

Resolution on male violence against women. (1999). Available at: http://www.apa.org/pi/wpo/maleviol.html

National Coalition Against Domestic Violence: http://www.ncadv.org

National Domestic Violence Hotline:
1-800-799-SAFE
1-800-787-3224 TDD
http://www.ndvh.org/

EATING DISORDERS

American Psychiatric Association. (2006). *Practice guideline for the treatment of patients with eating disorders* (3rd Ed.). Available at: www.psych.org

Grabe, S., & Hyde, J. S. (2006). Ethnicity and body dissatisfaction among women in the United States: A meta-analysis. *Psychological Bulletin, 132,* 622–640.

Kilbourne, J. (2000). *Killing us softly III.* [Videotape]. Northampton, MA: Media Education Association.

National Eating Disorders Association: http://www.nationaleatingdisorders.org/

Renfrew Center Foundation: http://www.renfrew.org/

Wildes, J. E., Emery, R. E., & Simons, A. D. (2001). The roles of ethnicity and culture in the development of eating disturbance and body dissatisfaction: A meta-analytic review. *Clinical Psychology Review, 21,* 521–551.

VIDEO AND DVD RESOURCES FROM APA

Brown, L. S. (1994). *Feminist therapy.* [Videotape]. Washington, DC: American Psychological Association.

Fouad, N. A. (2009). *Culturally oriented career counseling.* [DVD]. Washington, DC: American Psychological Association.

Jordon, J. V. (2009). *Relational-cultural therapy.* [DVD]. Washington, DC: American Psychological Association.

McDaniel, S. H. (2009). *Counseling clients who have trouble conceiving.* [DVD]. Washington, DC: American Psychological Association.

Savin-Williams, R. C. (2009). *Coming out in adulthood.* [DVD]. Washington, DC: American Psychological Association.

Root, M. P. P. (2009). *Mixed-race identities.* [DVD]. Washington, DC: American Psychological Association.

PRACTICE GUIDELINES

American Counseling Association Multicultural Competencies and Standards. Available at: http://www.counseling.org/Publications/.

American Psychological Association. (2000). Guidelines for psychotherapy with lesbian, gay, and bisexual clients. *American Psychologist, 55,* 1440–1451.

American Psychological Association. (2003). Guidelines for multicultural education, training, research, practice, and organizational change for psychologists. *American Psychologist, 58,* 377–402.

American Psychological Association. (2004). Guidelines for psychological practice with older adults. *American Psychologist, 59,* 236–260.

American Psychological Association. (2007). Guidelines for psychological practice with girls and women. *American Psychologist, 62,* 949–949.

National Committee on Women's Issues: http://www.socialworkers.org/governance/cmtes/ncowi.asp

SUPERVISION AND ETHICS

American Association of Marriage and Family Counseling. (2001). *Code of ethics.* Available at: http://www

.aamft.org/resources/lrm_plan/Ethics/ethicscode2001
.asp

American Counseling Association. (2005). *ACA code of ethics*. Alexandria, VA: Author. Available at: http://www.counseling.org/

American Psychological Association. (2002). *Ethical principles of psychologists and code of conduct*. Washington, DC: Author. Available at: http://www.apa.org/ethics/code2002.html

American Psychological Association. (2002). *Guidelines and principles for accreditation of programs in professional psychology*. Available at: http://www.apa.org/ed/G&P2.pdf

Assessment of Competency Benchmarks Work Group: Competencies Benchmark Document. (2007). American Psychological Association Board of Educational Affairs in collaboration with the Council of Chairs of Training Councils.

Barnes, K. L., & Bernard, J. M. (2003). Women in counseling and psychotherapy supervision. In M. Kopala & M. A. Keitel (Eds.), *Handbook of counseling women*, (pp. 535–545). Thousand Oaks, CA: Sage.

Council for Accreditation of Counseling and Related Educational Programs (CACREP). (2009). *2009 standards*. Available at: http://www.cacrep.org/2009standards.pdf

Council on Social Work Education (CSWE). (2008). *Education policy and accreditation standards*. Available at: http://www.cswe.org/CSWE/.

Feminist Therapy Institute. (1999). *A code of ethics for feminists*. Retrieved February 15, 2009, from http://www.feminist-therapy-institute.org/ethics.htm

National Association of Social Workers. (1996). *Code of ethics*. Available at: http://www.socialworkers.org/pubs/code/default.asp

Nelson, M. L., & Friedlander, M. L. (2001). A close look at conflictual supervisory relationships: The trainee's perspective. *Journal of Counseling Psychology, 48*, 384–395.

Owens-Patterson, M. (2000). The African American supervisor: Racial transference and countertransference in interracial psychotherapy supervision. In L. C. Jackson & B. Greene (Eds.), *Psychotherapy with African American women: Innovations in psychodynamic perspectives and practice* (pp. 145–165). New York: Guilford Press.

JOURNALS

Feminist Family Therapy
Journal of Women and Social Work
Journal of Women in Culture and Society
Sex Roles
The Psychology of Women Quarterly
Women and Therapy

ORGANIZATIONS SPECIFIC TO WOMEN'S ISSUES

American Psychological Association

Division 35: Society for the Psychology of Women: http://www.apa.org/divisions/div35/

Division 44: Society for the Psychological Study of Lesbian, Gay, and Bisexual Issues: http://www.apadivision44.org/

Division 45: Society for the Psychological Study of Ethnic Minority Issues: http://www.apa.org/about/division/div45.html

Women's Programs Office: http://www.apa.org/pi/wpo/aboutus.htm

Association for Women in Psychology: http://www.awpsych.org/

Feminist Therapy Institute: http://www.feminist-therapy-institute.org/

EXERCISE 13.1: SELF–AWARENESS EXERCISE: YOU AS A GENDERED BEING

This can be conducted as an individual or group exercise. For group exercises, it is important to create a safe learning environment, with clear communication and confidentiality guidelines, and to debrief with participants afterwards.

A. How would you describe yourself?

B. How important is gender to who you believe you are?

C. What do you like or dislike about being a woman or a man?

(continued)

(continued)

D. Regardless of whether you follow them or not, what do you understand to be the "rules" of your gender? Do these remain constant or do they change depending on your environment?

E. How did you learn the "rules?"

F. Are you aware of any rules that seem to conflict with each other?

G. Which rules do you accept without question? Which ones do you question? Which ones are you not sure of? In what ways have you benefited or suffered as a result?

H. What are the benefits of your gender, as it intersects with other parts of you (e.g., religion, culture, sexual orientation)?

I. What are the drawbacks?

J. What did you learn from your early caregivers about being your gender?

K. Who in your personal life, if anyone, has been a gender role model for you? (Is there someone that you would like to emulate in terms of how they are as a man or woman or otherwise identified?)

L. Who, in your personal life, if anyone, has represented something you do not want to be, in terms of how they are as a man or woman or otherwise identified?

M. Are there any famous people (dead or living) that you would like to emulate in terms of how they are as a man or woman or otherwise identified?

N. Are there any characters in history, fiction, film, or other media that you admire in this way?

O. If you were to have a child tomorrow, what gender would you want the child to be, and why?

P. If you were to have a child tomorrow, what concerns would you have about a boy? What concerns would you have about a girl?

PSYCHOLOGY OF WOMEN SEMINAR

Topics and Activities

Trainers and practitioners may select from among the following suggestions.

A. Knowledge gained through didactic training and independent study:

1. Relation of gender to multicultural competency

2. Intersection of gender with multiple levels of identity (e.g., culture, ability/disability, economic status, religion, sexual orientation)

3. Connection between women's gender and mental health

4. Connection between women's physical and mental health

5. Definitions of gender socialization, gender role, gender identity

6. Definitions of patriarchy, sexism, multiple oppressions

7. Gender role socializations across cultures

8. Benefits and risks of gender role conformity and nonconformity

9. Impact of media on girls and women

10. Developmental theories of girls and women, including lifespan development into older age

11. Pros and cons of "difference" theory (differences between men and women)

12. Identity models

13. Assessment and case conceptualization: guarding against bias; recognizing environmental and socialization impacts on coping

14. Theoretical orientations and models of therapy: making adaptations in order to provide non-sexist therapy

15. Components of gender-aware therapy

16. Common therapeutic issues: abuse, assault, and domestic violence; body dissatisfaction and eating disorders; depression; anxiety

17. Ethical and legal standards

B. Awareness of one's own values and attitudes:

1. Use Table 16.5 and the questions that go with it (earlier in this chapter).

2. Use Exercise 13.1.

3. Work with one or more of the identity models (e.g., feminist identity, womanist identity).

4. Use journaling, paper-writing, and group discussion to process the above three issues.

5. Engage in activities that increase media literacy for women: Watch Jean Kilbourne videos or attend a lecture; analyze a selection of women's magazines or TV commercials for mixed messages about women's appetites and sexuality.

6. Invite a cross-section of women to speak about their experiences.

7. Participate in or visit a women's group.

8. Discuss in groups some of the issues common to women: self-consciousness, body dissatisfaction, self-esteem, romantic relationships, work and family balance, role changes and conflicts, caretaking.

9. Visit groups or treatment centers that deal primarily with women's issues: overeaters anonymous (also anorexia and bulimia subgroups); substance abuse; domestic violence.

10. Discuss transference and countertransference.

11. Discuss case examples and work through assessment, diagnosis, conceptualization, treatment planning; discuss potential for gender bias.

12. Choose a therapeutic issue, such as partner abuse or bulimia, and consider it from a variety of women's identities (e.g., culture, sexual orientation).

13. Interview an older woman about her life: what privileges and restrictions she grew up with; how she views herself as a woman; what things she has seen change or not change.

COMPETENCY BENCHMARK TABLES

The purpose of the Competency Benchmarks (Tables 16.1–16.4) is to create developmental models for defining and measuring competencies in professional psychology; each chapter in this *Handbook* applies the diversity competence for mental health practitioners in their work with a particular diverse population.

Table 16.1 Developmental-Level Competencies I

READINESS LEVEL—ENTRY TO PRACTICUM	
Competencies	Learning Process and Activities
Knowledge Students are gaining knowledge in: • Core counseling skills and theories. • Ethics codes. • Multiculturalism and guidelines for practice. • History of women in psychology and society. • The role of gender within biological, psychological, and sociopolitical realities and its effects on mental health. • The role of gender in their own lives.	At this stage of development, education of mental health practitioners focuses on the foundational knowledge, skills, and values and attitudes of their particular discipline. Students at this stage become aware of the principles and practices of the field, but they are only beginning to apply their knowledge to practice. Therefore, the training curriculum is focused on knowledge of core areas, including literature on multiculturalism, ethics, basic counseling skills, scientific knowledge, and the importance of reflective practice and self-awareness.
Skills Skills in the following areas are beginning to develop: • The ability to demonstrate empathic listening skills, respect, and interest when talking with women from a variety of backgrounds. • The ability to know when to seek supervision, particularly regarding crisis issues that affect women predominantly (e.g., rape, eating disorders). • The ability to formulate basic case conceptualizations.	It is important that throughout the curriculum, trainers and teachers incorporate an analysis of gender (even briefly) as they discuss theory, assessment, diagnosis, treatment planning, and treatment modalities. Discussion and analysis of gender should be embedded with other identities; that is, if possible, avoid broad references to "women" without anchoring women within other contexts. This models for students the understanding that all people have multiple dimensions of identity.
Values and Attitudes Students demonstrate: • Willingness to engage in self-exploration about their own gender beliefs and gender role socializations. • Willingness to engage in self-exploration about their stereotypes and biases (negative and positive) regarding women. • Intellectual curiosity and flexibility. • Ability to value expressions of diverse viewpoints and belief systems. • Willingness to examine how their own gender may impact women clients.	Given that all students have a gendered experience, they can often easily engage in exploration of their own gender socializations, intersections of identity, and biases regarding gender. Reflection papers, journaling, and experiential exercises can help them explore this. Help students understand the *social construction* of gender. Students may need help from readings, videos, movies, novels, and the psychological literature to broaden their perspectives. They may have difficulty understanding the more subtle but equally pernicious forms of sexism that exist (which they perhaps experience or inflict on others). An examination of gender often affects family and partner dynamics and students may need support regarding this.

Table 16.2 Developmental-Level Competencies II

READINESS LEVEL—ENTRY TO INTERNSHIP	
Competencies	Learning Process and Activities

Knowledge	Students have:	At this stage of development, students are building on their education and applied experiences (such as supervised practicum experiences) to attain a core set of foundational competencies. They can then begin applying this knowledge to professional practice. As a result of being exposed to didactic training and close supervision, students attain the multicultural values and attitudes appropriate to their level of development. Foundational knowledge and multicultural values and attitudes are becoming well established, but more specific skill in work with women is not likely at this point.

Knowledge — Students have:

- Knowledge of the following concepts: social construction of gender; gendered power dynamics; and sexism, oppression, patriarchy, gender norms, gender role socialization, gender role conflict.
- General understanding that there are multiple gender role socializations and that these vary according to many other dimensions of identity.
- General understanding of current and historic oppressive factors for women in society.
- General understanding of sexist elements in psychological assessment, diagnosis, theory, and treatment modalities.
- General understanding of the role of women's gender in depression, anxiety, trauma, and eating disorders.
- Understanding of the importance of the ethics of nonmaleficence, beneficence, and non-exploitation of women clients.
- Awareness of the general principles of non-sexist counseling.
- Awareness of APA's *Guidelines for Psychological Practice with Girls and Women*.

At this stage of development, students are building on their education and applied experiences (such as supervised practicum experiences) to attain a core set of foundational competencies. They can then begin applying this knowledge to professional practice. As a result of being exposed to didactic training and close supervision, students attain the multicultural values and attitudes appropriate to their level of development. Foundational knowledge and multicultural values and attitudes are becoming well established, but more specific skill in work with women is not likely at this point.

Learning occurs through multiple modalities:

- Some students may choose to train in clinical settings geared primarily for women (e.g., domestic violence shelters, eating disorder clinics, rape crisis centers). This can be beneficial to their overall understanding of gender in women's issues; however, it may also narrow their perceptions of women's issues.
- Receiving didactic training in gender and women's clinical issues can occur in academic programs (e.g., multicultural courses, courses in women's and GLBT [gay, lesbian, bisexual, and transgender] issues) and it may be infused into the core curriculum (e.g., ethics, assessment, multicultural, career counseling, research, human growth and development, and clinical courses).
- Providing therapy, under supervision, to women clients.
- Receiving supervision from psychotherapists knowledgeable and skilled in working with women's issues.
- Seeking additional study and professional development opportunities (e.g., trauma, eating disorders, addictions, couples work).
- Working on research projects related to women's issues.

Skills — Skills in the following areas are beginning to develop:

- The ability to enact the basic elements of non-sexist counseling.
- The ability to conceptualize women clients' issues within the context of gender and other sociopolitical and diverse factors.
- The ability to more fluidly establish a therapeutic alliance with women by integrating an understanding of gender into their basic counseling skills.
- The ability to assess for histories of trauma and abuse and remain respectful of the client's desired boundaries.
- The ability to formulate treatment plans that empower women to have more choices in their lives, while at the same time not imposing their own values on the client.
- The ability to illuminate strengths in the client and utilize these in therapy.
- The ability to critically examine the literature on women.
- The ability to recognize how their own gender and dimensions of identity may be impacting their women clients.

Topics to be covered in didactic training include:

- Relation of gender to multicultural competency.
- Relationship of gender to individual and cultural differences.
- Basic research literature describing the relevance of women's gender to wellness, physical health, mental health.

(continued)

Table 16.2 Developmental-Level Competencies II (*continued*)

READINESS LEVEL—ENTRY TO INTERNSHIP	
Competencies	Learning Process and Activities
Values and Attitudes	Students demonstrate: • An understanding that gender is an aspect of multicultural diversity. • Awareness of their own intersecting dimensions of identity (ethnicity, socioeconomic status [SES], sexual orientation, ability, etc.) and ability to discern clients' intersecting dimensions. • An awareness of their own and others' sexist assumptions. • A commitment to engage in self-exploration about their own gender beliefs and gender role socialization. • A commitment to engage in self-exploration about their stereotypes and biases (negative and positive) regarding women.	• The social construction of gender. • Basic definitions of patriarchy, sexism, gender role socialization, power, and oppression.

Table 16.3 Developmental-Level Competencies III

READINESS LEVEL—ENTRY TO PROFESSIONAL PRACTICE	
Competencies	Learning Process and Activities
Knowledge	Practitioners have: • Knowledge of the literature on the relationship between sexism and other forms of oppression on women's mental and physical health. • A good understanding of multiple dimensions of identity and how gender interacts with those for women across different backgrounds and cultures. • A good understanding of sexist elements in psychological assessment, diagnosis, theory, and treatment modalities. • A good understanding of the general principles of non-sexist counseling. • Knowledge of lifespan development issues for women (e.g., fertility and pregnancy; menopause). • Knowledge of the range of possible mental health issues for women. • Increasing knowledge of specific subgroups of women and how gender impacts their issues. • Knowledge of community resources (e.g., domestic violence shelters, legal aid for undocumented women, rape crisis, child care).	In the earlier stages of training, students solidified their professional knowledge base and attained appropriate values and attitudes while developing increasingly sophisticated clinical skills. At the level of Entry to Professional Practice, mental health practitioners have attained the full range of competencies in the domains expected of all independent practitioners. Preparation for this level of competency takes place through closely supervised clinical work, augmented by professional reading, personal exploration, and training opportunities such as professional development and training seminars. Clinical supervisors observe students' clinical work, provide training in assessment, case conceptualization, and treatment planning, and challenge supervisees to examine their countertransference reactions, biases, and values to develop their supervisees' clinical competency with gender issues.

READINESS LEVEL—ENTRY TO PROFESSIONAL PRACTICE	
Competencies	**Learning Process and Activities**
Skills Skills are demonstrated by the ability to: • Perform the basics of non-sexist therapy with greater ease. • Perform a basic gender role analysis within the context of multiple dimensions of identity and a broader assessment. • Form diagnostic impressions with the awareness that bias exists in the *DSM*. • Utilize diagnoses to assist and empower clients. • Formulate appropriate treatment plans that are sensitive to the client's gendered experience. • Identify the limits of their own competency with certain issues that affect women, and refer appropriately. • Form a trusting therapeutic relationship with clients. • Use supervision/consultation to enhance gender-aware skills. • Avoid boundary violations, but recognize that some boundaries might appropriately be crossed, specifically because of gender/multicultural dynamics. • Establish effective consultation relationships with treatment centers for women. • Create a climate in which supervisees and trainees feel safe to talk about gender issues, their own and their clients'.	Additional methods by which practitioners can attain competency with women at this level include: • Seeking opportunities to provide therapy to a diverse range of women clients. • Supervision/consultation provided by supervisors knowledgeable and skilled in working with women's issues. • Self-directed study and professional development opportunities. • Internship and postdoctoral seminar training in women's issues. • Presenting and participating in clinical case conferences that include discussion of women's gender.
Values and Attitudes Practitioners have: • Increased understanding of the complexity of multiple dimensions of people's identity, and how gender intersects with these dimensions. • Increased awareness of their own intersecting dimensions (ethnicity, SES, sexual orientation, ability, etc.) and ability to discern clients' intersecting dimensions. • Increased awareness of their own and others' sexist assumptions. • Increased awareness of how their own experience, culture, and gender socializations impact their approach to clients. • Commitment to lifelong learning and self-knowledge regarding gender. • Awareness that when they are supervisors, there are now three levels (supervisor, therapist, client) with their own unique socializations and dimensions of identity.	

Table 16.4 Developmental-Level Competencies IV

READINESS LEVEL—ADVANCED PRACTICE AND SPECIALIZATION	
Competencies	Learning Process and Activities
Knowledge Extensive knowledge of: • A range of women's gender roles socializations and gender role conflicts. • The intersection of multiple dimensions of identity. • Identity models: women, GLBT, ethnic, cultural, acculturation. • Impact of gendered experiences on human development. • The connection between women's gender and mental health. • Women and depression, anxiety, trauma, and eating disorders. • Women and self-esteem, shame, and guilt. • The impact of media on women's socialization.	Almost all mental health practitioners will work with some women and need basic levels of competency (see Table 16.3). Others will specialize in women's issues (e.g., sexual abuse trauma, eating disorders) or practice in a setting that primarily serves women (e.g., a community women's clinic, a women's substance abuse center). Learning activities will vary depending on the practitioner's unique background, established competencies, and interest areas. Regardless of the focus area, learning activities can include:
Skills Advanced skills in: • Incorporating gender role analysis seamlessly into assessment and diagnosis. • Providing therapy that is non-sexist and gender aware. • Providing therapy that takes into consideration the multiple realities of a woman's life and the intersection of her many dimensions of identity. • Finding respectful ways in which to promote and encourage women's choices. • Managing boundary issues in a nuanced manner that takes women's needs and experience into account. • Helping supervisees to process their own gender as it relates to their work with clients.	• Professional reading (information about diverse gender role norms and socializations across cultures; empirical studies, and literature on feminist and multicultural theory and practice). • Professional reading in related but different disciplines: women's studies, sociology, feminist studies, gender, political science, history and biography. • Teaching. • Attending and leading educational workshops. • Peer consultation groups. • Consultation with knowledgeable mental health professionals.
Values and Attitudes Well-integrated values and attitudes are demonstrated by the following: • Independently monitors own gender identity in relation to work with others. • Continually assesses and reassesses own biases and expectations of women clients. • Continually engages in broadening knowledge of resources for women and for continuing professional development.	

Table 16.5 Stereotypes and Gender Role Socializations

Culture/Ethnic Group	Traditional Family Structure	Intersecting Factors	Stereotypes	Gender Role Socialization and Conflicting Messages and "Rules about How to Be a Woman"
People often are descended from a mix of groups, and most people have to contend with the dominant culture's values to some degree.	Each family has unique features and many are now divorced, never married, blended, with gay or lesbian parents, or are separated by immigration issues.	Religious affiliation, economic status, disability and health, education, life events, strengths and resiliency, personality factors, genetic factors	These often derive from historical prejudice of the dominant culture, and many emerged based on White males' perspectives and fantasies. They are used between and among groups and are perpetuated in the media.	Most women have to contend with dominant cultural messages about what it means to be a woman, but also have their own cultural group influences, as well as various sub-group influences.
European Americans (particularly the historically dominant Anglo culture descended from Northern Europe)	• Patriarchal • Nuclear family • Individualistic • Emphasis on autonomy and competition • Protestant work ethic • Future-focus • Historically men were providers and this continues • Women often work outside the home but are still responsible for caregiving • Heterosexist	• Racial privilege • Increasing economic and educational power for some • Some also have access to more power (though White men) • Rapid change in gender roles over the past four decades • Intense media sexualization of girls and women	• Nurturing and communal • Relational and good at communicating • Warm, expressive • Intuitive • Dainty, passive, childlike, pure, weak, illogical • Overly emotional (hysterical) • "Sirens and shrews" • Manipulative, cold	• Be communal and nurturing • Women are responsible for relationships • Do not be selfish: others' needs come first • Be competent but not dominant • Be nice • Exercise self-control (of food, body, sex, emotions, aging) • Real women are married with children • "Superwomen" succeed at career, love, sex, and marriage, and are thin and fit • Show sympathy, love, sadness • Do not show anger, pride
Native Americans (keeping in mind great variability across hundreds of tribes)	• Extended family systems • Collectivist, but differs by tribe • Urbanization has impacted clan systems	• Genocide, colonization, discrimination, racism • Enforced Christianity • Trauma	• Stoic • "Primitive" • Exotic • Beautiful, "sacrificing princess" (gentle and noble)	• Female spiritual beings in the historical lore greatly valued • Often flexible roles and considerable power

(continued)

Table 16.5 Stereotypes and Gender Role Socializations (*continued*)

Culture/Ethnic Group	Traditional Family Structure	Intersecting factors	Stereotypes	Gender Role Socialization and Conflicting Messages and "Rules about How to Be a Woman"
	• Spirituality • Emphasis on the present • Historically tolerant of a range of gender identities, but increasingly heterosexist	• History of federal boarding school enforcement • Acculturation stress with increased contact with mainstream culture • Low life expectancy in women compared to other U.S. groups: violence, obesity, alcoholism, abuse, suicide	• Squaw (overly sexual, lazy, alcoholic)	• (depending on the tribe), but less so with acculturation to European American values • Some increase in power in recent years: "retraditionalization," an attempt to recapture egalitarian roles and integrate traditional values with modern culture • Aging is valued
African Americans (primarily descendants of slaves but also includes African immigrants and their descendants)	• Extended kinship networks and bonds • Collectivistic • Evidence of patriarchy, but generally flexible and egalitarian roles within the family • Heterosexist	• Slavery, discrimination • Stereotype of lower intelligence • Racist practices meant African American men struggled to find work • Religion and spirituality • Racial identity	• Independent • Loud • "Strength of the family" • Sexually promiscuous or aggressive • "Angry, hostile Sapphire" (angry at Black men) • "Nurturing mammy" (asexual and nonthreatening)	• Caretaking and mothering (others' children as well as one's own biological children) • Teach children how to navigate a racist society • Be strong, show pride • Forgive and do not challenge AA men for infidelity, unemployment, etc., because they suffer enough from a racist society • Correct negative stereotypes
Latinas/os (keeping in mind numerous countries of origin and enormous variability)	• Patriarchal • Collectivist • Hierarchical • Large and extended family networks • Importance of social harmony, • Catholicism	• Colonization • Immigration experience (legal or undocumented) • Acculturation and ethnic identity • Country of origin • Discrimination	• Submissive, dependent, powerless, naive, irresponsible • Romantic, exotic, sensual • "Hot Latina," dangerously sexual • "Good domestic worker"	• Maintain the family: nurturance • *Marianismo:* be self-sacrificing • Show love (but don't be sexual) • Do not show pride or anger

	Familismo *Personalismo* *Machismo* *Marianismo* *Respeto* *Heterosexist*	Language difficulties Women immigrants often find work sooner than the men do	• Even if you suffer, do not contribute to your men's "emasculation" in a racist society • Acculturation stress as gender roles change: pressure to maintain harmony
East Asian American (Japan, China, South Korea; keeping in mind enormous variability)	• Collectivist, • Hierarchical • Emphasis on social harmony • Emotional restraint • Confucianist influences include filial piety and women's obedience to father, husband, and then son • Heterosexist	• A visible minority, resulting in "forever-foreigner" status in some areas • Different waves of immigration • Western colonization of some Asian countries • "Model minority" stereotype • Acculturation and identity	• "Perfect" woman: obedient, beautiful, sensual • "Dragon Lady" Conniving • "Worker bees" • "Dolls": erotic/exotic, passive • Inscrutable • Intelligent	• Obedience to male authority • Acculturation stress as gender roles change: pressure to maintain harmony • Family-focused • Self-restraint • Personal sacrifice • Show shyness • Do not show pride

Sources:

Abrams, L. S. (2003). Contextual variations in young women's gender identity negotiations. *Psychology of Women Quarterly, 27,* 64–74.

Bernal, G., & Shapiro, E. (2005). Cuban families. In M. McGoldrick, J. Giordano, & N. Garcia-Preto (Eds.), *Ethnicity and family therapy* (3rd ed., pp. 202–215). New York: Guilford Press.

Bird, S. E. (1999). Gendered construction of the American Indian in popular media. *Journal of Communication, Summer,* 61–83.

Bradshaw, C. K. (1994). Asian and Asian American women: Historical and political considerations in psychotherapy. In L. Comaz-Diaz & B. Greene (Eds.), *Women of color: Integrating ethnic and gender identities in psychotherapy* (pp. 72–113). New York: Guilford Press.

Chrisler, J. C. (2008). 2007 Presidential address: Power, perfectionism, and the psychology of women. *Psychology of Women Quarterly, 32,* 1–12.

Comaz-Diaz, L., & Greene, B. (1994). (Eds.). *Women of color: Integrating ethnic and gender identities in psychotherapy.* New York: Guilford Press.

Durik, A. M., Hyde, S. J., Marks, A. C., Roy, A. L., Anaya, D., & Schultz, G. (2006). Ethnicity and gender stereotypes of emotion. *Sex Roles, 54,* 429–445.

Falicov, C. J. (2005). Mexican families. In M. McGoldrick, J. Giordano, & N. Garcia-Preto (Eds.), *Ethnicity and family therapy* (3rd ed., pp. 229–241). New York: Guilford Press.

Garcia-Preto, N. (2005). Latino families: An overview. In M. McGoldrick, J. Giordano, & N. Garcia-Preto (Eds.), *Ethnicity and family therapy* (3rd ed., pp. 153–165). New York: Guilford Press.

Goodwin, S. A., & Fiske, S. T. (2001). Power and gender: The double-edged sword of ambivalence. In R. K. Unger (Ed.), *Handbook of the psychology of women and gender* (pp. 358–366). New York: Wiley.

Greene, B. (1990). What has gone before: The legacy of racism and sexism in the lives of black mothers and daughters. In L. S. Brown & M. P. P. Root (Eds.), *Diversity and complexity in feminist theory* (pp. 207–230). New York: Harrington Park Press.

Greene, B. (1994). African American women. In L. Comaz-Diaz & B. Greene (Eds.), *Women of color: Integrating ethnic and gender identities in psychotherapy* (pp. 10–29). New York: Guilford Press.

Hall, C. C. I. (1995). Asian eyes: Body image and eating disorders of Asian and Asian American women. *Eating Disorders, 3,* 8–19.

Kite, M. E. (2001). Changing times, changing gender roles: Who do we want men and women to be? In R. K. Unger (Ed.), *Handbook of the psychology of women and gender* (pp. 215–227). New York: Wiley.

LaFromboise, T. D., Berman, J. S., & Sohi, B. K. (1994). American Indian women. In L Comaz-Diaz & B. Greene (Eds.), *Women of color: Integrating ethnic and gender identities in psychotherapy* (pp. 30–71). New York: Guilford Press.

McGill, D. W., & Pearce, J. K. (2005). American families with English ancestors from the Colonial Era: Anglo Americans. In M. McGoldrick, J. Giordano, & N. Garcia-Preto (Eds.), *Ethnicity and family therapy* (3rd ed., pp. 520–533). New York: Guilford Press.

Moore-Hines, P., & Boyd-Franklin, N. (2005). African American families. In M. McGoldrick, J. Giordano, & N. Garcia-Preto (Eds.), *Ethnicity and family therapy* (3rd ed., pp. 87–100). New York: Guilford Press.

Paludi, M. A., Paludi, C. A., & DeFour, D. C. (2004). Introduction: Plus ca change, plus c'est la meme chose (The more things change, the more they stay the same). In M. A. Paludi (Ed.), *Praeger guide to the psychology of gender* (pp. ix–xxxi). Westport, CT: Praeger.

Root, M.P.P. (1990). Disordered eating in women of color. *Sex Roles, 22,* 525–536.

Rudman, L. A., & Glick, P. (2001). Prescriptive gender stereotypes and backlash toward agentic women. *Journal of Social Issues, 57,* 743–762.

Smolak, L., & Murnen, S. K. (2001). Gender and eating problems. In R. H. Striegel-Moore & L Smolak (Eds.), *Eating disorders: Innovative directions in research and practice* (pp. 91–110). Washington DC: American Psychological Association.

Sue, D. W., & Sue, D. (2003). *Counseling the culturally diverse: Theory and practice* (4th ed.). New York: Wiley.

Sutton, C. T., & Broken Nose, M. A. (2005). American Indian families: An overview. In M. McGoldrick, J. Giordano, & N. Garcia-Preto (Eds.), *Ethnicity and family therapy* (3rd ed., pp. 43–54). New York: Guilford Press.

Tafoya, N. (2005). Native American women: Fostering resiliency through community. In M. P. Mirkin, K. L. Suyemoto, & B. F. Okun (Eds.), *Psychotherapy with women: Exploring diverse contexts and identities* (pp. 297–312). New York: Guilford Press.

Vasquez, M. T. (1994). Latinas. In L. Comaz-Diaz & B. Greene (Eds.), *Women of color: Integrating ethnic and gender identities in psychotherapy* (pp. 114–138). New York: Guilford Press.

REFERENCES

American Counseling Association. (2005). *ACA code of ethics*. Alexandria, VA: Author. Available at: http://www.counseling.org/.

American Psychiatric Association. (1994). *American Psychiatric Association: Diagnostic and statistical manual of mental disorders*, (4th ed.). Washington, DC.

American Psychological Association. (1975). Report of the task force on sex bias and sex-role stereotyping in psychotherapeutic practice. *American Psychologist, 30*, 1169–1175.

American Psychological Association. (2000). Guidelines for psychotherapy with lesbian, gay, and bisexual clients. *American Psychologist, 55*, 1440–1451.

American Psychological Association. (2002). *Ethical principles of psychologists and code of conduct*. Washington, DC: Author. Available at: http://www.apa.org/ethics/code2002.html

American Psychological Association. (2003). Guidelines for multicultural education, training, research, practice, and organizational change for psychologists. *American Psychologist, 58*, 377–402.

American Psychological Association. (2004). Guidelines for psychological practice with older adults. *American Psychologist, 59*, 236–260.

American Psychological Association. (2007). Guidelines for psychological practice with girls and women. *American Psychologist, 62*, 949–949.

American Psychological Association, Task Force on the Sexualization of Girls. (2007). *Report of the APA Task Force on the sexualization of girls*. Washington, DC: American Psychological Association. Available at http://www.apa.org/pi/wpo/sexualization.html

American Psychological Association, Task Force on Mental Health and Abortion. (2008). *Report of the Task Force on mental health and abortion*. Washington, DC: Author. Available at http://www.apa.org/pi/wpo/mental-health-abortion-report.pdf

Assessment of Competency Benchmarks Work Group: Competencies Benchmark Document. (2007). American Psychological Association Board of Educational Affairs in collaboration with the Council of Chairs of Training Councils.

Barnes, K. L., & Bernard, J. M. (2003). Women in counseling and psychotherapy supervision. In M. Kopala & M. A. Keitel (Eds.), *Handbook of counseling women* (pp. 535–545). Thousand Oaks, CA: Sage.

Bem, S. L. (1981). Gender schema theory: A cognitive account of sex typing. *Psychological Review, 88*, 354–364.

Black, B., & Joiner, J. M. (2008). Gender and social work practice. In D. M. DiNitto & C. A. McNeece (Eds.), *Social work issues and opportunities in a challenging profession* (pp. 99–120).

Bordo, S. (1993). *Unbearable weight: Feminism, Western culture, and the body*. Berkeley, CA: University of California Press.

Bradshaw, C. K. (1994). Asian and Asian American women: Historical and political considerations in psychotherapy. In L. Comaz-Díaz & B. Greene (Eds.), *Women of color* (pp. 72–113). New York: Guilford Press.

Broverman, I. K., Broverman, D. M., Clarkson, F. E., Rosenkrantz, P. S., & Vogel, S. R. (1970). Sex-role stereotypes and clinical judgments of mental health. *Journal of Consulting and Clinical Psychology, 34*, 1–7.

Brown, L. S. (1990a). Taking account of gender in the clinical assessment interview. *Professional Psychology: Research and Practice, 21*, 12–17.

Brown, L. S. (1990b). The meaning of a multicultural perspective for theory-building in feminist therapy. In L. S. Brown & M. P. P. Root (Eds.), *Diversity and complexity in feminist theory* (pp. 1–21). New York: Harrington Park Press.

Brown, L. S., & Root, M. P. P. (Eds.). (1990). *Diversity and complexity in feminist theory*. New York: Harrington Park Press.

Bussey, K., & Bandura, A. (1999). Social cognitive theory of gender development and differentiation. *Psychological Review, 106*, 676–713.

Chrisler, J. C. (2001). Gendered bodies and physical health. In R. K. Unger (Ed.), *Handbook of the psychology of women and gender* (pp. 289–302). New York: Wiley.

Chrisler, J. C. (2008). 2007 Presidential address: Fear of losing control: Power, perfectionism, and the psychology of women. *Psychology of Women Quarterly, 32*, 1–12.

Comaz-Díaz, L., & Greene, B. (1994). Overview: An ethnocultural mosaic. In L. Comaz-Díaz & B. Greene (Eds.), *Women of color* (pp. 3–9). New York: Guilford Press.

Constantine, M. G., Greer, T. M., & Kindaichi, M. M. (2003). Theoretical and cultural considerations in counseling women of color. In M. Kopala & M. A. Keitel (Eds.), *Handbook of counseling women* (pp. 40–53). Thousand Oaks, CA: Sage.

Council for Accreditation of Counseling and Related Educational Programs (CACREP). (2009). *2009 standards*. Available at: http://www.cacrep.org/2009standards.pdf

Council on Social Work Education (CSWE). (2008). *Education policy and accreditation standards*. Available at: http://www.cswe.org/CSWE/.

Cummins, L. H., Simmons, A. M., & Zane, N. W. S. (2005). Eating disorders in Asian populations: A critique of current approaches to the study of culture, ethnicity, and eating disorders. *American Journal of Orthopsychiatry, 75*, 553–574.

Danzinger, P. R., & Welfel, E. R. (2000). Age, gender, and health bias in counselors: An empirical analysis. *Journal of Mental Health Counseling, 22*, 135–149.

Davis, S. N., & Gergen, M. (1997). Toward a new psychology of gender: Opening conversations. In S. N. Davis & M. Gergen (Eds.), *Toward a new psychology of gender: A reader* (pp. 1–27). New York: Routledge.

Deaux, K., & Stewart, A. J. (2001). Framing gendered identities. In R. K. Unger (Ed.), *Handbook of the psychology of women and gender* (pp. 84–97). New York: Wiley.

de Beauvoir, S. (1989). *The second sex*. (H. M. Parshley, Trans. and Ed.). New York: Vintage. [Original work published 1949].

Downing, N. E., & Roush, K. L. (1985). From passive acceptance to active commitment: A model of feminist identity development for women. *The Counseling Psychologist, 13*, 695–709.

Durik, A. M., Hyde, S. J., Marks, A. C., Roy, A. L., Anaya, D., & Schultz, G. (2006). Ethnicity and gender stereotypes of emotion. *Sex Roles, 54*, 429–445.

Enns, C. Z. (2003). Contemporary adaptations of traditional approaches to the counseling of women. In M. Kopala & M. A. Keitel (Eds.), *Handbook of counseling women* (pp. 3–22). Thousand Oaks, CA: Sage.

Enns, C. Z. (2004). *Feminist theories and feminist psychotherapies: Origin, themes, and diversity* (2nd ed.). New York: Hayworth Press.

Eriksen, K., & Kress, V. E. (2008). Gender and diagnosis: Struggles and suggestions for counselors. *Journal of Counseling and Development, 86*, 152–162.

Evans, K. M., Kincade, E. A., Marbley, A. F., & Seem, S. R. (2005). Feminism and feminist therapy: Lessons from the past and hopes for the future. *Journal of Counseling and Development, 83*, 269–277.

Fallon, P., Katzman, M. A., & Wooley, S. C. (Eds.). (1994). *Feminist perspectives on eating disorders*. New York: Guilford Press.

Fischer, A. R., & Holz, K. B. (2007). Perceived discrimination and women's psychological distress: The roles of collective and personal self-esteem. *Journal of Counseling Psychology, 54*, 154–164.

Fredrickson, B. L., & Roberts, T. (1997). Objectification theory: Toward understanding women's lived experiences and mental health risks. *Psychology of Women Quarterly, 21*, 173–206.

Gilbert, L. A. (1994). Reclaiming and returning gender to context: Examples from studies of heterosexual dual-earner families. *Psychology of Women Quarterly, 18*, 539–558.

Gilbert, L. A., & Rader, J. (2001). Current perspectives on women's adult roles: Work, family, and life. In R. K. Unger (Ed.), *Handbook of the psychology of women and gender* (pp. 156–169). New York: Wiley.

Gilligan, C. (1982). *In a different voice: Psychological theory and women's development*. Harvard University Press.

Gilligan, C., Lyons, N. P., & Hanmer, T. J. (Eds.). (1990). *Making connections: The relational worlds of adolescent girls at Emma Willard School*. Harvard University Press.

Gilligan, C., Rogers, A. G., & Tolman, D. L. (Eds.). (1991). *Women, girls, and psychotherapy: Reframing resistance*. New York: Harrington Park Press.

Good, G. E., Gilbert, L. A., & Scher, M. (1990). Gender aware therapy: A synthesis of feminist therapy and knowledge about gender. *Journal of Counseling and Clinical Development, 68*, 376–380.

Goodwin, S. A., & Fiske, S. T. (2001). Power and gender: The double-edged sword of ambivalence. In R. K. Unger (Ed.), *Handbook of the psychology of women and gender* (pp. 358–366). New York: Wiley.

Gordon, R. A. (2001). Eating disorders East and West: A culture-bound syndrome unbound. In M. Nasser, M. A. Katzman, & R. A. Gordon (Eds.), *Eating disorders and cultures in transition* (pp. 1–16). New York: Taylor & Francis.

Greene, S. (2003). *The psychological development of girls and women: Rethinking change in time*. New York: Routledge.

Hare-Mustin, R. T. (1997). Discourse in the mirrored room: A postmodern analysis of therapy. In M. M. Gergen & S. N. Davis (Eds.), *Toward a new psychology of gender: A reader* (pp. 553–574). New York: Routledge.

Hare-Mustin, R. T., & Marecek, J. (1988). The meaning of difference: Gender theory, post-modernism, and psychology. *American Psychologist*, *43*, 455–464.

Hoffman, M. A., & Baker, L. M. (2003). Women and sexually transmitted diseases: A biopsychosocial perspective. In M. Kopala & M. A. Keitel (Eds.), *Handbook of counseling women* (pp. 411–426). Thousand Oaks, CA: Sage.

hooks, b. (1981). *Ain't I a woman: Black women and feminism*. Boston: South End Press.

Jones, L. S. (2003). Power and women in the counseling relationship. In M. Kopala & M. A. Keitel (Eds.), *Handbook of counseling women* (pp. 31–39). Thousand Oaks, CA: Sage.

Kanuha, V. (1990). Compounding the triple jeopardy: Battering in Lesbian of color relationships. In L. S. Brown & M. P. P. Root (Eds.), *Diversity and complexity in feminist theory* (pp. 169–185). New York: Harrington Park Press.

Kimball, M. M. (2001). Gender similarities and differences as feminist contradictions. In R. K. Unger (Ed.), *Handbook of the psychology of women and gender* (pp. 66–83). New York: Wiley.

Kirst-Ashman, K. K., & Hull, Jr., G. H. (Eds.). (2002). *Understanding generalist practice* (3rd ed.). Pacific Grove, CA: Brooks/Cole.

Kite, M. E. (2001). Changing times, changing gender roles: Who do we want women and men to be? In R. K. Unger (Ed.), *Handbook of the psychology of women and gender* (pp. 215–227). New York: Wiley.

Kitzinger, C. (2001). Sexualities. In R. K. Unger (Ed.), *Handbook of the psychology of women and gender* (pp. 272–285). New York: Wiley.

Kopala, M., Keitel, M. A. (Eds.). (2003). *Handbook of counseling women*. Thousand Oaks, CA: Sage.

Kress, V.E.W., Eriksen, K. P., Rayle, A. D., & Ford, S. J.W. (2005). The DSM-IV-TR and culture: Considerations for counselors. *Journal of Counseling and Development*, *83*, 97–104.

Marecek, J. (2001). Disorderly constructs: Feminist frameworks for clinical psychology. In R. K. Unger (Ed.), *Handbook of the psychology of women and gender* (pp. 303–316). New York: Wiley.

McGill, D. W., & Pearce, J. K. (2005). American families with English ancestors from the Colonial Era: Anglo Americans. In M. McGoldrick, J. Giordano, & N. Garcia-Preto (Eds.), *Ethnicity and family therapy* (3rd ed., pp. 520–533). New York: Guilford Press.

Merskin, D. (2007). Three faces of Eva: Perpetuation of the hot Latina stereotype in Desperate Housewives. *The Howard Journal of Communications*, *18*, 133–151.

Mirkin, M. P., Suyemoto, K. L., & Okun, B. F. (Eds.). (2005). *Psychotherapy with women: Exploring diverse contexts and identities*. New York: Guilford Press.

National Association of Social Workers (1996). Code of Ethics. Available at: http://www.naswdc.org/pubs/code/code.asp

Nelson, M. L., & Friedlander, M. L. (2001). A close look at conflictual supervisory relationships: The trainee's perspective. *Journal of Counseling Psychology*, *48*, 384–395.

Ossana, S. M., Helms, J. E., & Leonard, M. M. (1992). Do "womanist" identity attitudes influence college women's self-esteem and perceptions of environmental bias? *Journal of Counseling and Development*, *70*, 402–408.

Owens-Patterson, M. (2000). The African American supervisor: Racial transference and counter-transference in interracial psychotherapy supervision. In L. C. Jackson & B. Greene (Eds.), *Psychotherapy with African American women: Innovations in psychodynamic perspectives and practice* (pp. 145–165). New York: Guilford Press.

Powlishta, K. K., Sen, M. G., Serbin, L. A., Poulin-Dubois, D., & Eichstedt, J. A. (2001). From infancy through middle childhood: The role of cognitive and social factors in becoming gendered. In R. K. Unger (Ed.), *Handbook of the psychology of women and gender* (pp. 116–132). New York: Wiley.

Rudman, L. A., & Glick, P. (2001). Prescriptive gender stereotypes and backlash toward agentic women. *Journal of Social Issues*, *57*, 743–762.

Seem, S., & Johnson, E. (1998). Gender bias among counseling trainees: A study of case conceptualization. *Counselor Education & Supervision*, *37*(4), 257. Retrieved October 18, 2008, from Academic Search Premier database.

Sommers-Flanagan, J., & Sommers-Flanagan, R. (2004). *Counseling and psychotherapy theories in context and practice: Skills, strategies, and techniques*. Hoboken, NJ: Wiley.

Tavris, C. (1992). *The mismeasure of woman*. New York: Simon & Schuster.

Unger, R. K. (2001). Women as subjects, actors, and agents in the history of psychology. In R. K. Unger (Ed.), *Handbook of the psychology of women and gender* (pp. 3–16). New York: Wiley.

Vasquez, M. T. (1994). Latinas. In L. Comaz-Díaz & B. Greene (Eds.), *Women of color: Integrating ethnic and gender identities in psychotherapy* (pp. 114–138). New York: Guilford Press.

Vasquez, M. T. (2003). Ethical responsibilities in therapy. In M. Kopala & M. A. Keitel (Eds.), *Handbook of counseling women* (pp. 557–573). Thousand Oaks, CA: Sage.

Wooley, O. W. (1994). . . . And man created "woman": Representations of women's bodies in Western culture. In P. Fallon, M. A. Katzman, & S. C. Wooley (Eds.), *Feminist perspectives on eating disorders* (pp. 17–52). New York: Guilford Press.

Woollett, A., & Marshall, H. (2001). Motherhood and mothering. In R. K. Unger (Ed.), *Handbook of the psychology of women and gender* (pp. 170–182). New York: Wiley.

Worell, J., & Johnson, D. (2001). Therapy with women: Feminist frameworks. In R. K. Unger (Ed.), *Handbook of the psychology of women and gender* (pp. 317–329). New York: Wiley.

Wyche, K. F. (2001). Sociocultural issues in counseling for women of color. In R. K. Unger (Ed.), *Handbook of the psychology of women and gender* (pp. 330–340). New York: Wiley.

CONTRIBUTORS

Roki Abakoui, PhD, is the Assistant Director for Clinical Services at Northwestern University's Counseling and Psychological Services. She earned her doctorate in counseling psychology at the University of North Texas. She has presented regionally and nationally on Health at Every Size and working with people of size. She is also a member of the Association for Size Diversity and Health, a national organization devoted to promoting size-acceptance and health for everyone. Other interests include trauma, using Dialectical Behavior Therapy in university counseling centers, and multicultural counseling.

Sarah K. Armstrong, PsyD, earned her doctorate in clinical psychology and is currently the Director of the Pre-doctoral Internship at the University of St. Thomas in St. Paul. She is a licensed psychologist in the state of Minnesota, and is an active member of the Association of Counseling Center Training Agencies, where she has served as a board member, conference planner, listserv survey coordinator, and member of the research committee. She is a member of the Minnesota Psychological Association's education and training committee and currently serves as a reviewer for *Training and Education in Professional Psychology* and *Professional Psychology: Research and Practice*. Her professional interests include training and supervision, spirituality in counseling, and multicultural competencies.

Cyndy Boyd, PhD, is the Associate Director for Training at the Counseling Center at the University of Illinois at Chicago. She has served on several national committees and boards, including the American Counseling Association's Association of Lesbian, Gay, Bisexual, and Transgender Issues in Counseling. Her professional interests, publications, and presentations include the topics of training, multicultural competence, sexual orientation, and gender identity. She volunteers as an activist with the Illinois Safe Schools Alliance to promote social equality in the public school system.

Julie Corkery, PhD, is currently the Director of Training at the University Counseling Service, University of Iowa. She received her PhD in counseling psychology from Iowa State University in 1991. She is excited about helping psychologists develop multicultural competencies.

Claytie Davis III, PhD, is the Director of Training in Counseling and Psychological Services at the University of California, Berkeley. He earned his PhD in counseling psychology from the University of Texas at Austin. He is an Associate Editor of *Training and Education in Professional Psychology* and an editorial board member for *The Counseling Psychologist*. His professional interests include supervision, ethics, multicultural competence (development and assessment), and internship and postdoctoral training.

Alicia del Prado, PhD, is an Assistant Professor at the Wright Institute in Berkeley, CA. She earned her PhD in counseling psychology from Washington State University. Her primary professional interests include acculturation, ethnic identity, Filipino culture, and multiracial identity development.

Aisha Dixon-Peters, PsyD, is Staff Psychologist for University Counseling Services at California State University at Northridge. Dr. Dixon-Peters has a doctoral degree in clinical-community psychology from the University of La Verne. Dr. Dixon-Peters is a Psychology Summer Institute Fellow of the American Psychological Association's Minority Fellowship Program. Her professional interests include trauma, grief, integrating mindfulness and meditation in clinical practice, women and women of color, mixed ancestry, domestic/intimate partner violence, underserved communities, and trainings in multicultural competency and social justice education.

Jeana L. Dressel, PhD, is a licensed psychologist in California and earned her PhD from Michigan State University in counseling psychology. She was Training Coordinator at University of California at Santa Barbara for 25 years prior to her retirement. Her professional interests include training and supervision, with a particular interest in multicultural supervision, secondary trauma, and disaster mental health. She has served on the boards of the Association of Counseling Center Training Agencies (ACCTA), Division 17 Section on College and University Counseling Centers, and her local psychological association. She has also served ACCTA as its Historian and Archivist for 15 years.

Matt Englar-Carlson, PhD, is Associate Professor of Counseling at the California State University at Fullerton. He received his doctoral degree in counseling psychology from the Pennsylvania State University and completed his APA accredited predoctoral internship in psychology at the University of Southern California Student Counseling Center. Matt co-edited the books *In the Room with Men: A Casebook of Therapeutic Change* (APA, 2006) and *Counseling Troubled Boys* (Routledge, 2008) and the upcoming book series *Theories of Psychotherapy* to be published by APA Books, and developed the APA DVD, *Engaging Men in Psychotherapy* (2009).

Jennifer A. Erickson Cornish, PhD, ABPP, is Assistant Professor and Director of Clinical Training at the University of Denver's Graduate School of Professional Psychology. Her professional interests include supervision and training, ethics, multiculturalism, and group modalities. Dr. Cornish sits on several editorial boards and has served in a variety of leadership positions, including her current membership on the APA Ethics Committee. She is a licensed psychologist in Colorado, listed with the National Register of Health Service Providers in Psychology, board certified in counseling psychology by the American Board of Professional Psychology, and a fellow of the American Psychological Association.

Lynett Henderson Metzger, JD, PsyD, is a Clinical Assistant Professor at the University of Denver Graduate School of Professional Psychology and maintains a small private psychotherapy practice serving the needs of adults with developmental differences. Her professional interests focus on the intersection between law and mental health, including issues related to social justice, intimate violence, and forensic psychology.

Arpana G. Inman received her PhD in counseling psychology from Temple University. Currently, she is an Associate Professor in Counseling Psychology at Lehigh University. Her areas of research include South Asian identity, Asian American coping and mental health, international counseling and psychology, and multicultural competencies in supervision and training.

Shelly Kerr, PhD, is a licensed psychologist and the Director of the University of Oregon Counseling and Testing Center. Dr. Kerr earned her doctorate in counseling psychology from Washington State University. She previously co-edited *Preventive Health Measures for Lesbian and Bisexual Women* (Haworth, 2006*)* and *Lesbian and Bisexual Women's Mental Health* (Haworth, 2003). Her professional interests include training and supervision, multicultural organizational development and multicultural issues, and campus mental health issues.

Kim Dudley Lassiter, PhD, earned her PhD in clinical psychology from Ohio University. After seven years as Director of the Ohio University Psychology and Social Work Clinic in Athens, Ohio she has relocated to North Carolina. Her areas of professional interest include clinical training, clinical competencies, and clinical supervision. She is co-author with Dr. Bob Hatcher of the 2007 publication, "Initial Training in Professional Psychology: The Practicum Competencies Outline."

William Ming Liu, PhD, is Associate Professor and Program Coordinator for the Counseling Psychology program at the University of Iowa. He received his counseling psychology doctorate at the University of Maryland in 2000. His research and clinical interests are in social class and classism and men's issues. He is the editor of *The Handbook of Multicultural Competencies in Counseling and Psychology* (Sage, 2003), an editor for the forthcoming *Culturally Responsive Counseling with Asian American Men* (Routledge), and the author of the forthcoming *Social Class and Classism in the Helping Professions: Research, Theory, and Practice* (Sage). He also received the Award for Emerging Leadership, Committee on Socioeconomic Status, American Psychological Association (2008). He is the associate editor for *The Psychology of Men and Masculinity,* and is on the editorial boards of *Cultural Diversity and Ethnic Minority Psychology,* and *Men and Masculinities.*

Lavita I. Nadkarni, PhD, is the Director of Forensic Studies at the University of Denver's Graduate School of Professional Psychology, and is currently licensed as a clinical psychologist in New York and Colorado. She has an MA in forensic psychology from John Jay College of Criminal Justice and earned her PhD from Adelphi University Derner Institute of Advanced Psychological Studies. She has been working with forensic populations for over 20 years, primarily providing clinical services (therapy, assessment, expert testimony, and consultation) and training. Her research interests lie in the area of interpersonal violence and trauma in both domestic and international arenas, entitlement, clinical training, and diversity issues within psychology. In addition to publications in these areas, Dr. Nadkarni is a textbook, manuscript, and proposal reviewer for several publishers and is the associate editor for *Psychotherapy Bulletin*. She actively reaches out to diverse communities as a clinician, and has been a Human Rights Clinic volunteer for Doctors of the World for over five years. Dr. Nadkarni is an active member of the American Psychology–Law Society (AP-LS) and the National Council of Schools and Programs in Professional Psychology (NCSPP), and has leadership positions within these organizations.

Barbara J. Palombi, PhD, ABPP, is the Director of the Counseling and Career Development Center at Grand Valley State University. She received her PhD in counseling psychology from Michigan State University. She is board certified in counseling psychology by the American Board of Professional Psychology. She serves as a board member of the American Psychological Association's Board for the Advancement of Psychology in the Public Interest (BAPPI) and on the board of Counseling Psychology, American Board of Professional Psychology. Her areas of professional interest include students with personality disorders, campus wellness, and issues related to disability.

Henrietta Pazos, PsyD, is a Cuban American clinical and school psychologist in Denver, Colorado. She is married to Joseph Knight and has two boys, Gabriel and Samuel Pazos-Knight. Dr. Pazos grew up in Miami, Florida and is the daughter of Cuban refugees. She graduated from the University of Denver in 1999 with a doctorate in school psychology and later obtained her post doctoral degree in child and adolescent psychology from the University of Miami/Jackson Memorial Medical Center. Dr. Pazos has worked in the areas of outpatient and inpatient child and adult mental health, behavioral medicine, and most recently in the schools. She has made it a mission to work with immigrant and refugee populations as well as focusing on multicultural and multilingual psychology.

Emil Rodolfa, PhD, is the Director of the University of California, Davis Counseling and Psychological Services. He is a fellow of the American Psychological Association, a member of the State of California Board of Psychology, President of the Association of State and Provincial Psychology Boards (ASPPB), and the editor of *Training and Education in Professional Psychology (TEPP)*. He is a former President of the Association of Counseling Center Training Agencies (ACCTA), a former Chair of the Association of Psychology Postdoctoral and Internship Centers (APPIC), and a former Chair of the Council of Chairs of Training Councils (CCTC). Dr. Rodolfa has received awards for his contributions to psychology education, practice, and advocacy.

Delida Sanchez, PhD, is an Assistant Professor in School Counseling at Brooklyn College of the City University of New York. She earned her PhD in counseling psychology from Columbia University Teachers College. She's a National Institutes of Health grant recipient for her research on racism-related stress, health risk factors, and psychological outcomes among adolescents of color. Her professional interests include supervision, multicultural training, school counseling, and consultation.

Julie Savage, PhD, served as the Training Director at Counseling and Consultation, Arizona State University, for seventeen years and she is currently a Senior Psychologist at the center. She is a licensed psychologist in Arizona, and has served on committees and boards of several professional psychology organizations. Her professional interests include supervision, training, working with spiritual issues in counseling, and multicultural competencies in professional training.

Barry A. Schreier, PhD, is the Director of Counseling and Mental Health Services at the University of Connecticut. Dr. Schreier was previously the Coordinator of Training at Purdue University's Counseling and Psychological Services for 11 years. Dr. Schreier has served on numerous psychology training organizational boards and journal editorial boards. Dr. Schreier is extensively published in the areas of sexual orientation and gender identity. Dr. Schreier is also founder and senior consultant for BRIDGE PARTNERS, a private consulting firm on LGBTQ issues and concerns.

Rosemary E. Simmons, PhD, is the Director of the Counseling Center at Southern Illinois University at Carbondale. Prior to this position, she was the Assistant Director/Director of Training at SIUC for 11 years. Her professional interests include supervision and training, trauma survivors, disordered eating, and size acceptance. She is a local, regional, and national presenter on the topics of clinical intervention with trauma survivors, dialectical behavioral therapy in university counseling centers, size acceptance, and health at every size.

Anneliese Singh, PhD, LPC, NCC, is an Assistant Professor in the Department of Counseling and Human Development Services at the University of Georgia. She received her doctorate in counseling psychology from Georgia State University in 2007. Her clinical, research, and advocacy interests include: LGBTQ youth, Asian American/Pacific Islander counseling and psychology, multicultural counseling and social justice training, qualitative methodology with historically marginalized groups (e.g., people of color, LGBTQ, immigrants), feminist theory and practice, and empowerment interventions with survivors of trauma. Dr. Singh has been the President of the Association of Lesbian, Gay, Bisexual, and Transgender Issues (ALGBTIC) and led on establishing counseling competencies with transgender people. She is the recipient of the 2007 Ramesh and Vijaya Bakshi Community Change Award and the 2008 O'Hana award from Counselors for Social Justice (CSJ) for her organizing work to end child sexual abuse in South Asian communities and to increase visibility of South Asian LGBTQ people.

Rebekah Smart, PhD, is an Assistant Professor of Counseling at the California State University at Fullerton. She has a doctoral degree in counseling psychology and a certificate in gender studies from the University of Southern California. Prior to her academic position, she worked as a staff psychologist at a large university counseling center for a number of years, focusing on women's issues and treatment of eating disorders. Her research interests include gender and social justice issues across cultures, disordered eating and body dissatisfaction in women and men across cultures, and multicultural competency in counselor development.

Hal Stevens, PsyD, is the Coordinator of Training at Clemson University Counseling and Psychological Services. His interests include diversity, multiculturalism, social justice, and white privilege.

Mark Stevens, PhD, is the Director of the University Counseling Services at California State University at Northridge (CSUN). His latest edited book with Matt Englar-Carlson is titled *In the Room with Men: A Casebook of Therapeutic Change* (2006), and is published by the American Psychological Association. Dr. Stevens is also the featured therapist in an APA-produced video (APA, 2003) on *Counseling and Psychotherapy with Men*. He is the past President of APA Division 51 of the Society for the Psychological Study of Men and Masculinity.

Jenni Thome, PhD, received her PhD in counseling psychology at the University of Illinois at Urbana-Champaign. She currently works as a Licensed Clinical Psychologist at Illinois State University Student Counseling Services. Her professional interests include clinical work, outreach, and training, particularly as they relate to first-generation college students and social class issues. Dr. Thome has presented at several regional and national conferences on these topics. She authored a self-help brochure for first-generation college students that is published by the University of Illinois at Urbana-Champaign Counseling Center. Dr. Thome also has a strong research, outreach, and clinical background in the treatment and prevention of eating disorders.

Pratyusha Tummala-Narra, PhD, is a clinical psychologist, a faculty member and Director of Integrative Research at the Michigan School of Professional Psychology, and Teaching Associate at Cambridge Health Alliance/Harvard Medical School. She is also in private practice in Farmington Hills, MI. She founded and directed the Asian Mental Health Clinic at the Cambridge Health Alliance (1997–2003), and was on faculty at Georgetown University School of medicine (2003–2005). She has presented nationally and authored several publications on multicultural psychology, trauma, and psychotherapy.

Carmen Inoa Vazquez Ph.D, ABPP, is a board-certified clinical and forensic clinical psychologist with over 25 years of experience as a distinguished clinician, teacher, researcher, author, and program presenter with both Spanish/English bilingual and English-speaking populations. Dr. Vazquez is author of *Parenting with Pride Latino Style* (Rayo, 2004) and co-author of *The Maria Paradox* (Perigree, 1997). She has also published in the area of aging. Dr. Vazquez consults, supervises, and teaches at Bellevue Hospital, where she was Director of the Institute for Multicultural Behavioral Health and Director of the New York University Bellevue Clinical Psychology Internship training program for 16 years. She was also Founder and Director of the Bilingual Treatment Program Clinic. Dr. Vazquez is a Clinical Professor in Psychiatry at New York University School of Medicine and also has a private practice in New York City. Dr. Vazquez has received many honors, including Outstanding Career Achievement from Nassau County Medical Center, and One of the Most Outstanding Women of 1997 from *El Diario–La Prensa*.

Joy Whitman, PhD, is a Licensed Clinical Professional Counselor and Associate Professor and Program Director in the Human Services and Counseling Program at DePaul University in Chicago. She is past president of the Association for Lesbian, Gay, Bisexual, and Transgender Issues in Counseling and has served on the American Counseling Association's Ethics Committee. She has written and presented nationally on clinical issues for lesbian, gay, bisexual, and transgender clients, counselor education for working with LGBT clients, and positive aspects of lesbian and gay identities. She advocates for safe schools for LGBT students through workshops and trainings for school personnel and maintains a small private practice in Chicago that serves the lesbian communities.

AUTHOR INDEX

SUBJECT INDEX